Lecture Notes in Computer Science 14383

Founding Editors

Gerhard Goos
Juris Hartmanis

Editorial Board Members

Elisa Bertino, *Purdue University, West Lafayette, IN, USA*
Wen Gao, *Peking University, Beijing, China*
Bernhard Steffen ⑩, *TU Dortmund University, Dortmund, Germany*
Moti Yung ⑩, *Columbia University, New York, NY, USA*

The series Lecture Notes in Computer Science (LNCS), including its subseries Lecture Notes in Artificial Intelligence (LNAI) and Lecture Notes in Bioinformatics (LNBI), has established itself as a medium for the publication of new developments in computer science and information technology research, teaching, and education.

LNCS enjoys close cooperation with the computer science R & D community, the series counts many renowned academics among its volume editors and paper authors, and collaborates with prestigious societies. Its mission is to serve this international community by providing an invaluable service, mainly focused on the publication of conference and workshop proceedings and postproceedings. LNCS commenced publication in 1973.

Lissa Holloway-Attaway · John T. Murray
Editors

Interactive Storytelling

16th International Conference
on Interactive Digital Storytelling, ICIDS 2023
Kobe, Japan, November 11–15, 2023
Proceedings, Part I

 Springer

Editors
Lissa Holloway-Attaway 🆔
University of Skövde
Skövde, Sweden

John T. Murray 🆔
University of Central Florida
Orlando, FL, USA

ISSN 0302-9743   ISSN 1611-3349 (electronic)
Lecture Notes in Computer Science
ISBN 978-3-031-47654-9   ISBN 978-3-031-47655-6 (eBook)
https://doi.org/10.1007/978-3-031-47655-6

This Springer imprint is published by the registered company Springer Nature Switzerland AG
The registered company address is: Gewerbestrasse 11, 6330 Cham, Switzerland

Paper in this product is recyclable.

Preface

This volume constitutes the proceedings of the 16th International Conference on Interactive Digital Storytelling (ICIDS 2023). ICIDS is the premier conference for researchers and practitioners concerned with studying digital interactive narrative forms from various perspectives, including theoretical, technological, and applied design lenses. The annual conference is an interdisciplinary gathering that combines technology-focused approaches with humanities-inspired theoretical inquiry, empirical research, and artistic expression.

The theme for the conference this year was "Traversing Boundaries, Barriers and Borders." We were motivated to consider the varied border and boundary crossings enabled by the current state of Interactive Digital Storytelling. At a time when our fields for reflection and making have matured and deepened, particularly in the complex intra-disciplinary modes of creative/critical design and research within our ICIDS communities, we asked authors to reflect on their own situated-ness, displacements, and modes and means of travel. We asked in particular for them to reflect on key questions: "Where are you located in relation to interactive digital story-making and reflection, and how does that enable or hinder your perspectives? In what ways, and how, do you navigate around and through disciplinary fields, making-practices, users, nations, cultures, and other environments for engagement? Who is included and excluded from these bounded territories, freshly mapped worlds, and/or open sites for play and interaction?" We suggested they might consider maps and mapping as a strategic entry point to the topic. Maps can describe a variety of features from different perspectives of physical, social, and economic significance. We envision the act of traversing as both wayfinding and trailblazing and cartography of a burgeoning field that requires multiple, intersectional perspectives, and we invited authors also to consider how they might act as cartographers of the disciplines from which they come. We asked them, "What are your cartographic tools and how do they allow you to map-make to find new routes and passages that are open for all?" We encouraged contributions from diverse perspectives, including but not limited to: decolonial thinking, cross-disciplinary collaboration or resistance, multinational design as well as development critique and practice, and/or around issues of diversity and inclusion across communities and tools.

These proceedings represent the latest work from a wide range of researchers, with representation from around the world. The program was divided into six main areas based on the tracks to which authors submitted their research: Applications and Case Studies; Interactive Narrative Design; Social and Cultural Contexts; Theory, History and Foundations; Tools and Systems; and Virtual Worlds, Performance, Games and Play. Each subject area represents an important domain for exploring the theories, contexts, histories, practices, and designs for interactive digital storytelling. Collectively the papers in this volume present a range of intriguing and thoughtful reflections on how these unique digital narrative forms may be critiqued, developed, and designed.

ICIDS 2023 was hosted in Kobe, Japan, and sponsored by Kansai University and Ritsumeikan University, but it was also organized as a hybrid event, with participants either attending on-site, or joining the conference remotely. Care was taken to ensure that all aspects of the program were equally accessible to those who were attending physically and virtually.

This year, we received 101 submissions (45 full papers, 22 short papers and 34 Late Breaking Works papers). Following the review process, the Program Committee accepted 30 full papers, 9 short papers, and 22 Late Breaking Works (61 total). The total acceptance rate was 0.61. We also accepted 15 submissions to the Doctoral Consortium.

As in the past, the review process for Papers and Late Breaking Works was strictly double-blind and used a structured and detailed review form. A minimum of three reviews per paper were requested before the decision, with additional reviews solicited on the recommendations of reviewers. In addition, we included a rebuttal phase for long and short papers, and final decisions were made at virtual program chairs' meetings, which included the area chairs. However, we still welcome feedback from both authors and reviewers to help us continue to refine and strengthen the way that we run the conference. We want to thank our area chairs for their hard work and participation in the meta-review process: Mattia Bellini, Colette Daiute, Joshua Fisher, Emily Johnson, Hartmut Koenitz, Vincenzo Lombardo, Sandy Louchart, Mark Marino, Frank Nack, Christian Roth, Rebecca Rouse, and Anastasia Salter.

Finally, we want to thank the members of the ICIDS community who served as reviewers this year. The commitment of our reviewers to provide high-quality reviews and constructive and insightful discussions is a credit to our community, and helps to maintain the rigor and integrity of the ongoing development of this exciting and growing field.

November 2023

Lissa Holloway-Attaway
John T. Murray

ARDIN, The Association for Research in Interactive Digital Narratives

ARDIN's purpose is to support research in Interactive Digital Narratives (IDN), in a wide range of forms, be that video and computer games, interactive documentaries and fiction, journalistic interactives, art projects, educational titles, transmedia, virtual reality and augmented reality titles, or any emerging novel forms of IDN.

ARDIN provides a home for an interdisciplinary community and for various activities that connect, support, grow, and validate said community. The long- term vision for the suite of activities hosted by ARDIN includes membership services, such as a community platform, job postings, and support for local gatherings, but also conferences, publication opportunities, research fellowships, and academic/professional awards. ARDIN publishes a monthly newsletter and holds a monthly online social, where both established researchers and graduate students share their ongoing work in an informal setting. A new journal (Journal for Interactive Narrative Research), published in collaboration with ETC press, is currently being prepared, with a first issue planned to be available soon. There are also several committees and task forces, listed below.

ICIDS is the main academic conference of ARDIN. Additional international and local conferences are welcome to join the organization. The Zip-Scene conference, focused on eastern Europe, is the first associated conference.

Diversity is important to ARDIN. The organization will strive towards gender balance and the representation of different people from different origins. Diversity also means to represent scholars at different levels of their careers.

No ARDIN member shall discriminate against any other ARDIN member or others outside of the organization in any way, including but not limited to gender, nationality, race, religion, sexuality, or ability. Discrimination against these principles will not be tolerated and membership in ARDIN can be withdrawn based on evidence of such behavior.

The association is incorporated as a legal entity in Amsterdam, the Netherlands. First proposed during the ICIDS 2017 conference in Madeira, Portugal, the association was officially announced at ICIDS 2018 in Dublin, Ireland. During its foundational year, members of the former ICIDS Steering Committee continued to serve as the ARDIN board as approved by the first general assembly at ICIDS 2018. The current board structure and membership were approved at the second general assembly at ICIDS 2019 in Utah, and, as of October 2023, ARDIN has more than 160 members.

More information about ARDIN can be found at https://ardin.online/. ARDIN is also on Facebook (https://www.facebook.com/ARDINassociation), X (@ARDIN_online), and Discord (https://discord.gg/jNg5b5dWP4).

Committees

The Promotion and Advancement committee is led by Hartmut Koenitz and Josh Fisher with the help of Luis Bruni and Colette Daiute. The aim of this committee is to create a tenure equivalency document and recruit a team of expert reviewers for tenure and examination. Those interested should reach out to Hartmut Koenitz (hkoenitz at gmail.com). The IDN in Education committee is led by Jonathon Barbara. This committee will be looking into how IDN can become a part of school (K-12) curricula and will be producing a white paper with recommendations. Students are also welcome to join as task force members! Those interested should reach out to Jonathon Barbara (barbaraj at tcd.ie).

Task Forces

The Task Force on Inclusive Pricing Structure is led by Agnes Bakk. This task force will be looking into how to adjust registration for membership and conference registration according to GDP. Those interested should reach out to Agnes Bakk (bakk at mome.hu). The Task Force on ARDIN Outreach is led by Maria Cecilia Reyes. Aims of this task force are to create awareness about IDN and around ARDIN, and to build partnerships with industry, art, and education institutions, among others key stakeholders. Contact Maria Cecilia Reyes (mariaceciliareyesr at gmail.com) for more information or to get involved.

Organization

Organization Committee

General Chairs

Ryosuke Yamanishi	Kansai University, Japan
Ruck Thawonmas	Ritsumeikan University, Japan

Program Committee Chairs

Lissa Holloway-Attaway	University of Skövde, Sweden
John T. Murray	University of Central Florida, USA

Financial Management Chairs

Akiko Yamanobe	May Project, Japan
Frank Nack	University of Amsterdam, The Netherlands

Art Exhibition Chairs

Iva Georgieva	Bulgarian Academy of Sciences, Bulgaria
Mondheera Pituxcoosuvarn	Ritsumeikan University, Japan

Workshop Chair

Frederic Seraphine	University of Tokyo, Japan

Doctoral Consortium Chairs

Hartmut Koenitz	Södertörn University, Sweden
Ágnes Bakk Moholy-Nagy	University of Art and Design, Hungary

Online Chair

Liang Li	Ritsumeikan University, Japan

ARDIN Officers and Board

Executive Board

Hartmut Koenitz (President)	Södertörn University, Sweden
Frank Nack	University of Amsterdam, The Netherlands
Lissa Holloway-Attaway	University of Skövde, Sweden
Alex Mitchell	National University of Singapore, Singapore
Ágnes Bakk Moholy-Nagy	University of Art and Design, Hungary

General Board

Luis Bruni	Aalborg University, Denmark
Clara Fernandez-Vara	NYU, USA
Josh Fisher	Columbia College Chicago, USA
Andrew Gordon	University of Southern California, USA
Mads Haahr	Trinity College Dublin, Ireland
Michael Mateas	UC Santa Cruz, USA
Valentina Nisi	University of Madeira, Portugal, and Carnegie Mellon University, USA
Mirjam Palosaari Eladhari	Södertörn University, Sweden
Tess Tanenbaum	UC Irvine, USA
David Thue	Carleton University, Canada, and Reykjavik University, Iceland

ICIDS Program Committee Area Chairs

Theory, History, and Foundations

Hartmut Koenitz	Södertörn University, Sweden
Mattia Bellini	University of Tartu, Latvia

Social and Cultural Contexts

Anastasia Salter	University of Central Florida, USA
Rebecca Rouse	University of Skövde, Sweden

Tools and Systems

Frank Nack	University of Amsterdam, The Netherlands
Vincenzo Lombardo	University of Torino, Italy

Interactive Narrative Design

Mark Marino	University of Southern California, USA
Christian Roth	HKU University of the Arts, The Netherlands

Virtual Worlds, Performance, Games and Play

Sandy Louchart	Glasgow School of Art, UK
Emily Johnson	University of Central Florida, USA

Applications and Case Studies

Colette Daiute	City University of New York, USA
Joshua Fisher	Ball State University, USA

Late Breaking Works

Hartmut Koenitz	Södertörn University, Sweden
Joshua Fisher	Ball State University, USA

Program Committee

Febri Abdullah	Ritsumeikan University, Japan
Alberto Alvarez	Malmö University, Sweden
Gabriele Aroni	Manchester Metropolitan University, UK
Pratama Atmaja	University of Pembangunan Nasional "Veteran" Jawa Timur, Indonesia
Byung-Chull Bae	Hongik University, South Korea
Sojung Bahng	Queen's University, Canada
Agnes Bakk	Moholy-Nagy University of Art and Design, Hungary
Jonathan Barbara	Saint Martin's Institute of Higher Education, Malta
Mattia Bellini	University of Tartu, Estonia
Jessica L. Bitter	Hochschule RheinMain, Germany
Alex Calderwood	Montana State University, USA

Jack Murray	University of Texas at Dallas, USA
Frank Nack	University of Amsterdam, The Netherlands
Daniel Peniche	Tallinn University, Estonia
Andy Phelps	American University, USA
Antonio Pizzo	University of Turin, Italy
Derek Reilly	Dalhousie University, Canada
María Cecilia Reyes	Universidad del Norte, Colombia
Joellyn Rock	University of Minnesota, USA
Christian Roth	HKU University of the Arts Utrecht, The Netherlands
Rebecca Rouse	University of Skövde, Sweden
Svetlana Rudenko	Bray Institute of Further Education, Ireland
Anastasia Salter	University of Central Florida, USA
Morgan Sammut	Independent, USA
Despoina Sampatakou	University of York, UK
Frédéric Seraphine	University of Tokyo, Japan
Digdem Sezen	Teesside University, UK
Tonguç Sezen	Teesside University, UK
Yotam Shibolet	Utrecht University, The Netherlands
Claudia Silva	Technical University of Lisbon, Portugal
Shweta Sisodiya	University of California Santa Cruz, USA
Lyle Skains	Bournemouth University, UK
Andy Smith	North Carolina State University, USA
Caighlan Smith	Memorial University of Newfoundland, Canada
Gabriele Sofia	Université Paul Valéry Montpellier, France
Ulrike Spierling	RheinMain University of Applied Sciences, Germany
Claire Stricklin	Rutgers University—Camden, USA
Stella Sung	University of Central Florida, USA
Nicolas Szilas	University of Geneva, Switzerland
Alexandra Teixeira Riggs	Georgia Institute of Technology, USA
Rui Torres	Universidade Fernando Pessoa, Portugal
Renske van Enschot	Tilburg University, The Netherlands
Jasper Van Vught	Utrecht University, The Netherlands
Jessica Vandenberg	North Carolina State University, USA
Ruoyu Wen	Uppsala University, Sweden
Rob Wittig	University of Minnesota Duluth, USA
David Thomas Henry Wright	Nagoya University, Japan
Hongwei Zhou	University of California, Santa Cruz, USA

Contents – Part I

Tools and Systems

Interactive Narrative Design

Virtual Worlds, Performance, Games and Play

Contents – Part II

Theory, History and Foundations

Interpretation as Play: A Cognitive Psychological Model of Inference and Situation Model Construction

Matthew Higgins[✉] (iD)

University of Portsmouth, Portsmouth, UK
`matthew.higgins@port.ac.uk`

Abstract. Interpretation of narrative can itself be considered a form of play that is psychologically engaging and effortful. Previous work has provided initial considerations of the cognitive psychology of narrative interpretation, particularly of how players derive pleasure from understanding story. This paper elaborates on the specific processes involved in the comprehension of narrative, providing a review of discourse comprehension theories that culminates in a synthesised summary model of inference and situation model construction. The applicability of this psychological model to players of digital games is considered through comparison to participant descriptions of playing Gone Home. Prevalent themes reflect the relevance-determination of inference and demonstrate the activation of long-term memory in recall of expectations from personal experiences, games, and other media. This is briefly considered in application to storytelling in games and IDN. Future work in this area will focus on the operationalisation of this psychological understanding in practice in game design and storytelling.

Keywords: storytelling · digital games · psychology

1 Interpretation as Play and Cognitive Psychology

Scholars in digital games and interactive digital storytelling have considered interpretation of narrative as a form of play [1–3]. Upton [1] summarises this in discussion of story-focused digital games such as Dear Esther [4] and Proteus [5], offering that in the absence of expected gameplay mechanisms there is a compensatory complexity in their 'interpretive play' spaces. Comparisons can be made between narrative interpretation and play. Caillois' [6] understanding of play, for example, involves the acceptance of a temporary 'imaginary universe', akin to Huizinga's [7] 'temporary world' or Gray's [8] mental removal from the 'real-world'. Research on the experience of spatial presence in digital games has also argued for the construction, acceptance, and prioritisation of mental models [9]. In comparison to story, as discussed in this paper, perspectives on narrative interpretation broadly agree that comprehension of story also involves the creation and acceptance of mental models. Where play is considered to involve the creation and acceptance of a mental model, so is narrative interpretation. It is therefore argued that narrative interpretation can be considered a form of play in itself. In consideration

L. Holloway-Attaway and J. T. Murray (Eds.): ICIDS 2023, LNCS 14383, pp. 3–20, 2023.
https://doi.org/10.1007/978-3-031-47655-6_1

of IDNs and story-focused games, this casts their prioritisation of narrative as a focus on facilitating interpretation as play as compared to facilitating strategic thinking in real-time strategies or tactical thinking in shooters.

These perspectives together indicate the cognitively involving and playful nature of narrative interpretation. Consequently, it has been previously argued that understanding the specific cognitive processes involved in narrative interpretation can assist with the design of games and interactive digital narratives (IDNs) that prioritise narrative interpretation as play [10]. A psychological understanding of narrative interpretation may also further discussion surrounding player response and critical reception. It is therefore important to explore relevant cognitive psychological theories, but to also convey them accessibly for academics and practitioners from other fields (such as game design and IDN).

This psychological approach to understanding games and IDNs builds on similar perspectives that utilise cognitive psychology such as working memory and schema theory in application to games research and design, such as Howell's use of learning theories towards 'disruptive' game design [11–13] and Pinchbeck's use of schema theory in understanding and designing story-focused digital games [14–17]. This also relates to cognitive narratology, which similarly considers narrative to pertain to the construction of mental models [18–20], though the present paper draws from discourse comprehension theories to elaborate on how these mental models are specifically constructed. In digital games and IDN, the present discussion of mental model construction is comparative to Young and Cardona-Rivera's work in the same area, drawing from similar theories of discourse comprehension theory to understand player experience of narrative [21, 22]. However, Young and Cardona-Rivera's work in this area has focused on the interplay of comprehension with affordances and player agency, and on the creation of computational models of salience for generative narrative systems. The present paper intends to elucidate on the cognition involved in narrative interpretation in the context of its facilitation as play in games and IDN. Comparisons may also be drawn between this discussion of narrative interpretation and Koenitz' perspective on IDN, where this paper can be considered to elaborate on the 'process' of Koenitz' SPP model of IDN [23, 24], bringing a psychological perspective to IDN that Koenitz' has previously encouraged [25].

Previous work has provided a summary of perspectives on how narrative information is understood through inference and stored in long-term memory, but then specifically investigated the psychological processes related to the experience of pleasure during interpretation [10], offering an understanding of how audiences enjoy story. This paper focuses on compiling and reviewing discourse comprehension theories in more detail to better elaborate on how narrative information triggers inference and is consequently sorted into mental models (or 'situation models') in long-term memory. This culminates in a summarised model of inference and situation model construction. However, theories of discourse comprehension pertain to text and film, with no explicit consideration of games or interactive digital narratives. The applicability of this model to players of digital games is therefore considered through analysis of participant descriptions of experience of playing Gone Home [26] and comparison to the proposed psychological model, resulting in a more specific, novel model of inference and situation model construction contextualised in games and IDNs.

2 Reviewing and Comparing Discourse Comprehension Theories

Earlier work summarised that new narrative information is initially processed by a 'working' memory [27] (a temporary memory store that sorts incoming stimuli and directs attention) that assesses its relevance and determines how it may integrate into existing understanding in long-term memory. Many psychological theories agree that narrative information is integrated into mental models in long-term memory [28–34]. Long-term memory is also typically considered to consist of 'schemas' [35–37]; associative clusters of relevant memories that may collectively activate in response to stimuli. For example, individuals may have schemas associated with specific genres (horror, fantasy etc.) or mediums (games, film etc.) that represent expectations informed by experiences of those genres or mediums that can be activated in response to associated stimuli. Gone Home's initial ambience (the darkness, the storm, the empty house), for example, may likely activate schemas related to horror, priming players' expectations of typical horror games or media.

While earlier theories considered how text and its meaning were cognitively represented in mental models [29], further research established the more specific concept of situation models. Situation models are posited to represent the discourse as a whole, as compared to purely textual or 'surface' representations, representing concepts in the text and their interrelations, integrated with prior knowledge [31, 32, 34]. For example, the text representation of the novelisation of The Hitchhiker's Guide to the Galaxy [38] would be the words themselves. Their interpreted meaning would then be represented in situation models, including events and characters and their interrelations, such as Arthur's relationship with Ford, Ford's alien identity, and their escape of Earth's demolition on an alien spaceship. The usage of the term 'situation models' persists in more contemporary discussion of discourse comprehension [31, 39, 40], as does their proposed applicability to narrative media generally [41], and is therefore a commonly accepted perspective with which to understand how narrative information is stored in long-term memory.

Van Dijk and Kintsch's [32, 42] Construction-Integration model lays many of the foundations of discourse comprehension theories, elaborating on the activation of relevant memory (and suppression of irrelevant memory) in current narrative understanding and broader long-term memory in response to new stimuli. This activation of memory, or inference, determines how information is then integrated in the construction of a coherent situation model of the discourse. A lack of activation is associated with incoherence and may result in more effortful ('controlled') inference with wider activation.

Gernsbacher's [43, 44] more medium-agnostic Structure-Building model (as compared to Construction-Integration's focus on textual discourse) elaborates on the same concept, focusing on the dynamics of activation in response to stimuli. Gernsbacher discusses the enhancement of the strength of association between activated memories in response to relevant stimuli, and the suppression of irrelevant memory and stimuli.

This broadly suggests that activated memory is more likely to be activated again, with increased activation resulting in a stronger association between memory and stimuli. This is echoed by neurological perspectives on brain plasticity that indicate that neural pathways between memories are strengthened when activated [45, 46]. Gernsbacher further posits three processes for mental representation creation: laying the foundation of the structure; mapping new information into the structure (comparable to van Dijk and Kintsch's integration); shifting to new structures when mapping is insufficient. Gernsbacher's key addition to van Dijk and Kintsch's model here is the proposal of a network of multiple mental models, being substructures within a larger structure, that collectively represent a broader narrative.

Zwaan et al.'s Event-Indexing model [33, 34] adopts the concept of situation models and similarly proposes successive connected situation models for larger narratives with multiple, more distinct events akin to Gernsbacher's model. In contrast to Construction-Integration and Structure-Building, in that situation models may contain multiple events and information (termed as 'entities' and their respective 'properties'), the Event-Indexing model focuses more on how coherence is established through the monitoring of five 'event indices' that link events: temporality, spatiality, protagonist, causality, and intentionality. Any discontinuity detected in these indices in the current situation results in the situation model being updated. If multiple changes are detected, this may indicate a new event has been encountered, resulting in construction of a new situation model. Discussion of the segmentation of a narrative into events also suggests that situation models may contain predictive information of how events may change [47].

In comparison to Event-Indexing's prioritised indices, additional studies and theories suggest that causality is typically prioritised in the determination of coherence. In comparison to the event indices, the Causal Network model [48–50] suggests more broadly that situation model construction is primarily achieved through causal inferences. This is further suggested in studies that show causally connected information is more likely to activate in response to stimuli [41, 51, 52]. Causally relevant information may be events that are causes or consequences of other events. However, aspects such as where and when events occur, or characters goals and intentions and how they may influence or react to events can also be causally relevant [49, 53], hence the Event-Indexing model's five event indices are still potentially relevant to causality.

Lastly, Hofer et al.'s [9] 'book problem' acknowledges that audiences can experience spatial presence in more traditional media. Considering that the construction and prioritisation of mental models of a virtual environment are proposed by Hofer et al. as key to the experience of spatial presence, the construction of situation models during narrative interpretation is directly comparable. In comparison to Zwaan's 'spatiality' event index, and studies that suggest that situation models contain spatial information [54, 55], narrative situation models and spatial mental models can be considered significantly associated, though it is uncertain if they are interchangeable.

Although these discourse comprehension models differ, their shared focus on mental representations (most commonly 'situation models') suggests a significant degree of compatibility, as demonstrated in similar syntheses of discourse comprehension models in cognitive psychology [53]. The widely discussed process of activating memory to determine the relevance and coherence of stimuli for integration into existing or new situation models can be generalised and synthesised into a combined model of inference and situation model construction.

2.1 Summarising and Integrating Theories of Discourse Comprehension

Discourse comprehension theories can here be summarised and integrated into a singular understanding of narrative interpretation. Situation models are constructed through the combination of information provided by the discourse (e.g., novel, film, game), existing narrative understanding, and long-term memory more broadly. Situation models can contain a large amount of complex information, such as the speaker or narrator, character intentions, relationships, opinions, emotions (as suggested by van Dijk and Kintsch [32]) or events, entities, and properties suggested by Zwaan et al. [34]).

When constructing situation models, audiences are aiming to establish a coherent understanding of the discourse [56–58]. Certain kinds of information are posited to be prioritised in establishing coherence. For example, Zwaan et al.'s [33] five 'event indices' that are monitored and updated when any change occurs (temporality, spatiality, protagonist, causality, intentionality). Alternative perspectives, such as the Causal Network model, emphasise the importance of causality specifically during the construction of coherent mental representations of discourse [49]. Memory that is causally-relevant is more likely to activate in response to new narrative information [41, 52], suggesting that causal narrative information that connects the events, characters, and properties of a narrative is prioritised during interpretation.

Situation models can be constructed incrementally and gradually, as new information is introduced and integrated into current understanding, or globally when new situation models are required when new information cannot be easily integrated [32, 33]. For example, Zwaan's event indices and theories of event segmentation [47, 59, 60] propose that the detection of changes in the current situation would result in updating that aspect of the situation model, although the Causal Network model would suggest a more general consideration of limited causality, and Gernsbacher's Structure-Building model would abstract this more broadly to limited activation and poor mapping of the new information to the existing stored information. Conversely, significant changes to a narrative situation may indicate that a new situation is being perceived, such as between levels of a game or chapters in a novel, resulting in the construction of new situation models, or recall of a prior, more relevant situation model. In conjunction with Gernsbacher's substructures [43, 44] and the similar events of the Event-Indexing model, this suggests the construction of successive, connected situation models that collectively represent a larger narrative, with the current narrative situation being the focus of attention and retrieved in working memory.

Various perspectives on situation models delineate how the activation of memory dictates how new information is integrated and how situation models are therefore constructed and updated [32, 43, 44, 53, 58, 61]. When encountering stimuli, this triggers a spreading activation of memory (of both current narrative understanding and broader long-term memory schemas) that is cohesive or associated with the stimuli to determine the coherence and relevance of new information for its potential integration into current narrative understanding. As discussed, information that is causally connected to the incoming stimuli [50, 56] or was more recently encoded [62] is more likely to be activated. The activation of relevant memory also increases its likelihood of further activation in response to additional stimuli and inhibits the future activation of less relevant memory [32, 44, 63].

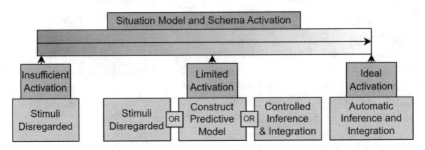

Fig. 1. Ideal, Limited, and Insufficient Activation of Memory

If there is ideal activation, in which enough memory is activated to determine relevance, this new information is then successfully integrated into the situation model (see Ideal Activation in Fig. 1 above). Limited activation may result in the creation of a new situation model. Given prior discussion of event segmentation [59], event-indexing [33], and structure-building [43, 44], this may result in a series of related situation models representing current narrative understanding in long-term memory. For example, a significant change, such as a new scene in a film or level in a game, may be less immediately relevant, result in less activation, and trigger the construction of a new situation model. Theories also suggest that with limited activation, predictive situation models may be created that can be later confirmed or disregarded when new information is found [47, 64, 65]. However, if activation of memory is inadequate for automated inference and integration of narrative information, then an effortful process of controlled inference involving the purposeful and conscious activation of memory may occur [53, 66]. This more controlled inference triggers additional activation that may therefore allow for the integration of the narrative information. Lastly, if activation of memory is particularly insufficient, then the stimuli may instead be considered irrelevant, and ignored without integration or further controlled inference. The determination of when controlled inference is attempted when activation is limited varies based on individual differences between audiences, such as in their specific experiences and expectations with games or stories. Van den Broek [57] further suggests individual, personal standards of coherence. The potential activation of memory and the likely outcomes are depicted in Fig. 1 above.

2.2 Summary Model of Inference and Situation Model Construction

The model of inference and situation model construction (Fig. 2) integrates and summarises these theories of discourse comprehension as an extension of Baddeley's model of working memory [27]. This provides an understanding of how individuals engage with and interpret narrative information, integrating numerous existing psychology theories into a more accessible model for scholars and practitioners in the fields of digital games and IDN. In this summary and integration, some specificity of prior models of discourse comprehension are abstracted.

Stimuli, or narrative information in this specific context, is coordinated via working memory, here shown with a central executive that organises incoming stimuli into short-term stores (i.e., visuospatial sketchpad, episodic buffer, phonological loop) for further processing and sorting into long-term memory. As suggested by van Dijk and Kintsch [32], Gernsbacher [43], and Zwaan et al. [33], this triggers the currently relevant situation model to be recalled in working memory. Abiding van Dijk and Kintsch's initial model, and echoed in following models, working memory and long-term memory is activated to determine the potential relevance of the incoming stimuli. Insufficient memory activation determines the stimuli as completely irrelevant or incoherent and is ignored or forgotten. Ideal activation of memory determines relevance, and the information is integrated into the situation model (here shown as a nested structure within long-term memory). The specific information that may be considered, or prioritised, as relevant may differ and is uncertain, and so the event indices offered by Zwaan et al. are not specified in this summary model, opting for a broader causal prioritisation as suggested in the Causal Network model.

If activation is limited, then more controlled activation of memory may occur and result in additional activation (controlled inference) and consequent integration into the situation model (as posited by van Dijk and Kintsch and Gernsbacher), or the creation of a new situation model (e.g., if activation was less optimal because the situation had changed as posited by Zwaan et al. and Gernsbacher). Alternatively, limited activation of long-term memory may result in the construction of predictive situation models for later activation, confirmation, and integration into the situation models [65].

For example, when playing Gone Home, a player may encounter a new piece of information in a letter. This information triggers activation of their understanding of Gone Home's narrative so far, and their memory pertaining to experiences of similar games and stories, personal experiences, and other relevant long-term memories. First, this may result in ideal activation and allow for the new information to be determined as relevant, and thus sorted into situation models. Second, it may result in insufficient activation and be disregarded. Third, it may result in limited activation and trigger controlled inference, activating more memory with more effort. In relation to the model of optimal arousal regulation [10], controlled inference is suggested to result in greater shifts in arousal, and thus potentially more pleasure.

3   Assessing the Relevance of the Model and Theories

Theories of discourse comprehension largely pertain to text or film, with no consideration of comprehension of narrative in games or IDN. While the same psychological processes are likely utilised in understanding story in a game or IDN, it is not guaranteed. Consequently, a study of players' experiences of Gone Home can assist in providing an initial indication of the relevance of the reviewed psychology.

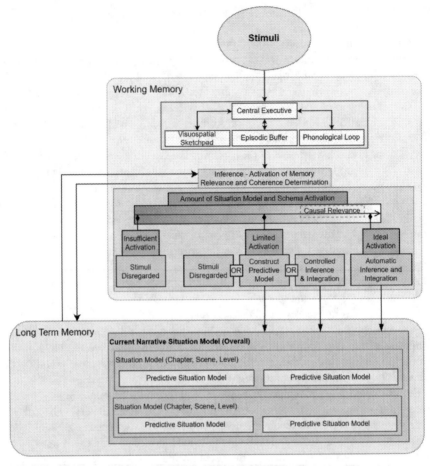

Fig. 2. Model of Inference and Situation Model Construction

3.1 Method

Fifteen participants each played fifteen minutes of Gone Home, a game that encourages players to explore an empty family home filled with environmental clues as to the events of the story and whereabouts of the family. Gone Home tells a story of an American family, particularly the youngest daughter Sam, through a variety of methods, with audio narration, environmental storytelling, and through letters, diaries, and notes. Gone Home was chosen as a story-focused digital game with a short enough length that participants would be able to experience a reasonable portion of the story in 15 min.

Data was collected with stimulated recall [67, 68], and retrospective think-aloud. Participants watched a recording of their play and described their experience. Stimulated recall and retrospective think-aloud are methods encouraged in games studies [67] and UX [69] that were chosen here to ensure proximity to the lived experience but avoid impacts on user experience found in situated think-aloud strategies [70–72] due to splitting participant attention between multiple cognitively involved activities (playing Gone Home while vocalising their thoughts and feelings).

These experiences were thematically analysed [73–76], resulting in 11 themes and 40 sub-themes. Themes were considered significant due to the frequency of their codes across the participant group, or due to the number of relevant codes and sub-themes within a particular theme.

3.2 Results

The most prevalent theme was Forming Expectations, with frequent discussion amongst participants (f = 241) about their predictions of the story. These involved multiple potential outcomes being considered ("…she either died, or was kidnapped, or possessed"), and also often centred around uncertainties discovered in the game, such as a school locker in a bedroom or a TV left on in the living room, potentially indicative of the limited, non-ideal activation of memory [65] and the predictive situation models proposed by Zacks et al. [47].

Engaging with Story was also a prominent theme, both in determining relevance and understanding the story as a cohesive whole. 10 participants (f = 20) discussed their attempts to determine the relevance of new information ("…even though it's like such an irrelevance thing and irrelevant piece of information…") ("there's little bits of things that I keep finding everywhere which don't have any use other than just to show you what your family is like"). This is likely indicative of the process of inference, with the activation of memory being utilised to determine the relevance of stimuli. Similarly, seven participants (f = 30) recalled, in detail, their understanding of the story as they'd discerned so far. This is also reflected in the discussion of establishing context, with seven participants (f = 12) similarly attempting to attain a broader understanding of the game ("I needed the context of who they were, what their relationship was to my character and to the world that this was building"). The desire for context pertained to what was occurring in the story and why, but also to their specific purpose in the story, such as why they were there and what they were meant to be doing as part of this. This reflects the discussion of a desire for coherence in discourse comprehension theories [56–58], but also indicates some additional aspects to players' desires for coherence in the context of digital games and IDNs.

Much of the focus in 14 participants recall of the story centred on the characters (f = 165), with information such as their emotional state ("…she's shying away from it, but she knows it's important, she's just embarrassed"), their relationships ("Janice is probably the mother", "I know the sister is Sam"), and of who the protagonist or player character may be ("I'm starting to think I'm Katie now"). This is reflective of Zwaan et al.'s [33] protagonist and intentionality (with emotional states often being related to a character's actions), and also demonstrates proposed priority of causal relevance during inference [27–31].

In discussion of characters and forming expectations, participants also frequently refer to their own personal experiences and expectations, indicating a frequent recall of their long-term memory during interpretation. When discussing characters, five participants (f = 14) considered their own personal experiences in relation to those characters ("I can relate to that, how that feels, you know my parents said to me, just try to make friends"). Participants recall of long-term memory ranged from broader semantic connotations ("it was like a caution or warning, a radioactivity sign, I knew that it was important"), to other media ("I found myself thinking, is this the Cabin in the Woods?"), to games more specifically ("I've played so many games, I've seen the set-up before"). Recall of games was the most likely relevant experience to draw from, with ten participants (f = 27) discussing their expectations informed by their experience with games.

3.3 Discussion

Results indicate the relevance of the proposed psychological model of inference and situation model construction. The theme Determining Relevance is immediately comparable to the process of the relevance-determining inference central to discourse comprehension theories and the summarised model of inference and situation model construction. The prevalence of this theme demonstrates the activation of memory in attempt to integrate new information. The theme Recalling from Memory similarly demonstrates the activation of long-term memory specifically, but also elucidates the memory and schemas that are likely recalled during gameplay. Firstly, participants discuss personal experiences, such as specific life experiences or specific related games and media. However, participants also recall their broader expectations stemming from specific experiences, with frequent recall of semantic connotations as well as expectations of genre and medium. In contrast to the discussed discourse comprehension theories, and the resulting summary model of interpretation and situation model recall, this data offers much more specificity as compared to the more indistinct reference to long-term memory activation.

Participants' desire for context tentatively reflects the underlying need for coherence suggested in discourse comprehension theories. Van Dijk and Kintsch's Construction-Integration and the Casual Network model are of particularly relevance here, each suggesting a desire for coherence during discourse comprehension, though the latter offering prioritised causality. Participants' recall of Gone Home's story does reflect this prioritisation of causality as proposed in the Causal Network model, but also does elucidate on the kinds of memory typically considered as causally relevant. Given Gone Home's focus on character, it is unsurprising that much of participants' recall of the story pertains to its characters – however, there is frequent focus on character emotions and their relations to one-another. This is comparable to Zwaan's proposed event index of intentionality. Similarly, participants often discussed the identity of the central character, prompting discussion of Sam and Katie alongside consideration of their player-character. Participants' consideration of context also often involved an understanding (and recall) of the game's setting, with common discussion around the time in which it is set, and on the house in which the characters reside. Firstly, this lends support for Zwaan's event indices (temporality, spatiality, protagonist, causality, and intentionality), with each of these being subject to discussion by participants, though some more than others (particularly causality, protagonist, and intentionality). Secondly, the common consideration of the player-character indicates additional 'index' that players of games and IDNs may prioritise during inference and situation model construction.

Forming Expectations also reflects the common sources of participants predictions, such as recall of comparable media and games, but is further indicative of limited activation of participant memory during inference. As emphasised in Construction-Integration and Structure Building, and as represented in the summary model, limited activation of memory may result in either more effortful, controlled inference to activate additional memory, or in the creation of predictive situation models. The expectations formed by participants reflects the latter, with expectations often being predictions of the story of Gone Home. The discussion of expectations alongside uncertainties found in Gone Home may also reflect controlled inference.

In comparing the results of the study with prior models of discourse comprehension and the integration of these models in a summarised model of inference and situation model construction, the various processes and aspects of discourse comprehension theories can be seen in participants' experiences of Gone Home. While this firstly contextualises these theories in games and IDN, participants experiences have also provided additional specificity as to how these cognitive processes operate during play of games and IDN. These can be integrated into a final, novel model that aggregates prior theories of discourse comprehension theory with games and IDN-specific considerations found in the study.

Amending the prior summarised model of inference and situation model construction, Zwaan's event indices are included as part of inference to indicate the type of memory that may be prioritised during activation of memory. The commonly recalled forms of long-term memory have also been integrated, both with episode-specific memories and their schematic counterparts. For example, specific game experiences may be recalled, as can game-related schemas. Broader semantic connotations here indicate the schematisation of more specific life experiences; as demonstrated in participant response to Gone Home, for example, recognition of a radioactivity sign can lead to recall of broader connotations of danger.

3.4 Limitations

It is acknowledged that retroactive think-aloud may result in memory decay in participants as their recall occurs after the lived experience [77, 78]. Stimulated recall was employed to assist with recall, but this may still result in inaccuracies in participant descriptions.

While the use of Gone Home has provided useful comparisons to theories of discourse comprehension, this is only so far representative of the experience of one game. While these findings may be generalisable outside of the context of Gone Home, this is still limited, and further studies should examine this psychology in the context of other narrative games and IDNs. Similarly, the study examines participants experience of a story-focused digital game, and therefore unsurprising that responses are reflective of experiences of narrative. Further research should also compare experiences of games that are not story-focused to allow for the comparison of the presently discussed psychological models in scenarios in which it would be less likely reflected.

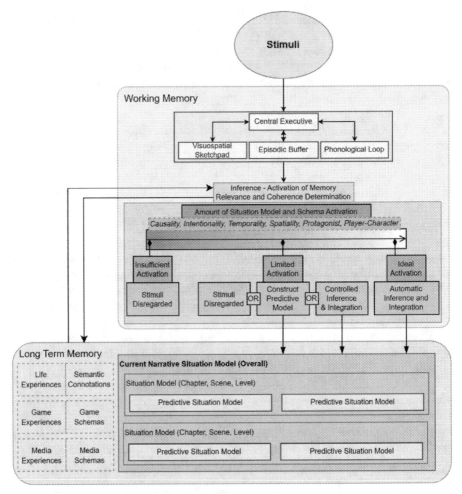

Fig. 3. Updated, novel Model of Inference and Situation Model Construction

4   Relevance of Discourse Comprehension Theories to Game/IDN Design

The model of inference and situation model construction, in conjunction with the prior proposed model of optimal arousal regulation [10], offers an understanding of how players interpret narrative and how this process is pleasurable. Research suggests that mediating the activation of memory during inference to encourage controlled inference should result in larger shifts in arousal that trigger a pleasure response in players. The practicality of this psychology can therefore be considered in approaches to game and IDN design that encourage controlled inference to facilitate interpretation as play.

Mediating the activation of memory to encourage controlled inference largely pertains to limiting the memory available to be activated, or providing incoherent stimuli that will result in limited activation. For example, omitting pertinent narrative information results in less available memory, central to narrative techniques such as twists and mystery. This can be seen in Gone Home, with the reason behind the absence of Katie's family being initially omitted. When their whereabouts are instead gradually implied through the letters and notes within the environment, the limited information provided therefore has little corresponding cohesive memories to activate in current situation models. Controlled inference is instead required to piece together these smaller incoherent narrative fragments into a more salient situation model, as demonstrated in the varied recall and predictions in participants' responses. Omission, limitation, and ambiguity of narrative information are therefore common to existing approaches to design, such as in the environmental storytelling (in which context is deprived and requires the collective interpretation of disparate aspects of an environment) and epistolary narrative (in which limited information is spread between multiple correspondences) utilised in Gone Home.

Omission and ambiguity are key to approaches to storytelling, as has been previously discussed in regard to arousal regulation [10]. For example, Pinchbeck discusses withholding narrative events in Dear Esther, with the intent to encourage players to 'fill the gaps' [79]. As players explore the Hebridean island, the semi-randomised narration of letters to Esther avoids communicating specific narrative events and instead provides descriptors of characters. Instead of explaining the fate of the character Paul, Paul is instead described in conflicting ways, such as 'Paul was drunk' or 'Paul was sober', but never indicating what Paul does or how he connects to Esther. Barlow [80] demonstrates this in his approach to telling a story 'using the player's imagination' in Her Story [81] (a crime fiction game that involves sifting through a police database of interview footage), noting approaches such as omission (by withholding the detective's questions), twists (omitting key details to later confuse and surprise), non-chronology (showing interviews in non-chronological order and therefore withholding causality), and contradiction to challenge the player's narrative understanding. As with Dear Esther's Paul, contradiction is a seemingly effective method for providing intentionally incohesive, conflicting information that would require further inference to resolve.

The examined psychology can be seen in approaches to storytelling, both old and new. Hemingway's iceberg theory [82, 83] similarly purports for the withholding of information which would also likely result in limited memory activation. More recent perspectives also echo this, such as Glinblat et al.'s [84] reparative play and the provision of intentionally incomplete or disparate artefacts that invite players to 'repair' and assemble meaning for themselves. Arjoranta's 'interpretive challenges' [85] likewise discusses ambiguity and contextuality to make narrative interpretation more challenging, comparable to the effortful controlled inference presently proposed, with ambiguity and withheld context again limiting activation during inference. Discourse surrounding poetic games [86–90] proposes the use of 'defamiliarization' to subvert expectations of narrative, structure, and interaction to facilitate poetic gameplay and encourage narrative interpretation. In comparison to discourse comprehension theories, this can again be seen as a method for encouraging controlled inference, with the subversion of expectations here resulting in limited activation of expectations in long-term memory and relevant schemas specifically (such as expectations of genre or medium).

A full review of approaches to game and IDN design that relate to the proposed psychological understanding of narrative interpretation is beyond the scope of this paper, but these examples emphasise the relevance of this psychology to understanding approaches to practice and its potential use in game and IDN design. Further research should consider how the proposed psychological models can inform approaches to storytelling in games and IDN in future.

5   Conclusion and Future Work

Considering interpretation as a form of play is a potentially useful perspective with which to examine existing media and creating new stories. A significant aspect of furthering this perspective is therefore developing a greater understanding of how audiences specifically interpret narrative, particularly in the context of digital games and IDN in which existing theories of discourse comprehension do not explicitly consider.

This paper has offered a review of existing perspectives on discourse comprehension. This initially provided a summarised, aggregated psychological model of inference and situation model construction, conveying how new narrative information triggers an activation of existing understanding and long-term memory to determine its relevance for integration into existing understanding. Analysis of participants' experiences with Gone Home has provided a tentative indication of the relevance and applicability of this psychology to digital games and IDN specifically, with much of the themes and specific discussion reflecting the reviewed discourse comprehension theories and the resulting model of inference and situation model construction. This has resulted in a novel version of the model that includes games and IDN-specific aspects provided by participant experiences. In summary the key contribution of this paper is the review of discourse comprehension theories, their comparison to the experience of a story-focused digital game, the novel model of inference and situation model construction that integrates the findings of each of these, and finally the initial consideration of how this psychology may influence game and IDN design.

In conjunction with the model of optimal arousal regulation, these provide a more accessible and relevant assimilation of cognitive psychology that outline how players seek and interpret new narrative information, and how this may be enjoyable. Future work should further endeavour to understand the psychology of narrative interpretation, but also seek to better operationalise this psychology for the context of both practice and critical analysis. Further work will investigate specific approaches for intentionally facilitating interpretation as a form of play, particularly methods for encouraging more effortful controlled inference to increase shifts in arousal and consequent pleasure. While this is more immediately relevant to practitioners in storytelling, IDN, and game design, this would also be of benefit to understanding existing approaches to practice.

It is also argued that theoretical approaches to practice should then be contextualised in the active design and development of real-world artefacts, such as digital games or IDNs. There are a variety of potential influences, caveats, or constraints that apply in practice, particularly in commercial game development, and it is useful to assess the applicability of findings and proposals pertaining to practice in their intended environment. Presently, this is being explored through the development of White Lake, a story-focused digital game set in an ambiguous white void, that intends to facilitate interpretation as play by encouraging controlled inference in players. The ongoing aim of this research is to understand the psychological experiences of players with which to develop approaches to storytelling in game and IDN design, and to contextualise findings in commercial games development.

References

1. Upton, B.: The Aesthetic of Play. MIT Press (2015)
2. Bozdog, M., Galloway, D.: Worlds at our fingertips: Reading (in) what remains of Edith Finch. Games Cult. 1555412019844631 (2019)
3. Muscat, A.: Mechanics & Materialities: WORLD4 and the Effort of Looking in Videogames. University of the Sunshine Coast, Queensland (2020)
4. The Chinese Room: Dear Esther. The Chinese Room, Curve Digital, Brighton, United Kingdom and London, United Kingdom (2012)
5. Key, E., Kanaga, D.: Proteus. Self-published (2013)
6. Caillois, R.: Man, Play, and Games. Uiversity of Illinois Press, Illinois (1961)
7. Huizinga, J.: Homo Ludens: A Study of the Play Element in Culture. Routledge, Switzerland (1944)
8. Gray, P.: Free to Learn: Why Unleashing the Instinct to Play Will Make our Children Happier, More Self-Reliant, and Better Students for Life. Basic Books (2013)
9. Hofer, M., Wirth, W., Kuehne, R., Schramm, H., Sacau, A.: Structural equation modeling of spatial presence: the influence of cognitive processes and traits. Media Psychol. **15**, 373–395 (2012)
10. Higgins, M., Howell, P.: Interpretive play and the player psychology of optimal arousal regulation. In: Bosser, AG., Millard, D.E., Hargood, C. (eds) Interactive Storytelling. ICIDS 2020. Lecture Notes in Computer Science, vol. 12497, pp. 243–257. Springer, Cham (2020). https://doi.org/10.1007/978-3-030-62516-0_22
11. Howell, P.: A theoretical framework of ludic knowledge: a case study in disruption and cognitive engagement. In: 10th International Conference in the Philosophy of Computer Games, Valletta, Malta, October (2016)
12. Howell, P., Stevens, B., Eyles, M.: Disrupting the player's schematised knowledge of game components. In: DiGRA 2014: <Active Noun> the <Verb> of game. Digital Games Research Association (2014)
13. Howell, P.: Schematically disruptive game design. In: DiGRA 2011: Think Design Play (2011)
14. Pinchbeck, D.: Story as a function of gameplay in First Person Shooters: an analysis of FPS diegetic content 1998–2007. Creative Technologies, vol. PhD. University of Portsmouth (2009)
15. Pinchbeck, D.: Dear esther: an interactive ghost story built using the source engine. In: Spierling, U., Szilas, N. (eds.) ICIDS 2008. LNCS, vol. 5334, pp. 51–54. Springer, Heidelberg (2008). https://doi.org/10.1007/978-3-540-89454-4_9
16. Pinchbeck, D.: Story and recall in first-person shooters. Int. J. Comput. Games Technol. **2008**, 6 (2008)
17. Pinchbeck, D., Stevens, B., Van Laar, S., Hand, S., Newman, K.: Narrative, agency and observational behaviour in a first person shooter environment. In: Proceedings of Narrative AI and Games Symposium: Society for the Study of Artificial Intelligence and the Simulation of Behaviour (AISOB'06), pp. 53–61. SSAISB (2006)
18. Thon, J.-N.: Transmedial Narratology and Contemporary Media Culture. U of Nebraska Press (2016)

19. Herman, D.: Cognitive narratology. Handbook of Narratology, vol. 1, pp. 30-43 (2009)
20. Herman, D.: Story logic: Problems and Possibilities of Narrative. U of Nebraska Press (2004)
21. Cardona-Rivera, R.E., Cassell, B.A., Ware, S.G., Young, R.M.: Indexter: a computational model of the event-indexing situation model for characterizing narratives. In: Proceedings of the 3rd Workshop on Computational Models of Narrative, pp. 34–43 (2012)
22. Young, R.M., Cardona-Rivera, R.: Approaching a player model of game story comprehension through affordance in interactive narrative. In: Proceedings of the AAAI Conference on Artificial Intelligence and Interactive Digital Entertainment, pp. 123–130. (2011)
23. Koenitz, H.: Understanding Interactive Digital Narrative: Immersive Expressions for a Complex Time. Taylor & Francis (2023)
24. Koenitz, H.: Towards a specific theory of interactive digital narrative. In: Interactive Digital Narrative, pp. 91–105. Routledge (2015)
25. Koenitz, H.: Interactive storytelling paradigms and representations: a humanities-based perspective. In: Handbook of Digital Games and Entertainment Technologies, pp. 1–15 (2016)
26. The Fullbright Company, M.C.: Gone Home. The Fullbright Company and Majesco Entertainment, Portland, OR and Hazlet, NJ (2013)
27. Baddeley, A.: Working memory: theories, models, and controversies. Annu. Rev. Psychol. **63**, 1–29 (2012)
28. Graesser, A.C., Millis, K., Zwaan, R.A.: Discourse comprehension. Annu. Rev. Psychol. **48**, 163–189 (1997)
29. Johnson-Laird, P.N.: Mental Models: Towards a Cognitive Science of Language, Inference, and Consciousness. Harvard University Press (1983)
30. Perfetti, C., Stafura, J.: Word knowledge in a theory of reading comprehension. Sci. Stud. Read. **18**, 22–37 (2014)
31. Raudszus, H., Segers, E., Verhoeven, L.: Situation model building ability uniquely predicts first and second language reading comprehension. J. Neurolinguistics **50**, 106–119 (2019)
32. Van Dijk, T.A., Kintsch, W.: Strategies of Discourse Comprehension (1983)
33. Zwaan, R.A., Langston, M.C., Graesser, A.C.: The construction of situation models in narrative comprehension: an event-indexing model. Psychol. Sci. **6**, 292–297 (1995)
34. Zwaan, R.A., Radvansky, G.A.: Situation models in language comprehension and memory. Psychol. Bull. **123**, 162 (1998)
35. Liu, Y.: An empirical study of schema theory and its role in reading comprehension. J. Lang. Teach. Res. **6**, 1349 (2015)
36. Mandler, J.M.: Stories, Scripts, and Scenes: Aspects of Schema Theory. Psychology Press (2014)
37. An, S.: Schema Theory in Reading. Theory & Practice in Language Studies, vol. 3 (2013)
38. Adams, D.: The Hitchhiker's Guide to the Galaxy. Pan Books (1979)
39. Hoeben Mannaert, L., Dijkstra, K.: Situation model updating in young and older adults. Int. J. Behav. Dev. 0165025419874125 (2020)
40. Kendeou, P., McMaster, K.L., Christ, T.J.: Reading comprehension: core components and processes. Policy Insights Behav. Brain Sci. **3**, 62–69 (2016)
41. Zwaan, R.A., Rapp, D.: Discourse comprehension. In: Traxler, M.J., Gernsbacher, M.A. (eds.) Handbook of Psycholinguistics, pp. 725–764. Elsevier Inc. (2006)
42. Kintsch, W.: Comprehension: A Paradigm for Cognition. Cambridge University Press (1998)
43. Gernsbacher, M.A.: Two decades of structure building. Discourse Process. **23**, 265–304 (1997)
44. Gernsbacher, M.A.: Language Comprehension as Structure Building. Lawrence Erlbaum Associates Inc, Hillsdale, NJ (1990)
45. Bruel-Jungerman, E., Davis, S., Laroche, S.: Brain plasticity mechanisms and memory: a party of four. Neuroscientist **13**, 492–505 (2007)
46. Kolb, B.: Brain Plasticity and Behavior. Psychology Press (2013)

47. Zacks, J.M., Speer, N.K., Swallow, K.M., Braver, T.S., Reynolds, J.R.: Event perception: a mind-brain perspective. Psychol. Bull. **133**, 273 (2007)
48. Suh, S.u., Trabasso, T.: Inferences during reading: converging evidence from discourse analysis, talk-aloud protocols, and recognition priming. J. Memory Lang. **32**, 279–300 (1993)
49. Trabasso, T., van den Broek, P., Suh, S.Y.: Logical necessity and transitivity of causal relations in stories. Discourse Process. **12**, 1–25 (1989)
50. Trabasso, T., van den Broek, P.: Causal thinking and the representation of narrative events. J. Mem. Lang. **24**, 612–630 (1985)
51. Sundermeier, B.A., van der Broek, P., Zwaan, R.A.: Causal coherence and the availability of locations and objects during narrative comprehension. Mem. Cognit. **33**, 462–470 (2005)
52. van den Broek, P., et al.: Assessment of comprehension abilities in young children. Children's Read. Comprehension Assess. 107–130 (2005)
53. McNamara, D.S., Magliano, J.: Toward a comprehensive model of comprehension. Psychol. Learn. Motiv. **51**, 297–384 (2009)
54. Curiel, J.M., Radvansky, G.A.: Spatial and character situation model updating. J. Cogn. Psychol. **26**, 205–212 (2014)
55. Smith, E.R., Stiegler-Balfour, J., Williams, C.R., Walsh, E.K., O'Brien, E.J.: Access to prior spatial information. Mem. Cognit. **48**, 1234–1248 (2020)
56. Todaro, S., Millis, K., Dandotkar, S.: The impact of semantic and causal relatedness and reading skill on standards of coherence. Discourse Process. **47**, 421–446 (2010)
57. van den Broek, P., Bohn-Gettler, C.M., Kendeou, P., Carlson, S., White, M.J.: When a reader meets a text: the role of standards of coherence in reading comprehension (2011)
58. van den Broek, P.: Comprehension and memory of narrative texts: inferences and coherence (1994)
59. Zacks, J.M., Speer, N.K., Reynolds, J.R.: Segmentation in reading and film comprehension. J. Exp. Psychol. Gen. **138**, 307 (2009)
60. Zacks, J.M., Swallow, K.M.: Event segmentation. Curr. Dir. Psychol. Sci. **16**, 80–84 (2007)
61. van den Broek, P., Helder, A.: Cognitive processes in discourse comprehension: passive processes, reader-initiated processes, and evolving mental representations. Discourse Process. **54**, 360–372 (2017)
62. van den Broek, P., Beker, K., Oudega, M.: Inference generation in text comprehension: automatic and strategic processes in the construction of a mental representation. Interences During Reading (2015)
63. Weingarten, E., Chen, Q., McAdams, M., Yi, J., Hepler, J., Albarracín, D.: From primed concepts to action: a meta-analysis of the behavioral effects of incidentally presented words. Psychol. Bull. **142**, 472 (2016)
64. Linderholm, T.: Predictive inference generation as a function of working memory capacity and causal text constraints. Discourse Process. **34**, 259–280 (2002)
65. Schmalhofer, F., McDaniel, M.A., Keefe, D.: A unified model for predictive and bridging inferences. Discourse Process. **33**, 105–132 (2002)
66. Kintsch, W.: Information accretion and reduction in text processing: inferences. Discourse Process. **16**, 193–202 (1993)
67. Pitkänen, J.: Studying thoughts: stimulated recall as a game research method. Game Research Methods, pp. 117–132 (2015)
68. Rowe, V.C.: Using video-stimulated recall as a basis for interviews: some experiences from the field. Music. Educ. Res. **11**, 425–437 (2009)
69. Fierley, R., Engl, S.: User experience methods and games: lessons learned. Proc. HCI **2010**(24), 204–210 (2010)
70. Hsu, K.J., Babeva, K.N., Feng, M.C., Hummer, J.F., Davison, G.C.: Experimentally induced distraction impacts cognitive but not emotional processes in think-aloud cognitive assessment. Front. Psychol. **5**, 474 (2014)

71. Van Den Haak, M., De Jong, M., Jan Schellens, P.: Retrospective vs. concurrent think-aloud protocols: testing the usability of an online library catalogue. Behav. Inf. Technol. **22**, 339–351 (2003)

72. Nielsen, J., Clemmensen, T., Yssing, C.: Getting access to what goes on in people's heads? reflections on the think-aloud technique. In: Proceedings of the Second Nordic Conference on Human-Computer Interaction, pp. 101–110 (2002)

73. Braun, V., Clarke, V.: One size fits all? what counts as quality practice in (reflexive) thematic analysis?. Qual. Res. Psychol. 1–25 (2020)

74. Braun, V., Clarke, V., Terry, G.: Thematic analysis. In: Liamputtong, P. (ed.) Handbook of Research Methods in Health Social Sciences, pp. 843–860. Springer Nature Singapore (2019)

75. Braun, V., Clarke, V.: Thematic Analysis - An Introduction. Bristol, UK (2018)

76. Braun, V., Clarke, V.: Using thematic analysis in psychology. Qual. Res. Psychol. **3**, 77–101 (2006)

77. Furman, O., Mendelsohn, A., Dudai, Y.: The episodic engram transformed: time reduces retrieval-related brain activity but correlates it with memory accuracy. Learn. Mem. **19**, 575–587 (2012)

78. Sekeres, M.J., et al.: Recovering and preventing loss of detailed memory: differential rates of forgetting for detail types in episodic memory. Learn. Mem. **23**, 72–82 (2016)

79. Pinchbeck, D.: Ambiguity and abstraction in game writing: lessons from dear esther. In: Game Developers Conference. (2012)

80. Barlow, S.: Making her story - telling a story using the player's imagination. In: Game Developers Conference (2016). [https://www.gdcvault.com/play/1023430/Making-Her-Story-Telling-a]

81. Barlow, S.: Her Story. Self-published (2015)

82. Smith, P.: Hemingway's early manuscripts: the theory and practice of omission. J. Mod. Lit. **10**, 268–288 (1983)

83. Hemingway, E.: A Moveable Feast. Scribner's, Jonathan Cape, New York, London (1964)

84. Grinblat, J., Manning, C., Kreminski, M.: Emergent narrative and reparative play. In: Mitchell, A., Vosmeer, M. (eds.) ICIDS 2021. LNCS, vol. 13138, pp. 208–216. Springer, Cham (2021). https://doi.org/10.1007/978-3-030-92300-6_19

85. Arjoranta, J.: Interpretive Challenges in Games. Digital Games Research Assocation 2018, Turin, Italy (2018)

86. Wong, J., Foong, P.S., Mitchell, A.: Contemplative interactions: exploring the use of defamiliarization in a serious game to promote reflective thinking about personal health. In: Designing Interactive Systems Conference 2021, pp. 984–998. (2021)

87. Mitchell, A., Kway, L., Neo, T., Sim, Y.T.: A preliminary categorization of techniques for creating poetic gameplay. Game Stud. **20**(2) (2020)

88. Mitchell, A.: Antimimetic rereading and defamiliarization in save the date. In: DiGRA Conference (2018)

89. Mitchell, A.: Making the familiar unfamiliar: techniques for creating poetic gameplay. In: DiGRA/FDG (2016)

90. Mitchell, A.: Defamiliarization and poetic interaction in Kentucky route zero. Well Played J. **3**, 161–178 (2014)

When Has Theory Ever Failed Us? - Identifying Issues with the Application of Theory in Interactive Digital Narrative Analysis and Design

Hartmut Koenitz[1]([✉]) [ID] and Mirjam Palosaari Eladhari[2] [ID]

[1] Södertörn University, Alfred Nobels allé 7,141 89 Huddinge, Sweden
hartmut.koenitz@sh.se
[2] Stockholm University, SE-106 91Stockholm, Sweden
mirjam@dsv.su.se

Abstract. In this paper, we discuss how theories can fail us in analysis and design of interactive digital narrative (IDN) works. We demonstrate a range of theoretical failures using the milestone IDN work *Façade*. To this end, we demonstrate the effect of different theoretical lenses, treating *Façade* as an interactive drama, as a game, as a work of hypertext fiction, and as general IDN work. We identify different types of theory failures with regards to analysis, creation and audience reception: miscatogorization, blind transfer, bogus theory, semantic creep, analytical blur, out of date, lack of problematization, fallacy of universality, analysis-productive mistakes, inappropriate conventions, out of context, over-pragmatization, and setting the wrong expectations for audiences. Finally we propose a way to prevent theoretical failures and call for more work in this respective area.

Keywords: interactive digital narrative theory · interactive digital narrative design · interactive digital narrative authoring · interactive storytelling theory and design · theoretical failures · application areas of theory

'To a man with a hammer, everything looks like a nail' (Abraham Maslow)

1 Introduction

The creation and analysis of interactive digital narrative (IDN) works contains a question of theory, as the choice of theory effects both understanding and design. Therefore, which theory should be used? And what are the consequence of picking a theory? Is there a 'wrong' use of theory? Can theory mislead us? Even fail us? We propose a clear answer to this question: theory fails regularly and this is by design as any given theory is always limited in its scope. Yet, often

L. Holloway-Attaway and J. T. Murray (Eds.): ICIDS 2023, LNCS 14383, pp. 21–37, 2023.
https://doi.org/10.1007/978-3-031-47655-6_2

we do not notice, and this describes the real problem - that the nature of theory is widely misunderstood and its influence often ignored.

In this paper, we will consider the status of theory in interactive digital narrative research and development, its application, and the problems that we encounter as a result. In particular, we want to draw attention to 'theory failures,' a notion we will expand on.

When it comes to available theory for understanding IDNs, several options exist. There is a well-established body of narrative theory with roots in literary studies and film studies. As alternatives, there are proposals for specific theory, e.g. in the form of Murray's affordances and experiential qualities [38], Joyce's understanding of hypertext fiction [20], Montfort's perspective on interactive fiction [36], or Koenitz' SPP framework [24]. In practice we frequently see applications of theoretical frameworks inherited from legacy media such as drama, film and print, e.g. Propp's morphology [39], Aristotelian poetics [3] or Coleridge's concept of the "suspension of disbelief" [11]. The reliance on legacy lenses - theoretical perspectives originating with non-interactive works - has been denounced as "theoretical imperialism" [1] and we have described this practice previously as a forever repeating seemingly inescapable "Groundhog day" of interactive digital narrative research and teaching [27]. However, the consequences of using legacy theory have yet to be fully demonstrated, leading to the provocative question "when has theory ever failed us?" asked by a participant at ICIDS 2022 as a reaction to an earlier paper by us [25]. Indeed, we agree that our argument for "novel approaches" was lacking such a demonstration. In this paper, we pick up the gauntlet, discuss types of 'theory failures' and examine the results obtained by analyzing one of the most groundbreaking IDN works - *Façade* [33], with different theoretical lenses.

2   What Is Theory?

When we are asked to explain theory, we might resort to terms like "concepts," but after some reflection we can arrive at a provisional definition: Theory is the use of language to describe a phenomenon in an abstract manner so that it is applicable to more than a single instance and its explanatory capacity includes identification of elements, provision of vocabulary, classification, and the description of relationships between elements. Furthermore, theory facilitates the comparison of different instances of the same phenomenon. This is to say that theory provides insights that exceed direct observation and description.

It is worth noting that theory has different meanings in different academic areas. For example, in the natural sciences, a theory is an unverified hypotheses, which assumes the status of a law (of physics for example) once verified. For example, Einstein's theory of general relativity (developed between 1907 and 1915) was unverified until the British astronomer Arthur Eddington proved one of its central predictions, the deflection of light by gravity in 1919.

Theories in the context of human-created artistic artifacts such as narratives are different. They are heuristic, 'rules of thumb' and they draw their legitimacy from critical consideration by fellow scholars and continued application to analyze works, but not from verification through observation or repeat experiments. Such crucial differences in the status of theory are not pointed out often and clearly enough, especially in teaching. Yet, in a multidisciplinary effort such as interactive digital narrative, an understanding of the respective status of theory is crucial. Training in the humanities is mindful of the status of narrative theory, but academics and professionals with a background in the natural sciences might be tempted to misunderstand narratological approaches as proven laws of nature. Yet, neither Propp's "Morphology of the Folk Tale" [39] nor Aristotle's Poetics [3] are verified natural laws. Hence, their application as a foundation for work in computer science is non-trivial and can be problematic, in particular when the nature of such a framework is changed from analytical to productive. The effects of this conversion process are mostly overlooked so far.

3   What Is a Failure of Theory?

Theory is designed to cover particular phenomena and thus its scope is limited. What we call a 'failure' in this paper is thus technically an 'out of scope' problem which becomes a failure not because of the theory itself, but because of problematic applications which fail to recognize these limits. In this way, different things can go wrong. Maybe the most obvious failure of the application of theory is a categorical failure, when theory makes us see a type of artifact as different than it is. At the same time, theory can fail us in different contexts - for analysis, in the process of creating an IDN work and also, in its use by audiences. When an audience member approaches an interactive artifact in a particular manner, for example as a computer game, they apply an implicit theory of what a video game is.

Taking these three contexts (analysis, creation, audiences) as a basis, we distinguish the following failures of the application of theory.

Failures of theory for analysis

- Miscategorization (framing a work as something it is not)
- Blind transfer (application of models from different fields without adaptation)
- Bogus theory (claiming something which does not exist)
- Semantic creep (increasing vagueness of terms)
- Analytical blur (increasing vagueness of categories)
- Out of date (using outdated perspectives)
- Lack of problematization (failing to address theoretical issues)

In the analysis context, there is *miscategorization*, which happens when we understand for example an educational XR-experience as a video game and consequently misunderstand its specific qualities. A related issue is *blind transfer* - the direct application for example of literary theory to interactive digital narrative analysis without adapting to the changed affordances and context. *Bogus theory* applies when claims are made about non-existing aspects of works, e.g. freedom of movement or decision-making when these qualities do not exist. *Semantic creep* [25] is the failure to preserve the precise meaning of terms by applying it to cover more and more aspects. *Analytical blur* [25] describes the related failure to preserve the precise meaning of categories. *Out of date* refers to the failure of applying obsolescent theoretical perspectives, e.g. ones that have been superseded because of novel insights, fallacies or because of racist or misogynistic content. Finally, the failure of *lack of problematization* means to ignore theoretical issues and thus facilitate confusion and undeclared implicit theories.

Failures of theory for creation

- Fallacy of universality (the belief in universally applicable 'laws' of design)
- Blind transfer (application of models from different fields without adaptation)
- Analysis-productive mistake (taking an analytical framework as a productive one)
- Inappropriate conventions (use of conventions inappropriate for the design vision)
- Out of context (use of terminology/concepts valid in a different context)
- Over-pragmatization (theoretical framework is declared but mostly ignored)

In the context of creation (a term we take to include the notion of design and of authoring), *fallacy of universality* describes the failure to understand the specificity of a particular design context which is expressed in sentences such as this: 'the universal laws of narrative always apply.' *Blind transfer* is an aspect which also effects creators, e.g. by approaching an interactive production as a film production. The *analysis-productive mistake* is the failure of applying an analytical framework as a productive one, without understanding the different needs of production and analytical contexts. The failure of *inappropriate conventions* happens for example when stage drama conventions are applied to an interactive work without realizing that these run counter the design vision. *Out of context* describes the use of terminology or concepts without regard for the changed context of IDN. Finally, *over-pragmatization* describes the use of theory in a mostly ornamental role, meaning that theoretical positions are declared as a basis for creation, but are not realized during development.

Failures of theory for audiences

- Wrong expectations (setting expectations inappropriate for the type of work)

In the context of audience, the failure of *wrong expectations* means to trigger an inappropriate implicit theoretical framework in the audience. This issue can be caused by either side in the triadic relationship between creator, audience and work. A creator can produce incorrect expectations, the work can invite misunderstandings and audiences can project an incorrect framing onto a work.

4   A Test Case for Theory: *Façade*

Façade [33] is an IDN work created by Michael Mateas and Andrew Stern. In *Façade*, the interactor [38] visits friends Trip and Grace, whose marriage is falling apart. The interactor engages in conversations with the virtual characters and encounters significant objects in the 3D space of their living room. The experience proceeds depending on how the interactor chooses to react to the distraught couple, using textual input for conversations, movements within the 3D space as well as interactions with the available objects and the characters. *Façade* is a milestone work in the field of interactive digital narrative research and a good text case to investigate the effect of different theoretical lenses. As we will show, different theoretical approaches do not only produce different results, but also the theoretical failures we have previously described.

4.1   The Context of *Façade*'s Creation

Façade has been studied across a broad range of fields. At the times of it release, game studies had only recently been formed as a new research field of its own, and sub-fields of computer science interested in natural language processing (NLP) had emerged. The area of AI for games was developing to broader applications from a narrower focus on methods concerned with deep search for classical zero-sum games such as *Chess* and *Go*. *Façade* was created in this unique context, by developers who were concerned with using computation for artistic expression. Mateas had previously created *Office Plant no 1*, an AI-powered reactive art piece [6]. In addition, he had worked with the OZ project at Carnegie Mellon University [5] which was concerned with believable characters. At the time, the standard application of AI in games was to develop computational processes that would create the smartest possible opponent. Yet, in the case of *Façade*, the aim was to create character believability in Bates' sense [4] and in this regard, *Façade* succeeded, winning several awards and becoming an ubiquitous example at conferences on AI for games and interactive media. *Façade* was - and still is - a flagship for research endeavors in computational expression, especially for the way its underlying system processes interactors' typed input. Noah Wardrip-Fruin lauded the work as the realization of the "true dream of interactive drama," [47] creating "[...] an emotionally engaging, if frequently uncomfortable, interactive experience about the relationships between people." [47]

Façade's strongest impact in legacy disciplines is as a demonstration how a computational system can be used for artistic expression. This in turn paved the way for systems such as Versu [16] and Comme il Faut [35] , making works such as *Blood and Laurels* [44] and *Prom Week* [34] possible. With *Façade*, Mateas and Stern delivered an irrefutable proof that computation can indeed be used for artistic expression.

4.2 The Use of Theory During Creation: From the Poetics to Interactive Drama

The creators of *Façade* provide an explicit framing for the work as an interactive drama, a category of works first conceptualized by Brenda Laurel [30]. Michael Mateas came into contact with Laurel as a member of the OZ group at Carnegie Mellon University and was subsequently influenced by her work.

As we have pointed out previously [25], conceptualizing the structure of *Façade* as an "Aristotelian tension arc," [31] is problematic and represents both the theoretical failures of 'semantic creep' and 'analytical blur.' Aristotle confines his theoretical perspective to a particular form of Athenian drama, the tragedy, while neither the terms "tension," nor "arc" exist in the Poetics. In addition, the idea of a tension arc is more related to Freytag's dramatic pyramid [17]. Yet, in contrast to our earlier, more abstract criticism, we are now concerned with a more concrete question: what are the consequences of this theoretical framing for the creation of *Façade*?

First, we want to better understand Michael Mateas' conceptual framing for *Façade*, which he spells out explicitly [32]. Mateas traces the lineage of his framework from Aristotle to Brenda Laurel's conception of interactive drama and general interactivity as well as to Janet Murray's experiential qualities before detailing his integration of agency into Laurel's neo-Aristotelian interpretation of the Poetics. On this foundation Mateas lays out the plan for *Façade* as follows: "[...] a short one-act play [...] that provides the player with 15 to 20 min of emotionally intense, unified, dramatic action. The story should have the intensity, economy and catharsis of traditional drama." [32]

From a critical perspective on theory, there are several interesting aspects here: First, there is no distinction between 'interactive drama' and 'play' - which is an an *analytical blur* theory failure, as the theatrical play differs in many ways from an interactive experience on a computer or an AR installation. Secondly, aspects of 'traditional drama' are designated as goals for 'interactive drama' - a theory failure of the category of *blind transfer* - the application of models from another field without adaptation.

Furthermore, the creation of catharsis as an explicit goal for *Façade* is problematic. Aristotle understood this effect as the result of a particular relationship between the drama content and the audience. Catharsis is a product of the pity and fear the audience experiences when they see a tragic protagonist fail. According the Aristotle, audiences fear that what they see could happen to them too, and experience pity as the audience knows long before the protagonist that they are doomed, but is incapable to change the course toward their fate. It is difficult to reconcile this concept with interactive drama, where the audience is no longer in the role of an observer but are an active participant. An essential element of catharsis is in the inability to do anything but watch. We see this as a theoretical misconception - a theoretical failure of the type *out of context* - as Aristotle's conception of catharsis is not compatible with interactive conditions. In sum, we detect several issues when we apply our framework of theory failures to Mateas and Stern's conceptualization for the creation of *Façade*. This might be surprising, given the wide acclaim of the work and its deserved masterpiece status. This leads us to see *over-pragmatization* as the overarching theoretical failure in the creation process of *Façade*. We can say that the work is brilliant - somewhat counter intuitively - because at important junctures during its development the creators abandoned their own theoretical positions. However, this means that the creator's own theoretical framing is problematic and in terms of theory it would have been more productive to create a specific perspective, less dependent on earlier - and as we have shown - incompatible positions. In this regard, Brenda Laurel's original description of interactive drama as an an "experience [which] would afford the user pleasures that are both similar to and distinct from those offered by viewing or writing a play or by playing a video game" [30] is instructive. In terms of theory "both similar and distinct" means that according to Laurel, neither the theoretical frameworks of drama nor video games provide the full perspective on interactive drama.

4.3   How Do Others Conceptualize *Façade*?

The next step in our investigation of the effects of theory is the Wikipedia article on *Façade* [48]. The current Wikipedia entry describes it as "an artificial-intelligence-based interactive story." However, in the same Wikipedia article, *Façade* is also categorized as a video game in its very title "*Façade* (video game)," and labeled in the 'facts' sidebar as "interactive drama, interactive fiction, social simulation," where it is also assigned the mode of "single player."

Both 'video game' and 'interactive fiction' are theoretical failures of the type *miscategorizations* when seen in contrast to the authors' own conceptualization of the work as an "interactive drama" [31]. To understand how this categorical confusion came to pass, we need to consider the context of the time of *Façade*'s release in 2005. Research fields and genres we take for granted now in the 2020s had not yet formed. In the early 2000s, the field of digital games was much more in flux and new genres emerged frequently. First person shooters (FPS), massively multiplayer online games - MMOs - were already in their heyday. At the same time, mobile games that could be played on cell phones existed only in an nascent state (Apple's iPhone was introduced two years later), and casual games played via social platforms such as Facebook became popular. During this period, games emerged as a mainstream medium, and the game studies field was still in formation. This temporal connection is certainly one factor why *Façade* is so often categorized as a game even though its authors explicitly understood it as something different - an interactive drama. Another reason why *Façade* was often categorized as a game is probably because it was exhibited at venues where games were shown such as the 2004 Independent Games Festival and the 2003 Game Developers Conference.

A second issue from our list of theory failures is the lack of *problematization*. The mix of different categories is not addressed in the wikipedia article and thus no attempt is made to explain the confusing situation and what it means to apply these different categories for the understanding of the work. If we apply the theoretical lens of "video game" then we take the work for something it is not according to its creators. Yet, the editors of the Wikipedia page are not alone in disregarding the theoretical framing of the creators, since we can find a number of papers and articles which refer to *Façade* as a game [2,40,43].

4.4   *Façade* as a Video Game

So what does it mean to apply the theoretical lens of "game" to *Façade*?

We are keenly aware that no generally accepted, universal theory of games exist. Game theorists like Huizinga [19], Calois [10] or Sutton-Smith [45] rather provide elements towards a theoretical understanding and later theorists such as Katie Salen and Eric Zimmerman or Jesper Juul further add their perspectives and understanding to this canon.

An often used definition of 'game' is by Salen and Zimmerman from 2003: "A game is a system in which players engage in an artificial conflict, defined by rules, that results in a quantifiable outcome." [42]. A "quantifiable outcome" is usually tied to what players need to achieve in a game in order to win (a winning condition). Juul [21] expanded on the notion of quantifiable outcome in the same year. As a step toward understanding the nature of the rapidly emerging new form of computer games he proposed a narrowed-down definition of what a game is by looking at "classical" games such as chess. Juul defines a classic game as "a rule-based formal system with a variable and quantifiable outcome, where different outcomes are assigned different values, the player exerts effort in order to influence the outcome, the player feels attached to the outcome, and the consequences of the activity are optional and negotiable." (ibid)

If we apply these definitions to *Façade* and ask whether *Façade* is a game in the sense of Salen/Zimmerman or Juul, then the answer is a clear "no": Facade does not have an explicit quantifiable outcome. The relationship drama in *Façade* can end in several ways. As Michael Mateas described it: "How the facade of their marriage cracks, what is revealed, and the final disposition of Grace and Trip's marriage, and Grace and the player's relationship, depends on the actions of the player." [32] Mateas also explicitly rejects a particular pre-scipted role for the interactor as it exists in many video games:

> The player should not have the feeling of playing a role, of actively having to think about how the character they are playing would react. Rather, the player should be able to be themselves as they explore the dramatic situation. Any role-related scripting of the interactor (Murray 1998) [38] should occur as a natural by-product of their interaction in the world. The player should "ease into" their role; the role should be the "natural" way to act in the environment, given the dramatic situation.

These aspects paint a clear picture of "video game" as an theoretical failure of analytical *miscateogrization*, however, things become more complicated once we realize that a source of miscategorization is with the creators' own use of the term "player." An alternative for "player" was available with Murray's term interactor and if used, would have prevented some confusion. We can only speculate, but maybe the term player seemed to have a broader appeal, an important consideration given that Mataes and Stern attempted to commercialize their technology at the time.

The theoretical/conceptual framing as a video game also effects audiences in regard to expectations and resulting experience. By providing an opening for framing *Façade* as a game, some members of the audience will instead approach the activity of interacting with *Façade* as 'playing a game' and consequently add the 'missing' winning condition by setting their own goal, meaning they would consider to have "won" once they achieve their goal, for example that Trip and Grace get together again.

When *Façade* is played like a game, interactors don't let the drama unfold in the same way as when it is experienced like a drama, and they don't do whatever comes naturally to them as acting in their role as a guest - as intended by *Façade*'s creators. Instead, they consider every move they make, and the likelihood that their move might lead Trip and Grace to stay together. Hence, *Façade* can be a game if it is played as such, however this means the interactor is losing out on what makes *Façade* special. What we have here is the type of theoretical failure of *wrong expectations*.

Indeed, Nick Montford explicitly categorized *Façade* as not a game but "something closely related to it." [37] He sees the work as a significant advance in interactive digital narrative:

> [...] when things go right, which isn't all that difficult to achieve, they can go brilliantly right. Your conversation can take you in an exhilarating free ride over the Freytag diagram of Trip and Grace's soul-searching and their coming to terms with their relationship, a ride that is not just funny, but manages to be touching. And, it's a ride that you get to steer: once a good typist is keyed into the way to talk to Trip and Grace, he or she can provoke reactions, draw the conversation to different topics, side with one or the other character, and nudge the drama in different directions. [37]

4.5 *Façade* as Hypertext Fiction

We will now investigate the effects of the lens of constructive hyper fiction, a theoretical position first developed by Michael Joyce in 1995 [20], to *Façade*. This theoretical position is interesting for two reasons: first, because it is a well-developed, fully spelled-out specific theory of a form of IDN in contrast to the many different strands of video game theory. Secondly, this frameworks helps us to demonstrate the effects of a 'foreign' theory that is predicated on digital interaction and not simply an adaptation of more traditional perspectives.

Early on, Hypertext Fiction (HF) aligned itself with the 20th century literary Avant Garde and theories of poststructuralism. Specifically, HF theorists saw the digital medium as a means to overcome limitations inherent in the traditional forms of print literature [9].

Robert Coover further emphasized the participant's role as "co-writers" in the meaning-making process: "Hypertext reader and writer are said to become co-learners or co-writers, as it were, fellow-travelers in the mapping and remapping of textual (and visual, kinetic and aural) components." [12] Even closer to poststructuralist concepts is Bolter's later description of HF as disrupting "traditional views of the author as authority and of literature as an expression of mimesis." [8]

These statements align quite well with Mateas and Stern's stated goals for *Façade* (see Sect. 4.2) when it comes to the impact of the interactor on the experience and the variable outcome.

Joyce describes his theoretical vision of "constructive hypertext" as aspiring "to its own reshaping" where the audience is turned into "scriptors" (Roland Barthes' term for an author without the connotations of authority) empowered to create "oriented insertions" [13] - additions to the fictional world of an HF artifact. In more concrete terms, the interactor of a constructive HF would be able to change both the structure and the content, creating a contour, the "emerging surface of constructive text as it is shaped by its reading" [20]. This vision provides a theoretical framework to analyze and evaluate IDN works by asking whether they allow changes to both structure and content.

To answer this question in the case of *Façade*, we need to consider the elements provided by this work. *Façade* uses an AI framework to understand textual input and map it to available "beats" - narrative units containing pre- and postconditions and featuring pre-recorded voice acting. Beats are controlled by a drama manager function which fires up beats depending on their pre-conditions, as well as the current position in a predefined "Aristotelian tension arc" [31].

Mateas and Stern's beats might be related to Joyce's understanding of textual units or lexias. In the case of *Façade*, the interactor's textual input plays a major role in shaping the experience, in line with Joyce' vision, but this is where the similarities end. The existence of a predefined story arc means that the structure cannot be re-shaped. There are certainly varied individual trajectories, but no contours that emerge. To claim so would be a failure of *analytical blur* in terms of the mapping of lexias to beats. In addition, the relationship between textual input and pre-recorded voice acting in the beats is less flexible than what Joyce envisions for constructive hypertext.

Further, the HF-focused analysis emphasizes textual segmentation and linking as well as navigation in the resulting map of links and thus misses many important aspects of *Façade*. For example, visual representation of the location and characters, as well as navigation and non-verbal interaction with objects and the two characters in a 3d space. Even if we understand text in a specific humanities tradition to denote representation, Joyce HF theory lacks the granular understanding necessary to distinguish between the navigational choices of HF maps and the intricate movements and interactions of *Façade*'s intimate 3d space. Its application would thus create the theoretical failures of *miscategorization* (*Façade* is not a constructive HF) and *analytical blur* by blurring the difference between lexias and beats.

To make Joyce's theory productive for the analysis of a work like *Façade*, its categories would need to be redefined to include aspects beyond textual representation such as visuals and movement in 3D space.

5   A Specific Approach: The SPP Model

Finally, we consider a theoretical framework, which is positioned by its author (a co-author of this paper) as a general theory for different varieties of interactive digital narrative works: Koenitz' SPP (System, Process, Product) model [23,24] (See Fig. 1). Koenitz emphasizes the dynamic aspects of IDN works and thus understands them as *systems*. *Process* describes the engagement of the interactor with work, while *product* is the output. Further, he distinguishes between *objective product* (recording/playtrace) and *subjective product*, incorporating Eladhari's understanding of "retellings" [14]. Koenitz describes the system content as *protostory*; the sum of all potential narratives a given interactive digital narrative work contains. In addition, *instantiation* is described as a foundational aspect, since interactive digital narrative works require interaction to generate products - each product being an instantiated narrative. The SPP model understands narrative as used in cognitive narratology, as a mental frame for "mentally projected worlds" [18], open in principle to novel narrative expressions such as IDNs.

We will now consider whether the SPP model produces theoretical failures. Koenitz provides an analysis of *Façade* in his book [24, pp. 87–90], where he describes *Façade*'s protostory as an IDN system with the basic elements: *procedural components*, *assets*, *user interface (UI)*, and *narrative design*. According to Koenitz, *procedural components* here consist of a three-dimensional space of the apartment (in the sense of the rules which define what movements are possible), with a physics system. The AI functions responsible for recognizing textual input are also a procedural component as are the "beats" [31]. *Assets* are the 3D model of the apartment, as well as the graphics for props and the characters of Grace and Trip. Pre-recorded utterances provide additional material. The *user interface* affords movement in space as well as interactions with objects and characters through gestures. Finally, textual input enables the communication with the characters and the AI system behind it.

The *narrative design* in *Façade* combines a story arc implemented in the form of a drama manager program as well as the pre- and post- conditions of the different beats. *Narrative vectors*, an element of narrative design, are formed by the drama manager component as a response to the interactor's input and by consulting previously authored pre/post goals and distinct phases in the story. A narrative vector is completed for example when an interactor is kicked out, or when Grace and Trip reach the therapy part of the experience in which they can rescue their marriage (Fig. 1).

In terms of theoretical failures, the SPP model fares well - there is no miscategorization or blind transfer, due to the framework's more abstract position.

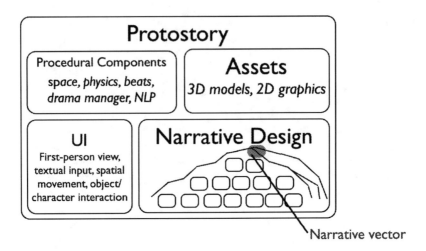

Fig. 1. Protostory Elements in *Façade*

Potential issues here are whether the model's categories might create analytical blur in specific cases, for example when the distinction between procedural components and UI becomes problematic.

6   Discussion

As we have shown, different theoretical approaches create different perspectives on the same work and can result in different types of failures (see Fig. 2). Adapted theoretical perspectives are especially susceptible to this effect, as terminology and categories originating in the analysis of non-interactive, traditional works are difficult to adapt and transfer to a novel context.

The point we are making is that regardless how we pass judgement on a theoretical question such as whether *Façade* is a video game or not, it is important to realize that the applied theoretical lens has consequences for creation, analysis and experience by audiences. A 'game' lens would differ from a drama lens for example, and the nature of the respective 'game lens' would also yield different perspectives.

Façade is an important milestone in field of IDN studies and game studies alike, and as such a work worthwhile of investigation in both fields. In this regard, we need to be aware of the considerable consequences from applying different theoretical perspectives. *Façade*, the interactive drama, is not the same construct as *Façade*, the video game.

In our analysis, the interactive digital narrative 'meta-framework' of the SPP model produces no theoretical failures for three reasons; first, it is designed from the onset to accommodate different types of IDN works. Secondly, it attempts to avoid the theoretical baggage of legacy frameworks. Third, the framework has been continuously developed since 2010 [22,23,41] - for example by the

Theoretical approach	Type of Application (Analysis, Creation, Audience)	Theoretical Failures regarding Façade
Interactive Drama	Creation	- Analytical blur: no distinction between 'interactive drama' and 'play', also "Aristotelian tension arc" (which also represent the failure of semantic creep) - Blind transfer: aspects of 'traditional drama' are declared the goal for 'interactive drama' - Out of context: Catharsis requires a different context - Over-pragmatization: theoretical positions are declared, but ultimately ignored
Wikipedia article (multiple theories)	Analysis	- Miscategorization: Façade is described as a video game and an interactive fiction work and as a social simulation - No problematization: the different theoretical approaches are not problematized and simply stated
Video game	Analysis, Audience	- For analysis: Miscategorization: the work is not a game according to the creators, but an interactive drama. The aspect of a missing winning condition further emphasizes this failure - For audiences: wrong expectations, due to 'playing to win' instead of experiencing as intended
Hypertext Fiction	Analysis	- Analytical blur: there are important differences between lexias and beats - Miscategorization: Façade is not a constructive hypertext fiction
SPP model	Analysis	No failures detected

Fig. 2. Overview of failures in different theoretical approaches to *Façade*

integration of the aspect of "re-tellings" [14] - to improve its usability, scope and precision as well as to incorporate feedback. However, this assessment does not mean that we consider the SPP model to be perfect. As any other theory, it can and will fail when applied to out of scope phenomena and it can only produce the insights it is designed to deliver.

6.1 Preventing Theoretical Failure

Maybe the best method to avoid theoretical failure would be to assess several theoretical perspectives in parallel. Such an approach would help to understand the respective shortcomings and provide a corrective to failures. Here, the multi-method analysis we proposed previously [15] is a promising approach.

The MMA approach entails gathering a number of experts who in a "jam" format analyze an artifact in groups, where each group uses a particular analytical approach for a few hours, and then compare their results. While an MMA jam is dependent on the collected expertise of its participants, it would certainly give a broader palette of theories to apply to a work than that of a single person. In 2022, an MMA workshop was hosted at the DiGRA Conference. Lenses used [26] include:

– Formal analysis of games, where the study of a game's specific elements are examined closely, and the relations of the elements are described in detail [29].
– Game Design Praxiology, that focuses on the actions of making a game [28].
– Analysis of play-experience, such as by close-playing [7], and [46] where the playing is part of the analysis method, carefully reflecting on how to whether to approach the the game as an object or a process, and specifying the context.
– Study of retellings, that is to examine what experiences from an IDN work that interactors find important enough to tell someone about in order to understand what about a game is meaningful to its audience [14].
– IDN theory, by examining the interactive narrative components of a work in terms of system, process and product [24]

So far, the MMA approach is missing any provisions to avoid unnecessary theoretical failures. In the light of the present discussion, the unqualified use of theoretical perspectives is problematic. The theories chosen for an MMA effort should be carefully selected and ideally produce the least amount of theoretical failures possible. What we propose is that MMA should add a first step of "vetting theoretical approaches" to avoid analytical methods which will result in a high number of theoretical failures. For example, the direct application of Aristotelian Poetics to IDN works would as a theory produce the theoretical failures of *miscategorization*, but would also be a *blind transfer*, is *out of date* and would produce both *semantic creep* and *analytical blur*.

7 Conclusion

So far, the capacity of theory to 'fail us,' to introduce a variety of issues in analysis, creation and audience reception has been under-researched. We acknowledge, that in principle, theory is never perfect, but rather an imperfect abstraction. Consequently, there is a need for increased awareness of the limits of theory in the IDN field and its status as designed frameworks with a particular explanatory aim, granularity, and scope. In this paper, we demonstrated how theories - or to be more precise: the application of theories - can fail us in analysis and design of IDN works. We first identified different categories of theory failures with regards to analysis, creation and audience: *miscatogorization, blind transfer, bogus theory, semantic creep, analytical blur, out of date, lack of problematization, fallacy of universality, analysis-productive mistakes, inappropriate conventions, out of context, over-pragamatization*, and setting the *wrong expectations* for audiences. Then, using *Façade* as an exemplar, we identified theoretical failures and applied our categories. As we have shown, the choice of theory has considerable consequences. We can only understand what the respective framework lets us understand and the limitations of any given framework will limit our understanding. We have made this point in a more abstract way before [25,27], but this paper contributes two crucial additions. First, a categorization of different types of theoretical failures in different application areas that facilitates a methodological reflection. Secondly, a concrete analysis of such failures using the milestone IDN work *Façade*. Our contributions are meant as first steps in this direction and a basis for application by other scholars. Our intention with this paper is to raise awareness of the issues and encourage others to follow up with further analysis and proposals for revision of our categories of failures. Another aspect ripe for future treatment is the question of the implicit use of theoretical positions by audiences. More work is needed this area to better understand how the framing of an IDN work affects its audiences.

References

1. Aarseth, E.J.: Cybertext. Johns Hopkins University Press (Sep, Perspectives on Ergodic Literature (1997)
2. Adams, E.: You Must Play Facade, Now! (Jul 2005), https://www.gamedeveloper.com/design/the-designer-s-notebook-you-must-play-i-fa-ade-i-now-
3. Aristotle: Poetics (c 335 BCE)
4. Bates, J.: The role of emotion in believable agents. Commun. ACM **37**(7), 122–125 (1994). https://doi.org/10.1145/176789.176803
5. Bates, J., et al.: OZ Project (1989)
6. Böhlen, M., Mateas, M.: Office plant #1: intimate space and contemplative entertainment. Leonardo **31**, 345 (1998). https://doi.org/10.2307/1576593
7. Bizzocchi, J., Tanenbaum, J.: Well read: applying close reading techniques to gameplay experiences. In: Well Played 3.0, pp. 262–290. ETC Press (2011)
8. Bolter, J.D.: Writing Space: The Computer, Hypertext, and the History of Writing. Lawrence Erlbaum Associates (1991)
9. Bolter, J.D., Joyce, M.: Hypertext and creative writing. In: Proceeding of the ACM conference on Hypertext - HYPERTEXT '87, pp. 41–50. ACM Press, Chapel Hill, North Carolina, United States (1987). https://doi.org/10.1145/317426.317431
10. Caillois, R.: Man, Play, and Games. The Free Press, Sociology/Sport (1961)
11. Coleridge, S.T.: Biographia Literaria; or, Biographical Sketches of My Literary Life and Opinions; and Two Lay Sermons. I. - the Statesman's Manual: II. - Blessed Are Ye That Sow beside All Waters, George Bell and Sons (1894)
12. Coover, R.: The End of Books. New York Times Literary Review (1992)
13. Eco, U.: The Open Work. Harvard University Press, Cambridge, MA, USA (1989)

14. Eladhari, M.P.: Re-Tellings: The Fourth Layer of Narrative as an Instrument for Critique. In: Rouse, R., Koenitz, H., Haahr, M. (eds.) ICIDS 2018. LNCS, vol. 11318, pp. 65–78. Springer, Cham (2018). https://doi.org/10.1007/978-3-030-04028-4_5

15. Eladhari, P.M., Koentiz, H.: MMAJams - Multi-Method Analysis of Games in Research and Education. In: Proceedings of the 2020 DiGRA International Conference: Play Everywhere. Tampere, Finland (2020)

16. Evans, R., Short, E.: Versu-A simulationist storytelling system. IEEE Trans. Comput. Intell. AI Games **6**(2), 113–130 (2014). https://doi.org/10.1109/TCIAIG.2013.2287297

17. Freytag, G.: Die Technik des Dramas. S. Hirzel, Leipzig, Germany (1863)

18. Herman, D.: Story Logic. U of Nebraska Press, Problems and Possibilities of Narrative (2002)

19. Huizinga, J.: Homo Ludens. Random House (1938)

20. Joyce, M.: Of Two Minds. Hypertext Pedagogy and Poetics, University of Michigan Press (1995), http://press.umich.edu/script/press/10599

21. Juul, J.: The Game, the Player, the World: Looking for a Heart of Gameness. In: Level Up: Digital Games Research Conference Proceedings, pp. 30–45. Utrecht University, Utrecht (2003)

22. Koenitz, H.: Towards a Theoretical Framework for Interactive Digital Narrative. In: Aylett, R., Lim, M.Y., Louchart, S., Petta, P., Riedl, M. (eds.) ICIDS 2010. LNCS, vol. 6432, pp. 176–185. Springer, Heidelberg (2010). https://doi.org/10.1007/978-3-642-16638-9_22

23. Koenitz, H.: Towards a specific theory of interactive digital narrative. In: Interactive Digital Narrative: History, Theory and Practice (2015)

24. Koenitz, H.: Understanding interactive digital narrative: immersive expressions for a complex time. Routledge (2023). https://doi.org/10.4324/9781003106425

25. Koenitz, H., Eladhari, M.P.: Approaches Towards Novel Phenomena. a Reflection on Issues in IDN Research, Teaching and Practice. In: Interactive Storytelling. LNCS, Springer (2022). https://doi.org/10.1007/978-3-031-22298-6_28

26. Koenitz, H., et al.: MMA Workshop Description. Krakow, Poland (2022), https://drive.google.com/file/d/1sCbAeprvJtDYNn2vgKbBLZwRtPKYMWpB/view

27. Koenitz, H., Eladhari, M.P.: Challenges of IDN Research and Teaching. In: Cardona-Rivera, R.E., Sullivan, A., Young, R.M. (eds.) ICIDS 2019. LNCS, vol. 11869, pp. 26–39. Springer, Cham (2019). https://doi.org/10.1007/978-3-030-33894-7_4

28. Kultima, A.: Game design praxiology. Ph.D. thesis, Tampere University, Finland (2018)

29. Lankoski, P., Björk, S.: Formal analysis of gameplay. In: Game Research Methods, pp. 23–35. ETC Press, Pittsburgh, PA, USA (2015)

30. Laurel, B.: Toward the design of a computer-based interactive fantasy system (1986)

31. Mateas, M., Stern, A.: Structuring content in the façade interactive drama architecture. In: AIIDE'05 Proceedings of the First AAAI Conference on Artificial Intelligence and Interactive Digital Entertainment, pp. 93–98. AAAI Press, Marina del Rey, California (2005)

32. Mateas, M.: A preliminary poetics for interactive drama and games **12**(3), 140–152 (2001). https://doi.org/10.1076/digc.12.3.140.3224

33. Mateas, M., Stern, A.: FACADE Project (2002)

34. McCoy, J., Treanor, M., Samuel, B., Mateas, M., Wardrip-Fruin, N.: Prom week: social physics as gameplay. In: Proceedings of the 6th International Conference on Foundations of Digital Games, pp. 319–321. ACM (2011)
35. McCoy, J., Treanor, M., Samuel, B., Wardrip, N., Mateas, M.: Comme il Faut : a System for Authoring Playable Social Models, pp. 158–163 (2010)
36. Montfort, N.: Twisty little passages: an approach to interactive fiction. The MIT Press (2003–12)
37. Montfort, N.: Not another one-room game set in an apartment! the society for the promotion of adventure games (2005)
38. Murray, J.H.: Hamlet on the Holodeck. The Free Press (1997)
39. Propp, V.: Morphology of the folktale. University of Texas Press (1968)
40. Rejack, B.: Toward a virtual reenactment of history: video games and the recreation of the past 11(3), 411–425 (2007). https://doi.org/10.1080/13642520701353652
41. Roth, C., van Nuenen, T., Koenitz, H.: Ludonarrative hermeneutics: a way out and the narrative paradox. In: Rouse, R., Koenitz, H., Haahr, M. (eds.) Interactive storytelling: 11th international conference for interactive digital storytelling, ICIDS 2018, pp. 93–106. The 3rd International Conference for Interactive Digital Storytelling (2018)
42. Salen, K., Zimmerman, E.: Rules of play: game design fundamentals. MIT Press (2003)
43. Schiesel, S.: Redefining the Power of the Gamer - The New York Times (2005), https://www.nytimes.com/2005/06/07/arts/redefining-the-power-of-the-gamer.html
44. Short, E.: Blood & Laurels. Linden Lab (2014)
45. Sutton-Smith, B.: The Ambiguity of Play. Harvard University Press (2001)
46. Van Vught, J., Glas, R.: Considering play: from method to analysis. Trans. Digital Games Res. Assoc. 4(2) (2018). https://doi.org/10.26503/todigra.v4i2.94
47. Wardrip-Fruin, N.: Expressive processing: digital fictions, computer games, and software studies. The MIT Press (2009)
48. Wikipedia: Façade entry. Page Version ID: 1161157295 (2023)

A Refinement-Based Narrative Model
for Escape Games

Mirek Stolee[✉]

University of Central Florida, Orlando, FL 32816, USA
`mirek.stolee@ucf.edu`

Abstract. This paper presents a model for comparing narratives in digital and non-digital escape games. The live-action escape room is a massive industry, but theoretical academic research on the games is lacking. Other forms of the escape game, including point-and-click games and portable escape boxes, are generally understudied. The cross-media genre of escape games has two parallel stories: the backstory embedded in the game's setting, and the player narrative that unfolds during play. These stories can be individually refined to different levels, creating four categories of escape games: puzzle games, thematic games, narrative games, and the newly identified setting-agnostic games. The model demonstrates how existing interactive narrative models can be expanded to include non-digital games, revealing commonalities and differences between escape game formats and illuminating future directions for escape game narratives. This work lays the foundation for future research investigating the relationships between narrative and space in various game formats. Finally, the narrative model has additional applications outside of the escape game genre. It can be used to analyze any interactive narrative's relationship with its fictional space, as well as the relationships between fictional and non-fictional space more broadly.

Keywords: Ontologies · Digital Narratives · Game Design · Analog Games

1 Introduction

In the genre of escape games, players are confined to a limited space and complete challenges that culminate in escape. Although there were earlier text adventure games with a similar format [1], the genre label seems to have been first applied to free point-and-click games produced in Flash. Escape games have now become a massive commercial industry in the form of the live-action escape room. In these analog games, players physically enter a designed space and use their bodies to directly interact with the game's challenges. A 2022 industry report found more than 1900 facilities in United States alone, and an international directory includes many more games [2]. Following the popularization of the escape room, new forms of escape games have emerged. The geenre has been adapted for virtual reality systems and portable formats have been designed to be played in homes and classrooms. Live-action escape rooms have become an increasingly common object of study, with many studies exploring their educational

L. Holloway-Attaway and J. T. Murray (Eds.): ICIDS 2023, LNCS 14383, pp. 38–53, 2023.
https://doi.org/10.1007/978-3-031-47655-6_3

potential [3–6]. Educational work has been applied to other escape games, such as virtual reality (VR) [7] games and escape boxes [8]. However, escape games, both digital and non-digital, are still understudied by scholars.

Despite industry interest in using escape rooms to tell stories, including an annual convention discussing the relationships between narrative, puzzles, and technology in these games [9], there is little scholarly work examining narrative in escape games. What work exists focuses on a single medium, most often live-action rooms [10, 11] or virtual reality games [7]. Even within the analog categories, however, escape games exhibit various degrees of digital integration. The escape game's proliferation onto a wide variety of digital and non-digital media offers an opportunity to build on existing IDN work exploring how narrative can be implemented within the constraints of specific games media [12–14].

This paper presents a method of categorizing digital and non-digital escape games that places scholarship on interactive storytelling in conversation with existing research on escape game narratives. The archetypal escape game narrative is a tale of escape from the game space. The term "escape room" contains the two crucial elements here: the room, or space, and the process of escape. This paper presents a narrative model for categorizing escape games based on these two components, providing insight not only into the various escape games, but also into the relationship between any interactive narrative and its setting.

2 Interactive Narratives Across Media

Narrative models differ in the media they attempt to cover. As a starting point, Koenitz et al. [15] provide a useful definition of Interactive Digital Narrative (IDN). They distinguish between the possible stories a computational system can generate, or protostory, and the instantiated stories, or products, that result from the interactive process [15]. Although the name itself excludes non-digital interactive narratives, IDN can accommodate non-digital works by expanding the purview of the term "computational system". In search of commonalities between digital and non-digital games, Jesper Juul [16] defines computation as the ways in which game rules are enforced. Non-digital games are computational systems powered by human thought, and therefore can be analyzed through the lens of IDN.

Marie Laure-Ryan's [17] broader view explores the commonalities between IDN and other narrative media. She draws on Aristotelian drama when defining what she calls "type[s] of story" [17]. She contrasts the epic plot, which follows a solitary hero as they perform physical actions to complete a quest, with the dramatic plot, which instead is concerned with the changing relationships between characters. A common structure for the epic plot is the Hero's Journey, which has specific tropes such as traversal of a larger world and a final confrontation with an antagonist [15]. The epic plot, although originating in other media, is commonly seen in video games following structures like the hero's journey [18]. The epic plot's myopic focus upon a single character and their ordeals means the other characters and their relationships are often shallow. The dramatic plot instead foregrounds these relationships and how they change over time.

To these two Aristotelian types, Ryan adds the epistemic plot, which is a combination of two stories. The first occurs before the events of the other, and the later story follows characters as they uncover those past events. The archetypical form of the epistemic plot is the mystery story. Existing mystery stories have been adapted to games, and there are many original detective games [19]. In interactive epistemic plots, the player often takes on the role of an investigator who needs to piece together past events to solve a mystery. Understanding the backstory is crucial for the player to succeed in the present. All three plots described by Ryan can be applied to both interactive and non-interactive narratives, but it is the epistemic narrative that serves as the foundation for this project's narrative model for escape games due to its emphasis on both space and narrative.

As the term "narrative" has historically been used to study non-interactive storytelling, however, it may carry unwanted connotations if applied wholesale to IDNs like escape games. Koenitz et al. thus warn against relying on story structures originally developed in non-interactive narratives [15]. Rather than attempting to develop frameworks that perfectly encompass narratives in all media, they argue, scholars should acknowledge the specific capabilities of different storytelling media. Some models focus on digital games exclusively, considering the complex interactions between narrative and gameplay that arise when designing computational systems [20]. Another model categorizes the ways in which players can interact with IDNs [21].

Espen Aarseth's narrative theory of games model [22] strikes a good balance between universality and medium-specificity by focusing on both analog and digital interactive media. Narratives in his model, regardless of medium, share four components: world, objects, agents, and events. A fictional world is populated with objects upon which agents can act. Events are moments of action in this world that form a narrative when strung together. Aarseth divides those events into kernels and satellites. Kernels are important events that define the story, whereas satellites are details that can be changed without making the story unrecognizable. These events are directly authored in non-interactive media, but in an IDN, a player may be able to influence satellites, kernels, or both. While Aarseth's theory includes both interactive and non-interactive narratives, his primary focus is on how these components change when interactivity is introduced.

In an interactive narrative, the events that take place are shaped by the player's influence over agents, objects, and the world. Players typically compel an agent to act on objects in the world. Aarseth's "world", hereafter referred to as the gameworld, describes concrete spatial structures that can be navigated by these agents. Such a world can be either physical or virtual extensions of what we might call a fictional universe, which contains all spaces that exist in a fictional reality. Within the gameworld, Aarseth further distinguishes ludic space from extra-ludic space. Ludic space is explicitly navigable by the player, versus extra-ludic space whose structure is modeled but is inaccessible to the player. Aarseth's four components will be considered the building blocks of narrative in the escape game model, but of particular importance is the ways in which the gameworld interacts with narrative.

3   Narrative and Space

Previous research has explored narrative's relationship to space in IDNs, considering how players can inhabit a gameworld and manipulate its objects. Studies of immersion and presence have been conducted both for virtual reality experiences [23] and analog games [24]. Hameed's and Perkis' theory [25] seeks to explain how players may feel immersed and present within a narrative space from an interdisciplinary perspective. Other research emphasizes the role of objects in storytelling. Echeverri and Wei describe "tangible storytelling", a IDN method that expresses its narrative through digital content mapped to physical space and objects [26]. Their project demonstrates that IDN theories can be applied to hybridized spaces that include both digital and non-digital components.

Ryan and Foote's study [27] analyzes several relationships between narrative and space. They examine how "narrative spaces," the settings in which a story takes place, are used in both static and interactive narratives [27]. The space occupied by the audience's bodies is the contextual space, which may or may not be the same as the narrative space. Ryan and Foote make a further distinction between the concepts of space and place. Space refers to physical properties of an environment, such as "location, position, arrangement, distance, direction, orientation, and movement" [27]. Space becomes a place when it has been shaped by human intervention. A gameworld has spatial properties, but not all parts of the gameworld are places. Fictional places have a history, shaped by past agents.

The history of a place can be revealed through traces of past events. The way a theatre set is arranged, its *mise-en-scene*, can tell the audience things about the characters who act within that space. In what Henry Jenkins calls "environmental storytelling," spaces can contribute to stories through their spatial arrangement, the objects that are included, and how those objects are positioned [28]. In his "embedded narratives", ones that use environmental storytelling, the gameworld and its objects are infused with narrative meaning through careful curation and arrangement [28]. The spaces have traces of human activity that indicate that activity to the present observer. Both professional narrative designers and scholars [29] are interested in the uses of environmental storytelling in traditional digital games. Environmental storytelling has also been applied to other games media, such as virtual reality games [30] and live-action experiences including escape rooms [31]. Environmental storytelling is especially useful for epistemic narratives. In an interactive epistemic plot, interactors "enact their narrative curiosity through the navigation of fixed narrative fragments of an unchangeable event" [19]. The plot requires the player to read into the properties of a place to determine past events within that place.

4 Escape Game Narratives

We may now use these frameworks to understand how escape games present narratives using their world, objects, agents, and events. Escape games are a cross-media genre of games that typically require players to complete a series of challenges within a specific space, using the objects within that space [10, 32–34].

I have previously distinguished between four subgenres of escape games based on the ways in which players relate to the game's objects: live-action, point-and-click, virtual reality, and tabletop escape games. [32]. I now prefer the term "escape boxes" [8] rather than "tabletop escape games" to describe tangible games that are not designed to be played in a specific physical space, including but not limited to tabletop games. A narrative framework for escape games would need to include each of these subgenres, both digital and non-digital, but this distinction is increasingly blurred. Shawn Fischtein's [35] generational taxonomy describes the degree to which digital technology is embedded within a live-action escape game. The most advanced Generation 4 rooms use digital sensors and computing software to automate game processes and enable new kinds of challenges. Even analog escape boxes may include digital elements. The *Unlock!* [36, 37] series of card games requires a mobile app to play. As the game's physical components include only cards, along with other paper objects, the app allows for challenges that those components do not afford.

Nicholson [10] builds on Fisctein's taxonomy with a four-stage "generational model" for narrative in escape rooms. In puzzle rooms, the focus is entirely on solving a series of puzzles – there is no specific setting, and the player takes on only the role of puzzle-solver. In the next stage, thematic rooms, the narrative is a story of escape from a specific place, like a prison. In the following generation, narrative rooms, players have defined diegetic roles and follow a quest-based structure toward a narrative resolution. Nicholson's final stage, hypernarrative rooms, may be a future direction for the industry. These games have not a single definitive narrative but instead branch based on player choices. Nicholson's framework is designed specifically for live-action escape rooms but can be applied to the broader genre of escape games by integrating it with Ryan's epistemic plot, Aarseth's theory of narrative games, and scholarship on space and narrative.

5   Refinement in Escape Game Narratives

Consider the two juxtaposed stories in Ryan's epistemic plot: the immutable backstory and the interactive story in the present. Although not every escape game's narrative is explicitly an epistemic plot, these elements are still present. The backstory is a narrative embedded in the game's space, while the player narrative unravels during play. The degree to which an escape game refines each of these stories drives the narrative experience of the game. Refinement, as described by Wardrip-Fruin, is a process through which an abstract concept becomes specific and concrete [38]. It is not a binary operation, but one with several stopping points. The backstory and player narrative can to an extent be refined individually, and each to varying degrees. Thus, we can create a model that categorizes escape games on two axes:

Escape games can be compared with one another based on the processes of *setting refinement* and *player narrative refinement*. These processes may occur individually or in tandem, resulting in games with strikingly different narrative experiences. This approach contextualizes Nicholson's generational categories and expands his model to include more forms of escape games, including a new category.

A puzzle game makes no attempt at refinement of either the setting or the player narrative. The players are in a generic room, and the narrative is that they must escape from that room for no other reason than the fact that it is an escape game. A thematic game is one in which the game's setting is defined but the game's narrative is comparatively vague. These games' settings fit within a particular type of space (pyramid, tomb, prison, etc.) but the narrative is simply escaping from that space. Narrative games feature both refined settings and refined player narratives. Players act within a defined world according to their roles and narrative goals.

Setting-agnostic games are a new category illuminated by this model. These games may give players roles and a clear objective to work toward, but the setting itself is not

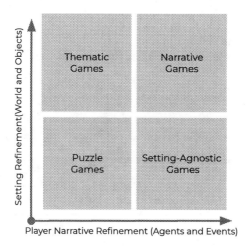

Fig. 1. A refinement-based model for escape game narratives.

especially important. *Escape Room in a Box: The Werewolf Experiment* [39], acknowledges that the game may be played in any setting. The box itself is framed as a diegetic package that upon opening releases a deadly toxin into the players' contextual space. The players must then complete challenges to retrieve the antidote. While each category in the model may appear to be monolithic, detailing the processes of refinement will illuminate the variations within the quadrants.

5.1 Setting Refinement

In an abstract sense, an escape game occurs in a room. Through refinement, that room shifts from space to a defined place. Both Nicholson and Hanssen et al. have previously used Henry Jenkins' narrative architecture to explore how a live-action escape room's space can contribute to a game's backstory [10, 11]. This paper further develops how backstory is expressed to the players through Aarseth's world and object components.

Moving along the world refinement axis requires supplying information that helps players interpret the gameworld. Contrary to the binary quadrants in the diagram, world refinement has at least two steps. Using genre conventions, the world can be refined to a category of place such as a bedroom, office, or bank vault. In this way, the setting becomes what Jenkins calls an "evocative space," one that relies on outside knowledge to contextualize itself [11, 28]. Such a place can be defined further by contextualizing that place in a broader geographic and temporal continuity. Setting refinement can occur in at least two ways: through the objects and the gameworld.

Refinement Through Objects. Objects in escape games act as signs that refine the game's setting. Fernández-Vara [40] builds on Jenkins' concept of environmental storytelling using Peirce's semiotic model. She describes how icons and signs communicate information to the player. The "Labyrinths of Egypt" level in the video game *Escape Simulator* [41] is marked with decontextualized hieroglyphs and sphinxes that convey a vague exoticist "Egyptness". Using icons and signs helps develop space into a more specific place by using markers with which the audience is assumedly familiar. One step of refinement is establishing the game's setting as a place that belongs to a particular category. The presence of cobwebs might evoke the concept of "haunted house," along with its associated cultural conventions. In these games, objects prompt players to interpret their surroundings as what Jenkins calls an "evocative space," which relies on outside knowledge of similar spaces to characterize itself [28]. The creators of the escape game *Sister Jill* reference evocative spaces to describe how their game's setting draws on genre conventions of horror movies to characterize their space as an unsettling church [11].

Objects can be used to go a step further. The third type of Peircean sign, the index, can make a game's sense of place more specific by implying past activity [40]. Hansson et al. differentiate between prospective objects which are used as clues during the escape room, and retrospective objects that act as fragments for the game's embedded narrative [11]. Retrospective objects serve as traces of activity in the fictional past of the game world. The selection of books on a shelf, for example, may invite the player to consider what kind of person curated that collection and why. These objects provide information that players can use to reconstruct the past actions taken by agents in the gameworld. Learning about the haunted house's tormented inhabitants through indices invites players to turn the game's setting into place. Through the players' interpretation of past events, a generic haunted house can become an inhabited place.

As creating place is a process of interpretation, the legibility of signs is important to setting refinement. The markers of a kind of place will be legible to some players and not to others. The way two people experience the same place, then, may be quite different. McDowell and Nicholson provide guidelines for reducing the "cultural bias" that limits an escape game's legibility and accessibility to players outside of the expected audience [42]. They provide guidelines for reducing ambiguity for players outside of the target audience. However, that does not mean designers cannot use signs from their locality. The design of some live-action escape rooms have been influenced by objects from the local region, such as Ameli's Roman cistern escape room [43]. These games take advantage of their physical location to tell local stories.

Refinement Through the Fictional Universe. The ludic gameworld is not the only way to refine a game's setting. Like Aarseth, Nicholson distinguishes between the accessible parts of a gameworld and the fictional universe [10, 22]. Information both inside and outside the room can contribute to the players' understanding of the gameworld and its place in its universe. Escape games take place in a small slice of a larger fictional universe, and defining that universe refines the setting. Before players see any of the game's objects, the process of creating place has already begun.

The game's name sets the stage. Some names refine the game's setting to only the broad categorical level, such as The Escape Game: Orlando's room *Prison Break* [44]. Others are more specific. The Great Escape Room's *Poker Night at the President's Bunker* [45] implies both the place's owner and perhaps a history of events that have taken place in the game's space. Paratexts like marketing descriptions also provide material for interpretation. *President's Bunker*'s description reads: "You must work together in a 60-min, high-stakes race to prevent nuclear Armageddon" [45]. This example addresses the universe outside of the gameworld, which is under threat of nuclear war, Nicholson identifies other factors like "customer service and the elements of the lobby" that can contribute to setting refinement [10]. The place that players create upon entering an escape game is thus pre-shaped by a myriad of texts and experiences surrounding the game.

The broad world of an escape game's setting might also be known by the players prior to playing the game. Escape games that are transmedia extensions of existing franchises may borrow the visual language of that franchise. Paul Booth describes how the *Doctor Who Experience*, a branded escape room, includes in-universe objects familiar to *Doctor Who* fans, such as the "iconic scarf" belonging to the Fourth Doctor [46]. As the successful communication of placeness in these cases relies on these past experiences, however, the signs may be interpreted entirely differently by non-fans.

Spatial properties of the gameworld itself also communicate information. The dimensions and shape of a room's layout may resemble places the player recognizes, such as a western saloon or a bank vault. Implications of events and areas outside of the gameworld can also expand the player's understanding of the fictional world. Nicholson describes how a telephone without a dial tone in the escape room, accompanied by a note suggesting that a nearby explosion cut the phone line, could develop places outside of the room [10]. The gameworld becomes more specific by defining its relationship to the rest of the fictional universe.

5.2 Player Narrative Refinement

As the player narrative is the series of events that the players experience during the game, even the most simplistic puzzle rooms have a narrative. This is a narrative only in the most abstract sense. The typical escape game narrative is a barebones epic plot: there is a room, and players must escape from it. In his 2015 survey of escape room facilities, only 16% of respondents had abstract rooms in which escaping the room is the only narrative goal [47]. We can categorize these as simple epic plots. The point-and-click game's solitary hero takes physical action, completing several tests and then being rewarded through escape. Refining the player narrative means imbuing these story beats with meaning. Like setting refinement, player narrative refinement begins with vague ideas, continues into genre-level refinement, and ends with a more specific narrative. Nicholson [10] invites designers to "ask why" the players must complete each challenge, and answering this question using the game's events and agents refines the player narrative.

Refinement Through Events. Each challenge the players overcome constitutes an event in the player narrative. The basic kernels of these stories include the players entering a space, completing challenges, and ultimately exiting the space. These events are given narrative meaning through framing and structure.

One method of refining the player narrative is by framing it within a fictional genre that may replace these generic kernels with more specific ones. Nicholson argues that establishing a fictional genre sets player expectations for what they will have to do in the room [10]. Framing the narrative within a genre provides the game's kernels with basic meaning. Genres identified by Nicholson's 2015 survey respondents [47] include "be[ing] an adventurer" (4%), conducting a heist (4%), and carrying out a military operation (2%). Perhaps unintuitively, escape is not always the primary narrative goal.

In Nicholson's sample, 30% of the games did not include escaping the room as part of its narrative [47]. As "escape" is only one of many possible narratives to refine the generic epic plot, designers are stretching the limits of the "escape" genre label itself.

Leading up to the game's narrative goal, the sequence of challenges determines the story's pacing and narrative structure. In Nicholson's model, advancing from a thematic room to a narrative room requires the implementation of a quest-based structure. This structure requires the interplay of game design and narrative design. The players complete a series of increasingly difficult challenges that culminate in a dramatic climax, following the dramatic arc. This structure satisfies basics of both game design and narrative; scaling difficulty is typical in video games, and the Western narrative arc is common in storytelling.

Positioning the typical Western narrative structure as the most "refined," however, incorrectly imply that other structures are inferior [15]. Other structures may be more appropriate in certain contexts. Epistemic plots were also common in Nicholson's survey: 9% of games had players investigating a crime or mystery, 5% solving a murder, and 4% gathering intelligence or espionage [47]. Other than the open structure, in which all content is accessible from the beginning, the structures Nicholson [47] identifies follow what Gasque et al. refer to as a "gated story structure" [19]. Challenges and narrative fragments are not available until previous challenges have been completed. The gradual discovery of past events is central to the epistemic plot, and a gated structure controls when revelations occur. Escape games also need not adhere to Western conceptions of narrative. Koenitz et al. [15] provide several story structures from beyond the Western literary tradition that could be applied in future escape games.

Refinement Through Agents. Defining the role of the player is key to providing narrative context for the story's kernels. As agents, the players drive the progression of the player story. In digital games, players typically take on the role of an avatar to act in the story, but the relationship between the player and the avatar can differ across forms of escape game. Nicholson claims that in live-action escape rooms, the player and the avatar are one and the same [10]. Players might play as themselves, or as a generic captive or adventurer. Similarly, point-and-click escape games similarly do not include much information about the player character. Some games like Takagi's *Crimson Room* [48] include a bit of first-person narration as they explore the room, but even in those cases the character's traits are not well defined. These characters resemble the unnamed protagonists of some adventure games in their lack of age, face, gender, or race [49].

The player's role as an agent can first be refined to an archetype. Players might take on roles such as detectives, robbers, adventurers, and other archetypes directly pertaining to the goal of the room. The player's role as a spy in the VR *I Expect You To Die 2* [50] drives that game's events, requiring players to disguise themselves and complete challenges such as protecting a prime minister during a theater show. In scriptwelder's point-and-click *Don't Escape* [51], the player takes on the role of a werewolf who must securely lock themselves within a room before they transform and destroy a nearby village Non-live-action escape games can cast the player as an agent whose body does not match their own. In VR game *A Fisherman's Tale* [52], players take on the role of a small puppet who can change sizes to explore a surreal lighthouse. The protagonist of point-and-click *A Ruff Day* [53] is a dog who wants to go outside for a nap. These examples demonstrate that refinement in escape games is influenced by the medium.

The player's role may also be refined into a more established character. The short duration of the games can make it difficult to develop these characters, however. In one solution, transmedia extensions of existing franchises can draw on outside information for defining their characters. Card game *Unlock! The Adventurers of Oz* [54], for example, casts the players as the protagonists in L. Frank Baum's *The Wonderful Wizard of Oz* [55]. Like branded escape rooms that rely on players' understanding of the fictional world from related media, the characterization of these protagonists occurs primarily outside of the game.

Including agents other than the players can also add depth to the narrative, but this too differs across media. Escape games often do not include active characters beyond the players' avatar. When present, however, non-playable agents can be placed on their own spectrum of refinement. Aarseth distinguishes between generic bots with no individuality, shallow characters who have identities but simple personalities, and fleshed-out deep characters [22]. VR escape game *I Expect You to Die* [56] includes named allies that provide context for the mission, such as the player's handler, and antagonists like assassins, who have no individual identities. These characters are still limited by their programming, however. In live-action rooms, non-playable agents may be played by staff members that can react to player behavior more organically than current AI NPCs [34]. Similar to Aarseth's categorization of digital non-playable agents, Donley uses the categories of "observers," "bit characters," and "key characters" to describe the degrees to which these live-action agents are developed as characters and to which they are integrated into the narrative. Key characters, especially, can add emotional depth to a narrative. In a time-travel themed room Donley describes, players interact frequently with an actor playing a pop star. As "[t]he central narrative of the game was built around the pop star and their seemingly inevitable doom," attempting to save the character as they repeatedly face death may provoke an emotional attachment from the players [34].

6   The Future of Escape Game Narratives

As the settings and narratives of escape games continue to change, this model will still provide valuable insight. The range of stories told in escape games can expand by refining to unusual settings and player narratives. Wardrip-Fruin [38] sees a vast expansion of the topics video games are about as new tools have made games more accessible to create and easier to distribute. Escape games might take what he calls an alternative approach, which takes familiar game actions and places them in an uncommon domain.

An alternative approach may address Sawyer Kemp's [57] critique of patterns in live-action escape room narratives. Kemp argues that the prevalence of games set in prisons or life-threatening scenarios shows a tendency toward tragic, masochistic stories. They suggest that escape rooms tend toward "masculine endings," in the words of escape room designers they interviewed. Although the typical story tends toward "masculine endings" and settings, Kemp argues that escape games can tell stories that are neither tragic nor based around entrapment. They point to Aviki Games' *Escape the Dressing Room* [58], in which players play as actors who have a limited time to get dressed up and ready for their performance [57]. As "escape" as a narrative becomes less important in the live-action escape game space, new possibilities emerge. Escape games might also be used for social critique. Risa Puno's *The Privilege of Escape* [59] was an escape room art installation that attempted to explain social privilege using its mechanics. As two groups solved the same set of puzzles in parallel, one group had arbitrary rules constraining their actions that made it more difficult to complete the challenges [60].

The escape game structure may also change drastically. Nicholson is concerned with the replayability of live-action escape rooms [10]. Both the backstory and the kernels of the player narrative are static in the typically linear escape game. Additionally, facing the same puzzles for a second playthrough can be trivial. Live-action escape rooms are expensive to create and change, so if each player can only play each game once, escape rooms need a constant influx of new players to remain profitable.

Nicholson suggests the branching narratives of hypernarrative rooms as a possible solution to the linearity of escape games. Escape games with variable narratives do exist. *Unlock! The Adventurers of Oz* [54] ends with a choice that determines the ending, and even includes optional side content as variable satellites between playthroughs. These games require the creation of more content than a player will see in one play. In IDN terms, the protostory of the room must expand. This structure has implications for both the setting and player narrative of escape games.

As the player narrative is told through the sequence of challenges, the challenges themselves will have to change between playthroughs. Nicholson points to artificial intelligence technology that generates new puzzles every time as a potential solution. IDN research projects demonstrate methods for procedurally generating puzzles that integrate with a game's narrative [61]. A system like Fernández-Vara and Thomson's puzzle-dice system, designed specifically for adventure game puzzles, may be used to make an escape game's challenges unique to each playthrough [62].

Space could play a major role in branching escape games. Chris Hales describes how Cincera's interactive cinema piece *Cinelabyrinth*, set in a physical labyrinth, asks the audience to make choices by physically following the path corresponding to their decision [63]. This approach is a physical manifestation of what Murray and Salter call spatial mapping, a visualization of IDN that relies on the physical relationships between parts of the gameworld [64]. An escape game might include branching in its narrative through selectively extending the game's ludic space. The setting might also change over multiple playthroughs. Fernández-Vara suggests that indexical storytelling can provide new ways for players to engage with interactive narratives. Rather than only interpreting the signs included by the game's designers, players might be able to leave their own indices. Live-action escape game players leave traces like opened locked and drawers, but these are reset for the next group [11]. What kind of stories might be told using escape games that do not reset?

This paper's model also suggests new narrative directions for future games. Escape games might take on less common narrative structures. This paper, and Western narrative theory as a whole, has relied heavily on Aristotelian dramatic arcs for plot analysis, but other structures may be used [25]. Games could also be designed around the concept of replay, considering what the player experience might be like on subsequent playthroughs [65]. In a time-travel story, for example, the narrative structure could incorporate the actions of time-travelers over multiple playthroughs into one extended player narrative. Generative research may also be useful in generating escape game spaces. Existing projects present implementations of systems that generate gameworlds and populate those spaces with environmental storytelling objects [29, 66]. As escape games change, designers will still need to consider the refinement of the game's setting and narrative. Procedural generation requires careful consideration when designing the generator as that will influence the output. Generating settings and puzzles with separate systems may fail to produce consistency between them.

7   Future Work

This project applies theories from IDN to expand knowledge of the understudied escape game genre. Placing differently mediated escape games in direct comparison rather than in a generational model avoids the historiographical pitfalls of an evolutionary framing. Escape game history narratives [67, 68] tend to position the point-and-click games as a mere predecessor to the live-action games, but these games continue to be made and played. It also advocates for consideration of escape boxes and VR escape games, which are understudied in comparison to the live-action games. Future work on space and place in escape games can build on this framework by considering issues like immersion, presence, and embodiment. Its introduction of setting-agnostic games also invites analyses of the relationships between fictional and non-fictional settings. How might games recontextualize the spaces in which they are played?

This formal framework can also be a foundation for critical research. For live-action games, future work should consider more closely the relationship between the game's fictional space and its physical location. Silva [69] describes an inequitable spatial participation gap occurring in games that take place in existing spaces. Similar bias might occur in the case of geographically located live-action escape rooms. Stuit describes the experience of playing *Prison Escape*, which takes place in a former prison [70]. The fictional backstory of the escape game's place intertwines uncomfortably with the actual history of the game's building. Non-escape VR experiences counter similar ethical concerns when using real-life places [71, 72].

The refinement-based narrative model for escape games contributes to our understanding of storytelling across games media. Continuing to examine analog games and live-action entertainment in conjunction with digital games may provide insights for IDN. The model can also be used to analyze and design games outside of the escape genre. The "escape room" label becomes less descriptive as games present new narrative goals and format, but the relationship between other interactive narratives and their respective settings may be analyzed through this lens.

References

1. Wilson, J.: Behind Closed Doors (1988)
2. World of Escapes: All escape rooms in the world on the map. https://worldofescapes.com/countries. Accessed 06 July 2023

3. Friedrich, C., Teaford, H., Taubenheim, A., Boland, P., Sick, B.: Escaping the professional silo: an escape room implemented in an interprofessional education curriculum. J. Interprof. Care , 1–3 (2018). https://doi.org/10.1080/13561820.2018.1538941

4. Nicholson, S.: Creating engaging escape rooms for the classroom. Child. Educ. **94**, 44–49 (2018). https://doi.org/10.1080/00094056.2018.1420363

5. Vörös, A.I.V., Sárközi, Z.: Physics escape room as an educational tool. AIP Conf. Proc. **1916**, 050002 (2017). https://doi.org/10.1063/1.5017455

6. López-Pernas, S., Gordillo, A., Barra, E., Quemada, J.: Examining the use of an educational escape room for teaching programming in a higher education setting. IEEE Access. **7**, 31723–31737 (2019). https://doi.org/10.1109/ACCESS.2019.2902976

7. Pendit, U.C., Mahzan, M.B., Fadzly Bin Mohd Basir, M.D., Bin Mahadzir, M., binti Musa, S.N.: Virtual reality escape room: the last breakout. In: 2017 2nd International Conference on Information Technology (INCIT), pp. 1–4 (2017). https://doi.org/10.1109/INCIT.2017.825 7884

8. Veldkamp, A., Daemen, J., Teekens, S., Koelewijn, S., Knippels, M.-C.P.J., van Joolingen, W.R.: Escape boxes: Bringing escape room experience into the classroom. Br. J. Educ. Technol. **51**, 1220–1239 (2020). https://doi.org/10.1111/bjet.12935

9. Event Overview. https://realityescapecon.com/event-overview/. Accessed 05 July 2023

10. Nicholson, S.: Ask Why: Creating a Better Player Experience Through Environmental Storytelling and Consistency in Escape Room Design. Meaingful Play (2016)

11. Hansson, J., Eklund, M., Hellgren, J., Hlina, M., Perez, S.P., Niedenthal, S.: Sister Jill. Well Play. J. Video Games Value Mean. **10**, 81–108 (2021). https://doi.org/10.1184/R1/143769 74.V1

12. Eladhari, M.P., Lopes, P.L., Yannakakis, G.N.: Interweaving story coherence and player creativity through story-making games. In: Mitchell, A., Fernández-Vara, C., Thue, D. (eds.) Interactive Storytelling, pp. 73–80. Springer International Publishing, Cham (2014). https://doi.org/10.1007/978-3-319-12337-0_7

13. van Velsen, M., Williams, J., Verhulsdonck, G.: Table-top gaming narratology for digital interactive storytelling. In: Iurgel, I.A., Zagalo, N., and Petta, P. (eds.) Interactive Storytelling, pp. 109–120. Springer, Berlin, Heidelberg (2009). https://doi.org/10.1007/978-3-642-10643-9_15

14. Acharya, D., Mateas, M., Wardrip-Fruin, N.: Interviews towards designing support tools for TTRPG game masters. In: Mitchell, A., Vosmeer, M. (eds.) Interactive Storytelling, pp. 283–287. Springer International Publishing, Cham (2021). https://doi.org/10.1007/978-3-030-92300-6_26

15. Koenitz, H., Di Pastena, A., Jansen, D., de Lint, B., Moss, A.: The myth of 'universal' narrative models. In: Rouse, R., Koenitz, H., Haahr, M. (eds.) Interactive Storytelling, pp. 107–120. Springer International Publishing, Cham (2018). https://doi.org/10.1007/978-3-030-040 28-4_8

16. Juul, J.: The game, the player, the world: looking for a heart of gameness. level digit. Games Res. Conf. Proc. 30–45 (2003)

17. Ryan, M.-L.: Interactive narrative, plot types, and interpersonal relations. In: Spierling, U., Szilas, N. (eds.) Interactive Storytelling. pp. 6–13. Springer, Berlin, Heidelberg (2008). https://doi.org/10.1007/978-3-540-89454-4_2

18. Vosmeer, M., Schouten, B.: Interactive cinema: engagement and interaction. In: Mitchell, A., Fernández-Vara, C., Thue, D. (eds.) Interactive Storytelling: 13th International Conference on Interactive Digital Storytelling, ICIDS 2020, Bournemouth, UK, November 3–6, 2020, Proceedings, pp. 140–147 (2014). https://doi.org/10.1007/978-3-319-12337-0_14

19. Gasque, T.M., Tang, K., Rittenhouse, B., Murray, J.: Gated story structure and dramatic agency in Sam Barlow's telling lies. In: Interactive Storytelling: 13th International Conference on Interactive Digital Storytelling, ICIDS 2020, Bournemouth, UK, November 3–6, 2020, Proceedings, pp. 314–326. Springer-Verlag, Berlin, Heidelberg (2020). https://doi.org/10. 1007/978-3-030-62516-0_28

20. Cardona-Rivera, R.E., Zagal, J.P., Debus, M.S.: GFI: a formal approach to narrative design and game research. In: Interactive Storytelling: 13th International Conference on Interactive Digital Storytelling, ICIDS 2020, Bournemouth, UK, November 3–6, 2020, Proceedings, pp. 133–148. Springer-Verlag, Berlin, Heidelberg (2020). https://doi.org/10.1007/978-3-030-62516-0_13

21. Carstensdottir, E., Kleinman, E., Seif El-Nasr, M.: Towards an interaction model for interactive narratives. In: Nunes, N., Oakley, I., Nisi, V. (eds.) Interactive Storytelling, pp. 274–277. Springer International Publishing, Cham (2017). https://doi.org/10.1007/978-3-319-71027-3_24

22. Aarseth, E.: A narrative theory of games. In: Proceedings of the International Conference on the Foundations of Digital Games, pp. 129–133. Association for Computing Machinery, New York, NY, USA (2012). https://doi.org/10.1145/2282338.2282365

23. Lum, H.C., Greatbatch, R., Waldfogle, G., Benedict, J.: How immersion, presence, emotion, & workload differ in virtual reality and traditional game mediums. In: Proceedings of the Human Factors and Ergonomics Society Annual Meeting, vol. 62, pp. 1474–1478 (2018). https://doi. org/10.1177/1541931218621334

24. Farkas, T., Wiseman, S., Cairns, P., Fiebrink, R.: A grounded analysis of player-described board game immersion. In: Proceedings of the Annual Symposium on Computer-Human Interaction in Play, pp. 427–437. Association for Computing Machinery, New York, NY (2020). https://doi.org/10.1145/3410404.3414224

25. Hameed, A., Perkis, A.: Spatial storytelling: finding interdisciplinary immersion. In: Rouse, R., Koenitz, H., Haahr, M. (eds.) Interactive Storytelling, pp. 323–332. Springer International Publishing, Cham (2018). https://doi.org/10.1007/978-3-030-04028-4_35

26. Echeverri, D., Wei, H.: Letters to José: a design case for building tangible interactive narratives. In: Bosser, A.-G., Millard, D.E., Hargood, C. (eds.) ICIDS 2020. LNCS, vol. 12497, pp. 15–29. Springer, Cham (2020). https://doi.org/10.1007/978-3-030-62516-0_2

27. Ryan, M.-L., Foote, K.E., Azaryahu, M.: Narrating Space/Spatializing Narrative: Where Narrative Theory and Geography Meet. Ohio State University Press (2016)

28. Jenkins, H.: Game design as narrative architecture. In: Wardrip-Fruin, N., Harrigan, P. (eds.) First Person: New Media as Story, Performance, and Game, pp. 118–130. MIT, Cambridge; Mass (2004)

29. Nielsen, T.L., Rafferty, E.I., Schoenau-Fog, H., Palamas, G.: Embedded narratives in procedurally generated environments. In: Bosser, A.-G., Millard, D.E., Hargood, C. (eds.) ICIDS 2020. LNCS, vol. 12497, pp. 30–43. Springer, Cham (2020). https://doi.org/10.1007/978-3-030-62516-0_3

30. Feng, R., Gao, M.: Videnda: Environmental Storytelling in Virtual Reality

31. Hall, L.E.: Environmental Narrative: Telling Stories in Spaces Without Saying Anything Aloud. Game Developers Conference (2019)

32. Stolee, M.: A Descriptive schema for escape games. Well Play. J. Video Games Value Mean. **10**, 5–28 (2021). https://doi.org/10.1184/R1/14376974.V1

33. Wiemker, M., Elumir, E., Clare, A.: Escape room games. Game Based Learn. **55**, 55–75 (2015)

34. Donley, R.: Character is key. well play. J. Video Games Value Mean. **10**, 55–72 (2021). https:// doi.org/10.1184/R1/14376974.V1

35. Spira, L., Fischtein, S.: Escape Game Technological Generations: Interview with Shawn Fischtein [Interview]. https://roomescapeartist.com/2016/06/05/escape-game-technological-generations-interview-with-shawn-fischtein-interview/. Accessed 12 Dec 2018
36. Bruyant, A., Demaegd, C., Servais, Y.: Unlock! The Noside Show (2019)
37. Malone, A.: Unlock! Expedition: Challenger (2019)
38. Wardrip-Fruin, N.: How Pac-Man Eats. The MIT Press (2020)
39. Patel, J.M., Rubin, A.: Escape Room in a Box: The Werewolf Experiment (2016)
40. Fernandez-Vara, C.: Game Spaces Speak Volumes: Indexical Storytelling. MIT Web Domain (2011)
41. Studio, P.: Escape Simulator (2021)
42. McDowell, S., Nicholson, S.: Players' accounts of cultural bias in escape rooms. Well Play. J. Video Games Value Mean. **10**, 29–54 (2021). https://doi.org/10.1184/R1/14376974.V1
43. Richardson, J.: Creating an Escape Room in a Heritage Site. https://www.museumnext.com/article/creating-an-escape-room-in-a-heritage-site/. Accessed 02 July 2023
44. The Escape Game: Orlando: The Escape Game Orlando. https://theescapegame.com/orlando/, https://theescapegame.com/orlando/escape-rooms/prison-break/. Accessed 25 Apr 2023
45. The Great Escape Room: Poker Night at The President's Bunker Providence Escape Room. https://thegreatescaperoom.com/providence/rooms/bunker. Accessed 25 Apr 2023
46. Booth, P.: Between fan and player. Pop. Commun. **20**, 16–28 (2022). https://doi.org/10.1080/15405702.2020.1772972
47. Nicholson, S.: The State of Escape: Escape Room Design and Facilities. Meaningful Play (2016)
48. Takagi, T.: Crimson Room. https://www.addictinggames.com/strategy/crimson-room (2004)
49. Reed, A.A., Murray, J., Salter, A.: Adventure Games: Playing the Outsider. Bloomsbury Publishing USA (2020)
50. Schell Games: I Expect You To Die 2 (2021)
51. scriptwelder: Don't Escape (2019)
52. InnerspaceVR: A Fisherman's Tale, (Oculus Quest 2)
53. Yurika! A Ruff Day (2023)
54. Cauët, T.: Unlock! The Adventurers of Oz (2018)
55. Baum, L.F.: The Wonderful Wizard of Oz. G.M. Hill Company (1900)
56. Schell, G.: I Expect You To Die (2017)
57. Kemp, S.: Escape Rooms and the Seductive Ubiquity of Capture. Analog Game Stud. X, (2017)
58. Aviki Games: Escape the Dressing Room (2017)
59. Puno, R.: The Privilege of Escape (2019)
60. The Privilege of Escape. https://creativetime.org/the-privilege-of-escape/. Accessed 06 July 2023
61. De Kegel, B., Haahr, M.: Procedural puzzle generation: a survey. IEEE Trans. Games. **12**, 21–40 (2020). https://doi.org/10.1109/TG.2019.2917792
62. Fernández-Vara, C., Thomson, A.: Procedural generation of narrative puzzles in adventure games: the puzzle-dice system. In: Proceedings of the the third workshop on Procedural Content Generation in Games - PCG'12, pp. 1–6. ACM Press, Raleigh, NC, USA (2012). https://doi.org/10.1145/2538528.2538538
63. Cinelabyrinth: The Pavilion of Forking Paths. https://www.springerprofessional.de/en/cinelabyrinth-the-pavilion-of-forking-paths/15220776. Accessed 06 July 2023
64. Murray, J.T., Salter, A.: Mapping the unmappable: reimagining visual representations of interactive narrative. In: Hargood, C., Millard, D.E., Mitchell, A., Spierling, U. (eds.) The Authoring Problem: Challenges in Supporting Authoring for Interactive Digital Narratives, pp. 171–190. Springer International Publishing, Cham (2022). https://doi.org/10.1007/978-3-031-05214-9_11

65. Mitchell, A.: Writing for replay: supporting the authoring of kaleidoscopic interactive narratives. In: Hargood, C., Millard, D.E., Mitchell, A., Spierling, U. (eds.) The Authoring Problem: Challenges in Supporting Authoring for Interactive Digital Narratives, pp. 131–145. Springer International Publishing, Cham (2022). https://doi.org/10.1007/978-3-031-05214-9_9

66. Smith Nicholls, F., Cook, M.: That darned sandstorm: a study of procedural generation through archaeological storytelling. In: Proceedings of the 18th International Conference on the Foundations of Digital Games, pp. 1–8. Association for Computing Machinery, New York, NY (2023). https://doi.org/10.1145/3582437.3587207

67. Escape the Room: History of Escape Room Games. https://escapetheroom.com/blog/history-of-escape-room-games/. Accessed 25 Nov 2018

68. 5th Street Escape Room: The History of Escape Games. https://5thstreetescaperoom.com/the-history-of-escape-games/. Accessed 06 Mar 2023

69. Silva, C.: Spatial participation gap: towards a conceptual perspective on locative storytelling creation. In: Rouse, R., Koenitz, H., Haahr, M. (eds.) ICIDS 2018. LNCS, vol. 11318, pp. 563–576. Springer, Cham (2018). https://doi.org/10.1007/978-3-030-04028-4_67

70. Stuit, H.: Carceral projections: the lure of the cell and the heterotopia of play in prison escape. In: Turner, J., Knight, V. (eds.) The Prison Cell. PSPP, pp. 305–325. Springer, Cham (2020). https://doi.org/10.1007/978-3-030-39911-5_14

71. Barbara, J., Koenitz, H., Bakk, Á.K.: The ethics of virtual reality interactive digital narratives in cultural heritage. In: Mitchell, A., Vosmeer, M. (eds.) ICIDS 2021. LNCS, vol. 13138, pp. 288–292. Springer, Cham (2021). https://doi.org/10.1007/978-3-030-92300-6_27

72. Fisher, J.A., Schoemann, S.: Toward an ethics of interactive storytelling at dark tourism sites in virtual reality. In: Rouse, R., Koenitz, H., Haahr, M. (eds.) ICIDS 2018. LNCS, vol. 11318, pp. 577–590. Springer, Cham (2018). https://doi.org/10.1007/978-3-030-04028-4_68

Social and Cultural Contexts

IDNs in Education: Skills for Future Generations

Jonathan Barbara[1,3](✉) ⓘ, Hartmut Koenitz[2] ⓘ, Breanne Pitt[3] ⓘ, Colette Daiute[4] ⓘ, Cristina Sylla[5] ⓘ, Serge Bouchardon[6] ⓘ, and Samira Soltani[7] ⓘ

[1] St. Martin's Institute of Higher Education, Hamrun, Malta
jbarbara@stmartins.edu
[2] Södertörn University, Huddinge, Sweden
hartmut.koenitz@sh.se
[3] School of Computer Science and Statistics, Trinity College Dublin, Dublin, Ireland
pittb@tcd.ie
[4] Graduate Center, City University of New York, New York, USA
cdaiute@gc.cuny.edu
[5] Research Centre On Child Studies; ITI/LARSyS, University of Minho, Braga, Portugal
cristina.sylla@ie.uminho.pt
[6] Université de Technologie de Compiègne, Compiegne, France
serge.bouchardon@utc.fr
[7] Toronto Metropolitan University, Toronto, Canada
samira.soltaani@torontomu.ca

Abstract. Interactive Digital Narrative (IDN) literacy and authoring skills are being gained too late along a typical student's educational journey and only by a niche subset of learners while such skills are crucial to consume modern day media communications reporting on complex phenomena from multiple perspectives. This paper acknowledges the impact of technology on teaching and learning methods as well as the current status of digital media in education and uses them to explain how IDN can be used to teach K-12 subjects with the aim of helping students attain IDN literacy skills. It also suggests ways to expand IDN literacy by adding authoring skills. The paper connects these overarching goals with current initiatives in establishing IDN literacy and authoring skills in the K-12 curriculum and presents short-, medium- and long-term objectives towards the above two aims.

Keyword: Interactive Digital Narratives · K-12 Education · literacy · authoring

1 Introduction

The World Economic Forum is intent on providing better education and new skills to 1 billion people by 2030[1]. Amongst their initiatives is the *Schools of the Future* report [1] which identified eight critical characteristics of high quality future-proof learning.

---

[1] https://initiatives.weforum.org/reskilling-revolution/

L. Holloway-Attaway and J. T. Murray (Eds.): ICIDS 2023, LNCS 14383, pp. 57–72, 2023.
https://doi.org/10.1007/978-3-031-47655-6_4

Among these are *global citizenship skills*, *innovation* and *creativity*, *technology*, *personalized* and *self-paced learning*, and *accessible* and *inclusive learning*. With today's complex narratives and underlying problems, traditional storytelling techniques fall short of conveying the multiple perspectives necessary to understand the systemic nature of modern society. On the other hand, Interactive Digital Narratives (IDNs) are better equipped to provide an experiential understanding of the complex narratives of modern society [2]. On this background, we might wonder why exposure to IDN literacy and authoring education is delayed until the final years of undergraduate study or even at postgraduate level after many years of education through single-perspective narratives. If K-12 education (i.e. Kindergarten to 12th Grade) has unilinear 'creative', informative, and argumentative writing as the pillars of literacy, why are IDNs not part of every learner's skill set in order to help them cope with modern society and its complex narratives?

During the Association for Research in Digital Interactive Narratives (ARDIN) general meeting held as part of the ICIDS online conference in Bournemouth, 2020, an idea emerged to push IDN literacy further down the education curriculum to help produce IDN analysts, scholars, and designers that can assist future generations cope with the complex realities that surround them. This idea attracted the interest of IDN scholars engaged in education as well as IDN students and undergraduate alumni who focused on IDNs in their final year projects, to form a committee and push this idea forward.

In this paper, we present the vision of the committee and work of its members seeking to engage with the ICIDS community whose collaboration we seek to push IDNs down the K-12 curriculum. We first contextualize the use of IDNs in education within related research. Then we describe some existing applications of IDNs in K-12 education that serve as starting points and further motivations for the committee. Finally, we share the short- and long-term objectives that were discussed during meetings of this committee in order to spread this initiative further and invite conversations that may further steer the direction of this endeavor.

1.1 Aims

The committee presents two general aims that have short-term and long-term objectives. The aims revolve around K-12 skills in consumption (experiencing and reflecting upon) as well as authoring IDNs. Both are elements of IDN literacy [2] and have been shown as being highly interlinked [3]. They should thus be addressed together while clearly demarcating these roles and their contributions in education. These aims are:

Aim #1: To identify ways how we can use IDN to teach K-12 subjects in order to help students attain skills in consuming IDN,

Aim #2: To identify ways how we can teach IDN skills to K-12 students in order to help them attain IDN authoring skills.

2 Related Research

Novel methods and technology are regularly introduced in formal educational settings. Examples include "flipped classrooms" [4] and "blended learning" [5, 6] methods, as well as the introduction of laptops and tablets alongside gamification and adaptive learning systems. At the same time, new technology by itself does not result in improved education. Instead, new technology needs to be paired with matching educational concepts and implemented together.

2.1 Teaching with Technology

The flipped classroom shifts the content delivery to home studying before and after the lesson, leaving contact hours for problem solving and application of the main ideas [4]. Blended learning combines face-to-face learning with online learning [5] allowing learning to scale out while providing individuals with the ability to pace their learning [6], especially with the development of MOOCs in 2008 [7] and the response to challenges offered by the COVID-19 pandemic [8], particularly in non-Western cultures [9, 10]. The use of technology in and outside the classroom facilitates novel approaches, for example gamified learning, by incorporating game elements and mechanics into the learning process to build upon the learners' experiences with such technology for leisure and entertainment purposes. Gamification includes the use of educational video games, simulations and interactive activities designed for more immersive and enjoyable learning. Gamification does not always succeed however, with at least one research study identifying negative effects such as loss of performance, declining effects across time, indifference and undesired behavior [11]. Indeed, introducing technology into the classroom is not just about adding a 'magic ingredient'. It turns out that the use of technology in the classroom often does not live up to the hype and rhetoric surrounding it, hampered also by the teachers' lack of alignment of pedagogical models with the technology's potential [12].

Thus, adopting technology in education requires careful planning and design of impactful applications of interactive techniques afforded through technology that allows for self-paced and personalized learning. Adaptive learning systems use technology and algorithms to build a model of goals, preferences and knowledge of each individual learner in order to personalize their learning experience [13, 14]. These systems assess a student's strengths and weaknesses and provide customized content, feedback, and recommendations to optimize their learning journey. While such systems lend themselves more easily towards computer science programmes as the subject being taught is native to the medium through which it is being delivered, technology is a means that is available in all subjects. Indeed, with educators of different subjects across the globe having to adapt and shift their lessons online during the COVID-19 pandemic [15–18] and general applicability of technology in education has become apparent. In addition, as technology pervades all aspects of daily life, an increased need for digital literacy exists for the 21st century citizens, and many related initiatives already exist in the educational sector [19].

This context presents a fertile ground for the application of IDNs to education at different levels and in different subjects. Building on the flipped classroom concept, IDNs can replace or complement recorded lectures and video clips with interactive experiences of the subject matter, allowing the learner to delve deeper into subject areas allowing for a personalized learning experience. Blended learning affords a guided navigation of the subject matter as students are led through the educational content in class for more in-depth and slow-paced revision outside the classroom. Using the fictional nature of IDN artifacts to present simulations of real-world scenarios, these works can provide a safe exploratory experience of the subject matter at hand, be it a physics experiment, a biology dissection lesson or a historical re-enactment of a cultural ceremony. Through their interactive nature, IDNs offer an adaptive learning platform that can provide personalized learning opportunities that can be customized according to education level and accessibility requirements.

However, IDNs offer opportunities beyond those offered by gamification, role playing, and other types of simulations in education. IDNs as systemic, dynamic, and reactive narrative expressions [2] can make use of these approaches, by combining and extending them under a unified perspective. IDNs, through their ability to portray multiple perspectives, can provide holistic representations of a subject matter without trivializing its complexity or falsely projecting a singular truth. IDNs afford replays that reveal more information with each session, allowing the student to engage deeper with the subject free from the bias of a singular perspective. Thus IDNs should be given priority in the classroom as they help create future citizens with the ability to negotiate the complex times ahead [2].

2.2 Teaching about IDN

Teaching with IDN is only one side of the equation. The other side is teaching about IDN, enabling a critical understanding of the advantages and limitations of this mediated expression by educators and learners alike. This involves engaging with a number of key IDN artifacts that are appropriate for the learners' age and subject, but also includes IDN authoring to gain full IDN literacy. This aspect has been a gap in education and members of the committee have been particularly active to address it. Their work is presented next.

IDN use in education can integrate and adapt learning principles to this novel context. Interacting principles of IDN pedagogy design include identifying digital media affordances as relevant to learning capacities and challenges in relation to societal circumstances [20]. Implementing innovative learning activities with such interacting principles may be more feasible than formal mainstream educational settings. However, interactive education may be also transferrable to mainstream education. Examples in this regard are dynamic storytelling workshops across countries separated by a decade of wars which illustrate this integration of digital affordances to address learning capacity/challenges in relation to societal circumstances [20].

Education in divided societies, such as during and after war, political revolution, or changing socio-political ideologies can draw on teens' intense social motivations, willingness to experiment, curiosity about diversity, and desire to right wrongs they perceive in society, as well as their often-unchallenged abilities for symbolic manipulation such as required with digital media creation. Dynamic storytelling workshops occurred in community education centers across the former Yugoslavia with a range of digitally-mediated narrative and other communication activities, implemented across the settings and adaptable to each local situation, such as with the diverse access to computers, internet connections, and young people's availability to engage in several hours of activities [21]. The workshops involved a variety of interactive digital tools for verbal and visual narrating, creating surveys, publishing, letter writing, and research. Although not IDN authoring in regard to using the full facilities of the interactive medium, the activity nevertheless shows the potential of related narrative-focused activities. The compilation of different youth collaborative expressions fostered non-linear sense making about challenges to youths' lives in their post-war contexts. One hundred thirty-seven youths in Bosnia and Herzegovina, Croatia, Serbia, and the United States participated in several activities to create local newsletter entries about problems and possibilities in daily life from the youth perspective.

A IDN authoring activity designed and implemented with science undergraduates [22] is also adaptable for use with students from middle school onward, depending on their prior work with digital media. To study the development of IDN design learning by undergraduates without prior digital design experience, a two-hour workshop was devised which involved a brief introduction to Twine[2] and subsequent turns in which participants designed an IDN and shared their experience playing a peer's emerging IDN design. Transcriptions of the player experience reflections and the final IDN designs indicated the students' ability to learn basic IDN design tools and the benefits from a player's reflections about the design [22]. College students were able to work through the process relatively independently, and younger students who may need a structured environment could benefit from doing such a process in lab or classroom settings. This will be possible in the near future based on an online implementation [22].

Several studies show the relevance of linking IDN consumption skills with IDN authoring skills, namely the analysis and interpretation of an IDN with its creation. For instance, in their study conducted in France with seven teachers in literature classes (11 year old to 16 year old students), Bouchardon and Brunel [3] show the mutual reinforcement of the analysis/writing links (links between IDN consumption skills and IDN authoring skills). The authors emphasize that the experience of production is called upon more than for other types of works. The conduct of a pedagogical sequence, with its various sessions, shows that the creation of a short IDN is an important part of the sequence and is directly linked to the resources worked on during the analysis phase of an IDN. The tools used are very different, and a considerable diversity of creative practices and formats can be observed: e-books, slideshows, hierarchical or branching narratives created with Twine, etc. But for each teacher, the chosen format is directly associated with the digital piece studied. The teachers aimed to encourage their students to transfer the various contents and forms studied in the digital works to their own production, and to do this using similar writing forms to those of the studied works. Overall, three main notions were transferred from the students' analysis of the IDNs to their own creation of an IDN: a sensorial and multimedia universe, animation and temporality (the different ways of playing with the notion of time), interactivity and author-reader relationship (between control and loss of control, grasp and loss of grasp).

---

[2] https://twinery.org/

2.3   Current Status of Digital Media in Education

Teaching digital media and incorporating digital media in education has become increasingly important in recent years. By integrating these aspects into the curriculum, schools can equip students with the skills, knowledge, and competencies necessary for success in the digital era [23]. These skills empower them to become responsible, informed, and ethical digital citizens who can navigate, contribute, and thrive in our increasingly digital and interconnected world.

Digital Media and Literacy Skills.   Digital Media is currently used as a tool to teach traditional literacy skills (reading and writing) in many K-12 schools. There are different regional and national standards around the globe for literacy, but oftentimes reading and writing falls under one of the following categories across disciplines: expository, argumentative, and creative writing. For example, the United States has adopted the Common Core State Standards (CCSS), a set of academic standards created to streamline learning across the States in Mathematics and English language arts/literacy in which the following Text Types and Purposes are specified for Grade 6:

> *"Write arguments to support claims with clear reasons and relevant evidence.*
>
> *Write informative/explanatory texts to examine a topic and convey ideas, concepts and information through the selection, organization, and analysis of relevant content.*
>
> *Write narratives to develop real or imagined experiences or events using effective technique, relevant descriptive details, and well-structured event sequences."* [24]

The anchors of CCSS literacy instruction involve developing informative, argumentative, and narrative writing skills. The focus is placed primarily on augmentative and informative writing, with narrative writing supported in the younger grades but ancillary in the upper levels.

Digital Media is used as an aid for teaching these literacy skills, and is recognized within the standards of the CCSS framework itself under Production and Distribution of Writing for Grade 6:

> *"Use technology, including the Internet, to produce and publish writing as well as to interact and collaborate with others; demonstrate sufficient command of keyboarding skills to type a minimum of three pages in a single sitting"* [24]

The CCSS places importance on using technology to produce and publish writing as well as to interact and collaborate with other students [25]. Therefore, digital media can be used as a tool to bridge the gap between more traditional methods of teaching and the contemporary student, making literacy skills more accessible to 21st century learners. Examples include digital filmmaking as a means to teach writing skills, the creation of customized learning materials through iBook Author, and more.

IDN has the potential to further support all three of these strands of traditional literacy, especially through the production and distribution of writing. Specifically, it can boost the production and publishing standard beyond simple "digital" aids, and instead help students become more creative and less linear in their writing process. Streamlining standards can lead to rigid writing structures, and IDN provides a means of countering this and encouraging higher-level learning.

At the same time, IDN's specific affordances and aesthetic qualities would be underused in this capacity. As a digital native form of expression, it can boost production and publishing standards beyond a simplistic use of "digital aids", and instead help students become more creative and explore interactive and dynamic forms of narration as means of representation for their own projects. In addition, streamlining standards can lead to rigid writing structures, and IDN provides a means of countering this and encouraging higher-level learning.

Use of Digital Media in Education during COVID-19. During the COVID-19 lockdowns schools across the world were forced to move to distance learning, transforming the teaching style from legacy, in-person teaching to digital, online learning practically overnight in the first quarter of 2020. This sudden and unexpected shift towards digital approaches in education brought about a multitude of challenges for teaching staff as well as students and parents who had to adapt to the technical requirement of virtual classrooms. With that, the discrepancy between households and individual students from different social backgrounds widened regarding conditions of confinement as well as access to equipment and secure internet connection, leaving many students disadvantaged compared to their peers [26, 27]. This shift highlights the pressing need for future educational programs to include teacher's training for producing online educational materials, and for online teaching styles that are more accessible.

IDN usage in digital education has the potential to bridge the digital gap to a certain extent, as they do not require specific, powerful devices or strong internet connectivity and allow students to experience them in their own time, thereby minimizing potential problems that occur when students share devices with other members of their household. IDNs created in software like Twine can even be consumed on mobile devices, making them accessible to a wider range of students whilst offering educators novel and powerful teaching tools.

The challenges of digital media in education are not limited to technological issues. For instance, teachers indicate that the presence of parents in the background has been a disturbance in the educational process and sometimes students felt disconnected from an online class discussion compared to their performance during in-person classes[3]. Furthermore, a research study in developing countries such as Palestine, Afghanistan, and Libya, demonstrates that unclear and limited concepts of digital inequity and digital ethics negatively impact students' engagement in online classes. Thus, education authorities need to develop a clear vision about digital privacy and accessibility which can alleviate parents' worries while their children access mobile phones for online education [28] but also provide access for all students.

However, even with the promotion of using digital media for teaching, pedagogical approaches are in need of improvements to fully capitalize on the potential of digital learning. To date, more than a third of classrooms are expected to be equipped with digital equipment for daily instruction in China[4]. Since 2010, the Chinese government

---

[3] https://media.shafaqna.com/news/498301/

[4] https://ncee.org/country/shanghai-china/

has piloted electronic school bags (e-SchoolBag) for educational tasks [13]. Initially, the e-SchoolBag plan was just the digitalization of textbooks. It has turned out to have more functionalities with the development of the "learning store" (similar to the App Store) [29]. However, teachers in China are critical to this new initiative as they normally evaluate students based on their traditional academic performance (scores) and prefer traditional teaching methods. The design of an IDN-based application could help students improve their grades in certain areas (e.g., academic writing) while providing instant feedback to assist both students and teachers in achieving their aims.

IDNs and Resultant Innovative Teaching Methods. Studies have shown how an innovative teaching object (namely an IDN) encourages and leads to innovative teaching methods. For instance, Brunel, Acerra and Lacelle [30] have recently conducted an exploratory study which describes how four French and Quebec high-school teachers have explored new teaching practices, by discovering and teaching an IDN (Florence, Annapurna 2018), which was a new object for them. The authors of the study looked at whether teaching a digital work can lead to the development of IDN literacy skills. The results showed that after studying the work *"the students developed specific skills, such as the ability to justify their choices of text animations in a production context or to identify possible gestures and actions depending on the technological environments"* (our translation).

Moreover, the study analyzed how the teachers considered the specific features of the digital work in their didactic sequences and how their choices have also led to evolutions, intended as innovations and recompositions, in their didactic plans and pedagogical implementations: "the approach to this innovative object has led to innovations: new teaching methods have been envisaged, more open to intermediality, subjectivity and reflexivity" (our translation).

Another project that took advantage of IDNs and introduced them into the K-12 classroom was the You&CO2 project which used the lesson-in-a-box concept to teach about climate change [31]. Lessons-in-a-box are a pre-designed set of lesson plans, activities, assessments, and rubrics according to a region's established curriculum framework that teachers can easily make use of in their classroom. Thus, even teachers with minimal technological training and environments resistant to "pilot projects" were able to implement it in their classrooms.

Artificial Intelligence and IDNs in Education. Artificial Intelligence (AI) has gained widespread popularity as a prominent digital technology in recent years [32]. However, it is currently seen as more of a hindrance to teaching, rather than an asset, as teachers cite issues with accuracy and plagiarism through the use of intelligent agents like ChatGPT [33]. However, we argue that this technology has the ability to assist in the mainstream integration of IDNs in the classroom. A significant issue regarding IDNs, specifically the creation of IDNs, is the time it takes to build an IDN system. Since IDNs involve interaction, system builders [34] are tasked with creating enough content for a user to explore multiple different perspectives/stories within a single system. Teachers notoriously cite time as a reason for not using digital technologies in the classroom [35]. While educators consider interactive digital storytelling as advantageous since it provides meaningful learning and is fun and motivational, a major disadvantage is that it is time-consuming and requires technological knowledge [36]. Therefore, the "time" it may take for a teacher or student to create an IDN system can provide a potential roadblock to integrating this technology in the classroom.

By using AI in IDNs, it is possible to cut back on the time-consuming IDN creation process. Specifically, AI can help generate dynamic and adaptive narratives based on user interactions, simulate intelligent and believable character behavior, generate and populate game worlds, levels, and narrative elements procedurally, and provide intelligent tutoring and feedback. Further research is required in this domain, highlighting the importance of interdisciplinary collaboration among researchers, authors, and software developers. This collaboration should prioritize user-centered design, incorporating user participation, and offering expressive tools that empower authors to craft impactful narrative experiences [37].

The incorporation of AI in education can have both reductionist and holistic effects, depending on how students and educators integrate these tools into the learning process. It is crucial to recognize this distinction, as an excessive reliance on generative AI may impede the development of critical thinking, analytical reasoning, and problem-solving skills [38]. However, the integration of AI in IDNs holds promise for addressing complex challenges and positively transforming education.

Finally, we need to be aware of the ethical aspects of the use of AI in IDN creation and thus adhere to and engage in the further development of ethics standards in the area [39].

3   Examples of IDNs in K-12 Education and Communities

In this section, we look at some projects that serve as proof of concept for the use of IDNs in K-12 education. These projects include communal and tertiary education settings that may be applied to K-12 through adaptation.

The *Mobeybou* materials are among some relevant examples of functioning IDN systems that are being used at school with pre- and primary school children [40]. The materials consist of (i) a tangible digital manipulative (DM) that uses tangible blocks to change digital story elements, (ii) a storyMaker, a fully digital version of the DM (that works without the physical blocks), and (iii) a set of interactive story apps. The materials are designed to work together and complement each other. Whereas the DM and the storyMaker are authoring tools, the apps provide information about the different elements represented in the authoring tools, feeding children's curiosity and narrative creation. Presently, the DM is composed of a total of 60 blocks (however this number can be easily extended) that represent eight cultures from around the world (Germany, Portugal, Turkey, Brazil, China, Cape Verde, and Angola). Each block represents a story element and has the respective visual representation on the upper face (see Fig. 1, left). Each cultural set is composed of seven elements, - a landscape, a girl and a boy protagonist, an animal, an antagonist, a musical instrument, and a magical object - that are representative of the depicted culture. There are also five blocks that trigger different atmospheric conditions (rain, snow, wind, thunder, and night), as well as music, sounds of the instruments and the characters (laughing, humming, yelling, shivering), and ambient sounds.

The blocks communicate with a computer or tablet via Bluetooth, and with each other through magnets embedded on the sides of each block (Fig. 1 left). Connecting the blocks to each other triggers its digital representation on a device screen. Each element has specific animations that display different actions, and animated narratives unfold according to the combination of blocks that the users connect to each other. The interactions between the narrative elements are defined based on Propps' structure of traditional Russian fairy tales [2]. The story world is modeled using behavior trees, such that different combinations of blocks result in the creation of a myriad of original narratives.

Fig. 1. The digital manipulative (left), and the storyMaker (right).

Children can change the scenario, mix, and remix all the elements across cultures, try out different plots, shift direction and start all over again. As the system provides visual and aural feedback in the form of sounds from the characters and music from the instruments, every child can imagine, and create their own spoken narratives, irrespective of their culture or language. A recording button allows recording/playing children's verbal narratives. The storyMaker is a digital version of the DM, and was developed to overcome the need of having the physical digital manipulative, this way boosting access to the tool.

Although related to the authoring tools, the interactive story apps can be used autonomously, offering themselves as full animated narrative experiences for children's meaning making. Each app presents a geographical map that locates the story in the world map, a 360° environment that incentivizes the children to move their device around to explore and visualize the full environment, a puzzle, a small game related to the cultural elements, an augmented reality (AR) page that offers children the possibility to print their own AR markers and bring the protagonists to life in their environment, and an incorporated glossary with keywords from the story and detailed information about the represented culture. The apps also help to provide context to the visual universe of the stories, informing the children about the country and feeding their imagination and promoting the construction of intercultural stories. The tools have been successfully used at school with primary school children (see Fig. 2).

Beyond attempts targeted at K-12 education, some pilot projects that aim to use IDN for educational purposes have been created in universities such as The *Gaming for Peace* project[5] which works towards conflict prevention and peace building. By role-playing

---

[5] https://gap-project.eu/

Fig. 2. Children using one of the apps (a) at school with the *Mobeybou* materials using a projection (b).

and making choices in a narrative-focused game, players are able to understand the challenges of a particular societal context, e.g., in terms of cultural norms and gender roles. As a result, people can gain soft-skills (e.g., gender awareness [7]) when working in environments other than the ones they grew up in. Another example could be the *Digital Humanities* + initiative [8], where media practitioners, researchers, local residences and audiences, as the online community for digital heritage, built an interactive documentary (i-doc). I-docs also have an educational function; through interactive video and gamification, people can participate in the learning of local history, for example by designing the batik (a particular Indonesian piece of clothing) motif. Adapting these ideas to the younger audience of the K-12 stage, some concerns such as ethical issues, customization, and policy adoption, would need to be addressed.

All of the above projects offer the opportunity for analysis in order to generate principles and evaluation techniques for future IDNs at K-12 level.

4 Next Steps for IDN in K-12 Education

Given the potential of IDN for education, and the concrete applications as described in the examples section, as well as existing efforts towards digitization in school systems worldwide, there is a considerable opportunity for IDN in education. In the following section, we sketch out a strategy for installing IDN in K-12 education.

4.1 Objectives

Short-term objectives include a rationale for introducing IDN in Education, identifying the target audience for such an endeavor, and a strategy on how the teaching staff would be involved.

A medium-term objective is to bring IDN literacy into K-12 education by providing early exposure to the notion of Interactive Narratives and fostering literacy in the education system. Currently there exists some work with pre-school children but then there is a big gap of no exposure until undergraduate and postgraduate levels. It is understood that prior to starting the teaching of pupils, their teachers need to be taught and trained on the matter, possibly through an IDN on how to use IDN in education.

A long-term objective is to develop a full Degree program in Interactive Narratives. Such programs need not be entirely supported by any one university but may also be a collaboration between institutions, such as falling under the EU Erasmus Mundus[6] program for joint master's programmes, for example, as well as international exchange programs.

4.2 Short-term Objectives

We start the conversation with a few points that address the short-term objectives and help situate, justify, and parametrize the committee's endeavor.

Rationale. A rationale needs to be built that caters to our target audience. It can be used to present our ideas to the policymakers and lay down the principles of Interactive Education to address educators (both teachers and parents). Presenting the transformative value of IDN for teaching and learning would go a long way in justifying its take-up in the K-12 curriculum, and this can be put into practice through activities that help us understand the dynamics of teaching and learning.

A driving motivation is the need for new narratives that represent the complexity of today's times. The Eurocentric universal story-arc is limited in its representational capacity and a new form of narrative is needed that affords dynamic mapping between cause and effect. This motivates the use of the IDN process for complex learning and thinking, allowing for playfulness, for discovery and for multiplicity in perspectives.

Different forms of storytelling need to be distinguished from the overused narrative structure so popular in films and should instead look at children's play-acting and how they negotiate around improvisations as contribution to child development [15]. IDNs can thus serve as scaffolding for constructivist learning teaching techniques wherein a pseudo-story can start off the lesson with initial content and then provide the students the opportunity to add content - both in class and outside school hours on an online community platform such as Discord, say.

While the introduction of IDN in K-12 education prepares the next generations to be conversant with such a medium, IDNs are also relevant to contemporary complex issues that merit multiperspectivity such as the capitalist construction industry vs environmental activists attempting to safeguard green areas and cultural heritage.

Target Audience. Identifying our target audience will help us articulate what we need as a convincing argument. Candidate members of our target audience are the policy makers and their advisory boards, if a top-down approach is to be taken, and teachers (existing and in-training, who might be more likely to carry the work forward) in case of a bottom-up approach. This may be possible with educational institutions that are flexible enough to allow teachers to perform pilot projects with students, who are the net recipients of this endeavor. Consequently, the third target audience will be their parents, especially in cultures where they are well involved in their children's educational development.

---

[6] https://erasmus-plus.ec.europa.eu/opportunities/opportunities-for-individuals/students/erasmus-mundus-joint-masters-scholarships

One must also consider the social dimension and seek target audiences that can benefit from having future generations educated in IDN literacy. These include situations where having multiple perspectives helps oppressive situations and their results to be better understood, such as the motivation of Somali pirates in *The Last Hijack Interactive* [16] and topics that are related to global warming such as responsible development in *Fort McMoney* [17]. Reframing the past is also a task in which IDNs can help today's generations re-interpret established history by looking at it from multiple perspectives.

4.3 Medium-term Objectives

Possible approaches that could facilitate the integration of IDN into the official school curriculum could be facilitated through the Official National Reading Initiatives (Reading Lists for schools), which are common in some countries. This is a strategy that the authors of the *Mobeybou* materials (the first example mentioned in Sect. 2 above) are pursuing, as the materials also include a series of dedicated story apps for children. Their strategy consists of contacting the responsible official authorities to include the story apps in the official Reading list for schools. Integration in the list provides an 'official quality stamp' promoting their use and integration in schools as well as their adaptation by informed and engaged parents. This then opens the door to using the other *Mobeybou* materials for IDN such as the digital manipulative and the *StoryMaker* since they dialogue and complement each other. Such could be a possible way to contribute to the integration of IDN in the school curriculum.

It would be presumptuous to think that IDNs can be applied to any topic in any subject, and thus one needs to explore how to go about applying IDNs into K-12 education. Which subjects, which lessons can best take advantage of IDNs? What changes are needed for existing lesson plans to integrate IDNs? What is the return on investment for the teacher's efforts? The better these questions will be answered the more people may become engaged with this approach and make it easier to adopt.

IDNs are a storytelling tool for multi-perspectivity and narrative complexity. They can therefore be conveniently used for subjects such as political studies, religious education, ethics, history, geography, and economics. These subjects in particular have the potential to benefit greatly from multilinear educational narratives, which consider different belief systems, ideologies, and points of view and would consequently allow for more diverse opinions that can generate engaging in-class discussions. Furthermore, by offering a multilinear teaching approach for commonly argued topics, teaching materials can become more inclusive. For instance, world history is likely to be taught through a Eurocentric lens in Western schools, however this approach cannot capture the complexity of the topics [18, 19]. This was for instance observed during an experiment in history classes in Norwegian schools where the result was that non-European history was often taught only in the context of European imperialism and colonialism [20]. Offering alternative narratives in teaching would allow topics to be dissected through multiple different critical lenses and thereby allow for other viewpoints to be amplified in the classroom. IDNs therefore have the potential to offer a device towards the inclusion of students of marginalized backgrounds, as their voices, heritage, and beliefs would be given more space within the curriculum and align with efforts in decolonization [41].

4.4 Long-term Objectives

The way forward is long and challenging but at the start of this endeavor it is important to identify routes that will help make IDNs a viable educational tool. These include reaching out to the educational research community as well as seeking collaborations and sponsorships from the technology industry to assist in dissemination.

Interdisciplinarity. The closure of schools to contain the COVID-19 pandemic in 2020 and in certain regions also in 2021 has forced the learning science community to focus their attention on the role of digital media in online learning [21–23]. Some drew their inspiration from the ICAP framework for designing learners' engagement with activities which lists interactivity as the most engaging mode of overt engagement behavior [24] while others took inspiration from the use of Narrative-centered learning environments in constructivist learning [25]. Such work lays the foundation for future attempts at reaching out to the learning science community, but their evidence-based approach suggests the need for increased efforts in empirical studies before attempting to approach that academic field.

Dissemination. In an ideal world there would be a roadmap in educational systems [42], which demonstrates what can be done in order to provide digital infrastructures for schools to harness the potential of digital media and IDN. This can be facilitated with the help of technology corporations to bridge the current digital gap across the world, because so far governments and educational systems seem unable to reach this goal by themselves. Furthermore, as mentioned, there is a need for trained technical staff to produce digital content and to aid progress in IDN related materials for schools, helping other teachers and employees to learn faster and to reach a better solution while facing challenges. As shortages in schools' budgets, which lead schools to neglect the need for services including consultation services, basic facilities for classrooms, food packages for students from disadvantaged backgrounds and so forth, make these goals difficult to tackle, the proposal of assistance from technology corporations in this matter would make it easier and more achievable.

5 Conclusion

Using IDNs to teach complex or multi-perspective subjects in K-12 education would provide a more holistic understanding of the topics, as well as provide future generations with the skills to handle and understand complex issues that abound in the modern society. Other important areas of application exist, for example in terms of fostering prosocial behavior and emotional intelligence in difficult situations. In order for this to happen, teachers need to be trained in IDN authoring skills to develop such IDNs for their topics. Extending these IDN authoring skills to the students themselves will raise a generation who can express their multiple perspective stories fluently to an audience who themselves will have developed their own IDN skills to understand them, resulting in IDN literacy. This is the challenge that this committee is taking up. Inspired by existing proof-of-concept IDN projects with younger audiences, scaffolding upon constructivist pedagogical approaches, heartened by the agile up-take of technology by teachers and students alike during the shift to online learning due to the COVID-19 pandemic and driven by its members' motivation, we look forward to sharing developments with the ICIDS community in the long, medium and, hopefully, short-term future.

References

1. World Economic Forum: Schools of the Future: Defining New Models of Education for the Fourth Industrial Revolution. World Economic Forum, Geneva (2020)
2. Koenitz, H.: Understanding Interactive Digital Narrative: Immersive Expressions for a Complex Time. Taylor & Francis (2023)
3. Bouchardon, S., Brunel, M.: Teaching literary interactive digital narratives in secondary education: a French study. In: Vosmeer, M., Holloway-Attaway, L. (eds.) Interactive Storytelling. ICIDS 2022. Lecture Notes in Computer Science, vol. 13762, pp. 101–120. Springer, Cham (2022). https://doi.org/10.1007/978-3-031-22298-6_7
4. Tucker, B.: The flipped classroom. Educ. Next **12**, 82–83 (2012)
5. Graham, C.R.: Blended learning systems. Handb. Blended Learn. Glob. Perspect. Local Des. **1**, 3–21 (2006)
6. Castro, R.: Blended learning in higher education: trends and capabilities. Educ. Inf. Technol. **24**(4), 2523–2546 (2019). https://doi.org/10.1007/s10639-019-09886-3
7. Liyanagunawardena, T.R., Adams, A.A., Williams, S.A.: MOOCs: a systematic study of the published literature 2008–2012. Int. Rev. Res. Open Distrib. Learn. **14**, 202–227 (2013)
8. Ashraf, M.A., et al.: A systematic review of systematic reviews on blended learning: trends, gaps and future directions. Psychol. Res. Behav. Manag. 1525–1541 (2021)
9. Tupas, F.P., Linas-Laguda, M.: Blended learning–an approach in Philippine basic education curriculum in new normal: a review of. Univ. J. Educ. Res. **8**, 5505–5512 (2020)
10. Mhlanga, D.: The fourth industrial revolution and COVID-19 pandemic in South Africa: the opportunities and challenges of introducing blended learning in education. J. Afr. Educ. **2**, 15 (2021)
11. Toda, A.M., Valle, P.H., Isotani, S.: The dark side of gamification: an overview of negative effects of gamification in education. In: Cristea, A., Bittencourt, I., Lima, F. (eds.) Researcher Links Workshop: Higher Education for all, pp. 143–156. Springer (2017). https://doi.org/10.1007/978-3-319-97934-2_9
12. Falloon, G.: Young students using iPads: app design and content influences on their learning pathways. Comput. Educ. **68**, 505–521 (2013)
13. Weber, G.: Adaptive learning systems in the World Wide Web. In: Kay, J. (ed.) UM99 User Modeling. CICMS, vol. 407, pp. 371–377. Springer, Vienna (1999). https://doi.org/10.1007/978-3-7091-2490-1_49
14. Ennouamani, S., Mahani, Z.: An overview of adaptive e-learning systems. In: 2017 Eighth International Conference on Intelligent Computing and Information Systems (ICICIS), pp. 342–347. IEEE (2017)
15. McQuirter, R.: Lessons on change: shifting to online learning during COVID-19. Brock Educ. J. Educ. Res. Pract. **29**, 47–51 (2020)
16. Rafi, A.M., Varghese, P.R., Kuttichira, P.: The pedagogical shift during COVID 19 pandemic: online medical education, barriers and perceptions in central Kerala. J. Med. Educ. Curricular Dev. **7**, 2382120520951795 (2020)
17. Oducado, R.M.F., Soriano, G.P.: Shifting the education paradigm amid the COVID 19 pandemic: nursing students' attitude to E learning. Afr. J. Nurs. Midwifery. **23**, 1–14 (2021)
18. Li, D.: The shift to online classes during the COVID-19 pandemic: benefits, challenges, and required improvements from the students' perspective. Electron. J. E-Learn. **20**, 1–18 (2022)
19. Reddy, P., Sharma, B., Chaudhary, K.: Digital literacy: a review of literature. Int. J. Technoethics (IJT). **11**, 65–94 (2020)
20. Daiute, C.: Educational uses of the digital world for human development. Learn. Landscapes **6**, 63–83 (2013)

21. Daiute, C.: Critical narrating by adolescents growing up in war: Case study across the former Yugoslavia. In: Narrative Development in Adolescence, pp. 207–230. Springer (2010). https://doi.org/10.1007/978-0-387-89825-4_11
22. Daiute, C.: Imagining the other in interactive digital narrative design education. In: Proposal to the PSC-CUNY Grant Series (2019)
23. Jackman, J.A., Gentile, D.A., Cho, N.-J., Park, Y.: Addressing the digital skills gap for future education. Nat. Hum. Behav. **5**, 542–545 (2021)
24. Association, N.G., others: Common Core State Standards. Washington, DC (2010)
25. Drew, S.V.: Open up the ceiling on the common core state standards: preparing students for 21st-century literacy—now. J. Adolesc. Health. **56**, 321–330 (2012)
26. Bonal, X., González, S.: The impact of lockdown on the learning gap: family and school divisions in times of crisis. Int. Rev. Educ. **66**, 635–655 (2020)
27. Bayrakdar, S., Guveli, A.: Inequalities in home learning and schools' provision of distance teaching during school closure of COVID-19 lockdown in the UK. ISER Working Paper Series (2020)
28. Khlaif, Z.N., Salha, S., Fareed, S., Rashed, H.: The hidden shadow of Coronavirus on education in developing countries. Online Learn. **25**, 269–285 (2021)
29. Hoel, T.: e-Schoolbag in China–exploring research evidence for large scale deployment of e-textbooks and services. In: 2015 IEEE 15th International Conference on Advanced Learning Technologies, pp. 454–455. IEEE (2015)
30. Brunel, M., Acerra, E., Lacelle, N.: Enseigner la littérature numérique au secondaire, entre innovation et sédimentation: analyse de cas autour d'une recherche collaborative. Tréma. (2023)
31. Rudd, J.A., Horry, R., Skains, R.L.: You and CO2: a public engagement study to engage secondary school students with the issue of climate change. J. Sci. Educ. Technol. **29**, 230–241 (2020)
32. George, A.S., George, A.H.: A review of ChatGPT AI's impact on several business sectors. Partners Univ. Int. Innov. J. **1**, 9–23 (2023)
33. Cotton, D.R., Cotton, P.A., Shipway, J.R.: Chatting and cheating: ensuring academic integrity in the era of ChatGPT. Innov. Educ. Teach. Int. 1–12 (2023)
34. Koenitz, H., Eladhari, M.P.: The paradigm of game system building. Trans. Digit. Games Res. Assoc. **5** (2021)
35. Hyndman, B.: Ten reasons why teachers can struggle to use technology in the classroom. Sci. Educ. News **67**, 41–42 (2018)
36. Gürsoy, G.: Digital storytelling: developing 21st century skills in science education. Europ. J. Educ. Res. **10**, 97–113 (2021)
37. Szilas, N.: Reconsidering the role of AI in interactive digital narrative. In: Interactive Digital Narrative, pp. 136–150. Routledge (2015)
38. Chan, C.K.Y., Hu, W.: Students' Voices on Generative AI: Perceptions, Benefits, and Challenges in Higher Education. arXiv preprint arXiv:2305.00290 (2023)
39. Koenitz, H., Barbara, J., Bakk, A.K.: An ethics framework for interactive digital narrative authoring. In: Hargood, C., Millard, D.E., Mitchell, A., Spierling, U. (eds.) The Authoring Problem: Challenges in Supporting Authoring for Interactive Digital Narratives, pp. 335–351. Springer (2023). https://doi.org/10.1007/978-3-031-05214-9_21
40. Sylla, C., et al.: Mobeybou-a digital manipulative for multicultural narrative creation. In: Extended Abstracts of the 2019 CHI Conference on Human Factors in Computing Systems, pp. 1–2 (2019)
41. Silva, C., Reyes, M.C., Koenitz, H.: Towards a decolonial framework for IDN. In: Vosmeer, M., Holloway-Attaway, L. (eds.) International Conference on Interactive Digital Storytelling, vol. 13762, pp. 193–205. Springer (2022). https://doi.org/10.1007/978-3-031-22298-6_12
42. Woolf, B.P.: A Roadmap for Education Technology (2010)

Centering the Human: Digital Humanism and the Practice of Using Generative AI in the Authoring of Interactive Digital Narratives

Joshua A. Fisher[(⊠)] [ID]

Center for Emerging Media Design and Development,
Ball State University, Muncie IN 47306, USA
`joshua.fisher@bsu.edu`

Abstract. This paper explores the application of chat-based Generative AI (GenAI) in the Interactive Digital Narrative (IDN) authoring process, advocating for a human-centered approach rooted in a Digital Humanist perspective. It scrutinizes GenAI's capacity to augment human narrative creation and unveils the complexities inherent in its integration into IDN authoring. The potential risks tied to GenAI's incorporation, including data exploitation, displacement of human labor, and the potential diminishment of human agency and creativity, are thoroughly examined. Offering a precautionary viewpoint, this work outlines Digital Humanist principles to guide GenAI's use in authoring, which includes elevating organic creativity and human agency. Further, emphasizing the need for transparency and accountability, the author underscores the importance of maintaining a harmonious, human-led creation process to serve the social good. The aim is to center the human elements of authoring while ethically leveraging GenAI's capabilities, paving the way for a future where IDNs embody collective human values and uphold creative integrity.

Keywords: Interactive Digital Narrative · Authoring · Digital Humanism · Generative AI · Ethics

1 Introduction

As chat-based Generative AI (GenAI) tools such as OpeanAI's ChatGPT, Google's Bard, Microsoft's AI-powered Bing, Midjourney, and more have entered mainstream use, anxieties about their potential impact on the creative industries have increased [1]. One of these anxieties is that GenAI will replace humans that are creative professionals. While such concerns are mainly hyperbolic, they identify a need to reflect on the relationships humans have with their AI production tools and their impact on the creative processes [2]. This relationship, mixed-initiative co-creativity, "assume[s] an autonomous computational system that explores the possibility space in its own ways as guided by human lateral decisions during the creative process, realizing and fostering human-machine co-creativity." [3] This "possibility space" could be authoring the system [4, 5], process [6, 7], and product [8] of an Interactive Digital Narrative (IDN).

L. Holloway-Attaway and J. T. Murray (Eds.): ICIDS 2023, LNCS 14383, pp. 73–88, 2023.
https://doi.org/10.1007/978-3-031-47655-6_5

The author utilizes David Thue's definition of authoring "to be a process of making and acting upon decisions about how some elements of a narrative (or perhaps many possible narratives) should be"[9]. Scholars and practitioners IDN have a history of exploring GenAI in a mixed-initiative co-creative authoring process as part of authoring platforms [9–13] and Interactive Emergent Narratives [6]. IDN scholars have used GenAI to engineer dramatic beats [14, 15], narrative events and structures [16], and interactor models [17, 18]. However, new interoperable GenAI tools—integrated with development and design engines like Unity, Unreal, and Blender—scale the impacts of computational creative initiative and constitute a new IDN authoring practice. As more GenAI are utilized in the IDN authoring process of an IDN system, the human author is displaced.

Hargood and Green have discussed that the author's user experience using IDN authoring tools has received little attention [19]. Their insights come at a valuable moment when the products generated by GenAI tools can supplant human initiative in the co-creative process. When integrated with existing IDN authoring tools, GenAI can scale the efficiency of authors and their resultant experience's complexity [11]. In such an instance, the authorial burden of authoring IDNs [20] is eased as GenAI are used as an intelligent narrative technology [9] to overcome bottlenecks in production [13]. This use of GenAI can occur in all stages of IDN authoring, from ideation to post-production [21]. However, as a byproduct, less human authoring is required as various production tasks are automated. This shift in labor alters the creator's authoring experience and can diminish human creative initiative and the novelty of created experiences [2].

In response, the author outlines and positions a Digital Humanist perspective on creators using GenAI as part of their IDN authorship. A Digital Humanist perspective emphasizes humanity's active role in the digital age, harnessing technology while retaining a focus on human values and dignity. The position empowers IDN creators to use GenAI in their mixed-initiative co-creativity processes while upholding a commitment to human creativity, wellness, and experience. By navigating the relationship between the affordances of GenAI and the humanist aims of narrative, the author outlines a vision of IDN authoring that centers the human creative initiatives while displacing the creative processes of GenAI. The article's central contribution is establishing a Digital Humanist perspective on using GenAI as part of IDN authoring.

1.1 GenAI as an IDN Authoring Tools

The way the author has discussed using GenAI in an IDN authoring practice crosses traditionally understood definitions of IDN authoring tools [9–11, 19]. Extending upon previous work [10], Shibolet and Lombardo define IDN authoring tools with three criteria. One, an IDN authoring tool comprises an independent and comprehensive workspace for IDN creation; two, the tool simplifies the authoring process; and three, a community of practitioners actively uses it [11]. According to this framework, chat-based GenAI tools are not IDN authoring tools. They afford procedural authoring, creating, designing, and developing as part of the creative process but are not used solely for IDN.

Further, the author does not invoke GenAI as an authoring tool in the same context as Kreminski and Mateas when they discuss Interactive Emergent Narrative (IEN). Their perspective is that of player-authorship [6], wherein the interactor's engagement with the

IDN system produces narrative meaning-making through an emergent process. Thue's inclusive definition of intelligent narrative technologies encompasses GenAI when such tools are used toward narrative ends [9]. Scaling Thue's recognition, the author positions GenAI as influencing the entirety of IDN authoring practices in the IDN system [2, 13, 22].

The latest The COST Action INDCOR (Interactive Narrative Design for Complexity Representations) paper proposes an action-thinking author model [23] with five phases that can all be influenced or automated by multiple GenAI tools. Ideation, meaning-making, and interaction can all be aided or automated by OpenAI's GenAI tools and plugins for code and design generation. Unity's AI Muse and Sentis can generate code, art assets, animations, and more for IDN authors [24]. Authors can validate their IDN experiences through generated and synthetic interactors [25]. Distributing the experience into an audience's hands is moderated by recommendation machine learning algorithms [26]. GenAI tools can increasingly edge human creative labor out of the IDN authoring process. However, this does not have to occur. The potential to pervasively use GenAI across all aspects of the IDN authoring practice impacts the resulting narratives [19], the creative initiative of human authorship, and requires perspective.

2   The Digital Humanist Perspective

Humanism is a philosophical stance that emphasizes the value and agency of human beings. Enduring in Humanism, the freedom of narrative expression and its necessity situate storytelling and the creation of narrative as innately human. Humans use narrative to communicate ideas [27, 28], understand identities [29, 30], and claim values [31, 32]. As storytellers, humans use narrative to express themselves through their voices, exercising autonomy and agency [33, 34]. Through this process, humans use narrative to make sense of the world to produce knowledge [35, 36]. IDN helps humans explore even more complex information in their worlds [37, 38]. A Humanist perspective on narrative and interactive narrative recognizes the value in the human's centrality in the IDN authoring process. As GenAI tools alter this process, a Digital Humanist perspective seeks to elevate and valorize the human elements of narrative creation.

The Digital Humanist perspective arose in many ways because of dissatisfaction with the contemporary understanding of Humanism, the tensions between Post-humanism and Transhumanism, and the accelerated growth of digital technologies [39]. Published in 2019, the Vienna Manifesto on Digital Humanism succinctly names these challenges and puts forward principles [40]. Critically, Digital Humanism stresses "the active and transformative capacities of human beings in the digital age." Digital Humanists seek the "development of digital technologies and society that is focused on the need of humans to liberate themselves from digital class society, digital domination, and digital ideology […] to together create a good digital society" [39]. Digital Humanists work practically to develop knowledge that results in a humane digital society where all benefit. As a philosophy, Digital Humanism aligns in many ways with Data Feminism, which seeks to challenge structures and power dynamics in data practices [41] to promote a more equitable form of data science [42]. It follows then that authoring IDNs, "should be shaped and used in manners that do not harm society and humans, but rather support the establishment of a good, humane society" [43]. News organizations and other groups are already seeking to use IDN in the manner. Take, for example, INDCOR's work, "addressing complexity as a societal challenge by representing, experiencing and comprehending complex phenomena and thus also address the issue of 'fake news'" [44]. Such an example can be read as a Digital Humanist endeavor.

This approach contradicts Post-humanist or Transhumanist approaches to using GenAI in IDN authoring. These two philosophical positions engage with the relationship between humans and technology differently and provide different framing for GenAI's use in IDN authoring. Post-humanism challenges the centrality of humanity as a universal frame. For example, game developer Luden.io released a game that was made entirely using GenAI. The developers used, "all the generative systems we could find" [45]. Everything from dialogue to character art was generated. Reading the post-mortem of the project from Luden.io developer, Oleg Chumakov, they intentionally ceded creative agency to the GenAI tools [45]. They relied on prompts and fine-tuning but the major creative efforts were handled by GenAI.

Technological Post-humanists argue that human exclusivity is undermined as technologies become more integrated into humans and societies [43, 46]. This equalization shifts agency and authority toward GenAIs away from human creators. David Thue invokes a Post-humanist perspective on authoring when he states,

> It is common to say that an AI system 'decides' which output(s) it should produce as it operates. Since authoring is about making and acting upon decisions, we say that an authoring process can include a narrative AI system; in such cases, the decisions that are made during authoring will be shared between the author(s) and the system.

Contrarily, Digital Humanism would say that authoring is not shared but is directed and owned by the human creator. From a Transhumanist perspective, GenAI and human creators would not be separate entities but a single, technologically-enhanced creator with a shared agency in authoring the IDN. In this instance, the creative agency is collapsed into the cyborg that produces an IDN, not with, but through both organic and computational processes [47]. Transhumanist authoring may be many years off from being realized. Digital Humanism re-centers authorial agency and authority with humans, using digital technologies to expand human nature and human values rather than diminishing them (as in Post-humanism) or overstepping them (as in Transhumanism). For Digital Humanist IDN creators, GenAI is used with IDN authoring tools to scale human inclusivity, agency, creativity, values, dignity, and well-being—not diminish them.

3   The Digital Humanist Interactive Storyteller

The Digital Humanist IDN creator is empowered to use GenAI in their authoring as a material practice. Central to this practice is recognizing that storytelling and narrative are and always will be a human practice—that the creation and use of stories are central to human nature and the well-being of human society [48]. The following section outlines Digital Humanist principles for utilizing GenAI tools in an IDN authoring practice.

3.1 Elevating Organic Creativity

Central to a Digital Humanist's approach to IDN is an appreciation, respect, and elevation of organic creativity. Giovanni Emanuele Corazza, the founder of the Marconi Institute of Creativity and scholar of creativity and innovation, outlines organic creativity as "the potential for originality and effectiveness conducive to personal and social well-being" [49]. Corazza considers creativity and creative behaviors a productive practice in pursuing human happiness. Kreminski and Mateas have drawn a similar observation from the "play-pleasures of authorship" in some IENs [6]. Going further, Corazza couples joy with creative production to pursue well-being and human dignity. In response, but not condemnation, of computational creativity, Corazza states, "We should actively work to preserve and enhance the authentic, emotional, unique capacity of human minds to intentionally generate truly original and effective outcomes in our relational mesh leading to cultural accumulation. Authenticity is a fundamental element in establishing originality" [49]. This invocation is reminiscent of Walter Benjamin's observations on art and mechanical reproduction [50]. Corazza builds upon Benjamin's invocations by drawing a direct line between organic, authentic creative endeavors and the joy of producing something novel.

When discussing the relationship between AIs and humans, there is a tendency to either anthropomorphize the AI or technomorphize the human [51]. Understanding that each intelligence, human and artificial, progresses along unique routes of wildly different complexity underscores the fallacy of this parallelism [52]. In the first instance, humans get pleasure from creating narratives. A GenAI does not and cannot feel pleasure in the mechanistic creation of narrative assets or systems. Further, humans improve their social well-being when they share stories with others. AIs do not have a capacity for well-being, so producing or generating narrative content does not impact their underlying mechanisms or relationships with other entities. GenAI cannot imagine like a human; even machine hallucinations—aberrations in images, texts, and produced artifacts—are abstracted from the collective organic intelligence upon which a creator trains their GenAI. A Digital Humanist IDN author values the organic production of humans above material automated by tools. They celebrate the fundamental value of human storytelling and appreciate its beneficial influence on social well-being and human growth. A Digital Humanist IDN author chooses organic creativity over GenAI to scale the positive and pleasurable experiences of authoring IDNs for humans.

An example of supporting organic creativity while using GenAI to scale the human elements of IDN authoring is the immersive theater experience, *Bad News* [53]. Performed in 2016, *Bad News* placed interactors in a procedurally generated town with a simulated history. An improvisational actor took dialogue prompts generated by the system and engaged with interactors live. GenAI generates the characters, town, and knowledge before the experience begins. Each town in *Bad News* is unique. A live-coding programmer known as the "wizard" moves an avatar of the live interactor around town based on that interactor's voice commands. The wizard also engaged in story sifting [4], "the wizard queries the simulation to search for narrative intrigue and potential dramatic nuggets that may be nestled in all its accumulated data" [53]. The wizard uses their creative curiosity to key up dramatic moments for a human actor to perform. Indeed, the actor in *Bad News* had to bring considerable improvisational talents to the work.

While GenAI provided the raw data, human creatives utilized their talents to create an organic process of narrative meaning-making for their interactors. GenAI is integral to the system's authoring, but the process of narrative meaning-making is only given life with the wizard's and actor's organic creativity.

3.2 Protecting Human Agency: Augment Instead of Substitute

Recognizing the centrality of organic creativity and its necessity to human well-being encourages Digital Humanist IDN creators to be inclusive of human creative efforts as they use GenAI in their IDN authorship. However, existing structures challenge this inclusivity. Aleena Chia of Goldsmiths discusses how the procedural generation of game art and assets is resulting in an underclass of creatives [54]. This underclass's work on conditioning algorithmic outputs is denigrated as a less-than-creative practice. These human artists' dignity is impugned. What Chia describes involves the substitution of human creatives and creative work accelerated by ceding too much creative agency to algorithmic generation.

Sense of Agency (SoA) is a constructive term for understanding the appropriate amount of agency to give a GenAI in a mixed-initiative creative interface [55, 56]. It is best understood by an example: a human flipping a switch to turn on a light might respond when asked who turned the light on, "I turned the light on." This response expresses a robust SoA. In authoring IDNs, a strong SoA occurs when the author feels that their use of GenAI effectively translates their narrative intentions into reality. They should feel that their creative decisions and outcomes are rooted within themselves, not the GenAI, asserting their role as the human creator. When an author gives the GenAI more agency than themselves, creators can feel distance from a resultant experience and perceive it as less novel [2].

Authors use GenAI as an action augmentation: "The system assists the user's action to produce the intended outcome" [55]. For example, *CharacterChat* is a GenAI tool supporting writers' creation of fictional characters [57]. To this end, the GenAI tool uses guided prompts for character motivations and suggestions for attributes to progressively transform the tool into the character the human author seeks to develop. The tool turns into the character the author is developing the longer they engage. In this instance, the author's action (developing a new character) is augmented by the GenAI system. Throughout the process, the human does not feel like their creative agency is diminished: the character deepens as they develop it. Compare this to work by Guzidal and Riedel, where the interactor and GenAI take turns authoring an artifact [58]. In that instance, agency shifts back and forth from AI to a human creator in a Post-humanist authoring relationship. In *CharacterChat*, the human creator defines all attributes, and the AI cannot depart from them—the human maintains creative agency. Critically, a Digital Humanist does not see agency as shared with an AI—the IDN creator is the agential actor—so safeguarding, valorizing, and recognizing human creative agency is critical.

3.3 Obligations: Transparency and Trust

GenAI systems are perceived as trustworthy when their processes are transparent and interpretable [59, 60]. However, the complexity of these GenAI systems can make it difficult to be transparent about their reasoning and actions [61]. Interactors of IDN deserve to know how an author has used a GenAI in the same way they are aware of the development engines of their games and the cameras used to shoot their movies. These disclosures respect their agency as human consumers who care about production processes. Writing on computational creativity in 2009, Simon Colton and colleagues underscore that constructing AI systems for creativity involves social perceptions of the process as much as technical considerations [62]. A Digital Humanist approach to IDN production using a GenAI involves fully disclosing its use. Transparency in the production process makes it easier to discern how human elements and creative initiatives are implemented [61, 63]. This disclosure informs the Digital Humanist IDN creator's accountability to the dignity of their fellow human creators, communities, and society as they work to expand human agency and meaning-making through IDN.

Transparency regarding training data and how a GenAI renders that data for an IDN creator is also necessary. GenAIs are trained on the collective intelligence and production of humans. As such, they are biased, and those models trained on the open internet primarily represent the global north and west [64, 65]. Much like IDN, a concerted effort to call out and decolonize these models is critical [17]. In any case, the contemporary datasets have been sourced without direct consent from those individuals [66]. The lack of transparency and erosion of trust diminishes the value of human creativity and the resultant artifacts. IDN creators must be mindful of how their GenAI tools source their training data to maintain the dignity of their fellow creators and audiences.

Human efforts demand recognition as part of building trust through transparency. Recognizing this effort and being transparent about GenAI's use reduces the tool to a statistical abstractor. GenAIs find patterns in what has already been produced by humans. They do not develop what has been said or created but scrape together something similar to what others have published. Reducing GenAIs to this function cements the entity as a tool—nothing more—that authors can use in their process. It is not a collaborator on par with a human nor a divine muse.

3.4 GenAI as the Divine, the Muse, and Other False Narratives

In the contemporary moment, there is a tendency in scholarship and industry to conflate human creators and computational processes for creativity [16, 39]. Further, some members of the mainstream press glorify AI as divine [52]. An article by Stephen Marche of the Atlantic claims that "an encounter with the superhuman is at hand" [52]. Technocrats tend to frame GenAI as a demonic or an angelic savior. Both parallels run counter to Digital Humanist thought. Andrews wrote in 2015, "Humanism is a 'philosophy or set of beliefs, that holds that human beings achieve a system of morality through their own reasoning rather than through a belief in any divine being" [67]. Humanism has long rejected concepts of the divine as vehicles to make meaning of human situations. Such analogizing and semantic work contradicts "human reason applied to evidence in contrast with theism, theological speculation, and revelation" [67]. Beyond stultifying intellectual engagement, these claims simplify or abstract implementation into some sorcery while diminishing technical literacy in the underlying systems of GenAI.

The Digital Humanist IDN creator rejects these false narratives and does not use them to explain authoring processes, inspiration, or the resulting artifacts. For example,

Digital Humanist IDN creators would dismiss the Transhumanist theological assertion that Gen AI is a "created co-creator" and that "God is working through the human creatures to develop robust technologies, for good" [68]. Digital Humanism pursues a secular approach to avoid the abuses made in the name of the divine. Such a rejection is critical for maintaining an IDN author's ethical, social, and cultural accountability [69]. This accountability is essential when considering how IDNs can transform [37, 70] and influence the behavior of interactors. Roth and Koenitz discuss how interactors construct "personal meaning from a story or piece of art" through eudaimonic appreciation [71].

> Media users with eudaimonic motivations seek entertainment offerings that deal with decisive and meaningful life events. By observing how characters cope with hardship or how they emerge victorious from a difficult challenge, they hope to deduce general life lessons, even insights into the meaning of life.

In the IDN authoring process, deferring to an AI-as-Divine-Creator or AI-as-Agential-Collaborator—instead of as a tool—shifts these "entertainment offerings" to illuminated texts. Meaningful life events are not defined by human minds but are said to be handed down to them by divine AI-like revelations. The responses to decisive life events are not originated through the design of an IDN creator but are claimed to be developed at the behest of an inscrutable GenAI. The false narrative becomes a rhetorical mechanism for the author to avoid the harmful effects of an IDN system. As discussed by IDN scholars, IDN can be used for ill ends [69, 72], and the authority of the divine associated with a GenAI tool may scale those negative impacts. This technochauvinism is a step backward and contradicts Digital Humanism's secular foundation.

4   Counter Arguments to a Digital Humanist Approach to GenAI's use in IDN Authoring

There are limitations and critiques to the Digital Humanist approach to using GenAI in IDN authoring. The author wishes to address these to expand the position and invite further deliberation. As societal, cultural, political, technological, and economic factors interact, these debates will evolve. The author is writing from a particular time-slice in a quickly changing space.

4.1 IDN has Always been a Digital Humanist Endeavor

One of the earliest forms of IDN was a teaching tool [73]. INDCOR explores IDN's use in comprehending complex issues [38]. These are ostensibly applications that can be understood through a Digital Humanist lens. However, as Bernstein discusses, IDN can be used for domination and villainous intent [72]. Henry Jenkins referred to the 2016 presidential campaign of Donald Trump as a deviously successful transmedia campaign [74]. While there is an inclination to use IDN toward humanist ends, there are ways in which the field's research and artifacts can be used for ill. Much like Digital Humanism is a response to Humanism's failings, as a field, IDN must grapple with how the systems we have explored and designed might be used to dimmish human well-being. Moreover, while previously procedural content generation tools were used as part of larger human-led production efforts [75], interoperable GenAI tools can displace more of that creative effort in the authoring practice. It is increasingly essential to center the human in this authoring process to keep creative minds working together to produce IDNs that improve the lives of interactors.

4.2 Digital Humanism is a Luddite Approach to AI in IDN

In the face of Post-humanism and Transhumanism, the author recognizes that Digital Humanism is a relatively conservative or precautionary approach to the relationships between humans and their creative tools. However, the idea that Post-humanism and Transhumanism will surpass the Digital Humanist position speaks to a tech determinism and fatalism that diminishes human agency. The approach is not Luddism because it embraces the "human being and its abilities and uses digital technology to expand them, not defeat them" [39, 76]. Technochauvinism, technological determinism, or belief in the divine providence of GenAI works against the humanization of the world for all. Post-humanism and Transhumanism would speed technology integration at the cost of human nature to achieve a romantic vision of human equity. In such an instance, the Digital Humanist is skeptical that structures of oppression would not stretch their tentacles in new ways to dehumanize the world through emerging technology [77, 78]. Indeed, more technology and computation may not solve the social and ethical challenges of using GenAI in the process of IDN authoring [79, 80]. Instead, maintaining a human-centered approach in the relationship with GenAI keeps our focus on liberating, empowering, and elevating humanity to build a "humane digital society where all humans lead a good life, flourish, and can realize their potential." [39].

4.3 AI Supplementation of Creativity

Critics of Digital Humanism's approach to GenAI in IDN might suggest that the tools be used to supplement human production so that human authors can focus on larger and more complex narrative systems, processes, or products. As Chia discussed, the supplementation of human creativity by GenAI in the name of efficiency often displaces human creative labor along geographic and racial lines. This use runs counter to a Digital Humanist approach. Additionally, as GenAI models begin to be trained on data created by other GenAI models, the novel quality of the creative work recedes, and errors perpetuate [81]. Organic creativity is ever diminished when an IDN creator supplements their content with increasingly lower quality material at the expense of human well-being. A Digital Humanist perspective maintains all human creative behaviors in the production loop. This inclusion maintains the dignity of those creative artists, programmers, sound designers, musicians, 3D modelers, and writers.

5 Moving Forward with Digital Humanism, GenAI, and Interactive Digital Narrative

Protecting and elevating human creative agency is of paramount concern. A practical approach is for an IDN creator to reflect on their GenAI usage and ask themselves, "Did I do this?" If the answer is yes, they then perceive their use of GenAI as aligned with the principles of Digital Humanism. For a more informed assessment, Thue presents a series of questions IDN authors might consider as they use GenAI [9].

- **How does the AI system behave?** Answers can be found via experimentation with a system or examining its underlying code to understand how it works.
- **How can I influence the AI system's behavior?** By determining its inputs and the effect of those inputs.
- **How can I determine the AI system's inputs?** By identifying collections of content being used, an AI's settings, the parameters being used, and any utilities used to define operations.
- **What of the AI system itself can I change?** Access to and understanding the underlying code enables the technical literacy to edit the AI system.
- **How can I refine or repurpose the AI system's outputs?** By identifying outputs and patterns that are particularly valuable

Understanding the answers to the questions provides a more substantial basis for understanding a human's SoA in the IDN authoring process. Further, an IDN author, answering these questions and becoming literate in the underpinning systems of a GenAI, enables them to make informed decisions about how they are using their tools and the effect of their creative initiative. With this information, they can more rightly claim their creative autonomy and agency. Lastly, providing this level of transparency in how a GenAI works is critical for critique and building trust with audiences. Such questions should be built into the necessary UX evaluations of IDN authoring tools [19].

Educators of IDN need to teach students how GenAI works, where their training data comes from, and why its use can be problematic when creating their experiences. While institutional panic has rocked higher education over the last year, cooler heads prevail, and educators are finding constructive ways to use the tools. Teaching students that human and organic creativity is critical and necessary for the well-being of society should be highlighted. This approach can help students engage in a provocateur relationship with the GenAI system, choosing to dismiss some or all of the tool's suggestions in preference for their organic creative choices [82].

Educators can also teach different forms of prompt engineering that align with Digital Humanist values. One such form is called Chain of Thought engineering [83]. It involves modeling one's creative process as a series of discrete steps. These discrete steps are then given to the GenAI to follow as part of its computational processes. The benefit of this approach is two-fold. First, it encourages authors to reflect on their creative practices. This reflection includes their creative intentions, steps to achieve those intentions, and expected outcomes. Such reflection can result in a more significant SoA in the creative process. Second, the Chain of Thought engineering forces the GenAI to conform to the human creator's authoring process and their creative steps. Human authorship and creativity shape the use of GenAI, not the other way around.

Protecting the livelihood and well-being of human artists, writers, and creatives whose work can be exploited is a priority. A sustainable GenAI practice that protects organic creativity must shift from contemporary large-language models that use data scraped from the internet to more finite data sets that individual creators have opted into. Alternatively, chat-based GenAI can block the names of artists, existing artifacts, and more to keep individuals from co-opting a creative's style and brand as their own. For example, Adobe keeps its GenAI Firefly from utilizing the names of visual artists [84]. If consent cannot be established, GenAI tools should automatically opt out creatives of all kinds from being included. Doing so exemplifies the Digital Humanist perspective on human dignity and appreciation for organic creativity.

To maintain a personal aesthetic and support the dignity of other creators, IDN creators might compile their creative material as training data for a personal GenAI tool. Training a GenAI in this manner augments the creator's action with their material. The IDN author's voice is extended, their style perhaps deepened through a reflection on their work parsed and remixed by their GenAI tool. The IDN author that pursues this approach demonstrates respect for the work of others. This approach might be an extension of authoring groups or studios compiling multiple individual creators' efforts as training data for a GenAI representative of their groups' talents. In this manner, a community or development studio's brand or style is augmented and extended by GenAI. It might provide a new baseline or composite understanding of the studio's creative efforts, aesthetic, voice, and style. Human creators can then use this GenAI as they experiment and expand on their community's efforts through their organic creativity. An example of this would be Stephanie Dinkin's *Not the Only One*, an "AI entity is trained on oral histories (data) supplied by three generations of women from a single-family" [85]. The data, given freely, generates a composite memoir from these women's experiences. From the site, "This project works toward the creation of culturally-specific, natural language-based AI that reflects the goals of the communities making them" [85]. *Not the Only One* is exemplary of an IDN author using GenAI toward Digital Humanist ends.

6 Final Thoughts

Interoperable chat-based GenAI's capacity to scale the affordances of traditional IDN authoring tools provides an exciting new horizon, offering a transformative shift in how IDNs are conceived, authored, and enjoyed. However, their capacity to supplant human creativity through the scale of their production requires a precautionary approach. The author has put forward Digital Humanism as a perspective to critically investigate the new scale and complexity of this shift in authoring while maintaining a human-centric position. This positioning means elevating organic creativity above computational creativity, seeking wherever possible to employ human creators in the production loop. Further, it means maintaining human initiative and agency in the authoring process. Maintaining this initiative requires transparency in how GenAI data is sourced and how the tool uses that data at the behest of an IDN author. Lastly, to maintain human accountability and support human dignity, the Digital Humanist perspective denies myths of the divine and the anthropomorphizing of GenAI tools.

As scholars of IDN, the power of telling stories and using narrative to create meaning is central to the field. As a Digital Humanist, one recognizes that creating IDNs and experiences gives human creators a sense of joy, well-being, and accomplishment. GenAI should be implemented in an authoring practice that assists in creating compelling and engaging narratives rather than as an independent entity that marginalizes the human creator. To that end, scholars and creators employing a Digital Humanist perspective on IDN authoring need to develop a deep understanding of GenAI tools' processes, source consent for inclusive training data, and utilize prompt engineering to extend human approaches to creative processes.

Through this human-centric approach to IDN authoring, the field can nurture a truly humane digital society where GenAI assists and augments human creativity rather than displaces or dominates. In this effort, IDN scholars and practitioners find themselves allied with educators who are seeking to integrate GenAI toward similar ends. A Digital Humanist approach to the use of GenAI in authorship supports the IDNs of tomorrow that reflect our shared human values, enrich our collective narrative tradition, and uplift, rather than erode, our dignity as human storytellers.

References

1. Nowotny, H.: Digital humanism: navigating the tensions ahead. In: Werthner, H., Prem, E., Lee, E.A., Ghezzi, C. (eds.) Perspectives on Digital Humanism, pp. 317–321. Springer, Cham (2022). https://doi.org/10.1007/978-3-030-86144-5_43
2. Figoli, F.A., Rampino, L., Mattioli, F.: AI in design idea development: a workshop on creativity and human-AI collaboration. Presented at the June 16 (2022). https://doi.org/10.21606/drs.2022.414
3. Liapis, A., Yannakakis, G.N., Alexopoulos, C., Lopes, P.: Can computers foster human users' creativity? theory and praxis of mixed-initiative co-creativity (2016)
4. Kreminski, M., Wardrip-Fruin, N., Mateas, M.: Authoring for Story Sifters
5. Gravina, D., Khalifa, A., Liapis, A., Togelius, J., Yannakakis, G.N.: Procedural content generation through quality diversity. In: 2019 IEEE Conference on Games (CoG), pp. 1–8. IEEE (2019)
6. Kreminski, M., Mateas, M.: A coauthorship-centric history of interactive emergent narrative. In: Mitchell, A., Vosmeer, M. (eds.) ICIDS 2021. LNCS, vol. 13138, pp. 222–235. Springer, Cham (2021). https://doi.org/10.1007/978-3-030-92300-6_21
7. Kreminski, M., Dickinson, M., Wardrip-Fruin, N., Mateas, M.: A demonstration of loose ends, a mixed-initiative narrative instrument. In: International Conference on Interactive Digital Storytelling, pp. 91–97 (2022). https://doi.org/10.1007/978-3-031-22298-6_6
8. Adams, T.: Emergent narrative in dwarf fortress. In: Procedural Storytelling in Game Design, pp. 149–158. AK Peters/CRC Press (2019)
9. Thue, D.: Working with intelligent narrative technologies. In: Hargood, C., Millard, D.E., Mitchell, A., Spierling, U. (eds.) The Authoring Problem: Challenges in Supporting Authoring for Interactive Digital Narratives, pp. 271–284. Springer International Publishing, Cham (2023). https://doi.org/10.1007/978-3-031-05214-9_17
10. Shibolet, Y., Knoller, N., Koenitz, H.: A framework for classifying and describing authoring tools for interactive digital narrative. In: Rouse, R., Koenitz, H., Haahr, M. (eds.) ICIDS 2018. LNCS, vol. 11318, pp. 523–533. Springer, Cham (2018). https://doi.org/10.1007/978-3-030-04028-4_61
11. Shibolet, Y., Lombardo, V.: Resources for comparative analysis of IDN authoring Tools. In: Vosmeer, M., Holloway-Attaway, L. (eds.) Lecture Notes in Computer Science (including subseries Lecture Notes in Artificial Intelligence and Lecture Notes in Bioinformatics), vol. 13762, pp. 513–528. Springer Science and Business Media Deutschland GmbH (2022). https://doi.org/10.1007/978-3-031-22298-6_33
12. Thue, D., Bulitko, V., Spetch, M., Wasylishen, E.: Interactive storytelling: a player modelling approach. In: Proceedings of the Third Artificial Intelligence and Interactive Digital Entertainment Conference. Associatio, pp. 43–48 (2007).https://doi.org/10.1007/978-3-642-106 43-9

13. Spierling, U., Szilas, N.: Authoring issues beyond tools. In: Iurgel, I.A., Zagalo, N., Petta, P. (eds.) ICIDS 2009. LNCS, vol. 5915, pp. 50–61. Springer, Heidelberg (2009). https://doi.org/10.1007/978-3-642-10643-9_9

14. Dow, S., Mehta, M., Lausier, A., MacIntyre, B., Mateas, M.: Initial lessons from AR Façade, an interactive augmented reality drama. In: Proceedings of the 2006 ACM SIGCHI international conference on Advances in computer entertainment technology. Article No.: 28-Article No.: 28 (2006). https://doi.org/10.1145/1178823.1178858

15. Mateas, M., Stern, A.: Façade: an experiment in building a fully-realized interactive drama. In: Game Developers Conference, pp. 4–8 (2003)

16. Shaker, N., Togelius, J., Nelson, M.J., Liapis, A., Smith, G., Shaker, N.: Mixed-initiative content creation. Procedural Content Gen. Games. 195–214 (2016)

17. Thue, D.J.: Generalized Experience Management. (2015)

18. Riedl, M.O., Stern, A., Dini, D., Alderman, J.: Dynamic experience management in virtual worlds for entertainment, education, and training. Int. Trans. Syst. Sci. Appl. Spec. Issue Agent Based Syst. Hum. Learn. **4**, 23–42 (2008)

19. Hargood, C., Green, D.: The authoring tool evaluation problem. In: Hargood, C., Millard, D.E., Mitchell, A., and Spierling, U. (eds.) The Authoring Problem. Springer Cham (2023). https://doi.org/10.1007/978-3-031-05214-9_19

20. Jones, J.: The Authorial Burden. Presented at the

21. Kitromili, S., Reyes, M.C.: Understanding the process of authoring. In: Hargood, C., Millard, D.E., Mitchell, A., Spierling, U. (eds.) The Authoring Problem. Human–Computer Interaction Series. Springer, Cham. pp. 17–30. Springer (2023). https://doi.org/10.1007/978-3-031-052 14-9_2

22. Koenitz, H.: Towards a theoretical framework for interactive digital narrative. In: Aylett, R., Lim, M.Y., Louchart, S., Petta, P., Riedl, M. (eds.) ICIDS 2010. LNCS, vol. 6432, pp. 176–185. Springer, Heidelberg (2010). https://doi.org/10.1007/978-3-642-16638-9_22

23. Nack, F., et al.: INDCOR white paper 3: Interactive Digital Narratives and Interaction. 1–17 (2023)

24. Whitten, M.: Introducing Unity Muse and Unity Sentis, AI-powered creativity. https://blog.unity.com/engine-platform/introducing-unity-muse-and-unity-sentis-ai. Accessed 28 June 2023

25. Stahlke, S., Nova, A., Mirza-Babaei, P.: Artificial playfulness: a tool for automated agent-based playtesting. In: Extended Abstracts of the 2019 CHI Conference on Human Factors in Computing Systems, pp. 1–6 (2019)

26. Cheuque, G., Guzmán, J., Parra, D.: Recommender systems for online video game platforms: the case of steam. In: The Web Conference 2019 - Companion of the World Wide Web Conference, WWW 2019. pp. 763–771. Association for Computing Machinery, Inc (2019). https://doi.org/10.1145/3308560.3316457

27. Fisher, W.R.: Human Communication as Narration: Toward a Philosophy of Reason, Value, and Action. Univ of South Carolina Press (2021)

28. Fisher, W.R.: Narration as a human communication paradigm: the case of public moral argument. Commun Monogr. **51**(1), 1–22, (1984)

29. Rogers, B.A., et al.: Seeing your life story as a Hero's journey increases meaning in life. J. Pers. Soc. Psychol. (2023). https://doi.org/10.1037/pspa0000341

30. Monteiro, J., Morais, C., Carvalhais, M.: Interactive Storytelling for the Maintenance of Cultural Identity: The Potential of Affinity Spaces for the Exchange and Continuity of Inter-generational Cultural Knowledge. Lecture Notes in Computer Science (including subseries Lecture Notes in Artificial Intelligence and Lecture Notes in Bioinformatics). 10690 LNCS, pp. 299–302 (2017). https://doi.org/10.1007/978-3-319-71027-3_30

31. Hutto, D.D.: Narrative and understanding persons. R. Inst. Philos. Suppl. **60**, 1–15 (2007)

32. Goodson, I., Gill, S.R.: Narrative Pedagogy: Life History and Learning. Peter Lang (2011)
33. Anderson, T.S.: Goal reasoning and narrative cognition. In: Goal Reasoning: Papers from the ACS Workshop, pp. 1-9 (2015)
34. Bruni, L.E., Dini, H., Simonetti, A.: Narrative cognition in mixed reality systems: towards an empirical framework. In: Chen, J.Y.C., Fragomeni, G. (eds.) Virtual, Augmented and Mixed Reality, pp. 3–17. Springer International Publishing, Cham (2021)
35. Knoller, N.: Complexity and the userly text. Narrative Complex. Cogn. Embodiment Evol. 98–122 (2019)
36. Herman, D.: Cognitive narratology. Handb. Narratol. **1**, 30–43 (2009)
37. Koenitz, H., Eladhari, M.P., Louchart, S., Nack, F.: INDCOR white paper 1: A shared vocabulary for IDN (Interactive Digital Narratives) (2020)
38. Koenitz, H., Barbara, J., Eladhari, M.P.: Interactive digital narratives (IDN) as representations of complexity: lineage, opportunities and future work. In: Mitchell, A., Vosmeer, M. (eds.) Interactive Storytelling, pp. 488–498. Springer International Publishing, Cham (2021)
39. Fuchs, C.: Digital Humanism: A Philosophy for 21st Century Digital Society. Emerald Group Publishing (2022)
40. Werthner, H., et al.: Vienna Manifesto on Digital Humanism (2019)
41. D'ignazio, C., Klein, L.F.: Data Feminism. MIT press (2023)
42. Shukla, P.: Book Review: Data Feminism by Catherine D'Ignazio and Lauren F. LSE Review of Books, Klein (2020)
43. Fuchs, C.: Digital Humanism. Emerald Publishing, Bingley (2022)
44. INDCOR – COST Action CA18230: About. https://indcor.eu/about/. Accessed 28 June 2023
45. Chumakov, O.: Generated Adventure — The Postmortem of a Game Made With chatGPT and Midjourney (Prompts Included). https://blog.luden.io/generated-adventure-the-postmortem-of-a-game-made-with-chatgpt-and-midjourney-prompts-included-f87e7e615204. Accessed 11 Sept 2023
46. Serbanescu, A., Ciancia, M., Piredda, F., Bertolo, M.: Narrative-based human–artificial collaboration. a reflection on narratives as a framework for enhancing human–machine social relations. In: Proceedings of Pivot 2021: Dismantling/Reassembling Tools for Alternative Futures, pp. 397–408. Design Research Society (DRS) (2022)
47. Vita-More, N.: Aesthetics: bringing the arts & design into the discussion of transhumanism. Transhumanist Reader Class. Contemp. Essays Sci. Technol. Philos. Hum. Future, 18–27 (2013)
48. Latar, N.L., Herzliya, I., Nordfors, I.D.: The Future of Journalism: Artificial Intelligence and Digital Identities (2011)
49. Corazza, G.E.: Organic creativity for well-being in the post-information society. Europ. J. Psychol. **13**(4), 599 (2017). https://doi.org/10.5964/ejop.v13i4.1547
50. Benjamin, W., Benjamin, W.: The Work of Art in the Age of Mechanical Reproduction (1935)
51. Hofkirchner, W.: Digital humanism: epistemological, ontological and praxiological foundations. In: AI for Everyone? Critical Perspectives, pp. 33–47. University of Westminster Press (2021). https://doi.org/10.16997/book55.c
52. Bender, E.M.: Emily M. Bender on Stephen Marche's of God and Machines in the Atlantic. Critical AI. 1 (2022)
53. Samuel, B., Ryan, J., Summerville, A.J., Mateas, M., Wardrip-Fruin, N.: Bad News: An Experiment in Computationally Assisted Performance. Presented at the
54. Chia, A.: The artist and the automaton in digital game production. Convergence **28**, 389–412 (2022). https://doi.org/10.1177/13548565221076434
55. Cornelio, P., Haggard, P., Hornbaek, K., Georgiou, O., Bergström, J., Subramanian, S., Obrist, M.: The sense of agency in emerging technologies for human–computer integration: a review. Front. Neurosci. **16**, 949138 (2022). https://doi.org/10.3389/fnins.2022.949138

56. Kreminski, M., Dickinson, M., Wardrip-Fruin, N., Mateas, M.: Loose ends: a mixed-initiative creative interface for playful storytelling. In: Proceedings of the AAAI Conference on Artificial Intelligence and Interactive Digital Entertainment, vol. 18, no. 1, pp. 120–128 (2022)

57. Schmitt, O., Buschek, D.: CharacterChat: Supporting the Creation of Fictional Characters through Conversation and Progressive Manifestation with a Chatbot. In: ACM International Conference Proceeding Series. Association for Computing Machinery (2021). https://doi.org/10.1145/3450741.3465253

58. Guzidal, M., Riedl, M.: An interaction framework for studying co-creative AI. In: Human-Centered Machine Learning Perspectives Workshop, pp. 1–6. IEEE Computer Society (2019). https://doi.org/10.48550/arXiv.1903.09709

59. Shin, D.: Why does explainability matter in news analytic systems? Proposing Explain. Anal. Journalism. J. Stud. **22**, 1047–1065 (2021)

60. Kim, S.S.Y., Watkins, E.A., Russakovsky, O., Fong, R., Monroy-Hernández, A.: Help me help the AI: understanding how explainability can support human-AI interaction (2022). https://doi.org/10.1145/3544548.3581001

61. Bertino, E., Doshi-Velez, F., Gini, M., Lopresti, D., Parkes, D.: Artificial Intelligence & Cooperation (2020)

62. Colton, S., de Màntaras, R.L., Stock, O.: Computational Creativity: Coming of Age (2009)

63. Hadfield-Menell, D., Russell, S.J., Abbeel, P., Dragan, A.: Cooperative inverse reinforcement learning. Adv. Neural Inf. Process Syst. **29** (2016)

64. Navigli, R., Conia, S., Ross, B.: Biases in large language models: origins, inventory and discussion. ACM J. Data Inf. Qual. (2023)

65. Abid, A., Farooqi, M., Zou, J.: Persistent anti-muslim bias in large language models. In: Proceedings of the 2021 AAAI/ACM Conference on AI, Ethics, and Society, pp. 298–306 (2021)

66. Baio, A.: Exploring 12 Million of the 2.3 Billion Images Used to Train Stable Diffusion's Image Generator - Waxy.org. https://waxy.org/2022/08/exploring-12-million-of-the-images-used-to-train-stable-diffusions-image-generator/. Accessed 22 June 2023

67. Copson, A.: What is Humanism? The Wiley Blackwell Handbook of Humanism, pp. 1–33 (2015)

68. Mocan, R.: From co-creator to demiurge. a theological and philosophical perspective. J. Study Religions Ideologies **9**, 110–123 (2020)

69. Koenitz, H., Barbara, J., Bakk, A.K.: An ethics framework for interactive digital narrative authoring. In: The Authoring Problem: Challenges in Supporting Authoring for Interactive Digital Narratives, pp. 335-351. Presented at the (2023). https://doi.org/10.1007/978-3-031-05214-9_21

70. Murray, J.H.: Hamlet on the Holodeck: The Future of Narrative in Cyberspace. MIT Press (2017)

71. Roth, C., Koenitz, H.: Towards creating a body of evidence-based interactive digital narrative design knowledge: approaches and challenges. In: AltMM 2017 - Proceedings of the 2nd International Workshop on Multimedia Alternate Realities, co-located with MM 2017, pp. 19–24 (2017). https://doi.org/10.1145/3132361.3133942

72. Bernstein, M., Hooper, C.: A Villain's guide to social media and interactive digital storytelling. In: Rouse, R., Koenitz, H., Haahr, M. (eds.) ICIDS 2018. LNCS, vol. 11318, pp. 50–61. Springer, Cham (2018). https://doi.org/10.1007/978-3-030-04028-4_4

73. Ryan, J.: Grimes' fairy tales: a 1960s story generator. In: Nunes, N., Oakley, I., Nisi, V. (eds.) ICIDS 2017. LNCS, vol. 10690, pp. 89–103. Springer, Cham (2017). https://doi.org/10.1007/978-3-319-71027-3_8

74. Galili, D.: A conversation with Henry Jenkins. NECSUS_Europ. J. Media Stud. **9**, 5–19 (2020). https://doi.org/10.25969/mediarep/15316

75. Kreminski, M., Wardrip-Fruin, N., Wardrip, N.: Gardening games: an alternative philosophy of PCG in games. In: Proceedings of the 13th International Conference on the Foundations of Digital Games (2018)
76. Nida-Rümelin, J., Weidenfeld, N.: Digitaler Humanismus: eine Ethik für das Zeitalter der künstlichen Intelligenz. Piper ebooks (2018)
77. Braun, M., Bleher, H., Hille, E.M., Krutzinna, J.: Tackling structural injustices: on the entanglement of visibility and justice in emerging technologies. Am. J. Bioeth. **23**, 100–102 (2023)
78. Zimmermann, A., Di Rosa, E., Kim, H.: Technology can't fix algorithmic injustice. Boston Rev. **9** (2020)
79. Rouse, R., Barba, E.: Design for emerging media: how MR designers think about storytelling, process, and defining the field. In: Nunes, N., Oakley, I., Nisi, V. (eds.) ICIDS 2017. LNCS, vol. 10690, pp. 245–258. Springer, Cham (2017). https://doi.org/10.1007/978-3-319-71027-3_20
80. Rouse, R.: Against the instrumentalization of empathy: immersive technologies and social change. In: Fisher, J.A. (ed.) Augmented and Mixed Reality for Communities, pp. 3–19. CRC Press, Boca Raton (2021)
81. Williams, R.: The People Paid to Train AI are Outsourcing their Work to AI. MIT Technology Review. (2023)
82. Denning, P.J.: Can generative AI bots be trusted? Commun. ACM **66**, 24–27 (2023). https://doi.org/10.1145/3592981
83. Wei, J., et al.: Chain-of-thought prompting elicits reasoning in large language models. Adv. Neural Inf. Process. Syst. **35**, 24824–24837 (2022)
84. Foley, J.: Just how ethical is Adobe's Firefly AI image generator?. https://www.creativebloq.com/news/adobe-firefly-stock-images. Accessed 29 June 2023
85. Dinkins, S.: Not the Only One. https://www.stephaniedinkins.com/ntoo.html. Accessed 28 June 2023

Digital Storytelling by Women in Tech Communities

Renata Loureiro Frade(✉) and Mário Vairinhos

Universidade de Aveiro, Campus Universitário de Santiago, 3810-193 Aveiro, Portugal
{renatafrade,mariov}@ua.pt

Abstract. Women have found in communities a safe space to learn and develop skills in STEM (Science, Technology, Engineering, Mathematics). These groups bring together specific operational and communicational characteristics related to feminist, design and interaction aspects. They share common goals of inclusion, empowerment and education. They are formed by leaders and founders, work team and target audience. One of the strategies for increasing members is the use of narratives by female role models in technology, successful people such as researchers, entrepreneurs or occupants of jobs in technology companies in face-to-face and online events. Testimonials are also present on the digital platforms used by these collectives.

This work aims to present results obtained in a focus group carried out with people impacted by the female community in IT (Information Technology), São Paulo WiMLDS. It was verified that the use of narratives and storytelling strategies in digital environments can become an important catalyst for the achievements of these collectives. This case study, inserted in a context of digital ethnography in online platforms and interviews carried out in this community for two years, in addition to two other case studies (Minas Programam and Geek Girls Portugal), integrates a broad empirical work of an ongoing doctoral research which involved more than 100 female IT communities in Brazil and Portugal. This work will present preliminary results of the potential of digital storytelling in initiatives already formed in the communication and interaction of these groups.

Keywords: Storytelling · Online Communities · Women in Tech

1 Introduction

Gender equality in IT (Information Technologies) is still a major challenge to be overcome, including the measurement of indices related to women's work. According to the World Economic Forum [1], technology is an industry that predominantly hires men (30%) in leadership positions. Women and girls are underrepresented in all digital technology; UN Women believes that around $1 trillion could be added to the GDP of low and middle-income countries if this problem was ended [2]. Men are 52% more likely to be online than women in the world's least developed countries [3].

The still scarce statistics on the presence of women in the technology job market reveal the gender disparity far from being solved. In addition to the need to promote

© The Author(s), under exclusive license to Springer Nature Switzerland AG 2023
L. Holloway-Attaway and J. T. Murray (Eds.): ICIDS 2023, LNCS 14383, pp. 89–102, 2023.
https://doi.org/10.1007/978-3-031-47655-6_6

greater education, inclusion, and awareness of empowerment among females, there is a lack of knowledge about the historical importance of women in technological development, from the first person considered a programmer in the world, Ada Lovelace, to countless role models worldwide. Women have been erased not just from the hardware and software development industry, but from the history books.

Narratives of important female characters in technology have been taken up again as an instrument for the inclusion of young people and women. Almost 15 years ago, female IT communities emerged in Brazil and Portugal with similar goals, seeking to expand access to professional opportunities in companies, but also to promote entrepreneurial and academic skills in STEM careers. Most of these collectives followed communicational and organizational models developed by pioneering groups, created in the USA between the 80s and 80s, such as Systers (now AnitaB.org). This emergence can be attributed to a natural evolution of the Web, whose emergence led to the creation of online communities and activism [4, 5]. Minorities such as women began to use digital platforms to access information. The development of devices and computational and computer programs became more accessible to women in an unprecedented way, now gathered in a network of connections beyond geographic borders.

Having a hybrid space (face-to-face and online), learning about IT and networking, female technology communities found an ideal space for introducing and improving a woman in technological careers, as well as obtaining empowered narratives of overcoming and conquering opportunities. These groups have been incorporating digital platforms developed by Big Techs such as Meta (Facebook, Instagram, WhatsApp), Slack, X (Twitter), LinkedIn and Telegram for sharing institutional, educational and other information for the exercise of their work. These platforms are free and used worldwide but have limited to interaction and participation rules defined by these companies, which consequently generates an impact on activism, engagement and the results obtained in promoting computing literacy related to STEM.

Based on an ongoing doctoral research which intends to propose solutions for inclusion, education and female empowerment in technology on the work of more than 100 Brazilian and Portuguese women in IT communities, it was found that narratives are used as a resource for engagement and the development of a critical awareness of gender equality in technology, in face-to-face events with speakers who report their success stories (with defeats), as well as spontaneous and sporadic testimonials published on the timelines of these online platforms. However, despite the use of narratives there is no regular storytelling strategy (digital and interactive) as part of their communicational ecosystem.

Women in tech groups study have a complex nature due to the superposition of layers and factors related to their emergence and development. The Social Sciences are used to contextualize motivations and phenomena that occur in these communities and in STEM domains, essentially related to the Exact Sciences, Computer Science. There is an intersection of perspectives and theoretical bases between sciences to configure these collectives in organizational and communicational terms and threats to be faced in the activist exercise.

Most of the communities' members, whether they are leaders, volunteer workers or the target audience to be impacted, have a background in exact sciences, IT, computational knowledge not related to training and communication skills, above all. Therefore, this work aims to characterize contexts of narratives use in digital environments of these groups, based specially on data obtained in a focus group in the São Paulo WiMLDS community, a case study in which a digital ethnographic work on digital platforms had been developed for two years. This work also aims to point out suggestions for digital storytelling strategies based on communication, organizational and interaction characteristics. It is intended to understand whether narratives - from leaders, volunteers and target audience - predominantly shared on digital platforms have potential in strategic planning of actions aimed at increasing and maintaining participants.

This research aims to evaluate the impact of narratives on female communities in technology as an empowerment and work instrument from a theoretical and empirical communication perspective. Therefore, raising positive narratives within the community, from the bottom up, are fundamental for proposing a communication intervention and a storytelling strategy to improve the work of inclusion and training of women in IT.

2   Theoretical Contributions

Studies of technofeminism [6, 7], transmedia [8] and human-computer interaction [9] form a necessary theoretical triad to perceive traces of feminism and activism, as well as potentials of engagement and communication, and characteristics of interaction and survey of functionalities on digital platforms that can catalyze the achievement of results by these communities. When analyzing the exchanges on the communities' platforms (whose empirical work will be discussed in the Methods section), it was noticed that the digital narratives generated commotion and impact, but their sharing could be improved to further expand the reach of the communities' initiatives.

Civic participation, social inclusion and justice, community engagement and feminism have become HCI research and development studies. Through digital communities and platforms, feminism had reached new contours due to the wide and multifaceted interactions between women. Online feminism and the collective female activism in Technology emerged [10, 11].

A participatory culture [12] embraces values of diversity and democracy based on interactions and shows we can make individual and collective decisions, as well as expressing ourselves through a wide range of forms and practices. Individuals participate in something, interact with something. Cultures also exercise their participation through technological means. Carpentier [13] relates the participatory culture to the exercises of power, implicit and explicit. There are privileged and non-privileged actors "in formal or informal decision-making processes". Media engagement is understood to be internal forces that lead people to act in society (or, in this case, in communities) as citizens, motivated by affection and identity similarities. Engagement would be a prerequisite for participation [14].

Human-computer interaction (HCI) studies the communication mediated between the end-user and the system designer, who must structure the system so that it can be understood by the user and so that the user can be guided by a sequence of actions to achieve results [15]. Social computing has become one of the fastest-growing areas in HCI. It is related to systems that support the collection, processing and dissemination of information distributed among social collectives [16]. Information is the main link between people, it mirrors and represents identities in common. Social computing systems can generate value by integrating knowledge among participants, by carrying out tasks based on human skills and by producing legitimate results from a community.

Despite these scientific domains occupying a central place in women in tech collectives study, there is an important link in the informational component exchanged, above all, on digital platforms (environments where most of the communication and interaction between leaders, voluntary workers and the public are concentrated): narratives. Narratives are shared in online environments are relevant to understanding the participants' engagement and participation in non-fiction content.

Narratives shared by women in technology groups members contain life stories based on overcoming obstacles, heroic moments, and defeats, but also important education and technological training information, allowing the development of a computer literacy transmitted from woman to woman. This feature is about the power of engagement through a broader literacy, also developed and combined with storytelling skills and the use of media. As will be addressed in this work, the narratives of stories in female IT communities, such as São Paulo WiMLDS, are not part of a storytelling system or interactive strategy. Narratives are dispersed on digital platforms in audio recordings, video and text timelines. However, they provoke interaction and interest between members when appear on digital platforms. There are no features on these social platforms that allow them to be highlighted or easily found in a specific area. On the platforms developed by the communities there is also no such emphasis. However, it is a rule to find these testimonials in all online and face-to-face events in this research, as role models are still a way of making success tangible in the job market in technology, even with scarce evaluation statistics on inclusion and performance of women.

Stories that bring together potential interactive narratives allow developments between readers, to navigate between various platforms, being able to share new authorial stories [17]. In this sense, Crawford's concept of interactivity [18] fits perfectly with the dynamics of producing and receiving testimonials from members of these communities, "a cyclic process between two or more active agents in which each agent alternately listens, thinks, and speaks".

Because they are shared in online environments, above all, it can be considered that women in technology groups narratives can be incorporated in the characterization of what digital storytelling is beyond fiction, because agents are not passive to the exposure of stories, but also play an authorial role. Within the classification of characteristics of digital storytelling [19], the participatory character, the fluidity of navigation through which stories are produced and transmitted, the possibility of present role models becoming characters (or a set of characteristics of these members provide the creation of personas and avatars), offer a shared experience in the community, enable changes in points of view, are an element of empathy that leads to increased interaction between participants.

A still small number of communities have developed their own digital platforms, which will be discussed later. These media also do not have storytelling features and strategies. Therefore, in addition to the importance of narratives in the collective work of female inclusion in IT, it is important to consider the incorporation of elements that enhance interaction. Interactive Digital Narratives (IDN) can serve this purpose, through a digital medium in which participants influence the production and continuation of the unfolding experience in new stories [18].

In addition to the affordances raised by Murray in digital media (procedural, participatory, spatial, encyclopedic), according to Koenitz, Barbara and Eladhari [20], "IDN allows dealing with limitless amounts of data (encyclopedic), enabling the exploration of a space (spatial), which reacts (procedural) to decisions by the audience (participatory) to create a narrative experience". It is possible to refer, in an analogous way to the female communities in IT, to what Brown & Chu [21] propose for therapeutic processes, allowing patients (or audience) the ability to build non-linear narratives because our lives do not follow a defined timeline, which can open up possibilities for new stories.

3 Related Work

There are few specific studies on storytelling in female technology communities around the world. There are two cases that apply to this work related to digital storytelling: groups that used online environments and platforms with storytelling as a strategy for engagement and success of initiatives (not necessarily feminine or feminist) and groups of women in technology that created their digital platforms, share narratives but without a storytelling strategy present in the communicational and organizational dynamics expressed in shared content.

Despite being a proper and specific space for exchanging information and developing activities, the dimensions of transmedia and storytelling were not verified, as well as attributes present in the Feminist HCI frameworks studied in the investigation.

A – More Women in Tech

Created by WomakersCode Brasil, which calls itself the largest community of women in technology in Latin America, Mais Mulheres em Tech is a platform with essentially educational objectives, training in IT. The online page mentions that it is "the first Brazilian platform created by women, with the mission of training women in technology and innovation".

The site brings together live and recorded courses, free of charge, with certification, aimed at training in the areas of Cloud Computing, Infrastructure, Information Security, DevOps, Development and Data Science and Artificial Intelligence. There are links to the community's social profiles on Twitter, Facebook, Instagram and LinkedIn, newsletter registration, and the community's online page.

The Mais Mulheres em Tech platform acts as a depository for these courses, as well as a reserve of data on enrolled students, in particular.

B – Professions Game

Gamified content platform created by Raparigas do Código, in partnership with the Women in Tech Portugal community, Portuguese Republic, Center for Social Studies of the University of Coimbra, among others. The Portuguese community developed an online memory game in order to provide simple, interactive, inclusive and educational games, as well as content and information on these topics to the educational community and families.

C – PWIT Community Platform

Private online platform created by Portuguese Women in Tech, with an interface like Facebook (hybrid of individual and professional page, and group) and Slack (division by subject channels). There is a timeline of posts where any member can share content, as well as areas reserved for job opportunities, sources of content such as reports and scientific articles.

Admission to the platform takes place according to the authorization of the community managers through registration. There are rules of interaction, communication, and socialization. This is an opportunity to promote more networking with the target audience, capture information about members, test initiatives based on surveys. An online environment whose dynamism is guided, above all, by content proposed by the managers. There is no emphasis on theoretical content related to feminism, as well as the extension of information from there to other platforms in a transmedia logic, without storytelling.

4 Method

This doctoral research from which this work originated is part of the interpretive paradigm, of a qualitative nature, but will use quantitative data, such as statistics. A bibliographic survey was carried out for three years to define the theoretical-conceptual field, objectives, and hypotheses of the thesis [22]. For the development of the fieldwork in particular, the adopted design methodology integrates ethnographic nature, experience design, participatory design.

Despite the author having been the leader of a female community in technology for 3 years and having been a technological entrepreneur for more than 10 years, the author assumed a stance of neutrality as a scientific researcher, adopting an observant participation when following content published on digital platforms, thus as a presence in online and in-person events of these groups. However, the author's experiences can enrich the content analysis of the phenomena observed due to a greater knowledge about the founding and development collectives contexts, such as social, economic, cultural and educational. It is also possible to have a clearer understanding of the intentions and meanings of focus group statements from volunteer members. Impartiality is also important for ethical reasons.

More than 100 groups were surveyed in these countries and informal monitoring was carried out in them for a year on the respective digital platforms (DP) to perceive organizational, operational and communicational characteristics. After this period, for about two years, case studies had been developed with São Paulo Women in Machine Learning and Data Science (full internal and external DP access), Minas Programam (focused on transmedia storytelling approach and proposed model) and Geek Girls Portugal (interaction design study focused on Slack platform related to other DP of the community) in order to deepen the analysis in an ethnographic research method on internal and external DP, associated with participant observation, interviews and focus group. Fundamentals of Design Based Research (DBR) and design methodology guided the fieldwork. The communities were chosen to become case studies due to their relevance and scope in technology activism, and the number of members present on digital platforms.

The investigation was divided into 5 phases, as shown in Table 1: 1 (Community´s Digital Platforms Survey); 2 (Case Studies Planning and Development); 3 (Conceptual model construction); 4 (Participatory design of a tech proposal impact evaluation); 5 (Results analysis and thesis writing).

In phase 1, Communities' Digital Platforms Survey, more than 100 Portuguese and Brazilian female communities were surveyed and informally monitored on their digital platforms for one year. After online follow-up and observational participation in some events in some communities, three were chosen for case studies. Exploratory interviews were conducted with some community leaders to understand the profile of leaders, volunteers, and the target audience.

In phase 2, Case Studies Planning and Development, three case studies were chosen for bringing together aspects related to the theoretical framework of the investigation and the characteristics of the work they carry out. Another selection criterion was the possibility of accessing all platforms for internal use to understand how the operational and communication strategies of these groups were set up. Monitoring began using the ethnographic method of Geek Girls Portugal and Minas Program communities, where interaction potentials were evaluated, with emphasis on the Slack platform and engagement potential via transmedia storytelling.

After the beginning of this work with the first two communities, a third one, São Paulo WiMLDS, was incorporated. Only this one allowed access to digital platforms for internal use (institutional email and WhatsApp group), which enabled a daily ethnographic immersion in the group's routine, before and during the covid pandemic.

Phase 3, Conceptual model construction, is being developed after surveying problems and opportunities, classifying groups by similar objectives, proposing models of communicational and organizational functioning. Phase 4, Participatory design of a feminist tech proposal impact evaluation, is also ongoing.

The stages of the two-year ethnographic work in the São Paulo WiMLDS community and case study are divided, in chronological order, into definition of topics to investigate, identification and selection of community, participant observation of the community (immersion), data collection (guarantee ethical procedures) and data analysis and interpretation of results. The collection of all data from the São Paulo WiMLDS ethnographic case study was carried out manually. Despite the variety of data collection and analysis tools in social media, it was a choice with the proposal of immersion and integration of the researcher into the group's observing coexistence. 3,188 media were collected and verified, published in text spaces on the group's internal digital platforms (WhatsApp, Telegram, Email).

Ten hours per week were spent extracting and archiving data on WhatsApp and Telegram from São Paulo WiMLDS during the seven months of collecting work, totaling 280 h. Data analysis for each month took place in the week following the end: 320 h per month (4 full days), 2,240 h.

In May 2023 a new community, Mulheres em Inteligência Artificial (Women in Artificial Intelligence), became the fourth case study as the São Paulo WiMLDS community, the main case study community, had its activities suspended due to the impact of the covid-19 pandemic. It aims to raise features that help activism on a new platform. For this, transmedia storytelling will still be tested in a communication campaign on the group's digital platforms.

Investigation methods and techniques used were:

A – Interviews: more than 15 with female community leaders in IT;

B – Focus Group: carried out with the target public of São Paulo WiMLDS. There will also be sessions to be held with the Women in Artificial Intelligence community to design a communication campaign with storytelling and a tech prototype.

C – Ethnography: two communities had their digital platforms monitored for a period of 7 months (Minas Programam and Geek Girls Portugal) to perceive aspects related to transmedia storytelling and interaction design, respectively. The São Paulo WiMLDS community had been monitored for 2 years, ending in December 2022, in order to understand organizational, hierarchical, communicational and interactional elements among all members, in order to perceive opportunities and problems, how information and initiatives are developed, objectives and impacts obtained.

D – Three case studies were finished. A new case study under development with Women in Artificial Intelligence is going to test a storytelling strategy on a digital platform communication campaign. Its results will be tested and part of a tech prototype which will be designed and developed to propose tools to help women in tech communities work with storytelling as a tool and part of routine strategy.

E – Participatory design: co-creation of a communication campaign and prototype of a technological proposal for communities with Women in AI, which incorporates elements of HCI, feminism, transmedia and storytelling.

F – Observant participation in more than 50 events in Brazilian communities and on technology with content related to topics studied in the investigation.

5   São Paulo WiMLDS: Focus Group in a Case Study

On July 9, 2022, a focus group was held with six participants from São Paulo WiMLDS. The selection criterion is to integrate the target audience, without any kind of active participation as a leader or volunteer until the day of the dynamic. The participant should consider the community to be extremely important for professional growth. These people were recruited on the Telegram group, which brings together the largest number of members among the group's platforms, through posts published by the researcher and the leaders with the invitation. The meeting was held on the Zoom platform and recorded on video, lasting one hour. After the focus group, a questionnaire was applied with questions about more subjective and personal aspects related to the trajectory of the members in the technological career, to identify a common profile.

Despite being a proper and specific space for exchanging information and developing activities, the dimensions of transmedia and storytelling were not verified, as well as attributes present in Feminist HCI frameworks.

The following Table 1 gather the questions asked and a summary of the participants' responses, which will be anonymized as Person 1, Person 2, Person 3, Person 4, Person 5, Person 6.

1 - How is your involvement with women's technology communities, especially SP WiMLDS? How did you find out about this community?

Person 1	Person 2	Person 3	Person 4	Person 5	Person 6
I was already following the community because I am part of several communities. I follow it mainly on Telegram; the first contact was in 2019	A friend recommenda-tion who was part of women data science communities. I didn't know any other machine learning community. I was interested in following this career. I joined the Telegram group. I follow more on Telegram than on Instagram profile	I follow several more communities on Telegram. In addition to workshops and lectures, it also has a lot of publicity for affirmative vacancies for women	I met the girls from the community at an event in 2019. My path is a little different because I participated since 2019 helping to organize the events. Now I have been following the vacancies on Telegram	I started participating in the community in 2019 at an event. I am currently active in other women's communities	I started participa-ting in the middle of the pandemic, in 2020. I think the PyLadies girls nominated me. As I wanted to go into the data area, I started to participate. I follow on Telegram, sometimes I post vacancies

2 - How could communication with this community have contributed to your work and study in technology?

Person 1	Person 2	Person 3	Person 4	Person 5	Person 6
My first contact with the community was because of its dataton, which was worldwide. I believe the community has helped me to open the range of options and take a closer look at what is happening out there. I think this expansion of perspective from the technical and social part adds a lot	I worked in technology; I was interested in machine learning. A data science friend recommended the community. It made possible to participate in worldwide workshops Since 2020 I haven't actively participated but I see vacancies and studies on Telegram	I participate in Telegram. I found it very interesting in the pandemic, classes from a book on Machine learning were broadcast on YouTube. Feminine communities empower us. We meet other women who are going through what we live. One supports each other	I think more empower-ment and networking. Being in a position of leadership, of creating, of organizing these things, you get to know the data community in general in São Paulo a lot. You end up knowing how relationships work. Empower-ment in the sense of being leading. I was very young, but I was there. I felt very empowered	When I joined the community, I didn't work with develop-ment and IT. Opened the mind to know new opportunities. It was through the community that I got my jobs. I learned a lot of things on Telegram. It brought me social and technical enrichment	I tend to look for new events, things not advertised in other commun-ities. I think it's a cool place to advertise vacancies, it has a lot of feedback

3 - What are the contents that are most engaging? Do you consider that testimonies and personal narratives make a difference in your life?

Person 1	Person 2	Person 3	Person 4	Person 5	Person 6
What interested me in this community were the advanced and more technical subjects. I also like testimonials	As a black woman, the testimony of another black woman empowers me to be able to enter a community, to feel embraced, to learn. The statement is very, very important because the woman feels: "wow, I didn't know I could do such a thing". I feel embraced. Here I can speak openly, feel heard It is essential to have these testimonials in a community. I joined this SP WiMLDS community based on a statement from a friend of mine who participated. This pushed me to join because I didn't know there was a community dedicated to ML and DS	Narratives are good for encouraging those at the back of the organization to be empowered to bring newer content. As much as these spontaneous testimonials do not happen on Telegram, in everyday life, when we are in person, they happen a lot. I've met women who are outside my bubble that I've been talking to has impacted me a lot. In the same way that I have impacted other women with my own story. I think that within the group itself, sometimes it ends up getting lost because women are much more interested in the technical issue than in the narratives of women who have succeeded. I think that the communities themselves are already giving this empowerment. Offline is where we really support each other	Testimonials add. I think that those who participate and want to spread the word, it can be through Telegram, it can be super interesting for sure, because it engages you to participate	I agree it really helps on the community engagement	I came from another profession. When I went to technology, I felt insecure. I was 38 years old. Testimonial make a lot of difference. Definitely to bring people to the area, to encourage to stay and become a developer. Testimonial is important

It was verified in the focus group the valorization of the testimonies, which consist of personal narratives about success or defeat trajectories that influence and inspire participants of the group or outside it to participate in it and attract new members. However, despite realizing the potential for empowerment and engagement, the focus group members fail to see where these narratives could be used in the context of existing digital platforms, as well as in the context of campaigns or specific initiatives related to them. Even participant 3, a former community leader, considers storytelling to be an important resource, but has not had the experience of developing engagement and empowerment strategies on digital platforms.

During the monitoring of digital platforms carried out for two years in São Paulo WiMLDS, it was found that whenever a testimony and statement were published by leaders, volunteers and target audiences, especially on Telegram (the most used platform), there were several associated comments also on the form of new narratives whose contents are related to overcoming obstacles in entering and growing in technological careers, to how the community was important for raising wages and more technical knowledge, for example.

It was not an objective for the focus group to assess the technical knowledge of the participants, but to see if communicational and storytelling dimensions could be proposed, which did not happen. However, the value of shared narratives on digital platforms has been proven as an element of unity, strengthening and growth of female technological communities.

6 Preliminary Results

The elaboration and incorporation of narratives by all members (leaders, volunteers, and target audiences) in the communication ecosystem of women in technology communities occurs spontaneously, sporadically, without measured reach in social networks, or regularly incorporated in the planning of actions.

In the Focus Group carried out with six members of the target public of São Paulo WiMLDS, as well as in the more than 15 interviews with leaders of female IT communities in Brazil and Portugal, it was verified that the testimonies content from the target public who represent engagement occurred in the form of acknowledgments, job promotions, job openings, improvement of technological knowledge by communities. These narratives usually yield prolonged interactions on the timelines of digital platforms, due to the commotion they provoke among the members. These are reports of a human, personal nature, full of authenticity and point out that, in fact, communities are an important catalyst for inclusion, training and empowerment of women in technology.

From the empirical work carried out and to be developed in the doctoral research in four case studies it was possible to outline some communication initiatives in the dimensions of storytelling and transmedia to be proposed.

Ciancia [23] highlights the concept of transmedia storytelling (TS) each medium makes distinctive contributions to our understanding of the world from stories spread across multiple media platforms. Pratten [24] believes "transmedia storytelling is a design philosophy". Gambarato, Alzamora, Tarcia [25] states TS "is a contemporary communication logic in social practices and in specific communication dynamics".

The concept of activist transmedia can be applied to the context of female communities in IT and storytelling and the use of its logic in a campaign or in the development of a technological and design proposal. According to Srivastava [26] it is a social impact framework with storytelling by authors who share and create content through media to influence social action. Gambarato, Alzamora, & Tarcia [25] define transmedia activism as a process related to collective in media connections that "foster awareness, engagement, and social change".

Stages of storytelling strategies to be incorporated into the ecosystem of digital platforms of female communities in technology:

1 – Immersion:

Raise which narratives were the most important, on which platforms, results for the community and individuals, if any work was carried out by the leaders in this regard. Evaluate the potential for action of the proposed narratives.

2 – Proposals for building a storytelling strategy:

Create personas from selected women in the target audience. Define a message for the campaign action. Evaluate the possibility of capturing and sharing narratives from the target audience on digital platforms.

3 – Execution of the transmedia storytelling strategy:

Build narratives from narratives: presentation of the characters, dramatic development, difficulties, and opportunities, when they joined the community as a milestone, group gains and elevation.

4 – Evaluation of the effectiveness of storytelling.

These stages will be tested in the communication campaign to be developed in the Women in Artificial Intelligence group and in the technology prototype for communities with an emphasis on storytelling as a feature in the design of digital platforms which will be codesigned with the community.

7   Conclusions

Ethnography on digital platforms in São Paulo WiMLDS, Focus Group and interviews with leaders and target audience showed testimonials generally take the form of personal narratives related to advances in their professional careers based on group interaction, whether in the form of a request for help with some information about programming, or in the form of winning job vacancies, insecurities in the career transition to IT, for example. These testimonies are usually the target of interactions in the form of emojis and also congratulations, sources of encouragement for women at different levels of knowledge in technology to gather strength for their own lives and even seek other women in support of the cause. However, despite the high level of engagement, as they represent participation at a deeper level, linked to the identification of stories and values, these testimonies are not used to be highlighted in communication on internal and external digital platforms, as well as in events.

In a face-to-face meeting that took place in August 2018 with one founder and leader, the question was raised about whether narratives as testimonies are relevant in communication. It was noticed that they are not perceived as relevant, contrary to what was demonstrated with the target audience in the focus group.

There were diverse reports about difficulties, fears and requests for help among members on Telegram about current discontent in jobs, trajectories in the transition from areas of professional activity to data science. The group acts as a social and solidarity protection network for these people; it is important for black women to have greater motivation to join and work in IT, especially reported by other black women from the same community. Knowing and communicating directly with leaders encourages them to create more and better content. Participating in the community allows you to meet women outside of the target audience's online and in-person social networks and the narratives around the construction of their life trajectories are an element of great inspiration and engagement. There has been a considerable increase in the exposure of personal narratives among community participants, which further encourages participation and engagement.

The empowerment narratives reinforce how fundamental São Paulo WiMLDS was in improving members in technology in digital platforms, focus group and interviews preliminary analysis. These are not praise for the group's work, but examples of social, professional, and personal transformations experienced by the people impacted. These narratives will still be compiled and analyzed in the final empirical work with the Women in Artificial Intelligence community in the communication campaign and in the technology prototype for communities that will be developed soon.

There is a communication and interaction space to be filled in female technology communities. Before creating transmedia systems, models, and frameworks for these communities, it´s to necessary establish verification, editing and treatment processes for narratives and storytelling that are disregarded by agents of the entire multiplatform communication chain of these groups. There are scattered stories of overcoming, conquests, losses, sisterhood, among many other personal stories of those involved, with stories of local role models (Brazil and Portugal) and international role models that today are wasted in their potential by the platforms, which will make the difference when inserted in a specific communication and transmedia proposal.

Acknowledgement. *This work is financially supported by national funds through FCT – Foundation for Science and Technology, I.P., under the project UIDB/05460/2020.* Renata Frade's PhD investigation is sponsored by Fundação para a Ciência e Tecnologia (FCT) doctorate scholarship (2020.06640.BD reference).

References

1. World Economic Forum: Global Gender Gap Report (2022). https://www3.weforum.org/docs/WEF_GGGR_2022.pdf
2. UN Women: Power on: How we can supercharge an equitable digital future (2023). https://www.unwomen.org/en/news-stories/explainer/2023/02/power-on-how-we-can-supercharge-an-equitable-digital-future
3. World Wide Web Foundation: Women's Rights Online: closing the digital gen- der gap for a more equal world (2020). https://webfoundation.org/research/womens-rights-online-2020/
4. Castells, M.: A sociedade em rede. Editora Paz e Terra, São Paulo (2002)
5. Castells, M.: O poder da identidade. Editora Paz e Terra, São Paulo (2018)
6. Wajcman, J.: El tecnofeminismo. Ediciones Cátedra, Madrid (2006)

7. Frade, R., Vairinhos, M.: Technofeminism: Multi and Transdisciplinary Contemporary Views on Women in Technology. UA Editora, Aveiro (2023)
8. Jenkins, H.: Cultura da convergência: a colisão entre os velhos e novos meios de comunicação. Aleph, São Paulo (2009)
9. Carroll, J.: Human computer interaction – brief intro. In: Soegaard, M., Dam, R.F. (eds.) The Encyclopedia of Human-Computer Interaction, 2nd edn. The Interaction Design Foundation, Aarhus (2013)
10. Dimond, J.P.: Feminist HCI for Real: Designing Technology in Support of a Social Movement. Georgia Institute of Technology, Atlanta, Ga (2012)
11. Riera, T.: Online Feminisms: Feminist Community Building and Activism in a Digital Age. Claremon Graduate University, Claremont (2015)
12. Jenkins, H., Shresthova, S., Gamber-Thompson, L., Kligler-Vilenchik, N., Zimmerman, A., Soep, E.: By Any Media Necessary: The New Youth Activism. New York University Press, New York (2019)
13. Carpentier, N.: Além da escada da participação: Ferramentas analíticas para a análise crítica dos processos midiáticos participativos. Revista Mídia e Cotidiano 12(3), 245–274 (2018)
14. Dahlgren, P., Hill, A.: Media Engagement. Routledge, Abingdon Oxon (2023)
15. de Souza, C., Preece, J.: A framework for analyzing and understanding online communities. Interact. Comput. 16(3), 579–610 (2004)
16. Erickson, T.: SocialComputing. In: Soegaard, M., Dam. (eds.) The Encyclopedia of Human-Computer Interaction. Interaction-Design.org Foundation, Aarhus (2013)
17. Gupta, S., Tanenbaum, T.: Shiva's Rangoli: tangible interactive storytelling in ambient environments, pp . 29–32 (2019). https://doi.org/10.1145/3301019.3325145
18. Crawford, C.: Chris Crawford on Interactive Storytelling. New Riders, Berkeley Calif (2013)
19. Miller, C.: Digital Storytelling: A Creator's Guide to Interactive Entertainment. CRC Press, Boca Raton, FL (2020)
20. Koenitz, H., Barbara, J., Eladhari, M.: Interactive digital narrative (IDN)—new ways to represent complexity and facilitate digitally empowered citizens. New Rev. Hypermedia Multimedia 28(3–4), 76–96 (2022). https://doi.org/10.1080/13614568.2023.2181503
21. Brown, S.A., Chu, S.L.: "You write your own story": design implications for an interactive narrative authoring tool to support reflection for mental health in college students. In: Mitchell, A., Vosmeer, M. (eds.) ICIDS 2021. LNCS, vol. 13138, pp. 312–321. Springer, Cham (2021). https://doi.org/10.1007/978-3-030-92300-6_30
22. Coutinho, C.: Metodologia de investigação em ciências sociais e humanas: Teoria e prática. Almedina, Coimbra (2013)
23. Ciancia, M.: Transmedia design framework: design-oriented approach to transmedia research. Int. J. Transmedia Lit. 1(1), 131–145 (2015)
24. Pratten, R.: Getting Started with Transmedia Storytelling: A Practical Guide for Beginners, 2nd edn. CreateSpace, London (2015)
25. Gambarato, R., Alzamora, G., Tarcia, L.: Theory, Development, and Strategy in Transmedia Storytelling. Routledge, New York (2020)
26. Srivastava, L.: Transmedia Activism: Telling Your Story Across Media Platforms to Create Effective Social Change (2009). https://web.archive.org/web/20130515174049/, http://www.namac.org/node/6925. Accessed 06 July 2023

VR Storytelling to Prime Uncertainty Avoidance

Zhengya Gong[1(✉)] ⓘ, Milene Gonçalves[2] ⓘ, Vijayakumar Nanjappan[1] ⓘ, and Georgi V. Georgiev[1] ⓘ

[1] Center for Ubiquitous Computing, University of Oulu, Oulu, Finland
{Zhengya.Gong,Vijayakumar.Nanjappan,Georgi.Georgiev}@oulu.fi
[2] Department of Design, Organisation and Strategy, Faculty of Industrial Design Engineering, Delft University of Technology, Delft, The Netherlands
m.guerreirogoncalves@tudelft.nl

Abstract. In recent years, there has been a growing interest among researchers in the field of virtual reality (VR) storytelling. There is a lack of studies on using VR storytelling to prime culture-related content. The cultural aspects, particularly the tendency to avoid uncertainty, have yet to be thoroughly examined within VR. Therefore, we developed VR storytelling intending to prime individuals' uncertainty avoidance values. An experiment was conducted to assess the efficacy of VR storytelling in priming individuals' uncertainty avoidance values. The participants' encounter with VR storytelling was assessed through various parameters, including but not limited to their experience of presence and engagement in the virtual environment. The study provides evidence that VR storytelling has the capacity to influence individuals' cultural values, particularly their inclination to uncertainty avoidance. Furthermore, the feedback provided by the participants revealed that they had positive emotions, a feeling of being present, engagement, and immersion while engaging with such VR storytelling.

Keywords: VR storytelling · cultural value · uncertainty avoidance · priming

1 Introduction

Numerous scholarly investigations have examined the impact of storytelling on the formation of individuals' values (e.g., [14,25,29,37,39,41,44]). Narratives were employed to elicit cognitive and intentional responses in individuals, specifically in relation to their self-construal [14] and their intention to utilize safety belts [36]. Furthermore, it has been suggested by scholars that the incorporation of virtual reality (VR) technology into the realm of storytelling, commonly referred to as VR storytelling, has the potential to act as a mechanism for activating individuals' cultural values and offering benefits such as heightened feelings of immersion and engagement, in contrast to traditional storytelling methods [16]. To date, there has been a lack of empirical research examining the impact

© The Author(s), under exclusive license to Springer Nature Switzerland AG 2023
L. Holloway-Attaway and J. T. Murray (Eds.): ICIDS 2023, LNCS 14383, pp. 103–116, 2023.
https://doi.org/10.1007/978-3-031-47655-6_7

of VR storytelling on priming the cultural values of individuals. Drawing inspiration from the aforementioned studies, we devised VR narratives and proceeded to conduct an empirical investigation to assess the efficacy of utilizing VR storytelling as a means of priming individuals' cultural values. Furthermore, an analysis was conducted on the affective experiences of the participants during VR storytelling. Our objectives in implementing VR in the realm of storytelling are twofold. Firstly, we seek to comprehend the impact of VR storytelling on priming individuals' cultural values, specifically their inclination towards uncertainty avoidance (UA). Secondly, we aim to explore various outcomes that arise from VR storytelling, including participants' experience of immersive, engagement, presence and the positive emotions it evokes in participants.

2   Background and Related Work

2.1   Storytelling

The custom of telling stories has been passed down for millennia. Storytelling is how people tell stories for entertainment, knowledge sharing, or maintaining cultural heritage [28]. "Storytelling is a uniquely human experience that enables us to convey, through the language of words, aspects of ourselves and others, and the worlds, real or imagined, that we inhabit" [4, p.31]. We follow this definition of storytelling as the term of storytelling in our study.

The primary objective of storytelling is to elicit emotional and cognitive responses from the audience, as noted by Lugmayr et al. [28]. The utilization of storytelling is prevalent within the field of education, as it facilitates the dissemination of knowledge to students [8,42]. The utilization of storytelling within organizations is a common practice [9,12] with the purpose of transmitting organizational culture and fostering a strong sense of affiliation between employees and the organization [12]. Furthermore, it has potential applications in the realm of design education, serving as a catalyst to motivate novice designers to enhance the originality of their ideas in incubation [3]. The significance of storytelling in the advancement and dissemination of culture has been widely acknowledged [7]. This is exemplified in tribal societies where oral narratives serve as a means to safeguard crucial aspects of myths and legends for posterity. Tribal cultures employ the practice of repeatedly sharing purposeful stories over an extended period to effectively transmit the essential components and significance of their values, beliefs, and governing structures. This process serves to enhance the cohesion of their communities [8,20].

2.2   Stories for Priming Cultural Values

The concept of priming is associated with the unconscious component of human memory, which involves the enhancement of cognitive processes [38] and influences social behaviours and intentions [11]. The phenomenon of priming refers to the increased accessibility of a specific category of information when individuals are exposed to a particular stimulus, such as an event [25]. The length of the priming effect may be influenced by many variables, including the characteristics of the priming itself, the strength of the priming stimulus, and individual differences in cognitive processes [32]. The temporal extent of short-term priming effects may vary from milliseconds to several minutes, during which they possess the capacity to influence immediate perceptual or cognitive processes [32]. Numerous narratives were employed to prime cultural values and assessed the subsequent behaviours and intentions of participants [25,29,37,39,41]. The narrative of the warrior Sostoras has been extensively employed to effectively prime cultural values, as evidenced by various iterations of the story that elicit either individualistic or collectivistic responses [14,37,43]. Hence, it has been demonstrated that narratives, when presented in written form, serve as a pragmatic method for activating cultural values.

2.3   VR Storytelling Priming Cultural Values

Virtual reality (VR) refers to a computer-generated simulation environment that enables individuals to experience a sense of presence, immersion, and engagement with a simulated world, facilitated by specialized electronic equipment such as a head-mounted display [15]. Several scholars have put forth the idea of utilizing VR as a means to prime cultural values through storytelling [16,17]. Presenting a story in a vivid and immersive way provides opportunities for priming individuals' subconscious and influencing their subsequent behaviours and responses [16,17,34]. In contrast to alternative narrative mediums such as written texts or videos, VR offers a heightened level of immersion by constructing a virtual environment that engenders increased arousal and presence, thereby evoking a profound sense of presence or "being there," [6]. Furthermore, it has been suggested that the utilization of VR immersive environments may lead to heightened levels of engagement among participants [2], in contrast to conventional methods of storytelling. Furthermore, it is possible to create virtual environments that incorporate contextual cues with the intention of aligning them with the narrative or priming objectives [17]. This approach has the potential to elicit anticipated behaviours in individuals that align with the intended priming objectives [21].

2.4   Research Aim

Notwithstanding the potentially effective approaches delineated in previous scholarly examinations regarding the utilization of VR storytelling to prime cultural values [16], the existing body of empirical research is insufficient to substantiate these assertions. Hence, the objective of our research is to develop a VR narrative and evaluate the efficacy of VR storytelling in priming the cultural values of individuals. Our research focus and previous investigations have led us to be particularly interested in the UA value. It has been observed that individuals' UA values have a significant influence on their experiences and outcomes in the field of creativity [19]. In a previous study conducted by authors, it was observed that individuals with a low UA value exhibited a commensurately low level of workability in the ideas they generated. As a result, our study aimed to prime individuals' UA values by utilizing a VR narrative. Subsequently, we sought to evaluate any changes in their UA values following the VR storytelling experience, serving as the preliminary pilot investigation. The present pilot study will establish a foundation for our forthcoming research endeavours in the domains of design and creativity to address and mitigate the adverse cultural impact. Furthermore, our research endeavours to investigate individuals' subjective experience in VR storytelling, encompassing aspects such as engagement, immersion, and emotional responses.

3   Experiment

In order to evaluate the efficacy of VR storytelling in priming individuals' UA values, the initial step involved the development of a VR narrative. An experimental investigation was conducted to evaluate the efficacy of a particular intervention (VR storytelling) within a controlled laboratory setting equipped with tables, chairs, and displays.

3.1   Designing the VR Storytelling

UA is one of the cultural dimensions analyzed by Hofstede [24], which refers to the degree of anxiety and risk aversion that people feel during uncertain situations [24]. According to Hofstede's research, individuals with a higher level of UA tend to avoid situations characterized by uncertainty, perceiving uncertainty as a potential threat. Conversely, individuals with a lower level of UA tend to embrace risk-taking behaviours and believe life is inherently unpredictable [24]. The malleability of individuals' UA values and associated attitudes has been demonstrated in several studies [16,17,29,36]. As an illustration, researchers conducted a study to prime UA-related concepts (risk-taking), which demonstrated that individuals increased their risk-taking attitudes when they saw others win gambling games (a highly uncertain activity) because of their gambling knowledge and skills [29]. We designed the VR story for priming UA value by considering several elements: the story aimed to prime UA, the way of presenting the story, the VR avatars, the virtual environment, the interaction methods, and the position and movement of participants, inspired by Fisher et al., (2022) [13] and Wolfe et al., (2022) [40].

We adopted the Sostoras story from the previous studies [14,37] and modified the story to be used for priming UA value based on the description of UA and priming theory [23,38]. The story was further polished by an English editor. The background of the story describes a coming war: *"Sostoras, a warrior in ancient Sumer, was largely responsible for the success of Sargon I in conquering all of Mesopotamia. As a result, he was rewarded with a small kingdom of his own to rule. About 10 years later, Sargon I was conscripting warriors for a new war. Sostoras was obligated to send a detachment of soldiers to aid Sargon I"*

Fig. 1. The screenshots of the VR story.

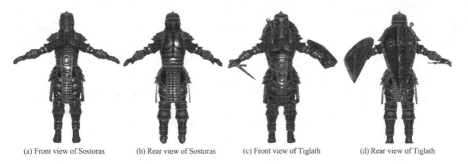

(a) Front view of Sostoras   (b) Rear view of Sostoras   (c) Front view of Tiglath   (d) Rear view of Tiglath

Fig. 2. The views of avatars.

[37, p.652]. From this point, the story is divided into two branches. One is used for priming a higher value of UA, in which Sostoras decided to put Tiglath in command of the war, who is older and the best general, considering his vast war experience. As Tiglath has won many battles, choosing him increases the chances of winning the war. After cautious consideration, Sostoras decided to put Tiglath in command of the army. In the other branch, the story aims to prime a lower UA value: Sostoras decided to put Tiglath in command of the war. Tiglath is young and does not have much war experience, but he shows tactical skills. Although choosing him is risky, Sostoras wants to give him a chance to train to be an excellent general. Note that in both branches, the name of Tiglath is the same, but participants only see one version of the story. Both branches led to the same result: they won the war, their country received a large amount of compensation and land, and the country prospered. We built the VR story with the game engine Unity 3D, and the required items for the design could be purchased from the Unity Asset Store. We divided the story into two sections for **presenting the story**. The first section focuses on the background of the story, as illustrated in Fig. 1 (a); the next section is composed of the two-story branches, showing different content, but both are designed as an inner narration of King Sostoras (Fig. 1 (b)). After clicking start, one branch aims to prime higher UA values, while the other primes lower UA values. In addition, two distinct voice styles were developed for the story's narration. Specifically, the first involved a female voice which provided an account of the background, while the second comprised a male voice narrating the monarch's monologue.

For **designing the avatars**, the original story has three characters: Sostoras, Sargon I, and Tiglath; however, Sargon I is only mentioned twice in the story's background; thus, we only included two characters in the VR story, which were purchased from Unity Asset Store, and modified. In addition, to create the tense atmosphere of impending war, the characters were dressed in military uniforms, and the difference between Sostoras and Tiglath is that Tiglath has a sword and shield on his back. Moreover, the avatars are covered by armour and helmet, which attempt to hide the avatar's race, and geographic characteristics to avoid potential biases [30], as shown in Fig. 2. To create a **virtual environment**, we have determined that the setting should be an ancient period with a tense atmosphere due to impending war, and the scene should feature an imperial palace. However, we have excluded several keywords, such as "Mesopotamia," as it may evoke different emotions in participants from diverse backgrounds. To enhance the experience, we have also selected intense background music that matches the story from the Unity Asset Store. For **interaction**, we designed a simple interaction in VR storytelling. Because the reading speed may vary among participants, we presented the story in sentences rather than paragraphs and designed two buttons to click forward and backward (Fig. 1 (b)). We attempted to design participants' initial **locations** and **movements** differently in the VR storytelling and tested this with fellow researchers. This resulted in further iterations on the initial location of the VR storytelling. As such, participants start in a broad platform (Fig. 1 (c)) to observe the whole environment and characters. The platform allows participants to walk and run there naturally, depending on the scale of the lab room. However, they do not have an avatar to represent them, as self-identification plays a crucial role for the participants, and previous studies propose the use of a non-protagonist narrative [5]. Therefore, they are bystanders in the story.

3.2   Participants

A total of 24 participants were recruited through the utilization of posters. The individuals in question were enrolled as graduate students, primarily hailing from the Department of industrial design. The participants' mean age was 25.04, with a standard deviation of 3. In terms of gender distribution, 41.7% of the participants identified as male, while 58.3% identified as female. Before being assigned to the two experimental conditions, participants were instructed to fill out a questionnaire that gathered information about their demographics, hand preference, and uncertainty avoidance scales. Based on their UA value, they were divided into two conditions in a between-subjected study, as depicted in Fig. 3. Participants with a higher UA value were placed in the low priming UA condition (LPUA) in order to enhance their tolerance for ambiguity and promote risk-taking behaviour. This was exemplified by the selection of Tiglath, a young and inexperienced individual, as the chosen candidate by the king. In contrast, individuals exhibiting a lower level of UA were divided into the high priming UA condition (HPUA), where Tiglath is chosen based on his war experience and established competence, thereby reducing the level of risk, as shown in Fig. 3.

Each condition includes 12 participants, five male and seven female, and there is no significant difference in age between the two conditions.

3.3   Procedure

The experiment was partitioned into five sequential stages, as depicted in Fig. 3. During the experimental procedure, participants were requested to complete the informed consent form, which was followed by an invitation to utilize a VR headset, specifically the Oculus Quest 2, to engage with VR storytelling on two occasions, with a total duration of fewer than 10 min. The initial session served as a preparatory exercise, during which individuals were encouraged to engage in walking, observing, and exploring the virtual environment, with the purpose of familiarizing themselves with the capabilities of VR. During the subsequent iteration, participants were instructed to observe and attentively engage with the VR story presented in Sect. 3.1. Subsequently, a task of ideation was administered, wherein participants were instructed to generate ideas. Given that the focus of this paper does not revolve around the ideation task, we refrain from engaging in a discussion or providing an explanation of it. The last two steps included questionnaires (to measure the uncertainty avoidance again) and a short interview. One aspect of the interview process was designed to ensure that the participants remained unaware of any priming influences, as noted by Molden (2014) [31].

Fig. 3. The experiment's procedure.

3.4   Measurements

The **uncertainty avoidance scale** was adopted in the study to measure individuals' UA values on a Likert-type scale. This has been previously developed by Jung & Kellaris (2004) [27] based on the description of cultural dimension [23]. The original scale consisted of eight items; however, one item *"I would prefer to stay with one employer as long as possible"* was excluded from the analysis. This decision was made due to the fact that the participants in our study consisted of students, the majority of whom lacked prior work experience. The uncertainty avoidance scale has been utilized in prior research to gather data on individuals' UA values and has demonstrated strong reliability and validity [1,27].

The **user experience in immersive virtual environments** was developed by the utilization of existing questionnaires [35]. The original questionnaire consisted of 82 items that were designed to assess various aspects of users' experiences, including presence and immersion within immersive virtual environments. Nevertheless, the initial survey is of considerable length, potentially leading respondents to develop a reduced sensitivity or responsiveness when providing answers [33]. Furthermore, a considerable number of items included in the initial questionnaire were deemed inappropriate for the purposes of our research. For example, participants observed the story from a platform as a whole rather than conducting a detailed examination of objects. Hence, the incorporation of the statement *"I had the capacity to closely analyze objects,"* was considered irrelevant. Consequently, a limited number of questions was chosen to examine the participants' experiences with VR storytelling, focusing on the dimensions of presence, immersion, engagement, and emotion [35].

4   Results

4.1   The Effectiveness of Priming UA Values by VR Storytelling

The UA values of participants were collected on two occasions, both before and after the VR storytelling experience, in order to assess the efficacy of using VR storytelling as a means of priming individuals' UA values. A paired sample t-test was employed to assess whether there is a statistically significant difference in the mean between paired observations. These observations consist of either the same individuals tested at two different time points or individuals tested under two distinct conditions on the same dependent variable. It is appropriate for our research to conduct repeated testing on the same individuals.

In the **HPUA condition** (participants with a low UA value in the condition to prime their UA values high), one outlier was detected; therefore, we replaced the outlier's value with one that is less extreme (median value) [26]. The difference scores for the first UA value and second UA value were normally distributed, as assessed by Shapiro-Wilk's test ($p = .506$). Data are mean $\pm$ standard deviation unless otherwise stated. Participants' UA values increased after VR storytelling in the HPUA condition (17.5 ± 3.06) as opposed to before (16.08 ± 3.60), a statistically significant increase of 1.41 (95% CI, 2.81 to 0.02), $t(12) = 2.24$, $p = .047$, as shown in Table 1.

In the **LPUA condition** (participants with a high UA value in the condition to prime their UA values low) there were no outliers in the data. The difference scores for the first UA value and second UA value were normally distributed, as assessed by Shapiro-Wilk's test ($p = .443$). Participants' UA values decreased after VR storytelling in the LPUA condition (21.25 ± 2.77) as opposed to before (24.75 ± 2.83), a statistically significant decrease of 3.5 (95% CI, -4.57 to -2.43), $t(12) = -7.22$, $p < .0005$ (Table 1).

Table 1. Paired samples test.

Conditions	Paired Samples	Mean	Std. Deviation	t	Sig. (2-tailed)
HPUA	After VR storytelling	17.50	3.06	-	-
	Before VR storytelling	16.08	3.60	-	-
	After - Before VR storytelling	1.42	2.19	2.24	.047
LPUA	After VR storytelling	21.25	2.77	-	-
	Before VR storytelling	24.75	2.83	-	-
	After - Before VR storytelling	-3.50	1.68	− 7.22	0.000

4.2   User Experience in Immersive Virtual Environments

This study examined four distinct factors pertaining to users' experience in VR storytelling. Specifically, we employed a 5-point Likert scale to measure participants' perceptions of presence, engagement, immersion, and emotion. Concerning the presence factor, approximately 80% of the participants demonstrated a positive attitude towards the feelings of being in the virtual environment. Regarding engagement, 60% of participants reported feeling involved in the virtual environment experience. Additionally, roughly half of the participants reported feeling stimulated by the virtual environment and becoming less aware of their surroundings because they were immersed in the virtual world. Regarding the emotional factor, 75% of the participants indicated they enjoyed and relaxed while engaging with the virtual experience.

5   Discussion

The results showed that the difference scores abstracted in the two times questionnaires (before and after VR storytelling) in two conditions differed, 3.5 in LPUA and 1.42 in HPUA, which means the priming lower UA values is more effective than priming higher UA values. These results suggest that participants were more easily to be primed with lower UA values than higher ones. The interviews provided further insights into this: participants, especially from the design area, tend to be risk-taking and more adventurous (characteristics that people with low UA value usually exhibit) in study and design. For example, when we explained our research aim and told one participant that he has a higher UA value (i.e., demonstrates risk-averse characteristics), he looked unhappy, directly expressing his disagreement with the UA questionnaire results. Another example is a female participant who indirectly referenced her preference for remaining within her comfort zone and aversion to taking risks. However, when engaged in the process of studying and designing, she actively challenges and takes risks herself to produce unconventional and daring ideas. Conversely, when we explained our research aim and told participants with a lower score of UA their questionnaire results, they expressed pride and pleasure in being risk-takers. In another example, a participant reported how his ideas surprised team members and were curious about how he came up with a solution they had never considered. Nevertheless, he believed it was everyday thinking and uncertainty that triggered creativity.

Although a few individuals expressed dissenting opinions, the majority of participants reported positive experiences with VR storytelling, including the sense of being present in the virtual environment, high levels of engagement, complete immersion in the story, and the elicitation of positive emotions. We endeavoured to extract and identify the underlying reasons for these disagreements. This may be because the scale of the lab room limited their movement in a virtual environment. When they were near physical objects in the lab room, purple border lines in the virtual environment reminded them and potentially disturbed the immersive experience of VR storytelling. Notwithstanding this fact, VR storytelling persists in providing a sense of presence, immersion, engagement, and pleasure, thereby affording a prospect to foster cultural values among individuals through VR storytelling, in contrast to other customary forms of storytelling, such as oral or textual [6,10].

6   Limitations

Similar to other studies, we have several limitations. The research encompasses a cohort of 24 individuals, and the limited sample size may impact the extent to which the findings can be applied to a broader population. In addition, it is advisable to incorporate a control group into our research design in order to assess the disparity between the two priming conditions and a neutral condition. Concurrently, doing a comparative experimental study between VR storytelling and other storytelling mediums has considerable potential to substantiate the advantages of VR storytelling by acquiring more robust empirical data. Moreover, the duration of the priming effect remains uncertain since our testing only included a limited timeframe. Furthermore, it is important to highlight that the VR story was predominantly developed with the purpose of priming UA values, while neglecting to adequately address alternative viewpoints, such as the aesthetics and visual representation of avatars and the virtual environment.

7   Conclusion and Future Work

Researchers have proposed methods to prime individuals' cultural values through VR storytelling, drawing on priming theory and Hofstede's cultural dimensions [17]. Consequently, we developed a VR story to prime individuals' cultural values, particularly in uncertainty avoidance (UA). Subsequently, we conducted an assessment to confirm that individuals' UA values could be successfully primed to be either higher or lower than their initial UA values through the use of VR storytelling. To the best of our knowledge, our study is the first empirical study to show that VR storytelling could be used to prime individuals' cultural values and demonstrated that such primed individuals' UA values were significantly different. Furthermore, the participants expressed a sense of enjoyment towards VR storytelling and exhibited positive attitudes towards the presence, engagement, and immersion experienced during the VR narrative.

Our study contributes to various disciplines in education and industries, such as design practice. Creativity is an essential element for design students and employees that could positively affect various academic and social outcomes, such as scholastic performance and breakthrough products [18,19,22]. Priming individuals' UA values to become lower may inspire designers to take risks in the design process, potentially increasing the chances of novel outcomes. Oppositely, priming individuals' UA values to increase may lead designers to become cautious and favour useful solutions rather than novel solutions in ideation. In industry, collaborative teamwork is a ubiquitous modality of work that involves a group of individuals pooling expertise, resources, and effort toward achieving a common objective. Within teamwork, team members are tasked with jointly planning and executing a product development process, which may encompass activities ranging from the generation of the initial idea to the screening of prototypes, and ultimately culminating in the delivery of a final product. During ideation, team members could be primed with a lower UA value to generate wild and novel ideas. In the ideas selection phases, individuals could be more thoughtful in selecting practical and workable ideas by priming them with a higher UA value.

The present study represents a novel avenue of inquiry in VR research, wherein built VR stories based on the priming theory, is employed to influence individuals' cultural values. In accordance with the priming theory, their subsequent behaviours and intentions could be influenced [38]. Therefore, our future objective is to investigate the impact of VR stories on the outputs and creativity of individuals in design processes. Specifically, we plan to examine the effects of VR storytelling on individuals who have been primed to balance their UA values. It aims to determine whether such priming can reduce the negative influence of UA values or enhance the positive influence of UA values in design and creative performances. Our study might inspire researchers to explore priming individuals' cultural values, which might affect their subsequent behaviours. Moreover, it is promising to compare VR storytelling with other forms of storytelling, such as oral and video storytelling, which will help researchers understand the benefits of VR in storytelling than other forms of storytelling.

Acknowledgements. This work was supported by the Research Council of Finland (former Academy of Finland) 6G Flagship Programme [Grant Number: 346208]; China Scholarship Council: [Grant Number 202107960006]; Opetushallitus (Finnish National Agency for Education): [Grant Number TM-20-11342]; and European Union's Horizon 2020 research and innovation programme [Grant Number H2020-856998].

References

1. Adair, W.L., Xiong, T.X.: How Chinese and Caucasian Canadians conceptualize creativity: the mediating role of uncertainty avoidance. J. Cross Cult. Psychol. **49**, 223–238 (2018)
2. Allcoat, D., von Mühlenen, A.: Learning in virtual reality: effects on performance, emotion and engagement. Res. Learn. Technol. **26** (2018)

3. Al-Shorachi, E., Sasasmit, K., Gonçalves, M: Creativity intervention: Using storytelling and math problems as intervening tasks for inducing incubation. In: DS 80–11 Proceedings of the 20th International Conference on Engineering Design (ICED 15), pp. 81–90. Design Society, Milan, Italy (2015)

4. Alterio, M., McDrury, J.: Learning through storytelling in higher education (2003)

5. Barbara, J., Haahr, M.: *Who Am I that Acts?* the use of voice in virtual reality interactive narratives. In: Mitchell, A., Vosmeer, M. (eds.) ICIDS 2021. LNCS, vol. 13138, pp. 3–12. Springer, Cham (2021). https://doi.org/10.1007/978-3-030-92300-6_1

6. Barreda-Ángeles, M., Aleix-Guillaume, S., Pereda-Baños, A.: Virtual reality storytelling as a double-edged sword: immersive presentation of nonfiction 360°-video is associated with impaired cognitive information processing. Commun. Monogr. **88**, 154–173 (2021)

7. Bietti, L.M., Tilston, O., Bangerter, A.: Storytelling as adaptive collective sensemaking. Top. Cogn. Sci. **11**, 710–732 (2019)

8. Bowman, R.F.: Teaching and learning in a storytelling culture. Clearing House A J. Educ. Strat. Issues Ideas **91**, 97–102 (2018)

9. Brady, W.H., Shar Haley, R.N.: Storytelling defines your organizational culture. Phys. Exec. **39**(1), 40 (2013)

10. Choo, Y.B., Abdullah, T., Nawi, A.M.: Digital Storytelling vs. oral storytelling: an analysis of the art of telling stories now and then. Univ. J. Educ. Res. **8**, 46–50 (2020)

11. Dijksterhuis, A., Bargh, J.A.: The perception-behavior expressway: automatic effects of social perception on social behavior. Adv. Exp. Soc. Psychol. **33**, 1–40 (2001)

12. Driscoll, C., McKee, M.: Restorying a culture of ethical and spiritual values: a role for leader storytelling. J. Bus. Ethics **73**, 205–217 (2007)

13. Fisher, J.A., Vosmeer, M., Barbara, J.: A new research agenda: Writing for virtual reality interactive narratives. Interactive Storytelling. 673–683 (2022). https://doi.org/10.1007/978-3-031-22298-6_43

14. Gardner, W.L., Gabriel, S., Lee, A.Y.: "I" value freedom, but "we" value relationships: self-construal priming mirrors cultural differences in judgment. Psychol. Sci. **10**, 321–326 (1999)

15. Georgiev, D., Georgieva, I., Gong, Z., Nanjappan, V., Georgiev, G.: Virtual reality for neurorehabilitation and cognitive enhancement. Brain Sci. **11**, 221 (2021)

16. Gong, Z., Wang, M., Nanjappan, V., Georgiev, G.V.: Instrumenting virtual reality for priming cultural differences in design creativity. In: Proceedings of the 14th Conference on Creativity and Cognition, pp. 510–514 (2022)

17. Gong, Z., Wang, M., Nanjappan, V., Georgiev, G.V.: Effects of digital technologies on cultural factors in creativity enhancement. Design in the Era of Industry 4.0, Volume 3. 383–394 (2023). https://doi.org/10.1007/978-981-99-0428-0_32

18. Gong, Z., Lee, L.-H., Soomro, S.A., Nanjappan, V., Georgiev, G.V.: A systematic review of virtual brainstorming from the perspective of creativity: affordances, framework, and outlook. Digital Creativity **33**, 96–127 (2022)

19. Gong, Z., Nanjappan, V., Lee, L.-H., Soomro, S.A., Georgiev, G.V.: Exploration of the relationship between culture and experience of creativity at the individual level: a case study based on two design tasks. Int. J. Design Creativity Innov. **11**, 185–208 (2023)

20. Guber, P.: Tell to win: Connect, persuade, and triumph with the hidden power of story. Crown Business, New York (2011)

21. Guegan, J., Nelson, J., Lubart, T.: The relationship between contextual cues in virtual environments and creative processes. Cyberpsychol. Behav. Soc. Netw. **20**, 202–206 (2017)
22. Hernández-Torrano, D., Ibrayeva, L.: Creativity and education: A Bibliometric mapping of the Research Literature (1975–2019). Thinking Skills Creativity **35**, 100625 (2020)
23. Hofstede, G.: Culture's consequences: Comparing values, behaviors, institutions, and organizations across nations. Sage, Thousand Oaks, CA (2001)
24. Hofstede, G.: Dimensionalizing cultures: The Hofstede model in context. Online Readings in Psychology and Culture. 2, (2011)
25. Israel, A., Rosenboim, M., Shavit, T.: Using priming manipulations to affect time preferences and risk aversion: an experimental study. J. Behav. Exp. Econ. **53**, 36–43 (2014)
26. Jain, A.K., Dubes, R.C.: Algorithms for clustering data. Prentice Hall, Englewood Cliffs, NJ (1988)
27. Jung, J.M., Kellaris, J.J.: Cross-national differences in proneness to scarcity effects: the moderating roles of familiarity, uncertainty avoidance, and need for cognitive closure. Psychol. Mark. **21**, 739–753 (2004)
28. Lugmayr, A., Sutinen, E., Suhonen, J., Sedano, C.I., Hlavacs, H., Montero, C.S.: Serious storytelling - a first definition and Review. Multimedia Tools Appl. **76**, 15707–15733 (2017)
29. Martinez, F., Le Floch, V., Gaffié, B., Villejoubert, G.: Reports of wins and risk taking: an investigation of the mediating effect of the illusion of Control. J. Gambl. Stud. **27**, 271–285 (2011)
30. McCabe, A.: Cultural background and storytelling: a review and implications for schooling. Elem. Sch. J. **97**, 453–473 (1997)
31. Molden, D.C.: Understanding priming effects in social psychology: What is "social priming" and how does it occur? Social Cognition**32**, 1–11 (2014)
32. Preiss, R.W., et al.: Mass media effects research: advances through meta-analysis. Routledge, New York (2010)
33. Sahlqvist, S., Song, Y., Bull, F., Adams, E., Preston, J., Ogilvie, D.: Effect of questionnaire length, personalisation and reminder type on response rate to a complex postal survey: randomised controlled trial. BMC Med. Res. Methodol. **11**, 62 (2011)
34. She, J., Seepersad, C.C., Holtta-Otto, K., MacDonald, E.F.: Priming designers leads to prime designs. In: Plattner, H., Meinel, C., Leifer, L. (eds.) Design Thinking Research. UI, pp. 251–273. Springer, Cham (2018). https://doi.org/10.1007/978-3-319-60967-6_13
35. Tcha-Tokey, K., Christmann, O., Loup-Escande, E., Richir, S.: Proposition and validation of a questionnaire to measure the user experience in immersive virtual environments. Int. J. Virtual Reality. **16**, 33–48 (2016)
36. Trafimow, D., Fishbein, M.: The importance of risk in determining the extent to which attitudes affect intentions to wear seat belts1. J. Appl. Soc. Psychol. **24**, 1–11 (1994)
37. Trafimow, D., Triandis, H.C., Goto, S.G.: Some tests of the distinction between the private self and the collective self. J. Pers. Soc. Psychol. **60**, 649–655 (1991)
38. Tulving, E., Schacter, D.L.: Priming and human memory systems. Science **247**, 301–306 (1990)
39. van den Bos, K., Brockner, J., Stein, J.H., Steiner, D.D., Van Yperen, N.W., Dekker, D.M.: The psychology of voice and performance capabilities in masculine and feminine cultures and contexts. J. Pers. Soc. Psychol. **99**, 638–648 (2010)

40. Wolfe, A., Louchart, S., Loranger, B.: The impacts of design elements in interactive storytelling in VR on emotion, mood, and self-reflection. Interactive Storytelling, pp. 616–633 (2022). https://doi.org/10.1007/978-3-031-22298-6_40

41. Wong, V.C., Wyer, R.S.: Mental traveling along psychological distances: the effects of cultural syndromes, perspective flexibility, and construal level. J. Pers. Soc. Psychol. **111**, 17–33 (2016)

42. Wu, J., Chen, D.-T.V.: A systematic review of educational digital storytelling. Comput. Educ. **147**, 103786 (2020)

43. Ybarra, O., Trafimow, D.: How priming the private self or collective self affects the relative weights of attitudes and subjective norms. Pers. Soc. Psychol. Bull. **24**, 362–370 (1998)

44. Yoder-Wise, P.S., Kowalski, K.: The power of storytelling. Nurs. Outlook **51**, 37–42 (2003)

Inclusive Digital Storytelling: Artificial Intelligence and Augmented Reality to Re-centre Stories from the Margins

Valentina Nisi[1]([✉]) [iD], Stuart James[2] [iD], Paulo Bala[1] [iD], Alessio Del Bue[2] [iD], and Nuno Jardim Nunes[1] [iD]

[1] ITI/LARSyS, IST-U., Lisbon, Portugal
{valentina.nisi,paulo.bala,nunojnunes}@tecnico.ulisboa.pt
[2] Pattern Analysis and Computer Vision (PAVIS), Fondazione Istituto Italiano di Tecnologia (IIT), Genoa, Italy
{stuart.james,Alessio.DelBue}@iit.it
http://iti.larsys.pt

Abstract. As the concept of the Metaverse becomes a reality, storytelling tools sharpen their teeth to include Artificial Intelligence and Augmented Reality as prominent enabling features. While digitally savvy and privileged populations are well-positioned to use technology, marginalized groups risk being left behind and excluded from societal progress, deepening the digital divide. In this paper, we describe MEMEX, an interactive digital storytelling tool where Artificial Intelligence and Augmented Reality play enabling roles in support of the cultural integration of communities at risk of exclusion. The tool was developed in the context of 3 years EU-funded project, and in this paper, we focus on describing its final working prototype with its pilot study.

Keywords: Interactive Digital storytelling tool · Marginalised Communities · Connectedness

1 Introduction

As computing technologies advance, Interactive Digital Storytelling (IDS) researchers anticipate how the field will evolve [57]. With the rise of the Metaverse, a fully immersive virtual world that blurs the lines between the digital and physical realms, exciting avenues open up [3]. The Metaverse uses various technologies across Extended Reality (XR), including Virtual (VR) and Augmented Reality (AR), increasingly combined with Artificial Intelligence (AI), among others, to build virtual spaces and simulate real-world factors. Further, it integrates the physical components in the digital world for users to experience, create, and interact with people and places.

As technologies continue to shape our futures, researchers come forward with inclusive strategies, designs, and applications, mindful of broadening access and

L. Holloway-Attaway and J. T. Murray (Eds.): ICIDS 2023, LNCS 14383, pp. 117–137, 2023.
https://doi.org/10.1007/978-3-031-47655-6_8

striving to keep all kinds of communities included and engaged. A large body of work already exists focusing on social equity and injustices to address social imbalances [39]. Research communities such as Participatory Design (PDC) and Computer Supported Collaborative Work (CSCW), to name a few, devote much of their research efforts to further inclusiveness. In times of continuous global crisis, changes, and increasing migrations, cultural inclusion becomes a pillar to guarantee a cohesive and open future for our societies. Therefore, technology must support **traversing such borders, boundaries, and barriers**.

In the spirit of the ICIDS 2023 conference theme, this paper describes MEMEX, an IDS tool designed and developed to promote social inclusion through collaborative access to tangible and intangible Cultural Heritage (CH). MEMEX facilitates encounters, discussions, and interactions between communities at risk of social exclusion. It allows people to combine their fragmented experiences and memories into compelling and geolocalized storylines. Using new personalized digital content linked to the pre-existent Cultural Heritage, MEMEX allows people to tell their stories and engage with society through cultural participation. To this end, MEMEX nurtures actions that contribute to practices of recognition of differences by giving voice to individuals to promote cultural diversity. The technological embodiment of MEMEX is a smartphone app allowing non-expert users to create and visualize stories related to their memories and experiences digitally linked to the geographical locations of either an intangible (e.g., an event) or a tangible cultural place/object. The app allows users to use AR to annotate the surrounding space or any physical object or location to which their stories and memories are connected. The stories are digital images, videos, audio recordings, or textual input and can be visualized using a smartphone. Then, the users connect their experiences and memories with a specific AI tool, namely a Knowledge Graph (KG), linking CH items and places with stories bound and entangled within history. Effectively, the users of MEMEX become active actors in shaping contemporary and historical content, including new material from their experiences and memories, and personalizing cultural heritage and creative media content in a meaningful and socially inclusive manner. The target communities of the MEMEX storytelling tool are socially fragile people, sometimes blocked from participating in cultural opportunities and blocked from resources ordinarily available to members of a different group, which are fundamental to social integration. Once it reached the stage of a final working prototype, MEMEX was successfully deployed in three distinct pilot cities and communities, representing a very heterogeneous user sample particularly distinct from each other:

- in **Barcelona**, community participants were migrant women, mainly working as domestic workers. Their shared experiences skewed towards women/worker rights activism and the city spaces in which they happened.
- in **Paris**, community participants were inhabitants of priority neighborhoods currently in the process of urban renewal. Their shared experiences often reflected barriers (financial, cultural, etc.) of living in the neighborhood and the ongoing changes to the space.

– in **Lisbon**, community participants were descendants of migrants from Portuguese ex-colonies. Their experiences reflected their heritage and its traces in the city spaces.

As we describe the MEMEX design and study results, we highlight the theme of **Connectedness** [7] as an empowering concept across various layers of the storytelling tool:

– through the use of AI and automatic KG interaction to write, view, and connect stories;
– through journeys to manually curate the trajectory of the experience in exploring the stories in the real world;
– through AR to explore the stories as they connect to the local cultural heritage in its real-world context.

2   Related Work

Storytelling is a way to record life [11], and memories are one of the most versatile materials for stories [42]. The potential of storytelling as a crucial strategy for scaffolding meaningful experiences through time and place is long known and studied [55,66]. Embracing Roland Barthes's postmodern theories [4] about texts requiring different levels of the reader's involvement (Readerly and Writerly), Interactive Digital Storytelling allows readers to be cast as both readers and authors of the same works [16,31,35,56]. As technology advances, AI and AR make their way into the fabric of our everyday lives and become central features for digital storytelling tools. Designers and researchers in this field must consider how to design IDS for positive social impact. This section exposes the intersection of storytelling with AI and AR, highlighting the potential of advancing IDS to support inclusion and overcoming cultural, economic, and digital divides. The collection of studies and tools presented in this section is not meant to be exhaustive but merely to trace the backdrop of our line of investigation.

2.1   Space, Place, and Storytelling

Space has long been explored as a strategy to support storytelling and learning practices [19]. Harrison and Dourish further distinguish the notions of space and place, positing space as the structural foundation of a world. In contrast, the place is a culturally invested space, serving as a distinctive frame for spatial interaction. The two concepts are the products of social practices and jointly shape computer-mediated spatial experiences [28]. In storytelling, the concepts of space and place influence evolve the notions of Interactive Digital Storytelling, from hypertext into Sculptural Hypertext [27], from Interactive Web pages to Digital Mediascapes [59] and Location-Aware Multimedia Storytelling [46,50] where authors and researchers design and distribute content in the 3-dimensional worlds. Moreover, in the last few decades, locative media has been deployed to champion disadvantaged neighbourhoods and communities, giving voice to the grassroots and often enhancing culture and heritage. Projects such as Urban and Social Tapestries, by Proboscis research group [36], the Media Portrait of the Liberties [54], Placewear and Storybank [22,53] are some of the early pioneering projects that bring the power of annotating space with stories memories and content supporting activism and participation, developing a form of distributed bottom up storytelling, transforming a spatial construct into a socially relevant place. Our work builds on these efforts, learning and extending the use of technologies to include recent cutting-edge developments such as AI and AR.

2.2   AR Storytelling and Heritage

The notion of narratives as spatial experiences often takes advantage of site-specific technologies. Benford et al. [6] propose the notion of trajectory to guide the design of site-specific storytelling journeys. While authors structure the narrative's spatial, temporal, and performative elements [52], the audience can traverse the space through spatial trajectories that result in specific experiential journeys. Extended Reality (XR), Virtual Reality (VR), Mixed and Augmented Realities (MR and AR) often feature to augment cultural heritage sites and museum visits with storytelling [1,5,15]. Kampa and Spierling developed a location-based AR prototype for outdoor museums [33] through which they identified and applied author requirements in designing multiple site-specific AR storytelling tools. Haahr et al. explore the space of gaming and locative stories in heritage contexts [26], highlighting the potential of AR for historical recollection. Shin and Woo [60] worked with local storytelling experts to understand the author's motivations, goals, and needs in creating AR narratives for historic outdoor locations. Extending on the trajectories concepts of Benford, Zhang et al. [68] developed a mobile AR application prototype that guides users to the physical locations of a story using AR flags. Although much research covers digital storytelling tools engaging with site-specific Heritage, very few engage in co-designing with disadvantaged and marginalized participants [46,49,54]. To the best of our knowledge, this area of research still presents a rich space for investigation.

2.3   AI, KG and Storytelling Tools

In Interactive Digital Storytelling, AI techniques include (but are not limited to) decisions about characters and objects of the narrative, dramatic plotting, character agency, dialogues, and interactivity in response to players' actions [63]. Curiosity and experimentation with AI and storytelling go back a long time. From the early 1960s experiments with the Eliza system, [64], a natural language processing computer program created to explore communication between humans and machines, Artificial Intelligence (AI) has been used to generate narrative structures, progress dramatic plots and virtual characters across both academia and industry. Research extends from the pioneering efforts of the CMU

Oz Project, building interactive agent-driven Drama [41], to interactive non-linear narratives [62] and architectures [40] to balance interactive plot adaptations and character believability [13,61,67], to the use of AI for story generation and presentation [14]. Recently, AI has seen a rise in coupling its potential with storytelling and children's [69] involving chat boxes, agents, and robots [9,20]. As AI technologies evolve and get entangled with our lives [24,45], decisions on how these technologies support us are made by those with the knowledge of how to develop them (e.g., engineers); most end users struggle to understand how AI supports them and have no influence on the design of such digital tools [2]. Lately, HCI research has strived to include AI in a human-centered approach and to empower creative processes [32]. The latest AI Natural Language Processes (NLP) models (such as Chat GPT) are opening up possibilities and inspiring authors and audiences to experiment with what could be the future of interactive narratives [10]. ChatGPT is an AI-powered chatbot that uses NLP to generate original story ideas. While ChatGPT is not a writing tool, and it is not going to write stories in place of the author, it can help create ideas. AI responses can be used as a jumping-off point for story writing. By understanding how a narrative AI system behaves, authors can benefit from the generative capabilities of AI systems to generate the stories they wish to tell [63]. Therefore, tools become partners, not only manipulable but responsive and supportive to the user's workflow [25]. As pointed out by recent research, future work in this area should look at how AI can inspire and empower users to write the stories they want [12,23,37]. Finally, aligning AI and crowd-generated content allows recasting the creative process as "reading-writing" [17], where a user can influence and be influenced in a collaborative partnership with digital tools [2].

2.4   Summary

In summary, IDS research combining storytelling with life stories, locative technologies, AI, and AR, is abundant. IDS tools have often been deployed to support cultural heritage, sometimes covering disadvantaged areas and serving marginalized communities. Nevertheless, very little has been (co-)designed directly with and to engage with those inhabiting the fringe of society, exposing them to cutting-edge technologies such as AI and AR. MEMEX covers this ground, promoting the use of AI and AR as storytelling tools to support marginalized communities to bond, share, and participate and, in doing so, traverse borders, boundaries, and barriers. MEMEX approaches this issue by harnessing the user's experiences through AI-supported authorship and site-specific AR storytelling. Moreover, it contributes to widening audiences' inclusive participation in Cultural Heritage by diversifying and enriching digital content for Cultural Heritage. It identifies and supports authors' motivations to engage with the sites as a creative resource, enhancing their socio-cultural significance [21].

3   MEMEX Storytelling Tool

The MEMEX EU project, of which the MEMEX IDS tool is the output, comprises a technological and a societal concept. MEMEX technology is instrumental in achieving the project's societal objectives. In the scope of this paper, we describe the technological concept and the digital storytelling tool in detail, concluding with the results of a study conducted at three pilot destinations involving users from three examples of communities at risk of exclusion.

3.1   Overview of the Tool

MEMEX considers storytelling a stepping stone for cultural inclusion. Therefore, the resulting MEMEX storytelling application is intended to:

- Gather memories of communities at risk of exclusion, connecting these with physical places, locations, and objects to promote social cohesion.
- Create assisted augmented reality experiences in the form of stories that intertwine the memories of participating communities.
- Develop techniques to semi-automatically link images to a location and connect to a new open-source knowledge graph to facilitate assisted storytelling.

Prominent in the MEMEX tool is the concept of "connectedness", which emerged during co-design with the communities at risk [49]. It is used as a common unifying thread among these different goals: connecting stories to physical environments, to virtual environments, and to information (external to the app and within the app). "Connectedness" is at the heart of the storytelling activity enabled by the tool, connecting authors among themselves and their audiences, as well as their stories and memories with the surrounding heritage. Finally, "connectedness" extends to MEMEX as a socio-technical system, as it requires understanding social structures, roles, and rights to derive hardware, software, personal, and community requirements. Regular activities involving the participation of various combinations of stakeholders took place during the ideation, design, and development of the application to achieve a consensus between the different consortium members and co-design parts of its features.

3.2   Basic Interactions, Story Writing, and Viewing

The tool's story writing and viewing aspects were developed over three iterations of user feedback moving towards a mature state. These functionalities include a guest option and authenticated users for authors. A story authoring interface (as shown in Fig. 1a) facilitating authoring with a set of inputs to structure stories: i) cover image; ii) story title; iii) story body text (optionally split into sections) with WYSIWYG interface; iv) linked cultural content suggestions (see Sect. 3.3); v) geographic location; and vi) a set of tags (from an expert-curated list). The interface then provides viewing of the stories as a list or on a map.

3.3 Connectedness Thread Embodied in the Tool

The MEMEX storytelling tool embraces the notion of connectedness at various levels. At a macro level, two different dimensions of connectedness come together: firstly, regarding interlinking cultural Heritage content with personal stories and memories of the marginalized community participants (Content Connectedness); and secondly, the tool connects different locations geospatial through journeys within physical space, taking the audience from one story (location) to another, following threads of memories or cultural topics (Geographical connectedness).

A graph structure provides the realization of both kinds of connectedness with content provided by WikiData [18]. We follow the approach of [43] for constructing a *Knowledge Graph* (KG) to provide content suggestions in the form of textual information and images [44].

Content Connectedness: Content can be connected in several ways, from during the authoring processing to post-processing using AI techniques. The KG can be searched for textual and image suggestions to support the authoring process. We frame this as an explicit process providing semi-curated content. The user can then add content to the stories, intertwining with their narrative. The High-fidelity wire-frames for the content suggestion process are shown in Fig. 1.

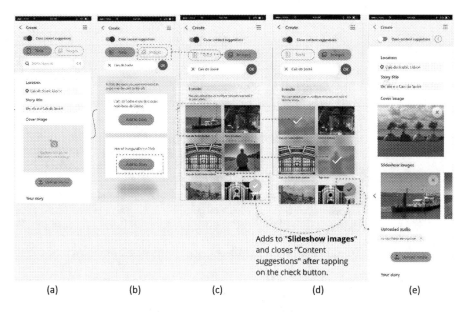

Adds to **"Slideshow images"** and closes "Content suggestions" after tapping on the check button.

(a)   (b)   (c)   (d)   (e)

Fig. 1. Hi-Fi Content Suggestion Design: We design a workflow from a story (a) facilitating search within the Knowledge Graph for both (b) intangible details (c) images of objects and places as a slideshow (d) and included in the story (e).

Moreover, stories are associated with meaningful tags that connect each story to one or more common themes. Common themes within stories are, therefore, automatically connected. The tags provide one way of interlinking stories based on expert-curated topics. However, they lack fine-grained details of the specific elements of the story. Therefore, we use Natural Language Processing (NLP) to enhance story connectivity.

We utilize the Named Entity Recognition (NER) technique to extract important keywords from a story. More precisely, we use SpaCy [30] with wide linguistic features. SpaCy annotates the story text with different types of named entities. We focus on the following types: i) Geopolitical entity (GPE), i.e., countries, cities, states; ii) Non-GPE locations, mountain ranges, bodies of water; iii) Buildings, airports, highways, bridges, etc.; iv) People, including fictional ones.

Once a user has completed and submitted for publishing a story, the MEMEX platform then performs the following steps:

1. NER tool extracts named entities (i.e., keywords), filtered by language, from the story text.
2. Where there is a match between an extracted named entity and the KG entities' labels, a link named "related to" will be added between the story and the KG entity.
3. Where the story has at least one common KG entity or common keyword with another published story, a link named "similar to" will be created between the two stories.

Geographical Connectedness (Journeys): In the context of MEMEX we define a journey as a set of several stories that form a geo-spatial narrative. We consider that a journey can be either sequential, allowing a path through the space, or unordered, allowing starting at any point. Each journey has a title, a description, and a list of stories, where the stories included in the journey may or may not belong to the user creating the journey. Each story in the set has an optional text component that the user can use to describe why the story was included in the journey. A user creates a journey by choosing a story as a starting point and then sequentially adds stories (irrespective of whether the journey is ordered). In addition, the journey creation and editing interface allows for configuring several graphical parameters of how the journey appears for the viewer (e.g., color). The process of the journey creation is shown in Fig. 2.

3.4   Bringing Connected Storytelling into Augmented Reality

A simple but scalable approach to AR content brings the stories and tangible content into reality. During the setup phase, virtual markers of the MEMEX icon (as shown in Fig. 3) are placed within environments. Each environment is created using Google AR Core[1] to position an (easily recognizable location) and virtual element(s) in the scene, which is linked to nodes within the KG. This article focuses more on visualization, as the creation can be approached in many ways with the rapid acceleration of AR technologies.

---

[1] https://developers.google.com/ar.

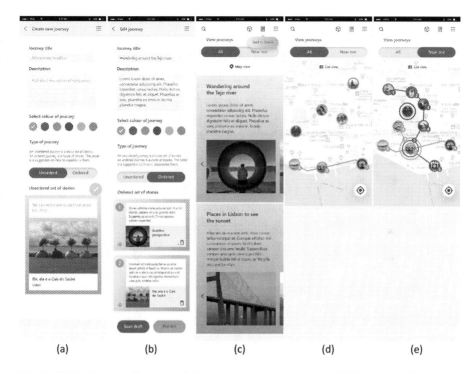

(a)   (b)   (c)   (d)   (e)

Fig. 2. Hi-Fi Journey Design: (a) Journey creation interface; (b) Selection of stories to be included in the journey; (c) list of journeys; (d) Visualisation of an ordered journey; (e) visualization of the unordered journey.

Given the graph structure within the KG, we would like to express the connectedness within the finite space of a mobile display while remaining usable for users. Displaying graph data within AR is a fleetingly addressed problem, with most approaches focusing on displaying a whole graph [38] or complex full-screen navigation around the graph as a content management system [34]. Displaying our large KG is not plausible, and complex UIs result in a loss of immersion, so we opt to display only immediate connections to the node to which the virtual element in AR is connected. We design an interface where once a virtual element is selected (Fig. 3b), a cloud of connections is displayed as icons in anti-clockwise ordering (Fig. 1c). The user can then click on either the central virtual element or any of its surrounding icons to view more information or, in the case of stories, drop out of AR to read the story in a standard 2D display (Fig. 3d). We opt for this approach as visualizing a story as a virtual text in AR is cumbersome to read, and also, reading stories takes time, which will have significant implications on battery and device temperature for a task that does not benefit from being in AR.

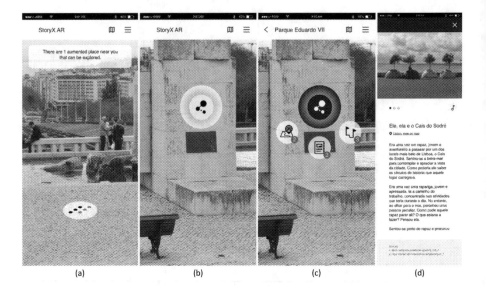

Fig. 3. Hi-Fi AR: (a) Place marker in location; (b) Object marker on a monument (c) Expanded marker showing connectivity to tangible and intangible content as well as stories (script) (d) A story visualized as a 2D interface for comfortable reading.

4   Study

Local NGOs associated with the project recruited participants from communities at risk of social exclusion in three pilot cities (Barcelona, Paris, and Lisbon). The participants' engagement was motivated by exploring public heritage through storytelling. It took multiple forms and iterations, which were the focus of other publications (exploration of needs and requirements [49], the creation of stories about their experience of living in these cities [47], co-creation and evaluation of prototypes [48]). The stories produced by the participants were geolocated multimedia stories (with text, photos, videos, and audio) and connected to the heritage of each pilot city.

In this section, we report on an "in the wild" study across the three pilot locations (N = 15) to test the third and last version of the MEMEX prototype in the locations where the marginalized communities live and provide stories about it. The study is designed to capture the user's experience with the tool through the Attrakdiff scale [29] and probes participants' expectations for the system, how they would change it, and how it would fit into their lives or workflow through a final semi-structured interview. The authors of this article developed the prototype, the study protocol, and the analysis; local NGOs were tasked with recruiting participants, setting up the AR experience, and evaluating the prototype (following the established protocol).

Participants Demographics: The recruitment for this study included community participants (who did and did not participate in previous activities), cultural operators stakeholders (such as museum and cultural professionals) and community operators (local social partners and NGOs), as well as some general audiences (who live or are visiting the pilot area). Of the 15 participants involved, three were from Barcelona, seven were from Paris, and five were from Lisbon. The sample was equally distributed in gender and typology; most participants were between 25 and 34. While most participants were experienced with smartphones, most reported no or very little experience with AR applications. To preserve anonymity, participants are identified by the first letter of the pilot city and a total number (e.g., P1 is Participant 1 in Paris, and B3 is Participant 3 in Barcelona).

Setup: The local social partners of the project selected two to three representative stories (from a corpus created earlier in the project during several digital storytelling workshops). With the help of technical experts, the Social partners situated the story content in real work by manually placing some AR anchors. The local social partners verified the integrity of the Knowledge Graph (KG) information related to the chosen area. They curated the creation of journeys, which manifested as specific paths through the corpus of stories, connecting stories.

Procedure: Before the experience, participants signed an informed consent form and filled out their demographic data (including previous experience with smartphones and AR applications). A local partner facilitated the experience at the location by providing the participant with a mobile with the prototype installed and a list of tasks. These tasks included: (1) exploring the physical surrounding location to find the story content; (2) visualizing the story as Augmented Reality media in the space where it is anchored; (3) visualizing the information provided by the KG and connecting to the Heritage connected to the story out to the physical location; and (4) use the journey feature by exploring the vicinity to find other stories which are connected to the first one visualized.

During the study, facilitators took notes and observed participants' interaction with the prototype. After the experience, participants filled out a form with the AttrakDiff scale, a tool designed to gauge the user experience through usability and design of an interactive product [29]. When no validated scale translations existed (e.g., Spanish), local partners translated the scale to the users on the fly. The scale has 28 word pair items that can be combined into 4 component dimensions:

- **Pragmatic quality** refers to the prototype's usability (ability to achieve tasks).
- **Hedonic stimulation quality** refers to the prototype's potential to provide a positive emotional experience.
- **Hedonic identification quality** refers to the prototype's potential to provide ownership (e.g., a social function or self-identification).
- **Attractiveness quality** refers to the overall attractiveness of the prototype based on pragmatic and hedonic qualities.

Finally, the facilitators conducted a short semi-structured interview with participants (audio recorded, transcribed, and translated by native speakers). The interview included questions about the experience of using MEMEX, and changes desired/needed, awareness of locations, and how data was connected to the physical location.

Analysis: The quantitative data from the AttrakDiff scale was analyzed in R [58], with figures produced using the ggplot2 package [65]. Analysis of qualitative data was conducted using thematic analysis [8] with NVivo (1.6.2),[2] a qualitative data analysis package.

4.1   Results

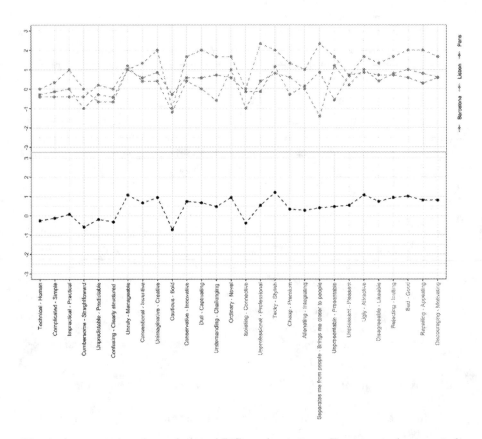

Fig. 4. Average values for each AttrakDiff word-pair item. From top to bottom: individual values per pilot location and combined values.

---

[2] https://www.qsrinternational.com/nvivo-qualitative-data-analysis-software/home.

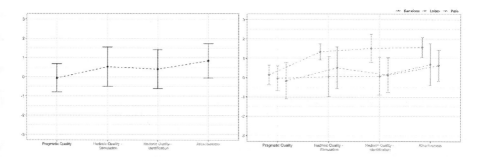

Fig. 5. Average values for AttrakDiff dimensions. From left to right: combined values and individual values per pilot location.

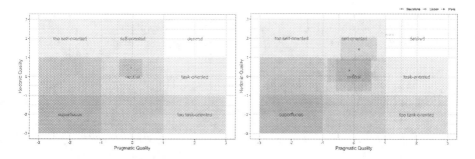

Fig. 6. Portfolio-presentation with average values of the Pragmatic Quality (PQ) and Hedonic Quality (HQ) dimensions, and confidence rectangle. From left to right: combined values and individual values per pilot location.

The analysis of the quantitative data from the AttrakDiff scale positions the user's experience of the prototype in the average scoring range for all four items of the scale (Pragmatic quality or Usability; Positive emotional experience or Hedonic stimulation quality; Ownership or Hedonic identification quality: and Attractiveness). The results are described and represented through three different visualizations below:

– **The usability of the product.** MEMEX usability (Pragmatic quality) scored average values according to the AttrakDiff word-pair items. See Fig. 4. Values between -3 and -2 are critiques needing improvement; values between 2 and 3 are strong points of the system. Average values for the MEMEX prototype are between -1 and 1, indicating no pressing issues exist, but there is space for improvement. In particular, lower scores are more prevalent for items connected to pragmatic quality, indicating usability issues in using the prototype in public.
– **Positive emotional response and ownership.** MEMEX scored average values for its ability to trigger positive emotional responses and ownership of the tool (Hedonic stimulation and identification qualities). See Fig. 5. Values between -3 and 0 are negative opinions of the system; values between 0 and 1

are standard opinions of the system and values between 1 and 3 are positive opinions of the system. While the values differ slightly for each pilot community, the combined scores for all the pilots across dimensions are between 0 and 1, representing a perception of the prototype in the standard range.

– **Attractiveness.** Based on the combination of the values from the pragmatic and hedonic quality, the attractiveness of the prototype is centrally placed in the scoring system, represented through a rectangle. See Fig. 6. The center of the rectangle represents the mean value, while the rectangle area represents the confidence level. For MEMEX, scores place our prototype in the "neutral" sector.

From the interviews, through the thematic analysis, researchers highlighted the following themes:

– **Novelty of the tool** - Several participants praised the novelty of using AR aligned with heritage (e.g., P1 *"This is the first time I have used augmented reality, in this context it allows the discovery of places/histories in the neighborhood based on heritage elements. AR allows the territory to be highlighted."*, P2 *"An enjoyable experience, it's fun to work with augmented reality [...] a great idea to discover areas"*, L2 *"I thought it was innovative, this thing of augmented reality. It's not that it is more interesting, but it is cool. It's creative."*). Lack of experience with the technology was not a hindrance to enjoying it as they quickly learn how to use it (e.g., L5 *"Once you start using it, you get used to the app's language. There is a first barrier from being something new that doesn't come with an instruction manual, but once you enter with something, it becomes easy."*).

– **Valuing the sharing of personal stories** - Several participants praised the prototype's connection to personal stories (e.g., L5 *"[...] attempt to create a bridge between the history of the place and the history of someone connected to the place."*, L2 *"I think that if we see many people doing it, I would probably spend an afternoon in Lisbon checking where there are stories."*).

– **Valuing the KG in providing extra information about CH** - Regarding the heritage-related information provided by the KG, participants cherished the connections made by the AI-supported system (e.g., L1 *"What I liked is the knowledge and the historical background about the place that I can retrieve from the MEMEX application (enabled by the KG feature)."*, L2 *"One thing that would be cool, aside from the story the person has written, is to know historical facts about the building or monument."*); participants also point out the need to further curate the information provided by the KG, as sometimes the reported information is very basic, sometimes banal, or too convoluted to make sense of (e.g., P7 *"[...] not very interesting information, hard to understand"*, L4 *"[...] I'm a local, so it's mostly information I already know about the places. I didn't want to read because it seemed too much text. I think the information could be (delivered) through a more visual language"*. Such reactions indicate a need for granularity and different levels of detail depending on the use case, as residents know greater detail than what the

MEMEX can provide. However, such participants were not the overall target of the project.

- **Navigation of the physical space** - Participants described navigating the space with the MEMEX prototype in hand as cognitively overloading. They expressed the need for more balance between the app's demands and the surrounding space. They were aware of what was happening around them and unaware of how the app would work (e.g., L5 *"[...] it was a compromise. I was alert because this plaza was lively, with many people and a lot of movement, and I was here. But at the same time, I was in the plaza and focused on how this app works. So it was a compromise between being present while understanding how this is operated"*). Resonating with many locative media experiences literature [50], the app screen requiring too much focus, and the action of pointing the phone to locate content [51] led to uncomfortable interactions in the space (e.g., L4 *"I wasn't very conscious, I was too much in my bubble. I even forgot I was in a tourist place. Amid it, I even touched my bag to check if I had everything [because of potential theft] but I was looking at the screen the whole time. I only looked at the area through the screen. And suddenly, I was on top of people and they looked into the camera, which is a bit invasive, and I realized I was pointing to people and it wasn't supposed to. So, no, I was not aware at all."*). The tension of striving for immersion while remaining sufficiently present is a fine line and proved to be a mixed experience and highly dependent on the participant's background.

- **Usability issues** - The study highlighted several usability issues with the prototype. As is common with AR experience, the participants sometimes had difficulty locating AR content in space. They expected the MEMEX prototype to facilitate the exploration of the space and the location of the markers by providing more information on the map through vibrations or visual feedback. Participants also reported issues in understanding the icons related to the KG. Highlighting the challenge of the finite space and clear communication of meaning. Naturally, this problem subsequently affected the use and testing of the KG feature in-depth, as some users could not figure out how to engage with the feature. In addition, internet connectivity proved challenging as the responsiveness and speed of the prototype (particularly in loading and playing videos were often a source of frustration and complaint. However, such could be overcome by local caching of the data.

5   Conclusions, Limitations and Future Work

While location-based narratives are not new topics for IDS researchers and practitioners, when brought to the margins of society, such interventions are still praised for their novelty, particularly in conjunction with cutting-edge technologies such as AI and AR. The AI future of the Knowledge Graph, supporting authoring and connecting stories to the surrounding CH, was perceived as potentially helpful and exciting but needing customization to individual users in usability and content curation. The combination of AR with the navigation of the surrounding space, augmenting the space with personal stories and heritage information, was well received. Nevertheless, users accused a certain lack of balance of attention between the application and the surrounding space, echoing much locative media literature. The opportunity to connect with others and share personal stories was one of the most celebrated features that overcame the usability challenges and lack of familiarity with the new technologies. Overall, results confirm that there is much value in bringing cutting-edge storytelling tools to the margins, exposing a wide variety of public to viewing, sharing, and authoring tasks, and wielding together their stories and memories with existing cultural discourses. MEMEX can be seen as a successful example of technology connecting people, places, and experiences to traverse borders, boundaries, and barriers, with exciting challenges still open for research investigation.

Limitations and Future Work. We are aware of several limitations of this work. More consistent and wider testing is needed to confirm its usefulness and appreciation from the communities at the margins. As the testing comprised a mixture of stakeholders, focusing on the single communities can highlight useful customizable features within the app. Specifically, it can be seen that participants with a rich knowledge of the local area require more detailed information to be presented than was provided within MEMEX, while visitors to the area can be satisfied with higher levels of overviews and historical details. Moreover, the participants' age range and technology literacy can also be harnessed to personalize app features. Finally, as the project ended, the iterative development of the tool ended with it. Using the tools within other research contexts can provide opportunities for further iterations of the prototype, improve usability, and incorporate user suggestions. In fact, after its final deployment, the MEMEX app has been adopted by two EU-funded projects[3] geared towards supporting citizens inclusion with digital tools in the face of climate change and sustainability, social and ecological alike. The tool will be used as a test bed for further explorations of storytelling in the context of marginalized communities, such as refugees, thanks to the interest and involvement of the Portuguese Association for Refugees (CPR) in continuing to provide support and context for further research. The Italian Institute of Technology, in partnership with Genova municipality, is exploring the use of MEMEX to co-create with local communities and non-humans whose voices within the community of the fishermen of Vernazzola village in the context of the Bauhaus of the Seas - New European Bauhaus (NEB) lighthouse project.

Acknowledgements. This research was supported by MEMEX (MEMories and EXperiences for Inclusive Digital Storytelling) Horizon Europe under GA 870743, by LARSyS (Project UIDB/50009/2020), and by the Portuguese Recovery and Resilience Program (PRR), IAPMEI/ANI/FCT under Agenda no.26, C645022399-00000057 (eGamesLab).

---

[3] Bauhaus of the Seas Sails - https://cordis.europa.eu/project/id/101079995 and DCitizens - https://cordis.europa.eu/project/id/101079116.

Specifically, we acknowledge the partners of MEMEX, including EY Advisory SpA (EY), NOHO Limited (Noho), University Ca'Foscari di Venezia (UNIVE), for their support in technological developments and documentation. As well as Michael Culture Association (MCA), Fundacio Interarts per a la Cooperacio Cultural Internacional (IA), Mapa das Ideias (MDI), Dédale (DED), and European Centre for Cultural Organisation & Management (ECCOM) for their support in evaluation. Full team members are available on the MEMEX project website (https://memexproject.eu/en/partners/consortium).

References

1. Aliprantis, J., Caridakis, G.: A survey of augmented reality applications in cultural heritage. Int. J. Comput. Methods Herit. Sci. (IJCMHS) **3**(2), 118–147 (2019)
2. Bala, P., James, S., Del Bue, A., Nisi, V.: Writing with (digital) scissors: designing a text editing tool for assisted storytelling using crowd-generated content. In: Vosmeer, M., Holloway-Attaway, L. (eds.) ICIDS 2022. LNCS, vol. 13762, pp. 139–158. Springer, Cham (2022). https://doi.org/10.1007/978-3-031-22298-6_9
3. Barbara, J., Haahr, M.: Identification and IDNs in the metaverse: who would we like to be? In: Vosmeer, M., Holloway-Attaway, L. (eds.) ICIDS 2022. LNCS, vol. 13762, pp. 601–615. Springer, Cham (2022). https://doi.org/10.1007/978-3-031-22298-6_39
4. Barthes, R., Howard, R., Barthes, R.: S/Z, repr edn. Blackwell, Oxford (1998)
5. Bekele, M.K., Pierdicca, R., Frontoni, E., Malinverni, E.S., Gain, J.: A survey of augmented, virtual, and mixed reality for cultural heritage. J. Comput. Cult. Herit. (JOCCH) **11**(2), 1–36 (2018)
6. Benford, S., Giannachi, G., Koleva, B., Rodden, T.: From interaction to trajectories: designing coherent journeys through user experiences. In: Proceedings of the SIGCHI Conference on Human Factors in Computing Systems, pp. 709–718 (2009)
7. Bleecker, J., Knowlton, J.: Locative media: a brief bibliography and taxonomy of GPS-enabled locative media. Leonardo Electron. Almanac **14** ,3 (Locative Media Special Issue) (2006)
8. Braun, V., Clarke, V.: Using thematic analysis in psychology. Qual. Res. Psychol. **3**(2), 77–101 (2006). https://doi.org/10.1191/1478088706qp063oa, http://www.tandfonline.com/doi/abs/10.1191/1478088706qp063oa
9. Bravo, F.A., Hurtado, J.A., González, E.: Using robots with storytelling and drama activities in science education. Educ. Sci. **11**(7), 329 (2021)
10. Brown, T., et al.: Language models are few-shot learners. In: Advances in Neural Information Processing Systems, vol. 33, pp. 1877–1901 (2020)
11. Bruner, J.: Life as narrative. Soc. Res. **54**(1), 11–32 (1987). http://www.jstor.org/stable/40970444, publisher: The New School
12. Calderwood, A., Qiu, V., Gero, K.I., Chilton, L.B.: How novelists use generative language models: an exploratory user study. In: HAI-GEN+ user2agent@ IUI (2020)
13. Cavazza, M., Charles, F., Mead, S.J.: Character-based interactive storytelling. IEEE Intell. Syst. **17**(4), 17–24 (2002)
14. Cavazza, M., Charles, F., Mead, S.J.: Interactive storytelling: from AI experiment to new media. In: Proceedings of the Second International Conference on Entertainment Computing, pp. 1–8 (2003)

15. Cesário, V., Petrelli, D., Nisi, V.: Teenage visitor experience: classification of behavioral dynamics in museums. In: Bernhaupt, R., et al. (eds.) CHI '20: CHI Conference on Human Factors in Computing Systems, Honolulu, HI, USA, 25–30 April 2020, pp. 1–13. ACM (2020). https://doi.org/10.1145/3313831.3376334

16. Cosley, D., Sosik, V.S., Schultz, J., Peesapati, S.T., Lee, S.: Experiences with designing tools for everyday reminiscing. Hum.-Comput. Interact. **27**(1–2), 175–198 (2012)

17. Emerson, L.: Reading Writing Interfaces: From the Digital to the Bookbound, vol. 44. U of Minnesota Press, Minneapolis (2014)

18. Erxleben, F., Günther, M., Krötzsch, M., Mendez, J., Vrandečić, D.: Introducing Wikidata to the linked data web. In: Mika, P., et al. (eds.) ISWC 2014. LNCS, vol. 8796, pp. 50–65. Springer, Cham (2014). https://doi.org/10.1007/978-3-319-11964-9_4

19. Farman, J.: Site-specificity, pervasive computing, and the reading interface. AoIR Sel. Papers Internet Res. **3**(0) (2013). https://spir.aoir.org/ojs/index.php/spir/article/view/8857

20. Ferreira, M.J., Paradeda, R.B., Oliveira, R., Nisi, V., Paiva, A.: Using storytelling to teach children biodiversity. In: Vosmeer, M., Holloway-Attaway, L. (eds.) ICIDS 2022. LNCS, vol. 13762, pp. 3–27. Springer, Cham (2022). https://doi.org/10.1007/978-3-031-22298-6_1

21. Floch, J., Jiang, S.: One place, many stories digital storytelling for cultural heritage discovery in the landscape. In: 2015 Digital Heritage, vol. 2, pp. 503–510. IEEE (2015)

22. Frohlich, D.M., et al.:: StoryBank: mobile digital storytelling in a development context. In: Proceedings of the SIGCHI Conference on Human Factors in Computing Systems, Boston, MA, USA, pp. 1761–1770. ACM, April 2009. https://doi.org/10.1145/1518701.1518972, https://dl.acm.org/doi/10.1145/1518701.1518972

23. Gero, K.I., Liu, V., Chilton, L.: Sparks: Inspiration for science writing using language models. In: Designing Interactive Systems Conference. DIS '22, pp. 1002–1019. Association for Computing Machinery, New York, NY, USA (2022). https://doi.org/10.1145/3532106.3533533

24. Giaccardi, E., Speed, C., Redström, J., Ben Allouch, S., Shklovski, I., Smith, R.C.: AI and the conditions of design: towards a new set of design ideals. In: Proceedings of the Design Research Society, Bilbao, Spain, June 2022. https://doi.org/10.21606/drs.2022.1078, https://dl.designresearchsociety.org/drs-conference-papers/drs2022/editorials/27

25. Grudin, J.: From Tool to Partner: The Evolution of Human-Computer Interaction. Springer, Cham (2022). https://doi.org/10.1007/978-3-031-02218-0

26. Haahr, M., Wiil, P.H.: A lens to the past: using site-specific augmented reality for historical interpretation. In: Söbke, H., Spangenberger, P., Göbel, S. (eds.) JCSG 2022. LNCS, vol. 13476, pp. 259–265. Springer, Cham (2022). https://doi.org/10.1007/978-3-031-15325-9_19

27. Hargood, C., Hunt, V., Weal, M.J., Millard, D.E.: Patterns of sculptural hypertext in location based narratives. In: Proceedings of the 27th ACM Conference on Hypertext and Social Media. HT '16, pp. 61–70. Association for Computing Machinery, New York, NY, USA (2016). https://doi.org/10.1145/2914586.2914595

28. Harrison, S., Dourish, P.: Re-Place-Ing space: the roles of place and space in collaborative systems. In: Proceedings of the 1996 ACM Conference on Computer Supported Cooperative Work. CSCW '96, Boston, Massachusetts, USA, pp. 67–76. Association for Computing Machinery, New York, NY, USA (1996). https://doi.org/10.1145/240080.240193

29. Hassenzahl, M., Burmester, M., Koller, F.: AttrakDiff: Ein Fragebogen zur Messung wahrgenommener hedonischer und pragmatischer Qualität. In: Szwillus, G., Ziegler, J. (eds.) Mensch & Computer 2003: Interaktion in Bewegung, vol. 57, pp. 187–196. Springer (2003). https://doi.org/10.1007/978-3-322-80058-9_19

30. Honnibal, M., Montani, I.: spaCy 2: Natural language understanding with Bloom embeddings, convolutional neural networks and incremental parsing (2017, to appear)

31. van den Hoven, E., Eggen, J.: The design of a recollection supporting device: a study into triggering personal recollections. In: 10th International Conference on Human-Computer Interaction (HCI International 2003), pp. 1034–1038. Lawrence Erlbaum (2003)

32. Hwang, A.H.C.: Too late to be creative? AI-empowered tools in creative processes. In: Extended Abstracts of the 2022 CHI Conference on Human Factors in Computing Systems. CHI EA '22. Association for Computing Machinery, New York, NY, USA (2022). https://doi.org/10.1145/3491101.3503549

33. Kampa, A., Spierling, U.: Smart authoring for location-based augmented reality storytelling applications. In: INFORMATIK 2017 (2017)

34. Lam, K.Y., Hang Lee, L., Braud, T., Hui, P.: M2A: a framework for visualizing information from mobile web to mobile augmented reality. In: 2019 IEEE International Conference on Pervasive Computing and Communications (PerCom), pp. 1–10 (2019). https://doi.org/10.1109/PERCOM.2019.8767388

35. Lambert, J., Hessler, H.B.: Digital Storytelling: Capturing Lives, Creating Community, 5th edn, revised and updated edn. Routledge, Taylor & Francis Group, New York (2018)

36. Lane, G.: Urban tapestries: wireless networking, public authoring and social knowledge. Pers. Ubiquit. Comput. **7**, 169–175 (2003). https://doi.org/10.1007/s00779-003-0229-8

37. Lee, M., Liang, P., Yang, Q.: Coauthor: designing a human-AI collaborative writing dataset for exploring language model capabilities. In: Proceedings of the 2022 CHI Conference on Human Factors in Computing Systems. CHI '22. Association for Computing Machinery, New York, NY, USA (2022). https://doi.org/10.1145/3491102.3502030

38. Li, J., Wang, Z.: An interactive augmented reality graph visualization for Chinese painters. Electronics **11**(15) (2022). https://doi.org/10.3390/electronics11152367, https://www.mdpi.com/2079-9292/11/15/2367

39. Liang, C.A., Munson, S.A., Kientz, J.A.: Embracing four tensions in human-computer interaction research with marginalized people. ACM Trans. Comput.-Hum. Interact. **28**(2) (2021). https://doi.org/10.1145/3443686

40. Magerko, B.: A proposal for an interactive drama architecture. In: AAAI 2002 Spring Symposium Series: Artificial Intelligence and Interactive Entertainment (2002)

41. Mateas, M.: An Oz-centric review of interactive drama and believable agents. In: Wooldridge, M.J., Veloso, M. (eds.) Artificial Intelligence Today. LNCS (LNAI), vol. 1600, pp. 297–328. Springer, Heidelberg (1999). https://doi.org/10.1007/3-540-48317-9_12

42. McAdams, D.P.: The psychology of life stories. Rev. General Psychol. **5**(2), 100–122 (2001). SAGE Publications, Sage CA: Los Angeles, CA

43. Mohamed, H.A., et al.: Geolocation of cultural heritage using multi-view knowledge graph embedding. arXiv preprint arXiv:2209.03638 (2022)

44. Mohamed, H.A., Vascon, S., Pilutti, D., James, S.: Memex-kg (2021). https://github.com/MEMEXProject/MEMEX-KG

45. Nicenboim, I., Giaccardi, E., Redström, J.: From explanations to shared understandings of AI. In: Proceedings of the Design Research Conference. Bilbao, Spain, June 2022. https://doi.org/10.21606/drs.2022.773, https://dl.designresearchsociety.org/drs-conference-papers/drs2022/researchpapers/293
46. Nisi, V.: Location Aware Multimedia Stories: A Location Based View of Interactive Narrative. Lambert Academic Publishing, Saarbrücken (2011)
47. Nisi, V., Bala, P., Bostock, H., Cesário, V., Nunes, N.J.: "before gentrification, we claim for habitation": Eliciting values and assets through cultural heritage storytelling. In: Proceedings of the 2023 ACM Designing Interactive Systems Conference. DIS '23, pp. 2423–2436. Association for Computing Machinery, New York, NY, USA (2023). https://doi.org/10.1145/3563657.3596124
48. Nisi, V., Bala, P., Cesário, V., Stuart, J., Bue, A.D., Nunes, N.J.: "connected to the people": Social Inclusion & Cohesion in Action Through a cultural heritage digital tool, vol. 7. Association for Computing Machinery, New York, NY, USA (2023). https://doi.org/10.1145/3610168
49. Nisi, V., Bostock, H., Cesário, V., Acedo, A., Nunes, N.: Impalpable narratives: how to capture intangible cultural heritage of migrant communities. In: Proceedings of the 10th International Conference on Communities and Technologies - Wicked Problems in the Age of Tech. C&T '21, pp. 109–120. Association for Computing Machinery, New York, NY, USA (2021). https://doi.org/10.1145/3461564.3461575
50. Nisi, V., Costanza, E., Dionisio, M.: Placing location-based narratives in context through a narrator and visual markers. Interact. Comput. **29**(3), 287–305 (2017). https://doi.org/10.1093/iwc/iww020
51. Nisi, V., Dionisio, M., Hanna, J., Ferreira, L., Nunes, N.: Yasmine's adventures: an interactive urban experience exploring the sociocultural potential of digital entertainment. In: Chorianopoulos, K., Divitini, M., Hauge, J.B., Jaccheri, L., Malaka, R. (eds.) ICEC 2015. LNCS, vol. 9353, pp. 343–356. Springer, Cham (2015). https://doi.org/10.1007/978-3-319-24589-8_26
52. Nisi, V., Haahr, M.: Weird view: interactive multilinear narratives and real-life community stories, **2**, 27 (2006)
53. Nisi, V., Oakley, I., Boer, M.d.: Locative narratives as experience: a new perspective on location aware multimedia stories. In: Proceedings of ArTech 2010, Porto, Portugal (2010)
54. Nisi, V., Oakley, I., Haahr, M.: Inner city locative media: design and experience of a location-aware mobile narrative for the Dublin liberties neighborhood. Intell. Agent **6**(2) (2006)
55. Nisi, V., Wood, A., Davenport, G., Oakley, I.: Hopstory: an interactive, location-based narrative distributed in space and time. In: Göbel, S., et al. (eds.) TIDSE 2004. LNCS, vol. 3105, pp. 132–141. Springer, Heidelberg (2004). https://doi.org/10.1007/978-3-540-27797-2_18
56. O'hara, K., Tuffield, M.M., Shadbolt, N.: Lifelogging: privacy and empowerment with memories for life. Identity Inf. Soc. **1**, 155–172 (2008)
57. Perkis, A., et al.: INDCOR White Paper 2: Interactive Narrative Design for Representing Complexity (2023). _eprint: 2305.01925
58. R Core Team: R: A Language and Environment for Statistical Computing. R Foundation for Statistical Computing, Vienna, Austria (2021). https://www.R-project.org/

59. Reid, J., Hull, R., Cater, K., Fleuriot, C.: Magic moments in situated mediascapes. In: Proceedings of the 2005 ACM SIGCHI International Conference on Advances in Computer Entertainment Technology. ACE '05, pp. 290–293. Association for Computing Machinery, New York, NY, USA (2005). https://doi.org/10.1145/1178477. 1178529

60. Shin, J.e., Woo, W.: Design guidelines for a location-based digital heritage storytelling tool to support author intent. In: 2018 3rd Digital Heritage International Congress (DigitalHERITAGE) held jointly with 2018 24th International Conference on Virtual Systems & Multimedia (VSMM 2018), pp. 1–8. IEEE (2018)

61. Szilas, N.: Interactive drama on computer: beyond linear narrative. In: AAAI Fall Symposium on Narrative Intelligence, vol. 144, pp. 150–156 (1999)

62. Szilas, N.: Stepping into the interactive drama. In: Göbel, S., et al. (eds.) TIDSE 2004. LNCS, vol. 3105, pp. 14–25. Springer, Heidelberg (2004). https://doi.org/10. 1007/978-3-540-27797-2_3

63. Thue, D.: Working with intelligent narrative technologies. In: Hargood, C., Millard, D.E., Mitchell, A., Spierling, U. (eds.) The Authoring Problem. Human–Computer Interaction Series, pp. 271–284. Springer, Cham (2023). https://doi.org/10.1007/ 978-3-031-05214-9_17

64. Weizenbaum, J.: Eliza-a computer program for the study of natural language communication between man and machine. Commun. ACM **9**(1), 36–45 (1966)

65. Wickham, H.: ggplot2: Elegant Graphics for Data Analysis. Springer, New York (2009). https://doi.org/10.1007/978-0-387-98141-3, http://ggplot2.org

66. Yates, F.A.: The Art of Memory. University of Chicago Press, Chicago (2001). https://press.uchicago.edu/ucp/books/book/chicago/A/bo91674300.html

67. Young, R.M.: Creating interactive narrative structures: the potential for AI approaches. Psychology **13**, 1–26 (2000)

68. Zhang, Q., Hinze, A., Vanderschantz, N.: Narrative navigation: visualizing story order and locations in augmented reality. In: Proceedings of the ACM/IEEE Joint Conference on Digital Libraries in 2020, pp. 541–542 (2020)

69. Zhang, Z., et al.: Storybuddy: a human-AI collaborative chatbot for parent-child interactive storytelling with flexible parental involvement. In: Proceedings of the 2022 CHI Conference on Human Factors in Computing Systems, pp. 1–21 (2022)

Decolonizing IDN Pedagogy *From* and *with* Global South: A Cross-Cultural Case Study

María Cecilia Reyes[1(✉)] ⓘ, Cláudia Silva[2] ⓘ, and Hartmut Koenitz[3] ⓘ

[1] Universidad del Norte, Barranquilla, Colombia
mcreyes@uninorte.edu.co
[2] ITI-LARSyS, IST, University of Lisbon, Lisboa, Portugal
claudiasilva01@tecnico.ulisboa.pt
[3] Södertörn University, Huddinge, Sweden
hartmut.koenitz@sh.se

Abstract. This paper presents a pedagogical activity with 120 students from two higher education institutions, one in the Global South and the other in the Global North. The objective was to incorporate decolonial thinking into analysing IDN artifacts through cross-cultural dialogue and collaboration. To achieve this, students were randomly divided into 20 groups comprising individuals from both countries and were assigned to work together across different time zones and geography. Students were prepared with an introduction to decolonial thinking and interactive digital narratives (IDNs). For the cross-cultural analysis, students used a methodology that merges the SPP model, the transformation aspect of IDN user experience, and the decoding position to reflect on how the artifacts perpetuate coloniality. Our results indicate that cross-cultural dialogue enabled students to counter colonial norms of universalism and Eurocentrism in IDNs through collaboration and interaction across the globe.

Keywords: Decoloniality · Decolonial Framework · Interactive Digital Narrative (IDN) · Cross-culturality · Cross-cultural Dialogue · Decolonial Pedagogy

1 Introduction

Media artifacts exist within cultural and societal situations. Simultaneously, the creation process of any such artifacts, and their design is deeply rooted in and influenced by this cultural context. During the past half century, our understanding of these mechanisms has increased considerably through scholarly work under headings such as decolonial and postcolonial theories, gender studies, critical race theory, and intersectionality. Consequently, awareness of structural oppression in artifacts such as Interactive Digital Narratives (IDNs) has increased considerably, and consequently, changes in the design have occurred, for example by adding women or racialized people as playable characters in some video games. Yet, these steps can only be the beginning of an ongoing process of decolonial thinking, a critical awareness of colonial elements and their effects which need to include both audiences and creators. Audiences need to be sensitized to

L. Holloway-Attaway and J. T. Murray (Eds.): ICIDS 2023, LNCS 14383, pp. 138–158, 2023.
https://doi.org/10.1007/978-3-031-47655-6_9

these issues and be enabled to identify them, voice criticism, and act - for example by protesting stereotypical depictions and by withdrawing support from works that contain "coloniality," - reproduction of hierarchies of race, gender, and geopolitics [24] and embedded in structures, depictions, and perspectives continuing the colonial legacy of oppression. On the other hand, creators should approach their work with a sensibility that does not exist yet - an awareness of how 'deep' coloniality runs and that it is by no means enough to simply replace visual appearances. For example, a Black character in an IDN work can be the digital equivalent of the problematic practice of "blackface" if it is just a white character masquerading as a black one if nothing has changed but the appearance. Hence, in this research endeavor, we intend to bring coloniality to the forefront to confront it, and hopefully complicate its perpetuating cycle. In this direction, our contribution has two aspects - the development of a workshop for students in higher education, implemented in a cross-cultural setting to enable a decolonial reflection by students and the insights we gained from this experiment.

This paper will first discuss motivation and context before providing a theoretical framing for decolonization and analyzing IDN works. Then, we will describe the workshop we conducted in the first semester of 2023 and report on its results. Finally, we will reflect on the experiment and lay out future steps.

2   Motivation, Context, and Theoretical Framing

This paper is aligned with a growing number of studies [28, 35, 47] calling for the decolonization of media There is no alternative to decolonization if we want to create a global dialogue and end the practice of oppression that hinders shared solutions to global challenges such as climate change, migration, armed conflict, and poverty. As simple as it sounds, communication is key here, but many levels of coloniality and problematic power structures in media representations are a considerable hindrance that needs to be addressed urgently.

An important related concept targeting education is *Critical Media Literacy (CML)*, [19] offering "a critique of mainstream approaches to literacy and a political project for democratic social change" (p.61). CML goes beyond traditional notions of media literacy to involve a multi-perspectival critical inquiry of popular culture and the cultural industries that address issues of class, race, gender, and power and promote the production of alternative counter hegemonic media" [19]. This concept is key for us, because it grounds our work in the politics of representation, avoiding apolitical notions of media education. Besides, it feeds into our cross-cultural approach, engaging students in the Global South and Global North, lending us a conceptual tool that facilitates a dialogue with the decolonial framework for IDN [41].

The premise of the CML-related studies [28, 35, 47] is that the classrooms and pedagogy are overwhelmingly defined by whiteness, upper/middle class, and male bodies, and no perspectives from outside this narrow scope are included in teaching. This educational setting and content shape the understanding and expectation of media representations and messages. To be more precise, "dominant white perspectives" in media classrooms may be translated into "tendencies to normalize white culture, advocate colourblind ideology, and promote individualistic values" evoking oftentimes a neoliberal education

[1]. To counter this problematic situation, and to establish an anti-racist and decolonial educational environment, Romero Walker argues that "educators must reevaluate their personal teaching philosophies by being reflexive per their chosen classroom material and the formed classroom rules and expectations" [35]. Our pedagogical activity is an attempt to establish such a decolonial environment.

2.1 Decolonizing Media

In this paper, we use the term "decolonial" as opposed to "postcolonial". Although related, these terms emerged in different geographical/historical contexts and time periods. In addition, we want to draw attention to the distinction between decolonization and decoloniality. While decolonization gained prominence in the 1950s, decoloniality emerged in Latin America during the 1990s [12]. South American scholars focusing on decoloniality address European incursions on American territories from the 15th century onwards. They draw upon world-systems theory and conceptual frameworks such as the modernity/coloniality dichotomy proposed by Anibal Quijano and María Lugones [5]. On the other hand, postcolonial approaches have their roots in South Asian and Middle Eastern diasporic scholarship, with a focus on European colonialism and its cultural impact. Considering this background, we align ourselves theoretically mostly with decoloniality. Yet, we position ourselves more broadly with efforts for decolonizing IDN recently emerging from South America, e.g., by the Brazilian researcher Bettocchi and colleagues [4], but also with collaborations between South scholars and North scholars [see 43], and with efforts by the South-Asian diaspora [see the talk 17 or 31] who both use the term postcolonial.

Bettocchi et al. [4] have proposed a decolonial pedagogy to teach students in Brazil to counter-hegemonic narratives, particularly in game design. The authors involved 10 game design students and introduced them to ludo narrative and decolonial concepts to identify problematic colonial aspects within games. In their study, they identified how Eurocentric perspectives shape narrative structures and visual representations in many popular games (1. Minecraft and the metaphor of colonization; 2. The Hero Journey and the archetypal point of view by Carl Jung; 3. Messianism and Dualism cosmology; 4. The Fibonacci Number, the Vitruvian Man, and the Golden Ratio).

The most interesting result from Bettocchi et al.'s work [4] is that students were asked to offer an alternative for those Eurocentric perspectives, challenging students to decolonize their minds, which is the first step towards decolonization [44] for those who were colonized. Those who resisted colonial practices such as enslavement, practice counter-colonization, as proposed by the Brazilian author Antonio Bispo (2015) when talking about *quilombolas* (enslaved Africans who resisted and escaped enslavement).

To counter the Eurocentric paradigm of colonization, Bettocchi and her students [4] proposed "Terra Nova" as an alternative, a fantasy setting where the colonizer was defeated by the colonized. As a contraposition to the Eurocentric paradigm of the Hero's Journey, they developed the Incorporeal Cardgame, a cooperative card game where characters must develop their relationships with other characters. As an alternative to the Messianic perspective of Good vs Evil for plots, they explored "Living Colors: what ship is This?" a point-and-click game composed of 16 mini-games that allow the exploration of different points of view in a plot that deals with conspiracy. Characters are created with basis on their deities of West Africa and religions of the African diaspora as an alternative to the Judeo-Christian model.

Despite the call for decolonizing IDN being recent [4, 43], other IDN-related fields such as media studies had related discussions at least since the 1980s [10, 25, 26]. In Latin America, liberation processes started in the 1960's with the works of the Brazilian pedagogue Paulo Freire [40], or the Argentinian-Mexican philosopher Enrique Dussel [8]. More recently, in media and communication studies, Moyo [28] has advocated for a decolonial pedagogy that "foregrounds race, culture, and colonial difference without ignoring class where and when class matters".

Considering decolonization as "a process and context" [12], we need to acknowledge some factors in the literature that informed the design of our study. First, we agree that there is an unequal intellectual dominance of USA and European academics that need to be challenged, understanding that the ideas and theories originating from these regions do not necessarily reflect or apply to the current debates and issues in the Global South. Therefore, there is a pressing need for an epistemic shift to incorporate a greater diversity of academic perspectives, which also applies to the IDN field [43]. Second, we draw upon Wasserman [46], who presents three major approaches to media studies: about, from, and with a region. The approach of researching "about" a region questions the tendency to treat Africa, for instance, as "just another" case study based on inherently biased Northern theory models, resulting in unethical and coloniality practices such as ethics dumping [28] or helicopter research [32]. The approach of researching "from" a region engages with diverse and inclusive scholarship. However, Global South may not offer innovative perspectives as well, as the author points out. Wasserman proposes that the most effective approach lies in researching "with" a region. We adapt Wasserman's [46] approach by decolonizing IDNs primarily from the Global South to challenge and disrupt power relations between South and North and then, with the Global North, as the title of this paper suggests.

Finally, our work has been also influenced by Moyo's proposition of a planetary curriculum, as a product of cross-cultural dialogue between knowledge archives, an epistemic dialogue. By drawing on Parek [33], Moyo emphasizes how important it is to counter our tendency to universalize our respective cultural values through dialogue. This is exactly what we tried to do in this study, by fostering connections, friendships, and collegiality between students from different sides of the globe.

2.2 Analyzing IDNs - SPP Model and Decolonial Thinking

As a basis for the analysis, the students were introduced to the SPP model [Koenitz 2023]. This framework is inspired by cybernetics and system theory and takes IDN works as consisting of *system* (the digital artifact), *process* (the interactive experience of the work by the audience), and *product* (the result as in recorded form - *objective product* - or as retellings [9] - *subjective products*). The audience assumes the role of "interactor" reflecting and acting at the same time in a double hermeneutic circle which becomes a triple hermeneutic circle during replay with the added reflection of previous playthroughs. SPP framework is built on earlier insights about the specificity of the digital medium by Brenda Laurel [23] as well as Janet Murray's fundamental insight about the medium's affordances (procedural, participatory, encyclopedic, spatial), and experiential qualities of immersion, agency, transformation [31] and the meta quality of the kaleidoscopic.

The SPP framework has three important advantages for our project. First, it is free of obvious legacy narrative perspectives (e.g. particular narrative structures). Second, it facilitates the granular separation and analysis of the different elements of an IDN, meaning that for example, particular computational rule systems can be analyzed for coloniality separately from narrative structures. Third, this framework enables an analysis of the audience's influence on the experience (as interactors) and the output in its tripartite separation of artifact, experience, and output. The framework allows the use of decolonial thinking in the analysis on several levels - in the construction of the artifact, its experience by interactors bringing in their respective cultural background and resulting objective/subjective products. On all these levels, hegemonic and oppressive aspects can be detected and analyzed, for example, visual representations, societal rule systems, and narrative structures in the protostory (the content of the system), but also aspects of the experience (e.g., subversive, and transgressive approaches countering oppressive aspects during the experience).

The quality of transformation is particularly relevant to our project. It has a dual meaning as it refers to changes in the IDN work which is transformed by the actions of the interactor, but also refers to changes in the interactor due to their experience. In that sense, IDN works can be deeply transformative for interactors and can change who we are [31]. In 2016, Roth and Koenitz [37] mapped Murray's initial three qualities of immersion, agency, and transformation to Roth's evaluation toolbox [36]. Enjoyment as the simple aspect, positive and negative affect (the overall feeling in the interactor created by the experience, either sad or happy which also lingers after the experience ends), and eudaimonic appreciation (a deep emotional and aesthetic appreciation of an IDN tied to personal experience). Based on Schoenau Fog [40], we can explicitly add the continuation desire to the transformation category [34].

In the past years, the concept of "transformative games" or "transformative play", defined by Rusch as "games that contribute to a meaningful life" [38] has gained attention from the academic community [3, 42], acknowledging the potential interactive narratives to have a deep impact on their interactors, after the interactive experience is over.

To further improve the understanding of the experience of IDN works, it is illustrative to consider basic tenets from communication and cultural studies, such as positionality and the encoding/decoding of power structures [14]. Interactive media complicates the status of both creators as system builders [22] and audiences as interactors and thus the linear relationships between sender and receptor as well as their status are changed. Yet, the questions of positionality and of power structures embedded into a *work*, and subsequently processed and reflected by audiences, remain. In mainstream non-interactive media, artifacts often embed hegemonic and oppressive structures. In principle, IDNs are no exception in this regard.

Interactors, therefore, can fully accept embedded hegemonic structures; they can negotiate with it, accept/reject some of their elements; or have a completely oppositional posture toward it. Understanding their own social position can help interactors understand where they stand when confronted with oppressive structures. Once we are aware of our own position (in society, versus the IDN work) we can also be aware of how we embed structures into our own communication. The transformational aspect of experience complicates the process in contrast to non-interactive reception but does not invalidate the overarching question of power structures and positionality. Insights into these aspects are an important step toward a developed IDN literacy and crucial in improving the creation of IDN works.

To make this theoretical framework practical, the students were given an introduction to the framework and were provided with a five-step analysis approach and examples detailed in Koenitz's book [20]:

Step 1. Identify the material.
Step 2. Categorize the material.
Step 3. Identify Narrative Design.
Step 4. Add Developer Information.
Step 5. Apply System, Process, and Product Progression.

The students were then asked to put their insights into slides and present these during a seminar.

3 Working Together Across the Globe - A Cross-Cultural Workshop

To integrate decolonial thinking in analyzing interactive digital narrative in a higher education setting, the study employed a cross-cultural activity approach, bringing together Global South and Global North BA students in a week-long workshop to analyze interactive digital narrative artifacts. Participants engaged in an introductory session where the educators (and authors of this contribution) presented the activity. The assignment for the students was to work together in groups that contained students from both institutions. Their assignment was to work together in analyzing an IDN artifact, to prepare a slide deck and present it during a final seminar at the end of the workshop.

To assess the perception of young audiences on how coloniality exists in IDNs and the impact of this activity on their way of analyzing interactive artifacts, we designed a dual-set survey to capture data both before and after the activity. An entry survey assessed initial perceptions, while a post-survey gathered feedback on the collaborative experience, decolonial media literacy growth, and cultural awareness.

3.1 Setup

120 students joined the workshop:

Global South (GS). 40 students enrolled in the second semester of the Communication and Journalism BA-level program at Universidad del Norte in Barranquilla, Colombia. The activity was developed in their "Communication Theory II" class.

Global North (GN). 80 students, enrolled in the second year of a Digital Media Design BA-level program at Södertörn University in Stockholm, Sweden. The activity was framed within their "Media Design Research" class.

Students were organized into 20 groups of six participants each: two from GS University and four from GN University. Students were assigned randomly to the 20 groups in Discord and were given the freedom to choose any other collaboration tool to work together, schedule their own meetings, and agree on the best workflow for all the members of the team. The activity was carried out in English. Between the introductory class and the final seminar, participants had three days to interact with the artifact, meet, discuss, and prepare a 5-slide presentation. Figure 1 shows an overview of the methodology of the workshop.

Fig. 1. Methodology overview of the workshop.

The goals and learning outcomes of the workshop were shared with the students during the introductory seminar:

- To analyze an interactive digital narrative from a decolonial point of view.
- To reflect on the media we consume and how they perpetuate or not oppressive structures.
- To cross borders in academia from a learning, teaching, and research perspective.
- To work together with students from another continent to create a shared experience.

Learning outcomes:

- Applying research methods.
- Recognizing oppressive structures in media artifacts.
- Comprehend our positionality.

3.2 Selected IDNs

We selected five IDN works for the students to analyze, considering the following factors: 1. Accessibility: all artifacts needed to be free or easily accessible through the web browser 2. Language: all artifacts needed to be (at least) available in English and 3 variety of form: the selected works include interactive documentaries, an interactive movie, a game, and a gamified training simulation. The selection also took the topic of power structures into account: while three of them address social issues, the other two propose altered hero's journeys, a narrative structure that has been criticized for perpetuating stereotypes [15]. Table 1 shows a breakdown of the selected IDNs, and the criteria applied for their selection.

Table 1. Breakdown of the selected IDNs criteria

Title	Produced by	Criteria
How to create a financial crisis	Created by Charles Trahan, Léon Courville, and Folklore (Canada, 2017)	The project was selected because of its topic, and the ironic way in which the information is presented
Bandersnatch	Produced by Netflix (USA, 2018)	This project introduced IDNs to the large audience of the Netflix streaming service. It presents a choose-your-own-adventure structure in the form of an interactive film, with a male character as protagonist
Save the date	Produced by Paper Dino	This project provides a satirical perspective of the hero's journey, a male hero in general and the expectation of winning a game
Mission Zhobia	Developed by &RANJ. (Netherlands, 2020)	This serious game is billed as a training simulation for a Global North aid worker to be sent to an African country
Last Hijack Interactive	Mirka Duijn (Interactive director) using material from Femke Wolting - Tommy Pallotta's Last Hijack. (Netherlands, 2014)	This work's narrative is driven by the complex social issues of a Global South country and their violent encounter with the Global North. It presents different perspective, including the pirate's and a hijacked captain

3.3 Analyzing IDNs From a Decolonial Standpoint

The analysis of the selected artifacts was developed in five moments: (1) Creation of the mixed workgroups and assignment; (2) Choosing the angle; (3) IDN analysis using SPP, and (4) Transformation aspect; and (5) Design Improvements.

Creation of Mixed Workgroups and Assignments. The mixed groups were set up on Discord and worked together to create a 5-slide presentation using the following structure: 1. Insights from Global South students; 2. Insights by Global North students; 3. 4. What did you learn in your discussion regarding the transformational aspect; and 5. What does the whole group think needs to be changed or improved in the IDN?

Choose an Analysis Perspective. Students could choose one of the following perspectives from which to analyze the artifact: (1) narrative content (NC), (2) aesthetic/mechanics (A/M), or (3) social context (SC). For each one of these perspectives, students were provided with guiding questions as shown in Table 2. But were free to develop their own questions.

Table 2. Analysis perspectives' guiding questions

Narrative Content (NC)	• Identify who are the characters, their socioeconomic status, gender, and stereotypes • Identify the narrative structure (how the story unfolds, what triggers the narrative, what are the narrative vectors?) • How do characters interact with each other? • Where does the story take place (location, period, cultural context, societal rules)?
Social Context (SC)	• Who are the story's creators, and how does that affect the narrative? • Is it a fictional or a real story? • To whom is the story told? • Can this IDN have an effect in real life?
Aesthetics/ Mechanics (A/M)	• How do I interact with the narrative? • How do my interactions affect the story? • How do the visuals, colors, text, and sounds affect the story?

Analyze the IDN Using the SPP Model. Students analyzed the artifact before and during the interaction and used the SPP model to isolate specific aspects with the aim of focusing on how colonial oppressive structures are embedded in that specific aspect of the artifact. The students were asked to reflect on their own position and approach in the experience of the artifact.

Transformation. Students were asked to identify their reception position and the transformational aspects. They reflected on whether they found themselves in a dominant, negotiation, or oppositional position. They should also reflect on whether the IDN affected them in a positive or negative way, and whether they found it enjoyable.

Design Improvements. Finally, the student groups discussed what could be improved in each IDN from a decolonial point of view, and how these insights can inform the design.

3.4   Surveys

Taking a step back from our theoretical framing, we want to understand to what extent the aspects we aim to address with our decolonization approach resonate with audiences outside the circle of academic researchers. To achieve this, we designed two surveys: one to establish a baseline prior to our activity, and the other to evaluate potential changes after the workshop. The surveys were anonymous and developed and distributed via Google Forms. Participants were asked to create a unique identifier for both surveys to contrast the before and after of the cross-cultural activity.

In the baseline survey, we asked questions such as: Where were you born, where were your parents born? Did you grow up in the place where you were born? Where do you currently study? Do you self-identify as a member of a historically marginalized group? What is your gender identity? In what languages are the media artifacts you consume on a regular basis originally produced? Which kind of digital media artifacts do you use regularly? What kind of devices do you use regularly? Furthermore, we asked questions related to media representation using five-point Likert scales, such as: 'How well do the depictions/representation in the digital media artifacts you use match your own experiences?'; 'Are the characters, habits, and societal structures in digital media artifacts similar to your own environment?' and 'If you feel that there is a misrepresentation of your environment in digital media artifacts, where do you perceive it? Be aware the misrepresentation can be both positive and negative (e.g., a nation presented in too positive light is also a misrepresentation).'

The post-survey considered aspects related to the media (mis)representation; decolonial thinking; the assigned IDN artifact appreciation; and their thoughts on the workshop. For the scope of this paper, we are presenting the profiles of the students and the results from the Media (mis)Representation section to analyze whether their perspectives evolved after the workshop. The questions of the Media (mis)Representation section were the same in the pre- and post-survey.

4 Results

4.1 Students' IDN Analysis

The cross-cultural workshop allowed the researchers to explore how students from different cultural backgrounds understand and interpret IDNs. In this section, we will analyze relevant insights from the presentations developed by the workgroups. The artifacts were randomly assigned to the groups. Table 3 shows the breakdown of the perspectives that the WGs chose.

Table 3. Breakdown of analysis perspectives (Narrative Content, Societal Context, Aesthetics/Mechanics) per workgroup

	Save the Date (StD)	Bandersnatch (B)	Financial Crisis (FC)	Mission Zhobia (MZ)	Last Hijack (LH)	Total
NC	4	1	2	1	0	8
SC	0	2	1	3	2	8
A/M	1	1	1	0	1	4

Table 4 shows the main reflections of the WGs for each IDN, according to the topics given by the instructors. For each category, we summarized the most relevant comments made by the WGs who chose the same perspective. The analysis from their slides and the presentations during the final seminar were considered. For this analysis, we video-recorded the presentations on Zoom. Although it is worth noticing that the GS reflections were undertaken by only half as many students as the GN perspectives, we believe that it does not affect the depth of the analysis.

4.2   Initial Results of the Pre- and Post-Survey

The surveys provided quantitative data on the students' social identities, digital media usage, and perceptions of coloniality in IDN work and the impact of the activity on their decolonial media literacy.

Social Positions.   71 BA-level students responded to our initial survey, 47 from GN aged between 19 and 22, and 26 from GS, aged between 17 and 19. 80,30% (n = 57) were raised in the place they were born, while 19, 7% were not (n = 14). When asked if they self-identified as a member of a historically marginalized group, 71,8% (n = 51) responded negatively, while 28,2% said yes (n = 20). As for the latter, the LGBTQA + group is the most represented minority community in our sample, considering that 8 out of 20 (33,3%) self-identified as part of such a group, while 3 identified as a person of African descent, 2 as a person of Asian descent, and one as Middle Eastern. Some of those social identities overlap Afro-descendant + LGBT or migrant + Afro-descendant. As for gender identity, one person self-identified as non-binary, 43 as females, and 29 as males.

Language of Media Artifacts.   Language is an important aspect of coloniality in media consumption. We asked the students in what languages the media artifacts are produced they consume on a regular basis. As a result, not surprisingly we found that the five most represented languages and their variations are:

–   95,8% of students said American English (n = 68)
–   69% said British English (n = 49)
–   38% said Spanish from Latin America (n = 27),
–   25,4% said Spanish from Spain (n = 18)
–   62% said Swedish (n = 44)

Besides those, Japanese appeared four times, Russian, and French appeared three times (4,2%) Mandarin Chinese and German appeared twice (2,8%), and several other languages appeared only once (Arabic, Brazilian Portuguese, Japanese, Thai, Norwegian, Syrian, Italian, Serbian).

Digital Media Use.   Regarding the type of digital media artifacts, the students use regularly, most of our respondents are heavy social media users, considering that 98,6% (n = 70) said that this is the medium they mostly use. 64, 8% of them also consume online news either on desktop or mobile devices (n = 46), while 46,5% play video games (on computers or consoles) and 45, 1% (n = 32) play casual games (on mobile phones). What it is interesting to highlight here is that emerging media formats such as VR/AR/XR are used only by 4,2% of our respondents (n = 3), interactive documentaries

Table 4. Work groups' reflections on IDN artifacts from a decolonial point of view

		Global South	Global North	Transformation	Improvements
NC	FC	The characters in the artifact are mostly stereotypes and lack diversity, such as the bald overweight banker... The focus is the American economic model. The narrative is boring for some people.	The characters are mostly white and middle class. The setting is modern, but it could be more diverse. The narrative is eurocentric and could be more critical of colonialism.	The IDN can more educational and could teach players about the effects of colonialism. The artifact could incorporate more diverse characters and perspectives. The artifact could be more challenging and could offer players more choices.	More inclusive representation when it comes to characters, different ethnicities, social and economic statuses should be in charge. The IDN could benefit from better visuals and music, a clearer conclusion, and it could be more inclusive and diverse.
	B	The interactor makes the decisions for the main character. From decolonial point of view, making the decisions for him, is an analogy of how oppressed people follow the decisions that others make for them. The setting shows the growing trend of consumerism, gender roles are traditional. Social issues related to drug abuse, criminality and immigration are presented.	Characters are predominately white and upper-middle class. Main character has access to a big house and a therapist. All programmers are male. Receptionist was portrayed by a woman, where women were excluded from leadership roles. The role of the mentor was not the traditional old man, but a young-rich man.	Making more immoral and extreme decisions as the movie played out. If you make moral/good decisions the movie rewinds. The work promotes bad decision-making.	Have actors from various background. Remove all the stereotypes. There was a time with a lot of immigration in the UK, they could have had a bigger role.
	StD	Experimental game that allows players to explore different emotions, such as tragedy and mortality. Unpredictable plot that can be triggering for some players. Different choices throughout the game determine the progression of the narrative and lead to different outcomes. Various unexpected events and challenges occur as the game progresses.	Stereotypical representations in the game.	The game does not show a Western perspective. The game does not guarantee a happy ending. The game allows players to explore different paths and outcomes. Players learn more about the character's emotions and characteristics as they try different paths. Players form an understanding of how the character views them based on their choices.	The game could provide more context to the story by explaining what happened before the events of the game as well provide more information about the main characters (backgrounds, personalities, and goals). The game could have a clearer conclusion that helps players understand the impact of their choices. It could use more visuals and better music.
	MZ	It is an experiment, and it is not known if it will work. One person is sent to an unsafe place, and you don't know how that will turn out. f the experiment goes wrong, there could be a revolution on the part of the citizens or the government itself. Seeks the justice of Zhobia. Seeks to change the government for the country to evolve. Seeks to give citizens more freedom.	False sense of inclusivity and choice. White saviorism rooted in western ideals. Continuation of narrative where Africa is poor, when in fact the continent is rich. Encouraged to learn the culture and the history. It attempts to portray reality. Shows the diversity within the country of Zhobia, which may act as a realistic depiction of other African countries and the issues they face	Appreciative of contribution to rule of law, but critical of white savior narrative. Shift in perspectives: Reflected on post-conflict complexities, questioned imposition of Western concepts and maintained open-minded perspective, acknowledged micro problems. Expressed concerns about neocolonial tendencies, questioned perpetuation of harmful narratives. Nuanced and culturally sensitive approach, avoided power dynamics.	More features and better performance will make the experience better. Some bugs and glitches need to be fixed. Critically examine and eliminate the white saviorism phenomenon. Counteract stereotypes by highlighting diversity. Celebrate the wealth and diversity of African cultures.
SC	FC	Students found stereotypes such as unequal pay for women, the typical white figure of power and emigrants occupying lower positions on the process.	Targets Western/North European audiences with higher education. Primarily uses English, with limited representation of other languages. Women in leading political roles, but less representation in economic roles. Highlights the importance of regulations for stability. It raises awareness of financial complexities	Seeing our artifact, the negotiating positionality, the game is educational, it teaches us how life works in many economic aspects. However, we did not agree with the stereotypes and the difference in pay gap between genders.	Diverse characters and non-Western visuals. Alternative viewpoints and beyond win/lose. Cultural influences and empathy. Decolonial storytelling and understanding. Active exploration and decolonial learning.

(continued)

Table 4. (*continued*)

B	Small decisions can lead to different outcomes and invites replay, so audiences can see outcomes from different choices. Each interactor can have a different interpretation of the ending. The production team made each ending feel different. To motivated continuous exploration. Some audience members prefer the conspiracy ending, while others prefer the action-packed ending.	choices affect the outcome. The work is set in the 1980s UK and features a predominantly white male cast. The work explores themes of free will, determinism, and the nature of reality. Bandersnatch has been praised for its innovative storytelling and its exploration of complex themes. The work has issues in its lack of diversity and representation.	Our social backgrounds and personal contexts can affect our choices and interpretations. The work uses implicit meaning about freedom and destiny. Ultimately, interactors don't really have free will if there are only two choices. The artifact gives viewers the opportunity to reflect on important themes. The work's exploration of authorship can be seen through a decolonial lens.	Increase interactor agency by giving them more options. Use AI and extended reality to create interactive films with multiple story paths. Remove irrelevant paths and keep the narrative towards a clear ending. Challenge the Western narrative by including a more diverse cast and crew. Engage with artists, writers, and consultants from diverse backgrounds.
MZ	IDNs can be used to study ethnicities, tribes, culture, history as well as develop peacemaking and conversation skills. The game's social context has similarities to our Global South country. International intervention is a sensitive topic that should be handled with care, but the portrayal of Zhobia and Africa is one-sided and reinforces stereotypes.	IDN can be used to practice peacemaking. The game imitates reality but is not completely realistic. It is unclear whether the game could make a difference in the real world. The game could be helpful for human rights studies. The game has a good concept but its execution is flawed.	The game can help players understand different perspectives and the nuances of language. The game can help players understand the complexities of social struggle. The game can help players connect with each other through shared experiences. The game perpetuates colonial thinking by presenting the Western journalist as the hero.	Instead of being a foreigner you could be a Zhobian peace maker which would rid the game of its white saviour complex issues. Avoid perpetuating colonial stereotypes and power dynamics and offer translations. Use multiple model options of justice. The game could add more playable characters and give players more freedom in their decision-making.
LHI	unsatisfied with the narrative presentation. The interface was a bit confusing at first. No info about the social contexts by which they ended up being pirates. There should be an intervention of both cultures in the way the story is told.	Mixing animation and interviews. Interesting to watch different views on the story. Autoplay mode. We recognize the narrative and the dramatic curve. Good vs bad story.	Not having context can be confusing and affects the interactor's experience and understanding. Can't make direct changes to the artifact but still learn through engagement. Personal growth, increased awareness, and advocacy for change in the real world	Draw attention to the Somali perspective. Address- and delve deeper into underlying causes/issues. Let the above points play a bigger role in the documentary
A/M FC	The interactions with the game were very simple and easy to understand. The interactions are needed for the progression of the IDN but they don't have a big impact, the outcomes are always the same. The written text prevails.	Neverending story. The graphical background was constantly moving, increasing with cursor interaction. Annoying sound effects. Informal language is useful.	The interactor gains knowledge, but it is too limited for the interactor, because they don't have a role.	Timeline to show start, current position, ending would be helpful. Simplify the graphical design to minimize distraction for the user. No sound effects during dialog
B	Ending spoilt from the beginning. The artifact makes you self-conscious and guilty of having a sense of control. The work tricks you into a false sense of control, tension through colored lights and shadows.	Your decisions can lead to different paths and outcomes. My choice making you become active. Music and photography can influence the interactor's decisions.	We should be mindful of the choices we make and their potential consequences. We should be aware of the ways in which technology can influence and even manipulate our decision-making. We assumed a Negotiation approach.	The character choose to work in isolation. It delivers a powerful message about team-work. When the main character chooses to work in a team the outcomes are better.
LHI	The narrative is enriching and thoughtful and is a reminder of the human cost of poverty and conflict. The work shows how lack of opportunities in Somalia as causes and consequences of maritime piracy. The story highlights the difference in socioeconomic status between the kidnappers and the kidnapped.	The story follows a three-act structure. The mix of animated frames and live footage affects the story's interpretation. The story allows users to explore different aspects of the story using maps and timelines. The autoplay function suggests that there is a "correct" way to watch the interactive narrative. The possibility to choose whose perspective to take first affects how the content is perceived.	The solidarity aspect in wanting to raise awareness among Somali youth as well as outsiders of the dangers of piracy. Hijacking gives Mohamed visibility and respect when he returns home, after getting all that money, and this is why he used to do it again. We choose paths in the documentary based on different interests and choices. This has given us in the group different perspectives on the story.	Create and persuade alternative jobs to encourage young people and keep them from becoming pirates. Establish a constant and concerned government for these new generations. Remove autoplay to further encourage choices. Highlight colonial traces. Amplify voices of marginalized communities

are used by 7% (n = 5), while eBooks are more often consumed, as 33,8% marked that option in the survey (n = 24). Hypertext fiction is a format only four students (5,6%) have engaged with.

Device Use. The most used device among our respondents is the smartphone (100%), while the laptop is the second one (88, 7%), desktop computer the third (35, 2%), the fourth video game consoles (22,5%), the fifth computer tablets (16, 9%) followed by mobile game consoles (14, 1%). As for emerging media devices such as VR headsets, only one respondent reported regular usage.

4.3   Pre- and Post-Survey on Media Representation

Figures 2, 3, and 4 illustrate changes in students' conceptions after the workshop, displaying both pre- and post-survey results on identical questions. It focuses on three questions related to how media portray or distort their environments and experiences, as well as the elements through which these representations can be uncovered.

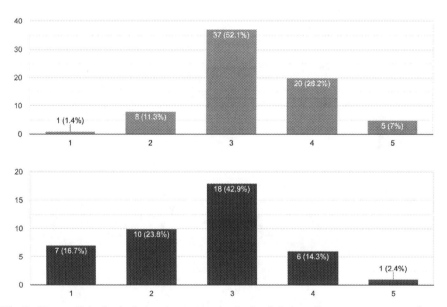

Fig. 2. How well do the depictions/representation in the digital media, you consume match your own experiences? (On the Likert scale 5 is "very alike" and 1 is "very different")

In general, we can see how the students became more critical of the media artifacts they consume. The responses from the pre- and post-survey in questions 1 and 2 show a significant change in recognizing colonial elements portrayed in the media and how media artifacts can portray environments that are distant from students' real environments and experiences. Question 3 shows another change of perspective in identifying colonial elements in the media artifacts. There is a significant increase in recognizing the misrepresentation of societal structures followed by how characters are built and

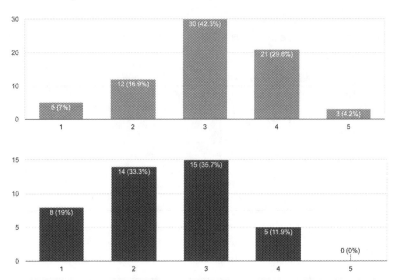

Fig. 3. The characters, habits, societal structures in the digital media that you consume are similar to your own environment? (On the Likert scale 5 is "very much" so and 1 is "not at all")

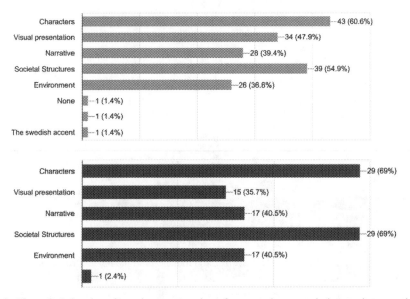

Fig. 4. If you feel that there is a misrepresentation of your environment in interactive narratives, where do you perceive it? Be aware that the misrepresentation can be both positive and negative (e.g., a nation presented in a too positive light is also a misrepresentation)

portrayed. Awareness of misrepresentation of narrative and environment also show an increase, although minor, both aspects are considered relevant in perpetuating coloniality. Misrepresentation of visual representation has decreased in significance. We take this as evidence that the students' increased understanding led them to detect misrepresentation beyond the visual surface e.g., in oppressive narrative structures which are embedded in IDN works.

5 Discussion

Our experimental workshop aimed to incorporate a decolonial framework into the practice of teaching IDN. We achieved this by facilitating collaboration between a GS and a GN institution, with the aim of creating a cross-cultural dialogue between the respective students, encouraging collaboration across the two nations. This approach aligns with Last Moyo's concept of a "planetary curriculum" [28] providing students with opportunities to engage with different knowledge sources and cultural perspectives, even across different time zones.

In general, we found that the respondents feel misrepresented in media, especially in terms of characters, and that they are aligned with Generation Z media consumption habits and the centrality of social media [48]. In addition, the main takeaway is the value of the cross-cultural dialogue that was fostered among the students. This dialogue is an important element of a decolonial pedagogy [28] and highlights the potential benefits of this cross-cultural dynamic, by enabling students to get out of their comfort zone and negotiate with the differences to achieve a common goal: their assignment. Here, the difference may be translated into struggles with finding a common schedule to work together despite a time difference of seven hours, to share and debate different views regarding the IDNs they chose, and cultural differences.

It is important to offer a reflection on the fact that this dialogue took place in the English language. This is a particularly problematic aspect since the language in the media reflects coloniality, with English remaining dominant in terms of media consumption among the students. It is deeply ironic that English, one of the main languages of colonialism in the past, has become the facilitator of cross-cultural dialogue in the 21st century. The cross-cultural dialogue resulted in a positive experience for GS students, who reported increased confidence in exchanging knowledge and proving their English proficiency with GN students. This outcome highlights a deeply ingrained colonial trait within GS culture, driven by the perception that everything in the GN is superior. Additionally, the students' spontaneous use of memes revealed another form of language that transcends cultural boundaries and encompasses shared global cultural references.

Another notable result is the set of students' suggestions for decolonizing IDN. One proposal is to incorporate a wider range of actors, art, and music into IDNs. Moreover, students stressed the importance of including artists, writers, and consultants from diverse cultural backgrounds, who possess direct experiences with colonialism/coloniality. Ensuring authentic representation is paramount, and this involves avoiding cultural appropriation and depicting characters from diverse backgrounds with respect and fairness. It is crucial to steer clear of stereotypical and exotic portrayals when representing non-Western cultures and characters (the most misrepresented aspects, according to the pre-survey results).

Beyond these highlighted results, below we also summarize some key insights based on the analysis elaborated by the students and presented in Table 4a:

- GS students arrived at the activity with a higher level of knowledge and sensibilization towards decolonial thinking. This might be explained by the nature of their careers and specifically, the course in which this activity took place that focuses on Critical Theory, Cultural Studies, and Decolonial Thinking.
- As Colombians, a country that has lived through a very complex internal war for decades, GS students found similarities between the depicted countries and their own, particularly regarding armed conflict, peace, and violence. Even though they do not share the same ethnicity with Africans, the Colombian participants in the study share a history of colonization, and as a result, coloniality with African countries. They criticized the portrayal of these aspects and noted a lack of depth in representing local citizens in *Mission Zhobia* and *The Last Hijack*. In the same way, they can recognize harmful stereotypes about Colombia, they perceived that these artifacts were reinforcing stereotypes about Africa.
- GS students demonstrated familiarity with the 'white savior' trope. Despite discussing this topic in class, they already had prior knowledge of the concept and were adept at identifying it in movies and video games.
- GN students displayed greater interest and expertise in media-related aspects, including interactive mechanics, bugs, usability, and narrative structure. Their proficiency in these areas can be attributed to their BA program in Interactive Media Design.
- Irony and satire proved to be challenging for both groups. Their mostly negative assessments of *How to Create a Financial Crisis* and *Save the Date* were based on a surface-level understanding that overlooked the satirical and ironic stances of these works.
- The messaging app Discord proved to be very efficient for exchanging written text and meeting in voice channels. Some groups chose ZOOM for their meetings. Google Slides and Canva were the most used apps for asynchronous collaboration. The shared knowledge of these tools by GS and GN students shows the availability of these platforms for this type of intercultural exercise.
- The environment was friendly and engaged. Students shared knowledge from the areas they felt most confident in and exchanged personal preferences (i.e., their favorite football team), or their personal social media accounts.

The data we collected through pre- and post-surveys permitted us to grasp that most of the students are native to their country and that the most represented minority community in our group of participants is LGBTQA+. The surveys provided interesting insights into the conceptions of media representation before and after the activity (Figs. 2, 3, and 4). In the first question, which assessed the alignment between digital media depictions and their own experiences, there was a noticeable decrease in the number of responses indicating a high level of agreement. Similarly, in the questions about the similarity between characters, habits, and societal structures in digital media artifacts and their environment, there was a shift towards lower agreement ratings in the post-survey. These changes in perception, whether perceiving media representations as similar or not, indicate that students developed a new or improved understanding of how coloniality is embedded in media artifacts. Regarding the specific elements where coloniality is detected in media artifacts, interesting shifts occurred: characters, narrative, societal structures, and environment gained more significance, while the importance of visual representation decreased.

6 Conclusions and Future Work

This paper presents a collaborative pedagogical endeavor involving two higher education institutions, courses, and student cohorts situated in diverse cultural geographies and time zones. It serves as an initial step in introducing decolonial thinking into IDN pedagogy, aiming to analyze the coloniality embedded within IDNs, as documented by [41]. Results show a successful cross-cultural dialogue and collaboration between GS and GN students, fostering the ability to negotiate differences and work towards a common goal. The overall activity proved to be a good strategy to raise awareness about how colonialism and coloniality permeate media artifacts, including IDNs.

After the activity, students were able to recognize elements related to the narrative, the social context, as well as the aesthetics and mechanics which embed harmful stereotypes and oppressive preconceptions. They were more critical of the representation gap between what the media shows and their own reality. Students also provided valuable suggestions for decolonizing IDN drawing attention to how the characters, narrative, and societal structures are portrayed in the media.

We are encouraged by these results and invite colleagues to join in the decolonization effort. Our own further work includes (1) a deeper analysis of the qualitative and quantitative data collected during the experiment and both surveys; (2) an improved methodology for future cross-cultural activities with an increased time span, as students felt that one week was very little time; (3) make the insights gained from this experience productive for the design of IDNs; and (4) to build bridges between IDN scholarship and Communication theories, with a focus on schools of thoughts from the Global South.

7 Positionality of the Authors

Positionality refers to an individual's worldview and the stance they take regarding a research task and its social and political context [16]. We recognize our positionality and the impossibility of complete objectivity in research. Our unique backgrounds provide us with a specific perspective through which we perceive the world. Therefore, this paper is a result of the first two authors' personal struggles and experiences stemming from the underrepresentation of their identities. Both first authors were born and raised in former colonized territories, are racialized early-career females, speak languages inherited from the colonizers, who developed their graduate studies as migrants in the Global North, and as such, belong to an often-marginalized minority in academia and society. While some may view the discussion of decolonial theories as a passing trend, for the first two authors, it is an essential pursuit rooted in the need to challenge power imbalances, historical and structural inequalities, and strive for visibility of historically marginalized groups in the world, and more specifically in academia in the related fields of digital media, IDN, and computing. This marginalization is exemplified by the authors' passports. European passports facilitate easy travel mobility and even the acquisition of a second citizenship [11]. Conversely, passports from countries in the Global South restrict individuals' freedom to travel globally. Academics from the Global South often face obstacles in attending international conferences due to visa restrictions, non-affordable registration fees, and the predominant location of such conferences in the Global North.

The third author is a privileged white male mid-career scholar who grew up and studied in the Global North. His awareness of marginalization started with his father, who was turned into a refugee by war and had to start his adult life from scratch in a foreign environment and as a dishwasher. The third author is a first-generation college graduate, he experienced age discrimination and topic-related marginalization and had to leave his home country to pursue a PhD. He is aware that these experiences do not compare to what many Global South citizens and his co-authors have experienced, yet his own trajectory has changed his awareness of oppression. An expat in his fourth country for professional reasons, he has had many experiences as a "foreigner" and understands himself as an ally to marginalized groups, he attempts to use his position to improve equality, foster dialogue and collaboration between Global North and Global South with decolonialization as an important vehicle.

References

1. Alemán, S.M.: Locating whiteness in journalism pedagogy. Crit. Stud. Media Commun. 31(1), 72–88 (2013)
2. Balme, C.B.: Decolonizing the Stage: Theatrical Syncretism and Post-colonial Drama. Clarendon Press (1999)
3. Barab, S.A., Gresalfi, M., Ingram-Goble, A.: Transformational play: using games to position person, content, and context. Educ. Res. 39(7), 525–536 (2010)
4. Bettocchi, E., Klimick, C., Perani, L.: Can the subaltern game design? An exploratory study about creating a decolonial ludology framework through ludonarratives. Cep 36036, 330 (2020)
5. Bhambra, G.K.: Postcolonial and decolonial dialogues. Postcolon. Stud. 17(2), 115–121 (2014)
6. Bispo, A.C.: Quilombos: modos e significados. INCTI/CNPq/UnB, Brasília, DF (2015)
7. Curran, J., Park, M.J.: De-Westernizing Media Studies. Routledge (2005)
8. Dussel, E.D.: América Latina: dependencia y liberación. Fernando García Cambeiro, Buenos Aires (1973)
9. Eladhari, M.P.: Re-tellings: the fourth layer of narrative as an instrument for critique. In: Rouse, R., Koenitz, H., Haahr, M. (eds.) ICIDS 2018. LNCS, vol. 11318, pp. 65–78. Springer, Cham (2018). https://doi.org/10.1007/978-3-030-04028-4_5
10. Foster, G.A.: Women Filmmakers of the African & Asian Diaspora: Decolonizing the Gaze, Locating Subjectivity. SIU Press (1997)
11. Global Citizen Solution, 30 March 2023. https://www.globalcitizensolutions.com/weakest-passport-in-the-world/?fbclid=IwAR3U-BSO-0RKIirxkVErGCSkPPZggaKkYoNsuu3l6a scmDuEoIOz2ywgevA
12. Glück, A.: De-Westernization and decolonization in media studies (2018)
13. Gunaratne, S.A.: De-Westernizing communication/social science research: opportunities and limitations. Media Cult. Soc. 32(3), 473–500 (2010)
14. Hall, S.: Encoding/decoding. Media Cult. Stud. Keyworks 2, 163–173 (2001)
15. Hambly, G.: The not so universal hero's journey. J. Screenwrit. 12(2), 135–150 (2021)
16. Holmes, A.G.D.: Researcher positionality–a consideration of its influence and place in qualitative research–a new researcher guide. Shanlax Int. J. Educ. 8(4), 1–10 (2020)

17. Jayanth, M.: White Protagonism and Imperial Pleaures in Game Design #DIGRA21 (2021). https://medium.com/@betterthemask/white-protagonism-and-imperial-pleasures-in-game-design-digra21-a4bdb3f5583c
18. Karam, T.: Tensiones para un giro decolonial en el pensamiento comunicológico. Abriendo la discusión. Chasqui Revista Latinoamericana de Comunicación **133**, 247–264 (2016)
19. Kellner, D., Share, J.: Critical media literacy: crucial policy choices for a twenty-first-century democracy. Policy Futures Educ. **5**(1), 59–69 (2007)
20. Koenitz, H.: Understanding Interactive Digital Narrative: Immersive Expressions for a Complex Time. Routledge, London and New York (2023). https://doi.org/10.4324/978100310 6425
21. Koenitz, H., Eladhari, M.P.: The paradigm of game system building. Trans. Digit. Games Res. Assoc. **5** (2021). https://doi.org/10.26503/todigra.v5i3.123
22. Laurel, B.: Toward the design of a computer-based interactive fantasy system, Ph.D. thesis, Ohio State (1986)
23. Laurel, B.: Computers as Theatre. Addison-Wesley, Boston (1991)
24. Maldonado-Torres, N.: On the coloniality of being: contributions to the development of a concept. Cult. Stud. **21**(2–3), 240–270 (2007)
25. Masha, F.L.: Decolonizing information: toward a new world information and communication order (NWICO). Polit. Commun. **1**, 337–342 (1982)
26. Maxwell, A.H., Davidson Buck, P.: Decolonizing media representations of race, ethnicity, and gender in the new world order. Transform. Anthropol. **3**, 1–3 (1992). https://doi.org/10.1525/tran.1992.3.1.1
27. Mohamed, S., Png, M.-T., Isaac, W.: Decolonial AI: decolonial theory as sociotechnical foresight in artificial intelligence. Philos. Technol. **33**, 659–684 (2020)
28. Moyo, L.: The Decolonial Turn in Media Studies in Africa and the Global South. Springer, Cham (2020). https://doi.org/10.1007/978-3-030-52832-4
29. Moyo, L., Mutsvairo, B.: Can the subaltern think? The decolonial turn in communication research in Africa. In: Mutsvairo, B. (eds.) The Palgrave Handbook of Media and Communication Research in Africa, pp. 19–40. Palgrave Macmillan, Cham (2018). https://doi.org/10.1007/978-3-319-70443-2_2
30. Mukherjee, S.: Playing subaltern: video games and postcolonialism. Games Cult. **13**(5), 504–520 (2018)
31. Murray, J.H.: Hamlet on the Holodeck: The Future of Narrative in Cyberspace. Free Press (1997)
32. Nature Publishing Group: Nature addresses helicopter research and ethics dumping. Nature News, 30 May 2022. https://www.nature.com/articles/d41586-022-01423-6
33. Parekh, B.: Rethinking Multiculturalism: Cultural Diversity and Political Theory-Palgrave. Macmillan, London (2000)
34. Reyes, M.C.: Measuring user experience on interactive fiction in cinematic virtual reality. In: Rouse, R., Koenitz, H., Haahr, M. (eds.) ICIDS 2018. LNCS, vol. 11318, pp. 295–307. Springer, Cham (2018). https://doi.org/10.1007/978-3-030-04028-4_33
35. Romero Walker, A.: Using critical media literacy to create a decolonial, anti-racist teaching philosophy. J. Media Lit. Educ. **13**(2), 86–93 (2021)
36. Roth, C.: Experiencing interactive storytelling, Ph.D. thesis, Vrije Universiteit Amsterdam (2016). https://research.vu.nl/en/publications/experiencing-interactive-storytelling
37. Roth, C., Koenitz, H.: Evaluating the user experience of interactive digital narrative. In: The 1st International Workshop, pp. 31–36. ACM Press, New York (2016). https://doi.org/10.1145/2983298.2983302
38. Rusch, D.C.: Existential, transformative game design. JGSS **2**, 1–39 (2020)
39. Schønau-Fog, H.: Sure, I would like to continue. Bull. Sci. Technol. Soc. **32**, 405–412 (2012). https://doi.org/10.1177/0270467612469068

40. Scocuglia, A.C.: Pedagogia do oprimido (1968–2018): da revolução ao reencontro da esperança. Educação em Perspectiva **9**(3), 576–591 (2018)
41. Silva, C., Reyes, M.C., Koenitz, H.: Towards a decolonial framework for IDN. In: Vosmeer, M., Holloway-Attaway, L. (eds.) ICIDS 2022. LNCS, vol. 13762, pp. 193–205. Springer, Cham (2022). https://doi.org/10.1007/978-3-031-22298-6_12
42. Tanenbaum, T.J., Tanenbaum, K.: Empathy and identity in digital games: towards a new theory of transformative play. In: FDG (2015)
43. Trammell, A., Cullen, A.L.L.: A cultural approach to algorithmic bias in games. New Media Soc. **23**(1), 159–174 (2021)
44. Wa Thiong'o, N.: Decolonising the mind. Diogenes **46**(184), pp. 101–104 (1998)
45. Wang, G. (ed.): De-Westernizing Communication Research: Altering Questions and Changing Frameworks, vol. 25. Routledge (2010)
46. Wasserman, H.: Media, Geopolitics, and Power: A View From the Global South. University of Illinois Press, Springfield (2018)
47. Zárate-Moedano, R.: Alfabetización mediática decolonial para la formación de miradas antirracistas en la Universidad. Ra Ximhai **14**(2), 201–224 (2018)
48. Young, S.: Media Consumption the Gen Z Way (2023). https://leaders.com/news/business/media-consumption-the-gen-z-way/

Fighting Against Hate Speech: A Case for Harnessing Interactive Digital Counter-Narratives

Cláudia Silva[✉] [ID]

ITI-LARSyS | IST, University of Lisbon, Lisbon, Portugal
claudiasilva01@tecnico.ulisboa.pt

Abstract. This paper delves into the pressing issue of hate speech (HS) by examining the potential of Interactive Digital Narratives (IDN) to develop Interactive Digital Counter-Narratives (IDCN), highlighting the limited research in this area. Drawing inspiration from two cases studies and other examples from the literature, the article explores the unique ways digital media have been used to address HS through counter-narratives. By incorporating principles of decolonial thinking and Critical Race Theory, IDCNs can leverage emerging formats like video games and VR/AR/XR to counter hate speech effectively. Pointing out the inadequacy of hate-speech laws in combating covert hate speech, the paper argues that interactive counter-narratives offer a powerful means to challenge this complex societal phenomenon. According to several studies on HS, counter-narratives may preserve freedom of speech, debunk stereotypes, encourage mutual understanding, and facilitate dialogue to de-escalate conversations.

Keywords: counter-narratives · online and offline hate speech · human rights · counter-hegemonic narratives · alternative narrative · social justice

1 Introduction

A couple of years ago, during a stroll through a quaint Swedish town, I came across an aged, torn yellow sticker that possessed a profound purpose of not merely alerting individuals to the presence of racism in public spaces; it invited people to actively engage with instances of racism by fostering empathy with the victims and inciting action, by incentivizing bystanders and witnesses to report such discriminatory acts (see Fig. 1). As a Black woman, this sticker resonated deeply with me, for it encapsulated several disturbing challenges and quests I face whenever confronted with racism: Should I react? And if so, how should I respond? Additionally, I pondered the reactions and responses expected from those who accompanied me in such situations. How can bystanders and witnesses of hate speech (HS) respond to it? From these specific questions, I engaged more broadly with the question: what the role of Interactive Digital Narrative (IDN) can play in countering HS and thus become 'counter-narratives'? IDN may be defined as "narrative experiences that can be changed by an audience, and which are created for the digital medium. What can be changed (for example outcome, progression, perspective)

© The Author(s), under exclusive license to Springer Nature Switzerland AG 2023
L. Holloway-Attaway and J. T. Murray (Eds.): ICIDS 2023, LNCS 14383, pp. 159–174, 2023.
https://doi.org/10.1007/978-3-031-47655-6_10

varies as does the particular form" [29]. To explore these questions, it is worth stressing two premises: 1) HS is based on prejudice and negative stereotypes, as well as positive ones [41]. HS is generically understood as

> all types of expression that incite, promote, spread or justify violence, hatred or discrimination against a person or group of persons, or that denigrates them, by reason of their real or attributed personal characteristics or status such as "race", colour, language, religion, nationality, national or ethnic origin, age, disability, sex, gender identity and sexual orientation[1].

2) Mainstream narratives and IDN (e.g., narrative-focused digital games, interactive documentaries, and journalistic stories) may reproduce prejudice and stereotypes, being quite often ripe with coloniality. In this sense, there is a need to decolonize the field of IDN, including production, processes, and cultural practices [42]. These enduring questions have transcended their original context, inspiring my investigation about online hate speech in Portugal in the context of EU-funded project KNOwHATE. In this project, we have found through focus group interviews that counter-narratives are scarce. Consequently, these questions as well as personal experiences and observations, such as this one about the sticker, motivate me to address this pressing societal issue within the community of IDN researchers. As to provide more information [3] about the anti-racist yellow stickers, they were created by the activist Linnéa Erisson (featured in the Fig. 1), who after witnessing racism in the subway in Stockholm, and also hearing from targets that they were being exposed to racism on the subway without anyone doing anything, she decided to create the sticker encouraging bystanders to act in case of racism by carrying out the following steps [our translation of the sticker's subheadings]:

Step 1: **Alert**. Make people in your surroundings aware, and join together.
Step 2: **Stop**. Intervene (or, "step in between") or find another way to stop the attack.
Step 3: **Support**. Talk to the person who were victimised/attacked and offer help and support.
Step 4: **Report**. Be a witness for the police, describe why the attack was a racially motivated hate crime.

From this sticker's case, we can infer several things: 1: it is targeted at the "silent crowd" [11] or bystanders, possibly White Swedish people who are not targets of racism, to become the so-called allies. 2) it fosters empathy (step 3), and 3) it requires people to have racism literacy and explain how racism operates (step 4), being it a crime in several countries [22]. As for the design of the stickers, it is insightful that the Linnéa Erisson drew on the aesthetics and color scheme of existing signs in public transportations to inform, for example, what a person should do in the event of a fire. This is the reason why they are yellow. Once I saw these stickers, I started wondering how an analogue piece could be turned digital, perhaps by harnessing on locative storytelling or AR allowing people to get information or storytelling through the sticker. This personal experience and observation of public space, along with my research in the scope of KNOwHATE[2],

---

[1] Definition provided by the Council of Europe: https://search.coe.int/cm/Pages/result_details. aspx?ObjectId=0900001680a67955.

[2] https://knowhate.eu/.

has inspired me to explore what can be done to fight against hate speech bridging offline and online worlds [3].

OHS has been consistently recognized as a significant societal challenge within the contemporary public and communication sphere by political bodies like the Council of Europe[3] and the United Nations[4]. This viewpoint is reinforced by numerous academic studies [4, 6, 12, 16]. To address this issue, various techniques, such as automatic detection on social networks to remove flagged hate speech content, have been implemented [2, 8]. However, scholars have raised concerns that the elimination of hate speech content alone is insufficient to combat the problem, as hate speech speakers can find ways to indirectly, subtly, or covertly reformulate their messages to evade automatic detection systems [4, 9]. Consequently, criticism has been directed towards a purely legal and punitive approach to HS [4].

Considering these factors, several scholars advocate for more research on counter-speech, counter-narratives, and educational activities to debunk and combat hate speech effectively [4, 9, 11, 45]. Therefore, the aim of this paper is to contribute to the advancement of the field of Interactive Digital Narratives (IDN) by emphasizing the need to develop Interactive Digital Counter-Narratives (IDCN).

Fig. 1. Screenshot of the website nyheter24. Source: https://nyheter24.se/nyheter/inrikes/882716-linnea-eriksson-anti-rasism-klisetermarken-aktion-tunnelbanan

Building upon these premises, this paper argues that IDN researchers have an opportunity to create IDCNs and I summarise several reasons to support this claim. Firstly, although research on hate speech is growing, studies on counter-narratives remain limited [2, 4, 14]. Secondly, within the IDN field, these counter-narratives may incorporate

---

[3] See the recommendations of the Council of Europe to combat hate speech here:https://www.coe.int/en/web/combating-hate-speech/council-of-europe-on-hate-speech.

[4] https://news.un.org/en/story/2023/01/1132232.

principles of decolonial thinking [42] and critical race theory by leveraging the potential to address hate speech in emerging formats like video games and VR/AR/XR [see, e.g., 15, 16]. Lastly, several scholars [9, 27] argue that hate-speech laws alone are inadequate for combating hate speech in cases where it does not directly incite imminent violence, referred to as covert hate speech [4]. In this sense, counter-narratives are presented as a powerful mean to tackle the complex phenomenon of hate in the contemporary society. Some scholars consider counter-narratives an effective way to combat HS, because they preserve the right to freedom of speech, counters stereotypes and misleading information with credible evidence. It can also alter the viewpoints of haters and bystanders, by encouraging the exchange of opinions and mutual understanding, and can help de-escalating the conversation [15, 28].

2   Context, Motivation and Conceptual Background

Over the last decade, OHS has become a growing research concern due to its increasing presence on social media and the Internet at large, being it a threat to stability of democratic and pluralistic societies. While hate speech is not a specific phenomenon of social media or the Internet, a large body of research has provided evidence that, due to user-generated content, HS is quite prevalent online, namely on social media [8, 12, 14, 37, 39]. This is the reason why most of the research on counter-narratives/counter-speech to tackle hate speech is related to the universe of social media, either by developing automated ways to moderate comments and tag hate content through AI and large language models [2, 14, 18] or through organized civil human rights organizations [21, 23, 46]. Although OHS is also present in IDNs, the research on the topic has not taken off yet in the field of IDN. Considering that one of the most powerful ways to tackle OHS is to generate counter-narratives [9], this paper discusses two case studies that exemplify counterspeech and counter-narratives within the scope of the Iberian Peninsula (Portugal and Spain), countries with an extensive history of colonization. This unique socio-historical-political context provides us with examples of counter-narratives against racism, xenophobia, and sexism with particular relevance for leveraging the intersectional dynamics of identity, diversity, colonial history, and consequently the legacy of coloniality.

Within the framework of decolonial theories, coloniality is defined as the perpetuation of hierarchies and concepts based on race, gender, and geopolitics, which were created or utilized as tools of colonial control [31]. Focusing momentarily exclusively on "race", it becomes apparent that the situation in Portugal is complex, as the state does not permit the collection of ethnic-racial data, even for research purposes [33]. The absence of data hinders researchers and policymakers from comprehensively understanding the demographic composition of the country, precisely identifying social inequalities based on race and gender, and developing policies to dismantle such inequities. At the same time, far-right wing parties have been gaining momentum in Portugal and Spain (as well as other European countries) and attracting followers, which is directly related to the increase of hate speech, as the Global Project Against Hate and Extremism (GPAHE) has documented as well as other studies [22]. Consequently, counter-narratives assume even greater significance and relevance in this context, as they serve as a vital means of resistance. Against this backdrop, this paper is rooted in the principals of the Decolonial Framework for IDN [42], Critical Race Theory [20, 24, 30, 36, 44], and Intersectionality theory [17, 19]. Thus, both case studies were chosen to stimulate reflection on counter-narratives that focus on gender, entanglements between migration and nationality, race, and class. These criteria informed the selection of the cases, ensuring a comprehensive exploration of the issues at hand.

3   Counter-Narratives and Counter-Speech

3.1   Definitions

This article explores narratives, which counter HS and the violence and discrimination it seeks to propagate, justify, or disseminate [10, 21, 37]. Before moving forward, it is important to highlight that counter-narratives have a long-standing tradition in several disciplines and professional fields. HS has been used in social work, psychology, political science, mediation, and education [24]. Broadly, counter-narratives, as per the Center for Intercultural Dialogue[5], refer to narratives opposing other narratives that resist messages from those in positions of power and privilege and therefore often go unchallenged. These narratives are often produced by marginalized communities.

While this definition assists us in understanding how the term "counter-narratives" is used in some fields, in the specific context of HS, more specific definitions are provided.

For instance, the Counter-narratives Handbook [28] defines them as messages providing positive alternatives to extremist propaganda or deconstructing and delegitimizing extremist narratives. For example, according to Tuck and Silverman, counter-narratives can involve:

Focusing on what we are *for* (rather than *against*) by offering positive stories about shared values, open-mindedness, freedom and democracy; Highlighting how extremist activities negatively impact on the people they claim to represent; Demonstrating the hypocrisy of extremist groups and how their actions are often inconsistent with their own stated beliefs; Emphasising factual inaccuracies used in extremist propaganda and setting the record straight; Mocking or satirising extremist propaganda to undermine its credibility [28].

Furthermore, a counter-narrative (sometimes called counter-comment or counter-speech) "is a response that provides nonnegative feedback through fact-bound arguments and is considered the most effective approach to withstand hate speech" [9]. Counter-narratives stories have been proven to be also an effective tool to fight anti-Black [7]. In addition, discursive devices, such as pleasure, rooted in Black feminism, have been also presented in the literature about IDN as an "anti-oppression counternarrative tactic" [38].

Besides counter-narratives, there is another common strategy to combat hate speech which is counterspeech, defined as a direct response/comment that counters the hateful or harmful speech" [9, 34]. A brief example of counter-speech is when someone replies

---

[5] https://centerforinterculturaldialogue.files.wordpress.com/2014/10/key-concept-counter-narrative.pdf.

to a comment on social media debunking discriminatory messages against a group. Other researchers define counter-speech as "a common, crowd-sourced response to extremism or hateful content. Extreme posts are often met with disagreement/conflicts, derision, counter campaigns" [6].

It is important to note that some authors use the term 'counter-speech' broadly, to refer to any content that counters or contradicts hateful or extremist content generally - not necessarily in response to any particular statement or speech act. Although counternarratives are sometimes called "counter-comment" or "counter-speech" [18, 21], there is no clear distinction between all those terms in the literature yet. As Poole et al. point out [37], while some scholars such as Blaya [5] and De Latour et al. [21] have started to distinguish between counter-narratives (that offer alternative frames) and counter-speech (that attacks or denies the original sentiment of a message but restages it in the process) others may use the terms interchangeably.

Similar to Chung [18], scholars in the Dangerous Speech Project, such as Susan Benesh et al. [9] and Cathy Buerger [11], differentiate those two terms. For them, counter-speech refers only to a direct response to HS. For expressions that counter another narrative or view in general - a much broader category that could include forms of education, propaganda, and public information – these authors use the term 'counter narrative' [9, 11]. In this paper, I use "counter-narratives", with a hyphen to highlight the notion of *narrative* in the field of IDN, as a broad term that encompasses any response, short-term or long-term, to combat HS against marginalized communities, following the latest definition provided by the Council of Europe.

3.2 Counternarratives in IDN

Despite the long tradition of counter-narratives in several areas, in the field of IDN, this type of narrative has been relatively underexplored and not closely systematized. For example, in Portugal, Costa et al. [15, 16] created a game-installation called "Enredo" in Portuguese (plot, in English), one of the few cases that explicitly mention "counternarratives" as a goal to combat OHS. The authors described their installation as a "gamified counter-narrative", but no clear definition of what they mean by counter-narratives is offered in their study, although they hint at the idea that counter-narratives may facilitate "changes in behavior" in the specific context of OHS. Enredo was developed to be experienced at schools. Like the "No More Haters" game, a case I will talk about later in this paper, there is a goal of educating youth about HS. Interactors are invited to enter a luminous cabin and find out why a website feed was discontinued. Once interactors choose to explore the system, they start encountering several hate messages, and learning through play why the feed was shut down. Costa et al. [15] motivated their work by explaining that due to the competitive nature of games, this medium is a sphere prone to dialogue that varies "between praise and negative or ironic comments about game performance, personal insults based on sexual orientation or ethnicity, harassment and attacks on minorities". In addition, the authors explain that HS speech in digital games is often the result of interactive dynamics between players, in unmoderated activities such as team building, sharing strategies and chats or live streaming on gaming platforms. The prevalence of HS in digital games has been documented in several studies [13, 48] and has also been recognized by the industry. For example, Intel has developed an AI accelerated speech filtering technology that enables users to filter HS in real time, while playing games. It is called Bleep[6] and the beta version is available for use. In 2021, the system was criticized for its interface design[7], as users could select how much HS they wanted to hear by using a sliding scale, which means that they could choose to hear no misogyny, some misogyny, most of it or all of it, raising ethical concerns about such choices. A video of the app showed that it would allow users to customize through a sliding scale what kind and how much hate speech they want to see, including "Racism" and "White Nationalism" sliders that can be set to "none," "some," "most," or "all," and a separate on and off toggle for the "N-word."

Besides these recent examples, over the last decade, there are additional IDNs like those pointed out by Gómez-García et al. [26] that have been created to challenge and to counter traditional/mainstream news outlets that reinforce or proliferate HS [41]. These IDNs are understood as newsgames by Gómez-García et al., as they were developed by media outlets following journalistic standards, to address the refugee crisis in Europe. This crisis has been a fertile ground for HS, the authors point out. Due to this crisis, refugees and migrants[8] are often portrayed as a dangerous threat. That message is often spread through social networks generating what it is called OHS. These IDNs are: "The Refugee Challenge" (The Guardian, 2014), "Two Billion Miles" (Channel 4, 2015), "Syrian Journey: Choose your own adventure" (BBC, 2015), "Bury Me, My Love" (ARTE, 2017) and "The Waiting Game" (ProPublica, 2017). By analyzing such cases, Gómez-García et al. have explored, among other things, the following RQ: How have narrative and game-based resources been used in newsgames to combat HS? One of the key answers to this question was that the games allow interactors an opportunity to deconstruct or recode, to use the authors' terms, the notion of the Other or "othering" [1, 48], meaning the use of language to express divisive opinions between the in-group (us) and the out-group (them). Othering has been found to be a rhetorical narrative surrounding hate speech [1], and the "we–they" dichotomy is commonly identified in racist discourse [10], as the desire to protect the in-group is the underlying motivation responsible for negative attitudes and discriminatory behavior. These IDNs, the authors argue, by allowing the interactor to play the role of a refugee, e.g. a parent caring for their family, create an immersive experience that is unlike in traditional media.

Amongst the cases chosen by these authors, "The Waiting Game" [26] is clearly related to HS, as the interactor has to face a number of threats due to social identities. This IDN also shows how to relate authorship of IDCN with official sources. For example, all the five characters' stories of this game were created based on the definition of what a refugee means, according to 1951 U.N. Refugee Convention and its 1967 protocol: a person fleeing persecution based on "race, religion, nationality, membership of a particular social group, or political opinion." To make interactors learn what refugee

---

[6] Source: https://game.intel.com/giveaway/bleepbeta/.

[7] https://www.vice.com/en/article/dyvgvk/intels-dystopian-anti-harassment-ai-lets-users-opt-in-for-some-racism.

[8] Refugees and migrants are different concepts and are treated very differently under modern international law. A refugee is a person fleeing wars, life threats, meaning that they are either preserving their lives or freedom. A migrant is often a person who wants to improve their lives for professional or financial reasons.

means, the game encompasses the 1951 UN Refugee Convention, which requires member states not to deport people fleeing persecution based on "race, religion, nationality, membership of a particular social group, or political opinion." Based on this, each of those criteria are represented by the game in a storyline:

– Race: An ethnically Tibetan man facing discrimination in Nepal
– Religion: A man who married outside his religion in Bangladesh
– Nationality: An Ethiopian deported to Eritrea because of his nationality
– Membership in a particular social group: A domestic violence survivor in El Salvador
– Political opinion: A student protester in the Democratic Republic of Congo.

This is a lesson to learn from the Waiting Game, and as such, this paper argues that IDCN should follow closely definitions of HS provided by official bodies like the UN.

Furthermore, there are also other efforts to increase representation of marginalized communities in IDN, which are often the main targets of HS in Europe and elsewhere. Examples in this regard are several IDNs created in Twine, which has a history of enabling the LGBT+ and Queer communities to create their own interactive digital narratives [40].

4   Case Studies of IDNs Against Hate Speech

4.1   *Counter-Speech:* **#Brasileirasnaosecalam #Brazilianswomendonotstayquiet**

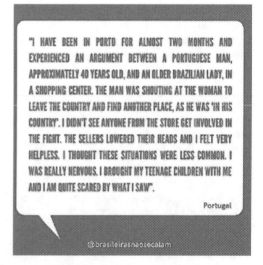

Fig. 2. Screenshots of the social media (Instagram and Facebook) pages of the project *Brasileiras não se calam* (Brazilian women do not stay quiet).

The Instagram and Facebook pages "*Brasileiras Não se Calam*" (in English, "Brazilian Women Do not Stay Quiet") have been recognized in the literature as a case of cyberfeminism, aiming to combat coloniality and long-standing stereotypes of Latin women, particularly Brazilian women who are often subjected to sexual objectification and stigmatization, especially when they are migrants in countries with a history of being colonisers like Portugal [31]. This campaign was initiated in July 2020 on the digital social network Instagram to anonymously report instances of harassment, discrimination, and prejudice experienced by Brazilian immigrant women in Portugal, following a discriminatory statement made against Brazilian women on a popular reality TV show. In response to this incident, a group of five Brazilian women residing in Portugal pondered upon what actions they could take to challenge the perpetuation of colonial stereotypes and bring about change. Their solution was to utilize social media platforms, starting with Instagram and later expanding to Facebook and Twitter. Over time, the project has evolved into an emotional support network for Brazilian women facing prejudice and discrimination including physical meetings, where women can share, tell their stories and look for advice and support [31]. This case demonstrates a significant trajectory, transitioning from being a counter-speech project as a direct response to specific discriminatory events (including stories and anecdotes of xenophobia and racism shared by numerous women) to becoming a long-term network and a counter-narrative project (Fig. 2).

In a study examining the motivations of counter-speakers—individuals who actively oppose hate speech—Buerger [11] explains that they aim to "bring content that they believe to be hateful into prominent public view so that more people become aware of it." Buerger [11] and her colleagues at the Dangerous Speech Project refer to this strategy as "amplification," which involves taking content from a small online forum and sharing it on a larger platform where a larger audience can access it. In the case of #Brasileirasnaosecalam, instances of HS that occur offline are collected and amplified online by sharing them in Portuguese and English to reach broader audiences. This amplification strategy can be effective because, as Buerger [11] suggests, it compels members of the dominant group to acknowledge how their society oppresses certain individuals, thereby prompting counter-speakers to "uphold or even shift norms against it."

This project is relevant for the purpose of this paper, as it provides the IDN research community with an empirical example which incorporates notions of counter-speech against HS that can stimulate discussions on how IDN can be integrated into counter-speech projects.

This case of social media activism can be understood as an IDN to the extent that it facilitates the interactive co-creating of an emerging narrative space of first-person accounts with different perspectives. The further sharing across different social media pages (Instagram, Facebook), generate more tales, commentary, and dialogues in the comments by active audience members who have become interactors. Arguably, this example is an IDN edge case, as there is no completed IDN system beforehand. However, the social media platforms can be seen as providing the interactive system, while the original post about the incident acts as a trigger for the creation of more and more narrative content in an interactive process, which then becomes available as product, encompassing all phases of the SPP model [29] as well as "interactivity 2," which means that the audience has an active participation in planning and execution of the narrative, as articulated by Koenitz [29].

4.2 No More Haters

While there is plenty of evidence about the pervasiveness and increase in volume of OHS [2, 4], there are not many cases of IDN fighting specifically and explicitly against HS or OHS, producing what in this paper is called IDCN.

One of the rare cases that could be conceptualized as IDCN is the game "No More Haters", which is focused on media literacy as its goal is to educate young people aged between 14 and 29 about how to detect and fight hate speech through a collection of games:

1. "The Hate Wheel", in which interactors have to compose words related to the universe of HS by choosing a letter of the alphabet. Some examples are "disparage" for D, "misogyny" for O, and "rage" for R.
2. "True or False" related to disinformation and HS. For example, the interactor has to decide whether the following statement "Muslims are suing Spain for the Holy Week Processions" is true or false. If the chosen answer is true, the interactor will get the following message: "It is false [repeat statement]. It's a case of HS towards that community". The same mechanics repeats, but the HS target groups and concepts are diverse, ranging from women, LGBT+, children from LGBT parents to debunking notions of heteronormativity ("Everything that is not heterosexuality is unnatural"). Regardless of the target or the concept, if the answer is wrong, the interactor gets a response saying that message is a case of hate speech.
3. An animated Quiz as a sort of mini-graphic adventure that poses a question very similar to the ones raised at the outset of this article: "how do you act if you are a victim or a witness of HS?" Here, the interactor is set in different narrative scenarios, (see Fig. 5).

No More Haters was developed by Maldita.es[9], a Spanish independent journalistic project that fights disinformation, with the support of Google.org and FAD[10], and it is available to be played on desktops or mobile devices here: https://play.nomorehaters. es/home, in Spanish or English. The IDN authors define the work as "educational", allowing interactors to test their knowledge about HS, as its description on the Google Play Store shows: *"Test yourself and identify hate messages with this app. Guess the words of the round of hate and learn to identify if a content is true or hoax. Also, you will have to respond to different hate situations. Collect points and become an expert. Help us break the chain of hate!"*.

4.2.1 Hate Speech Targets: Marginalized Communities

As the visuals below illustrate, interactors playing "No More Haters" are engaged in the first person (e.g., "You read a viral tweet…") to situate themselves in narrative scenarios and make choices about their actions, reaction, and dilemmas in the context of potential HS against historically marginalized communities such as transgender, Roma (referred in the game as "Gypsy"), and migrants. Besides that, the game also offers an answer

---

[9] https://maldita.es/.

[10] https://fad.es/notas-de-prensa/nace-no-more-haters-el-proyecto-de-fad-Y-maldita-es-contra-el-discurso-de-odio-en-redes/.

Fig. 3. Screenshots exemplifying the broad definitions of HS by the app No More Haters.

(correct or not correct) by having the right answer in green and the wrong answer in dark pink. Besides, when the answer is wrong, the interjection "Noooo!" pops up on the screen in light red. Aligned with the pedagogical goal of this IDN, the app also categorizes different variants of HS. For example, Fig. 3 shows a case, in which HS is categorized as prejudice and stereotype, while the Fig. 4 categorize it as transphobia.

Fig. 4. Screenshots exemplifying a playthrough showing the interactor choosing a wrong answer and the type of message he/she/they gets from the system.

This part of the game is quite effective in teaching the interactor that HS is a complex phenomenon which affects different social identities.

However, in some cases, it is not clear how the authors of this IDN define HS. This is because in some instances, such as in the examples below (see Fig. 5), linguistic discrimination against people from the South of Spain (e.g., Andalucía) is considered HS. Some scholars would argue those cases are not HS per se, but rather prejudice. This lack of clarity in how the authors define hate speech can be seen also in the example about a person being called "four eyes", and this situation exemplifies bullying and is not necessarily based on identity traces such as gender, race/ethnicity, religion.

Despite these inconsistencies, considering the literature on HS, "No More Haters" clearly exemplifies how IDN can be used to create counter-speech, and most importantly, to teach targets and bystanders how to respond directly to OHS on social media pages as well as offline. Below I outline a few key aspects of this game that makes it an IDCN.

Fig. 5. Screenshots exemplifying how the system defines HS to encompass non-historical marginalized communities.

1. Leverages social media content (e.g., tweets) to create the counter-narrative quiz, as the target audience of the game are young people, who consume content mainly through social media.
2. Offers a vocabulary through "The Hate Wheel" (Instruction: "Guess what word is related to the hate message that appear in the circle") to the interactors about the universe of HS, discrimination, and stereotypes.
3. Offers different perspectives and viewpoints in the quiz but offering conflicting answers and invites the interactor to play different roles, that of a hate speech/discrimination target or that of a witness. The interactor has the chance of learning through replay and revisit their choices.
4. Offers a true or false about disinformation, which includes HS. This is a simplistic way to approach disinformation, but may create awareness of what counts as disinformation, and how to debunk it.

5   Final Remarks

This paper presented two case studies which exemplify what has been done in the scope of interactive digital counter-narratives, including counter-speech. The first case was developed in the context of social media to "amplify" [11] the awareness of hate speech against Brazilian women, part of one of the largest migrants' communities living in Portugal [35] with the aim to counter narratives ripe with coloniality. The second case was developed as an educational game to educate youth about how to identify, act and counter HS in case they are either target or witness to it, in Spain. This work applies diverse examples that illustrate the range of digital content aimed at challenging dominant narratives. We have argued that IDN researchers, designers and authors can draw inspiration from such cases to develop more counter-narratives. To do so, one of the main aspects IDN creators and researchers should consider is the target groups the IDCN will address. In the examples presented in this paper, there are counter-narratives focused on refugees, Brazilian migrant women, and several other target groups like Roma and the LGBT+ community in the case of "No More Haters". In addition, several concepts can be incorporated into the IDCN to be countered such as heteronormativity, normativity, racism, Whiteness, social stereotypes, and Othering. In terms of design and character development, it is crucial to avoid gender and/or race/ethnicity stereotyping. The IDCN "No More Haters" has striven to do that by developing characters that do not have adhere to gender, skin color, or ethnicity stereotypes [47].

In terms of theoretical grounding, IDCN may be inspired by Critical Race Theory (CRT) [18, 22, 30, 37]. CRT acknowledges the empirical knowledge of racialized individuals as credible, highly valuable, and essential for comprehending, analyzing, and educating about the multifaceted aspects of racial subordination, as is notable in studies such as those of Ferreira in education [24], Ogbonnaya-Ogburu in academia, specifically in the field of HCI [36]. Notably, CRT actively seeks, analyzes, and listens to the lived experiences of racialized individuals through counterstorytelling methods, including family histories, parables, testimonies, and chronicles [24, 30, 36]. According to CRT, social reality is constructed through the exchange and formulation of stories about individual situations. These stories serve as interpretative frameworks that allow us to make sense of our experiences and how those experiences shape our understanding of the world [30]. Although HS encompasses more complexity, not being about only race or ethnicity, CRT may be helpful to an extent that it recognizes that narratives and stories [20, 32] play a crucial role in understanding personal experiences and providing confirmation or counterarguments about societal dynamics [30].

In this regard, CRT provides an excellent framework for developing counter-narratives [34] within IDCN. It highlights the significance of centering the stories of racialized individuals, positioning them as subjects, and recognizing their experiences as vital contributions to countering hegemonic narratives.

Furthermore, the case studies presented in this paper highlight an emergence of digital media content and platforms containing counter-narratives and counter-speech, what reveals a potential to leverage these formats with IDN procedures and participatory dynamics, resonating with Koenitz's arguments [29], highlighting the interactor's contributions in influencing the progress, perspective, content, and/or outcome of those counter-narratives.

Although the cases come from Portugal and Spain, and considering the decolonial lens this paper has taken on, the context of the selected cases may resonate with the history of other European countries such as England, Netherlands, France, and Germany, which are places with an extensive history of colonization of African countries, Latina American ones, and the Caribbean. Most of these countries share with the Iberian Peninsula current struggles with increasingly migration influx, increasing of the far-right wings, and as such an increase of hate speech [21, 23].

In this paper, I have argued that IDN, as a transformative field, has a role in pursuing prosocial change. It can do so by developing Interactive Digital Counter-narratives and incorporating insights from perspectives such as critical race theory.

While this paper constitutes an initial endeavor, as future steps to develop the case of IDCN, I intend to extend this study by conducting: 1) in-depth interviews with the creators of interactive counter-narratives (e.g., No More Haters), and 2) a more structured framework combing IDN theory with counter-narratives literature.

Acknowledgements. The author acknowledges the COST Action INDCOR (18230) for fostering an environment of reflection about IDN and societal issues, and the European Union in the scope of the EU-funded project KNOwHATE (101049306), which also enabled the research for this paper.

Disclaimer Funded by the European Union. Views and opinions expressed are however those of the author(s) only and do not necessarily reflect those of the European Union or CERV. Neither the European Union nor the granting authority can be held responsible for them.

References

1. Alorainy, W., Burnap, P., Liu, H., Williams, M.L.: "The enemy among us" detecting cyber hate speech with threats-based othering language embeddings. ACM Trans. Web (TWEB) **13**(3), 1–26 (2019)
2. Ashida, M., Komachi, M.: Towards automatic generation of messages countering online hate speech and microaggressions. In: Proceedings of the Sixth Workshop on Online Abuse and Harms (WOAH), pp. 11–23, July 2022
3. Backlund, A.: Linnéas klistermärken ska stoppa rasismen i tunnelbanan (2017). https://nyh eter24.se/nyheter/inrikes/882716-linnea-eriksson-anti-rasism-klisetermarken-aktion-tunnel banan
4. Baider, F.: Accountability issues, online covert hate speech, and the efficacy of counter-speech. Politics Gov. **11**(2) (2023). https://doi.org/10.17645/pag.v11i2.6465
5. Blaya, C.: Cyberhate: a review and content analysis of intervention strategies. Aggress. Violent Behav. **45**, 163–172 (2019)
6. Bartlett, J., Krasodomski-Jones, A.: Counter-speech examining content that challenges extremism online. DEMOS (2015)
7. Bell, L.A.: Telling tales: what stories can teach us about racism. Race Ethn. Educ. **6**(1), 3–28 (2003)
8. Ben-David, A., Fernández, A.M.: Hate speech and covert discrimination on social media: monitoring the Facebook pages of extreme-right political parties in Spain. Int. J. Commun. **10**, 27 (2016)
9. Benesch, S., Ruths, D., Dillon, K., Saleem, H.M., Wright, L.: Counterspeech on Twitter: a field study. A report for public safety Canada under the Kanishka project (2016)
10. Bonotti, M.: Religion, hate speech and non-domination. Ethnicities **17**(2), 259–274 (2017)
11. Buerger, C.: Why they do it: counterspeech theories of change, 26 September 2022. Dangerous Speech Project. DangerousSpeech.org
12. Breazu, P., Machin, D.: Racism is not just hate speech: ethnonationalist victimhood in YouTube comments about the Roma during COVID-19. Lang. Soc., 1–21 (2022). https://doi.org/10.1017/S0047404522000070
13. Breuer, J.: Hate speech in online games. In: Kaspar, K., Gräßer, L. (eds.) Online Hate Speech, pp. 107–112. Kopaed (2017)
14. Carvalho, P., et al.: The expression of hate speech against Afro-descendant, Roma, and LGBTQ+ communities in YouTube comments. J. Lang. Aggress. Confl. (2023)
15. Costa, S., Tavares, M., Bidarra, J., Mendes da Silva, B.: The Enredo game-installation: a proposal to counter hate speech online. In: Martins, N., Brandão, D. (eds.) DIGICOM 2022. SSDI, vol. 27, pp. 307–320. Springer, Cham (2023). https://doi.org/10.1007/978-3-031-20364-0_27

16. Costa, S., Tavares, M., Bidarra, J., da Silva, B.M.: IN[The Hate Booth]: a gamified installation to counteract hate speech. In: Brooks, A.L. (ed.) ArtsIT 2022. LNICS, SITE, vol. 479, pp. 161–173. Springer, Cham (2023). https://doi.org/10.1007/978-3-031-28993-4_12
17. Collins, P.H., Bilge, S.: Intersectionality. Wiley, New York (2020)
18. Chung, Y.L., Kuzmenko, E., Tekiroglu, S.S., Guerini, M.: CONAN–COunter NArratives through Nichesourcing: a Multilingual Dataset of Responses to Fight Online Hate Speech. arXiv preprint arXiv:1910.03270 (2019)
19. Crenshaw, K.: Demarginalizing the intersection of race and sex: a black feminist critique of antidiscrimination doctrine, feminist theory and antiracist politics. u. Chi. Legal f., 139 (1989)
20. Delgado, R., Stefancic, J. (eds.): Critical Race Theory: The Cutting Edge. Temple University Press (2000)
21. de Latour, A., Perger, N., Salag, R., Tocchi, C., Otero, P.V.: We Can!: Taking Action Against Hate Speech through Counter and Alternative Narratives (revised edition). Council of Europe (2017). Report
22. ENAR: Urgent Solidarity Call to Support Portuguese Anti-racist Activists (2020). https://www.enar-eu.org/urgent-solidarity-call-to-support-portuguese-anti-racist-activists/
23. Eu.MT: Counter-narratives: how to support civil society in delivering effective positive narratives against hate speech online. Report (2017)
24. Ferreira, A.J.: Teoria Racial Crítica e Letramento Racial Crítico: narrativas e contranarrativas de identidade racial de professores de línguas. Revista da Associação Brasileira de Pesquisadores/as Negros/as (ABPN) **6**(14), 236–263 (2014)
25. Global Project Against Hate and Extremism- GPAHE: Far-Right Hate and Extremist Groups, Portugal (2023). https://globalextremism.org/portugal/
26. Gómez-García, S., Paz-Rebollo, M.A., Cabeza-San-Deogracias, J.: Newsgames against hate speech in the refugee crisis. Comunicar **29**(67) (2021)
27. Heinze, E.: Hate Speech and Democratic Citizenship. Oxford University Press, Oxford (2016)
28. Tuck, H., Silverman, T.: The Counter-Narrative Handbook. Institute for Strategic Dialogue (2016). Report
29. Koenitz, H.: Understanding Interactive Digital Narrative: Immersive Expressions for a Complex Time. Routledge, London and New York (2023). https://doi.org/10.4324/9781003106425
30. Ladson-Billings, G.: Just what is critical race theory and what's it doing in a nice field like education? Int. J. Qual. Stud. Educ. **11**(1), 7–24 (1998)
31. Lamartine, C., da Silva, M.T.: Cyberspace as denunciation: harassment and discrimination linked to coloniality in the project Brasileiras Não Se Calam. Comunicação e sociedade **41**, 209–229 (2022)
32. Martins, S.: Repercussões da experiência de racismo nas ocupações maternais de mulheres negras: estratégias de enfrentamento (2021)
33. Maeso, S.R. (ed.): O estado do racismo em Portugal: Racismo antinegro e anticiganismo no direito e nas políticas públicas. Tinta-da-China (2021)
34. Mathew, B., et al.: Thou shalt not hate: countering online hate speech. In: Proceedings of the International AAAI Conference on Web and Social Media, vol. 13, pp. 369–380, July 2019
35. Neves, C.: 758 mil imigrantes: número de brasileiros e indianos é o que mais cresce (2023). https://www.dn.pt/sociedade/758-mil-imigrantes-numero-de-brasileiros-e-indianos-e-o-que-mais-cresce-15845644.html
36. Ogbonnaya-Ogburu, I.F., et al.: Critical race theory for HCI. In: Proceedings of the 2020 CHI Conference on Human Factors in Computing Systems (2020)
37. Poole, E., Giraud, E.H., de Quincey, E.: Tactical interventions in online hate speech: the case of #stopIslam. New Media Soc. **23**(6), 1415–1442 (2021)

38. Pettijohn, B.: Applying black feminist technopractice in digital storytelling at cultural sites. In: Vosmeer, M., Holloway-Attaway, L. (eds.) ICIDS 2022. LNCS, vol. 13762, pp. 206–213. Springer, Cham (2022). https://doi.org/10.1007/978-3-031-22298-6_13

39. Rieger, D., Kümpel, A.S., Wich, M., Kiening, T., Groh, G.: Assessing the extent and types of hate speech in fringe communities: a case study of alt-right communities on 8chan, 4chan, and Reddit. Social Media Soc. 7(4), 1–14 (2021). https://doi.org/10.1177/20563051211052906

40. Salter, A., Blodgett, B., Sullivan, A.: "Just because it's gay?" Transgressive design in queer coming of age visual novels. In: Proceedings of the 13th International Conference on the Foundations of Digital Games, pp. 1–9, August 2018

41. Silva, C., Carvalho, P.: When can compliments and humour be considered hate speech? A perspective from target groups in Portugal. Comunicação e Sociedade 43, e023006–e023006 (2023)

42. Silva, C., Reyes, M.C., Koenitz, H.:. Towards a decolonial framework for IDN. In: Vosmeer, M., Holloway-Attaway, L. (eds.) ICIDS 2022. LNCS, vol. 13762, pp. 193–205. Springer, Cham (2022). https://doi.org/10.1007/978-3-031-22298-6_12

43. Silva, L.: Immigrant population in Portugal increases to 750,000 (2023). https://www.portugal.com/news/immigrant-population-in-portugal-increases-to-750000/

44. Solorzano, D.G., Yosso, T.J.: Critical race and LatCrit theory and method: counter-storytelling. Int. J. Qual. Stud. Educ. 14(4), 471–495 (2001)

45. Tekiroglu, S.S., Chung, Y.L., Guerini, M.: Generating counter narratives against online hate speech: data and strategies. arXiv preprint arXiv:2004.04216 (2020)

46. Tuck, H., Silverman, T.: The Counter-Narrative Handbook. Institute for Strategic Dialogue, 1 (2016)

47. Vilches, I.: Fighting hate speech with... games? (2022). https://ivoriginal.com/work/no-more-haters. Accessed 17 Sept 2023

48. Zamri, N.A.K., Mohamad Nasir, N.A., Hassim, M.N., Ramli, S.M.: Digital hate speech and othering: the construction of hate speech from Malaysian perspectives. Cogent Arts Humanit. 10(1), 2229089 (2023)

VR for Diversity. The Seven Lives of a Research Project

Mirjam Vosmeer(⊠) ⓘ

Amsterdam University of Applied Sciences, Postbus 1025, 1000 BA Amsterdam, The Netherlands
m.s.vosmeer@hva.nl

Abstract. This paper gives an overview of the research project VR for Diversity that focused on the impact of interaction in VR on the user. For this purpose, a distinction is made between physical interaction, that can be achieved by using controllers, and para-social interaction, that refers to interacting with characters that inhabit the virtual world. In line with the perceived affordance of VR to serve as a perspective shifter, the topic of *diversity* was chosen as the theme for the narratives that were to be created for this the research project. The paper describes a number of different projects that all evolved around this theme and concludes by presenting insights on the impact of interactive VR.

Keywords: Virtual reality · diversity · inclusion · social presence

1 Introduction

Since the re-introduction of virtual reality (VR) in 2014 there has been a consistent exploration into the positive effects of the medium, with many initiatives investigating the ways VR may be used to contribute to a better world, such as *VR for Good* [1] and *VR for Impact* [2]. By 2023, a whole range of VR productions have been presented, that are intended to serve as an invitation to reflect on a particular theme, to contribute to a shift in world view, or simply a change in opinion or better understanding of an issue. This particular use of VR has been defined as 'VR as a perspective shifter' [3]. One of the affordances of the medium that is claimed to contribute to this characteristic is the way that VR allows the user to interact with the content. By interacting with the virtual world and its inhabitants, users are said to experience a heightened sense of engagement that would automatically lead to an increase in knowledge or a change of attitude. However, little theoretical knowledge is available that actually supports this claim. For the research project *VR for Diversity*, that is the topic of this paper, the aim therefore was to study the impact of interaction in VR: what effect does an interactive immersive experience have on the user's factual knowledge of and attitude towards the topic that is presented in the virtual world? For this purpose, a distinction is made between physical interaction, that can be achieved by using controllers, and parasocial interaction, that refers to interacting with characters that inhabit the virtual world.

L. Holloway-Attaway and J. T. Murray (Eds.): ICIDS 2023, LNCS 14383, pp. 175–183, 2023.
https://doi.org/10.1007/978-3-031-47655-6_11

In line with the perceived affordance of VR to serve as a perspective shifter, the topic of *diversity* was chosen as the theme for the narratives that were to be created for this the research project. Diversity is a comprehensive and sometimes even ambiguous notion that probably has as many interpretations as there are worldviews. According to the *Oxford English Dictionary*, the term is defined as "the practice or quality of including or involving people from a range of different social and ethnic backgrounds and of different genders, sexual orientations, etc. [4]. Diversity is increasingly stated as an entry condition, for instance in calls for media funding proposals, such as the *Videogames & Immersive Content Development*-call of the Creative Europe program [5]. In calls like that, the concept of diversity may be applied in many different ways: it could refer to diversity within the production team, but also to the topic of the media content itself. As there are probably also many other ways to embed a complex topic such as diversity in media production, the additional intention of the current research project therefore was to investigate what the interpretation of the concept might be, when different teams were invited to create a project that would be titled *VR for Diversity*. As it turned out, this eventually led to several different visualizations of the concept, as demonstrated in a number of separate projects. This paper presents those projects, describing how a research proposal ended up living seven different lives, leading to new insights into the impact of interaction in VR but also into the different ways that the concept of diversity may be embedded in media content.

1.1   Interaction in VR

The literature on the actual impact of interaction in VR is still sparse. In their exploration of the topic Ferguson et al. [6] claim that it may be expected that the attitude of players in a virtual reality serious games would benefit from active interaction, which could lead to better knowledge retention. However, they also point towards the discrepancy that players may recall more factual knowledge when they don't need to interact and therefore be less overwhelmed by the virtual experience. In their experiment, they found that participants in a passive interaction condition had higher percentage of correct answers on the test focusing on factual knowledge. Nevertheless, it was also shown that participants felt more present and showed more cognitive interest in an active interaction condition. The authors point out that this backs up the findings of Flowerday and Schraw [7]. While this study did not focus on VR, its results did also indicate that freedom of choice and interaction led to a negative effect on task performance (learning) but had a positive effect on attitude.

Apart from interacting with the environment, users in VR can also be invited to interact with the characters that they encounter in the virtual environments. One of the first industry accounts exploring the nature of the relation between users of VR technology and virtual characters was published on the blog of the Oculus Story Studio [8]. In his report, Matt Burdette described how the team noticed that in their first prototypes, there seemed to be a distinct lack of connection between users and the characters in the environment, and in turn, the story. Consequently, the team discovered that by having the VR protagonist 'lock eyes' with the user - by looking directly into the camera and seemingly acknowledging their existence – this effect could be partially eliminated. Since then, it has become clear that users in VR may develop dramatically different connections to the characters and the virtual environment they inhabit than they would with characters in traditional 'flat' media. The term 'social presence', that can simply be described as the "sense of being with another" [9] refers to the ability of a VR system to create the illusion that the user is actually inhabiting the virtual environment with someone else. Several experiments have shown that if the user feels social presence with another in VR, he or she will exhibit behavior similar to a real interaction [10].

2 The Seven Lives

2.1 The First Life: Narrative Novelties

The first life of *VR for Diversity* was a lonely life. The project had started in October 2020 and by that time life on earth had come to a relative standstill, due to the worldwide pandemic lockdown. Research was hard to set up, especially the kind of research that involves placing headsets on heads, making it impossible to keep a safe distance and thus risking contamination. Collaboration was exclusively possible online, from the safety of the researchers' own living rooms. In an effort to work towards a first outcome, an immersive desk research project was set up to examine the different ways that a number of VR experiences that were available in the oculus store use and explore the concept of interaction. For this project, four VR experiences were analyzed and it was concluded that theoretical conventions such as identification, parasocial interaction and 'breaking the fourth wall' may undergo a considerable shift in meaning when used for VR, thus giving way for new investigations into the interpretation of theoretical concepts from communication science and film- and media studies [11].

2.2 The Second Life: Amelia's Dream

VR for Diversity's second life was the main life, as it contained the central project that involved writing a script for VR with an embedded research plan, producing the actual VR experience and then conducting the research [12].

Writing a script for a VR experience comes with a multitude of challenges [13]. In this particular case, an extra challenge was added, namely that the VR experience did not only need to convey a message about gender equality - as was the interpretation of *VR for Diversity* in this project - but also be suitable for an academic experiment that would investigate the impact of physical and parasocial interaction on users. The script was written in close collaboration between the industry partner and the knowledge partners, in many iterations and in a constant exchange of technical, academic and narrative requirements.

The VR Experience
In the VR experience *Amelia's Dream*, the user enters the dream of a young woman. She will tease them a bit and have fun with her visitors, but also shares some of her dreams and concerns, that all relate to issues of gender equality in contemporary society. The first dream that Amelia confides the user in, is her ambition to become an aviator. While trying out an aviator helmet in front of a mirror however, she complains that it doesn't

fit very well. Amelia points out that the helmet has probably been designed according to male standard measurements, as is also often the case with medicine, telephones and even space suits [14]. After this first encounter Amelia is featured flying an airplane, but then decides that she needs to change the world and therefore wants to become a politician. When she is confronted with actual quotes that female politicians receive via social media however, she shies away. Her last dream is to become a dancer. The user is presented with a little musical box that features Amelia as a dancing ballerina when it opens. In the last sequence, Amelia confronts the user one last time and sweetly asks them to support her, as she has decided that she want to do it all: she intends to be fearless and will not let anyone in society stop her from pursuing her dreams.

The Experiment

The VR experience *Amelia's Dream* was meant to study different concepts, related to interactivity in VR, with the positive side-effect of raising awareness about gender inequality and eliciting interest in the topic. In Hartmann et al. [15] the theoretical background of the experiment, the experimental design, moderating factors and all outcomes and discussions are presented in full detail. The current text therefore gives an abbreviated overview of the study, for which two versions of the experience were produced. In version A the user needed to interact with the medium to continue the storyline after an episode ended, requiring them to perform little tasks such as opening the box to see Amelia perform as a miniature ballerina, or start a sequence by pushing a button. In version B, the storyline progressed autonomously, without user interaction. Additionally, some of Amelia's statements were made while she was looking the user in the eyes (i.e. speaking directly into the camera and thus establishing social interaction), while other statements were made while she was looking away, for instance as she was checking her reflection in a mirror.

Sample

The sample consisted of 103 participants (aged 18–60, mean age 26 years; 50 males, 45 females, 6 non-binary/other and 2 preferred not to say) who had been recruited at three universities in The Netherlands. The participants were assigned to either version A or version B of *Amelia's Dream*, after which they were requested to fill out a survey. Participation was on an anonymous, voluntary and non-paid basis, but participants could leave their email address in a separate file to enroll in a lottery[1].

Survey

The survey measured the variables such as transportation, persuasive appeal, interest and social presence, based on standardized scales. Some examples of items included:

> Transportation: "I was mentally involved in Amelia's story during the VR experience."

> Persuasive appeal: "The VR experience convinced me that gender inequality is a problem."

> Interest: "The VR experience made me interested in learning more about gender inequality."

---

[1] The grand prize in the lottery was the LEGO Amelia Earhart Tribute box.

Additionally, participants' recognition of information was examined by presenting them with 16 sentences, of which 8 were literal transcriptions of sentences said by Amelia during the VR experience, and 8 were faked. For each sentence, participants needed to judge whether it was said by Amelia or not.

Results

Analysis of the survey data showed that the interactive version lead to greater persuasive appeal and stronger interest and insight into the topic. However, recognition of the sentences was better in the non-interactive version, compared to the interactive version. Considering eye gaze, it was found that when Amelia looked the user in the eyes when conveying a message (i.e. when she was speaking directly into the camera), recognition was improved. With some caution, it can thus be concluded that while interaction in VR may heighten the users' interest for a topic, it may also cause them to be less aware of the actual facts that are conveyed within the medium. However, when a protagonist in a VR experience is actively making eye contact with the user while conveying a message, the information is remembered better.

2.3   The Third Life: The LHBTIQ+ Museum in VR

A team of students of the Master Digital Design interpreted the title *VR for Diversity* by building a LHBTIQ+ Museum in virtual reality, thus realizing the third life of the project. Wearing a VR headset, visitors are given a tour through a virtual space with various exhibitions that focus on different elements of queer culture. Upon entering a wall with flags of the different LGBTIQ+ communities is shown, and further on users can view and listen to personal experience stories, that have been shared by members of Pride communities. Another exhibition hall focuses on gay rights worldwide and on the concept of gender by introducing the virtual 'genderbread person' [16]. Furthermore, the museum features an exhibition of work from a Pride Photo Exhibition and a so-called 'Pride Experience Room', where users find themselves in virtual rendering of Canal Pride in Amsterdam, with canal houses, boats and people dancing on the quays.

The LHBTIQ+ Museum in VR was presented at multiple occasions such as museum events and queer festivals but was also accepted as a demo to be presented at the CHI conference in 2022 [17].

2.4   The Fourth Life: *Final Fantasy 7 Remake*

The fourth life of the project was a bit of an exception as it didn't involve VR but focused on diversity in a videogame. A master student from the New Media & Digital Culture program requested to do their internship within the scope of the project and proposed a study into diversity as it is reflected in a particular videogame: *Final Fantasy 7 Remake* [15].

For *Final Fantasy 7 Remake*, producer Square Enix developed a completely new version of the original *Final Fantasy 7* [19] that was launched in 1998 and that is still considered as one of the most famous games of all time, also because of its intricate and compelling narrative [20]. While the remake stays as close to the original as possible, it was clear that in terms of diversity, the narrative needed some careful updating, especially since some sequences in the original story had since long been the topic of debate because of the potential homophobic message that it conveyed [21, 22]. The internship study focused therefore on a close comparative analysis between the FF7 and FF7 Remake of two scenes, exploring how possibly homophobic content was transformed towards more inclusive narratives. Guided by an enthusiastic review on the Gayming website that states that "what was once an invitation to sneer at the idea of queerness has morphed into a celebration of it" [23], the analysis accurately points out how also classic game content can - and should - be transformed in such a way to meet current standards of inclusion and diversity. But while the reimagining of two of *Final Fantasy 7 Remake*'s classic but conflicting scenes show how, after more than twenty years, Square Enix transformed parts of their heteronormative past into a more considerate and ambiguous experience, both scenes fail to completely avoid heteronormative pitfalls in their narrative structures and gameplay dynamics, thus establishing the ongoing need to study the medium of videogames from a perspective of diversity [24].

2.5   The Fifth Life: Amstelpark VR

The fifth life of *VR for Diversity* blossomed from a collaboration between one of the SME partners and a group of students from the minor program Immersive Environments at the Amsterdam University of Applied Sciences. In this case, the students were challenged to create a VR experience that would benefit the residents of a nursing home, by presenting them with a lively rendition of a place that they were not able to visit anymore, because of physical inabilities. As an additional feature, the students were requested to create an immersive environment for the medium to be shown in, that would enhance the experience of what the users had seen in VR.

The VR experience that was thus created was titled *Amstelpark VR*. It featured a ride on the little train that runs through Amstelpark, a large park in Amsterdam. By placing a 360° camera in the front compartment of the train, the students had captured the experience of being in the park and enjoying its sights and colors. The experience was presented to the residents of the nursing home in a room that was prepared beforehand by decorating it with green leaves and garlands, thus making the transition easier from the real world to the virtual world, and vice versa. To enhance the feeling of the riding train, a gentle breeze was blown through the room with a fan. While there has been no official evaluation test of this projects, the students accounted of the emotional reactions of the residents, and how much the users had enjoyed being able to see and experience the park again.

2.6   The Sixth Life: Decolonialization

A meeting in Lisbon, organized by the Cost Action program INDCOR [25], that had focused on decolonialization inspired the sixth life of the research project. Two teams of students of the Master Digital Design at the Amsterdam University of Applied Sciences were requested to create interactive digital narratives to accompany a set of paintings of the Dutch colony in Brazil in Rijksmuseum in Amsterdam. The dominant narrative that has accompanied those paintings has long been that the Brazil was 'discovered', thereby neglecting the indigenous cultures that already existed there, and ignoring the fact that the original inhabitants were forced into slavery by the Dutch conquerors. The first group of students created an interactive audio tour called *Hidden History* that enables visitors to listen to stories from Brazilian descendants who tell about the role that the slavery past still plays in their daily lives.

The second student project created a VR experience named *Reframe*, in which the user stands in front of a virtual museum wall with the painting *View of the Island of Itamaracá* (1645) by Frans Post. Subsequently, various images on the canvas can be clicked on, followed by comments from contemporary Dutch, Brazilians and Ghanaians, who each see a different story in these paintings. This way, each viewer is confronted with the perspectives of others and thus with their own prejudices. On the other three virtual walls there are nine fictional paintings generated with the aid of artificial intelligence. While the assignment to the AI image generator had been neutral, in requesting paintings of a Brazilian plantation in 1600, the experiment showed that the image generator then automatically depicts the farm workers in black and places them in a rural landscape, showing how AI is not objective but instead full of prejudices.

2.7 The Seventh Life: Amelia Flies on

The last life of *VR for Diversity* continues to this day, as the main output of the project is still being requested for demos at various events. A recent notable occasion was GirlsDay, a yearly event that involves tech companies and institutions from all over the country opening their doors to girls aged 10 to 15, to elicit their interest in technical education and professions. Girls are invited to participate in all kinds of activities, meet female employees and learn more about working in technology. In April 2023, the VR experience *Amelia's Dream* was the main attraction on GirlsDay at the Amsterdam University of Applied Sciences. Young girls were dancing along with Amelia, commenting on her statements and agreeing loudly and wholeheartedly that girls can be and can do anything they want - thus once again demonstrating the impact on attitudes or even perspectives the medium of VR may convey.

3 Discussion and Conclusions

Conclusions from the *Amelia's Dream* experiment need to be presented with some caution. First of all, the sample was fairly small (103 participants) and the conditions under which the experiments were carried out varied, unfortunately: some participants were watching the VR experience in a busy hallway, while others were in a quieter environment. This of course may have influenced their experience. While none of the outcomes were extremely strong, the most significant effect was the self-reported measure about insight: being able to interact with the environment apparently lead to higher insight in the topic. However, when participants did not need to interact with the environment, they had better recollection of what had been said. This was also the case when the virtual character had looked participants in the eyes when conveying a message. The first outcome is in line with the earlier discussed work of Ferguson et al. [6] and while more research is certainly necessary to further confirm these findings, it may tentatively be concluded that an interactive VR environment may indeed help to shift a user's perspective on a topic, even by just helping them to better understand an issue. However, when it comes to conveying actual facts that need to be remembered, a non-interactive sequence may be a preferable choice for a VR producer. The second outcome, about the impact of eye-gaze, is a promising first exploration of a field that may prove to become more important in the future with the use of VR pointing towards social experiences. However, also future VR research that focuses on the study of interactive storytelling may benefit from insights like these that connect narrative design to user experiences.

As the description of the different lives of the project has shown, the concept of diversity can be embedded in media in a multitude of ways. Not only can the content of the medium itself focus on diversity, as is the case with *Amelia's Dream* and the LHBTIQ+ museum, but also the intended audience can direct the interpretation of diversity, as the Amstelpark VR experience has shown. In working towards an inclusive and diverse immersive media landscape, and a continuous search for ways that VR may be used to contribute to a better world, it is important to keep sharing insights like these with (future) content developers.

Acknowledgements. The research project VR for Diversity was led by the Amsterdam University of Applied Sciences. It ran from October 2020 until October 2022 and was funded by SIA RAAK.

References

1. VR for Good. https://www.oculus.com/vr-for-good/. Accessed 6 July 2023
2. VR for Impact. https://vr4impact.com/. Accessed 6 July 2023
3. Allen, C., Tucker, D.: Immersive content formats for future audiences. Digital Catapult (2019)
4. Oxford University Press: Oxford English Dictionary (2021). https://www.oed.com/
5. https://www.creativeeuropedesk.nl/nl/calls/videogames-immersive-content-development-2023
6. Ferguson, C., Van den Broek, E.L., Van Oostendorp, H.: On the role of interaction mode and story structure in virtual reality serious games. Comput. Educ. **143**, 103671 (2020)
7. Flowerday, T., Schraw, G.: Teacher beliefs about instructional choice: a phenomenological study. J. Educ. Psychol. **92**(4), 634–645 (2000)
8. Burdette, M.: The Swayze Effect (2015). https://www.oculus.com/story-studio/blog/the-swayze-effect/. Accessed 6 July 2023
9. Biocca, F., Burgoon, J., Harms, C., Stoner, M.: Criteria and scope conditions for a theory and measure of social presence. Presence Teleoper. Virtual Environ. **10**(01) (2001)
10. Sterna, R., Zibrek, K.: Psychology in virtual reality: toward a validated measure of social presence. Front. Psychol. **12**, 705448 (2021)
11. Vosmeer, M., Roth, C.: Exploring narrative novelties in VR. In: Mitchell, A., Vosmeer, M. (eds.) ICIDS 2021. LNCS, vol. 13138, pp. 435–444. Springer, Cham (2021). https://doi.org/10.1007/978-3-030-92300-6_44
12. Vosmeer, M.: VR for diversity: Amelia's Dream. In: Mitchell, A., Vosmeer, M. (eds.) ICIDS 2021. LNCS, vol. 13138, pp. 430–434. Springer, Cham (2021). https://doi.org/10.1007/978-3-030-92300-6_43
13. Fisher, J.A., Vosmeer, M., Barbara, J.: A new research agenda: writing for virtual reality interactive narratives. In: Vosmeer, M., Holloway-Attaway, L. (eds.) ICIDS 2022. LNCS, vol. 13762, pp. 673–683. Springer, Cham (2022). https://doi.org/10.1007/978-3-031-22298-6_43

14. Perez, C.C.: Invisible Women: Data Bias in a World Designed for Men. Abrams (2019)
15. Hartmann, T., Vosmeer, M., Roth, C.: (under review) Amelia's dream. An empirical study on shifting perspectives through interactive VR
16. Killerman, S.: (2011). https://www.samkillermann.com/work/genderbread-person/. Accessed 6 July 2023
17. Leslie, S., Vosmeer, M., Sterrenburg, C., Maimenscu, A., Catibovic, D., Matsjitadze, O.: VR for diversity: a virtual museum exhibition about LGBTIQ+. In: CHI Conference on Human Factors in Computing Systems Extended Abstracts, pp. 1–4, April 2022
18. Final Fantasy 7 Remake. Square Enix (2020)
19. Final Fantasy. Square Enix (1998)
20. https://www.cbr.com/final-fantasy-7-best-game-in-franchise/
21. Heinz, D.: Welcome to my fantasy: queer desires and digital utopias. GenderErträge V, 50 (2023)
22. Shaw, A., Friesem, E.: Where is the queerness in games?: types of lesbian, gay, bisexual, transgender, and queer content in digital games. Int. J. Commun. **10**, 13 (2016)
23. https://gaymingmag.com/2020/06/final-fantasy-vii-remake-complicates-its-queer-legacy/
24. Heijmen, N., Vosmeer, M.: Final fantasy VII remake: in search of queer celebration. In: Proceedings of the 2022 DiGRA International Conference, Kraków, Poland (2022)
25. https://indcor.eu/

Tools and Systems

Awash: Prospective Story Sifting Intervention for Emergent Narrative

Ben Clothier and David E. Millard[✉] ⓘ

University of Southamton, Southampton, UK
{bc2g20,dem}@soton.ac.uk

Abstract. Emergent Narrative (EN) affords extensive agency to participants but conflicts with the desire to guarantee compelling narrative. Recent work presents story sifting, an approach that curates simulation output, believing that intervention compromises the aesthetics of EN. However, this type of retrospective story sifting cannot improve narrative in participatory storyworlds, where the story emerges through play. We propose a new form of *prospective story sifting intervention*, that uses an incremental story sifter to identify possible stories during play, and passes these to a drama manager that intervenes in the simulation to make those stories more likely to complete. Our approach is incorporated into *Awash*, a pirate-themed EN game, and through qualitative analysis we find that the intervention increases narrative completeness and does not appear to compromise key EN aesthetics. Our work thus demonstrates a new technique that mixes generative and emergent approaches, and shows that intervention can be compatible with the aesthetics of emergent narrative.

Keywords: Story Sifting · Emergent Narrative · Intervention

1 Introduction

Interactive Digital Narrative (IDN) concerns itself with methodologies and technologies found within narratology, digital media, and computer science [16,26,28]. As well as Narrative Games it covers a broad range of forms including Interactive Cinema [10] and Hypertext Literature [6].

Within all of these forms the most common category of IDN is *Designed Narrative*. A typical designed narrative could be conceived as a tree or a graph representing a branching pre-authored story, often with alternative endings. This is traversed by the reader/player in order to experience a particular variation of the story and its outcome [15]. In hypertexts such as Joyce's *Afternoon: A Story* the nodes of the graph are textual [32], in *Black Mirror: Bandersnatch* [29] they are video fragments, in *Telltale's The Walking Dead* [7] they are playable sequences and cut-scenes.

An alternative approach is *Generative Narrative*. Here, there is no explicitly authored tree or graph structure. Approaches vary, but there is typically a *drama*

© The Author(s), under exclusive license to Springer Nature Switzerland AG 2023
L. Holloway-Attaway and J. T. Murray (Eds.): ICIDS 2023, LNCS 14383, pp. 187–207, 2023.
https://doi.org/10.1007/978-3-031-47655-6_12

manager that can realise the designer's narrative vision by unfolding the story in response to interactions [27]. In the interactive drama, *Façade*, the story is authored as a collection of plot points ('plot points' [14], 'story beats' [23], 'plot elements' [25]), and the drama manager interprets player actions and coherently constructs the narrative in response [14,23,25].

Finally, there is *Emergent Narrative* (EN). EN is a simulationist approach to IDN, exploiting the human proclivity for narrative sense-making [1], it is a bottom-up method by which the narrative is determined by the perceived coalescence of events in a simulated world [4,33]. EN affords extensive agency to the player (something that is challenging to accommodate in designed narratives) [31]. The disadvantage is that this is in conflict with the desire to guarantee compelling narrative, since the more control the player has, the less the author has – a tension known as the Narrative Paradox [3,21,22].

Some have attempted to resolve this paradox with a mixed-approach, introducing top-down intervention in EN simulations [5,21,34]. Others reject this method, arguing that EN has particular aesthetics that are damaged or eroded by intervention. Instead they prefer to curate EN after the fact in a process called *story sifting* [30], effectively drawing the players attention to any coherent narratives that have emerged naturally in the simulation.

In this paper we propose a novel mixed-approach to EN of *prospective story sifting intervention* that combines story sifting with a drama manager. With this approach the story sifter identifies possible narratives that are beginning to emerge in the storyworld, and the drama manager intervenes to make it more likely that they will continue. We demonstrate this approach in *Awash*, a short survival game set in an age of piracy, that uses an incremental story sifting engine coupled with a stage director for intervention. We use this to evaluate the player experience focusing on two key questions:

1. Can prospective story sifting intervention improve the narrative completeness of participatory storyworlds?
2. Can prospective story sifting intervention be employed whilst preserving the aesthetics of EN?

Section 2 explores story sifting further and defines what we mean by narrative completeness and the aesthetics of EN. Section 3 introduces *Awash* and uses it to explain how we have combined story sifting with a drama manager. Section 4 presents a qualitative comparative evaluation of the experience of playing *Awash* with and without the intervention component. Section 5 uses this to answer our two research questions. Finally, Sect. 6 summarises our findings and sets out the limitations and possible avenues of future work.

2   Background

2.1   Intervention and Emergent Aesthetics

Researchers in EN have taken various perspectives. Aylett adopts a *character-centric* stance focusing on interactions between intelligent characters [2,30].

Ryan instead emphasises the system as a whole, heralding EN as a phenomenon that can be attained by designing rich 'storyworlds' [30,31]. Although this perspective also recognises that narrative fundamentally emerges from the interaction between characters, it is strongly *world-centric*.

There is a disparity between the two perspectives in how they regard *intervention*. Those with a character-centric perspective seem to accept some level of intervention as a necessary treatment for the narrative paradox (take for example, the beats and narrative goals of *Façade* [24]) but Ryan dismisses the idea of intervention, asserting that it, 'kills the pleasure', of EN.

He goes on to describe a set of ten, 'aesthetics of emergent narrative' [30]. These are the aesthetics of the:

- **actual** (pleasure in stories 'based on true events')
- **personal** (pleasure in stories that relate to lived experience)
- **uncanny** (pleasure in the strangeness of simulation logic)
- **uncovered** (the thrill of discovery)
- **improbable** (the joy of unlikely events that were not fated)
- **vast** (the anticipation created by depth and breadth)
- **ephemeral** (the value of a unique story unseen by others)
- **unauthored** (the delight of non-human authored artefacts)
- **coauthored** (the satisfaction of participation in story creation)
- **larger context** (value of a larger storyworld as backdrop)

If a work lacks any of the aesthetics of EN then, Ryan claims, it is something different entirely from EN [30]. In our work we have concentrated on the first nine of these aesthetics. This is for practical reasons. The aesthetics of a 'larger context', has been left out, as it is harder to explore in an experimental game that is by necessity smaller in scope.

2.2   Curation and Story Sifting

Ryan's alternative to intervention is *curation*. One of Ryan's first works was, *Diol/Diel/Dial*, a vast encyclopedia generated from a chronicle of all the events that occurred in a storyworld simulation [30]. This work is an interface through which the user can explore the events of the simulation in search of compelling narrative. Searching through an encyclopedia of events manually does not constitute an engaging experience, so to counter this, Ryan proposed *story sifting*, a query-based approach to curating the vast outputs of simulated storyworlds by identifying interesting event sequences [30,31]. This has since received attention from other researchers who have typically aimed to improve *sifting pattern* authorship (the queries that search for the event sequences) [11,17–19].

Up until this point, story sifting had only been considered as a *retrospective* tool, sifting for narrative in events that have already occurred. However, in 2021 Kreminski proposed *incremental* sifting, which works by partially matching and progressing the queries as the events occur. These partially matched patterns provide the system with information that can facilitate foreshadowing of possible narrative futures (what Kreminski calls *prospective* stories) in real time [17].

We can thus expand the definition of story sifters to say that retrospective sifters look for completed patterns in the past, while prospective sifters look for patterns that might complete in the future. Sifting patterns are one approach that can be used to build a retrospective sifter, and incremental sifting modifies that approach to implement a prospective sifter.

2.3   Narrative Completeness

The completeness of a narrative has long been considered an important factor in its success [9] but completeness is not usually a strength of EN. Mateas compares, 'simulations', and, 'structured narratives', in three key areas [23]. His comparisons can be distilled into a set of desired features for EN:

– *Consistency*: compelling narrative should always occur,
– *Efficiency*: narratively irrelevant events should be minimised, and
– *Pacing*: dramatic tension should fluctuate appropriately throughout.

In our work we combine these elements under the umbrella of *narrative completeness*. Alternative definitions of narrative completeness, such as those found in psychology around recalled personal stories, emphasise additional aspects (such as meaning, clear responsibility, and developed characters) but share these key elements of coherent cause and effect over time [12]. Mateas' features also exclude narrative *closure* (the feeling of finality once all the threads of a narrative are resolved) [8,13], although this applies less to an emergent work which has no specific end state (the hypertext notion of *exhaustion* might be more appropriate [20]).

While a full exploration of narrative completeness is beyond the scope of this paper, we can say that our goal is to improve the narrative completeness of EN (in Mateas' terms) without compromising its aesthetics.

3   Design and Implementation of Awash

3.1   The Storyworld and Game

Awash is a survival game set in an age of piracy in which the player is the captain of a ship. They must navigate and survive in a procedurally generated ocean, managing their resources and interacting with other ships.

Our goal with Awash was to combine a prospective story sifter with a drama manager in order to explore the impact on narrative completeness and emergent narrative aesthetics. Figure 1 shows the overall architecture, which is inspired by Aylett and Louchart's 'Emergent Narrative Model' [22].

Awash is implemented in the Unity engine as a series of interacting state-machine characters and other simpler entities. Based on the states of these entities, a graphical representation of the world is created; a top-down, low-poly, 3D environment that the player can interact with (see Fig. 2).

The simulation of the world is driven by characters choosing and enacting actions. This forms a chain of events, named the *event stream* (as opposed to an event chronicle), that serves as material for the rest of the system.

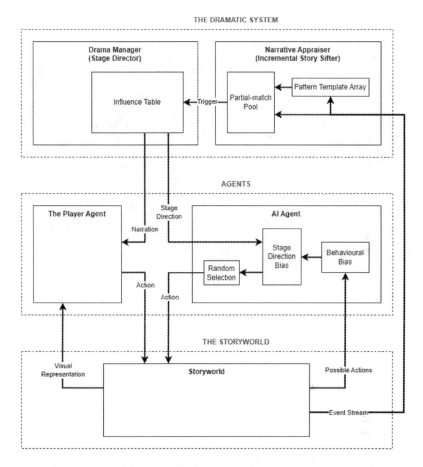

Fig. 1. The System Model (based on [22]), comprised of the *storyworld*, multiple *agents*, and the *dramatic system*.

3.2 The Agents

The storyworld is the world to be simulated, consisting of a map and various entities. It is character-centric in the sense that it is fundamentally driven by character action and interaction. That is to say that characters are given turns to act, and their actions become the events of the storyworld. A *storyworld character* is a type of entity in the storyworld that can perform actions. *The player* is an agent that controls a storyworld character. The player can act by interacting with the three-dimensional visual representation of the storyworld and a graphical interface. The player receives *narrations* in the form of simple text popups from a narrator-character. An *AI agent* is an instance of a class that also controls a storyworld character by retrieving the set of possible state machine actions and randomly choosing one according to its *behavioural bias* (a probability distribution over the possible actions).

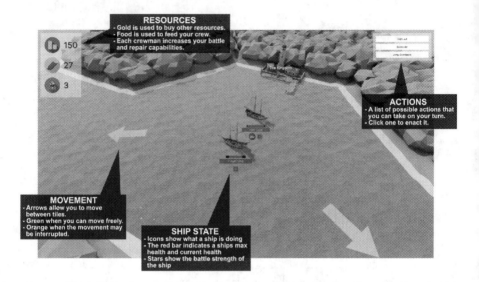

Fig. 2. The 3D graphical environment with interface descriptions.

3.3   The Narrative Appraiser

The Dramatic System in Awash is comprised of the Drama Manager and the Narrative Appraiser. The narrative appraiser monitors the stream of events emerging from the storyworld and identifies sequences that represent compelling narrative. This is achieved with incremental story sifting.

For this module to interpret the events of the storyworld, abstractions are necessary. A *narratable entity* is an abstraction of an entity (e.g., a character, ship, or settlement) consisting of a name and a unique entity ID. A *narratable event* is an abstraction of an event consisting of the event type, the acting entity, the target entity (if one exists), and tags (generic event descriptions associating them with other events and stage directions). An example of a narratable event is shown in Fig. 3.

[BigShip] started battle with [FastShip]

Type	Actor	Target	Tags
started_battle	BigShip	FastShip	aggressive

Fig. 3. Example of a narratable event (an abstraction of a storyworld event).

In order to recognise compelling narrative, sifting patterns are employed. These are represented in XML for simplicity. For example, Fig. 4 shows the *Revenging Ship* pattern: *a ship is fired upon by another ship, the fired-upon ship narrowly escapes and later comes back for revenge.* Other patterns in Awash deal with situations such as your crew running low on supplies, or saving another ship in a battle.

```
1   <?xml version="1.0"?>
2   <Pattern xmlns:xsd="http://www.w3.org/2001/XMLSchema" xmlns:xsi="http://www.w3.org/2001/XMLSchema-instance"
3       id="revenging-ship">
4       <EventSequence>
5           <Event type="started_battle" actor-var="ship_1" target-var="ship_2" />
6           <Event type="withdrew" actor-var="ship_2" influence-id="1" />
7           <Event type="started_battle" actor-var="ship_2" target-var="ship_1" influence-id="2" />
8       </EventSequence>
9       <Invalidations>
10          <Invalidation after="1">
11              <Event tag="defeated" target-var="ship_1" />
12          </Invalidation>
13          <Invalidation after="1">
14              <Event tag="defeated" target-var="ship_2" />
15          </Invalidation>
16      </Invalidations>
17  </Pattern>
```

Fig. 4. A pattern specification in XML: *Revenging Ship.*

A *pattern template* is a class representation of a sifting pattern. A *partial match* is a class representation of a sifting pattern that is queried and incrementally matched (i.e., strictly in sequence) as events are pushed to the event stream. It is this process that is distinctive of incremental story sifting [17]. The events of a partial match that have been matched represent the part of the micro-story that have already occurred, and the events yet to be matched represent the possible futures that would progress the micro-story. Figure 5 shows an example partial match pattern.

A partial match consists of the following:

- *Entity Bindings*: a mapping of narratable entities to variables to keep track of the entities/actors involved in the pattern,
- *Event Sequence*: a temporally-ordered list of event queries to specify the sequence of events to be matched, and
- *Invalidation Events*: a list of event queries that invalidate/discard the partial match if matched.

All pattern templates, representing all authored patterns, are held in the *pattern template array*. All partial matches, representing all partially-complete micro-stories, are held in the *partial match pool* (as in [17]). When an event occurs it is first queried over all pattern templates. A partial match is created from each matched template and is added to the partial match pool. The event is then queried over all partial matches, including any just added to the pool. Each matched partial match is progressed. Once a partial match is fully completed or one of its invalidation events is matched, it is removed from the pool and discarded. The pool represents the narrative appraiser's narrative information about the simulation at any given time. In pool design, Kreminski describes three strategies of, 'pool management' [17]:

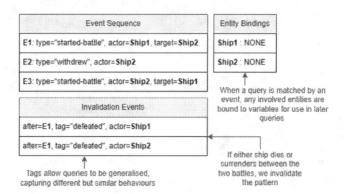

Fig. 5. The *Revenging Ship* partial match. It shows a sequence of event queries, a mapping of entities to variables, and a set of events that would invalidate the pattern.

- First, match behaviour: how the pattern is handled when an event is matched. This is either: 'fork and advance', or, 'advance directly', behaviour. The former duplicates the pattern before advancement, the latter simply advances the existing pattern.
- Secondly, pattern expiry: how long the pattern can remain in the pool without receiving any advancement.
- Thirdly, implied invalidation: the use of default invalidation conditions.

Our pool is designed to use advance-directly match behaviour by default, with the option to specify event queries with fork-and-advance behaviour. This way, the pool size is naturally bounded. It does not, however, use pattern expiry or implied invalidation, since they were deemed unlikely to provide a benefit given the limited scope of the storyworld.

3.4   The Drama Manager

The Drama Manager is the other half of the dramatic system. It utilises the narrative information of the narrative appraiser to provide narration and intervention. Intuitively, the more influence the dramatic system has on the storyworld, the more likely it is to diminish the aesthetics of EN. Three possible levels of intervention were considered:

- *Generative*: actions/events are spawned as required,
- *Direct*: existing action/event possibilities are chosen to occur, and
- *Indirect*: existing action/event possibilities are probabilistically encouraged.

In the interest of preserving the aesthetics of EN whilst demonstrating that narrative completeness can be enhanced, the intervention method chosen was *indirect*. Our drama manager employs a type of intervention that we term *stage direction*. This indirectly influences the decision-making policies of AI characters

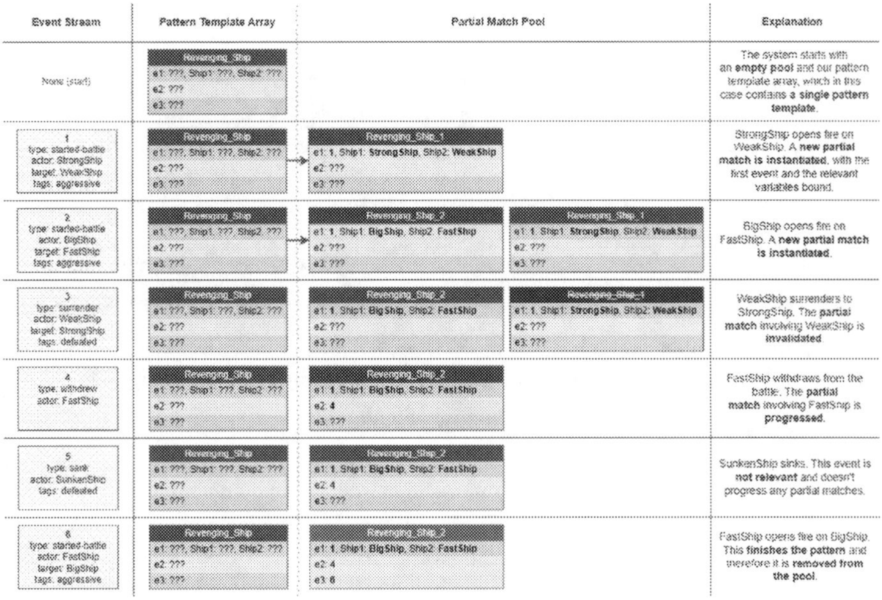

Fig. 6. A visualisation of incremental pattern matching for the *Revenging Ship* scenario. The diagram is a modification of Kreminski's [17] for the given example, although using advance-directly match behaviour.

to encourage the progression of partial matches. Additionally, the drama manager employs real-time narration, in a similar vein to *Winnow* [17]. Although narration itself can be viewed as a form of influence (it could influence the player), it is used here mainly as a sense making device working alongside the interventions of the drama manager.

To trigger stage directions or narrations (which together we call influences), patterns are authored with *influence IDs* associated with a specific event (see Fig. 4). When an event of a pattern is matched, its influence ID is looked up in a table for any associated narrations or stage directions (see Fig. 7).

This module can be illustrated by extending the Revenging Ship scenario (see Figs. 7 and 8). As shown, event matches sometimes trigger stage directions and narrations (Fig. 9 shows an example of how narration is delivered in the game). Stage directions will influence, but not dictate, an AI agent's action.

4 Evaluation

4.1 Methodology

Our goal with Awash was to use the game to explore the impact of prospective story sifting intervention on the narrative completeness of the experience and the aesthetics of emergent narrative. To this end we conducted a controlled qualitative comparative study looking at two conditions:

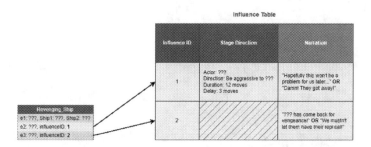

Fig. 7. Influence table example: *Revenging Ship*. Showing the set of influences that the drama manager module can perform, linked to Influence IDs in the pattern.

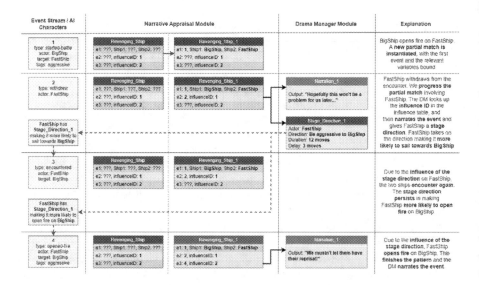

Fig. 8. Drama manager example: *Revenging Ship*. This is a modification of Fig. 6 to extend the *Revenging Ship* scenario. The pattern template array and partial match pool now make up the, 'Narrative Appraisal Module', column, and AI agent processes are now shown alongside the event stream.

There! *The Weak Spirit* again!

Fig. 9. An example of a narration given to the player.

1. Baseline Mode (BM) in which the story sifter drives only narration, this is in the form of the live commentary of a parrot character, resembling Kreminski's application of *Winnow* to *Blaseball* [17].
2. Influence Mode (IM) in which the story sifter drives narration as well as indirect intervention. This is identical to BM but with the addition of stage directions that influence the actions of the AI characters.

To analyse each participant's experience, interview questions were created with two frameworks in mind: the strength of the aesthetics of EN [30], and the narrative completeness of the experience [23] (discussed in Sect. 2).

In total twelve University students participated, each given the option to take part in person or online. All of the participants had some experience in emergent and narrative games. The study was conducted identically in each case. Each participant was informed about the study and game play. They played both modes of the game (conditions) for twenty minutes. The order of game mode was alternated so that half of the participants experienced BM first and the other half experienced IM first. Participants did not know what the difference was between the two conditions. Each participant then took part in a thirty minute semi-structured interview in which they were asked to recount some interesting stories that they experienced in each twenty minute play session. The questions that followed then deconstructed these stories in line with the aesthetics and narrative completeness variables described in Sect. 2.

The twelve interviews were inductively coded by one researcher, and the themes and codes were reviewed and iterated in discussion with a second researcher. For each code it was noted which condition it applied to (cross-referencing the story related by the participants with the system logs).

The study was approved by the University of Southampton ethics board, 'ERGO/FEPS/78677.v1').

4.2 Results and Analysis

During the sessions we recorded the activity of the story sifter and drama manager in an activity log. This captured: the number of events that occurred in the simulation, the number of patterns instantiated by the story sifter, the number of events that progressed a pattern, the number of patterns subsequently completed, the number of narration events that occurred, and the number of stage directions generated by the drama manager. Table 1 shows this data averaged across all twelve sessions, separated into the two conditions.

Table 1. Descriptive data from the twelve evaluation sessions

	Total Events	Patterns Instantiated	Events Pro-gressed	Patterns Com-pleted	Narrations Given	Stage Directions Given
BM Mean	3777	45	105	7	31	n/a
BM Std. Dev.	1170	19	50	2	13	n/a
IM Mean	4026	52	105	6	25	51
IM Std. Dev.	984	17	33	3	11	23

In both conditions the story sifter monitors events and attempts to match them against patterns, recording those patterns that are completed. In BM players are responsible for completing patterns (if possible), in IM the drama manager intervenes to make completion more likely. In both conditions the story sifter functioned well (instantiating an average of 45 patterns in BM, and 52 in IM), and that in the IM condition the drama manager also produced stage directions (51 in total). It also shows that in both cases players received narration (31 narration events in BM, 25 in IM) and that they completed a subset of those patterns (7 in BM, 6 in IM). It is interesting that in the IM case there was no significant difference in the number of events progressed or the number of patterns completed and we will explore this more in Sect. 5.

The qualitative analysis of the interviews resulted in three major themes (Artificiality, Vastness and Uniqueness, and Drama) and twelve codes (or subthemes), these are shown in Table 2 with counts split into each condition. In the Table, and subsequent sections, quotes are given with the participant number (P1-P12). In the following sections we will review each theme in turn.

4.3 Artificiality

Artificiality was reported when participants felt that an occurrence was enacted intentionally to create drama, whereas organicity was expressed when they felt an occurrence transpired by chance, or through reasonable character action.

Table 2. Interview themes, sub-themes, count per condition, and example quotations.

Theme	Sub-theme	BM	IM	Example Quote
Artificiality	Organic Moment Felt Organic	12	1	"I guess what I was expecting was a programmed response rather than them attacking me." (P7)
	Influenced Moment Felt Organic	n/a	19	"[It] felt like it was making a decision for itself rather than being programmed to do so." (P5)
	Organic Moment Felt Artificial	7	4	"It was kind of set out by the game that I had an arch-nemesis, because there was only one strong ship, sort of artificially there." (P4)
	Influenced Moment Felt Artificial	n/a	5	"It's almost trying too hard to make a story." (P5)
Vastness and Uniqueness	Rare	6	8	"The way it turned out was more surprising, like, I didn't expect it to happen." (P8)
	Likely	3	2	"I would say all of the choices felt fairly expected." (P5)
	Personal	2	12	"I also felt like a lot of stuff I had done led up to that moment. It didn't feel random, it felt like I deserved it." (P1)
	Funny or Strange	3	2	"I did chuckle at it a bit. It felt like it was strange to see." (P11)
Drama	Dramatic Presence	9	16	"I feel like there was a bit of tension when coming back after getting the artefact." (P4)
	Dramatic Absence	18	10	"I was just sailing through without issue." (P6)
	Dramatic Harmony	1	11	"Yeah, it felt almost less jittery. It felt like the interactions were longer and less frequently interrupted" (P4)
	Dramatic Discord	14	5	"I would not really expect it to follow me, because I feel like I would have to come across it by chance again to continue interacting with it." (P5)

As you might expect **organic moments felt organic** was a point that was raised significantly more for BM than IM (12 vs 1), this included causal story moments that occurred naturally:

> "I wasn't expecting to find that very same ship again. It wasn't hinted at and I didn't work it out ... It seemed really quite natural." (P11)

However, participants also reported that **influenced moments felt organic**, in other words that an event altered by the drama manager felt natural (this could only have happened in IM, and occurred 19 times). This was particularly notable in the case of the *revenge* pattern (where ships were more likely to run away, heal, upgrade, and come back for revenge).

> "the enemy re-appeared out of the blue and there were loads of enemies that could've re-appeared that had run away earlier." (P7)

Conversely we recorded occasions where **organic moments felt artificial** (7 for BM, 4 for IM). This was commonly expressed in both modes when the game randomly generated an unusual element.

There were relatively few comments around **influenced moments feeling artificial** (only possible in IM, there were 5 occurrences). Inspection of the logs reveals that all of these moments were caused by *artefact* or *bounty* interventions influencing unsuitable ships, or influencing too many ships uniformly.

> "Generally, it didn't feel artificial. The only exception would be the two weaker ships that attacked me. It's almost trying too hard to make a story." (P5)

Looking overall at the ratios of comments on organicity and artificiality they are similar in both conditions (BM is 12:7, IM is 20:9) despite the fact that IM was the only condition to feature artificiality.

4.4   Vastness and Uniqueness

This theme relates to the perceived qualities of the events experienced by players. The **rare** sub-theme was reported when participants felt occurrences were improbable or the possibilities were vast, whereas the **likely** sub-theme was expressed when they felt occurrences were expected or common.

Examples were identified as rare not just because they were encountered once, but because they seemed unusual and noteworthy:

> "I had not encountered something like that before. So that was very much an exclamatory moment for me that I was surprised by ... if I talked to someone about playing the game, that would be something that I bring up and recount." (P10)

A similar number of these instances occurred in both conditions. Even when intervention was involved participants still expressed that moments felt like they were unlikely and amongst many possibilities.

"It did make you wonder if this was an unlikely event that just happened to occur out of all the interactions." (P11)

The **personal** sub-theme was reported when participants felt occurrences were resultant of their previous choices, or they were being targeted by a character they had previously interacted with. Although these did occur in BM they were significantly more numerous in IM. This theme was often expressed when a participant experienced an interaction that was reinforced by a pre-existing interaction: a weakness of BM. For example, the bounty pattern which gave participants a sense of consequence for their actions.

"It definitely felt like a direct connection with the action of me betraying one of the trade ships earlier. It was definitely a connection between what I'm doing in the game." (P8)

Finally, participants also reported occurrences that were **funny or strange**. There was a fine line, however, between a strange occurrence being positively or negatively received.

"It was kind of funny, and it was plausible because it was a fairly strong ship that was fairly equally matched in a fight." (P12)

Occurrences of this theme are low in both conditions (3 in BM, 2 in IM) and there is thus no evidence that intervention influenced these perceptions.

4.5   Drama

This theme included comments on the dramatic quality (or lack of quality) of specific moments, as well as how well the different moments related to one another. Both IM and BM included a number of moments that could be described as having **Dramatic Presence**:

"I was convinced that I didn't stand a chance and was really trying to get away at every opportunity. So I was definitely under pressure, it was quite tense." (P8)

IM produced 16 such examples and BM 9. Perhaps where the game was most successful was in adding drama to important game elements (i.e. possessing the artefact, or being the target of a bounty).

Comments around **Dramatic Absence** were more common for BM (18 vs. 10 for IM), for example referring to lulls in the action that went on for to long:

"In terms of intensity it felt like there were moments where the sea felt very calm [in BM], and there was little resistance to me getting the artefact home." (P3)

Participants described feelings of more consistent or better flowing drama, what we have termed **Dramatic Harmony**, almost exclusively in IM (11 instances compared to just 1 in BM).

"It felt almost less jittery. It felt like the interactions were longer and less frequently interrupted." (P4)

The opposite of Harmony is **Dramatic Discord**, this was particularly prevalent in BM (14 instances) compared to IM (5 instances). For example, the participants expressed frustration towards their interactions with a nemesis in BM.

"I think it felt like there was an element of randomness to the [BM nemesis], in that, had that situation arisen, say I was similarly low on health and [this ship] was attacking me and I managed to run away, I would not really expect it to follow me, because I feel like I would have to come across it by chance again to continue interacting with it." (P5)

5 Discussion

5.1 Improving Narrative Completeness

Our first question was: *Can prospective story sifting intervention improve the narrative completeness of participatory storyworlds?* Narrative Completeness is defined in Sect. 2.3, and includes how consistent the narrative is, its efficiency in terms of including only relevant events, and its pacing.

The *Drama* theme reflects this for *Awash*. With the intervention (IM condition) participants express *dramatic presence* more often and *dramatic absence* less often. This tells us that moments of tension occur more often and expectations of drama are more often fulfilled, indicating that consistency (the first component of narrative completeness) is improved. Furthermore, participants often report *dramatic harmony* with intervention, but *dramatic discord* without. This is likely because characters interact with the player repeatedly, oftentimes more coherently, due to the intervention. As a result, the experiences produced appear to be of a higher dramatic quality, with enhanced efficiency and pacing (the final two components of narrative completeness). This is not necessarily pacing in the sense that drama is modulated over time, but rather that when tension builds it is less likely to be dissipated by incongruous events.

Despite the qualitative analysis demonstrating an increase in narrative completeness, the descriptive statistics presented in Sect. 4 show that the average number of event matches and partial patterns completed do not significantly change for the IM condition. So how can it be that the experience is qualitatively improved despite the same number of patterns being experienced? Firstly, there may be a specific set of patterns that lead to higher quality narrative. With the intervention, these may be progressed more frequently and less often invalidated. Secondly, more complex patterns may lead to higher quality narrative. With the intervention, more complex patterns may be progressed more frequently and less often invalidated.

Further analysis is required to determine the true explanation, as the data collected in our logs does not adequately explain which characteristics account for the improved experience revealed by the qualitative analysis.

5.2   Preserving the Aesthetics of EN

Our second question was: *Can prospective story sifting intervention be employed whilst preserving the aesthetics of EN?* The aesthetics are set out in Sect. 2.1; Ryan argues that these goals are mutually exclusive [30].

The *actual* and *unauthored* aesthetics can be analysed through the *Artificiality* theme. When comparing the sub-themes of artificiality and organicity a similar ratio is found regardless of the condition, this is evidence that intervention in Awash does not increase feelings that the experience is authored or unreal. Moreover, it demonstrates that a storyworld may provoke feelings of artificiality even when free from intervention.

The *personal, co-authored,* and *uncanny* aesthetics are related to the *Vastness and Uniqueness* theme. In IM, participants frequently describe experiences as feeling *personal*, far outnumbering those described without intervention. It could be that encouraging characters to interact with the player multiple times with harmonious actions leads participants to feel targeted due to their interaction history. Players also reported strong feelings of agency, indicating that they are driving the story in a process of *co-authorship*. Participants describe experiences as *funny or strange* at a similar frequency regardless of the intervention, indicating that the potential for uncanny occurrences is not reduced by the intervention. Overall these results indicate that the intervention does not diminish these aesthetics.

We did not see any evidence of the *uncovered* aesthetic in any of the interview responses. This may be due to the simplicity of the storyworld.

The remaining aesthetics concern the *vastness* of possibilities and the perception of *improbability* and *ephemerality* of occurrences, which we also see reported as part of the *Vastness and Uniqueness* theme. Participants report the *rare* sub-theme at a similar frequency regardless of the intervention. This is also the case for the *likely* sub-theme, indicating that the sense of vastness is not diminished and thus the intervention does not reduce these aesthetics.

6   Conclusions

This paper has proposed a new approach for intervening in emergent narratives through prospective story sifting, and we have presented an example game – Awash, an emergent narrative pirate game – that implements this through incremental story sifting linked to stage directions. Prospective story sifting has been used before for foreshadowing, but has never before been linked to interventions in this way in a participatory storyworld.

The work presented here aims to answer two research questions: *Can prospective story sifting intervention improve the narrative completeness of participatory storyworlds*, and, *Can prospective story sifting intervention be employed whilst preserving the aesthetics of EN?*

In answer to the first question our evidence suggests that completeness is improved by the intervention. Participants reported more occurrences of dramatic moments, and fewer occasions of dramatic absence (indicating *narrative consistency* is improved); they also reported more harmonious relationships between those moments more frequently when the intervention was in place (indicating *narrative efficiency* and *narrative pacing* are improved). However, our quantitative analysis showed no change in key statistics (105:105 event matches, 7:6 patterns completed, 80:82 patterns invalidated), which implies that there is some characteristic of the patterns being taken forward that creates this improved experience, rather than it just being the raw number of patterns.

In answer to the second question we judged that nine of the aesthetics identified by Ryan could be evaluated in our experimental set up: *actual, personal, uncanny, improbable, vast, ephemeral, unauthored, coauthored,* and *uncovered*. Evidence from our interviews suggests that Awash at least partially delivers on the first eight of these. Participants did not comment on *uncovered* (the thrill of discovery) in either condition, implying that it is perhaps lacking in the game itself (possibly due to the smaller scale). Importantly, for the eight aesthetics that we were able to measure there was no negetive impact from the intervention, despite the improvements reported for narrative completeness, and in fact we also see an improvement in the aesthetics of the personal.

Overall this is evidence that the prospective story sifting intervention in *Awash* successfully promotes narrative completeness without fundamentally diminishing the aesthetics of EN. This success might be due to manifesting the intervention through character action. These conclusions may point towards existing Distributed Drama Management work as another intervention strategy that preserves the aesthetics of EN [4, 34].

Our work has a number of limitations. First, Awash is a simple story world, and this already seems to have excluded two aesthetics. The intervention method employed here deserves to be explored further in richer simulations. Second, we have only used one intervention strategy – indirect 'stage directions' – and more forceful interventions may have impacted the aesthetics more. It may also be the case that the specific mechanics of *Awash* or our choice of patterns has impacted our evaluation. While this is still evidence that useful intervention is possible without damaging the aesthetics of EN, further work is needed to understand the interplay between different mechanics, patterns, and aesthetics.

Finally, there are some important ideas that could be expanded in future, including exploring rules systems around pattern selection, more complex pattern definitions and composition, and the definition of narrative completeness itself. We see Awash as a starting point to explore these ideas, and a template for future, more complex games, that follow the prospective story sifting intervention approach, further develop pattern languages and rules-based engines, and which can undertake more focused evaluations to understand the relationship between different interventions and the experience of emergent narratives.

Our work is the first to show prospective story sifting intervention (combining a story sifter with a drama manager) and intends to open the door to exploring further intervention strategies aimed at creating more complete narrative experiences that nevertheless remain strongly emergent in their aesthetic.

References

1. Andersen, D., Ravn, S., Thomson, R.: Narrative sense-making and prospective social action: methodological challenges and new directions. Int. J. Soc. Res. Methodol. **23**(4), 367–375 (2020). https://doi.org/10.1080/13645579.2020.1723204
2. Aylett, R.: Narrative in virtual environments-towards emergent narrative. In: Proceedings of the AAAI Fall Symposium on Narrative Intelligence, pp. 83–86. USA (1999)
3. Aylett, R.: Emergent narrative, social immersion and "storification". In: Proceedings of the 1st International Workshop on Narrative and Interactive Learning Environments, pp. 35–44 (2000)
4. Aylett, R., Truesdale, J., Suttie, N., Louchart, S.: Emergent narrative: past, present and future of an interactive storytelling approach. In: Interactive Digital Narrative. Routledge (2015)
5. Aylett, R.S., Louchart, S., Dias, J., Paiva, A., Vala, M.: FearNot! – an experiment in emergent narrative. In: Panayiotopoulos, T., Gratch, J., Aylett, R., Ballin, D., Olivier, P., Rist, T. (eds.) IVA 2005. LNCS (LNAI), vol. 3661, pp. 305–316. Springer, Heidelberg (2005). https://doi.org/10.1007/11550617_26
6. Bell, A.: The Possible Worlds of Hypertext Fiction. Palgrave Macmillan UK, London (2010). https://doi.org/10.1057/9780230281288
7. Bostan, B., Yönet, Ö., Sevdimaliyev, V.: Empathy and choice in story driven games: a case study of telltale games. In: Bostan, B. (ed.) Game User Experience And Player-Centered Design. ISCEMT, pp. 361–378. Springer, Cham (2020). https://doi.org/10.1007/978-3-030-37643-7_16
8. Carroll, N.: Narrative Closure. Philosophical studies: an international journal for philosophy in the analytic tradition **135**(1), 1–15 (2007)
9. Erler, M.: Detailed completeness and pleasure of the narrative. some remarks on the narrative tradition and plato. In: Plato's Styles and Characters: Between Literature and Philosophy, 2015, 103–119, ISBN 9783110444032, Págs, pp. 103-119. De Gruyter Recht (2015)
10. Hales, C.: Cinematic interaction: From kinoautomat to cause and effect. Digit. Creativity **16**(1), 54–64 (2005). https://doi.org/10.1080/14626260500147777
11. Johnson-Bey, S., Mateas, M.: Centrifuge: a visual tool for authoring sifting patterns for character-based Simulationist story worlds. In: The 17th AAAI Conference on Artificial Intelligence and Interactive Digital Entertainment: Programming Languages and Interactive Entertainment Workshop (2021)
12. Kellas, J.K., Manusov, V.: What's in a story? The relationship between narrative completeness and adjustment to relationship dissolution. J. Soc. Pers. Relat. **20**(3), 285–307 (2003). https://doi.org/10.1177/0265407503020003002
13. Klauk, T., Köppe, T., Onea, E.: More on narrative closure. J. Lit. Semant. **45**(1), 21–48 (2016). https://doi.org/10.1515/jls-2016-0003
14. Koenitz, H.: Towards a theoretical framework for interactive digital narrative. In: Aylett, R., Lim, M.Y., Louchart, S., Petta, P., Riedl, M. (eds.) ICIDS 2010. LNCS, vol. 6432, pp. 176–185. Springer, Heidelberg (2010). https://doi.org/10.1007/978-3-642-16638-9_22
15. Koenitz, H.: Towards a specific theory of interactive digital narrative. In: Interactive Digital Narrative. Routledge (2015)
16. Koenitz, H., Haahr, M., Ferri, G., Sezen, T.I.: First steps towards a unified theory for interactive digital narrative. In: Pan, Z., Cheok, A.D., Müller, W., Iurgel, I., Petta, P., Urban, B. (eds.) Transactions on Edutainment X. LNCS, vol. 7775, pp. 20–35. Springer, Heidelberg (2013). https://doi.org/10.1007/978-3-642-37919-2_2

17. Kreminski, M., Dickinson, M., Mateas, M.: Winnow: a domain-specific language for incremental story sifting. In: Proceedings of the AAAI Conference on Artificial Intelligence and Interactive Digital Entertainment, vol. 17, no. 1, pp. 156–163, October 2021. https://doi.org/10.1609/aiide.v17i1.18903, https://ojs.aaai.org/index.php/AIIDE/article/view/18903

18. Kreminski, M., Dickinson, M., Wardrip-Fruin, N.: Felt: a simple story sifter. In: Cardona-Rivera, R.E., Sullivan, A., Young, R.M. (eds.) ICIDS 2019. LNCS, vol. 11869, pp. 267–281. Springer, Cham (2019). https://doi.org/10.1007/978-3-030-33894-7_27

19. Kreminski, M., Wardrip-Fruin, N., Mateas, M.: Authoring for story sifters. In: Hargood, C., Millard, D.E., Mitchell, A., Spierling, U. (eds.) The Authoring Problem: Challenges in Supporting Authoring for Interactive Digital Narratives, pp. 207–220. Springer, Cham (2022). https://doi.org/10.1007/978-3-031-05214-9_13

20. Landow, G.P.: Hypertext 3.0: Critical Theory and New Media in an Era of Globalization. The Johns Hopkins University Press, Baltimore, MD, USA (2006)

21. Louchart, S., Aylett, R.: Solving the narrative paradox in VEs – lessons from RPGs. In: Rist, T., Aylett, R.S., Ballin, D., Rickel, J. (eds.) IVA 2003. LNCS (LNAI), vol. 2792, pp. 244–248. Springer, Heidelberg (2003). https://doi.org/10.1007/978-3-540-39396-2_41

22. Louchart, S., Aylett, R.: The emergent narrative theoretical investigation. In: the 2004 Conference on Narrative and Interactive Learning Environments, pp. 21–28 (2004)

23. Mateas, M., Stern, A.: Integrating plot, character and natural language processing in the interactive drama façade. In: Proceedings of the 1st International Conference on Technologies for Interactive Digital Storytelling and Entertainment (TIDSE-03), vol. 2 (2003)

24. Mateas, M., Stern, A.: Structuring content in the Façade interactive drama architecture. Proc. AAAI Conf. Artif. Intell. Interact. Digit. Entertainment 1(1), 93–98 (2005). https://doi.org/10.1609/aiide.v1i1.18722

25. Mott, B., Lee, S., Lester, J.: Probabilistic goal recognition in interactive narrative environments. In: Proceedings of the National Conference on Artificial Intelligence, vol. 21, p. 187. Menlo Park, CA; Cambridge, MA; London; AAAI Press; MIT Press, 1999 (2006)

26. Murray, J.H.: Research into interactive digital narrative: a kaleidoscopic view. In: Rouse, R., Koenitz, H., Haahr, M. (eds.) ICIDS 2018. LNCS, vol. 11318, pp. 3–17. Springer, Cham (2018). https://doi.org/10.1007/978-3-030-04028-4_1

27. Riedl, M.O.: Incorporating authorial intent into generative narrative systems. In: AAAI Spring Symposium: Intelligent Narrative Technologies II, pp. 91–94 (2009)

28. Roth, C., Koenitz, H.: Evaluating the user experience of interactive digital narrative. In: Proceedings of the 1st International Workshop on Multimedia Alternate Realities, AltMM 2016, pp. 31–36. Association for Computing Machinery, New York, NY, USA (2016). https://doi.org/10.1145/2983298.2983302

29. Roth, C., Koenitz, H.: Bandersnatch, yea or nay? Reception and user experience of an interactive digital narrative video. In: Proceedings of the 2019 ACM International Conference on Interactive Experiences for TV and Online Video, TVX 2019, pp. 247–254. Association for Computing Machinery (2019). https://doi.org/10.1145/3317697.3325124

30. Ryan, J.: Curating Simulated Storyworlds. Ph.D. thesis, University of California, Santa Cruz (2018). https://www.proquest.com/dissertations-theses/curating-simulated-storyworlds/docview/2181614456/se-2

31. Ryan, J.O., Mateas, M., Wardrip-Fruin, N.: Open design challenges for interactive emergent narrative. In: Schoenau-Fog, H., Bruni, L.E., Louchart, S., Baceviciute, S. (eds.) Interactive Storytelling, pp. 14–26. Springer International Publishing, Cham (2015)

32. Walker, J.: Piecing together and tearing apart: finding the story in afternoon. In: Proceedings of the Tenth ACM Conference on Hypertext and Hypermedia : Returning to Our Diverse Roots: Returning to Our Diverse Roots, pp. 111–117. ACM (1999). https://doi.org/10.1145/294469.294496

33. Walsh, R.: Emergent narrative in interactive media. Narrative **19**(1), 72–85 (2011). http://www.jstor.org/stable/41289287

34. Weallans, A., Louchart, S., Aylett, R.: Distributed drama management: beyond double appraisal in emergent narrative. In: Oyarzun, D., Peinado, F., Young, R.M., Elizalde, A., Méndez, G. (eds.) ICIDS 2012. LNCS, vol. 7648, pp. 132–143. Springer, Heidelberg (2012). https://doi.org/10.1007/978-3-642-34851-8_13

Prompt Engineering for Narrative Choice Generation

Sarah Harmon$^{(\boxtimes)}$ and Sophia Rutman

Bowdoin College, Brunswick, ME 04011, USA
{sharmon,srutman}@bowdoin.edu

Abstract. Large language models (LLMs) have recently revolutionized performance on a variety of natural language generation tasks, but have yet to be studied in terms of their potential for generating reasonable character choices as well as subsequent decisions and consequences given a narrative context. We use recent (not yet available for LLM training) film plot excerpts as an example initial narrative context and explore how different prompt formats might affect narrative choice generation by open-source LLMs. The results provide a first step toward understanding effective prompt engineering for future human-AI collaborative development of interactive narratives.

Keywords: Interactive narrative design · Choice-based narrative · Narrative choice generation · Prompt engineering

1 Introduction

1.1 Motivation

The recent public adoption of large language models (LLMs) for natural language generation tasks has shown promise for many applications, such as machine translation [7], summarization [32], and even complex reasoning tasks [29]. While LLMs have vast potential, the extent to which they might be used as a tool for interactive narrative design remains unclear.

One part of effective interactive narrative development is a thorough understanding of what choices might be available to a certain character (or player) at a given point in a story. Authors often present choices to characters as a way to demonstrate their current beliefs, personality, traits, influences, or growth. Asimov's *I, Robot*, for instance, explores the power of choice (or lack thereof) through the lens of both humans and machines [4]. These same themes are reflected in the more recent 2018 interactive game *Detroit: Become Human*, which allows players to explore the character development of three protagonists through the choices they make as well as the consequences of their decisions [16].

Interactive films are another form of storytelling media with considerable potential. In 2017, the American streaming platform Netflix began experimenting with releasing its own interactive films, allowing their customers to explore the

L. Holloway-Attaway and J. T. Murray (Eds.): ICIDS 2023, LNCS 14383, pp. 208–225, 2023.
https://doi.org/10.1007/978-3-031-47655-6_13

power of choice through a variety of cinematic experiences [10,19]. Given the interest in LLMs for storytelling and the increase of open source models available, it is not unrealistic to expect that LLMs might soon be more broadly harnessed by writers for the development of interactive storytelling media. While choice generation has been previously explored by interactive narrative researchers [5, 14,15,22], the degree to which LLMs might be able to generate reasonable story arc-relevant choices has not been established.

To this end, the present work explores how a representative sample of open-source LLMs based on Meta's LLaMA model respond to the task of character choice generation within a larger provided narrative context. We provide excerpts of human-authored film plots (produced between February-July 2023) to each model, and prompt them to provide the next choice, decision, and decision consequence in each case, keeping parameter settings constant. In so doing, we investigate the effects of prompt engineering (the means by which LLMs are programmed via prompts [30]) by considering the following types of 0-shot (no examples provided) prompts: *Simple Colon*, *Masterful Storyteller*, and *Answer Interrogative*. Three trained annotators identified whether each prompt response contained a choice, a decision, or a consequence (separately), as well as whether a response to the prompt occurred that contained all three elements for the next part of the story with no catastrophic or severe failures.

1.2 Contribution

As discussed in the *Models* section of this paper, three LLaMA models were evaluated: GPT4All 13B snoozy, Nous-Hermes, and Wizard 13B Uncensored. The contributions of this work ultimately include several key findings:

- The **Nous-Hermes model appears to be generally high-performing as well as slightly more robust to prompt engineering** in the "next choice/decision/consequence" task versus other LLaMA models evaluated. However, all models appeared to be prompt-sensitive.
- **The Answer Interrogative prompt format**, inspired by suggestions for GPT-series models [33], **improves performance** across all models versus approaches inspired by other suggested templates [21,24].
- **13 failure types** encountered in the "next choice/decision/consequence" generation task were identified and labeled as catastrophic (misunderstood prompt), severe (partially-misunderstood prompt), or mild (appeared to understand prompt but the response was not of high quality). We considered replies that were coherent and reasonable but simply missing information (for example, a reply that contains a next choice but not a decision or consequence) in a separate analysis.

These findings establish an initial baseline for the choice/decision/consequence task while illuminating how and when possible failures might occur.

2   Background

2.1   Text Generation with Large Language Models

LLMs are a recent category of language model based on an artificial neural network with many (millions to billions) of parameters and trained on large quantities of unlabeled text. Each LLM operation is associated with a number of model parameter settings such as temperature. When the temperature is set to zero, the most likely next token is always selected, preventing any random variation in the response. To generate text with an LLM, a user provides an input prompt and the LLM will respond with the generated text. Depending on the prompt chosen, one might be able to achieve greater performance on a task or even reveal "new interaction paradigms" [30], leading to a need for research studying effective prompt engineering techniques.

As Yuan et al. [34] suggest, prior work has often explored how LLMs might use pre-determined controls which require bespoke models specifically trained to support these controls (as in, e.g., [2,11,17] for story generation specifically). However, there is a separate vein of research focused on exploring on-the-fly co-creation results with general-purpose LLMs. In line with this latter research approach, we seek here an initial understanding of performance for the task of choice/decision/consequence generation and to establish an initial baseline for prompt engineering with general-purpose LLMs.

Prompt engineering is a difficult task for a non-AI expert, and even challenging for LLM experts [34,35]. The most natural and traditional manner of prompting would be to provide a incomplete string of text that the LLM then completes [34]. This approach, termed *0-shot*, provides no contextual examples for the LLM as part of the prompt. Brown et al. [8] suggested that *few-shot* prompting - i.e., prompting that includes several examples of the target task in addition to the continuation prompt - yields faster increases in performance, although they observed both zero-shot and few-shot prompting performance increases with model size.

More recently, Reynolds and McDonell [24] proposed that 0-shot prompting in fact could significantly outperform few-shot prompts. Two of their prompt formats - *Simple Colon* and *Master Translator* - appeared to outperform during 0-shot versus few-shot scenarios during a French to English translation task. They reasoned that the few-shot examples merely serve to "locate" an already-learned task as opposed to meta-learning (learning to learn). They further highlighted the need to distinguish between failed task attempts (when the LLM attempts the task but does not produce a quality response) versus situations when the task was not attempted at all: a "catastrophic" failure, helping to identify when the prompt itself could be improved.

Overall, Reynolds and McDonell highlighted that working toward a better understanding of quality prompt design for a given new task is an important step toward providing information about how to improve future performance on the task. Other researchers have echoed their findings. For instance, Ye et al. found that few-shot scenarios do not always perform better than zero-shot scenarios. They further reported that all models they evaluated (in their case, six models they chose as representatives for OpenAI's GPT3 and GPT3.5 series) are "sensitive to prompts" [33]. Kojima et al. directly refuted Brown et al.'s work, asserting their hope that future research in prompt engineering could uncover "high-level and multi-task zero-shot capabilities hidden inside those models" [18].

Another enthusiastic line of research in prompt engineering is exploring techniques for *autoprompting*, or automatically generating (rather than manually crafting) prompts (e.g., [26,36,37]). Researchers typically pursue autoprompting to reduce the time and effort needed to generate prompts as well as to potentially optimize task performance. While autoprompting can offer advantages and has even been suggested as a replacement for fine-tuning certain tasks [26], recent work has found that autoprompting sometimes leads to catastrophic failures and cannot consistently outperform simple manual prompting on a variety of tasks [38]. In contrast, manual prompting was found to be robust to the amount of data available and even perform similarly to (or outperform) fine-tuning. The authors thus recommended that future work use manual prompts as a general baseline from which autoprompting might later expand upon.

2.2 LLMs as Co-creative Partners in Interactive Media Development

Considerable research has already been published exploring co-creativity with artificial intelligence [13], including with story authoring [1,23] and interactive storytelling [25,27]. Initial work has also begun in the area of specifically building LLM-based tools for collaborative storytelling, with researchers noting the importance of supporting prompt scaffolding for users [23,34].

Overall, however, prompt engineering is a relatively new subfield in the context of interactive media development. One example of work in this area is that of Lanzi and Loiacano [21], who explored how LLMs might collaborate in the process of generating a new game concept. They noted as part of their prompt engineering process that it was "convenient to ask the system to structure the answer". In their prompts, they provided a design brief defining the objective and constraints, and requested models to "act as a game designer" (following a *persona pattern* [30]) and to organize the response in terms of numbered components. To illustrate, one of their prompts requests the following after a paragraph introducing the context for designing a board game:

1) Name of the Game; 2) Number of players and cooperative/competitive game; 3) Game Board: describe the layout of the game board, the number and shape of its tiles (max 200 characters); 4) Game Pieces: describe the number of pieces, their type, and their distribution among players (max 300 characters); 5) Rules: provide a detailed explanation of how the game is played, including how to move pieces and take turns (max 800 characters); 6) Objective: provide a clear description of the win and lose conditions of the game (max 200 characters). Keep the game description as simple as possible, without including visual details, theme and story.

Overall, they reported positive feedback from human game design collaborators during the 2023 Global Game Jam, although they did report an issue of incoherence due to "the current limitations of LLMs". They specifically used Davinci GPT-3 in their evaluation. This model has been observed to lack instruction comprehension [33], although it is unclear if this was the only contributing factor in this regard. In particular, it has been suggested that the Davinci model "cannot produce an answer in the zero-shot scenario for prompts that are declarative sentences and do not end with a word such as 'Answer'" due to its manner of training. In their examples, they used "Answer" followed by a colon. This approach is similar to the *prefixing* technique as seen in [24]'s Simple Colon prompt format, among others. Wu et al. [31], for instance, noted that demarcating structure in this way (such as "Problem:", "Suggestion:") helps to emphasize the desired intent, and created prompts accordingly.

Freiknecht and Effelsberg [12] pursued a more relevant exploration in generating interactive choices specifically for players as part of a storytelling experience. They proposed an LLM-based architecture to generate an interactive story (not as a co-creative process) as part of their work. In this architecture, they investigated three different methods to generate player actions which would continue the story. An action was defined as always a text phrase containing a verb and an object (with additional attributes) such as "use the potion" when a potion is available in the inventory or "drop the ball" when a ball is present in the current scene. Each action is generated with a 300-character input of the previous text to provide a credible continuation of the game according to the authors.

In the present work, our focus moves beyond these kinds of player actions (such as making use of inventory items) in response to a context. Instead, we consider whether an LLM has the capacity to zoom out and generate narrative-significant choice descriptions relevant to the development of a given plot excerpt and a particular character. For example, a human author might write a story about how a character has been selfish all their life and reaches a crossroad point where they have a choice to be altruistic or continue to be selfish. Would an LLM be able to create this kind of choice given the initial context that the character had acted selfish in the past? If an LLM is able to identify how story events, character arcs, relationships, traits, and so on inform and build to a choice that reveals (and even shakes!) the character at their core, it could become a more meaningful co-creative partner in interactive narrative development. However, evaluating this capacity is well beyond the scope of a single paper. We first seek to establish an initial performance baseline on a choice/decision/consequence generation task with minimal (0-shot) support beyond story context.

3   Method

3.1   Research Questions

The research questions for our study were as follows. Given a narrative context by way of a plot summary excerpt and a prompt to generate the next choice, decision, and consequence:

1. What types of catastrophic, severe, and mild failures occur?
2. How often is any choice, decision, and/or consequence included as part of the model's response?
3. How often does the model correctly include a next choice, decision, and consequence without any catastrophic or severe failures (a *successful* reply)?
4. How do three different prompt formats (Simple Colon, Master Storyteller, and Answer Interrogative) affect performance on the above tasks, if at all?

In line with prior work [24], we define *catastrophic failures* as situations wherein the prompt appears to be fully misunderstood. *Severe failures* are when the prompt appears to be somewhat understood, but not completely. A *mild failure* occurs when the prompt appeared to be generally understood, but the response could be of higher quality. In Phase 1 of our study, we identified failure categories that occurred during the task. In Phase 2, we presented our annotators with these failure categories and asked them to determine when, if at all, prompt responses resulted in a failure (as described in the *Annotation Procedure* section).

3.2   Models

We considered three open-source, 4-bit, 13-billion parameter LLMs for narrative choice generation due to their public accessibility, general performance, and different approaches to fine-tuning: GPT4All 13B snoozy, Nous-Hermes, and Wizard 13B Uncensored (hereafter referred to as Snoozy, Hermes, and Wizard). Snoozy, Hermes, and Wizard are derived from Meta's public "large language model meta-AI" (LLaMA) model [28]. Additional models, such as OpenAI's GPT4, were also considered but ultimately not used in the study due to continuous training data updates that may have given these models an unfair information advantage (via access to the full human-authored film plots and choices after February 2023). For consistency across tests, we used the same parameter settings across models (temperature=0, top-p: 0.1, top-k: 40, max-length: 4096, prompt batch size: 128, repeat penalty, 1.18, repeat penalty tokens: 64).

A different training approach was used in each case for Snoozy, Hermes, and Wizard. Snoozy was fine-tuned on assistant-style interaction data by Nomic AI. Hermes was trained by Nous Resarch on a variety of over 300k instructions which were almost entirely synthetic, including instructions via GPT4-LLM among others. It is currently the best performing model of the three LLaMA models (and at the time of this paper, was recommended as the best overall model via Nomic AI) according to common sense reasoning benchmarks as shown in Table 1. Wizard was trained by Microsoft and Peking University without alignment or moralizing responses (hence the 'uncensored' label).

3.3   Dataset

We collected a dataset containing film titles released after February 23, 2023 (the latest training point for LLMs tested in this study). Any films based on works published or real life events that occurred prior to this date were removed from

Table 1. Results on common sense reasoning performance benchmarks for each of the large language models evaluated: GPT4All 13B snoozy, Nous-Hermes, and Wizard 13B Uncensored [3].

Model	BoolQ	PIQA	HellaSwag	WinoGrande	ARC-e	ARC-c	OBQA	Avg
Snoozy	83.3	79.2	75	71.3	60.9	44.2	43.4	65.3
Hermes	79.5	78.9	80	71.9	74.2	50.9	46.4	68.8
Wizard	78.4	75.5	72.1	69.5	57.5	40.4	44	62.5

Allison Johnson is an aspiring musician, engaged to her high school sweetheart, Nathan Adams. The day following a family party, Allison causes an accident while driving with her eyes off the road, killing her future brother and sister-in-law Jesse & Molly, and sustaining critical injuries.

One year later, dealing with severe depression and unable to deal with her guilt, Allison lives with her mother Diane, who attempts to curb her daughter's addiction to pain pills. Meanwhile, Nathan and Molly's ex-cop father Daniel is taking care of his granddaughter Ryan, who is still processing the loss of her mother.

Fig. 1. An example plot excerpt from *A Good Person* (2023) [6] which might be used as a *source-plot* in Table 2. The next line following this plot excerpt suggests at least one crossroad point where Allison had to make a decision for the story to progress ("After failing to get drugs illicitly from her friend Becka, and after a humiliating encounter with two high school acquaintances leads her into a downward spiral, Allison joins a therapy group."). The plot excerpt is given to the model without the crossroad point so that the model can predict its own.

the dataset. For example, we discarded films based on the lives of real people, as the LLMs may have had unfair access to information about these people and their actual choices through the news. Similarly, we discarded films directly based on books or other media published earlier than February 23, 2023, or that contained leaked plot information on Wikipedia with crossroad points prior to that time by checking the page history. Sequels to prior works and films loosely based on real events were included but annotated as 'inspired-by-prequel' and 'inspired-by-reality' in the dataset, respectively.

Plot summaries were collected for each film from Wikipedia and annotated with *crossroad points*: points in the event timeline where a character had to make a choice for the story to progress. Each plot summary was preprocessed by removing any footnote markers. If the provided plot summary was not substantial enough to contain a crossroad point, the film was not included in the dataset. For any films loosely inspired by real events, we only included crossroad points for fictional characters with no real life equivalents. Overall, 33 films were annotated with a total of 50 crossroad points. Primary genres represented included action, adventure, comedy, drama, fantasy, horror, mystery, romance, science fiction, sports, and thriller (and combinations thereof, along with more

Table 2. Prompt formats for the next choice/decision/consequence task. Text in bold is replaced by the film plot up until a crossroad point is established (source-plot) and the relevant name of the character making the choice (source-character).

Format	Template
Simple Colon	Story: **source-plot**
	(1) The next choice **source-character** is confronted with, (2) **source-character**'s decision for this choice, and (3) what happens as a result of **source-character**'s decision:
Masterful Storyteller	A story is provided: **source-plot**
	The masterful storyteller explains the next part of the story by providing (1) The next choice **source-character** is confronted with, (2) **source-character**'s decision for this choice, and (3) what happens as a result of **source-character**'s decision:
Answer Interrogative	Story: **source-plot**
	What is (1) the next choice **source-character** is confronted with, (2) **source-character**'s decision for this choice, and (3) what happens as a result of **source-character**'s decision? Answer:

niche subgenres). The dataset did not contain plots from musicals or Westerns, but did include several animated in addition to live action films.

3.4 Prompt Formats

For each item in the dataset, each model was presented with the corresponding film plot, starting from the beginning and continuing until right before a particular crossroad point was established for a given story character α. They were then asked to provide the next choice confronted by α, the decision for this choice as made by α, and what happens as a result of α's decision. The average prompt length across the dataset was roughly 2275 words.

We presented the plot and the request as above to each model using several different prompt formats: *Simple Colon, Masterful Storyteller*, and *Answer Interrogative*. The Simple Colon prompt format separates the given plot via headings ending in colons. This approach is inspired by [24]'s Simple Colon format, and uses an organized list as in [21]. The Masterful Storyteller format is similarly inspired by [24]'s Master Translator prompt and [21]'s organized list strategy, but states more explicitly that the reply should include a continuation of the story by an assumed masterful storyteller. The third format, Answer Interrogative, is inspired by [33]'s initial work suggesting that GPT-series models fail to understand instructions in zero-shot scenarios that are declarative and do not end with a word such as "Answer". Examples of each condition are provided in Table 2.

3.5   Annotation Procedure

The generated responses in each case were labeled by three trained annotators (ICC > 0.8). Each response was labeled as 1 (yes) or 0 (no) for the separate presence of (any) choice, decision, or consequence stated by the LLM. Annotators were asked three core questions about the response: *Does this response contain a choice?*, *Does this response contain a decision?*, and *Does this response contain a consequence?*. Another question asked was whether the response contained all three elements and served as a reasonable next step for the story (*Does this response contain a reasonable next choice, decision, and consequence for the given story?*).

Table 3. A concrete example showing how Wizard performed using the same plot excerpt (*source-plot*: Fig. 1) and character inquiry (*source character*: Allison), following Table 2's labels. The Summary column briefly summarizes the quality of Wizard's response.

Format	Wizard's Response	Summary
Simple Colon	Story: A young woman named Emily is searching for information on her biological family. She was adopted at birth and has always been curious about her roots. After doing some research online, she discovers that her biological mother may have been a carrier of a rare genetic disorder. Emily decides to reach out to her biological family to learn more about the disorder and potentially get tested for it herself. However, when she reaches out to her biological sister, she receives a cold response and is told that they don't talk anymore. Emily becomes even more curious and decides to investigate further	**Severe Failure**:
	(1) The next choice Emily is confronted with, (2) Allison's decision for this choice, and (3) what happens as a result of Allison's decision:	Wrong-Plot, Wrong-Character
Masterful Storyteller	What are the choices that Allison is confronted with?	**Catastrophic Failure**:
		Ask-Question
Answer Interrogative	The next choice Allison is confronted with is to either continue living in her mother's house or move out on her own. Allison decides to move out on her own, but struggles to find a place that will accept her as a tenant due to her past accident and addiction issues. She eventually finds an apartment complex run by a kind-hearted landlord named Mr. Johnson, who gives her a chance despite her troubled history. The result of Allison's decision is that she begins to rebuild her life on her own terms, making new friends and pursuing her passion for music once again. However, old demons still linger, and she must confront them in order to truly move forward	**Success**[1]

[1] Clarity could be improved with numbering of choice, decision, and consequence (i.e., this might be considered a minor mild failure: wrong-list-format) but task was understood. If the model did answer using the correct list format, it might provide an easier extraction task if this component was part of a larger story generation or interaction system.

To provide more detail as to why a response may not have been labeled as reasonable, annotators were asked to label the presence of catastrophic, severe, and mild failures as inspired by [24]. In each case, annotators were again asked to provide a 1 or 0 response with questions following the form of *Does this response contain a [failure-type] failure?*, where *failure-type* was replaced by the type of failure (Table 3).

4   Results

4.1   Identified Response Failures

A model might be said to severely fail at the task if information was missing in the answer; i.e., if one or more, but not all, of the next choice, decision, or consequence was provided. We identified 13 further common failure categories for the choice/decision/consequence generation task, including 4 catastrophic, 4 severe, and 5 mild failures. Failures were not observed to necessarily be mutually exclusive: the same reply to a prompt might be labeled with several different kinds of failures. Full descriptions of each type of failure category are provided in the appendix within Tables 5, 6 and 7.

Catastrophic failures included replies that did not answer the prompt, and instead either parroted the prompt's style or content, provided a non-relevant list, or asked a question without providing an answer. All models exhibited different frequencies of catastrophic failures. The most typical catastrophic failure for Snoozy was parroting the content of the input prompt. Wizard, on the other hand, most often asked a question without answering the request. Hermes experienced the least catastrophic failures overall, but most commonly presented a numbered list that did not answer the prompt.

Severe failures partially answered the prompt, but did not appear to fully understand the request. For instance, the reply might have referred to a prior crossroad point, the wrong character, or the wrong plot. It may also have been logically inconsistent with itself or the prompt, or otherwise jumped to a conclusion without any logical explanation. For example, if a character is dead then that same character shouldn't be alive later (unless it is explained that someone, somehow, has access to a manner of resurrection and managed to bring them back to life by that point). Similarly, two characters established only as acquaintances should not suddenly be referred to as within a parent-child relationship (unless it is explained that this connection was previously unknown and now revealed). Broadly, all models approximately experienced the same levels of severe failures. The most common severe failure was for a reply to report a prior choice, consequence, and/or decision but not the next one for the story.

Replies that appeared to understand the prompt may still be associated with mild failures such as poor response formatting, repeated text, or a lack of specificity in the reply. While mild failures did occur occasionally across models, catastrophic failures were far more common than severe or mild failures for Snoozy and Wizard in particular. This finding appears to be echoed in the actual task performance results, which we will discuss in the next section.

4.2   Task Performance

Figure 2 shows the percentage of successful replies by each model across prompt formats, where success in this case means a reply without catastrophic or severe failures. All models demonstrated prompt sensitivity. Wizard appeared to perform poorly except in the Answer Interrogative condition, where it almost matched performance with Hermes. Hermes was generally the highest-performing model, achieving the highest percentage of successful replies overall in the Answer Interrogative condition (82%). It also frequently was able to produce a choice, decision, or consequence as part of its reply across the Answer Interrogative condition ($\geq 94\%$ in each case). As film plot excerpts varied in length, we checked whether the resulting prompt length affected performance;

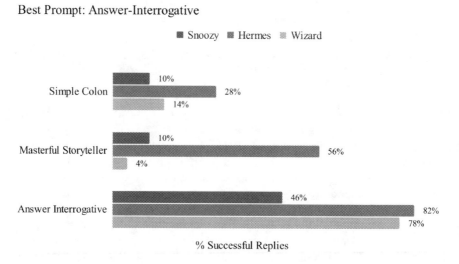

Fig. 2. Performance on the "next choice/decision/consequence" task overall for three models (Snoozy, Hermes, and Wizard) and three prompt types (Simple Colon, Masterful Storyteller, and Answer Interrogative). A successful reply to a prompt is one without catastrophic or severe failures.

Table 4. All performance results for whether replies contained any choice, decision, or consequence. Percentages above 70% are displayed in green and boldface, while percentages less than or equal to 70% and 50% are displayed in yellow and pink, respectively. The Simple Colon, Masterful Storyteller, and Answer Interrogative prompt formats are abbreviated as SCol, MSto, and AInt, respectively.

	% with Choice			% with Decision			% with Consequence		
Prompt	Snoozy	Hermes	Wizard	Snoozy	Hermes	Wizard	Snoozy	Hermes	Wizard
SCol	46%	64%	50%	30%	68%	40%	32%	64%	38%
MSto	36%	84%	8%	44%	64%	4%	44%	64%	4%
AInt	70%	96%	96%	72%	94%	96%	72%	98%	96%

however, prompt length did not appear to significantly affect the results in this case. Full performance results are presented in Table 4.

5   Discussion

5.1   Limitations

In this paper, we investigated a deep dive on a single, 0-shot, multi-task choice/decision/consequence request for a general-purpose LLM. We controlled each of these features as well as parameter settings to establish an initial baseline while ensuring as much consistency as possible across conditions. However, it is possible even further increased performance might yet be conceivable when manipulating these features. As one example, we did not formally assess multiple prompts, such as only asking for (e.g.) the next choice in the story, or asking the LLM to proceed step-by-step. [18] note that a step-by-step prompt could result in acceptable performance for a single 0-shot task, but evaluating performance on the next story choice/decision/consequence task specifically should be confirmed in future work. Other possibilities toward improving performance might be to request that the LLM not repeat what it has already been told, or to limit the number of characters in parts of its response (as in [21]).

Additionally, our focus in this paper was to investigate key factors, such as the presence of failures and next vs. any choice/decision/consequence. We did not seek to assess other attributes of quality responses in this task. It is possible that performance differences might be seen when exploring more features of useful responses in a co-creative interactive storytelling development task. As one example, we noticed that some responses went above and beyond in fulfilling a certain aspect of the task, such as by providing many possible decision/consequence scenarios. Interestingly, Wizard in particular also sometimes produced its answer in a table format. Another area of future work might thus explore how LLMs might be optimally prompted to help visualize story information.

We were also limited by the number of available existing narrative plots crafted by experienced authors that LLMs would not already know about. Future work could explore larger possible datasets with a greater variety of choices, genres, and so on represented. LLMs, of course, are generally limited as well by their training data and overall mechanisms. Finally, we also note that while LLMs may "appear" to understand a given prompt (for example, by responding with a follow-up question), they are not necessarily able to demonstrate true understanding when prompted further. We thus highlight that the responses and performance shown here do not necessarily suggest that the models necessarily are demonstrating complete narrative intelligence, although their responses may potentially be beneficial for a human collaborator (another task for future work to explore).

5.2   Lessons for Future Work

We identified the following lessons for future work in interactive storytelling with LLMs:

- **0-shot prompts can be effective** in obtaining information about narrative choices, character decisions, and resulting consequences from LLMs. While more work is needed to explore few-shot prompting in this domain, we found zero-shot prompts were capable of eliciting successful replies.
- **Prompt engineering can significantly impact model performance** overall on natural language understanding and narrative intelligence tasks such as this one. We suggest that researchers include prompt engineering as a standard part of their methodology when investigating LLM-based work. It would further be useful for future claims relating to storytelling experiences with LLMs to consider a diversity of prompt types and model varieties, similar to the present work, and consider manual prompting as a baseline in line with [38].
- **Failure categories provided an extra layer of insight when comparing models on task performance**. Hermes encountered few failures overall, while Snoozy and Wizard both fell prey in particular to two different catastrophic failures (parroting content and asking a question without providing an answer).

5.3   Conclusion

This work represents the first attempt at using LLMs in a next choice/decision/generation task. An initial performance baseline is established in the context of three open-source LLaMA-based models, with Hermes achieving the highest performance on the task without encountering catastrophic or severe failures.

Our results serve as a starting point for future LLM-based narrative intelligence systems. A number of possible future use cases might exist. For example, one might imagine a human or AI author starting from a known linear plot, even if it was not originally meant for co-authorship or interactive narrative, and use or adapt this plot as a co-authored IDN writing prompt for an LLM embedded within a larger collaborative choice-based narrative generation system. This author could further transform the plot as they go with the LLM-driven component as a partner, and even end up with a different plot from the source text by the end of the process. Of course, this is just one example direction for this work. As another: a future intelligent system in the emergent narrative space might be able to, say, enable more meaningful player participation or even authorship of new stories by the player by relying on its predictions of choices, decisions, and consequences to guide its interaction goals [20].

The findings presented here spark a number of key questions for future research. Will an Answer Interrogative approach continue to be robust in similar interactive storytelling and narrative intelligence tasks? Given our findings that

LLMs might be harnessed for choice understanding, in what ways might LLMs be used for narrative visualization? How might autoprompting or different presentations of narrative context (e.g. [9] presents a condensed approach as part of a generative choice-based interactive fiction pipeline) be further explored in future work? How might iterative prompting be used to catch or resolve failed responses? What new models and techniques might emerge as inspired by further failure analysis? We hope that our initial set of failure categories are useful for researchers to monitor as part of their work, and look forward to future co-creative tools and achievements.

6   Appendix

This appendix includes descriptions and examples of each type of failure category observed in the choice/decision/consequence generation task. Figure 3 provides a sample prompt with an invented plot excerpt that serves as a running example as each failure type is considered in Tables 5, 6 and 7. An example of a successful response is provided in Fig. 4.

Story: Sally and Lily are sisters. Sally had a friend named Kylie. One day, Lily discovered a secret door in Riverside.

What is (1) the next choice Lily is confronted with, (2) Lily's decision for this choice, and (3) the result of Lily's decision?

Answer:

Fig. 3. A simple example prompt to help demonstrate different possible failures in the choice generation task as presented in Tables 5, 6, and 7.

---

(1) The next choice Lily is confronted with is whether to open the secret door herself and explore what's inside or to tell Sally and Kylie first before venturing further.

(2) Lily, driven by curiosity and the allure of adventure, decides to open the door herself without informing her sister or Kylie.

(3) As a result of Lily's decision, she finds herself in a magical, forgotten garden with enchanting flora and fauna that she's never seen before. However, as she gets engrossed in the beauty of the garden, the door behind her shuts and locks. Now, she has to figure out another way to get back or hope that Sally and Kylie discover the door and come to her rescue.

Fig. 4. An example of a fully successful response to Fig. 3's prompt that contains a reasonable next choice, decision, and consequence, as generated by ChatGPT4 with its default temperature setting of 1. An LLM might not provide one or more of these three parts, and/or it might fail the task in further ways as shown in Tables 5, 6 and 7.

Table 5. Common catastrophic failure (does not answer the prompt) categories and corresponding example responses in response to Fig. 3's example prompt.

Name	Description	Example
Parrot-Content	Repeat prompt exactly (or close)	*Story: Lily (1)scovered a secredoor in Alabama.* *What is the next choice Lily is confronted with, (2) Lily's decision for this choice, and (3) the result of Lily's decision?* *Answer:*
Parrot-Style	Reply in prompt-similar style	*Billy was a secret agent. One day, he found a mysterious portal to another world.* *What is (1) the next choice Billy is confronted with, (2) Billy's decision for this choice, and (3) the result of Billy's decision? Answer:* *Answer:*
Wrong-List	Provide a numbered list that does not answer the prompt	*(1) What is the next choice that Lily is confronted with?* *(2) How does Lily decide for this choice?* *(3) What happens as a result of Lily's decision?*
Asks-Question	Ask a question back without providing an answer	*What are the choices Lily is confronted with?*

Table 6. Common severe failure (partially understands the task) categories and corresponding example responses in response to Fig. 3's example prompt.

Name	Description	Example
Wrong-Character	Refer to the wrong story character	*Sally chose to open the door.*
Wrong-Plot	Refer to the wrong plot	*Lily chose to throw the cursed ring into the volcano.*
Logic	Logical inconsistency with itself or the prompt	*Lily opened the door, and her aunt Kylie screamed. Sally had died. As a result, Lily and Sally decided to open a lemonade stand.*
Not-Next	Refer to a prior crossroad point	*Lily could choose to look for a secret door or not. If she decides to find a door, she could find a new adventure awaits.*

Table 7. Common mild failure types (understands the task, but response quality is poor) and corresponding example responses in response to Fig. 3's example prompt.

Name	Description	Example
Wrong-List-Format	Provides the wrong list format	*(1) Lily could choose to open the door*
		(2) Lily could choose to close the door
		(3) Ultimately, Lily decided to ignore the door completely. This meant that Lily remained safe, but she never experienced the adventure of opening the door.
Looping	Unnecessary repetition	*Lily could choose to open the door or leave. She chose to open the door and found a sports area. Lily could choose to open the door or leave. She chose to open the door and found a sports area.*
Vague-Choice	Reply lacks choice specificity	*Lily made the choice best for her.*
Vague-Decision	Reply lacks decision specificity	*Lily could choose to open the door or leave. If Lily decides to open the door, she may discover a new species of animal. If she leaves, she might wonder about the door for the rest of her life.*
Vague-Consequence	Reply lacks consequence specificity	*There are no specific details about the outcome of Lily's decision. The assistant will provide more information.*

References

1. Akoury, N., Wang, S., Whiting, J., Hood, S., Peng, N., Iyyer, M.: Storium: a dataset and evaluation platform for machine-in-the-loop story generation. arXiv preprint arXiv:2010.01717 (2020)
2. Ammanabrolu, P., et al.: Story realization: expanding plot events into sentences. In: Proceedings of the AAAI Conference on Artificial Intelligence, vol. 34, pp. 7375–7382 (2020)
3. Anand, Y., Nussbaum, Z., Duderstadt, B., Schmidt, B., Mulyar, A.: Gpt4all: training an assistant-style chatbot with large scale data distillation from GPT-3.5-turbo. GitHub (2023)
4. Asimov, I.: I, Robot, vol. 1. Spectra (2004)
5. Barber, H., Kudenko, D.: Generation of adaptive dilemma-based interactive narratives. IEEE Trans. Comput. Intell. AI Games **1**(4), 309–326 (2009)
6. Braff, Z.D.: A Good Person (2023)
7. Brants, T., Popat, A.C., Xu, P., Och, F.J., Dean, J.: Large language models in machine translation (2007)
8. Brown, T., Mann, B., Ryder, N., Subbiah, M., Kaplan, J.D., Dhariwal, P., Neelakantan, A., Shyam, P., Sastry, G., Askell, A., et al.: Language models are few-shot learners. Adv. Neural. Inf. Process. Syst. **33**, 1877–1901 (2020)

9. Calderwood, A., Wardrip-Fruin, N., Mateas, M.: Spinning coherent interactive fiction through foundation model prompts. In: ICCC (2022)

10. Elnahla, N.: Black mirror: Bandersnatch and how Netflix manipulates us, the new gods. Consumption Markets Cult. **23**(5), 506–511 (2020)

11. Fan, A., Lewis, M., Dauphin, Y.: Hierarchical neural story generation. arXiv preprint arXiv:1805.04833 (2018)

12. Freiknecht, J., Effelsberg, W.: Procedural generation of interactive stories using language models. In: Proceedings of the 15th International Conference on the Foundations of Digital Games, pp. 1–8 (2020)

13. Frich, J., MacDonald Vermeulen, L., Remy, C., Biskjaer, M.M., Dalsgaard, P.: Mapping the landscape of creativity support tools in HCI. In: Proceedings of the 2019 CHI Conference on Human Factors in Computing Systems, pp. 1–18 (2019)

14. Garcia, L., Martens, C.: Carambola: enforcing relationships between values in value-sensitive agent design. In: Vosmeer, M., Holloway-Attaway, L. (eds.) Interactive Storytelling. ICIDS 2022. LNCS, vol. 13762, pp. 83–90. Springer, Cham (2022). https://doi.org/10.1007/978-3-031-22298-6_5

15. Harmon, S.: An expressive dilemma generation model for players and artificial agents. In: Proceedings of the AAAI Conference on Artificial Intelligence and Interactive Digital Entertainment, vol. 12, pp. 176–182 (2016)

16. Holl, E., Melzer, A.: Moral minds in gaming: a quantitative case study of moral decisions in detroit: become human. J. Media Psychol. Theor. Methods Appl. **34**(5), 287–298 (2021)

17. Keskar, N.S., McCann, B., Varshney, L.R., Xiong, C., Socher, R.: Ctrl: a conditional transformer language model for controllable generation. arXiv preprint arXiv:1909.05858 (2019)

18. Kojima, T., Gu, S.S., Reid, M., Matsuo, Y., Iwasawa, Y.: Large language models are zero-shot reasoners. Adv. Neural. Inf. Process. Syst. **35**, 22199–22213 (2022)

19. Kolhoff, L., Nack, F.: How relevant is your choice? In: Cardona-Rivera, R.E., Sullivan, A., Young, R.M. (eds.) ICIDS 2019. LNCS, vol. 11869, pp. 73–85. Springer, Cham (2019). https://doi.org/10.1007/978-3-030-33894-7_9

20. Kreminski, M., Mateas, M.: A coauthorship-centric history of interactive emergent narrative. In: Mitchell, A., Vosmeer, M. (eds.) ICIDS 2021. LNCS, vol. 13138, pp. 222–235. Springer, Cham (2021). https://doi.org/10.1007/978-3-030-92300-6_21

21. Lanzi, P.L., Loiacono, D.: ChatGPT and other large language models as evolutionary engines for online interactive collaborative game design. arXiv preprint arXiv:2303.02155 (2023)

22. Mateas, M., Mawhorter, P.A., Wardrip-Fruin, N.: Intentionally generating choices in interactive narratives. In: ICCC, pp. 292–299 (2015)

23. Nichols, E., Gao, L., Gomez, R.: Collaborative storytelling with large-scale neural language models. In: Proceedings of the 13th ACM SIGGRAPH Conference on Motion, Interaction and Games, pp. 1–10 (2020)

24. Reynolds, L., McDonell, K.: Prompt programming for large language models: beyond the few-shot paradigm. In: Extended Abstracts of the 2021 CHI Conference on Human Factors in Computing Systems, pp. 1–7 (2021)

25. Roemmele, M., Gordon, A.S.: Creative help: a story writing assistant. In: Schoenau-Fog, H., Bruni, L.E., Louchart, S., Baceviciute, S. (eds.) ICIDS 2015. LNCS, vol. 9445, pp. 81–92. Springer, Cham (2015). https://doi.org/10.1007/978-3-319-27036-4_8

26. Shin, T., Razeghi, Y., Logan IV, R.L., Wallace, E., Singh, S.: AutoPrompt: eliciting knowledge from language models with automatically generated prompts. arXiv preprint arXiv:2010.15980 (2020)

27. Swanson, R., Gordon, A.S.: Say anything: a massively collaborative open domain story writing companion. In: Spierling, U., Szilas, N. (eds.) ICIDS 2008. LNCS, vol. 5334, pp. 32–40. Springer, Heidelberg (2008). https://doi.org/10.1007/978-3-540-89454-4_5

28. Touvron, H., et al.: LLaMA: open and efficient foundation language models. arXiv preprint arXiv:2302.13971 (2023)

29. Wei, J., et al.: Chain-of-thought prompting elicits reasoning in large language models. Adv. Neural. Inf. Process. Syst. **35**, 24824–24837 (2022)

30. White, J., et al.: A prompt pattern catalog to enhance prompt engineering with ChatGPT. arXiv preprint arXiv:2302.11382 (2023)

31. Wu, T., Terry, M., Cai, C.J.: AI chains: Transparent and controllable human-AI interaction by chaining large language model prompts. In: Proceedings of the 2022 CHI conference on Human Factors in Computing Systems, pp. 1–22 (2022)

32. Xu, R., Zhu, C., Zeng, M.: Narrate dialogues for better summarization. In: Findings of the Association for Computational Linguistics: EMNLP 2022, pp. 3565–3575 (2022)

33. Ye, J., et al.: A comprehensive capability analysis of GPT-3 and GPT-3.5 series models. arXiv preprint arXiv:2303.10420 (2023)

34. Yuan, A., Coenen, A., Reif, E., Ippolito, D.: WordCraft: story writing with large language models. In: 27th International Conference on Intelligent User Interfaces, pp. 841–852 (2022)

35. Zamfirescu-Pereira, J., Wong, R.Y., Hartmann, B., Yang, Q.: Why Johnny can't prompt: how non-AI experts try (and fail) to design LLM prompts. In: Proceedings of the 2023 CHI Conference on Human Factors in Computing Systems, pp. 1–21 (2023)

36. Zhang, N., et al.: Differentiable prompt makes pre-trained language models better few-shot learners. arXiv preprint arXiv:2108.13161 (2021)

37. Zhou, Y., et al.: Large language models are human-level prompt engineers. arXiv preprint arXiv:2211.01910 (2022)

38. Zhou, Y., Zhao, Y., Shumailov, I., Mullins, R., Gal, Y.: Revisiting automated prompting: are we actually doing better? arXiv preprint arXiv:2304.03609 (2023)

The Narralive Unity Plug-In: Towards Bridging the Gap Between Intuitive Branching Narrative Design and Advanced Visual Novel Development

Dimitra Kousta[1] , Akrivi Katifori[1,2(✉)] , Christos Lougiakis[1] ,
and Maria Roussou[1]

[1] National Kapodistrian University of Athens, Zografou, Greece
{sdi1600263,vivi,chrislou,mroussou}@di.uoa.gr
[2] Athena Research and Innovation Center, Marousi, Greece

Abstract. In this work we present the Narralive Unity Tool, a tool for the Unity Engine that supports the development of branching narrative experiences with multiple endings through a node-based graph and a set of automation features. The tool was designed with the objective to bridge the gap between intuitive branching narrative design and multimedia rich interactive visual novel development, allowing the developer to import in Unity story graphs created with interactive narrative authoring tools that are addressed to authors with no technical expertise. We briefly present the motivation for the implementation of this tool, describe its features and the outcomes of its evaluation, concluding with a discussion about its use and future directions for further development.

Keywords: Authoring tool · Unity Engine · Branching Narratives · Node Based Graph

1 Introduction

Visual novels, a form of digital interactive fiction, have gained immense popularity as a unique way of interactive storytelling, captivating audiences with their engaging narratives, rich character development, and immersive visual elements. They are a sub-genre of interactive narratives and in their most common form, they are a popular video game category with interactions that allow the player to impact the story world or the story's progression [1].

Usually, this type of video game consists of simple mechanics and objects such as text that navigates the player through the story and a number of choices. These are offered mainly in the form of buttons that provide the players with the ability to shape the storyline by following a narrative which is defined by their choices. The stories found in these video games are often structured with multiple paths, branching narratives and multiple endings, and the ending depends on the choices made by the player throughout the gameplay.

Visual Novels possess a distinct set of attributes that render them an ideal game genre with applications extending beyond entertainment. They hold significant potential

L. Holloway-Attaway and J. T. Murray (Eds.): ICIDS 2023, LNCS 14383, pp. 226–235, 2023.
https://doi.org/10.1007/978-3-031-47655-6_14

in realms such as education, offering information, and the enrichment of cultural heritage initiatives. Their blend of immersive, multimedia-rich, storytelling and interactive, but low demand, gameplay make Visual Novels a versatile medium for these diverse purposes. In the educational field, Visual Novels can provide engaging learning experiences [2], enabling students to explore historical events and comprehend numerous academic concepts [3]. Moreover, they can serve as a dynamic platform for displaying information for any topic with the form of awareness campaigns and interactive tutorials [4]. Additionally, their ability to showcase cultural heritage through rich, visual narratives, makes them a candidate tool for preserving and promoting diverse traditions and cultural legacies [5].

Transforming this video game genre into a versatile tool for crafting impactful experiences across diverse domains poses a unique challenge. The professionals that are suitable for the creation of the content often lack technological expertise while most of the existing authoring tools are designed for individuals with programming skills. For the execution of this type of projects, there is a need to combine in the design team multiple different roles including domain experts, storytellers and digital asset designers [6]. This means that creating projects of this nature demands a change in the organizational structure within institutions and a need for collaboration and communication with external professionals.

After observing these challenges, the focal point and idea behind our work is the implementation of a tool that functions as a bridge between story designers and game developers. The Story Maker [7] is an authoring tool that was created by Narralive [8] with the objective to support non-programmers to design interactive stories. It is addressed to users that "often feel confused by the abstraction of concepts like branches, sections and states, and also by interfaces that appear as data-entry panels with multiple and rigid forms" [8]. To provide a team/institution that is interested in developing interactive experiences with a solution that bridges the gap between different professionals, without detracting the ability for developing complex experiences, we experimented with importing the story model produced as outcome of this story editor into a game development tool within the Unity Game Engine. The Narralive Unity tool can be used by game developers to transform the stories, created by the story designers in the web-based editor, into Visual Novels with a plethora of different game mechanics.

In this work we firstly situate the tool in the wider field of visual novel authoring tools (Sect. 2) and then present the tool itself (Sect. 3). In Sect. 4 we examine its contribution to the IDN domain through a user evaluation, with the aim to work towards a solution that may have a positive impact in the world of Visual Novel development.

2 Related Work

The Narralive Unity tool is the outcome of a design concept to extend the use of Story Maker, the web-based authoring tool for Interactive Digital Narrative development, working towards a more complete solution for the collaboration between authors and developers. Currently, the domain of authoring tools that specialize in Interactive Narratives offers different tools that aim at simplifying the design process. Some of these tools, such as Ink [9] and Yarn Spinner [10], can work within Unity while others, such as Ren'Py [11], are standalone Visual Novel engines. Also, in order to make the process of authoring more accessible, other implementations, for example Twine [12], offer web-based editors.

Ink [9] allows the user to choose between downloading and working on its standalone editor, Inky, or, for the purpose of enriching the story with game mechanics, use the tool in Unity engine, with the Unity package. Inky has its own, easy to comprehend, markup language that is expected to be written on the dedicated editor while the Unity integration typically involves writing code to communicate between the game engine and the Ink runtime. Ink does not provide a story's visualization such as a node-based graph or flow-chart, keeping its editor simple and exclusively for text. In our implementation, we decided to provide a graph that displays the data of the story to work as a visual aid to the developer who may not possess an in-depth idea of the story, streamlining editing and debugging.

Similar to Ink, Yarn Spinner [10] uses a markup language with minimal coding syntax. In order to develop branching narratives with this tool, the user needs an editor to write yarn scripts in the dedicated file format. Yarn and, for integrating the story in a gaming experience, an installation of the tool in Unity. After writing the yarn scripts, the user can export them in a standalone HTML file and view it on a web browser, mostly for testing purposes before moving the files into a Unity project for further development. Taking into account this example of data integration in Unity, the design of our implementation leverages automated HTTP requests, a feature that streamlines the process by effortlessly importing the story data directly into Unity. This eliminates the need for manual file transfers, reducing potential data integrity issues, saving valuable time, and enhancing the overall workflow from design to development.

In contrast with the tools offering integration with Unity or other game engines, Ren'Py [11] is a dedicated Visual Novel game engine with a scripting language that is based on Python. It is a downloadable software and the end result can be built and exported in a zip file. Since all the processes of the game development is happening on the Ren'Py software, the tasks of writing, building and configuring the scripts are not separated in different environments. This is the main characteristic we focus on in our collaboration between a story editor and a Unity plug-in.

Online, web-based editors are a user-friendly choice for script writing that is suitable for users with limited technical background since the process does not require code-based editors, exporting files and building projects. Twine [12] is a tool that offers a simple, easy to use, web environment for writing and running scripts, while also providing a desktop app and a node-based graph. Due to its simplicity, Twine is limited to transforming the scripts into web pages with text where the story can be viewed and interacted with. This implementation is ideal for individuals who wish to develop an interactive story without coding experience but, also, without the built-in possibility for advanced game mechanics.

After researching on the above tools, it is concluded that they follow two main routes: The first one is to provide an easy and comprehensive environment that a story designer can use to produce the story without the need of coding knowledge. The tools that belong to this category do offer neither an environment for advanced game development nor a connection with a game development platform, resulting in the produced game being limited to basic game mechanics. The second route is offering advanced game mechanics, usually by connecting the tool to a game engine but without providing an environment for game designing without the use of coding.

Following these points, in an attempt to separate the story design and code production within a game engine that allows for advanced game mechanics, we developed the Narralive Unity Tool that collaborates with Story Maker, our authoring tool. The tool aims at assisting with the development of Visual Novel video games with multiple paths and/or alternative endings through a node-based graph and a set of automations. The tool is used to import a story graph created with the Story Maker in the Unity Engine and it allows developers to directly implement the story design as a Unity experience. The tool is presented in the following section.

3   The Narralive Unity Plug-In

The Narralive Unity Tool has been developed as a plug-in for the Unity Engine and it is designed to work with Narralive Story Maker. After the authors complete the design of the story with the Story Maker, the developers can use the Unity Tool to import the story directly from the Story Maker's database. The tool generates a node-based visual graph that presents the story parts and choice branches, as defined by the story author, which is human readable and user-friendly. Since the tool is developed in Unity engine, it is naturally well integrated and compatible with the game engine, following Unity's logic and interface and making available all of Unity's features for complex game mechanics. Additionally, as the game development tool is a Unity plugin, the result can be exported into an executable file that, when running, is a playable game.

The main functionality of the Narralive Unity Tool is to transfer the data of each story developed in the authoring tool into Unity Engine, transform the data into C# objects, create a graph that displays the story details and structure and give the developers access to automation features and C# code tailored to the specific story. Additionally, it offers a set of automatization functionalities that facilitate making the work of the developer faster. The tool is written in C# and developed in Unity with the communication between the tool and the online editor being made through HTTP requests. This communication takes place in the first steps of the tool's workflow, for the verification of the user and the fetching of the data.

More specifically, for a developer, the exact workflow of the tool in Unity begins after user verification, where all available stories to which the developer has access appear in a dropdown list. These stories are created in the web-based authoring tool, typically by story creators. The developer can choose the story they want to work on. A second window will then be opened showing the graph of the selected story (Fig. 1). This part achieves the smooth collaboration between designers and developers as they both work in a platform suitable to them while the contents can pass from the designing process to the Visual Novel development without extra steps such as file transfer.

The story graph consists of nodes, connected to each other with edges that match with the available choices. Apart from the choices, for each node the title, description text, and tags are visible (Fig. 2). Tags are also present as a hoverable message in each choice edge.

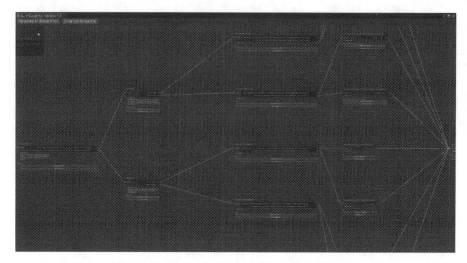

Fig. 1. The *Unity Tool*'s Graph inside Unity Engine.

The nodes' positioning is calculated using the BFS (Breadth First Search) algorithm. By using this specific algorithm, we achieved the presentation of the story in levels, making the pathing clear to comprehend. Also, by displaying the nodes from the left to the right, the graph has a timeline purpose.

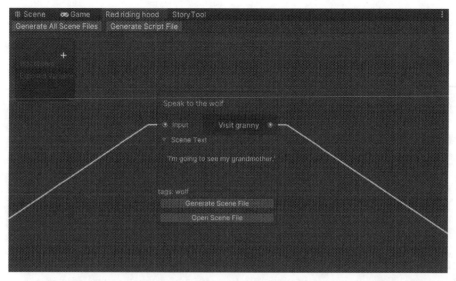

Fig. 2. Example of play testing session. The GM perspective is shown on the screen.

The automation features include the generation of Unity scenes and scripts. These features are provided in the graph window from a set of buttons. The user can find a

"Generate all Scene files" and a "Generate Script file" in the top of the graph window while each node contains a "Generate Scene file" as well.

The generation of scene files can be made either in bulk, by generating one scene for each node, or the user may decide to generate the scenes of specific nodes. The result is empty scenes files with the names of the nodes' titles that can be opened in Unity through another type of button that can be found in each node with the name "Open Scene".

The "Generate Script file" generates a C# file with a class that represents the specific story that is opened in the graph and gives access to the story's data in the form of C# objects.

The aforementioned files are organized in a specific folder structure (Fig. 3). Firstly, a folder with the tool's name is created and inside this folder there is a dedicated folder for every story that has scenes and/or scripts generated by the tool, with each folder having the title of the story it refers to. Inside every story's folder there may be two other folders, a "Scenes" and a "Scripts" and each of these folders will be created after the user chooses to use the tool's scene and/or script generation separately.

Fig. 3. The folder structure in Unity after using the Scenes generation feature.

4   Evaluation

In order to assess the effectiveness of the implemented software solution, we invited Unity developers for a comprehensive evaluation. Five participants selected, aiming for diverse background and expertise in both branching narrative design and programming in Unity. The participants' profile is presented in Table 1. In this section, we present the evaluation process and outcomes. The evaluation process has been approved by the Ethics Committee of the Department of Informatics and Telecommunications of the National and Kapodistrian University of Athens.

4.1   Evaluation Process

Regarding the selection of the participants, the goal was to ensure a diverse representation of different expertise and experience both in IDN and in Unity development. The first two participants are members of the Narralive team and they have experience with the authoring part of this workflow, making their review valuable as to how well the authoring and the developing tools cooperate. The third and fourth participants are Unity professionals and were able to review this tool from the perspective of a game developer that does not have an in-depth understanding of the story's design process. Lastly, the fifth participant is a developer that has experience with Unity from personal projects and they gave their opinion on this tool through the prism of it being an understandable Unity plug-in.

The selected participants were invited to the evaluation location at pre-arranged dates and times. They were presented with the objectives of the study and were asked to sign the consent forms. The evaluation process then involved introducing the software to the participants and providing them with ample time to explore its functionalities and features. The participants were encouraged to perform various tasks and use the software as they would in a real-world scenario, while being observed by the evaluator. A think-aloud protocol was followed, to directly record their comments throughout the evaluation. Detailed guidelines and instructions were provided to ensure consistency in their evaluations. Following the testing phase, the participants were asked to provide feedback and rate their experience using a standardized evaluation questionnaire [13]. This process is summarized in Fig. 5.

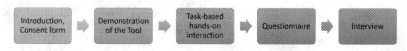

Fig. 5. Overview of the evaluation process

The tasks that the user was asked to execute during the evaluation were separated into numbered steps. The first group of steps was instructing the user to open the tool and provide the given credentials in order to get access to a list of stories that were previously designed in the web-based authoring tool. Next, the user was prompted to select a specific story. The story that was chosen for the purposes of the evaluation process had a complex graph, with multiple nodes, multiple branches and endings and, in general, higher complexity than the rest. The objective for this was to give the user an impression of the tool's possibilities, The user was free to navigate the graph that was generated after the story selection and explore the nodes information, including descriptive texts and tags. Then, the user was asked to use the scenes and script generation features. Finally, using the generated classes and script, they were asked to write code in order to print in the Unity's console a set of the story data such as the text of the first scene or a list of tags of every node. The last part was dedicated to give the user some experience with the advantages of the tool's automations.

Questionnaire
The evaluation questionnaire [13]. Encompassed aspects such as usability, performance, reliability, and overall satisfaction with the software. The first part of the questionnaire included the SUS model (System Usability Scale) [13], a widely used questionnaire-based tool used to evaluate the usability of a system, product, or interface. It was developed by John Brooke in 1986 and has since become one of the most commonly used usability evaluation methods as it covers aspects such as the system's complexity, ease

of use, user confidence, and overall satisfaction. The SUS consists of a 10-item questionnaire that aims to measure the perceived usability of a system. Each item is rated on a 1–5 scale ranging from "Strongly Disagree" to "Strongly Agree".

The second part of the questionnaire included open questions that were used to guide a semi-structured interview to record more in depth and qualitative feedback provided by the participants. These were the following:

1. What did you find more useful?
2. What did you find more difficult?
3. What kind of improvements, changes and future work would you suggest?

5   Results

As we can see from the SUS scores in Table 1, all participants appreciated the tool with a consistently high SUS score. A positive observation is that every user answered "Strongly disagree" in the question about the tool being complex, which provided the information that the tool is intuitive even for a user that is using it for the first time. This result is supported by the responses to the statement "I felt confident using the system". An aspect that we were concerned with was whether a user would choose to use this tool in the future for their work. Thus, we paid attention specifically to the SUS question "I think that I would like to use this system frequently", where the results were, again, positive, with the answers being between "Agree" and "Strongly agree" (Fig. 6).

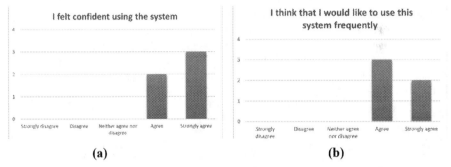

(a)   (b)

Fig. 6. Selected statements from the evaluation questionnaire. (a) "I felt confident using the system" and (b) "I think I would use this system frequently".

The feature of the tool that was described as particularly helpful by all the participants is the story visualization through the graph. The fact that "it gives the feeling of a timeline" (User 1) and that it contains the story's details provides the user an overview of the story: *"especially in a large, complex story, the user would definitely get lost without this feature"* (User 2). Another interesting characteristic that was pointed out was that since the tool was created in Unity's GUI environment it makes it "easy to understand as it keeps a UI/UX consistency inside Unity Engine" (User 3). Additionally, the users found the auto-generation of code and scenes useful with the main focus being on the ability to make massive scene generations and have the folders organized as *"this feature*

Table 1. Study participants profiles. The players with experience as GMs are noted with "GM"

	User 1	User 2	User 3	User 4	User 5
Age	24	27	28	25	26
Unity experience	Academic	Academic	Professional	Personal Projects	Professional
IDN Authoring Tool experience	Some	A lot	None	None	None
Visual Novel playing experience	Some	A lot	A lot	A lot	None
SUS score	87.5%	90%	85%	87.5%	90%

saves me, as a Unity developer, a lot of time" (User 5). When it comes to the logic behind the tool's workflow, the participants agreed that it simulates how a developer would work and that "*the structure of the C# classes is intuitive, clear and understandable*".

As to the difficulties faced while using the tool, all reported that there is a need for documentation to guide them on the generated code as, otherwise, there would be a need for "some time to view the code and start working on it" (User 4).

An important outcome of this evaluation were the ideas and suggestions for improvement and future development that were provided. An addition that was suggested by most of the users concerns the ability to edit the graph. For example, the graph could be enhanced with "some more actions inside the nodes, like a "Clear Scene" button" (User 2). Also, another interesting idea was the ability to "duplicate scene content and add scene objects in bulk" (User 2). Lastly, a suggestion was to include in the package a simple Unity scene with some objects that are likely to be used in a Visual Novel scene. These objects could be a background image, a text and a button that will act as a scene's choice. The point of this feature is to provide the developer with a basic scene to start working on, edit and copy to other scenes as, for a simple Visual Novel, this type of scene could be adequate to display all of the story.

6   Conclusions and Future Steps

In this work we presented the Narralive Unity plug-in, a tool for Unity Engine that facilitates and, in some cases, even automates the work of a game developer of visual novels, or branching narratives in general. The tool import functionality transforms it to the bridge between the story design created by a story author and the developer called to transform this design into a visual novel experience. With the implementation of this tool we aim to promote a simple and clear work-flow for the creation of interactive stories and facilitate the collaboration and communication of the authors and the software developers involved in the same project.

The collected data and feedback from the evaluation played a crucial role in analyzing the tool's strengths and weaknesses ultimately facilitating the improvement of its efficacy and usability. Conducting similar evaluations with more participants can assist with improving the tool further.

In the future we aim to evolve the tool by adding more automation features such as developing algorithms for the ready to use script that give the developers more functionalities, code-wise. An important improvement would be the implementation of an editing functionality for the graph so that the users can add and edit the stories' nodes and paths inside Unity. Lastly, the tool currently offers import functionality for the Story Maker tool, however, it could be extended to support other authoring tools which produce graph-based interactive narratives, taking into account that their story data is available.

References

1. Camingue, J., Carstensdottir, E., Melcer, E.: What is a visual novel? Proc. ACM Hum. Comput. Interact. **5**, 1–18 (2021). https://doi.org/10.1145/3474712
2. Oygardslia, K., Weitze, C.L., Shin, Jh.: The educational potential of visual novel games: principles for design. Replaying Japan, vol. 2 (2020)
3. Petousi, D., Katifori, A., Servi, K., Roussou, M., Ioannidis, Y.: History education done different: a collaborative interactive digital storytelling approach for remote learners (2022)
4. Parra, G., Klerkx, J., Duval, E.: Understanding engagement with interactive public displays: an awareness campaign in the wild (2014)
5. Katifori, A., Karvounis, M., Kourtis, V., Perry, S., Roussou, M., Ioannidis, Y.: Applying interactive storytelling in cultural heritage: opportunities, challenges and lessons learned. In: 11th International Conference on Interactive Digital Storytelling, ICIDS 2018, Dublin, Ireland, 5–8 December 2018
6. Spierling, U., Szilas, N.: Authoring issues beyond tools (2009)
7. Vrettakis, E., et al.: The story maker - an authoring tool for multimedia-rich interactive narratives. In: Bosser, A.G., Millard, D.E., Hargood, C. (eds.) ICIDS 2020. LNCS, vol. 12497, pp. 349–352. Springer, Cham (2020). https://doi.org/10.1007/978-3-030-62516-0_33
8. Vrettakis, E., Kourtis, V., Katifori, A., Karvounis, M., Lougiakis, C., Ioannidis, Y.: Narralive-creating and experiencing mobile digital storytelling in cultural heritage. Digit. Appl. Archaeol. Cult. Herit. **15** (2019)
9. Ink. https://www.inklestudios.com/ink/. Accessed 04 July 2023
10. Yarn Spinner. https://yarnspinner.dev/. Accessed 04 July 2023
11. Ren'Py. https://www.renpy.org/. Accessed 04 July 2023
12. Twine. https://twinery.org/. Accessed 04 July 2023
13. Brooke, J.: SUS: A quick and dirty usability scale (1995)

Interactive Narrative Design

Discovering IDN Authoring Strategies: Novices Anchor Choice Design Through Character Development with Player Feedback

Colette Daiute[1]($^{(⊠)}$) ⓘ, John T. Murray[2] ⓘ, and Jack Wright[3] ⓘ

[1] Graduate Center, City University of New York, New York, USA
cdaiute@gc.cuny.edu
[2] University of Central Florida, Orlando, USA
jtm@ucf.edu
[3] Queens College, City University of New York, New York, USA

Abstract. Shifting from narrating in everyday life and culture to designing an IDN is a major challenge. It requires rethinking the goals and elements of narrating, with a focus on the player's perspective. Yet, we know little about student designers' IDN composing processes, such as how they use digital techniques (like branching) and develop narrative qualities, like character, to create multiple story trajectories for player engagement. Novices' uptake of devices and narrative elements, such as character and choice poetics, is a process that can inform IDN theory and practice about the shift to this new genre. This paper presents a secondary analysis of interactive digital narrative (IDN) designs and player reflections created during a 2.5-h online workshop. Detailed analyses of narrative elements and digital devices in hundreds of design and reflection sequences trace uses and developments of novice authoring strategies. Four strands of analysis (narrative elements, choice poetics, player reflection, and Twine tree structure) offer a complementary picture of the IDN design learning process. Findings of our analysis show that, over time, student designers developed characters with increasing literary quality and with sophisticated choice options (socio-emotional and moral dilemmas) as pivots for narrative trajectories. Different character and choice development patterns related to player feedback suggest the importance of integrating these multiple dimensions into IDN research and pedagogy. Discussion highlights how the analysis captures the complexity of the IDN genre, provides a foundation for ongoing research into IDN designing as a developmental process, and offers a foundation for IDN pedagogy.

Keywords: Interactive Digital Narrative Design · Character Poetics · Choice Poetics · IDN Pedagogy · Twine

1 Introduction

While a major purpose of everyday storytelling is to make sense of the world and one's role in it [1], the purpose of IDN designing is to make sense of "the other," in particular, the player as potential co-author. In that process, the IDN designer becomes "a

© The Author(s), under exclusive license to Springer Nature Switzerland AG 2023
L. Holloway-Attaway and J. T. Murray (Eds.): ICIDS 2023, LNCS 14383, pp. 239–258, 2023.
https://doi.org/10.1007/978-3-031-47655-6_15

narrative architect creating a "protostory," which is "a digital template with narrative and digital elements that interacting players can work with in satisfying ways to create narratives" [2]. Creating such possible stories must also, thus, be aesthetically appealing to culturally diverse others. Because becoming part of a culture involves using the culture's storytelling aesthetics, such as what makes a narrative satisfying, we highlight the processes of novice IDN designers from a wide range of cultural backgrounds. We consider how these novice IDN designers used basic digital tools (like branching in Twine), narrative elements (such as character dialogue), and social interaction (such as a player's feedback) to create increasingly crafted protostories.

Although novice IDN designers have narrated in daily life, they must make a major shift to a very different kind of narrating. Managing the shift to IDN authoring involves unlearning the value of creating a single coherent storyline and learning to create player-sensitive options for multiple possible story trajectories. While practicing this new genre, the IDN designer must do so by integrating diverse complex symbol systems (digital tools, narrative elements, and players' interactions) into a concrete playable dynamic artifact. IDN authors must, moreover, assess the quality of their developing designs from the perspective of potential players at *specific* junctures of character development and plot possibilities, rather than primarily in terms of their authorial preferences. A database of designs by a culturally and linguistically diverse group of IDN authors provides unique insights into such character and choice poetics because multi-cultural experience requires attention to multiple forms and dissonant meanings [3–5].

We analyze a database from a previous study with undergraduates new to IDN design [6]. In that practice-based study, volunteers from college social science courses met up in the Authoring-Other System in Sherlock [6, 7], which (after consent and registration) guided them through four turns of designing, playing-reflecting on a peer's design, and continuing to work on one's own design. Sherlock recorded events generated from a modified version of Twine [8] and provided them via the server to each partner, who then shared reflections to passages using a chat interface. In addition to implementing the Authoring-Other Exchange workshop, the system stored and exported the data to a database system for coding with four complementary strands of analysis [6]. The present inquiry focuses on character and choice options as mediational tools for IDN authoring, the impact of player feedback on designing, and consequences for a measure of Twine tree structure.

Following are the research questions guiding this inquiry and then a review of related literature, the methodology, results of quantitative analyses, illustrative case studies, and a discussion connecting to IDN theory and pedagogy.

Research questions guiding the inquiry include:

- How did undergraduates new to IDN authoring use narrative elements and basic *Twine* tools to create player-oriented protostories during a 2.5-h online workshop?
- What patterns of character and choice use and development occurred over time? How did character and choice developments relate to player reflections and a measure of IDN structure?
- What are the implications of mediating functions of character, choice, and player interaction for IDN theory and pedagogy?

These questions were motivated by previous research into IDN pedagogy and extend it to further explore issues of narrative content development and process.

2 Research on Poetics in IDN Genres

Much prior research on character representation in IDN has focused on connections between player and character identity [9–13] or the consequences of game design on behavior, such as aggression [14] and cognitive skills [15]. In contrast, research on IDN poetics focuses on interactive devices mobilizing aesthetic forms to engage and deepen a player's narrative involvement [16, 17]. Highlighting language use, such as with poetics, is consistent with theory about the mediational role of formal systems, like language and digital tools, in the concrete enactment of meaning in social interaction [6].

2.1 Character Poetics

Given the importance of player engagement in IDN appeal and advancement (such as for increasingly complex modes like VR), research focuses on player identity as a bridge between author and player [9]. For example, researchers are examining diegesis - such as the use of "you" involving narrator and/or player characters affecting player agency [9]. Research has also explored mediational means of player characters, such as character indeterminacy [16]. For example, one study examined "shell characters," descriptively under-determined characters in over-determined social or political roles like the border controller in "Papers Please" [16]. Players can inhabit vague characters with empathy or critical moral stances more easily than they can inhabit fully formed ones.

Another study of interactive life narratives explored altering feedback loops to help convey protagonist experiences, thereby eliciting player emotions [17]. Gameplay poetics theory emphasizes formal qualities that draw interlocutors' attention away from meaning in ways that re-ignite engagement for expansive or transformational meaning [17]. The analysis found that structuring player actions, such as disrupting player expectations of control, evokes certain emotions that engage players to form new interpretations of the narrative. Such focus on crafting form and emotion is wrought of experience that novices may arrive at slowly while working with IDN tools with players. Observing that developmental process in action could offer insights into IDN genres and pedagogy. The focal point in this developmental process is choice poetics.

2.2 Choice Poetics

Choice poetics identifies diverse conceptual options from the designer's perspective in relation to players' expectations [18]. Choice poetics theory and research posit that "choices are an essential part of poetic effects like transportation, agency, autonomy, responsibility, and regret" when relative to player goals [18]. Research applying this theory with goal-based choice analysis can "dissect a player's perception of choice," thereby offering authors and scholars a way to analyze how choices work within narratives [18]. Prior empirical research on choice poetics uses an artificial intelligence tool to implement diverse conceptual options from the designer's perspective in relation to players' expectations as they engage with different options. We ask how novices use choice options when considering IDN authoring as a developmental process.

In addition to learning a technical device for creating choice options with the potential for multiple narrative sequences, planning for dissonance in a story may be a skill developed in multi-cultural or other challenging life experiences. Scholars who study literacy and literature development have found, for example, that attention to aesthetics occurs in multi-cultural experiences [3–5], such as among bilinguals and speakers of multiple dialects who have had to pay special attention to form and meaning as they manage communication. As Toni Morrison has explained: "If my work is faithfully to reflect the aesthetic tradition of Afro-American culture, it must make conscious use of the characteristics of its art forms and translate them into print: antiphony, the group nature of art, its functionality, its improvisational nature, its relationship to audience performance …" [4]. The uptake of IDN authoring by undergraduates from a wide range of cultural backgrounds and aesthetic traditions may, thus, be especially sensitive to multiple expressive devices, like those in interactive digital narratives.

3   Methodology

Four strands of analysis of IDN designs (narrative elements, choice poetics, player reflection, and Twine tree structure) together offer a complementary picture of this authoring learning process. Each strand of analysis has been established and tested in our previous research [6]. We drew on prior analysis of the IDN designs (narrative elements, choices, protostory tree structure) at the end of each design turn with peer playing and reflection sharing between the design turns for the present statistical analyses. Descriptive and analytic statistics (frequencies, means, Principal Components Analysis, factor analyses, and correlations) identified patterns within and across the IDN elements and player reflection categories. In addition, two qualitative case studies explored different approaches to crafting player engagement via character design and choice poetics in relation to narrative trajectories.

3.1   Database and Analyses

Data for this secondary analysis come from the study of college students working synchronously in real-time in the Authoring-Other Exchange System [6]. Data were deidentified, labeled with author demographic codes (race/ethnicity, gender, and native language), downloaded to ATLAS.ti 9 [19], analyzed with defined categories, and stored for ongoing study.

We analyzed coded data from 54 workshop participants who had volunteered through college social science courses. Based on demographics noted during registration and volunteers' declaration that they had no prior IDN authoring experience, the database represents the diversity of the large public university system; many authors identified as bi-(or tri+) lingual with native languages other than English (24 of 54) and as in diverse ethnic/racial groups including Asian (16), White (10), Hispanic (10), Black (8), South Asian (7), Middle Eastern (3), and female gender (37 of 54).

The database consists of 191 player reflection turn segments with (3 player reflection turns), resulting in 1187 expressive units (clauses, phrases, verbal emojis). IDN design data was available in text form with time stamps and Twine tool codes (e.g. [[…]] and ->) in 240 units in 4,140 expressive unit categories (sentences, clauses, phrases) over 4 design turns. The on-screen prompt for designing was "[t]hink of a story idea and use the Twine tools you learned to begin designing an IDN." The prompt provided for player reflection turns was "Share with your partner what you are thinking and feeling as you play their emerging design." After each player reflection turn, the designer prompt was "Consider your player's reflections and continue your IDN design". Figure 1 illustrates the four strands of data examined in the present study.

Fig. 1. Database Strands for Analysis of Character and Choice

3.2 IDN Elements

The IDN Elements analysis identified narrative qualities and choice node options, as added in each of the four design turns. Because of our interest in aesthetic forms and functions, this analysis focuses on the full range of detailed categories with attention to any prominent features and patterns. As presented in Table 1, the coding scheme identified character dynamics: character descriptions, actions, psychological states, and dialogue. Objects were also noted as described and animated. World elements included place (rooms, nature) and temporality. Character-independent events were also identified. This process yielded from 1 to 26 characters (with the character functions); 0–26 objects (with object functions).

Figure 2 illustrates how the character coding is applied using the ATLAS.ti tool.

For example, in Fig. 2 *Char1Dia* identifies the narrator, setting the scene; the "two squirrels" *(Char2Des)* who are at "a grassland beside a beautiful lake at a national park" *(WorSet)*. Entering next is "one visitor stops" *(Char3Act)*, who also "take a photo" *(Char3Act)*.

In addition to character enactment functions, we identified character roles in narrative trajectory(ies), such as protagonist or secondary roles. The roles of characters in the IDN composing process emerged from examining the character entry point into the design, frequencies, patterns in factor analyses, interactions in choice option types,

Table 1. IDN Element Categories

IDN Element Category	Example
Character Description	*You* (Player character)
Character Action	*You trip*
Character Psychological state	*You wake up*
Character Dialogue	*You say to yourself "Where am I?*
Object Description	*The wind is so strong*
Object Animation	*The wind is blowing like it's mad*
World Setting	*An enormous mansion*
World Setting Nature	*The woods*
World Setting Room	*The Bears' kitchen*
World Temporality	*All of a sudden*
Event (Event) – agentless activity	*#Departure*
	Bouldering is a process
Choice: Single-dimension decision	*[[The right path]] [[The left path]]*
Choice: Adventurous options	*[[You barely catch the hold and scramble to get both hands on it]] [[You miss entirely]]*
Choice: Socioemotional options	*[[You ask a question]] [[You suppress your anger]]*
Choice: Moral Dilemma involved	*[[stop and see what she needs]] [[ignore again to continue your journey]]*

Fig. 2. Excerpt of Design with IDN Narrative Element Analysis. Passage Titles indicated with # prefix, choices with [[]].

and protostory trajectory (such as in episodes of complicating actions and/or potential resolutions). Specific character enactments designed to engage the player diegetically, such as the use of a second-person perspective, were of interest, as indicated in previous research [9]. A majority of the IDN designs used the second person "you" as a player character (35), others created non-player characters (17), and some mixed (2). As described below, the factor analysis of the IDN elements and player reflections identified inter-relationships among variables.

3.3   Player Experience Reflection Analysis

Player experience reflections identified the expressive function of shared thought units (sentence or independent clause, phrase, word, verbal emojis such as "lol") over three 15-min turns playing their partner's IDN design. As shown in Table 2 with examples, coded categories in the database: "Player cognition/intention," "Player affect," "Negative evaluation," "Positive evaluation," "IDN feature," "Repeat narrative," "Suggest narrative" "Suggest procedure/process." The eight mutually exclusive categories accounted for all the player reflections, were defined in the project manual, and checked for consistency.

Table 2. Player Reflection Categories

Player Reflection Category	Examples
Player affect: expresses emotion, subjective experience, own or other's	*I liked* *The cat purred* *It's really fun to follow along;* *The situation gave me a sense of fear* *Hahaha; lol*
Player cognition/intention: Expressing thoughts, intentions, wondering, discovering, own or other's	*I'm confused;* *I'm getting really interested to see* *She enters cautiously*
Positive evaluation: Offers positive comment on the narrative or process	*This is great!* *Good job so far*
Negative evaluation: Player offers negative comment on the narrative or process	*This isn't interactive* *should be more interactive*
IDN feature: Refers to a digital quality or feature, often in their terms	*Option* *I like your hook,* *Click the first choice...* *[[...]]* *This IS interactive*
Repeat designer narrative: Repeats a narrative sequence from the design	*how Doe sounded strange on the call;* *The person fell deeper into the cave*
Suggest procedures/process: Suggests Twine or other IDN procedure or process	*Use [[...]] to create a branch* *Add more choices*
Suggest narrative: mentions a specific narrative sequence or structure	*How will this end? Who will she choose?* *You should punish their selfishness*

Descriptive statistics identified frequencies, means, and distributions of all the player reflection categories within and across turns. Factor analyses organized the player reflection data to examine interactions with IDN elements, choice types, and the tree structure metric.

3.4 IDN Tree Structure Metric

The IDN Tree Complexity Metric (TCM) describes the size and shape of a Twine story as it appears on a design screen [20]. For this study, the TCM provided information about Twine-internal features of the designs and an independent indicator of the design structure, as perceived by experts and modeled to apply to the many design images created over time in this study. This measure is relevant to the present analysis to quantify how IDN designs included the available technical features of the authoring program. Features scraped with transcribed symbols (e.g. [[]] = choice node) from the data export files at the end of 15-min design turns included nodes, branches, leaves (nodes with no posterior links), non-leaf nodes (nodes minus leaves), choice nodes (nodes with multiple exit branches), maximum path length (path length = number of nodes connected from the origin to a leaf), average path length, and recursive branch. The TCM was developed through 2500 pairwise comparisons of IDNs, with experts comparing pairs of design images for complexity [20]. A random forest machine learning model was then built to predict a complexity metric on tree pictures outside the training sample IDNs (R^2 = .75). The TCM provides a single metric that captures the size and growth of the tree structure.

3.5 Case Studies

Case studies illustrate patterns of character, choice, and player reflection use in the context of a developing protostory. Screen shots were aids for considering protostory trajectory and dynamics, such as how choice options or other devices provided multiple narrative possibilities. The protostory images also indicate the design structure space captured in the TCM. Selection of the cases was also based on the authors' different strategies for player immersion, particularly whether and how they implemented player characters or other techniques.

4 Results

Analyses offer information about IDN design learning processes. The novice IDN designs include a range of narrative elements (world, character, object, events) and digital devices (nodes, branches, choice nodes, recursion, etc.). Character development and choice complexity increased over turns and in relation to supportive and IDN-relevant player reflections with some patterns of connection to the TCM.

4.1 Novice IDN Designers Took up Narrative and Digital Devices

A Principal Components Analysis of the students' uses of Twine features indicated that the participants drew on the available digital and narrative devices.

The PCA showed that 70% of the variance is accounted for by features related to the volume of the tree structure. Principal component 1 is comprised of branches, nodes, non-leaf nodes, and path length. Principal component 2, accounting for 15% of the variance, is composed of variables with a more specific emphasis on leaves and recursion. The leaves and recursion component indicates that the size of the tree structures cannot be captured by volume alone. Moreover, the TCM offered concise evidence that the designs increased in complexity over time, based on the model with experts' judgments.

4.2   Character Rich Design Learning Strategy

While participants employed the range of Twine features available (as shown in the PCA results), the most frequently added narrative element was characters, accounting for 80% of added content (across node types). Figure 3 illustrates the frequencies of coded narrative and choice elements across turns. A common strategy was for the first character to be enacted relatively fully with psychological states (emotion, cognition, intention) and dialogue (direct quotes or reported speech). Setting elements were also relatively frequent, as was a second character with psychological states and a choice option.

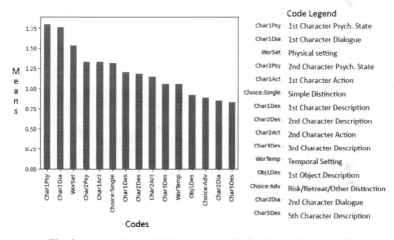

Fig. 3. Mean Values of Character and Choice Categories Overall

As shown in Fig. 3, the IDN protostories included new (choice nodes) and familiar elements (characters).

4.3   Characters Developed Over Time

To identify whether and how characters developed over the turns, we examined the distribution of basic enactments (character descriptions and character actions) compared to more elaborated character enactments (animated with psychological states and dialogue). Figure 4 presents percentages of the four character enactment functions: character psychological states and character dialogue increased over turns, while descriptions and actions decreased. We correlated basic character expressions (description and action) and elaborated character expression (psychological and dialogue) within all the IDN elements for all active design and play turns. The analysis showed basic character enactments and elaborated character enactments are inversely correlated ($r = 0.64$), indicating character development over time in the workshop.

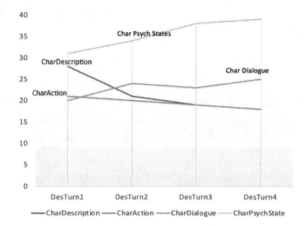

Fig. 4. Percentage of Character Enactments over Design Turns

4.4 From Character Enactments to Character Relations

Characters are not only plentiful, functional, and developing over the workshop but are also interrelated. We explored this construction of characters with interacting voices within the IDN design. If characters were forming a meaningful narrative fabric, they would interact, possibly as protagonist(s) (individual or comrades), protagonist/antagonist (hero/villain; primary point of view/secondary point of view), bystanders, or chorus. These relations can vary by frequency, time they emerge, development level, and whether they participate in choice interludes. We examined the introduction of characters by character enactments over design turns to assess such relationships among characters. Figure 5 presents character enactment over the turns.

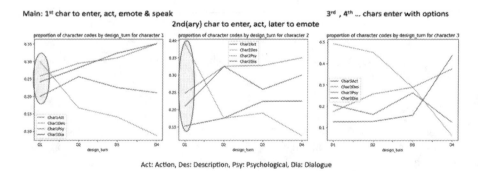

Fig. 5. Graphs Illustrating Character Roles in the IDN Designs

Figure 5 depicts the average introduction of character functions for Characters 1, 2, and 3 (as they entered the design). We observe that in the first turn, Character 1 tends to think and/or emote and to speak, as well as to be described (or named) and/or doing some action. That character is not alone, as a second enters via name or description and less frequently by action or psychological state. A third character remains primarily described across more design turns than the first or second while perking up notably with dialogue on turn four. We learn, thus, that in addition to anchoring the early IDN experience, characters occur in dynamic relation, certainly because exploring human relations is a narrative function, but also because characters provide the salient potential for growing IDN trajectories.

A factor analysis organized the many coded variables depicting character enactments and functions. Complementing the frequency and means data illustrated above, the factor analysis offered another way to identify possible character roles and relationships, as main characters (protagonists), secondary characters (interacting as antagonists, active bystanders), and tertiary characters designed into the narrative as foils).

Non-overlapping factors explain the maximum amount of variance in the data: agent-less Events (Factor 1); Characters 2, 4, 3 description (Factor 2) Objects (Factor 3); (Character 1 action, psychological state, description (Factor 4); Character 4 action, psychological state and Character 2 psych states (Factor 5). The scree plots indicate that Factor 4 captures protagonists, Factor 2 captures foils, and Factor 5 captures antagonists or bystanders.

Excerpts illustrate these character development patterns identified in the statistical analyses. For example, "The Journey Begins" depicts a protagonist with other characters entering later primarily as foils. "You" (Character 1, player) "have the day off" and Character 1 psychological state (you) "want to spend it in a fun way;" "You rack up your brain for some things to do throughout the day." In turn 3, character 1 continues to act, decide, and speak, as other characters are designed into the protostory, mostly as foils. For example, Character 2, a salesperson at "Footlocker" dialogues "asks you what type of shoe," "you would like to buy" (Character 1 psychological state). Later on, at Macy's, things get tense when "You enter the store" (Character 1 acts) "and you hear" (psychological state) new characters entering with psychological states: "a few people shouting." After a few more characters enter in various ways, the consequences for Character 1 are psychological: "You feel overwhelmed."

That pattern of a primary character who enters first in the design, with a relatively full complement of action, psychological states, description, and/or dialogue, then meets another who is described or responds minimally is a robust pattern, as indicated by the factor analysis. Case studies in Sect. 5 below illustrate some different variations of this pattern. This characterization resource, if not poetics, then interacts with the IDN device of choice to vary any individual storyline.

4.5 Choice Poetics

Like character development, choice options increased in sophistication during the IDN design learning workshop. Figure 6 shows how choice node option types changed over the design turns, with the single option decreasing (43 to 9), the adventure option decreasing less (23 to 13), and socioemotional options increasing (6 to 10). Options trading on moral decisions varied (7, 1, 6, 1).

Choice developments coincide with character development in the design titled "A Day Off." Choice types in that protostory begin simply, with choices requiring single distinctions and, gradually, over design-play turns, choices turn on more socioemotional

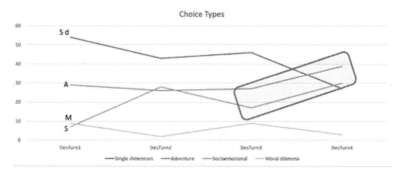

Fig. 6. Frequency of Choice Types Introduced over Design Turns

decisions. For example, in design turn 1, the narrator offers (*Char2Dia*) choices including [[Have a delicious breakfast at a small cafe->Choice 1]] or [[Go straight to the mall and grab a coffee there->Choice 2]]; [[Have a nice brunch with your family->Choice 3]]; [[Skip breakfast->Choice 4]] … [[An English muffin and black coffee]]; [[Vanilla latte]]; [[Blueberry scones]]; [[Something else entirely]]. After player reflection turns, choices become more socioemotional, such as in design turn 3 with [[SCREAMMM because it burns]]; [[Yell at the person who caused the accident]]; [[A bit of both]]; [[Demand a refund and a whole lot of tissues as you stomp out of the store]]. This pattern is also quite common.

Having described the significant character and choice design developments, we turn to player reflections, which occurred between design turns and proved to impact the designs over time.

4.6 Player Reflections Come into Play

Providing access to players during the novice IDN design process also has the potential to guide the designer with insights at the heart of IDN: player engagement. Table 3 presents the player reflection types related to changes in IDN elements, choice types, and an analysis of the TCM over time. As mentioned, the reflection prompt invited the player to share their thoughts and feelings while playing through the partner's design after each turn. Players did that with relative frequency: "Player Affect" = 276 and "Player cognition/intention" = 298, yet they also spontaneously offered other kinds of comments, as listed in Table 2. Among the other types was: "IDN feature" (155), which we expected to occur, as well as "Positive Evaluation" (115) and "Negative Evaluation" (49). As with "IDN feature," we expected that players might offer a peer struggling with the Twine tools to make procedural suggestions ("Suggest procedures/processes" = 70). Because the qualitative analysis to determine the player reflections was open to all comments, "Repeat Narrative" (161) and "Suggest narrative" (94) emerged.

The reflection type that related most often to changes in peers' IDN design qualities was "Repeat Narrative," followed by "Suggest Procedures/Practices" (Table 3). Results of the statistical analyses of the cross-strand effects (in Table 3) indicate that affirming a designer's work, especially by repeating exact sequences, made a difference in

Table 3. Player Reflection Types Related to Changes in Other IDN Measures

PLAYER REFLECTION TYPES	IDN FEATURE	CHOICE TYPES	TCM
Player Affect	-	-	-
Player Cognition/Intention	-	Choice: Single	-
Positive Evaluation	-	-	TCM +
IDN Feature	IDN Factor 4 – Main Character	-	TCM -
Repeat Narrative	IDN Factor 5 - Secondary Character	Choice: Single Choice: Socioemotional	-
Suggest Procedures/Processes	-	Choice: Adv Choice: MorDil	TCM +
Suggest Narrative	-	-	TCM +

certain kinds of design fluency and structure: creating secondary characters, that could, for example, elaborate a narrative and potential trajectories, as in the examples above. This use of choice connects significantly with the structural measure, TCM, not only as a digital feature (branching) but also in narrative quality, involving players' socioemotional decision-making. While "Repeat narrative" appears to fuel the design process, "Suggest procedure/process" also adds to structural development, as indicated in the positive correlation with the TCM and with the "Adventure" and "Moral Dilemma" choice types, which require the designer's and the player's deeper conceptual engagement. That "Negative evaluations" would be associated with stalling or shutting down the design development is not surprising. In contrast, that the design process increases with "Positive evaluation" is also not surprising but a dramatic indication of the robustness of these interacting measures.

Qualitative examinations of two designs follow to integrate these myriad findings.

5   Case Studies Showing Diverse Player Engagement Strategies

Thus far, the analysis has described how novice IDN designers approach the challenging new task of IDN designing, focusing on character development, choice offerings, and player reflections in relation to a measure of the overall tree structure. In this qualitative analysis, we further explore how students used narrative and digital devices to expand possibilities in the narrative trajectory. The tree structure measure captured growth in the overall shape of the designs, and this inquiry with Twine pictures further illuminates and examines the role of character development, choice options, and player reflection dynamics as junctures in the protostory structure.

Consistent with our consideration of how novice designers become IDN-player oriented, we chose one design (among the relatively many in this database) that invites the player as a character with the second person pronoun "you" and another design with characters depicted within the story world (almost completely). This critical examination considered, for example, whether a choice option would have consequences for qualitatively different character interactions, such as conflicts about a journey path or social relationships, and whether different choice options would lead to different resolution strategies. The increasing TCM throughout the study and its positive relation to character and choice types points to IDN design skill as a developing process with flexibility while also showing consistent patterns like those presented above.

5.1 "The Encounter," Mediated by Player Character, Socioemotional Choices, and Peer Player Affirmation

"The Encounter" was designed by a participant identifying as a Hispanic female whose first language was Spanish. The story begins on a rainy, windy day on an island, where a plane lands with only one passenger. *You* (the player) look up, and your umbrella flies away, so you chase it, OR you almost fly away, but the person waiting holds your hand. Chasing the umbrella leads you home to sleep. The person holding your hand IS the encounter with a past love, John. The encounter reminds you of your love for John and sets off a range of self-conversation you have as "you" shift to being "Melissa." This inner dialogue is punctuated by your/Melissa's leaving John with your Dad so you can go off to your job at the clinic. John shows up as a patient at the clinic to tell you he is engaged and wants to invite you to his wedding. This shifts to a linear sequence of Melissa's self-reflections about the disappointment and, ultimately, gratitude for hearing a truth that ends the false hope of being with John. A seemingly agentless statement of truth is followed by the author presenting outside the story to thank the player for reading her story.

This design develops characters in several ways, focusing on two main characters and a foil. The story develops through the protagonist (the most frequent, most psychologically and dialogically animated, and addressed by the other characters); the antagonist former boyfriend and unrequited love interest, John (less frequent, speaking/ emoting less and often the object of the protagonist's reflection); and a bystander/foil Dad, whom John visits and protagonist leaves to tend to John (mentioned less and with less animation).

The protagonist changes and develops over time in two major ways that interact minimally with choice options. "You" are later named "Melissa," and eventually seem to be the narrator and then the author, who thanks the peer player in the end. With these changes, you/Melissa/narrator/author use self-dialogue, conversations with the other characters, and the player, as in these examples: "you think to yourself, is he going to let me go? do I let him to let me go? why is my heart beating so fast. I thought I got over John a long time ago. My face! how's my face? with the rain it must be looking awful". Later, there's "the first conversation" between John and Melissa herself: "you: "thank you so much for saving me"; Him: "Melissa? is that you? I didn't recognized you. Wow! its been like what... 10 years?" you: "oh... Hey John! Yeah, 10 years I think". From beginning to end, characterization develops, as do the choice types, although there are only a few: "Adventure": [[you flew away with the umbrella]] or [[You almost flew away, but the person hold your hand]] and "Socioemotional": He says... [[Are you okay?]] or [[Melissa?]] (Fig. 7).

How, then, does character development interact with choice poetics aspects of the design? Fig. 8 shows three choice nodes that have consequences for interactions among the three main characters: the protagonist (you/Melissa…), the antagonist (John), and the facilitator (Dad).

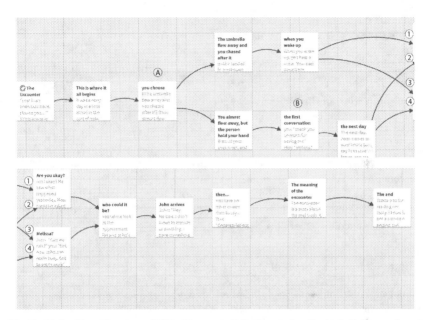

Fig. 7. Twine Tree Structure of "The Encounter" (in 2 parts for display), links numbered.

After a few choice options, the rest of the story is a linear protagonist self-conversation followed by a general statement of truth and a specific thank you to the player. A choice node on design turn 1 is "you choose" with two options: [[The umbrella flew away and you chased after it]] or [[You almost flew away, but the person hold your hand]].

On the first reflection turn, the peer player, also identifying as a Hispanic female whose first language is Spanish, asked "*who could this person be?*" as a comment linked to the passage "# You almost flew away, but the person hold your hand", as well as another another comment "*will they finally confess their feelings towards them?*" Then, in design turn 2, author implements another set of choices in design, although they provide minimal expansion of the narrative trajectory. The choice node: "when you wake up" invites the player to select [[Melissa?]] or [[Are you okay?]], as does the other choice node "the next day."

The author has used the technical feature and seems to be figuring out how to use this feature narratively, opting for a temporal marker and conversational uses of choice options. The player responds to this conversational strategy with these reflections to the passage titled "the first conversation": "wow ten years have gone by and it feels like it was only yesterday where John and Melissa had their last encounter". The player, who had been "you," now refers to Melissa by her name, yet expresses empathy, with affect ("wow, it feels like it was only yesterday…") and repeating sequences from the story "ten years have gone by," "John and Melissa" "last encounter." On the third reflection turn, the player responded to the final connection from the author to the storyline around the story, to the passage "the meaning of the encounter": "wow I really like the ending to the story because this is a realistic ending where sometimes you have to let go of someone to be happy even if it hurts."

This design draws on personal narrating abilities, the integration of some new digital literary devices and seems to serve a socioemotional purpose. Character anchors the design, beginning with a player character device and self-dialogue to create drama with questions that anticipate a story of unrequited love, which was obviously appealing to the player. The player reflections were of the kind that sparked fluency, character development, and attempts at trajectory amplification. The TCM independently identified this design as increasing in overall trajectory shape (764.5 after design turn 1, 1110.6 after design turn 2, and 1233.5 after design turn 3, where the designer and player signed off).

This design demonstrates IDN development and a foundation for student and faculty curriculum ideas. Subsequent examination of this design, possibly compared to others, provides a basis for describing what is there, what some issues might be, and what support would be needed next. While this author emphasized character development, another emphasized different dimensions of basic IDN authoring.

5.2   Emotional Engagement of Player Looking in, then Invited

The protostory design we titled "The Amulet" without an author title is by a Hispanic male whose native language is Spanish. This author's approach to character and choice development differs from "The Encounter," with consequences for potential player engagement.

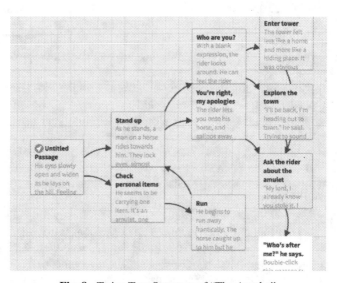

Fig. 8. Twine Tree Structure of "The Amulet"

The Twine picture in Fig. 8 shows the structure of "The Amulet." Different from "The Encounter", "The Amulet offers action-oriented choice options, such as [[Stand up to look around->Stand up]] or [[Check personal items]] and later on, [[Enter tower]] or [[Explore the town]] as well as conversational ones [[Who are you?]] or [[You're right, my apologies]]. The consequences of each also differ for the story trajectory. Options are also consequential, such as when one choice, "# Enter tower" leads to a conflict between the protagonist and the rider, who grabs his wrist reaching for the amulet, and the other, "Explore the town", leads to the rider violently smashing a mysteriously appearing hooded figure's face with a thick hammer. After the hooded figure falls back, the protagonist has his final awakening to "# Ask the rider about the amulet," finding that it has made him immortal. This design also has an increasing TCM (from 849.81 on design turn 1 to 1030.1, with a dip to 959.5 on design turn 3, and completing with 1122).

The different approaches to character and choice option development indicate the fertility of these devices for diverse learners as well as for IDN pedagogy and theory. These analyses introduce ideas about diversities and dynamics relevant to devices like character and choice, thereby adding to curricula and evaluations.

6   Discussion and Implications

This study with novice IDN designers' developments of characters and choices in relation to player feedback responds to the 2023 ICIDS conference theme is several ways. The Authoring-Other Exchange System workshop on the Sherlock platform blurs a boundary between beginning and experienced IDN designers and between the resources they bring to this fascinating complex creative genre. We asked students with no prior digital authoring experience to jump in as designers with exposure to a player, and they did. We also assumed that the undergraduates from the urban public university serving mostly ethnic/racial minority and bi-(tri+)-lingual students would bring resources especially relevant to a multi-symbolic aesthetic activity, like IDN designing, and they did.

Our workshop design included player engagement after design turns, and, as we learned in a previous study [6], that assisted novice IDN designers in positive ways. That these student designers used newly acquired digital devices to develop the quality of choice options from those involving more basic distinctions (here or there) to those involving more complex distinctions (hope or accept) while also animating characters to increase IDN narrative trajectories is remarkable. Although branching is only a first and basic device for taking up player-oriented narrating, these novice designers did so quickly and interactively with at least two other symbol systems – literary character and player subjectivity. Among numerous other possible uptake strategies, designers might have reduced character development while learning to use a digital mechanic and might have stuck to only simple choice options while taming the overall narrative structure. Making this learning process visible indicates that interactive digital narrative can build on prior narrative genres, with the introduction of a digital device to anchor the develop-ment of this complex conceptual/procedural system. In addition, the authors' different choice poetic strategies, such as one turning on character poetics and the other on action sequences, indicates the need to represent the IDN system with varying approaches.

IDN designing is, thus, a composing process and learning process to explore further for insights about theory and practice.

We learned with this quantitative and qualitative analysis that character and choice devices can anchor IDN design learning and that player interactions nudge peer authors to develop and provide bridges as well as foundations for ongoing authoring skill development. Analyses of interdependent strands of the IDN design process—narrative elements, digital devices, player engagement, and complex (non-linear) protostory construction – reveal shared and diverse design strategies. For example, some people used choice options to elaborate character development and character interactions, while others used choice options to expand possible story trajectories, such as with different conflicts, turning points, or resolutions. These and other approaches were fueled by player interactions and contributed to the growth of the Twine tree structure. With this systematic unification of four robust strands of analysis, we urge others to apply the workshop and analytic tools for future research projects with different IDN author groups, research questions, instructional time, and resources. Such future research can also offer validity checks and expansions of our methodology.

Patterns of character and choice poetics add to ongoing discoveries in the IDN field. For example, as highlighted in the diverse character enactments in the case studies as well as in the overall pattern of findings, players are engaged by diverse forms of character development, not only or primarily via identification with player characters, such as with "you." Consistent with other choice poetics research, we found that the development of choice options related to player feedback in terms of encouragement and other supports rather than to any apparent one-to-one matching of players' stated preferences/expectations for certain kinds of choices. Of course, a deeper understanding of IDN aesthetics will benefit from ongoing collaborative research.

We add to IDN pedagogy research [21–23] to suggest that a learning-by-doing introduction to authoring sets a foundation for subsequent examination by faculty and students themselves, as evidence of what they can do, what can't yet do, and insights about how they could advance their skills. In terms of poetics, these analyses indicated increasing attention to synergies of narrative and digital form. Prior linguistic and cultural resources come into play, including for students whose life histories may have prepared them especially for such poetics. Finally, because IDN integrates diverse kinds of functional symbolic tools, including digital mechanics, narrative elements, and expressive interaction, understanding how people learn this complex genre advances study of the mediated mind in human development and education research, as well as in IDN design pedagogy.

In summary, students' rapid uptake of a few digital tools (creating passages and linking options), sometimes seemingly spontaneously and at other times with the nudging of a player, anchored the development of characters and an increasingly complex story trajectory. As we stated at the onset of this article, IDN designing is a major challenge, yet the fact that it is so complex and, thus, can build on prior experience with language and social relations also makes the shift feasible and flexible. Including student designers as co-researchers with their teachers reflecting on their own beginning designs will further blur the boundary between research and practice.

References

1. Nelson, K.: Autobiographical Memory and the Construction of a Narrative Self. In: Fivush, R., Haden, C.A. (eds.) Developmental and Cultural Perspectives. Taylor & Francis Group (2003)
2. Koenitz, H.: Towards a specific theory of interactive digital narrative. In: Koenitz, H., Ferri, G., Haahr, M., Sezen, D., Sezen, T.I. (eds.) Interactive Digital Narrative, pp. 91–105. Routledge
3. Lee, C.D.: Toward a framework for culturally responsive design in multimedia computer environments: cultural modeling. Mind Cult. Act. **10**(1), 42–61 (2003)
4. Morrison, T.: The Source of Self-Regard, p. 264, Knopf (2019)
5. Gutiérrez, K.D., Baquedano-López, P., Alvarez, H.H., Chiu, M.M.: Building a culture of collaboration through hybrid language practices. Theory Into Pract. **38**(2), 87–93 (1999). https://doi.org/10.1080/00405849909543837
6. Daiute, C., Murray, J., Wright, J., Calistro, T.: Intersubjective picots in interactive digital narrative design learning. In: Vosmeer, M., Holloway-Attaway, L. (eds.) ICIDS 2022. LNCS 13762, vol. 13762, pp. 1–17 (2022). https://doi.org/10.1007/978-3-031-22298-6_22
7. Murray, J.T.: Telltale Hearts: Encoding Cinematic Choice-Based Adventure Games (2018). https://escholarship.org/uc/item/1n02n02z
8. Klimas, C.: Twinery: Twine Homepage (2009). https://twinery.org/
9. Barbara, J., Haahr, M.: Identification and IDNs in the metaverse: who would I like to be? In: Vosmeer, M., Holloway-Attaway (eds.) ICIDS 2022. LNCS, vol. 13762, pp. 601–615
10. Kukshinov, E., Shaw, A.: Playing with privilege: examining demographics in choosing player-characters in video games. Psychol. Popular Media **11**(1), 90–101 (2022). https://doi.org/10.1037/ppm0000378
11. Miles, A.P.: Jenkins, (Re)Born digital-trans-affirming research, curriculum, and pedagogy: an interactive multimodal story using Twine. Vis. Arts Res. **43**(1), 43–49 (2017)
12. Perreault, M.F., Perreault, G., Suarez, A.: What does it mean to be a female character in "Indie" game storytelling? Narrative framing and humanization in independently developed video games, games and culture **17**(2), 244–261 (2022). https://doi-org.ezproxy.gc.cuny.edu/10.1177/15554120211026279
13. Waddell, T.F., Moss, C.E., Holz, A., Ivory, J.D.: Character portrayals in digital games: a systematic review of more than three decades of existing research. J. Broadcast. Electron. Media **66**(4), 647–673 (2022). https://doi.org/10.1080/08838151.2022.2100376
14. Delhove, M., Greitemeyer, T.: The relationship between video game character preferences and aggressive and prosocial personality traits. Psychol. Popular Media **9**(1), 96–104 (2020)
15. Plass, J.L., et al.: Emotional design for digital games for learning: the effect of expression, color, shape, and dimensionality on the affective quality of game characters. Learn. Instr. **70** (2019) https://doi.org/10.1016/j.learninstruc.2019.01.005
16. Lee, T., Mitchell, A.: Filling the gaps: "shell" playable characters. In Rouse, R., Koenitz, H., Haahr, M. (eds). Interactive Digital Storytelling: ICIDS 2018, LNCS, vol. 11318, pp. 240–249. Springer, Cham (2018). https://doi.org/10.1007/978-3-030-04028-4_24
17. Chew, E.C., Mitchell, A.: Bringing art to life: examining poetic gameplay devices in interactive life stories. Games Cult **15**(5), 874–901 (2019)
18. Mawhorter, P., Mateas, M., Wardrip-Fruin, N.: Generating relaxed, obvious, and dilemma choices with Dunyazad. In: AAAI Conference on Artificial Intelligence and Interactive Digital Entertainment, pp. 58–64 (2015)
19. Atlas.ti. Scientific Software Development GmbH
20. Wright, J.J.: IDN tree complexity. MS thesis, School for Professional Studies, Graduate Center, City University of New York (2022). https://rpubs.com/JackJWright/902090Wirght, 2022

21. Barbara, J.: Authoring tools in teaching IDN: Design of LudoNarrative Dissonance. In: ICIDS (2020)
22. Bouchardon, S., Brunel, M.: Teaching literary interactive digital narratives in secondary education: a French study. In: Vosmeer, M., Holloway-Attaway, L. (eds.) ICIDS 2022. LNCS, vol. 13762, pp. 101–120 (2022)
23. Koenitz, H., Palosaari Eladhari, M.: Challenges of IDN Research and Teaching. In: ICIDS (2019)

On the Interactions Between Narrative Puzzles and Navigation Aids in Open World Games

Sam Davern$^{(\boxtimes)}$ and Mads Haahr

Trinity College Dublin, University of Dublin, Dublin, Ireland
{daverns,haahrm}@tcd.ie

Abstract. Narrative puzzles feature prominently in story-based open world video games where they form part of the progression of a narrative and require exploration and logical and creative thinking to solve. Open world games use navigation aids to help players solve narrative puzzles located across the vast worlds they provide. Narrative puzzles offer designers one of the most interactive methods of conveying a game's narrative, particularly in the action-adventure focused genre of open-world games. In this paper we discuss the interaction between narrative puzzles and navigation aids in open world games, highlighting in case studies of three different games how the amount of information a navigation aid provides impacts the intricacy and expansiveness of puzzles. Finally, we discuss the design implications of these interactions and suggest potential future analytical uses of the discussed framework.

Keywords: Navigation Aids · Narrative Puzzles · Open World · Video Games

1 Introduction

Open world games have emerged as one of the most popular forms of story-based video games over the last 20 years, such that open world video game franchises like *Assassin's Creed*, *Grand Theft Auto*, and *The Elder Scrolls* are some of the most successful franchises on the market. Moreover, video games are the most common and most popular medium for interactive storytelling, as reflected in the vast revenue generated by story-based games like *Grand Theft Auto V* [12] and in their significant cultural impact [19].

Open world games have previously been defined by Squire [35] (summarised by Min et al. [20]) as games that "enable players to explore and pursue gameplay objectives within expansive virtual worlds" (p. 2590). However this definition lacks precision and can also include games that are not typically considered to be open world such as The Legend of Zelda: Link's Awakening [25] (a fantasy action game), Sekiro: Shadows Die Twice [15] (a samurai action game) or games in the 'Metroidvania' genre. These games gradually grant access to their full worlds by gating this access behind narrative progression. Once the player has

© The Author(s), under exclusive license to Springer Nature Switzerland AG 2023
L. Holloway-Attaway and J. T. Murray (Eds.): ICIDS 2023, LNCS 14383, pp. 259–275, 2023.
https://doi.org/10.1007/978-3-031-47655-6_16

progressed through most of the narrative, they are free to traverse and explore the world at their leisure. The world is only truly open in the latter stages of the narrative, meaning that the majority of the game is spent in a world that is not freely explorable. Similarly, Aung and colleagues' [2] characterisation of open world games as "featuring large virtual worlds that can span hundreds of square kilometres of virtual real estate, with very few restrictions on the freedom of the player to go where they please; and a corresponding range of affordances" (p. 1) fails to account for game mechanics that are common across all open world games. As such, we will briefly discuss the core mechanics, design tenets, and narrative structure of open world games and arrive at a new definition.

In open world games, players typically have access to the game's entire world from the beginning (or after completing a short tutorial section) though it is also possible that access to a very limited number of large areas is only provided after completing key narrative content. While many open world games are also classified as role-playing games (RPGs) that focus on player customisation, a wide variety of other game genres have adopted the open world format such as racing games like *Forza Horizon 5* [29], survival games like *Subnautica* [38], 3D platformers like *Bowser's Fury* [27], and narrative adventure games like *Outer Wilds* [21]. Even though these genres of open world games can differ greatly from each other, they all focus on three key elements: exploration, autonomy and traversal. Exploration can be rewarded with narrative clues like records of conversations from lost ships in *Outer Wilds*, or collectable items like Korok seeds in *The Legend of Zelda: Breath of the Wild* (BOTW) [26] while autonomy rewards players' intrinsic motivation by allowing them to problem solve and choose how they want to play the game. Given that open world games contain large spaces to explore, most of them feature a variety of traversal mechanics. BOTW gives players a paraglider, horses, boats and a motorbike while also allowing players to climb almost every surface in the game. *Red Dead Redemption 2* [31] (an action game set in the 'Wild West') provides players with horses, boats, trains and carriages, while *Elden Ring* [16] (a fantasy RPG) has a 'spectral steed', fast travel points that allow players to respawn in a new location, and a number of portals scattered throughout the world.

Many open world games are designed for player autonomy by allowing players to complete certain key sections of the main narrative in whatever order they want; BOTW is a good example of this where the player can complete the four 'Divine Beast' dungeons in any order, or even not at all. However, while this feature is common in open world games, it is not universal. Story-based action games like *Grand Theft Auto V* [30] and *Red Dead Redemption 2* have linear main narratives that are supplemented by ancillary but ultimately optional side narrative content that can be completed in any order. Therefore, it cannot be said that a non-linear main narrative is a key feature of open world games but it can be said that smaller ancillary non-linear narratives that can be completed in any order are a very common feature. Whereas the main narrative can be linear or non-linear, optional ancillary narrative content is inherently non-linear. With the above in mind, we propose the following working definition of an open world game:

> "A game that takes place in a large, freely traversable world, rewards exploration, affords significant player autonomy, and can include non-linear ancillary narrative content."

This definition allows for flexibility in the structure and core mechanics of any type of open world game, not just story-based ones and is applicable to even the earliest open world games like *Hydlide* [36], *Ultima I* [17], and *Courageous Perseus* [8], all of which are fantasy RPGs that employ mechanics from tabletop RPGs like Dungeons & Dragons.

Players can progress through the core narrative and other optional narrative content by reaching particular milestones, watching animated cut-scenes, and completing narrative puzzles. As Murray [24] states, interactive digital narratives (IDN) exhibit both spatial and encyclopedic affordances, which open world games take full advantage of. When considering narrative puzzles specifically, the large size of game worlds in open world games requires that exploration and traversal be incorporated into a game's narrative and by extension are often instrumental in the solution of narrative puzzles in open world games. Designers of open world games can take advantage of their expansive landscapes to create narrative puzzles that span large sections of the world. However, if they are to do this successfully, they will need to take into account how navigation aids interact with narrative puzzles.

2   Narrative Puzzles

Puzzles in games refer to tasks that "provide the player with a challenge that has one solution, and requires thinking rather than skills" [13]. By extension, narrative puzzles have been defined as:

> "puzzles that form part of the progression of the narrative, whose solutions involve exploration and logical as well as creative thinking" (p. 1) [11].

Narrative puzzles represent one of the most interactive means of delivering narrative content given that they require players' actions to be the driving force behind a the progression of a narrative. In focusing on narrative puzzles forming part of the progression of the narrative rather than simply being a narrative event, the definition provided by De Kegel and Haahr [11] can be interpreted as narrative puzzles needing to be part of the main narrative of a game to be considered to be a narrative puzzle. In the case of story-based open world games, narrative puzzles can be used to progress *a* narrative rather than *the* narrative. Ancillary narrative content in particular is often experienced through narrative puzzles. Therefore, we will update this definition such that a narrative puzzles are puzzles that form part of the progression of a narrative, whose solutions involve exploration and logical as well as creative thinking.   The concept of

Fig. 1. A screen from *The Case of the Golden Idol.*

narrative puzzles is closely tied to Bogost's theory of procedural rhetoric wherein an idea is conveyed effectively through computational processes rather than audiovisual means [3]. Narrative puzzles challenge the player to understand a game's systems, how these systems interact with each other and how they can be manipulated by the player to create a desirable outcome. Bogost relates interactivity in the context of procedural rhetoric to the Arsitotelian enthymeme where a proposition in a logical argument is omitted and it is the responsibility of the listener (or player in the case of a game) to intuit this proposition and complete the argument. With regards to narrative puzzles, puzzles must be designed such that a player can intuit the solution based on their understanding of what the game's systems afford, i.e., the game's procedural rhetoric. A key must open a lock, water must quench a fire, a healing potion must heal, and so on.

Narrative puzzles have most commonly been found in the adventure game genre, dating back to *Colossal Cave Adventure* [9,10]. Adventure games are games wherein the player assumes the role of a character in a fantasy world and engages in exploration and puzzle solving to progress the narrative [32]. Fernández-Vara and Thomson [14] provide examples of the types of narrative puzzles found in adventure games; these include receiving a reward for giving someone an object, creating a new object by combining other objects, altering the state of an object, convincing characters to help the player, and finding keys to access new areas.

Adventure games' narratives are typically quite linear and progression through the narrative is only achievable by solving narrative puzzles. For example, in *The Case of the Golden Idol* [7], narrative progression is contingent on the player solving the murders of various characters that interact with the eponymous Golden Idol. Through solving the murders by exploring and manipulating items in the murder scene vignettes presented to the player, the overarching narrative of the game can be discerned. Solving these narrative puzzles focuses heavily on exploration and environmental manipulation and the diegetic environment in which players must solve the narrative puzzles is quite small at only a few screens/vignettes per puzzle (Fig. 1).

In 3D games with larger worlds, such as the survival horror game *Resident Evil 4* (RE4) [4], the proportion of the whole puzzle space visible per frame is significantly smaller than the visible puzzle spaces in 2D games like *The Case of the Golden Idol*. The expansiveness displayed by RE4 requires the player to explore more and highlights how traversal of a 3D space is necessary to solve a narrative puzzle in 3D games. However, games with larger worlds typically feature narrative puzzles that, while not serving as a key element in the progression of the main narrative, still reveal new aspects of the game's narrative that the player can choose to engage with or not. In the remake of *Dead Space* [22], a puzzle involving locating a specific tissue sample and placing it in a medical device gives the player more information about the game's narrative. This narrative content supplements the main plot but is not required for progression, highlighting how adventure games with large, explorable worlds can use narrative puzzles to present optional narrative content. Similarly in RE4, a puzzle involving paintings of sacrificial victims does not add to the main plot but reinforces the game's tone and the nature of the threat the player character faces.

As with larger adventure games, open world games feature narrative puzzles as both a means to progress the main narrative of the game and to present ancillary narrative content. In *Red Dead Redemption 2*, exploring the city of Saint Denis to map the locations of ominous graffiti leads players to finding and fighting a Nosferatu-like vampire that has been killing victims throughout the city. Similarly, in *The Legend of Zelda: Breath of the Wild*, a character named Kass will play folkloric songs containing riddles that must be interpreted to solve nearby puzzles by performing a particular action, waiting until a particular time of day, or combining different items. In both of these games, the solution to the narrative puzzles exists within a limited distance from the onset of the puzzle. However, as open world games usually allow players to explore at their leisure, they afford puzzle designers the opportunity to distribute puzzle components across the whole open world. In order to explore the open world and find all of the puzzle components, players need systems that allow them to navigate and traverse the world.

3   Navigation Aids

As we have discussed, story-based open world games can feature large game worlds with narrative puzzles that incorporate exploration and traversal into their solutions. Given that many people use navigation aids like GPS map smartphone apps to navigate familiar and unfamiliar areas, players too need tools to help them navigate large digital open worlds. In their meta-analysis of theories of spatial knowledge acquisition, Ahmadpoor and Shahab [1] highlight how the two external factors that influence cognitive mapping are the means/tools used in navigation, and the physical characteristics of the environment. When considering this in the context of open world games, physical characteristics of the environment can refer to the world's level design while means/tools can refer to navigation aids. For the purposes of this analysis, we will be focusing mainly on navigation aids, although the intersection between narrative puzzles and level design is also worthy of investigation.

Chittaro and Burigat [6] refer to navigation aids (NAs) in virtual environments as "electronic analogues of the tools commonly used by people to navigate unfamiliar real-world environments" (p. 2) and while this definition is applicable to video games, it does not allow for NAs that do not aim to emulate the functions of real-world navigation tools. Moura and El-Nasr [23] argue that video game navigation aids are any elements that give players directions, help them identify a location, or determine their current orientation such as maps, markers, directions from characters, GPS, a compass, and subtitles that state locations or directions. However, their definition is still limited especially when considering exploration in open world games where navigation can involve terrain assessment and the passive appraisal of players' surroundings (e.g., treacherousness of a terrain, or relative safety of a particular area).

In the case of open world games, they can refer to systems a game explicitly provides players to help them navigate in the world of the game. These can include maps, character dialogue, compasses, markers, tools to assess the environment, and HUD elements like mini-maps and location names. For the purposes of this analysis, techniques used to indirectly guide players through the world (e.g., lighting and landmarks) will not be included as navigational aids because they relate more to level design than the design of systems used to aid navigation. Not only is exploration a key aspect of open world games, but it is also a key aspect of narrative puzzles [14]. Therefore, the successful implementation of narrative puzzles in open world games requires the inclusion of effective navigation aids.

4   Case Studies from Open World Games

The following section provides examples of narrative puzzles from popular open world games and their accompanying navigation aids. The games detailed in these case studies were chosen from an ongoing survey of navigation aids in open world games that the authors are conducting. These particular games were chosen due to their recency, popularity, and level of accessibility on modern platforms to ensure that the maximum number of readers will have first-hand experience with them. The games and narrative puzzles chosen, alongside their respective navigation aids, are presented in Table 1.

4.1   Elden Ring

In *Elden Ring* (ER) [16], players must traverse a dangerous, dark fantasy realm to collect pieces of the 'Elden Ring' and restore order to the world. One of the core

Table 1. Games, narrative puzzles, and navigation aids used in this analysis.

Games	Narrative Puzzles	Navigation Aids
Elden Ring	'Grand Lift of Dectus' Puzzle	Main map
		Custom map markers
		Compass
		Item descriptions
		NPC Dialogue
Assassin's Creed: Valhalla	'The Doom Book of Cats'	Main map
		Quest markers
		Compass
		NPC Dialogue & Actions
		'Odin's Sight' filter
The Witcher 3: Wild Hunt	'Missing in Action' & 'Twisted Firestarter'	Main map
		Quest markers
		Compass
		NPC Dialogue & Actions
		'Witcher Senses' filter

narrative puzzles in ER concerns the Grand Lift of Dectus, an enormous elevator that grants players access to the Altus Plateau, a key area in the progression of the game's main narrative. This puzzle requires the player to find and present both the left and right halves of the 'Dectus Medallion' while standing on the Grand Lift of Dectus. Doing so will operate the Lift and transport the player to the Altus Plateau. The puzzle can be initiated at three different points: at the location of each medallion half, or at the Lift itself. Should players find a medallion half first, they must use the item description ("The right half is said to reside in Fort Faroth in the Dragonbarrow, far to the east.") and limited main map to find the second half and the Lift itself. Should they first find the Lift, NPC's dialogue will hint towards the nature of the Lift and that something is needed to operate it (Fig. 2).

Regarding the first two initiation points, the player may or may not have already discovered the forts that store the medallion halves. If they have found them, they need only travel back to the location of the fort shown on their map. If they have not found them, they need to use both the map and the medallion item description to find the location of each respective fort. The item description gives them the direction they need to travel from the discovered medallion to find the undiscovered one. The hand-drawn main map (Fig. 3) features simple sketches of walls where buildings are located. To find the second half of the medallion, the player would need to locate the buildings on the map in thedirection indicated

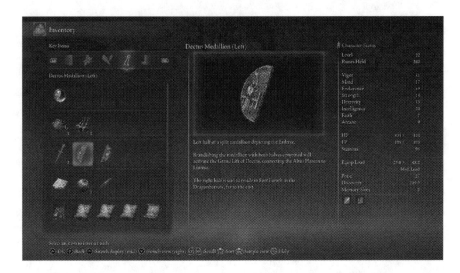

Fig. 2. Item description for Dectus Medallion (Left) in *Elden Ring*.

Fig. 3. The main map in *Elden Ring*.

by the item description. Doing so will eventually bring them to the relevant fort. They must also find the location of the Lift, which the item description notes is used to connect the Altus Plateau to Liurnia (the only area through which the Altus Plateau is accessible). To do this, they need to explore the border of Liurnia using the map or use the map to find locations that appear to be significant and investigating them.

If the player starts the puzzle by first finding the Grand Lift of Dectus, they still need to explore, unprompted, to find the medallions (an NPC's cryptic dialogue implies that there is some way to activate the Lift but no further information is given). It is also possible that a player may discover all three initiation points in any order through self-motivated exploration. Therefore, the potential for the player to find all components of the puzzle without realizing a puzzle exists is relatively high. However, if the player is to knowingly engage with the puzzle, they must make use of several navigation aids (e.g., the main map, the item descriptions, custom markers, compass etc.) to solve it. This puzzle spans a significant portion of the game's entire map, requiring players traverse great distances in search of the medallion halves. Conversely, while the hints provided by the item descriptions and NPC dialogue are cryptic and harder to intuit, the puzzle only requires three actions to be completed, i.e., collect each medallion half and then combine them. The mental challenge lies in finding the medallion halves using the limited amount of information that the navigation aids provide.

4.2   Assassin's Creed: Valhalla

In *Assassin's Creed: Valhalla* (ACV) [37], players play as Eivor, a Viking leader who invades and pillages England in the 9th Century and interacts with various historical figures from the period. A large number of small narrative puzzles are present throughout the game's world. They are labelled as 'World Events' and the initiation point of the puzzle is marked on the map with a blue rune quest marker. Players typically interact with an NPC and complete a small number of tasks that require logical reasoning, before returning to the NPC to conclude the puzzle. For instance, in the "The Doom Book of Cats" world event, the player meets a farmer who is trying to rid his fields of rats but has no effective means to do so. Further along the road, a woman is tending to a large number of cats. It is up to the player to deduce that the cats can be used to kill the rats and that the woman must be convinced to allow the player to use the cats for this purpose through the selection of specific dialogue options. Once the player has sent the cats to kill the rats, the farmer grants the player access to his home to take some valuable materials as thanks. All elements of the puzzle are located within a very small area (it only takes a matter of seconds to reach the house with the cats from the farmer's house) and scanning the environment with 'Odin's Sight' will place a filter over the world that highlights the location of interactable NPCs (Fig. 4). Similarly, the NPCs involved in the puzzle have a text box icon hovering above them when the player is within a close range. This formula is mirrored in most other 'World Events': the solution to the puzzle, or at least the area that contains the solution, is visible from the location of the puzzle's initiation. As players need only survey their immediate environment (sometimes with the aid of Odin's Sight or the presence of NPC icons) to find the solution to the puzzle, there is little need for any other navigation aids.

4.3   The Witcher 3: Wild Hunt

In *The Witcher 3: Wild Hunt* (TW3) [5], players take on the role of monster hunter-for-hire Geralt of Rivia as he travels across the fantasy world of the

Fig. 4. The Doom Book of Cats puzzle space; the farmer is in the middle ground and the woman is in the background. From *Assassin's Creed: Valhalla*.

Continent. One of the game's optional narrative puzzles involves finding a soldier who is missing in action. Players take on the request at a noticeboard in a village, track the puzzle in the HUD, and travel to the location marked on the mini-map. They will meet the brother of the missing soldier who will tell the player that solider was last seen on a nearby battlefield. A new quest marker directs the player towards the battlefield where the brother asks the player to find shields with the soldier's insignia on them. The player must use their Witcher Senses to find the shields. These 'Witcher Senses' constitute a filter placed over the world that highlights important interactable elements with a red glow. The map displays the area within which all the shields are located. Once the correct shield is found, the brother's dog catches the soldier's scent and guides the player to him. In this puzzle, all relevant areas, even the approximate location of the solution (the correct shield) are shown on the main map and mini-map. The maps also plot a route to each key location. The navigation aids direct the player to both the battlefield and the correct shield, reducing the difficulty of the puzzle. Another puzzle involves the player locating the arsonist who burned down the local blacksmith's workshop. After using the Geralt's Witcher Senses to follow the arsonist's footprints to a river (Fig. 5), it is discovered that the arsonist was attacked by a monster and lost his shoes in the struggle. The player must then follow the trail of blood to a house where they must look for an injured, barefoot man. In this instance, the main navigation aid used is the Witcher Senses ability that highlights the footprints and blood on the ground. The player must use these to solve the puzzle as opposed to travelling to a pre-determined location marked on the map. In both of these puzzles, the navigation aids provide players with enough information such that while they require more actions to solve than the puzzle in ER, the mental challenge presented is minimal.

Fig. 5. Footprints visible in the mud through use of the Witcher Senses. From *The Witcher 3: Wild Hunt.*

5   Interactions Between Narrative Puzzles and Navigation Aids in the Case Studies

Based on the case studies outlined above, it can be seen that the amount of information a navigation aid provides can affect how far a player must travel to complete a puzzle, and how complex and mentally challenging a puzzle is. As such, navigation aids interact with narrative puzzles to affect puzzle design on two different continua: intricacy, and expansiveness. Below, we will take examples of narrative puzzles and navigation aids from the three case studies outlined above and discuss how an open world game's navigation aids can impact the intricacy and expansiveness of its narrative puzzles.

5.1   Intricacy

We use the term intricacy to refer to the number of components in a narrative puzzle in concert with how mentally challenging it is. A component can be an action that needs to be taken or a tool that needs to be used. Mental challenge refers to how much logical and creative thinking is required to solve the puzzle. Out of the examples above, ER presents the most intricate puzzle while ACV presents the least intricate narrative puzzles.

For the purposes of this discussion, it is assumed the player intends to pursue the Grand Lift of Dectus puzzle after reaching one of the first two initiation points discussed above. After finding the first half of the medallion, they must use the navigation aids provided to find the second half and to find the location of the Grand Lift of Dectus. The main NAs used to solve this puzzle are the main map, the HUD compass, custom map/environment markers, and item descriptions. The main map is a full-colour, hand-drawn representation of the game's world onto which players can place blue custom map markers. Once a map marker is placed, a pillar of blue light is visible in the game's world at the corresponding location, as well as a blue marker on the HUD compass. To solve the Dectus puzzle, players need to plot a course to the second half of the medallion and the Dectus Lift itself. Map markers can be used to mark a route on the map that will be visible in the world. The map itself features rough outlines of buildings along with names of each main region in the game. To find the second half of the medallion, players must find the fort specified in the item description of the discovered medallion half. To achieve this, they can use the directions in the item description; for instance "The right half is said to reside in Fort Faroth in the Dragonbarrow, far to the east". They now must locate Dragonbarrow and then locate a specific fort within it. This involves searching the far east of the map for the outline of a building and travelling to it to determine if it is the correct one. Similarly, the item description states that the Dectus Lift connects Liurnia with the Altus Plateau and as such, players need to use the map to look for structures along the borders of Liurnia and then travel to them to determine which one is correct.

The lack of explicit instruction given to the player through the navigation aids is what makes it mentally challenging, and therefore intricate. Players need to consider the clues they are given in the context of the game world and use the NAs provided to act on them. The main map is relatively abstract when compared to main maps in most modern open world games; the main map in ACV features dynamic location markers for sites of interest, shops, bars, treasure etc. as well as the inclusion of location names that increase in granularity as the player zooms in. The top-down view of the world is so detailed that it is possible to discern individual trees and fields. If the same puzzle were present in ACV, the player need only scan the map for the name of the fort to find its exact location. In this way, the puzzle is not only less mentally challenging but also has less components (e.g., players can ignore details on the map, removing the need for them to solve the puzzle). The exploration and interpretation of the navigation aids required to complete the puzzle in ER is significantly diluted in ACV.

Similarly, in TW3, navigation aids are used as a means of explicitly directing players to each successive component of certain puzzles. In the case of the "Twisted Firestarter" puzzle, the player must use their Witcher Senses to follow a trail to a river, investigate the scene of an attack, and follow a trail of blood to a house. Only then does the player need to inspect NPCs to determine who is injured. Throughout the course of this puzzle, each area containing the next clue is highlighted on the mini map with an orange circle; each action the player needs to take is clearly signposted with the navigation aids. Guiding players in this way reduces how mentally challenging the puzzle is and in turn reduces its intricacy. The amount of information an NA gives to a player can significantly impact the intricacy of a game's narrative puzzles as engagement with and the interpretation of NAs are key elements in the solution of narrative puzzles in open world games.

5.2 Expansiveness

We use the term expansiveness to refer to the how much physical space must be traversed to complete the puzzle. From the examples, ER has the most expansive puzzle while ACV's puzzles are the least expansive. ACV provides particularly interesting examples as even though the game features very detailed navigation aids (the main map provides the locations of almost all points of interest) they are not implemented in its narrative puzzles. As such, the components of many of the game's narrative puzzles are located within a small radius of where the puzzle is initiated. In ACV, the solution to the puzzle, the woman who owns a lot of cats, is clearly visible from the location of the farmer who acts as the beginning of the puzzle (Fig. 4). Only two navigation aids can be used to aid the solution of this puzzle: floating point markers highlighting the location of interactable NPCs, and the 'Odin's Sight' ability that similarly highlights interactable NPCs. Given that this puzzle does not require the use of the more detailed navigation aids like the main map, it cannot have large distances between its components as players could easily lose track of their progress in the puzzle or lose track of the puzzle altogether due to the immense scale of the game's world. Had this puzzle, and other 'World Events' in ACV incorporated the navigation aids in the game into their solution, it would have allowed the puzzles to be more expansive and to take advantage of the affordances of the game's large explorable world. These puzzles adopt the approach taken by narrative puzzles in smaller adventure games wherein only a limited puzzle space needs to be explored to find the solution. As such, the narrative puzzles, or 'World Events', in ACV are presented as a series of small, discrete puzzle spaces dotted across a large open world. Players can find them using the blue dots that appear on the main map but once they have reached the puzzle space, the navigation aids are not required to solve the puzzle.

In contrast, the Dectus Lift puzzle in ER takes full advantage of the game's navigation aids to make the puzzle very expansive; in this instance, the puzzle space is approximately half of the game's full map. The design of this puzzle takes into account the fact that players can use the main map, custom map markers, and HUD compass to help them to interpret the clues in the medallion halves' item descriptions and aid them in exploring the world in search of the solution to the puzzle. Similarly, TW3 uses its navigation aids to make the "Twisted Firestarter" puzzle more expansive. As part of the puzzle, the player must follow tracks out of a village, across a river and back around to the village again. Throughout the course of this journey, the player is explicitly guided by the game's navigation aids; the Witcher Senses highlight the tracks and evidence that the player needs to follow, and the mini-map displays orange circles placed on the map to indicate the approximate area of the next part of the trail to investigate. The approach taken here allows the puzzle to be more expansive but does not afford the player a great deal of autonomy in how they approach solving the puzzle. As such, incorporating, or at least accounting for, NAs when designing narrative puzzles allows them to be much more expansive and takes full advantage of the exploratory affordances of open world games.

6   Design Implications

Based on the understanding that the information navigation aids provides impact narrative puzzles on the continua of intricacy and expansiveness, we present several design implications ground in IDN theory.

Regarding the design of narrative puzzles and navigation aids for expansiveness, it is worthwhile to consider Ryan's [33] discussion of the concept of 'flânerie' in relation to the emotional and strategic experience of digital space. Ryan argues that a digital space, like physical space, can be experienced both emotionally (where traversing a space elicits emotion in the traveler) and strategically (where a traversal is viewed as a means to an end in service of a seperate goal). 'Flânerie', as Ryan describes it, encapsulates the experience of "free wandering, open to chance meetings and random discoveries" wherein a space is traversed simply for the joy of traversal and the aesthetic opportunities this affords. In the case of the most expansive puzzle from the case studies above, the 'Dectus Lift' in ER, progress in the puzzle is contingent on the player discovering at least one of the three potential initiation points. Without these, the player is not aware that this puzzle even exists and as such, must explore the world to happen upon one. Therefore, designing for flânerie is a useful of way of encouraging this exploration. ER succeeds in this respect by not only providing a large world that is well designed and aesthetically pleasing but also in its relatively limited use of navigation aids, specifically the lack of quest markers. Players must rely on flânerie, rather than quest markers as in ACV and TW3, to guide them through the world in order to find the 'Dectus Lift' puzzle. In this way, considered world design coupled with navigation aids that don't provide excessive information can promote flânerie in players, allowing the design of expansive narrative puzzles whose solutions rely less on using information rich navigation aids to direct players across vast distances, and that are more mentally challenging.

As previously mentioned, the use of information rich navigation aids can reduce the mental challenge associated with a puzzle, thereby reducing its intricacy. Similarly, simply reducing the number of components of a puzzle will also reduce its intricacy. Designing for intricacy therefore requires a puzzle to not only be mentally challenging (e.g., less reliance on direct instruction from navigation aids) but to also have many components. Ensuring that players can successfully intuit or decipher the solution to a puzzle in a way that promotes agency and is satisfying to complete is important to the design of an intricate puzzle. Considering the procedural and encyclopedic affordances of IDNs [24] alongside their ability to instantiate a narrative based on a protostory [18], a focus on systems driven gameplay in concert with effective narrative framing could be beneficial. As Spierling [34] notes, the framing narrative of a game can be employed to give players an implicit understanding of what a game's systems afford, much like creating a mental model in interaction design [28]. Players implicitly understanding a game's affordances can allow puzzle designers to greatly increase both the number of puzzle components and the mental challenge associated with narrative puzzles; the responsibility of directing the player to each puzzle component is removed from information rich navigation aids and assigned to the player's mental model of the game's affordances. As a basic example, if a potion requires a fish that lives in the dark, players should be able to intuit that they can find a cave fish in the nearby cave that they heard about from an NPC or through their own flânerie-driven exploration. Constructing both an effective framing narrative and systems that can map interactions between a wide variety of items and actions can be complex an time consuming but can also afford the design of more sophisticated and intricate narrative puzzles.

7   Conclusions and Future Work

Narrative puzzles are an integral part of story-based open world video games and the ways in which they interact with navigation aids can significantly impact their intricacy and expansiveness. When designing narrative puzzles for open world games it is important to take the design of the game's navigation aids into account as not doing so could make the puzzles boring or frustrating or could limit their scope. Designing for flânerie and placing a focus on systemic and intuitive gameplay can help prevent a game's narrative puzzles becoming trivial and unsatisfying.

The categorization of narrative puzzles according to their intricacy and expansiveness could prove to be a useful analytical tool going forward. For instance, plotting puzzles on a graph with Intricacy and Expansiveness on its axes, as in Fig. 6, would allow one to analyze the structure of puzzles in a variety of open world games, or even the structure of puzzles in a single open world game. Clusters of points on the graph could be used to differentiate and categorize puzzles in different games and aid games studies researchers and game designers in their analyses of particular games. The question of how to quantify intricacy and expansiveness such that they can be represented on a graph remains an open question (the examples in Fig. 6 are represented relative to one another) but one that could no doubt be addressed in future work. Going forward, it could be useful to analyse narrative puzzles in story-based open world games along the continua of intricacy and expansiveness both during and after a game's development.

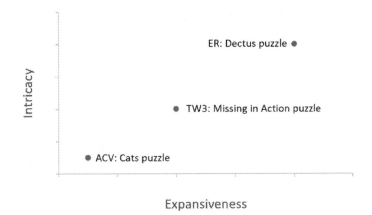

Acknowledgments. This work was conducted with the financial support of the Science Foundation Ireland (SFI) Centre for Research Training in Digitally-Enhanced Reality (d-real) under Grant No. 18/CRT/6224.

References

1. Ahmadpoor, N., Shahab, S.: Spatial knowledge acquisition in the process of navigation: a review. Curr. Urban Stud. **7**(1), 1–19 (2019)
2. Aung, M., et al.: The trails of just cause 2: spatio-temporal player profiling in open-world games. In: Proceedings of the 14th International Conference on the Foundations of Digital Games, pp. 1–11 (2019)
3. Bogost, I.: Persuasive Games: The Expressive Power of Videogames. MIT Press, Cambridge (2010)
4. Capcom Production Studio 4: Resident Evil 4 (2005)
5. CD Projekt Red: The Witcher 3: Wild Hunt (2015)
6. Chittaro, L., Burigat, S.: 3D location-pointing as a navigation aid in virtual environments. In: Proceedings of the Working Conference on Advanced Visual Interfaces, pp. 267–274 (2004)
7. Color Gray Games: The Case of the Golden Idol (2022)
8. Cosmos Computer: Courageous Perseus (1984)
9. Crowther, W.: Colossal Cave Adventure (1976)
10. Crowther, W., Woods, D.: Colossal Cave Adventure (1977)
11. De Kegel, B., Haahr, M.: Towards procedural generation of narrative puzzles for adventure games. In: Cardona-Rivera, R.E., Sullivan, A., Young, R.M. (eds.) ICIDS 2019. LNCS, vol. 11869, pp. 241–249. Springer, Cham (2019). https://doi.org/10.1007/978-3-030-33894-7_25
12. Donnelly, J.: GTA 5 estimated to be the most profitable entertainment product of all time (2018). https://www.pcgamer.com/gta-5-estimated-to-be-the-most-profitable-entertainment-product-of-all-time/
13. Fernández-Vara, C.: Introduction to Game Analysis. Routledge, Milton Park (2019)

14. Fernández-Vara, C., Thomson, A.: Procedural generation of narrative puzzles in adventure games: the puzzle-dice system. In: Proceedings of the The Third Workshop on Procedural Content Generation in Games, pp. 1–6 (2012)
15. FromSoftware Inc.: Sekiro: Shadows Die Twice (2019)
16. FromSoftware Inc.: Elden Ring (2022)
17. Garriot, R. and Origin Systems: Ultima 1 (1981)
18. Koenitz, H.: Understanding Interactive Digital Narrative: Immersive Expressions for a Complex Time. Taylor & Francis, Milton Park (2023)
19. MacCallum-Stewart, E., Stenros, J., Björk, S.: The impact of role-playing games on culture. In: Role-Playing Game Studies, pp. 172–187. Routledge (2018)
20. Min, W., Mott, B.W., Rowe, J.P., Liu, B., Lester, J.C.: Player goal recognition in open-world digital games with long short-term memory networks. In: IJCAI, pp. 2590–2596 (2016)
21. Mobius Digital: Outer Wilds (2019)
22. Motive: Dead Space (2023)
23. Moura, D., El-Nasr, M.S.: Design techniques for planning navigational systems in 3-D video games. Comput. Entertain. (CIE) 12(2), 1–25 (2015)
24. Murray, J.H.: Hamlet on the Holodeck, updated edition: The Future of Narrative in Cyberspace. MIT Press, Cambridge (2017)
25. Nintendo EAD: The Legend of Zelda: Link's Awakening (1993)
26. Nintendo EAD: The Legend of Zelda: Breath of the Wild (2017)
27. Nintendo EPD: Bowser's Fury (2021)
28. Norman, D.: The Design of Everyday Things: Revised and expanded edition. Basic Books, New York (2013)
29. Playground Games: Forza Horizon 5 (2021)
30. Rockstar Games: Grand Theft Auto V (2013)
31. Rockstar Games: Red Dead Redemption 2 (2018)
32. Rollings, A., Adams, E.: Andrew Rollings and Ernest Adams on game design. New Riders, Berkeley (2003)
33. Ryan, M.L.: Emotional and strategic conceptions of space in digital narratives. In: Interactive Digital Narrative, pp. 106–120. Routledge (2015)
34. Spierling, U.: Interaction design principles as narrative techniques for interactive digital storytelling. In: Interactive Digital Narrative: History, Theory, and Practice, pp. 159–173 (2015)
35. Squire, K.: Open-ended video games: A model for developing learning for the interactive age. MacArthur Foundation Digital Media and Learning Initiative (2007)
36. T&E Soft: Hydlide (1984)
37. Ubisoft Montreal: Assassin's Creed: Valhalla (2020)
38. Unknown Worlds Entertainment: Subnautica (2018)

Lovecraftian Horror in Story-Driven Games: Narrative Design Challenges and Solutions

Mads Haahr[✉] 🆔

Trinity College Dublin, University of Dublin, Dublin, Ireland
haahrm@tcd.ie

Abstract. Cosmic horror, or Lovecraftian horror, is an important subgenre in horror fiction, which is concerned with the horror of the unknowable and incomprehensible. In cosmic horror, the thin veil of human sense-making through which we ordinarily perceive the world is inevitably destroyed through a confrontation with a deep and terrible truth about the universe. For the story protagonists, the encounter with the true nature of things practically always results in madness or death, or at least denial of the events that took place. While cosmic horror originates in literature, significant works exist also in films, graphic novels and games. However, while many games include elements from cosmic horror, the themes and genre conventions of cosmic horror mean that it is far from trivial for games to engage genuinely with the genre. This paper explores the potential for games to capture the feelings of experience of a Lovecraft story authentically via their mechanics and design. We give an overview of the genre conventions of literary cosmic horror and identify six narrative design "challenges" where the genre conventions of narrative-driven games appear to be directly incompatible with those of literary cosmic horror. For each challenge, we discuss the depth and nature of the seemingly irreconcilable differences and use examples from narrative horror games (Lovecraftian and otherwise) to identify potential solutions. Can games and cosmic horror really be mixed? And, if so, how?

Keywords: Lovecraftian horror · Cosmic horror · Game narrative · Interactive narrative design

1 Introduction

Cosmic horror, or Lovecraftian horror, is an important subgenre in horror fiction, which is concerned with the horror of the unknowable and incomprehensible [1]. Genre conventions place the human protagonists against monstrous antagonists that are impossible to overcome, or even to understand. In cosmic horror, the thin veil of human sense-making through which we ordinarily perceive the world is inevitably destroyed through a confrontation with a deep and terrible truth about the universe; and the encounter with the true nature of things practically always results in madness or death.

While cosmic horror originates in literature, significant works exist also in films [6], TV series [22] and graphic novels [10]. An increasing number of games are also classified

© The Author(s), under exclusive license to Springer Nature Switzerland AG 2023
L. Holloway-Attaway and J. T. Murray (Eds.): ICIDS 2023, LNCS 14383, pp. 276–290, 2023.
https://doi.org/10.1007/978-3-031-47655-6_17

as Lovecraftian, by critics as well as gamers. For example, as of 14 June 2023, a Steam search for "Lovecraftian" returned 1163 results, and 620 games were specifically tagged as "Lovecraftian." However, even though many games include elements from cosmic horror, it is far from trivial for games to engage genuinely with the genre. In fact, I would argue that of the many supposedly Lovecraftian games, few offer a genuine engagement with the idea of cosmic horror as we know it from literature. Games often borrow surface level elements (e.g., tentacled monsters) rather than engage deeply with the genre (e.g., instilling a sense of cosmic dread). Kevin Flanagan has explored this in some detail, but his focus is on "the sheer variety of approaches" to Lovecraftian horror in games, rather than on the specific ability (or inability) of games to "capture the feelings of experience of a Lovecraft story via its mechanics and design" [5].

In this paper, cosmic horror is of interest to us exactly because of its ability to evoke feelings of a Lovecraft story, because these are not typically within range of game experiences. We consider the ability to evoke feelings of cosmic dread an expansion of the range of procedural rhetoric available to games as a medium, which is valuable for the narrative games to mature as a form of storytelling. In this fashion, we are concerned with the expressivity of games as a storytelling medium. It is for this reason, that the paper explores the potential for games to capture the feelings of experience of a Lovecraft story authentically via its mechanics and design. As a starting point, we argue that there seems to be a seemingly irreconcilable relationship between the most important cosmic horror conventions from literature and the genre conventions (perhaps even inherent characteristics) of story-driven games. Drawing upon a selection of horror games (Lovecraftian and otherwise) from the last three decades, our intention is to present a deep analysis of the challenges related to making cosmic horror work in games and chart the possible solutions. Can games and cosmic horror really be mixed? And, if so, how?

2 Cosmic Horror Conventions from Literature

The originator of cosmic horror is the American writer H. P. Lovecraft (1890–1937). Rather than being concerned with gore and shock as is known from many other sub-genres of horror, cosmic horror themes include cosmic dread, forbidden and dangerous knowledge, madness, non-human influences on humanity, religion and superstition, fate and inevitability, and the risks associated with scientific discoveries. While Lovecraft's contribution to the horror genre is very significant, his legacy is also encumbered by racism [22–24]. Fortunately, modern creative works in cosmic horror show that racism and racial anxieties are not integral to the genre, and that cosmic horror in fact can be used to *critique* racism, as Dan Hassler-Forest observes in his analysis of the TV series *Lovecraft Country* (2020) [22].

In relation to genre conventions, Donald Burleson [1] has identified five major themes in Lovecraft's writings:

1. *Denied primacy*: Humans are neither the first or last civilization on Earth and has never really been the foremost.
2. *Forbidden knowledge* (or *merciful ignorance*): Some types of knowledge are so terrible that wellbeing can only be maintained through avoidance or suppression.

3. *Illusory surface appearances*: Things are not as they seem, and underneath lies a deeper and more terrible reality.
4. *Unwholesome survival*: Some things and beings outlive their rightful existence and encroach on human existence.
5. *Oneiric objectivism*: Any distinction between reality and dreams is at best ambiguous, and deep dream may be as real (or more real) than the waking world and holds terrible secrets about the ultimate nature of the universe.

In terms of morphological conventions, cosmic horror stories are often short[1] and frequently take the form of personal accounts, often authored by people who are either dead or missing or otherwise distanced in time and/or space. An example can be found in "The Green Meadow" (1927) [15] in which a notebook written in classical Greek is found by scientists inside a meteorite (and hence separated from the story's characters by time as well as space) and is revealed to contain the account of a man trapped on a small, disintegrating island in an alien world. Even if a narrator is still alive, they must frequently distance themselves from the experience that is the subject of their account, such as in "Under the Pyramids" (also published as "Imprisoned with the Pharaohs") (1924) [16] in which the narrator attempts to retain his *merciful ignorance* by denying his terrible encounter with monstrous entities under the Sphinx of Giza as dream, hallucination or delirium. The possibility that the experience is true is impossible to bear, and only denial of the knowledge about it allows a modicum of sanity to persist. Vivienne Ralickas writes:

> Cosmic horror therefore amounts to an experience of the cataclysmic horror that the human subject experiences once it cognizes the finitude of its existence and realizes that, contrary to a humanist view which posits human life as intrinsically meaningful in relation not only to itself but to the cosmos, *there is neither anything distinctive nor significant about being human*. [19; emphasis added]

The *insignificance* of the protagonists is also identified by David McWilliam who observes that the characters in cosmic horror stories tend to experience "*insignificance and powerlessness* at the cosmic scale" [17; emphasis added]. As we will argue in this paper, these characteristics are not easily reconcilable with genre conventions of story-driven games.

While cosmic horror stories in this fashion deal with the *unknowable* and the *incomprehensible*, and also emphasise *insignificance* and *powerlessness* of their protagnists, the stories are also concerned with the *indescribable*. On this topic Kneale writes, "Lovecraft's stories are centrally concerned with the paradox of representing entities, things and places that are beyond representation" [12]. This has a marked effect on the vocabulary used in cosmic horror stories, and Philip Smith observes:

> A recurring theme in Lovecraft's prose is that which is beyond description. A collection of Lovecraft's work includes the following prose, 'unheard of,' 'inconceivable,' 'nameless,' 'indescribable,' 'unmentionable,' 'inexplicable,' 'unexplainable,' 'useless to describe,' 'no pen could even suggest' and 'unknown.' [21]

---

[1] H. P. Lovecraft wrote or co-write 73 short stories, six novellas and only one novel.

The challenge of showing the indescribable is of course of particular interest to a visual medium like story-based games, even if it is not unique to games *per se*.

3 Challenges for Cosmic Horror in Gaming

We have identified six characteristics of games (in particular, story-driven games) that appear to be in direct conflict with the genre conventions of cosmic horror. In the following sections, we will discuss each of these characteristics and identify why it seems irreconcilable with cosmic horror conventions and give examples of games that engage with the challenge, either successfully or unsuccessfully.

3.1 Agency

Nearly all game genres are defined by (and even named after) the core game mechanics, i.e., *what the player does*. Examples include *shooter* games, *fighting* games, *puzzle* games, *role-playing* games, etc. It is through these game mechanics that the player interacts with the gameworld and thereby experiences *agency*. Notably, *horror* games (along with *sport* simulations) is one of the few game genres named for its content (or, perhaps, the emotion that it aims to evoke), rather than a core mechanic. (Perhaps this indicates that horror games are "special" somehow and that the game mechanics and emotional affect serve a different purpose for horror than they do for many other game genres, but that is the topic of another paper.) In the context of interactive narrative, Janet Murray defines agency as "the power to take meaningful action and see the results of our own choices" [18]; and in the context of games, Carstensdottir et al. write,

> Broadly, agency in games can be described as the phenomenon where a player feels that the actions presented to them in the context of the game are *meaningful* and that their choice of action has a *meaningful impact* on the context in which they are engaging. [2; emphases added]

As Carstensdottir et al. observe, definitions of agency in games generally focus on whether the actions available to the player are meaningful; and agency is seen as a good (if not crucial) characteristic of games. More agency in a game is typically seen as better, and games are often lauded if the player has a wide range of actions available to them to which the game (and the gameworld) can respond meaningfully. Janet Murray's identification of the infinitely adaptable and endlessly flexible Holodeck as a guiding metaphor for interactive storytelling [18] shows that more agency is considered desirable in interactive digital narratives too, even agency in interactive narratives, as Noam Knoller has argued very convincingly [27], is always restricted.

In comparison with their counterparts in games, the protagonists of cosmic horror stories have little, if any, agency. Rather, such characters experience "insignificance and powerlessness at the cosmic scale" [17]. Their situation is fundamentally hopeless, and any perceived agency is soon revealed as illusory and, if attempted, outright dangerous. For example, in "The Horror at Martin's Beach" (1923) [14], the industrious Captain Orne attempts to land a monstrous sea creature using a heavy rope, but instead he and his men find themselves mysteriously unable to detach themselves from the rope and are slowly and painfully dragged into the sea. The agency Captain Orne expresses becomes his doom, and also the doom of others. The bystanders leave the scene while Orne's men are still being dragged into the sea, not only because it is too terrible to keep watching but also because the event is incomprehensible: How did the sea creature cause the men to stick to the rope? While the question is not answered (or even articulated) in the story, no plausible answer seems possible; there is no meaning to be found, and all the bystanders can do is walk away in a futile attempt to return to merciful ignorance. The unseen monster's powers are awesome and incomprehensible, and it retains its primacy over the humans with little or no effort. The question of *meaning making* is at the centre of this discussion. In story-driven games, exercising agency enables the players make sense of the world. In Lovecraftian horror, the characters come to realise that the world makes no sense. In this fashion, the character arcs used in the two forms are exactly the inverse of each other.

So how do games deal with this? It appears that few games do. Agency is so intrinsic to games that removing it, even for short periods of time, is a highly risky design decision that is likely to result in player frustration. An example can be found in the (non-Lovecraftian) *Haunting Ground* (2005) in which the playable character and protagonist Fiona under certain circumstances reaches a state of panic, causing the player to lose control of her, often resulting in the death of Fiona and severe frustration for the player. Perhaps the distinction made by Murray and Carstensdottir above offers some hope: As long as there is *gameplay* agency, perhaps we can dispense with *narrative* agency. There are many examples of (non-Lovecraftian) games that do this successfully, such as *The Last of Us* (2013), which is narratively completely linear (and hence, offers no narrative agency) but features a considerable amount of gameplay agency through its well-designed game mechanics. However, as we saw in "The Horror at Martin's Beach," it is exactly Captain Orne's *actions* (which would map to gameplay and mechanics in a game adaptation of this story) that turn out to be not only futile, but detrimental. The difference here seems irreconcilable: It is doubtful that a game in which the player takes on the role of Captain Orne and struggles on a rope for two hours before drowning (or worse) will be a rewarding game experience.

We have found two game/narrative design techniques that seem to result in less in conflict with literary Lovecraftian conventions around agency, even if they are closer to "workarounds" than create approaches to game design. The first technique is to use game mechanics that emphasise story, rather than gameplay. Many (non-Lovecraftian) titles already use such techniques, and common examples include environmental storytelling, in which the player uses game mechanics to navigate and examine the gameworld and its objects in order to piece the story together; or narrative puzzles that must be solved in order for the story to progress or for its elements to be revealed. Fernandez-Vara has identified five narrative puzzle patterns, e.g., figuring out which item a character desires and helping them, or combining and disassembling game objects to form new objects [4]. Nevertheless, narrative puzzles also rely on meaning making; they are generally assumed to "have a satisfying solution, i.e., one that ultimately makes sense to the puzzler" [3].

The second technique is to include (and place focus on) game mechanics that emphasise danger and powerlessness. Figure 1 shows two examples from *Song of Horror* (2020) in which the character must listen at doors to detect (and avoid) the presence of monsters in the next room and (less frequently) keep a door closed to keep the monster away, at least for a short while. The radio in the (non-Lovecraftian) game *Silent Hill 2* (2001) also falls into this category; it serves a gameplay function by alerting the player to the presence of monsters but its uncanny static also creates a feeling of danger and vulnerability. Survival horror games, like the *Silent Hill* series, frequently feature game mechanics that emphasise danger and powerlessness, even when they are not Lovecraftian, and these are straightforward to use also in Lovecraftian games.

Fig. 1. Game mechanics in *Song of Horror* (2020): listening at doors (left) and keeping the monsters out (right)

3.2 Opponents Can Be Defeated

Many games, including story-driven games, features opponents, and it is convention that these opponents can be defeated. Opponents of varying difficulty are frequently used to regulate or mark the progression of a game, such as a "boss fight" at the end of every chapter. For the purposes of this paper, we will consider the question of whether opponents can be defeated a special class of *gameplay agency*, which extends the discussion in the previous section.

Many games with Lovecraftian elements, such as the classic game *Quake* (1996), features killable enemies with Lovecraftian design, rather than the undefeatable undying monsters that are one of the hallmarks of literary cosmic horror (Fig. 2 left). Even *Call of Cthulhu: Dark Corners of the Earth* (2005), which is one of the more faithful attempts to use cosmic horror in games, sees the protagonist confronting the monstrous Dagon with a machine gun (Fig. 2 right). This type of agency works well in games, but as we saw in Sect. 3.1, it is directly at odds with the genre convention of *powerlessness* from cosmic horror. Any protagonist in cosmic horror literature who confronts a Great Old One with a gun would quickly come to dismal end, but not so in games. In games, the Lovecraftian monsters may bear a superficial resemblance to those from the literature, but for many games, the engagement with cosmic horror goes no deeper.

Some RPGs feature monstrous antagonists that appear multiple times and are designed to defeat the player repeatedly until the final encounter. An example is the monster Lavos in *Chrono Trigger* (1995) which defeats the player (although without killing the playable character) repeatedly until the final encounter in which it is finally possible for the player to win. Through the repeated (but non-fatal) defeats, the game emphasises the antagonist's power. *Chrono Trigger* is not a cosmic horror game, and it does let the player prevail in the end, but its repeated defeat structure is a useful approach that can be adopted by cosmic horror games to help show the overwhelming power of the opponents.

Fig. 2. Left: Lovecraftian monster from *Quake* (1996). Right: The monstrous Dagon from *Call of Cthulhu: Dark Corners of the Earth* (2005)

So, how do games deal with this? While many games (such as *Quake* mentioned above), do not attempt to create a feeling of powerlessness against invincible, incomprehensible opponents, there are games that adopt clever solutions to solve this problem. One approach is to introduce multiple monstrous antagonists that are equally powerful and pit them against each other: Cthulhu is not really after the puny humans – he is pitted against another Great Old One, and the humans just happen to be in the crossfire, or serve as pawns in the game between the two. *Eternal Darkness: Sanity's Requiem* (2002) does this expertly through a three-way structure of Great Old Ones (called Ancients) whose powers are also mapped to game resources. Another approach is to remove combat from the game altogether. This can be done by simply not including a game mechanic for fighting, such as *Song of Horror* (2020) or *The Terrible Old Man* (2019), or by making the monster obviously undefeatable, such as in *The Land of Pain* (2017). This approach combines well with the introduction of narrative-focused game mechanics discussed in Sect. 3.1.

3.3 Winning is Possible

Most games incorporate the idea of winning, or at the least overcoming obstacles and reaching a satisfying resolution. Victory (over a level, over an enemy, over other players) is something the player must strive for. We have already discussed the question of whether opponents can be defeated, but the question about whether the game can be "won" in any meaningful sense is a broader one. In many games, victory in one shape or another is typically used as requirement for game progression, through a level completion, boss fight, etc. The player may fail at first, but they get a second try, and a third, and a fourth, typically through checkpoints and saved games. While some games are punishingly hard, such as the *Dark Souls* series, there is always a path to victory, and players who are sufficiently adamant and skilled can achieve it. In addition, many story-based games feature a "good" ending and one or more "bad" endings, which are awarded depending on how well the player has played. When such multiple endings exist, there is a motivation for most players to reach the good ending, and for completionist players to reach all endings through repeated playthroughs.

For literary cosmic horror, however, the idea of a "win" or a "good ending" is alien. The characters always lose and there is no way that they could not. As we have seen, this is especially the case when characters exercise agency, like Captain Orne. Hence, games are nearly always winnable, and literary cosmic horror never lets the characters win in any meaningful sense. This convention of winning – even if it is hard and takes many tries – is one of the big challenges for making genuinely Lovecraftian games.

So, how do games deal with this? Many games, e.g., *Quake* as mentioned earlier, simply ignore this genre convention from literary cosmic horror, resulting in experiences that while they may look Lovecraftian on the surface, feel much less Lovecraftian when played. Other games The best approach we have found is to surprise the player with a narrative "defeat" snatched from the jaws of a gameplay "victory," as *The Land of Pain* (2017) does: After finally having returned from the alien world to their own, the player breathes a sigh of relief. But immediately, it becomes clear that the monsters have returned too. The subsequent ending is swift and merciless: the playable character is overpowered and transported to an alien world in which there is no choice but to become one with the Great Old One in the void, which of course means the destruction of the playable character. *Call of Cthulhu: Dark Corners of the Earth* also features the destruction of the playable character (through madness and suicide) at the end. In most games, narrative victory and gameplay victory go hand in hand, but by decoupling the two, games like *The Land of Pain* and *Call of Cthulhu: Dark Corners of the Earth* can reconcile the two seemingly incompatible genre conventions. The player gets a feeling of satisfaction from having completed the game, but at the same time, they understand that the playable character's defeat is inevitable, which honours the genre convention of narrative endings with no hope or victory. For the decoupling between narrative defeat and gameplay victory to work, it must be clear that the narrative defeat is inevitable, or the player will likely feel unfairly treated. *The Land of Pain* uses the almost instant capture of the player to make it clear that there is no escape; there is no better ending than that which was achieved. This removes the resonsibility for the defeat from the player and makes it acceptable. There is nothing the player could have done to avoid it – the playable character was doomed from the beginning.

The idea of decoupling narrative closure from gameplay (or "system") closure has been proposed by Alex Mitchell et al. [25] as a useful distinction between the player reaching a satisfying understanding of the story and a satisfying understanding of its underlying structure. In my analysis, the "narrative defeat" is largely equivalent to what Mitchell et al. consider "narrative closure," i.e., what Noël Carroll describes as a "feeling of finality that is generated when all the questions saliently posed by the narrative are answered" [26]. Interestingly, the cosmic horror titles discussed here are structurally simple, featuring no narrative branching, and do not appear to be designed for the player to achieve a "system closure," i.e., an understanding of the narrative's structure.

•

3.4 Knowledge is Good

Many games have complex mechanics and narratives that require the player to learn in order to develop the right strategies (for a gameplay heavy game) or make the right decisions (for a narrative game). In this way, games reward the player for achieving knowledge and understanding, such that they can complete the challenges. Steven Johnson [11] has observed that when players interact with games, they are using a probe-hypothesize-reprobe-rethink loop first proposed by James Gee in connection with learning experiences. Johnson has argued that games in this way essentially teach players the scientific method. The argument is that games are fundamentally about learning, and the entertainment value of the game is to learn to play the game, learning to understand how it works. In this fashion, games teach players that with careful attention, it is possible to understand the gameworld, and that this will lead to improvement in their skill and eventually to mastery. In other words: Knowledge is good.

At a first glance, this seems fundamentally irreconcilable with the cosmic horror genre convention that knowledge – especially scientific knowledge – can only lead to madness and death. As observed by Burleson [1] in the form of the *forbidden knowledge* theme and as discussed earlier in the context of "Under the Pyramids," denial is often the only way that a protagonist of a cosmic horror story can cope with their knowledge. While this may seem like an irreconcilable conflict at first, if we think deeper, the quest for knowledge in a cosmic horror game is only a problem if it leads to success. If the game has an ending that is consistent with cosmic horror, such as the death or incurable madness of the playable character, then the pursuit of knowledge can be depicted exactly as the reason for the dismal ending, which is completely compatible with cosmic horror and also the approach adopted by *Call of Cthulhu: Dark Corners of the Earth*. A game with multiple endings could even give the player an ending that is extra horrible if they have pursued knowledge with particular fervour, for example by finding and examining all story objects. I am not aware of any games that do this, but it is an interesting possibility.

3.5 (Prolonged) Survival of the Playable Character

We have already discussed whether the game is winnable or not. A related genre convention for games is that there generally is a way for the playable character to survive with their skin intact, and this is typically a requirement for a "good ending." A "bad ending" may feature the death of the playable character or one or more supporting characters, but other types of losses can also be used, such as the "nightmare ending" in *Fatal Frame 2* (2003) in which both sisters Mio and Mayu survive, but in which Mio has lost her sight (see Fig. 3). For this reason, we have classified the question of the survival of the playable character as separate from winning the game.

Generally, games use all sorts of methods to let the playable character ultimately prevail: Health bars and medkits, checkpoints and save points, respawns, etc. As discussed, even for the most difficult games, there exists a path through which the playable character can survive, and the most adamant players can find it. However, in cosmic horror, the genre convention is of course that the characters die horribly, go insane or at the very least survive considerably shaken. Furthermore, this tends to happen relatively quickly:

Fig. 3. The "nightmare ending" in Fatal Frame 2 (2003)

Cosmic horror stories tend to be short, perhaps because the horrors are so immense and so terrible that their effect is always quick and detrimental. It is rare to find a cosmic horror story that features a long, drawn-out survival of the protagonist, but prolonged survival is of course the convention in games, even for games that, like *Call of Cthulhu: Dark Corners of the Earth,* feature the ultimate demise of the playable character. In this fashion, the survival of the playable character is linked to the duration of the game.

How can these two genre conventions be reconciled? As mentioned, *Call of Cthulhu: Dark Corners of the Earth* admirably attempts to combine the long story form from the AAA game format (12–16 h) with the dismal ending from cosmic horror. From a story-telling perspective, it is challenging to justify the prolonged survival of the protagonist for a full-length AAA game, and it appears *Call of Cthulhu: Dark Corners of the Earth* compensates for its protagonist's prolonged survival by making his end extra horrible: not only madness, but also death, and sucide at that.

Perhaps the simplest approach to addressing this challenge is to make games that are short or very short, such as *The Land of Pain* (which takes 3–4 h) or *The Terrible Old Man* (which takes 20–30 min), and that features a fatal narrative ending, such as we discussed in Sect. 3.3. This lets the playable characters come to a dismal end rather quickly, which is in good accord with both genre conventions from Lovecraftian horror.

Another approach that allows the long game form is to have multiple playable characters that can be killed off or driven insane one at a time. *Eternal Darkness: Sanity's Requiem* does this very thoroughly, featuring a total of 12 characters, only one of whom prevails in the end, as shown in Fig. 4. This allows the two genre conventions to coexist. *Song of Horror* (2019) uses a similar approach, but its highly creative design allows the player to keep multiple characters alive if they play well. As long as one of the six playable characters survives, the game can be completed. In terms of gameplay, this works practically like having six "lives," but by making the characters different, *Song of*

Horror honours the cosmic horror convention of high character mortality and at the same time constructs a more complex and interesting storyworld than if only a single playable character had been used. *Song of Horror* and *Eternal Darkness: Sanity's Requiem* both use the deceased playable characters to reappear for extra creepiness. For example, Fig. 5 shows a scene from *Song of Horror* in which one playable character (Etienne Bertrand) encounters the rather physical ghost of the previous playable character (Alina Ramos) who was killed by the monsters and now stands in the kitchen, sobbing and asking what will become of her.

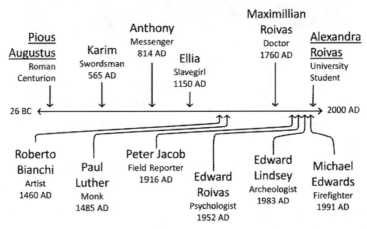

Fig. 4. Timeline with playable characters in Eternal Darkness: Sanity's Requiem

A third option is to adopt gameplay that features permanent death ("permadeath") of the playable character as an integral feature, such as known from Roguelikes [28]. This approach is taken by *Infra Arcana* (2011), which is set in the early 20th century (a genre convention from literary cosmic horror) and features the player repeatedly exploring a deadly procedurally generated underground complex in search of a mysterious object of non-terrestrial origin. The Roguelike genre conventions of permadeath and repeated attempts with different characters is a viable approach to reconciling games with cosmic horror.

3.6 Euclidean Space: A World that Makes Sense

Modern game engines, like *Unity* and *Unreal Engine*, are based around 3D (or sometimes 2D) models of the game world. When making a game, the designers create the entire game world – environment, levels, game objects, characters, everything – in a 3D modelling tool. Many of these are then animated and made to move according to the laws of physics, which like the 3D environment itself are built into the game engines. It is very difficult for a game developer to break free from the rigorous implementation of 3D Euclidean space and its associated physics, because it is hardwired into the game engines.

Fig. 5. Playable character Etienne Bertrand encountering deceased, previous playable character Alina Ramos sobbing in the kitchen (highlighted in red). Screenshot: Gab Smolders (YouTube) (Color figure online)

In comparison, cosmic horror deliberately eschews this orderly and familiar representation of the world. As noted earlier, cosmic horror frequently deals with the *indescribable*, and this also pertains to the perception of spaces and places in the stories. Perhaps the clearest example is from what is probably H. P. Lovecraft's most famous story "The Call of Cthulhu" in which he writes: "[T]he geometry of the dream-place [...] was abnormal, non-Euclidean, and loathsomely redolent of spheres and dimensions apart from ours" [13]. While Lovecraft only used the term "non-Euclidean" a couple of times in his stories, he returns to the subject in letters, such as the following:

> Straight lines do not exist, nor does theoretical infinity. What seems infinite extension is simply part of an inevitable returning curve, so that the effect of proceeding directly away from any given point in space is to return at length to that same point from the opposite direction. What lies ultimately beyond the deepest gulf of infinity is the very snot on which we stand. (Howard Phillips Lovecraft, Selected Letters III.388)

And:

> I have had many severe criticisms because of the concrete and tangible nature of some of my "cosmic horrors." Variants of the general theme include defeats of the visible laws of time ... And transcensions of the boundary-lines of Euclidean space. (Lovecraft, Selected Letters IV, 1932)

Moritz Ingwersen offers a deep analysis of H. P. Lovecraft's use of monstrous geometries [9], and Thomas Hull discusses Lovecraft's use of mathematical language in "The Call of Cthulhu" to observe that it can be seen as double-edged to have subtly different horror effects on mathematicians and non-mathematicians:

What better way to convey a sense of an unknown, alien, yet powerful landscape than to use mathematical language that, while just as unknown to most readers, simultaneously conveys levels of mystery and legitimacy to the environment? What's more, readers who do have an understanding of non-Euclidean geometry can also appreciate this effect. What would be more unsettling to one's sense of reality than to encounter physical examples of, say, hyperbolic geometry transplanted into our Euclidean world? Lovecraft's use of strange geometry is effective for both the mathematical literate and layman. [8]

The tyranny of Euclidean space in contemporary game engines is perhaps the biggest obstacle to anyone making Lovecraftian games. Game engines are specifically designed to model a comprehensible world and anyone (as some of my students) who have tried to bend them in a different direction is bound to struggle. Game engines are intrinsically unsuited to depicting the unfathomable mind-destroying hyperdimensional nature of the cosmos from cosmic horror. As Perry Ruhland puts it, "Lovecraft's mythos is, by nature, unadaptable into a visual medium. The Old Ones do not obey the laws of our universe, they aren't bound by how Earth works" [20].

A few games engage with this challenge by playing with perception through simple mechanisms like teleporting or inversion or visual effects. *Eternal Darkness: Sanity's Requiem* and *Call of Cthulhu: Dark Corners of the Earth* both do this well, but this is as far as is possible with current game engines. At present, the only other possibility for escaping the confinement of the 3D Euclidean space is by breaking through the fourth wall. *Eternal Darkness: Sanity's Requiem* also does this expertly as I have written about elsewhere [7], but it is a far cry from what cosmic horror literature can produce in our minds.

4   Conclusion

In this paper, we explored the challenges associated with making games that engage with cosmic horror as we know it from literature. We identified six specific challenges and discussed works that addressed them, and we identified the specific techniques used as well as challenges where few or no techniques were available. The discussion focused on story-driven horror games, either cosmic horror or survival horror games, even if the latter did not feature Lovecraftian elements. (Despite its name, survival horror is undoubtedly the horror game subgenre that is best suited for cosmic horror, even if not all the titles discussed here are cosmic horror games per se.)

We observed that several of the challenges had to do with *making sense* (of the events that take place, of the gameworld's geometry) in one way or another. Some of the six challenges could be addressed by a simple inversion of the genre conventions that most games use. For example, in cosmic horror games that are faithful to the literary tradition, agency and knowledge must both lead to failure, not to success as is otherwise the convention in games. In other cases, the challenge is more difficult to overcome and solutions are less obvious. In particular, the Euclidean space model that underlies game engines falls into this category. We found two particular areas where games and game technology could benefit from further work in order to capture the feelings of experience of a Lovecraft story authentically via mechanics and design: The potential for deliberately "punishing" players (or the playable characters) for pursuing knowledge with particular fervour (Sect. 3.4), and the need for a game engine that is free from the constraints of Euclidean space (Sect. 3.6). It is up to future game developers (and game technology developers) to develop solutions to this problem in order to support better interactive cosmic horror narratives.

References

1. Burleson, D.R.: On lovecraft's themes: touching the glass. In: David, E., Joshi, S.T. (eds.) Schultz, pp. 135–147. A Centennial Anthology of Essays in Honor of H. P. Lovecraft. Fairleigh Dickinson University Press, An Epicure in the Terrible (1991)
2. Carstensdottir, E., Kleinman, E., Williams, R., Seif El-Nasr, M.S.: Naked and on fire': examining player agency experiences in narrative-focused gameplay. In: Proceedings of the 2021 CHI Conference on Human Factors in Computing Systems, pp. 1–13 (2021)
3. De Kegel, B., Haahr, M.: Procedural puzzle generation: a survey. IEEE Trans. Games **12**(1), 21–40 (2019)
4. Fernández-Vara, C., Thomson, A.:Procedural generation of narrative puzzles in adventure games: the puzzle-dice system. In: Proceedings of the third Workshop on Procedural Content Generation in Games, pp. 1–6 (2012)
5. Flanagan, K.M.:Head games: adapting lovecraft beyond survival horror. In: Lanzendörfer, T., Dreysse Passos de Carvalho, M.J. (eds.) The Medial Afterlives of H.P. Lovecraft. Palgrave Studies in Adaptation and Visual Culture. Palgrave Macmillan, Cham, pp. 263–277 (2023). https://doi.org/10.1007/978-3-031-13765-5_15
6. Gibson, G.: The threshold of horror: indeterminate space, place and the material in film adaptations of Lovecraft's the colour out of space (1927). In: Lanzendörfer, T., Dreysse Passos de Carvalho, M.J. (eds.) The Medial Afterlives of H.P. Lovecraft. Palgrave Studies in Adaptation and Visual Culture. Palgrave Macmillan, Cham (2023). https://doi.org/10.1007/978-3-031-13765-5_8
7. Haahr, M.: Playing with vision: sight and seeing as narrative and game mechanics in survival horror. In: Rouse, R., Koenitz, H., Haahr, M. (eds.) Interactive Storytelling. ICIDS 2018. Lecture Notes in Computer Science, vol. 11318, pp. 193–205. Springer, Cham (2018). https://doi.org/10.1007/978-3-030-04028-4_20
8. Hull, T.: HP Lovecraft: a horror in higher dimensions. Math Horiz. **13**(3), 10–12 (2006)
9. Ingwersen, M.:Monstrous geometries in the fiction of Hp Lovecraft. In: Places and Spaces of Monstrosity, pp. 45-55. Interdisciplinary Press, Oxford (2014)
10. Janicker, R.: Conveying cosmicism: visual interpretations of Lovecraft. In: Lanzendörfer, T., Dreysse Passos de Carvalho, M.J. (eds.) The Medial Afterlives of H.P. Lovecraft. Palgrave Studies in Adaptation and Visual Culture, pp. 63–75. Palgrave Macmillan, Cham (2023). https://doi.org/10.1007/978-3-031-13765-5_4
11. Johnson, S.: Everything bad is good for you: How today's popular culture is actually making us smarter. Penguin (2006)
12. Kneale, J.: From beyond: HP Lovecraft and the place of horror. Cult. Geograph. **13**(1), 106–126 (2006)
13. Lovecraft, H.P.: 'The Call of Cthulhu.' 1926. The Call of Cthulhu and Other Weird Stories. Edited by S.T. Joshi, pp. 139–169. Penguin Books, London (1999)
14. Lovecraft, H.P.: The Horror at Martin's Beach. In: Weird Tales, vol. 2, no. 4, pp. 75–76, 83, November 1923
15. Lovecraft, H.P.: The Green Meadow. Spring. The Vagrant, pp. 188–195 (1927)

16. Lovecraft, H.P.: Under the Pyramids. In: Weird Tales, February 1924
17. McWilliam, D.: Beyond the mountains of madness: Lovecraftian cosmic horror and posthuman creationism in Ridley Scott's Prometheus (2012). J. Fant. Arts **26**(3) (2015). Accessed 21 Mar 2021
18. Murray, J.H.: Hamlet on the Holodeck: The Future of Narrative in Cyberspace, updated edition. MIT Press (2017)
19. Ralickas, V.: Art, cosmic horror, and the fetishizing gaze in the fiction of HP Lovecraft. J. Fant. Arts **19**(3), 297–316 (2008)
20. Ruhland, P.: What gaming gets wrong about Lovecraft. TechRaptor, April 2016. https://techraptor.net/gaming/opinions/what-gaming-gets-wrong-about-lovecraft
21. Smith, P.: Re-visioning romantic-era gothicism: an introduction to key works and themes in the study of HP Lovecraft. Literat. Compass **8**(11), 830–839 (2011)
22. Hassler-Forest, D.: Lovecraft country: horror, race, and the dark other. In: Lanzendörfer, T., Dreysse Passos de Carvalho, M.J. (eds.) The Medial Afterlives of H.P. Lovecraft. Palgrave Studies in Adaptation and Visual Culture, pp. 191-204. Palgrave Macmillan, Cham (2023). https://doi.org/10.1007/978-3-031-13765-5_11
23. Knopf, C.M.: Cthulhoo-Dooby-Doo!: the re-animation of Lovecraft (and Racism) through subcultural capital. In: Lanzendörfer, T., Dreysse Passos de Carvalho, M.J. (eds.) The Medial Afterlives of H.P. Lovecraft. Palgrave Studies in Adaptation and Visual Culture, pp. 159-172. Palgrave Macmillan, Cham (2023). https://doi.org/10.1007/978-3-031-13765-5_9
24. Sederholm, C., Weinstock, J.A.: Introduction: Lovecraft now. J. Fant. Arts **26**(3), 444 (2015)
25. Mitchell, A., Kway, L., Lee, B.J.: Storygameness: understanding repeat experience and the desire for closure in storygames. In: DiGRA 2020–Proceedings of the 2020 DiGRA International Conference (2020)
26. Carroll, N.: Narrative closure. Philos. Stud. **135**, 1–15 (2007)
27. Knoller, N.: Agency and the art of interactive digital storytelling. In: Aylett, R., Lim, M.Y., Louchart, S., Petta, P., Riedl, M. (eds.) Interactive Storytelling. ICIDS 2010. Lecture Notes in Computer Science, vol. 6432, pp. 264–267. Springer, Heidelberg (2010). https://doi.org/10.1007/978-3-642-16638-9_38
28. Parker, R.: The culture of permadeath: roguelikes and terror management theory. J. Gaming Virt. Worlds **9**(2), 123–141 (2017)

Designing *Sisters*: Creating Audio-Based Narratives to Generate Affective Connections and Material Story Worlds

Lissa Holloway-Attaway[✉] 🆔 and Jamie Fawcus 🆔

University of Skövde, Skövde, Sweden
{lissa.holloway-attaway,jamie.fawcus}@his.se

Abstract. In this paper, we reflect on the design of an interactive audio-based digital narrative experience called *Sisters*. This work is designed for a single interactor, constructed as a mobile AR experience using graphic illustrations on a deck of player cards in connection with abstract audio activated by trigger images on the cards. An interactor is asked to cluster series of cards together into different abstract environments, based on sounds associated with each card, meant to represent spaces in an interior/exterior domestic site, a house and its immediate surroundings. The work conveys experiences of 4 family members in a complex abusive household, mediating between scenes of normalcy, love, companionship, and violence. The core focus of the work is to explore fragmented and very personal states of being and memories derived from an outsider's perspective (the interactor), who co-experiences the complexities of the domestic spaces at a 'safe' distance, while also gaining empathy and affective connections to the characters. Connecting the content of the work and its fragmentary and elusive material audio and narrative design to our design model, the *New Material/Spectral Morphology Model*, we share how it may be used for aesthetic composition. Our model is based on feminist new material perspectives and foundational work from electroacoustic production and audio experimentation. *Sisters* extends our previous work with sound-based narrative, and we demonstrate how this work affirms our design strategies for novel interactive audio experiences.

Keywords: Feminist New Materialism · Electroacoustic Music · Agential Realism · Affect · Spectromorphology · Gestural Music

1 Introduction

1.1 Theoretical and Design Overview

In this article, we reflect on the design of an interactive audio-based digital narrative experience called *Sisters* created by the authors (Lissa Holloway-Attaway and Jamie Fawcus) along with an additional designer (Mio Jernström) who also served as a graphic

---

Trigger Warning: This paper includes descriptions of domestic violence, alcoholism, and mental illness.

© The Author(s), under exclusive license to Springer Nature Switzerland AG 2023
L. Holloway-Attaway and J. T. Murray (Eds.): ICIDS 2023, LNCS 14383, pp. 291–308, 2023.
https://doi.org/10.1007/978-3-031-47655-6_18

artist and who inspired the piece based on personal experiences. This work is designed for a single interactor and is constructed as a mobile Augmented Reality (AR) experience incorporating graphic illustrations on a deck of player cards in connection with abstract audio activated by trigger images on the cards. The interactor is asked to cluster series of cards together into different abstract environments, based on sounds they listen to that are meant to represent an interior and exterior domestic site, a house and its immediate surroundings. The work abstractly conveys the experiences of 4 family members in a complex abusive household that mediates between scenes of normalcy, love, companionship, and violence. In this paper, we share our design strategies for *Sisters* to illustrate our conceptual framework for our *New Material/Spectral Morphology Model* or *NM/SM Model* [1]. The model supports the creation of interactive digital narratives (IDNs) that feature complex material, acoustic phenomena to serve as the primary agents for activating story content. Our aim is both to describe our audio content and the design strategies for *Sisters*, but also to share our model as a basis for supporting other audio IDN design. In particular we hope to illustrate how our aesthetic design choices based on our theoretical influences may support affective connections among interactors to the challenging audio material that forms the basis for our often difficult and disturbing narrative content.

Our *NM/SM Model* draws from theoretical influences that critique and deconstruct notions of stable subjectivity and person-hood as necessary sites for establishing power and authority over more affective semiotic meaning-making within storytelling constructs. Specifically we are influenced by feminist new materialism—which in turn embraces posthuman and non-human influences and draws heavily on affect theory and emergent embodiment). In particular Karen Barad's theory of Agential Realism is core to our work as we explore the kinds of dynamic systems (or *apparatuses*) she describes as a model for knowing a world in a deeply material, phenomenological, and continuously changing set of interactions [2]. Our IDNs directly oppose content and delivery formats and systems intended to be rationally and cognitively decoded, hierarchically organized, and conclusively situated. In our previously published research, we outline in detail how Barad's theories, particularly of emergent apparatus constructions comprised of elements that form and uniform meaning making, may offer a useful model for supporting non-linear, non-representational audio content creation [1]. Our theoretical influences also draw from foundational research for electroacoustic music composition (EAM) and audio experimentation that complicate notions of sound- making and listening, as well as spatio-temporal perception and orientation for listeners [3, 26] .

Specifically, our design for *Sisters* and our *NM/SM Model* foreground Denis Smalley's influential work on dynamic aural spectra or spectromorphology [3] which we adapt and modify to include our more contemporary references to feminist new material philosophies. In combination with Smalley's notion of spectromorphology and gestural music, we illustrate how interactors may have specific un-natural (de-familiarized) encounters with sending and receiving agents, with sonic phenomena. These kinds of *other* material phenomenal agents and agencies (operational relata, following Barad, gathered in emergent assemblages, apparatuses, of meaning-making) defy more representational content for story making (characters, plots, settings, narrative arcs). They then also counter traditional concepts for creating stable linear narrative, as well as musical notation and composition. Instead, our designs support affective material and gestural audio-based IDNs, and they generate and circulate audio spectra and phenomena as operational agents to resist pure, stable, linear systems of organization while engaging with, and connecting to, interactors in novel ways.

1.2   Introducing *Sisters*: An Affective IDN Experience to Explore Complex Family Dynamics from a 'Safe' Distance

Fig. 1. A card depicting the 2 sisters in their shared bedroom, a key setting in the family house, used as a trigger image for sound content.

Sisters is an interactive digital narrative created as a mobile AR-based audio experience using black and white graphically designed trigger images on cards to engage a single user an interactor, with the story. (Our specific audio design is discussed in more detail in Section 3.) The interactor uses a mobile phone with headphones and uses the camera to activate sound files connected to trigger images on the cards. Each card has a unique sound file and image, although some are designed in ways to give clues to how they may be related or not to other sounds or images. (See Figures 1 and 2 below for graphical card details.) Interactors are asked to listen to the sounds and then place the cards into 9 different areas on a flat, clear tabletop. Each cluster corresponds to a different setting in our designed domestic space, which includes interior spaces (bedroom, living room, kitchen, for example) and outdoor spaces (spiral staircase, pond, sauna). The interactor can place any number of cards in each environment, and they do not have to equal in number. They receive little other information about the setting and characters. However, they are informed that the house that they will *construct* is inhabited by a family of 4—an older and a younger sister and their Mother and Father. But they are given no specific information about the characters or the family relationships. The aim is to encourage deep listening by the interactor when they activate the sound files with the cards, to find their own personal connections to the sounds, and to the sound relationships, one to each other, while they also attempt to construct the perceived environments. The story and its emerging environments are intended to be affectively organized by the interactor based on the way they discern and connect with the audio content, which in turn is strategically designed to create associations for users to orient them and to sustain an affective connection to the story. (See Figure 2 for a sample card layout, or cluster.)

Fig. 2. A series of cards from *Sisters* grouped together by an interactor on a tabletop. The interactor activates content by holding a mobile phone over the card to activate AR audio.

Our theoretical foundations are closely connected to the content and design of *Sisters* which supports and explores fragmentary and disorienting personal states of being and affective connections to others, both among the characters and for the interactor to the story. These inconclusive states, underscored by the audio, which is challenging to identify and order, come together to comprise the complex story world that abstractly depicts a troubled and sometimes violent and abusive domestic situation. The interactor is drawn to the story by careful listening to how the domestic world sounds from a distance, as an outsider, safe from the drama. By then reconstructing it, with the card placement, and based on perceptions of what one thinks is/has happened, and where, interactors are guided to find an affective association with the unfolding drama, The aim, however, is definitively *not* to exploit the trauma and violence at the center of the story as experienced by the characters. The *trouble* we engage is of the sort that Donna Haraway describes in *Staying With the Trouble*: one we must stir up and then stick close to, but never let it overwhelm or overpower us [4]. Our aim, as is Haraway's, "is to make kin in lines of inventive connection as a practice of learning to live and die well with each other in a thick present" (p. 1) [4]. Such openness, ironically perhaps, creates a *thickness* rich in semiotic experience, locating (non-)subjects in a dynamic, changing present while defying complete representation, offering an ambiguous time/place from where to gather and reflect. Our non-subjects (narrative subjects and characters, interactors) are then *permeable*, following an emergent digital humanities tradition that Holloway-Attaway describes as radically complex in terms of techno-human subjectivities and ontologies, creating space to re-inscribe the boundaries of the human through feminist genealogical critique [5]. In the case of *Sisters*, this geneology extends into audio design as an affordance towards thick permeability, an oxymoron to support our experimental feminist material aesthetics.

Designed as an aesthetic experience, we deliberately resist creating a kind of 'serious game' about mental illness, alcoholism, co-dependancy, or domestic violence, as in other kinds of therapeutic works designed to teach, support, or help users recover from their past or to inform others about such scenarios and the impacts [6, 7]. We want instead to experiment with narrative audio abstraction, affect, and generalized connection to themes which are discernable, close-up, but still hard to process or stabilize and which may be uncomfortable or disorienting, but never terrifying to those who interact. In that sense our work is definitively not inspired by "Horror" genres or games meant to immerse and terrify users (as with jump scares), in worlds without salvation or safety. Our core challenge is to engage listeners affectively to the complexities that define the troubled domestic space we create, while still allowing enough distance for them to listen deeply and organize their experiences into meaningful clusters (sounds and cards). Each interactor, in fact, is intended to have a somewhat unique experience indicated by the personalized ordering of their cards. However, *Sisters* is also designed so that there is some commonality to the experience so that interactors will ideally share many components and choices as well with other users, based on designed sound clues and sound signatures for each environment that should be recognizable to many, then, as belonging together. Following Haraway, we make odd-kin and find odd-kinship.

1.3   IDN Design and Affective New Material Reflections and Influences

Sisters draws on many transmedial influences and contemporary theoretical perspectives for IDNs that complicate perceptions of fixed, linear histories, complete narratives, and traditional representations and semiotics for world-building and meaning-making in storytelling contexts. It extends the work of foundational principles in interactive digital storytelling for supporting the unique affordances of the medium to promote engagement, re-playability and to support complex systems thinking [8–11] and to address complex contemporary issues ill-suited for linear narratives [12]. It also extends our own previous work creating audio-based content and using our compositional model, the *NM/SM Model* [1, 20]. The disruptions and disorientations, central to our narrative and audio

content and design in *Sisters* is influenced primarily by feminist new materialism, theoretically positioned to consider the body as a complex place positioned in-between
culture, nature, science, and the attendant politics that creates [13–15]. Related Posthuman critique overlaps in these theories focused on resisting and destabilizing subjectivity,
identifying it as a restrictive space in its relationship to power and authority [16–19].
And extending the notion of Posthuman critique, Non-Human studies further complicate
systemic thinking about what media (human bodies and otherwise) may communicate
about relations among themselves and others to decentralize power and political structures that denote truth and instead to embrace such dynamism and swarming resistance
[20, 21].

Core to these resistant aesthetics are what Gregg and Seigworth describe as co-
constitutive designs/systems, ones that embrace rhythmic, intense, and dynamic relations among agents: "Affect is found in those intensities that pass body to body (human,
nonhuman, part-body, and otherwise), in those resonances that circulate about, between,
and sometimes stick to bodies and worlds, and in the very passages or variations between
these intensities and resonances themselves" (p. 1). [22] Like the speculative fabulations,
or string figures, that Donna Haraway [4] describes, our design model and stories promote game-like play in their refusal to cohere entirely in meaning. But also in their
tactile responsiveness, as the interactor touches and manipulates the cards, our design
aligns with Haraway's childhood string game presented as a semiotic model for meaning-
making: "Playing games of string figures is about giving and receiving patterns, dropping
threads and failing but sometimes finding something that works . . . of relaying connections that matter. . . String figures require holding still in order to receive and pass on.
String figures can be played by many, on all sorts of limbs, as long as the rhythm of accepting and giving is sustained" (p. 10) [4]. Such figuration offer us a compelling framework
to consider intra-active narrative forces in our *Sisters* story world, told though touch and
listening and irrational organizing, and not. And unlike traditional semiotic systems (languages, musical notations, paintings), our systems deliberately resist coherence. They
trouble, and they connect.

2 Electroacoustic Music, Spectromorphology, and a New Material Design Model

Dennis Smalley's spectromorphology system is foundational to our design model and
our strategies for composing the audio as it offers a way to address the multidimensional
process or activity of listening, as well as the dynamic movements/shapes (morpholo-
gies) and the performative and emergent interrelationships of sound material in the act
of sending/receiving audio phenomena. [3]. Smalley's model, and his discussion of its
varied parts, illustrates how EAM technical interventions into traditional musical composition are radically and differently constructed by the nature of the content. Based
on electronic generation, they do not fit within traditional musical systems with clear
instrumental forms, using graphical representation and notation. Smalley's core aim in
creating his model is to determine how to keep a listener in process according to EAM
principles, avoiding the goal for concrete functional understanding of sound spectra,

while still gesturing toward comprehension of some variety. We offer a detailed discussion of Smalley and his spectromorphology model in earlier research where we outlined it as a basis of inspiration to create our *NM/SM Model* and to contextualize it in feminist new material principles [1]. From that earlier model design, and from pieces we made in tandem, *Patternings Apt 3B, 2020* for example [20], we now extend our practice in *Sisters*, particularly as we considered gestural compositions for narrative meaning-making.

In *Sisters*, gestural spectral spaces (the sites that connect audio content to the interactor through affective relation) are constructed to keep meaning- making active in interactors, but they are also deliberately elusive. Smalley, in fact, offers his spectromorphology model as a collection of tools for describing sound shapes, structures, and relationships, based on gestural aural perception, not on semiotic notation of pre-existing, recognizable spectra. He imagines it as flexible tool, one for "speculating and imagining" not as a way to organize materials into a single coherent and analytical or compositional action (p. 92) [3]. Smalley outlines forms of relationships (or gestures) between sound agents and listeners based on qualities such as, for example, spectral density and on other structural audio elements that unfold over time, without ever making perfect sense to listeners, who also may not have perfect rational models in the real world to which they may connect for reference.

We work to sustain these kind of irrational spectral gestures within each of our designed environments (our domestic interior and exterior places). The audio content specifically supports unique connections and relationships between sending and receiving agents. This kind of flexibility (a move toward Haraway's call for fabulations and Barad's for finding/making performative apparatuses) also compels us. Connecting these primary concepts from Smalley to key new material concepts and composing within emergent material-discursive systems of meaning, spectral spaces and systems, allows us to identify more precisely how experimental audio IDNs may be designed in ways to maximize their interpretive, intra-active material and narrative dimensions. Specifically, we draw on the interpretive and expectant tensions of a careful, strategic listener trying to make sense of spectral spaces, by, for example, measuring the density, opacity, transparency, directionality, and temporal ranges for local and global processes, usually unaware they are being guided to do so.

Our *NM/SM Model* is multi-layered and essentially defined by the way it allows for differently configured and relational forms of Baradian influences, apparatuses that frame, without clearly bounding, affective sound experiences into clustered arrangements based on their shared relationships. There are major and more minor apparatuses (*Interface Apparatuses, I-A,* and *Micro-Apparatuses, M-A*) and each can work in tandem with the others, although some may not be directly, overtly connected at all. Each apparatus supports a sort of "diary-like system" as it allows for textual notation, iteratively built through dense description of gestural activities to foreground and highlight different kinds of particular material, embodied and affective audio content in the design process. (See Figure 3 for an overview of primary functions of the *NM/SM Model* and apparatus functions. Figure 4 shows sample notations in an M-A.)

In our general model (Figure 3) relevant *M-As* that share common features (gestures) and that relate more directly to each other, are illustrated by purple arrows. Such arrows might increase or decrease based on design. They could be described more fully in a

I-A

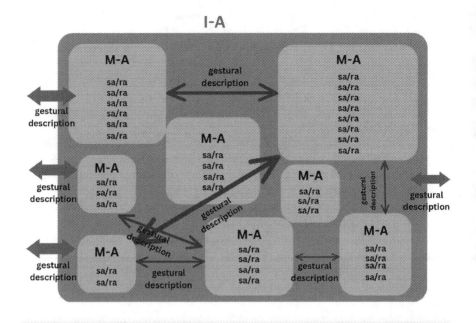

Fig. 3. The general outline of the Interface-Apparatus (*I-A*) with the Micro-Apparatuses (*M-A*) and the sending and receiving agents (*sa/ra*).

gestural notation. Gestures from the *I-A* to define the user experience are indicated by green arrows. Each kind of gesture, between *M-As* and between the *I- A* and the user could be customized to map each experience and might be described more fully in a notation (or gestural description).

As depicted in Figure 3, the *I-A* is the primary, major container for the work. It is not a technical system (a web browser or a mobile phone, for example). Rather it identifies the way users will connect with the work, highlighting the gestures that entice and invite them to the piece and determine the formal experience to engage them (as a single-user, via a web browser, with a mouse, as an AR application, as a sound walk in the woods, or as a fixed art installation experience in a gallery, for example). Within the primary *I-A*, multiple other more minor, *M-As* are constructed. Each of these is defined by sets of audio content paired with an anticipated listener, *sa/ra* (sending and receiving agents). Each of these *sa/ra* pairs offers particular modes of orienting or connecting to users with sound to align meaning-making while avoiding composing concrete representations: via audio provoking spatio-temporal dis/orientation or through depicting/discerning activities/actions/environments that are highly processed and thus difficult to comprehend. The *sa/ra* pairs are active, and they are both human and otherwise. Each pair is designed with a multidirectional desire for connection (a gesture) between the agents. That is they contain a type of audio agent (an *s-a*) that is formed to sustain an affective response to a listener in mind, one who is anticipated as a particular kind of recipient of that sound, and one who is moved to receive and engage with it, sometime iteratively, because of its abstract and complex compositional structure. To heighten the affect, they are composed strategically and then notated descriptively via identifying a number of differing qualities to dis/locate them in varied states of expression (sonically and materially). These processual, on-going gestural connections between *sa/ra* are also sustained among many of the *M-A*, and together they reverberate in the *I-A* overall, which is customized based on design content and implementation. As each *M-A* may contain any number/type of *sa/ra* content, some may be larger or smaller in composition, with more or fewer sounds. The gestures between the *M-A* (indicated by the purple arrows in Figure 3) are also multiply/infinitely configurable. Figure 4, a more graphical depiction of the general model we used in early designs for *Sisters*, presents another conceptual way to see the spaces. Here we began to sketch the *I-A* and *M-As* as a way to model our designs. Note, the sound relationships in each *sa/ra* are not consistent throughout each *M-A* and as such offer ways to create distinctive audio for each space.

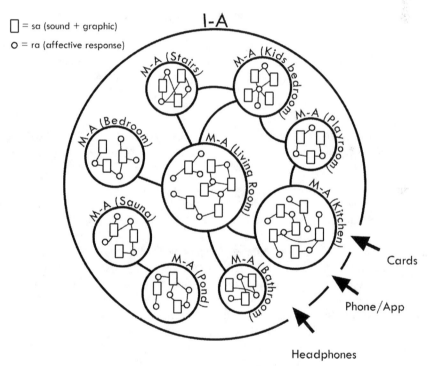

Fig. 4. This illustration offers a more specific design for *Sisters* according to the *NM/SM Model*. It was a starting point for us to begin to define specific sites/rooms (*M-As*) and to create spectral footprints for each room. Note the different relationships in each *M-A* among the *sa* (cards/graphics) and *ra* (affective responses) to support spectral distinctions for each space.

When considering Figure 3 and Figure 4 and in the case of *Sisters*, for example, the gestures from the *I-A* to the user (indicated by green arrows in Figure 3 and black ones in Figure 4) highlight our designed interaction for a single interactor, using a smart phone camera, wearing headphones, while activating AR content through trigger images on hand- held cards. Each of these is a unique form of sensory, tactile, material experience meant to engage a specific interactor. Additionally, the choice of a tabletop (as a kind of blank canvas), the use of a card deck (a familiar device for playing, which may be manipulated by touch, but which also has semiotic codes to discern), the handling of a phone, a personal and flexible device to connect and to support meaning, etc. could be further identified/elaborated as key to the material experience as a whole for the *I-A* we designed. As part of the gestural notation (exemplified in Figure 5), one could motivate the choices in any number of ways to foreground intentions: "There is a seated single user using headphones required to increase concentration and isolate focus. The table provides a stable surface and unstructured blank space for playing. It is purposefully abstract to encourage openness…" And so on. Descriptions of each *sa/ra* could also be further described and notated: "The low frequency and greatly slowed down pulsing heartbeat is barely recognizable to interactor, but the deep rhythmic beating is somehow familiar, technical yet human."

Figure 5 offers a more specific detailed framing of an *M-A*, in this case the Kitchen space, with notations. As indicated by notations, each specific *sa/ra* pair works together to build the basis for the sound content of a particular site in the domestic space. Because the Kitchen is a common site of threat and violence in our story, the audio agents are selected and described to specifically provide the narrative structural elements and to evoke the related responses from the interactor.

3   Designing *Sisters*: Engaging Audio Affect and Creating Material Phenomena

From an audio perspective *Sisters* is an interactive, narrative experiment intended to explore a number of concepts around sound, affect, the human voice, non-linear and interactive narrative as a multifaceted medium for participatory experience. In a pre-defined but flexible 'performance' space (an art installation, a small room, a café), the interactor is invited to engage with an AR experience via a mobile phone and a set of cards. On an instructional card, minimal guidance is offered: "Group the cards into 9 clusters based on what you listen to. Each cluster represents a space in a domestic setting, an interior and exterior of a small house in the countryside. 4 characters occupy the house, 2 sisters (one younger one older) a father and a mother. Listen carefully to explore the family relationships and realities." The experience is primarily individual, mediated through a mobile phone, and more importantly, closely audible through the headphones. The non-linear emergent narrative is created and mediated primarily by sound, but is framed and partially guided by a series of visual elements; cards consisting of monochrome sketches made by one of the project designers, someone whose personal experiences and familial relationships formed the starting point and inspiration for the work as a whole. (See Figure 6.)

As shared earlier, *Sisters* is based on the actual memories and recollections of one of its designers, Mio Jernström, who was raised in a strong religious upbringing in northern Sweden. Along with a sibling and a mentally ill, alcoholic father, they grew up in a remote house in the countryside, witnessing and experiencing both emotional trauma and physical violence. However, scattered throughout these experiences, they

Micro-Apparatus (M/A)

sa/ra (1)
[description/quality notation]
sa/ra (2)
[description/quality notation]
sa/ra (3)
[description/quality notation]
sa/ra (4)
[description/quality notation]
sa/ra (5)
[description/quality notation]

M-A: Kitchen
[focus on violence, fear, assault, embodied emotion, impending threats]

1. sa: Metal scraping - indistinct source but materialised in the aural space - close mic'ed. Referencing kitchen utensils, but not directly. Reference to knives and other implements used to threaten/attack// ra: Sound material invites attention from the listener through harsher frequency content, spectrally inharmonic/dissonant. Heightened arousal and attention from listener.

2. ra: Screaming 1,1 (father character) - low in amplitude, panned hard left or right, filtered or "muffled" to suggest distance but also to play with perception of the actual screaming-Complexity of father character and relationships. // ra: Ambiguity, is it threatening, aggressive and directed/associated with violence, or vocalisation and expression of distress, fear, pain, desperation? Fragmented and indiscernible/incomprehensible phrases/vocalisations.

3. sa: Rushing, pulsing + sustained texture. Indistinct "location" (not audibly materialized in the acoustic space). Suggestive of constricted blood flow, breathing, heartbeat. At the same time strong indicator of life, vitality, animal activity. Ambiguous. Try to convey and confuse if sound is internal to a character (expression of an inner voice or emotional state) or just something generally audible in the acoustic space. // ra: Is this about strangulation? Assault? Is this about power? Is it survival against all odds? Body awareness (breath, heartbeat) and perception of human, embodied presence is key.

4. sa: Rotational sound material exploiting HRTF or binaural techniques to generate 3D spatialisation in close proximity to listeners head. ASMR parallels. Suggesting the central point of the house (the kitchen) or central nature of certain events/material (narrated text, assault on mother by father, linking/overarching sounds that occur in different form in all rooms). Highly materialised frequency spectra through close mic recording and filtering, but abstracted or indistinct source material. // ra: Sound is confusing and immerses the listener who might feel trapped and afraid, but at the same time is highly alert and listening to cues, especially dialogue, to figure out what's happening. Intense listening is needed and heightened emotional state is anticipated.

5. sa: Repetitive mechanical ticking, clicking, tapping sound - occasionally accelerating or decelerating. Suggestive of machinery or timers, but indistinct. Ties in with material 1-4 themes of central point, crux of events, navigation. Sounds will be associated with Father, along with screams in other rooms, a signature. // ra: Suggestive of waiting, anticipation, time passing, inevitability, threat (ticking time-bomb) and possibly hope when sound slows after seeding. Regular, normal perception, except when not. Should evoke a sense of impending threat or danger, but not entirely clear.

Fig. 5. Outline of framework and detail for a *Micro-Apparatus* (*M-A*) construction. A generic framework for *M/A* is in upper left and then expanding in detailed notation on right. The description/notation and quality of each of the sending and receiving agents (*sa/ra*) are expanded during composition to offer a more fully elaborated model for each *M-A*. This kind of framing is a foundation to consider/identify/organize each *M-A* and then to help connect and elaborate relationships to other *M-As* through specific gestures, but also to the primary *I–A*. The detailed notation is based on the Kitchen space within the house, a common site of violence and threat.

also experienced some deep sibling and parental bonding, with moments of joy, play, and resonant connection, often through videogame play among the *Sisters* and the Father. In fact, the title of the piece (*Sisters*) is intended to underscore familial bonding, as in a close sibling relationship. It is also the basis of the affective one we hope to share with interactors.

Important to note, is that although the underlying interactive experience of *Sisters* is inspired to a degree by the memories and experiences of one designer, Jernström, the intention is not to document it precisely, or to tell it as a single linear story. Rather the final designed re-imagined experience (a troubling fabulation following Haraway) takes some inspiration and its thematic core from the bare memories and circular retellings of these events, discussed in conversations among all the designers and over a lifetime for the designer who experienced it first- hand. The piece uses this iterative expression as a rich source to explore the nature of memory, recollection, retelling and interactive

Fig. 6. A black and white card from *Sisters* depicting an encounter on the Spiral Staircase, one of the outdoor environments. The card also serves as a trigger image for the AR.

non-linear narrative forms— particularly as recalled through snapshot-like images (the art on our cards, also made by the artist/designer Jernström whose experiences we draw from) and key sounds designed to heighten affective responses (whispering, screaming, uncanny silence).

As such *Sisters* explores the nature of sound itself as both a substance and medium for the transmission and embodiment of emotion, memory and understanding. The four familial characters in the work inhabit and navigate a sonified and sonically delineated world along with the invited listener. Together the family are revealed as character-like, but not fully formed. They are ghostly inhabitants in a domestic space that slowly emerges. Formed by audible structures (audio apparatuses and agents) that deliver and organize the affective and affecting voices in the spaces, figures slowly take shape, become spectra, underscoring our *NM/SM Model* and its "spectral-morphological" roots. Whispered secrets, varied fragments of conversations, environmental sounds (videogame consoles, wind, steam from the sauna), and most notably screams, form the core of the work, along with the stark monochromatic images as evocative background, a resurfacing of the past in black and white. Sound is, then, the focal point of the experience, bringing the images to life and operating as cartographer of the remembered place, physical, emotional, conceptual and affective.

Screaming and whispering are resonant sounding, affective bodies, and they are prominent and key to the experience we design. These screams form both the voice of the

Father, but also operate as structuring processes that define the space in which the listener, and the sisters, inhabit and navigate. The screaming is particularly evident in the Living Room and Kitchen, for example, prominent and of a particular quality for each. But heard from the Sister's Bedroom, it is always just a distant threat. And it is never included in the outdoor spaces, the sauna and by the pond, places of solitude, of cleansing steam and watery heat, but also of companionship, laughter, and deep relaxation. Whispering features another important role in the narrative, both in manifesting and animating the two sisters, a kind of language shared only by them, but also then in defining, illustrating, expanding and constricting perceived physical space, emotional intensity and narrative movement (Fig. 7).

Fig. 7. A violent scene depicted on one of the cards. It is set in the Parent's Bedroom, as overseen by one of the sisters.

From an audio perspective, screams are a particularly evocative and interesting medium or aesthetic tool. The human scream triggers additional parts of the brain than "normal" loud noises and research has established certain common acoustic elements, namely amplitude modulation at certain rates that at least partially define the perceptual nature of screaming as an "affective" sound phenomena [23–25]. Socialisation, culture and psychology also play a part in decoding this kind of sensory input, and each individual may have a different experience, understanding and affective response to particular sounds like screams, but it is not unreasonable to present screams and whispers as approaching a common or universal sound experience for everyone. It is possible, then to listen to and process screams in ways that are not terrifying, but rather evocative and somehow even familiar.

The human voice, and in particular so-called "extended" vocal techniques (screams, for example) have been incorporated into many musical styles and formats that do not always terrify listeners. Two of the most relevant here are the numerous genres and sub-genres of metal music that employ screaming as a vocal style, and EAM with its continual experimentation and exploration of human vocalization through extended techniques and digital signal processing. EAM often employs traditionally "non- musical" sounds (recordings of physical objects, machinery, animals, field recordings and so on) as the foundation for deconstruction, reassembly, reapplication and re- contextualization. This acousmatic approach is employed in *Sisters*. Here, sound functions not just as literal, illustrative and navigational, but as a way of forming relationships and concepts [26]. Abstraction of the sound material was an important element in this work both due to the main sound designer's background (Jamie Fawcus) in acousmatic art, music and performance, but also as a way to explore the more ambiguous, multilayered and complicated psychological and emotional nature of the human experiences and recollections. Using techniques such as granulation, phase vocoding, spectral processing and other FFT treatments, the vocal material and other recordings are re- contextualised and explored without ignoring or removing contextual associations entirely. Working with sound can be a balancing act between comprehensibility and musical abstraction, and the grey areas between documentary/representative sound, spectromorphological gesture and spectra, and narrative/drama are explored intentionally in our work.

Because the screaming material in *Sisters* plays such an important role, we established early on that simply using stock screaming material from sound libraries or songs from more than one vocal performer would be inappropriate; the Father, in particular, the screamer, needed to have a distinct "voice." This led to the use of sound material provided from a professional vocalist from the extreme metal subgenre, who excels at expressing heightened emotional states that could be described as cathartic, primal and at the extremes edge of perceived emotional arousal, states such as despair, terror, anguish and emotional pain. Our vocalist provided separated vocal takes from a variety of projects that expressed or interpreted many of these extreme emotions, and the material was examined, discussed, and excerpts were selected based on the affective impression on the project designers, and in particular how much these vocalizations matched the memories and impressions of the one designer whose experiences form the foundation of our experience. The expert vocalist was able to reproduce a wide range of scream vocalizations whilst avoiding many of the risks of damage to the vocal chords associated with this kind of expression. Such work corresponds to others documentation and exploration of screaming as an highly affective emotional audio state for artistic expression focused on imitation, mimicry, de-contextualization and abstraction [27–30].

Other affective spaces are created through different forms of audio abstraction, such as in the Sisters' Bedroom, a space audibly defined by the creak of wooden floors, the motion of bodies in play, the brushing of hair, friction of clothes, and the actions/sounds of playing in the girls' dolls house. None of this is explicitly expressed visually in the interactive part of the experience (i.e., via the cards). The voices are mostly whispers of the sisters in play and communication combined with other sounds suggesting intimacy, activity and imagination.

Fig. 8. A card depicting a violent scene in the Kitchen. The whole family views the aftermath of a distressing encounter in the Kitchen.

Material is deliberately close-mic recorded, using varying techniques in order to create an aural experience similar to ASMR media: binaural methods such as with Jecklin discs, differing microphone placements and polar patterns in order to maximize feelings and impressions of closeness and physicality to the sound. This is where the sound through the combination of perceived proximity and rich spectral content (and possibly deep personal association) aims to induce deep affective responses in the interactor, the receiving agent. The room is one of safety, creativity and interaction. At the same time however the screams of the Father are audible at times, inescapable, distant yet integral to the experience. The Father's screams are treated with subtlety - filtered and presented at low amplitudes. Our intention was not to present the Father only as a threat or adversarial presence, as we wanted to include the humanity of the character without excusing any implicit and indefensible actions such as possible violence, and to present this part of the experience as fragmentary, often contradictory and complicated. This screamed material is treated, then, more like musical material and is deliberately used in a less conventional manner than traditional screams. It is also in direct contrast, however, to our characterization of him sometimes as mechanical, as a ticking clock working at different speeds to indicate calm or threat. Using the human and non-human associations, we make the Father a complex figure who defies simple ontological representation, human and not.

In the Kitchen space (described more fully in Figure 4 and graphically represented in Figure 8) audio content is abstract but relational. Here, metal scraping (utensil-like), breaking glass, ticking clocks, and screaming are perhaps the dominant sounds in this scenario. Some screams were sourced by our expert vocalist, and some were commissioned by others. But here they are presented both as disjointed sound events or gestures, shuffled, granulated or frozen in varying time frames, but also related in their sound recording to form an apparatus for memory in the form of the cards that the interactor should recognize and group together to construct the space. To help assist with the grouping, we created a simple associative spectral footprint for some sounds. For example, the Sisters' Bedroom consists of warm, organic sounds sourced from wood, fabric, whispers, paper and other materials with a rich and broad spectrum, with elements bordering on broadband white and pink noise. This signature is in direct contrast to the Kitchen where the screams, breaking glass, rolling, ringing metal pots and pans, as well as knives being sharpened or manipulated, formed a common basis. Collectively, the Kitchen sounds have a specific spectral footprint characterized by more pronounced and separated formants, both harmonic and inharmonic (both with regular and irregular separation and relative amplitudes) which are distinct from other spaces.

4　Final Reflections

Memory can behave as a repeating, linear loop, recalled in a fixed manner, but also as a fluid field of performative and emerging impressions developed over time. Through our sounding material in *Sisters*, impressionistic interpretations and fragments of memory offer the possibility to process and transform emotions, affects and understandings from a distance. We stress, our aim in *Sisters* is aesthetic and so psychiatric or therapeutic intent is intentionally not addressed. Through our work and our model, we offer the possibility for a compelling multifaceted experience at least partially steered by choice—that is by an interactor needed to engage and organize the materialities we deliver. (Of course all interactors can also stop at any time and withdraw form the experience. Purposefully, there is no predetermined end-state, or *win*.) The sound design we create, and the agents we offer to express the work, offer dynamic frameworks to support how a listener can participate in and organize audio-based IDNs into affective, impressionistic sources for engagement. In this way, interactors move through simultaneous enveloping screens of memory and impression and become integral to an IDN experience beyond words alone. As in *Sisters*, they are enticed to engage with what they may, or not, discern.

References

1. Holloway-Attaway, L., Fawcus, J.: Making COVID dis-connections: designing intra-active and transdisciplinary sound-based narratives for phenomenal new material worlds. New Rev. Hypermedia Multimedia **28**(3–4), 112–142 (2023)
2. Barad, K.: Meeting the Universe Halfway: Quantum Physics and The Entanglement of Matter and Meaning. Duke University Press, Durham (2007)
3. Smalley, D.: Spectromorphology: explaining sound shapes. Organised Sound **2**(2), 107–126 (1997)
4. Haraway, D.J.: Staying With the Trouble: Making Kin in the Chthulucene. Duke University Press, Durham (2016)

5. Holloway-Attaway, L.: Embodying the posthuman subject: digital humanities and permeable material practice. In: Åsberg, C., Braidotti, R. (eds.) A Feminist Companion to the Posthumanities. Springer, Cham (2018). https://doi.org/10.1007/978-3-319-62140-1_8

6. Fleming, T.M, et al.: Serious games and gamification for mental health: current status and promising directions. Front. Psychiatry **7**, 215 (2017)

7. Andrews, A.: Serious games for psychological health education. In: Shumaker, R. (eds) Virtual and Mixed Reality - Systems and Applications. VMR 2011. LNCS, vol. 6774, pp. 3–10. Springer, Berlin (2011). https://doi.org/10.1007/978-3-642-22024-1_1

8. Koenitz, H.: Towards a specific theory of interactive narrative. In: H. Koenitz, G.F., Haahr, M., Sezen, D., Sezen, T.I. (eds.). Interactive Digital Narrative: History, Theory, and Practice. Routledge, Milton Park (2015)

9. Knoller, N.: Complexity and the userly text. In: M. Grishakova, M., Poulaki (eds.). Narrative Complexity: Cognition, Embodiment, Evolution. University of Nebraska Press (2019)

10. Murray, J. Hamlet on the Holodeck. MIT Press, Cambridge (2017)

11. Murray, J.H.: Research into interactive digital narrative: a kaleidoscopic view. In: Rouse, R., Koenitz, H., Haahr, M. (eds.) Interactive Storytelling. ICIDS 2018. LNCS, vol. 11318, pp. 3–17. Springer, Cham (2018). https://doi.org/10.1007/978-3-030-04028-4_1

12. Koentiz, et al.: INDCOR white paper 0: interactive digital narratives (IDNs)—a solution to the challenge of representing complex issues. ArXiv (2023)

13. Alaimo, S., Hekman. S. (eds.) Material Feminisms. Indiana University Press, Bloomington (2008)

14. Alaimo, S.: Bodily Natures: Science the Environment and the Material Self. University of Indiana Press, Bloomington (2010)

15. Grosz, E.: Volatile Bodies: Towards a Corporeal Feminism. Indiana University Press, Bloomington (1994)

16. Alaimo, S.: Exposed: Environmental Politics and Pleasures in Posthuman Times. University of Minnesota Press, Minneapolis (2017)

17. Braidotti, R.: The Posthuman. Polity Press, Cambridge (2013)

18. Hayles, K.: How We Became Posthuman: Virtual Bodies, Cybernetics, Literature and Informatics. University of Chicago Press, Chicago (1997)

19. Wolfe, C.: What is Posthumanism? University of Minnesota Press, Chicago (2010)

20. Holloway-Attaway, L., Fawcus, J. Patternings, Apt. 3b. 2021. Sounds as Affective Space for World-Building. In: Reyes, M. Pope, J. (eds). Texts of Discomfort. Interactive Storytelling Art. ETC Press, pp. 282–313 (2022)

21. Parikka, J. Insect Media: An Archeology of Animals and Technology. University of Minnesota Press, Chicago (2010)

22. Gregg, M., Seigworth, G. (eds.) The Affect Theory Reader. Duke University Press, Durham (2010)

23. Arnal, et al.: Human screams occupy a privileged niche in the communication soundscape. Curr. Biol. **25**, 2051–2056 (2015)

24. Christensen, K.: A dynasty of screams: Jamie lee curtis and the reinterpretation of the maternal voice in scream queens. Crit. Stud. Media Commun. **36**(3), 272–288 (2019)

25. Ollivier, R., et al.: Enjoy the violence: is appreciation for extreme music the result of cognitive control over the threat response system? Music. Percept. **37**(2), 95–110 (2019)

26. Chion, M.: The sound object. Organised Sound **21**(1), 14–24 (2016)

27. Thompson, M.: Three screams. In: Thompson, M., Biddle, I. (eds.). Sound, Music, Affect: Theorising Sonic Experience. Bloomsbury. (2013)

28. Kassabian, A.: Music for sleeping. In: Thompson, M., Biddle, I. (eds.). Sound, Music, Affect: Theorising Sonic Experience. Bloomsbury. (2013)

29. Clough, T.: My mother's scream. In Thompson, M., Biddle, I. (eds.). Sound, Music, Affect: Theorising Sonic Experience. Bloomsbury (2013)
30. Thompson, M., Biddle, I. (eds.). Sound, Music, Affect: Theorising Sonic Experience. Bloomsbury (2013)

Bookwander: From Printed Fiction to Virtual Reality—Four Design Approaches for Enhanced VR Reading Experiences

Nikola Kunzova[(✉)] [iD] and Daniel Echeverri[(✉)] [iD]

Atelier of Graphic Design and Multimedia, Department of Visual Computing - Faculty of Informatics, Masaryk University, Brno, Czech Republic
{nikkun,Daniel.Echeverri}@mail.muni.cz

Abstract. This paper explores the transformation of traditional written fiction into an immersive virtual reality (VR) experience. By combining VR technology with specific design methods, the paper proposes creating an adaptable environment that prioritises the text over other perceptible stimuli. The paper introduces *Bookwander*, an experimental VR reading experience which incorporates four unique design approaches, namely, *The Power of Text, Selective Imagery, Scenic Reading, and Playful Reading*. Each approach contributes to immersion, interpretation, visualisation, and interaction in distinct ways. The preliminary results from a qualitative pilot study indicate that providing spatial-based content in a reactive environment to the text strikes a suitable balance between traditional reading and a VR experience. Participants felt immersed without compromising the reading experience, and the various visual representations did not hinder interpretation or imagination. The paper concludes with recommendations for further developments in immersive reading and future research directions in this field.

Keywords: Virtual Reality · Immersive reading · Reader experience · Speculative design

1 Introduction

Over the past four decades, virtual reality (VR) technology has transformed traditional and digital content into rich, immersive experiences, ultimately influencing how people engage with various contemporary forms of media. This paper focuses on transforming printed media, mainly works of written fiction, into immersive VR experiences. The challenge of this task lies in avoiding distractions that fragment the reader's attention and hinder a deep state of concentration and absorption while reading a text. We suggest that combining VR technology with specific design methods can enhance the enjoyment and fulfilment of the reading experience. In this paper, we consider *reading* as the process of being able to perceive, interpret, and comprehend written content, in this case, in a VR setting. The combination of VR and design can provide an adaptable environment that gives priority to the text. Addressing technical and conceptual questions is crucial in achieving this goal. This involves exploring optimal ways to visualise a text in VR,

L. Holloway-Attaway and J. T. Murray (Eds.): ICIDS 2023, LNCS 14383, pp. 309–328, 2023.
https://doi.org/10.1007/978-3-031-47655-6_19

preserving the original meaning of fiction in the transition to VR, and understanding the impact of visually rich virtual worlds on reader interpretation.

The paper is structured as follows: First, it examines changes in attitudes towards reading in the digital era and compares immersive VR experiences with reading works of fiction. It also briefly reviews critical concepts such as immersion, interpretation, visualisation, and interaction. Second, grounded on the shared concept of immersion between printed media and VR, the paper introduces *Bookwander*, an experimental VR reading experience.

Bookwander explores four unique design approaches: namely, *The Power of Text*, which focuses on kinetic typography, *Selective Imagery*, which imitates the visual representation of a page but constrains reader agency through scrollable paragraphs and anchored illustrations; *Scenic Reading*, which presents a text-driven experience augmented by reactive spatial-based narrative content, and *Playful Reading* which incorporates teleportation of the user and object manipulation to expand the narrative. Third, the paper presents the preliminary results from a qualitative pilot study that collected initial reactions and feedback on these four approaches.

While all approaches provided positive experiences, according to the study participants, offering spatial-based content in a reactive environment to the text provides a suitable balance between traditional reading and VR experience. Immersion was achieved without compromising reading, and various visuals did not hinder interpretation or imagination. We conclude the paper with recommendations to inspire new developments in immersive reading and future research paths in this field.

2 Related Work

Digital literature emerged in the mid-20th century and gave rise to interactive fiction, hypertext fiction, non-linear storytelling, expanding beyond printed books to interactive media like video games and interactive movies. Together with these novel forms of literature, the preferences of readers and their attitudes towards how they consume narrative content also evolved and changed, as we discuss below.

2.1 Attitudes and Preferences Towards Reading

Younger generations, such as Generation Z, read less for pleasure and more for educational and professional purposes [28], spending increased time with digital media. This has led to fragmented attention and reduced ability to focus deeply [1, 42]. Similarly, excessive use of digital technologies affects people of all ages, making it challenging to immerse in reading [1, 28]. Digital technology and information overload changed how people engage with books. However, borrowing from friends and family remains common [11, 24]. Changes in consumption trends, supported, for instance, by unlimited use of search engines, prioritise easy information access over its quality, potentially impacting the ability to synthesise information and analyse author intent. Immediate access can lead to viewing texts as authorless, overlooking critical background factors [1]. Digital reading is often perceived as less serious, leading to faster skimming and keyword searching [15]. Readers' limited time availability also hinders their ability to devote substantial time to reading [1].

Nonetheless, printed books—preferred across all generations [24]—are also favoured over digital, potentially due to habit and the tangible experience [8, 13, 23]. They are usually chosen for careful reading and note-taking, offering a better sense of overview [35]. Reading and learning from printed formats also tend to be more thorough and memorable, whereas digital reading can be more exhausting [4, 15].

2.2 VR as an Immersive Narrative Medium

The term *virtual reality* (VR) is connected to exploring an extended reality in such an immersive way that the virtuality completely absorbs the experiencer [22]. The immersive potential of VR as a storytelling medium is backed, for instance, by the current developments in VR games and VR cinema.

VR games are experiencing rapid growth supported by technological advancements [2, 48]. These games demonstrate VR's immersive potential, with ongoing research focused on improving immersion, embodiment, and presence [10, 41]. However, challenges like cyber-sickness and interaction-related concerns still hinder seamless immersion [5, 6, 10, 37].

In contrast, VR cinema provides a less interactive experience, requiring minimal movement from viewers [48]. Various approaches are employed, including dedicated physical spaces, virtual theatres, and exclusive VR-designed films featuring interactivity [48]. Production companies are pushing the boundaries of VR storytelling through live-action, computer graphics, and 360° videos.

While the boundary for VR cinema is empathy, and for VR games are explicit goals [49], these aspects can be considerably different when looking at the possibilities of reading works of fiction in a VR environment. For instance, current research explores integrating physical objects in virtual spaces for familiarity and spatial literacy [14], delves into concepts like identification, parasocial interaction, and 'breaking the fourth wall' to enhance narratives [38] and seeks ways to evoke emotional response in VR experiences through light, music, and colour [40].

Concepts and Principles

A better conceptual solution to reading fiction in a VR environment might be found in identifying not how they can be individually enhanced but how they are both similar and different. Both a book and a VR environment transport the reader into a fictional world (a concept closely related to *immersion* [10, 17]) and represent aspects of the narrative through different perceptible stimuli (a concept pertaining to *visualisation* [3]). There are also unique aspects of each medium, for instance, *interpretation* [9] in books and *interaction* [33] for VR. Failing to balance these aspects can negatively impact the VR reading experience. We discuss these concepts and how they are essential to the reading experience.

Immersion

This phenomenon involves deep engagement in an experience [10, 17]. In textual narratives, it encompasses attention, emotional engagement, mental imagery, and transportation [17]. In VR, it is divided into immersion, embodiment, and presence [25], with empathy for virtual characters enhancing immersion. While there are similarities between reading fiction and engaging in a VR environment, it is crucial to distinguish *narrative absorption* from *presence* [25].

Narrative absorption considers how a setting, plot, and characters stimulate mental imagery [20]. *Presence* correlates with immersion in VR, creating an illusion of "being there" [33]. This illusion can be attributed to the concepts of *place illusion* (PI) and *plausibility* (PSI). *Place illusion* is the sense of "being there," while *plausibility* is a deeper illusion formed by an interactive environment reacting to the person's actions, aligning with natural expectations and enhancing credibility. Balancing narrative absorption and presence while reading fiction in VR is crucial, ensuring neither overshadows the other, which can potentially alter the experience [25].

Interpretation
Interpreting the meaning of a text is a crucial mental activity while reading, and both mental imagery and embodied cognition influence this process [3, 20]. While mental imagery plays a role in interpretation by supporting and deepening the reading experience [9], embodied cognition considers the physical aspects surrounding the reader as integral to reading [3]. This involves the interface, environment, and the reader's body, encompassing both *spatio-temporal* and *imaginary dimensions*. The former relies on external factors for encoding and decoding information, like paper or screens, while the latter stimulates mental imagery based on the text, particularly during immersive reading. While the excessive use of audio and visual representations can negatively impact the imaginary dimension [3], 3D representation of objects facilitates the transfer of the spatio-temporal dimension into the VR space.

Visualisation
Adapting fiction to VR allows for enhancing visuals with sound effects, audio, or even virtual agents, though their impact on textual interpretation and mental imagery can vary [3]. VR visualisation can also provide readers with otherwise inaccessible environments, further stimulating their imagination [3]. However, in VR reading, *textual visualisation* should take priority over *pictorial visualisation* [16, 39]. Yet, hardware limitations like resolution and fixed eye distance constrain design solutions for visualising text in VR, but recent research has identified optimal parameters for comfortable reading, particularly benefiting readers with visual disabilities [16, 27, 31]. This optimisation considers factors such as font style, size, text segment length, contrast, and text positioning. VR reading can be slower and less accurate compared to traditional displays, but adjustments like a larger field of view and wider space to display content can enhance overall readability [27].

Interaction
This aspect of human behaviour is crucial for immersion in VR, fostering presence and connection to the virtual world [33]. While traditional books lack extensive interactivity, digital technologies have introduced interaction into textual narratives [32]. From the perspective of interactive storytelling, narrativity and interactivity can be combined in two ways: *narrative games* and *playable stories* [29]. Narrative games prioritise player actions over story content, while playable stories prioritise the story over player actions [29]. Narrative games have specific goals and winning and losing states, while playable

stories emphasise exploration and creativity without win-or-lose conditions [29]. Interactive narratives blur the boundaries between authors, readers, actors, and spectators [30]. In VR fiction, it is essential to explore how interaction can deepen immersion in textual narratives while creating a distinct interactive reading experience that adds value without becoming an obstacle [30].

Experiencing Works of Fiction in VR
Combining books with VR yields diverse reactions but presents challenges due to technology and conceptual limits. Some apps and platforms aim to imitate real-life reading experiences, offering traditional reading environments with virtual books like *Bibli-o-mat* (2022) [45] and *Chimera Reader* (2016) [46]. Others, such as *StoryVR* [26], enhance real-world reading with thematic 3D settings and audiobooks integration. A significant example is *Dear Angelica* (2017) [47], where in some passages, calligraphic text gradually appears alongside spoken words, guiding users through scenes. These passages create pauses between visually immersive sequences, allowing time for reflection and analysis.

Current VR solutions for reading fiction, while innovative and engaging, do not grasp the full potential of the technology. Adapting fiction to VR risks turning the narrative into VR movies with excessive audiovisual stimuli. We suggest that to maintain the essence of written fiction, an approach closer to real-life reading is the safest option. However, the challenge lies in combining the immersive and interactive aspects of VR with the qualities of real-life reading.

2.3 The Challenges and Opportunities of Reading in VR

Books and fiction have successfully overcome digital transformations, thus printed media remains the preferred choice for reading fiction. However, younger generations, accustomed to interactive digital entertainment, often find written fiction lacking immediate satisfaction, slow-paced and less entertaining [34, 42]. The association of reading with obligatory school activities further reduces its appeal [34].

Ironically, using VR can make reading fiction more appealing to young readers, creating immersive experiences that remove distractions and foster empathy [25]. Virtual environments can enhance attention and learning by incorporating props and providing stimulus-free settings [3]. However, it is crucial to ensure that VR does not compromise the content but instead enhances the reading experience using the medium's capabilities.

By embracing VR, it is possible to balance and respect the unique characteristics of printed and digital media while delivering unprecedented immersive experiences, especially captivating for new generations of readers. In the next section, we introduce *Bookwander*. This design exercise explored multiple authoring and design methods to provide an immersive reading experience in a VR environment.

3 Design of Bookwander

Bookwander, part of the master thesis and an original contribution of the first author of this paper [18], was developed in Unity for the Oculus Quest 2, following the Research through Design methodology. This methodology enabled the researcher to explore the making of design artefact, in this case, a series of experimental approaches to VR reading, while constructing theory not for the making but through the making [12, 43].

The title *Bookwander* originates from the idea that VR spaces allow the reader to wander around the reading environment. It includes an opening scene, four VR reading approaches, and a short tutorial for each approach. We named these approaches *Power of the Text*, *Selective Imagery*, *Scenic Reading*, and *Playful Reading*. The starting point for *Bookwander* was to shift from simulating the physical representation of books and instead focus on the narrative experience and fostering virtual absorption. *Bookwander* was designed to explore four distinct experiential approaches that transform a work of fiction into an enjoyable VR reading experience.

The narrative content of this prototype are extracts from Jules Verne's novel, *Twenty Thousand Leagues Under the Sea* (Verne, 1992) [36]. We used short fragments from the following passages. From the first part, Chapter 10, *The Man of the Seas* (pp. 44–56) and Chapter 15, *A Walk on the Bottom of the Sea* (pp. 77–81). From the second part, we used text from Chapter 9, *A Vanished Continent* (pp. 191–197), and Chapter 21, *A Hecatomb* (p. 273–280). Due to the widespread recognition of this science fiction story, including adaptations in theatre, film, and digital games, these story fragments spared participants in our user study from adapting to an entirely unfamiliar context.

Considering immersion, interaction, interpretation, and visualisation, we prioritised reading as the central activity in the experience. Interaction was primarily focused on moving forward or backwards through the text. The prototype featured three systems for the reader to progress in the story: an animated text moving line by line, scrollable paragraphs, and floating frames with paragraphs appearing around the reader. Some experimental approaches, like *Selective Imagery* and *Playful Reading* allowed readers to interact with virtual objects, supplementing traditional reading.

Merging immersive aspects of books and VR faced conceptual and technological limitations. Conceptually, it was crucial to strike a balance between the author's original intentions and the use of appropriate visuals that would support the reader's mental imagery. Furthermore, various methods were needed to enable readers to interact with the textual narrative in VR, such as recursive teleportation in *Playful Reading* and manipulating illustrations in *Selective Imagery*.

The colour schemes, crucial for setting the mood for the experience, were designed for legibility, avoiding high contrast like black and white. *Gelasio*, a versatile transitional serif typeface, was chosen due to its readability in digital and print media (Fig. 1). This choice aims to evoke an emotional connection and create a traditional reading experience, as transitional serif fonts are common in printed fiction.

Some paragraphs from the selected passages were divided into shorter blocks to display less text to the reader at a given moment. Even though those paragraphs do not match the ones in the printed novel, their content and order remain intact. The visual style was consistent throughout the entire experience, although there were variations across approaches (Fig. 2). Traditional book illustrations were the primary inspiration for the visuals, invoking readers' nostalgia for printed books. In some approaches, the visuals adopted a rather abstract form or combined illustrations with 3D objects (Fig. 3). The intention, in most cases, was to create visuals that conveyed the mood and dynamics of

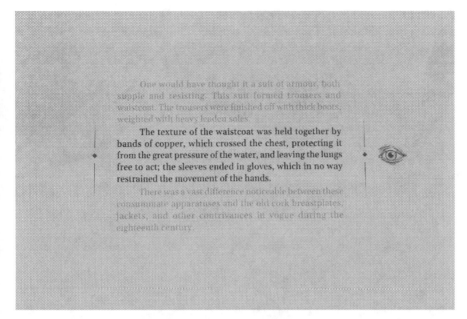

Fig. 1. *Gelasio*, the main typography in *Bookwander*.

the narrative rather than representing specific content. These intentional design choices aimed to explore how visuals would interfere with readers' subjective imagination.

All approaches featured an environment centred around the reader[1]. This design decision was based on the premise that people typically remain stationary while reading a book, and similar behaviour was anticipated in this scenario. Lastly, each approach incorporated ambient music with the purpose of enhancing the user's immersion. The selection of ambient music was carefully curated to align with the atmosphere of each passage in the respective approach.

3.1 Bookwander: Four Design Approaches

Bookwander delves into four distinct design approaches: *The Power of Text*, which explores kinetic typography; *Selective Imagery*, which replicates page aesthetics and illustrations; *Scenic Reading*, which provides reactive spatial-based content; and *Playful Reading*, which incorporates user teleportation and object manipulation to expand the narrative. Each approach has its distinct role in enhancing immersion, interpretation, visualisation, and interaction, as we discuss next.

Power of the Text
The first approach aimed to focus the entire experience around the textual content through kinetic typography [19, 21]. The main inspirations were typographic works such as

---

[1] We invite our readers to follow this link for a video sample of *Bookwander*: https://youtube.com/playlist?list=PL8fiaBDEkXrNu7xZIY-cYQdCuPVOKUmjd

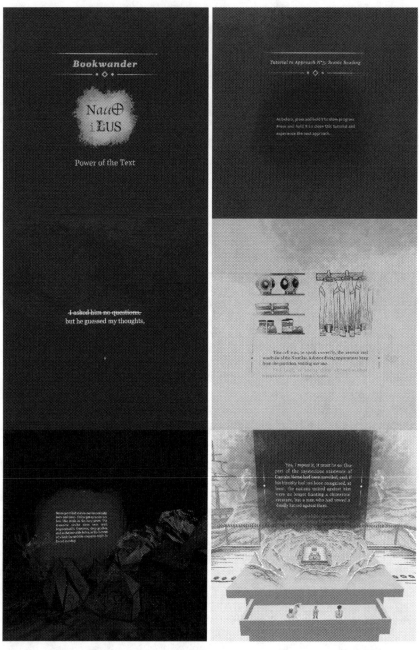

Fig. 2. General overview of *Bookwander* experiences. Top: Intro scene and tutorial. Middle: *Power of the Text* and *Selective Imagery*. Bottom: *Scenic Reading* and *Playful Reading*.

Apocalypse Rhyme [44]. Distinct animations were employed for dialogue and descriptions, ensuring consistency with the representations of the story throughout the passages

Fig. 3. Comparison between the abstract visual style in *Power of the Text* and a "specific" visual style in *Scenic Reading.*

(Fig. 4). Furthermore, these animations were based on the atmosphere and events of the virtual environment. To accommodate these animations, the text was displayed in lines instead of conventional paragraphs, departing from the usual novel format.

To ensure total concentration on the text and its animations, no additional visuals, like illustrations, were used in this approach. Considering the events of this passage, the environment draws inspiration from the Nautilus, offering an abstract setting with dark brown and red tones.

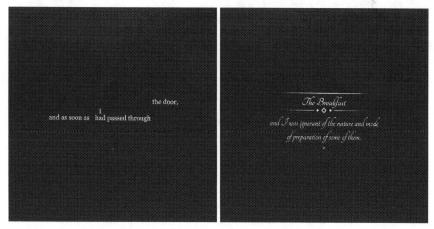

Fig. 4. Animations, special formatting of the text, and use of different fonts. Left: kinetic typographic play. Right: the text and layout mimic a menu, consistent with the story's events.

Selective Imagery

The second approach resembles the appearance of printed books by using scrollable paragraphs, showing only three paragraphs at a time to prevent an overwhelming amount of displayed text. The central paragraph is in the viewer's focus, accompanied by upper and lower paragraphs that hint at previous and upcoming events (Fig. 5). These peripheral paragraphs are typically within the reader's field of view during real-world reading. Some paragraphs are marked with an eye icon on the right side, which means they are complemented by an illustration. The reader can manually position the illustration anywhere around them (Fig. 5). As the reader progresses and the paragraph linked to an image disappears, the illustration fades away. The concept of placing images around the reader is inspired by appearing and disappearing thoughts and images through one's mind when reading.

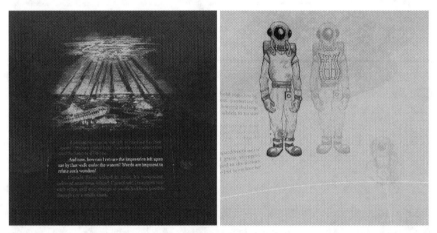

Fig. 5. The environment of Selective Imagery. Left: paragraph layout. Right: user placing an illustration.

The environment maintains an abstract nature rather than specific. The colour scheme of the environment changes to reflect shifts in scenery or the story's mood. Initially, it resembles that of printed books, with a light beige background—like paper—along with dark text and illustrations. When the events unwind, and a character, for instance, dives into the ocean, the colour scheme changes to dark blue with light blue text.

Scenic Reading

The third approach prioritises a high level of visual absorption compared to other approaches in *Bookwander*. To achieve this goal, a specially crafted environment was created to complement the story events using both textured 3D models and 2D sprites. Non-intrusive 2D animations were added to the background to introduce subtle move-ment. This combination ensures that the final experience does not "feel" like a movie but an environment (Fig. 6). To moderate the impact on readers' mental imagery, the priority was to capture the story's chromatic mood over detailed environments. Visual elements represent concepts rather than specific objects, offering readers a vague yet sufficient understanding of the surroundings. This approach aims to give readers enough conceptual space to imagine details while still feeling immersed in the spatial environment. In contrast to the second approach, there is no additional interaction with the surroundings beyond the progression of the story.

Fig. 6. The environment of Scenic Reading.

Playful Reading

The fourth approach combines reading and various mechanics found in digital games. Recognising that reading itself requires a cognitive effort, the aim of this approach, like playable stories [29], seeks to enhance the reading experience by providing game mechanics that allow a certain level of play without the presence of a winning or losing state. In this approach, readers solve puzzles while reading—by placing an object on a table, they establish a connection between the object and the current paragraph, indicated by matching colours (Fig. 7). This process encourages readers to observe, interpret, and link the object to the relevant paragraph. This cognitive activity could potentially improve the reader's retention of the events. In terms of visual style, unlike other approaches, this one leans towards concreteness, with illustrations being transformed into 3D objects, giving the impression that they have come to life within the experience (Fig. 7).

Due to its puzzle mechanic, this approach offers the highest level of interactivity, allowing readers to move around and manipulate objects. Thus, its interactive nature makes it the most experimental approach because it is the most distant experience from traditional reading.

Fig. 7. The environment of Playful Reading. Left: colour connection between the paragraph and the object. Right: general view.

4   User Study: The Pilot

This study aimed to explore how *Bookwander*'s four design approaches shaped the reading experience for VR users. With this in mind, we recruited 10 participants, four males and six females aged 23 to 28. Most of the participants had backgrounds in IT-related fields of study, while others were from fields related to the media industry. They were recruited based on *convenience sampling*—based on availability and accessibility, as well as through *snowball sampling*—referrals from other participants. In terms of reading habits, four participants stated they did not have as much time to read as they would like, and nearly half reported reading only one or two books annually. Many participants used alternative mediums for reading, mainly smartphones and tablets.

Before the pilot, the participants were briefed about the study and provided with a consent form as required by the research and ethics policies of our institution. This included details about their privacy and identity protection. During the study sessions, participants individually had the opportunity to experience all approaches sequentially (Table 1). Although a randomised sequence of approaches could have been possible for this study, the implications in the results, considering the sample size, would not have been considerable.

Table 1. Summary of participant sessions

Approach	Time in the Tutorial (avg.)	Time in the Approach (avg.)
Power of the Text	1.6 min	8.2 min
Selective Imagery	3.0 min	6.7 min
Scenic Reading	1.0 min	5.1 min
Playful Reading	6.8 min	12.5 min

After each experience, the participants shared their thoughts with the researcher, and their commentaries were audio recorded. They were encouraged to speak freely, and their conversations were generally uninterrupted. While direct questions about the research topic were not asked, participants sometimes provided hints about their experience, which led to additional questions for further clarification. Finally, after completing the fourth and final approach, participants shared their experiences, compared them, and selected their preferred one. In cases where certain topics were not addressed, such as immersion, visualisation, interpretation, interaction, readability, or controls, additional questions were formulated to gather insights on these aspects.

4.1 Summary of Findings

Following a grounded theory approach [7], the analysis of the information gathered was based on the following protocol. The interview recordings were transcribed, tagged with initial keywords, and later grouped into concepts and categories. Based on emerging patterns, we focused the analysis on the factors and aspects that contributed to immersive reading.

Seven out of ten participants preferred the third approach, *Scenic Reading*, as the most effective one for reading fiction in VR. A smaller group of participants (3) suggested a combination of the third and fourth approaches or the second and third approaches, while others (2) mentioned that they would choose the first approach due to its simplicity. For instance, Participant 2 mentioned:

> *"If I would go in the direction, like, really want to read a book through this media, I would go rather between the second and third approaches. I do have this surrounding which is helping me to merge into this world, but without any movement and interaction, because when I'm reading a book, I really just want to read. But if I want something more, some entertainment, then I would go something between the third and fourth approaches. It really depends on what my goal is* [for reading] *when I'm playing this."*

One participant suggested that each approach could be suitable for different contexts, for example, the first approach might work well for short stories or poems, the second approach for educational applications such as language learning, the third approach for longer texts, and the interactivity of the fourth approach might appeal to children.

The use of ambient music was generally well-received by the participants. Even those who do not typically listen to music while reading found that it enhanced their immersion and was not distracting. According to Participant 6,

> *"Often, when I read books, I have some music on in the background, and it sometimes irritates me that I read a slow scene in the book, and when the music is full of beats, it destroys my focus. But in this case, it is so nicely combined".*

Other participants expressed a desire for more sound effects aligned with the events in the story.

Another discussed feature was the controls used in the approaches. Overall, participants responded positively to the controls, finding them intuitive most of the time. More experienced VR users suggested minor improvements to enhance the user experience, such as using a different grabbing method. Below, we discuss in more detail the findings from this pilot study.

Power of the Text

Participants gave positive feedback on the first approach, specifically liking the short lines of text, kinetic typography, and overall simplicity. Interestingly, some participants suggested applying kinetic typography to the other approaches too. Opinions on using multiple fonts within the text varied, with many finding it interesting but cautioning against overuse due to potential confusion. For instance, Participant 2 mentioned, "...*when the text started to be in the different fonts and with some different animation, I was more curious about the animation and about these different changes than in the text itself.*" Calligraphic and highly detailed fonts were challenging for some participants to read. Displaying text in one or two lines, rather than a full paragraph, received mixed opinions. Some preferred having the previous line as a reminder of what they had read, while others liked seeing only the relevant lines at a given moment. This prevented them from skipping over lines as they would while reading a traditional book. Participant 4 illustrated this case:

I sometimes I get too confused by the text when I'm reading it, and I'm skipping lines. But now I feel that I cannot skip these lines because they are not there. So, I need to concentrate on the text. And when the text is also interactive, it catches your attention, and you can visualise [the ideas better].

Animations received overall positive feedback in this approach. For some readers, animations served as a validation of their understanding of the text, as they were played after relevant sections in the passage. However, four participants found animations distracting, diverting focus or altering mood. Some participants eventually skipped animations, preferring their own pace.

Selective Imagery

Participants thought the second approach successfully captured the essence of reading physical books with its use of paragraph layout and illustrations. They deemed it more suitable for longer texts than the first approach. The scrolling, similar to websites, felt natural to them due to their familiarity with this method of interaction. They valued that images acted as indicators of short pauses, allowing them to set their reading pace. According to Participant 1, "*In the second approach, whenever there was a picture, it fit really well with the text. It also provided this brief pause when I could think about what I just read*". Participants appreciated the illustrations in understanding specific paragraphs, particularly when their language proficiency was low or when recalling story events. They considered this a valuable enhancement to their reading experience. Participant 3 stated in this regard: "*...and in* [approach] *number two, I remember the illustrations more than the text. But because the illustrations were illustrating the text, I now remember the text as well.*"

Regarding the environment's colour combination, the transition from pale to dark colours did not significantly affect readability for participants. While most appreciated the change, some needed time to adjust to it and found it mildly distracting. Moreover, the insufficient colour difference between the current and adjacent paragraphs caused inadvertent reading of the "faded" paragraphs, impacting the experience negatively. The option to manually place illustrations also distracted almost half of the participants, leading to uncertainty about whether they should read or place illustrations first, which affected their sense of agency. Participant 6 mentioned, *"I felt this inner tension: do I want to read the paragraph first or show the picture, what should I do first? So that made me distracted a lot."* Although the manual placement of illustrations was not necessary, some participants felt that it made them focus more on the task of moving and looking at the illustration than they would in a traditional book.

Scenic Reading

The third approach received the highest favorability among participants, who agreed that it effectively used the potential of spatial immersion in VR while maintaining the act of reading as the primary activity. It was also regarded as the most immersive experience overall. Participant 5 stated, *"I really love to have the environment around me and then I really feel immersed to the story... I think this one resembles the most the feeling... when... what I have around me when I imagine what is around me, that it absorbs me and I have the feeling I am in the middle of the situation..."* The participants appreciated the balance between abstract and concrete visuals, as it immersed them in the story world while still allowing room for their subjective imagination. They enjoyed being able to simply appreciate the scenery without the need for additional interaction, distinguishing it from the second and fourth approaches.

However, the visuals and occasional animations raised expectations among participants; some desired more such events. The moving "text clouds" provided a refreshing change to static text placement in previous approaches. Participants liked how it directed their attention to relevant areas based on context. However, this approach also led some participants to skip paragraphs more often, as the visuals made them feel they could understand the story's content from the environment.

Playful Reading

The fourth approach elicited mixed reactions, largely due to its experimental nature. On the one hand, while many readers appreciated the main concept, some expressed strong negative opinions about it. The primary point of contention revolved around the interaction aspect. Some participants felt that the emphasis on interaction detracted from the reading experience and disrupted immersion. According to Participant 10, *"I was focusing a lot more on buttons and wanting to see more pictures and stuff like that and in the end focusing on pictures rather than the story.* They found themselves more attentive to remembering what to do or getting distracted by the playful elements instead of focusing on the reading itself. The prominence of interaction made them feel as if they were on a quest rather than engaging in a reading activity.

On the other hand, some participants enjoyed the entertainment value of this approach, particularly the interaction and the puzzle-solving aspect. They found that the puzzle component made them think about the paragraphs and enhanced their engagement with the text. In this regard, participant 9 stated, *"The fourth one was interesting because I had to decipher the picture, the object, and then I read the paragraph, of course, and then imagine the scene and then connect the scene with the picture, with the object. I think it made me think more about the paragraph."* This was an expected outcome considered in the design phase. The design of the puzzle aimed to minimise the reader's stress, but sometimes proved frustrating as objects weren't clearly visible, making accurate guesses difficult. Some mistakenly believed objects needed to be placed in specific locations, which added to the stress. Participant 8 remarked that *"It was a bit confusing for me if I'm supposed to place the object somehow correctly..."* Finally, a few participants voiced their interest in interacting with and changing the surroundings instead of solely focusing on the small table scene they teleported into.

In summary, while some participants desired interactive elements while reading, they suggested finding a middle ground between the third and fourth approaches. They prefer an interactive experience that does not have a quest-like structure. Participant 2 suggested, *"I am not sure if I was reading very properly in this chapter because most of the time it was kind of like a quest for me."* Avoiding such structure would allow them to engage with the content without alienating them from the actual reading experience.

5   Discussion

In the previous section, we presented findings from an empirical study on immersive reading using four design approaches: *Power of Text*, *Selective Imagery*, *Scenic Reading*, and *Playful Reading*. *Scenic Reading* emerged as the preferred approach due to its balanced use of abstract and concrete visuals, limited agency, and dynamic text placement that guided readers' attention through the environment. Spatial immersion was highly valued, as participants felt absorbed into the story environment. Yet, the most notable weakness was participants' inclination to skip or skim through content.

Nonetheless, the other approaches offered unique benefits. *Power of Text*, with kinetic typography, was praised for its simplicity, allowing readers to go at their own pace, while animations aided with text comprehension. However, participants cautioned against excessive typography complexity. *Selective Imagery*, the second approach, was considered suitable for longer texts, reminding participants of reading printed books. The scrolling feature in this approach allowed participants to read at their own pace, and the illustrations aided in understanding the meaning of specific paragraphs. Yet, the manual placement of illustrations was seen by some as distracting. *Playful Reading* generated mixed reactions; some liked the interactivity and puzzle-solving elements, while others felt that the emphasis on interaction disrupted immersion. Participants suggested combining interactivity and reading without a quest-like structure.

6   Conclusion

Overall, factors such as a well-balanced visual approach, limited agency, spatial immersion, simple interactivity, visuals aiding understanding, and moderation in interactive elements contributed to a positive immersive reading experience.

These factors were identified in the four different approaches for immersive reading of works of fiction in VR in the prototype *Bookwander*. The most significant outcome was that the participants of the pilot user study enjoyed reading a story the most in an environment resembling the events in the narrative without any additional interaction. This balance is the most optimal for the reading experience in VR. However, that does not mean that we need to suppress interaction completely. The most important finding regarding interaction is that it could be used, but it should not be a part of a quest-like system because it is more mentally demanding, thus causing unwanted distractions and stress.

The pilot study received positive feedback, but it also revealed controversial features, particularly interaction. A future user study aims to refine these findings for a deeper understanding of what makes reading in VR immersive. Results suggest VR can create a distraction-free environment that intensifies the feeling of transportation while reading fiction, which can be achieved by using various audiovisual elements. Future work can explore further ways in which interaction can be combined with various design approaches in a non-distractive manner so that it still enhances the reading experience. Additionally, it is intriguing to identify the possible effects of these audiovisual elements in VR on mental imagery, how they can intensify (or reduce) the impact of the written narrative, and how they influence the way the experiencers remember or comprehend the story.

Acknowledgements. We would like to thank Mgr.art. Helena Lukášová, ArtD. And Filip Opálený for their valuable input. We are also thankful to the participants for their time and insights. This research was part of a master's thesis at the Faculty of Informatics, Masaryk University in Brno, Czech Republic.

References

1. Alexander, P.A.: The disciplined reading and learning research laboratory: reading into the future: competence for the 21st century. Educ. Psychol. **47**(4), 259–280 (2012). https://doi.org/10.1080/00461520.2012.722511
2. Alsop, T.: Topic: Virtual reality (VR). https://www.statista.com/topics/2532/virtual-reality-vr/. Accessed 02 July 2023
3. Baceviciute, S., et al.: Remediating learning from non-immersive to immersive media: using EEG to investigate the effects of environmental embeddedness on reading in Virtual Reality. Comput. Educ. **164**, 104122 (2021). https://doi.org/10.1016/j.compedu.2020.104122
4. Barshay, J.: Evidence increases for reading on paper instead of screens. https://hechingerreport.org/evidence-increases-for-reading-on-paper-instead-of-screens/. Accessed 24 Apr 2023
5. Boletsis, C. et al.: HCI research in virtual reality: a discussion of problem-solving. In: International Conference on Interfaces and Human Computer Interaction, p. 5 IADIS, Portugal (2017)
6. Boletsis, C.: The new era of virtual reality locomotion: a systematic literature review of techniques and a proposed typology. Multimodal Technol. Interact. **1**(4), 24 (2017). https://doi.org/10.3390/mti1040024
7. Bryant, A.: The grounded theory method. In: Leavy, P. (ed.) The Oxford Handbook of Qualitative Research. Oxford University Press, Cambridge (2014). https://doi.org/10.1093/oxfordhb/9780199811755.013.016
8. Clinton, V.: Reading from paper compared to screens: a systematic review and meta-analysis. J. Res. Read. **42**(2), 288–325 (2019). https://doi.org/10.1111/1467-9817.12269
9. Douglas, J.Y.: Where the senses become a stage and reading is direction: performing the texts of virtual reality and interactive fiction. TDR 1988- **37**(4), 18–37 (1993). https://doi.org/10.2307/1146290

10. Evans, L., Rzeszewski, M.: Hermeneutic relations in VR: immersion, embodiment, presence and HCI in VR gaming. In: Fang, X. (ed.) HCI in Games: Second International Conference, HCI-Games 2020, Held as Part of the 22nd HCI International Conference, HCII 2020, Copenhagen, Denmark, July 19–24, 2020, Proceedings, pp. 23–38. Springer International Publishing, Cham (2020). https://doi.org/10.1007/978-3-030-50164-8_2

11. Faverio, M., Perrin, A.: Three-in-ten Americans now read e-books. https://www.pewresearch.org/short-reads/2022/01/06/three-in-ten-americans-now-read-e-books/. Accessed 28 June 2023

12. Frayling, C.: Research in art and design (royal college of art research papers, vol. 1, no. 1, 1993/4) (1994)

13. Gerlach, J., Buxmann, P.: Investigating the acceptance of electronic books – the impact of haptic dissonance on innovation adoption. In: ECIS 2011 Proceedings (2011)

14. Hameed, A., Perkis, A.: Spatial storytelling: finding interdisciplinary immersion. In: Rouse, R., Koenitz, H., Haahr, M. (eds.) Interactive Storytelling: 11th International Conference on Interactive Digital Storytelling, ICIDS 2018, Dublin, Ireland, December 5–8, 2018, Proceedings, pp. 323–332. Springer International Publishing, Cham (2018). https://doi.org/10.1007/978-3-030-04028-4_35

15. Jabr, F.: The Reading Brain in the Digital Age: The Science of Paper versus Screens. https://www.scientificamerican.com/article/reading-paper-screens/. Accessed 24 Apr 2023

16. Kojic, T., et al.: User experience of reading in virtual reality — finding values for text distance, size and contrast. In: 2020 Twelfth International Conference on Quality of Multimedia Experience (QoMEX), pp. 1–6 (2020). https://doi.org/10.1109/QoMEX48832.2020.9123091

17. Kuijpers, M.: Story world absorption scale (2020). https://doi.org/10.17605/OSF.IO/ZF439

18. Kunzová, N.: Immersive Reading in VR. Masaryk University, Faculty of Informatics (2023)

19. Kuraitytė, M., et al.: Impact of kinetic typography on readers' attention. Visible Lang. **54**, 1–2 (2020)

20. Kuzmičová, A.: Mental Imagery in the Experience of Literary Narrative: Views from Embodied Cognition. Stockholm University (2013)

21. Lee, J. et al.: Using kinetic typography to convey emotion in text-based interpersonal communication. In: Proceedings of the 6th Conference on Designing Interactive Systems, pp. 41–49 Association for Computing Machinery, New York (2006). https://doi.org/10.1145/1142405.1142414

22. Merriam-Webster: Experiencer (2023). https://www.merriam-webster.com/dictionary/experiencer

23. Noyes, J.M., Garland, K.J.: Computer- vs. paper-based tasks: are they equivalent? Ergonomics 51(9), 1352–1375 (2008). https://doi.org/10.1080/00140130802170387

24. Perrin, A.: Book Reading 2016. https://www.pewresearch.org/internet/2016/09/01/book-reading-2016/. Accessed 28 June 2023

25. Pianzola, F., et al.: Virtual reality as a tool for promoting reading via enhanced narrative absorption and empathy. Sci. Study Lit. **9**(2), 163–194 (2019). https://doi.org/10.1075/ssol.19013.pia

26. Pianzola, F., Deriu, L.: StoryVR: a virtual reality app for enhancing reading. In: Kubincová, Z., Lancia, L., Popescu, E., Nakayama, M., Scarano, V., Gil, A.B. (eds.) Methodologies and Intelligent Systems for Technology Enhanced Learning, 10th International Conference. Workshops: Volume 2, pp. 281–288. Springer International Publishing, Cham (2021). https://doi.org/10.1007/978-3-030-52287-2_29

27. Rau, P.-L.P., et al.: Immersive reading in virtual and augmented reality environment. Inf. Learn. Sci. **122**(7/8), 464–479 (2021). https://doi.org/10.1108/ILS-11-2020-0236

28. Rea, A.: Reading Through the Ages | Generational Reading Survey. https://www.libraryjournal.com/story/Reading-Through-the-Ages-Generational-Reading-Survey. Accessed 24 Apr 2023

29. Ryan, M.-L.: From narrative games to playable stories: toward a poetics of interactive narrative. Storyworlds J. Narrat. Stud. **1**, 43–59 (2009)
30. Ryan, M.-L.: Immersion vs. interactivity: virtual reality and literary theory. SubStance **28**(2), 110–137 (1999). https://doi.org/10.1353/sub.1999.0015
31. Rzayev, R., et al.: Reading in VR: the effect of text presentation type and location. In: Proceedings of the 2021 CHI Conference on Human Factors in Computing Systems (CHI 2021), pp. 1–10 Association for Computing Machinery, Online (2021). https://doi.org/10.1145/341 1764.3445606
32. Shetler, N.: Interactive Virtual Reality Reading Experience. Williams Honors Coll. Honors Res. Proj. (2021)
33. Slater, M., Sanchez-Vives, M.V.: Enhancing our lives with immersive virtual reality. Front. Robot. AI. **3** (2016). https://doi.org/10.3389/frobt.2016.00074
34. Stanica, I.-C., et al.: Emergent technologies to enrich reading outcomes through augmented reality. Rev. Roum. Sci. Tech. - Ser. Électrotechnique Énergétique. **64**, 95–100 (2019)
35. Torheim, M.G., Stavanger, U. of: Do we read differently on paper than on a screen?. https://phys.org/news/2017-09-differently-paper-screen.html. Accessed 24 Apr 2023
36. Verne, J.: Twenty thousand leagues under the sea. Wordsworth Editions, Ware (1992)
37. Vlahovic, S. et al.: The effect of VR gaming on discomfort, cybersickness, and reaction time. In: 2021 13th International Conference on Quality of Multimedia Experience (QoMEX), pp. 163–168 (2021). https://doi.org/10.1109/QoMEX51781.2021.9465470
38. Vosmeer, M., Roth, C.: Exploring narrative novelties in VR. In: Mitchell, A., Vosmeer, M. (eds.) Interactive Storytelling: 14th International Conference on Interactive Digital Storytelling, ICIDS 2021, Tallinn, Estonia, December 7–10, 2021, Proceedings, pp. 435–444. Springer, Cham (2021). https://doi.org/10.1007/978-3-030-92300-6_44
39. Weir, K., et al.: I see therefore i read: improving the reading capabilities of individuals with visual disabilities through immersive virtual reality. Univers. Access Inf. Soc. **22**, 387–413 (2021). https://doi.org/10.1007/s10209-021-00854-8
40. Wolfe, A., Louchart, S., Loranger, B.: The impacts of design elements in interactive storytelling in VR on emotion, mood, and self-reflection. In: Vosmeer, M., Holloway-Attaway, L. (eds.) Interactive Storytelling: 15th International Conference on Interactive Digital Storytelling, ICIDS 2022, Santa Cruz, CA, USA, December 4–7, 2022, Proceedings, pp. 616–633. Springer, Cham (2022). https://doi.org/10.1007/978-3-031-22298-6_40
41. Yao, S., Kim, G.: The effects of immersion in a virtual reality game: presence and physical activity. In: Fang, X. (ed.) HCI in Games: First International Conference, HCI-Games 2019, Held as Part of the 21st HCI International Conference, HCII 2019, Orlando, FL, USA, July 26–31, 2019, Proceedings, pp. 234–242. Springer International Publishing, Cham (2019). https://doi.org/10.1007/978-3-030-22602-2_18
42. Young, S.: Are We Losing the Ability to Read Books?. https://www.scotthyoung.com/blog/2023/03/21/reading-fewer-books/. Accessed 24 Apr 2023
43. Zimmerman, J., et al.: Research through design as a method for interaction design research in HCI. In: Proceedings of the 2007 Conference on Human Factors in Computing Systems, pp. 493–502. ACM, California (2007). https://doi.org/10.1145/1240624.1240704
44. Apocalypse Rhyme. Animate Projects, Lupus Films (2012)
45. Bibli-o-mat by artifactvideo. https://artifactvideo.itch.io/bibli-o-mat. Accessed 01 May 2023
46. Chimera Reader. https://devpost.com/software/chimera-reader. Accessed 01 May 2023
47. Dear Angelica | Oculus Story Studio | VR Story | Oculus. https://www.oculus.com/story-studio/films/dear-angelica/?utm_source=www.google.com&utm_medium=oculusredirect. Accessed 28 Apr 2023

48. How Virtual Reality Is Changing the Entertainment Industry. https://onix-systems.com/blog/revolutionizing-movie-industry-through-vr-movie-apps. Accessed 27 Apr 2023

49. What Distinguishes an Interactive VR Film from a VR Game?. https://vrgeschichten.de/en/what-distinguishes-an-interactive-vr-film-from-a-vr-game. Accessed 27 Apr 2023

Story-Without-End: A Narrative Structure for Open-World Cinematic VR

Mohammadreza Mazarei[✉][ID]

Staffordshire University, Stoke-On-Trent ST4 2DE, UK
mohammadreza.mazarei@research.staffs.ac.uk

Abstract. This article briefs a PhD project in creative arts in which the practices were shaped by research on Gilles Deleuze articulation of cinematic narrative in the books *Cinema1: movement-image (1986)* and *Cinema2: time-image (1989)*. The project intends to develop a narrative structure for interactive storytelling that is specific to the properties of Virtual Reality (VR) as a cinematic medium. The research focuses on developing a method for designing and integrating pre-recorded content into an interactive VR application. The outcome is an open-world Cinematic VR in which individuals can influence the VR system by wandering freely within the immersive setting of the movie.

Three different research projects are conducted to investigate the conventions for interactive storytelling that are compatible with the means of communication provided by VR technologies. The results utilise the principles of constructing a story-world and generating cinematic narratives through reciprocal acts of a "wanderer audience", a term used originally in this project, in exploring an original narrative structure, "story-without-end". The project also concludes to a design of interactive cinematic VR, *Déjà vu* that examine the feasibility of constructing a virtual story-world without any specific ending.

This article describes a standpoint over the terms of cinematic narrative and replicates Deleuzian ontology on relationship of time and space in an immersive cinematic experience to determine conventions for open-world cinematic VR. The project states perception condition for a "wanderer audience", and the principle of designing tools for a "virtual body", the avatar, who explore an "open story-world" and generate a "virtual duration" as the cinematic time that confirm a comprehensive story experience.

Keywords: Gilles Deleuze · Open-world Cinema · Story-without-end · VR

1 Deleuze as a VR Theorist

As a philosopher, Gilles Deleuze examines the history of cinema to define the concepts raised by cinematic narratives. According to him, a theory of cinema is not about cinema itself, "but about the concepts that cinema gives rise to, and which are themselves related to other practices" [1, p. 280].

Considerably, Deleuze's [2] discussions on the definition of "virtuality" relate to the interference of cinematic practices in an immersive medium such as VR. It provides an

© The Author(s), under exclusive license to Springer Nature Switzerland AG 2023
L. Holloway-Attaway and J. T. Murray (Eds.): ICIDS 2023, LNCS 14383, pp. 329–343, 2023.
https://doi.org/10.1007/978-3-031-47655-6_20

ontology for examining the relationship between filmmakers and spectators in a full-body immersion experience by stating that "the virtual is opposed not to the real but to the actual" [3].

Deleuze refers to Henri Bergson's philosophy which provides the foundation for the concept of virtuality and describes subjectivity in relation to "living matter" [4]. Bergson argues that a conscious being acquires virtual perception, virtual action, and virtual memory through interaction with the material universe's elements, while the universe as a whole is not a givable at once. Bergson considers subjectivity to be a subtraction from objective reality. The function of consciousness is not to shed more light on an object, but to obscure some of its characteristics. This is why he contends that "representation is always there, but always virtual" [4]. In this context, VR content is providing a layer of reality with its subject matter opposed to physical world, and users' immersion is causing a virtuality as they try to perceive the new reality in the surroundings.

Deleuze describes cinema's virtuality as the reader's virtual experience of pre-created content. However, his statement regarding the reversal of space's dominance over time is the most pertinent to an immersive experience. He believes "time is not the interior in us, but just the opposite, the interiority in which we are, in which we move, live and change" [1, p. 82]. In other words, consciousness is a vacuum filled by intervals that are fundamental to human perception. By watching movements and identifying its position in the surroundings, consciousness creates a virtuality. In the physical world, movements are organic, but non-isomorphic changes in a VR application interrupt consciousness and recreate a virtuality unique to the VR experience.

Deleuze's reference to Bergson's "living body" [4], which distinguishes the perceiver from the continuity of the universe, suggests that homogeneous space and time are "the work of solidification and division that a body effects on the moving continuity of real in order to assure itself a fulcrum for action and to introduce into it real change" [5]. Thus, a VR user's virtual body is the curator of freedom, breaking VR space continuity as it moves around settings. Bergson [4] defines perception as virtual acts of things and the body on each other. Hence, the delay in rethinking the virtual body's motion and interaction in a VR environment shapes the audience's experience of freedom.

In this respect, self-identification is required for perception in any virtual world. "No perception takes place in a mathematical instant in time" [5] because wanderer's virtual body is not a mathematical point in space. It is a characteristic of the human body that causes a delay in reaction to generate a perception of space's changes. "Perception measures the possible action of a body over things and vice versa" [5]. Thus, a greater degree of freedom for the virtual body within a VR system means a more expansive duration for the perception of the virtual world; however, this perception depends on putative virtual entities that can only be actualised by the audience's interaction.

Alternately, as discussed by Sermijn, et. al. [6] regarding the concept of "rhizome" [7], the self is neither a fixed nor a static entity, but rather a fluid and ever-changing story. The metaphor of the rhizome describes an approach to "self-as-a-story" as a rhizome, a plant with no central root but a network of interconnected roots. The rhizome demonstrates the thought process as an experiment in which rhizomatic thinking is applied to self-identification.

Sermijn, et al. [6] contend that the self-stories that have accumulated as memories have "monstrous" properties, including a non-linear organisation of time, unclear causality, and a non-fixed space, which makes them a rhizomatic, interconnected narrative of the self with an understanding of the whole as a "multiplicity" [7]. However, this process of identification takes place over time and is preserved as an experiment-specific memory.

Regarding the function of human mind, the notion of "multiplicity" in Deleuze's ontology could provide a framework for non-linear narratives. According to Deleuze and Guattari [7], there is no distinct hierarchy, structure, or specific order in the circulation of events within the multiplicity. In this regard, Deleuze and Guattari [7] state two main principles for a rhizomatic narrative: first, the principle of connection, which states that each point of a rhizome can be connected to any other point in the rhizome; and secondly, at whatever point a rhizome is ruptured or destroyed, it will always keep growing according to different lines or connections, indicating the principle of a signifying rupture.

In addition, Gaudenzi [8] examines the concept of "assemblage" [9] which describes a theory for integration of entities in a "machine assemblage" by explicating the function of Kafka's protagonists within their communities. Moreover, in "The Language of New Media" [10], Lev Manovich investigates the concept of the "fold" [11] in relation to virtual reality aesthetics and experiences. The concept of folding represents a complex comprehension of space, time, and multiplicity. The fold, according to Deleuze's interpretation, alludes to the fact that reality is composed of intricate folds and infoldings, where surfaces curve and overlap to create new dimensions and relationships. It implies a continuous and dynamic process in which multiple layers and perspectives coexist.

2 A Deleuzian Approach to Cinematic VR

2.1 Story-World

The approach of the current research is to reconstitute the terminology of Deleuze, redefine the function of concepts like fold and assemblage for a VR experience and restructure the rhizomatic representation in VR space to articulate the definition of open-world storytelling and introduce a unique story structure. As a result, the research defines an immersive story-world, based on Deleuze's definition of cinematic narrative, as a "mechanism of announcements and secrets" [12] in a regime of "movement-image" [12].

Deleuze distinguishes between movement, moving object, and "space-covered" [12]. Through the lens of a camera, he gives the movements that represent the narratives a cinematic quality as the actualisation of a "state of things" [12]. Deleuze argues that movements in the space do not refer to specific spectators because the camera continually shifts from a subjective to an objective viewpoint. It renders story-world movements immanent to the space and makes the cinema impersonal to any viewer.

In this approach, restructuring a story-world for an immersive experience begins with a covering space that is a "transparent world" [13] demonstrated by the mediation of a spectrum of Mixed Reality (MR) possibilities, ranging from a designated VR space at one end to a physical space with augmented virtual elements at the other. Second, it consists of moving objects that are part of the story's world but do not signify changes related to the story. They exist to demonstrate changes in the "whole" [12], the durations that circulate through space-covered to make it a "living matter" [2]. These moving objects transform the story-world into a place where dramatic events are possible.

Finally, the story-world has dramatic movements like moving characters or external interventions in space-covered modifications. The association between these motions suggests a causal relationship between occurrences and story progression. By connecting "parts" [12] of the story and expressing changes in the "whole" story-world, these dramatic movements provide dual information. Dramatic motions are meant to be open to others and build a "whole" as a multiplicity of stories in a predetermined order. Thus, story-world design involves creating dramatic events that endure cinematic durations and imply changes in the story. The connection of dramatic events proceeds a continuum of stories in an "acentred plain of immanence" [12].

However, in Deleuze's view, a cinematic narrative is generated the instant a camera captures a moving object in a "living image" [12]. In this instance, the camera is the centre of reference in this acentered plain of immanence. Thus, the cinematic narrative is created by the "spatio-temporal coordinate" [12] of the camera, which perceives the movements, brings some to life and executes others. In fact, the camera is cinema's consciousness, the "cine eye" [12] over the subject matter of cinema. Consequently, the moving camera is the founder of a "virtual duration", as it translates the continuity of the story-world's movements.

Conversely, in the case of cinematic VRs that facilitate real-body movement and interaction, the viewer becomes the space's interpreter while embarking on a personal narrative journey through the story's world. D'Armenio [13] describes this additional movement of the VR user as a "perceptual movement" [13]. He re-read the theory of movement-image as an "unbreakable relationship between the qualities of images and qualities of movements" [13]. In this context, virtual reality presupposes a correlation between the visual syntax of the designed story-world and a kinetic syntax based on the observers' interaction with a "transparent world" [13]. However, the VR apparatus (VR headset, controller, etc.) imposes its dynamic limitations and locomotion techniques over physical movements to create a unique motion experience for the user in the virtual world.

In other words, the immersive image provided by a VR system is referred to as an "environment-image" [14, 15] "for the way in which they break with the mimetic tradition of visual representation in order to become reprogrammable and, foremost, explorable." [13]. A reprogrammable story-world involves real-time interaction to regenerate the environment and its entities. It is the norm of VR role-playing games, which represent a "character-centric" interactive storytelling, while cinematic VR uses plot-centric interaction with the audience acts as an observer over pre-recorded content enabled to move within an "explorable" story-world.

According to Deleuze, for a wanderer the most essential change is in time representation. He describes the "wanderer camera" [1], as an emancipated viewpoint that creates a cinematic body with its virtual duration over the story. From this perspective, the possibilities for dynamic locomotion within a VR system translate to a duration of user movements in the virtual world. As a wanderer audience travels across a cinematic environment-image, relative shifts create a "virtual duration." This virtual duration reflects the cinematic duration created by camera movement and the application of montage in conventional cinema.

In this instance, the wanderer audience is granted the freedom to explore the world of the narrative and generate a cinematic duration while remains constrained to the design of story-world. In other words, the spatial and temporal journey of a cinematic body is determined by the story-world's design and the user's ability to move within the environment. This collaboration between designer and audience defines the story-world consistency by allowing wanderer audience has access to various parts of an open story-world at once.

In a Deleuzian re-reading of virtual duration for immersive experience, it is a "virtual co-existence" [1] of the present as the mechanical time of experiencing pre-made contents and the past as personal memories of the experienced contents that are still accessible. In contrast to the present, which contains time fragments caused by the movement of a virtual body, the past can be recollected outside of normal successive time and perceived differently each time.

Recollection of the past in a virtual coexistence with the present, according to Deleuze, is an actualisation of memories in the form of a "crystal-image" [1] that is a circuit of virtual image of the past and actual image of the present. Thus, time is not sequential, as perception operates outside of successive time in the coexistence of two timelines, one of which is toward the past by transforming the present into the "past-in-general" [1] and the other of which anticipates the future by bringing a virtual memory of the past into the present.

This point of view sees the story's indeterminacy in the virtual body's perception. Thus, residing in an avatar turns the wanderer audience into a continuous creator of narrative as it experiences a rhizomatic exploration within the story-world. Exploring memories that are digitally actualised creates a distinctive virtual life. In this regard, audience participation in the creation of a cinematic experience indicates a quality of kinetic and visual syntax perceived by wanderer audiences as a "temporal perspective" [12] over story-world. The kinetic syntax translates viewer locations into space-time blocks that constitute a virtual duration, the cinematic timeframe the audience controls to explore the virtual story-world.

The quantity of "virtual duration" is the actual amount of time a wanderer audience spends interacting with the story-world. However, the audience's perception of the duration for the entire experience is influenced by alterations in the environment. Thus, the quality of virtual duration is perceived as a "feeling of duration" [16] which is generated by the collision between the mechanical time of the experience and the qualitative change of psychological states in the consciousness of the wanderer audience, as it engages in perceiving and interacting with the narratives.

In this regard, the duration a wanderer audience experiences for the entire virtual journey is directly proportional to the temporal perspectives obtained during the experience. On the one hand, the feeling of duration correlates with the quality of engagement with the narratives, as the wanderer audience makes a concerted effort to reveal the layers of virtual reality.

On the other hand, it pertains to the enjoyment of the VR immersion as the commonplace and intellectual relationship with the physical world is suspended due to the immersion in a surrounded image. The enjoyment of this condition derives from Deleuze's concept of "involuntary memory" [2], which brings us pleasure because it is not experienced in continuity with the past sensations, but rather as an event that has no equivalent in empirical reality, thereby preventing the concept of death from arising over time. Thus, an immersive experience provides a moment of pleasure whenever the reader is liberated from the order of time and perceives a variety of virtual timelines that are "real without being actual, ideal without being abstract" [5].

2.2 A Narrative Theory for Cinematic VR

In Deleuzian reconstruction, an immersive cinematic narrative adds a quality of perception that interprets story-world changes in relation to a "presupposed whole" [12]. Alternatively, the wanderer audience perceives a cinematic consciousness from the virtual body's cooperation over time and location. In this view, for all types of immersive media, a cinematic narrative is a designated event, an interaction of spatial movements conveying a duration. Virtual entities interact to create kinetic and audio-visual aesthetics. Newer technologies add haptic feedback and other sense-interactive features to this list.

However, designated events require a reciprocal act of interaction from the perceiver, an additional action by a consciousness to mature the event. It becomes accessible through a virtual cinematic body, a designated virtual avatar that immerses the audience in the story-world and gives them the freedom to explore it.

Consequently, the interaction patterns incorporated in the VR cinema are a component of the narrative's structure, functioning as tools to apply a montage to the multiple durations that flow in the virtual space. The objective of interaction and the act of engagement is for the wanderer audience to figure out causality over the changes in the story-world, and the interaction tools are intended to assist them in this endeavor. This notion of emerging narratives by moving within the virtual environments derived the approach of this research to design a structure for interactive storytelling as it utilises a condition of the real-time generation of cinematic narrative through interaction between wanderer audience and pre-recorded contents.

In this instance, the first step in designing methods to guide wanderer audiences was to research[1] narrative engagement conditions, considering various factors that could affect wanderer audiences' perception of content durations. It concluded with a perception theory for immersive cinematic experiences that argues wanderer audiences' emotional participation moves from empathy to self-directed emotions due to immersion in a real-life simulation.

---

[1] This PhD research involves human. The ethics committee at Staffordshire University, UK, approved the project. All participants completed a consent form to publish their data anonymously.

2.3 Perception Theory

Conventional cinema uses camera movement and montage to show the story's progression. The audience feels the duration of the real world; however, cinematic time representation indirectly creates a perception condition. Immersive storytelling gives a living consciousness translation and expression tools and replaces indirect time representation with direct time representation. A fully immersive VR experience that allows users to explore the film's 3D virtual location beyond its timeframe, changes the perception condition. It suggests a presence in a multiplicity of accessible timelines perceivable in real-time.

The research project "How do you feel it?" [17] studied the "feeling of duration" as an indicator of narrative engagement in VR films. It examined determinants, including, level of presence, the rate of previous VR experiences, memory-retrieving process of participants to find their correlation with the feeling of duration. Participants experienced a 360 film and a cross-media questionnaire, ICT-SOPI [18], measured the "virtual presence" score [19–21] using four determinants: "spatial presence, engagement, ecological validity (naturalness), and adverse effects" [18]. These parameters measured how much VR content distracted participants from the actual world, indicating their objective presence in virtual space.

In an isolated situation, a seated 3-DoF experience provided 360 films (Fig. 1) with no camera movement, showing dramatic movements like time-lapses of sunset and sunrise and a still frame with movement sounds. In this case, pre-recorded content was the only creator of duration that assisted in clarifying how external movements affect the perception of duration in immersive environments. The study used an analysis of variance (ANOVA) to compare the time participants spent in VR simulation and their reported feeling of duration.

Fig. 1. (left) A 360 video- from a fast-rolling sunset in reverse speed. (center) A 360 still-image of a graveyard. (right) A 360 video of a fast-rolling sunrise tipped upside down.

This design was based on the idea that experiencing non-isomorphic movements in an immersive environment makes events more interesting than in real life. Thus, the perception of a novel movement releases consciousness from its chronology and brings enjoyment. Bergson's [16] theory of perception states that the novelty of a real-life occurrence creates a specific duration for the "inner world" [16] of consciousness, which can differentiate each conscious being's ability to interpret the phenomenon. For this research, this proposition of Bergson suggests the "feeling of duration" as an indicator of the quality of engagement for the VR audience.

The "Dual-Processing Model" [22, 23] was applied to assess memory-retrieving systems and specify the procedure each participant used to perceive and analyse the virtual environment. It showed the correlation of using a "theory-based" analysis of movements or a "similarity-based" [24] recognition of a phenomenon, with the feeling of duration. The research found that the feeling of duration can indicate the extent of emotional or intellectual involvement in interpreting movements for VR users.

The results also showed that the virtual body's proprioceptive condition is crucial to the feeling of duration. One of the immersive shots was shown in two conditions: normal and tipped upside down, resulting in different perceptions of duration. Thus, an immersive image differs from a flat image because the virtual body's position strongly affects duration. This immersion quality gives the immersive image the same perceptual condition as real-life perception, distinguishing it from the cinematic representation in conventional cinema.

2.4   The Conditions of Narrative Engagement in Cinematic VR

According to Mateer [25], "transportation" into the story is comparable to "suspension of disbelief" for cinematic narrative in VR. In this perspective, emotional contributions that retain the spectator's passive personality as an empathic observer of other characters drive narrative engagement in virtual reality. Bergson [16] explains it as a condition in which a perceiver predicts upcoming occurrences to experience a novelty, which engages them with narratives.

However, immersion in a story-world allows for freedom of exploration, marking a particular situation for "narrative engagement". The viewer's agency in looking at surroundings changes the perception condition even in a 3-DoF experience. In this situation, engaging with narratives is more of an effort of elaboration, but it comes from a mental image that is formed through an order of incidents to convince the observer that motions are causally related. In essence, the agency turns narrative engagement into an active role of analysis. Immersive environments provide the viewer with an existing virtual body, not a "ghost body behind the camera" [26]. The consciousness behind the user's avatar perceives the duration of story-world's movements, hence, whether it experiences a seated investigation of the environment or a full-body movement that engages many senses, the virtual body has a subjective existence with an emancipated viewpoint to experience the story-world.

In this respect, the second study hypothesized that a non-linear order of incidents with inorganic durations can encourage an active role to engage with narratives. It gives a joy distinct from the joyfulness of VR immersion. The audience's perception of the movie's duration distinguishes narrative engagement, which involves actively seeking causality, from virtual presence, which is a passive presence in an immersive environment.

This research involved viewing a 360 film, *The Man Who Disoriented in Time (2022)*, which challenges the credibility of a linear representation by reversing the order of video footages and/or attached sounds. A non-chronological timeline was shown in real time, forcing the audience to read narratives to determine the direction of time in the displayed environment. In this case, narrative engagement required comparing the present time in the virtual and real world. Thus, for each audience, the level of engagement with the narrative created a unique feeling of duration by showing the extent to which each event's direction was perceived.

The participants' actions, feelings, and interpretations of situations were coded inductively using "constructive grounded theory" [27]. It helps define narrative engagement as an active elaboration of dramatic occurrences. Different types of camera motion were designed and bonded for each direction of the timeline, as well as transition effects between each image, then the participants' reactions to predict and match the camera movement were assessed. In this case, better engagement meant a better prediction, which allowed for a more thorough exploration of the environment and recognition of dramatic components that signify the timeline's direction.

The comparison between participants' feelings about the duration and their behaviour during the experience revealed that a higher quality of reacting to camera movement and locating the narrative elements within the scene resulted in a more accurate feeling of duration compared to the mechanical time. In other words, participants' engagement in determining event timelines helped them understand real-world duration, and the ICT-SOPI questionnaire [18] showed high enjoyment in this group.

In addition, participants' enjoyment of immersion in a virtual environment for the entire experience was highest for those who felt a very short or very long duration. Interestingly, this group tried less to detect significant movements and incident causes. In this case, immersion in a simulated environment that displayed its non-isomorphic chronology in real-time, and disconnected audiences from the present provides enjoyment. It is the enjoyment of virtual presence in a VR simulation. These participants were passive observers, while the former group actively unfolded narratives. However, the novelty of the present chronology in the displayed environment delighted both groups, regardless of whether perceived it as a passive transportation or an active elaboration. Thus, as a design instruction for an immersive story-world, irregular durations increase enjoyment and encourage engagement with unfolding narratives.

Furthermore, another group of participants reported lower virtual presence and story engagement. Active participants who failed to match camera movements to uncover narrative elements. They reported camera motion and dramatic movements were disorienting them. It highlights the camera's motion as a narrative component in immersive images, creating duration for a virtual body in the story-world and influencing the audience's perception of duration.

Additionally, a second study examined camera motion's effects on the same group of participants. Four camera motions are observed: spinning or twirling, changing height, straight line, and still camera. The findings showed that participants' engagement with dramatic content was most negatively affected by the rotating camera and height level changing. The main drawback of a rotating camera is motion blur and image quality degradation, which disrupts virtual presence and causes motion sickness and eye strain. Alternately, adjusting the camera's height level during a straight movement did not affect image quality; however, the irregularity of this motion caused participants to experience motion sickness, which stopped them from exploring their environment. It proves that narrative engagement can be affected by irregular movements designed for a virtual body to explore the story-world.

3 The Principles of an Open-World Cinema

Deleuze states an "any-space-whatever" [12] as a situation that the perceiver can grasp all times at once, all the potential alternatives and the freedom of actualisation of a "state of things" [12]. Thus, an open-world cinematic experience gives the wanderer audience a virtual body with simultaneous access to all timelines and spaces and "degrees of interactivity" [28] set by the designer to determine the method of movement between blocks of space-time.

In this respect, open-world cinema is a plane of immanence, a continuous flow of durations in real time that changes the environment without referring to the reader's anchor. The story-world creates a depth-of-field by giving observers a perspective on space movements and an out-of-field by showing an event with a sequential spatial change that requires a "specific wait" [16] for the wanderer audience to comprehend it.

In other words, durations frame the field-of-view in space-time blocks; thus, in open-world cinema, the out-of-field is the movements that exist out of the spatial-temporal coordination of the wanderer audience. These unreachable movements provoke a tendency to interact with the story world resulting in the actualisation of a state of things. The storyteller designs a machine of announcements and secrets to encourage exploration. Hence, the generic element of design in a cinematic open-world story is "spatial-temporal coordination".

The VR filmmaker expands audience perception by decorating temporal elements into space blocks and controlling the distance and duration of dramatic elements upon each other. The designer guides the wanderer audience by establishing a "consciousness of alternative" [12] by linking parts of the story-world through adding aesthetic values like moving lighting or objects, colour, sound, and character activities to create threads. In contrast, the audience reads, interprets, and interacts with story parts in terms of its spatial-temporal coordination. Wanderer audiences' "feeling of indetermination" [16] is to regulate the interval to react to changes, prevent some possibilities, and open others. However, story impulses as uncontrollable occurrences encourage exploration of the story-world.

Regarding these concepts, an open-world cinematic VR can be seen as a mechanism of announcements and secrets. It incorporates a timeline that governs the sequence of events in a temporal manner, allowing for the presentation of a narrative to the user through its spatial-temporal coordination. In this regard, VR narrative representations such as *L.A. Noire: VR Case Files (2018)* and *Invisible Hours (2017)* can be regarded as examples of open-world cinema as they construct a story world by depicting various events and interconnecting them through narrative threads. For instance, in Invisible Hours, users follow different characters, while in L.A. Noire, they interact with objects, both of which lead to the exploration of new events. Ultimately, these VR experiences create a cohesive whole that can be comprehended as a chronological sequence identical to a movie timeline.

Cinematic virtual reality allows the audience to freely explore the story environment rather than create a narrative in real-time. In Invisible Hours (2017), the user is a passive observer who can freely roam the narrative area, track characters, and exert control over the temporal progression of events. This includes rewinding and fast-forwarding the story's timeline. In this case, a comprehensive understanding of the story-world is guaranteed as the movie's events are condensed in one place, an island, allowing the viewer to change their spatial and temporal coordination and interpret the story through a personal journey. This approach of consolidating the spatial aspects for cinematic storytelling, as also used in VR role-playing games like *No Man's Sky VR (2023)*, unites disparate worlds into a continuous narrative framework and serves as a mechanism for creating a coherent experience of a story that progresses over time.

4   Story-Without-End

This research offers the "Story-without-end" narrative structure for VR-specific open-world cinema. In this structure, a storyline is an order of events that represents a story's progression in a particular location which includes spatial shots in a space-time block. Like Invisible Hours (2017), a unified setting posits storylines in a comprehensive whole. While Invisible Hours' events unfold in three hours, the "story without end" represents a continuous "whole" by connecting locations through threads, in a way that eliminates the necessity to choose a final event for each location's story. Hence, since there is no beginning event, the story-world structure follows the first rhizome principle, the principle of connection.

In this structure, the journey of the story's characters through the world connects multiple storylines. Thus, events that happen to each character as they travel between locations are getting an extra order in addition to the order of events depicted in each location. This structure encourages the wanderer audience to explore the story-world as each character's journey implies a specific connection between the storylines in different locations.

Wanderer audiences can change their spatial-temporal coordination by following the characters; thus, they provide a temporal perspective on the order of events for characters and locations. It generates a causality at each moment that fractures as audiences follow different characters. It follows the second principle of rhizome, the principle of signifying rupture, since the wanderer audience can investigate a variety of occurrences, which can be ordered by the observer's path through the story-world.

Story-without-end presents an original design principle that makes the wanderer audience's journey endless. As long as each character's journey represents sensible causality in a circular order, the principle of infinity states that the loop in the journey of the story's characters within the story-world regulates events in each location in an infinite cycle. It is a design for a machine assemblage that considers a story's protagonist as an entity repeating a trajectory in a movement-image machine. Significantly, the character's journey within the story-world represents a character arc by involving a series of incidents; however, its relationship with space never changes. The journey's information only compels a character to advance to the subsequent spatial-temporal coordination.

The story progresses as characters navigate and modify the virtual world, creating a cinematic framing of the space through time. Their movements connect story-world parts and indicate space shifts. All character movements are pre-recorded and spread in 3D space, dictated by spatial-temporal coordination inside the story-world. Thus, wanderer audiences create interactive movie experiences by interpreting the plot based on their freedom of movement.

This design of the story-world allows for several causalities for each movement at any time, making it an any-space-whatever. It offers up all possibilities, and audiences' agency allows them to create a personal cinematic journey over an infinite story by exploring dramatic incidents that are impersonal to any observer and emanative of the story-world.

5 Déjà Vu Project

The project "Déjà vu" examined the feasibility of structuring a story-without-end for VR. It is a design of a story represented by branching the story-world into three concurrent timelines of past, present, and future, in each of which the relationships between the characters are distinct as each location occupies the same space at a different time (Fig. 2).

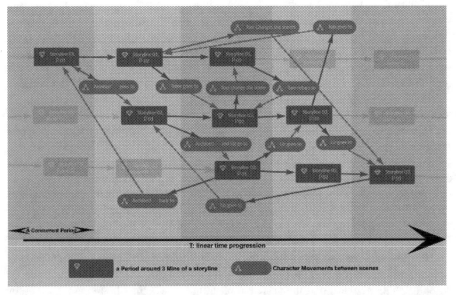

Fig. 2. Déjà vu's story map depicts the method of synchronization for three concurrent timelines.

Each timeline represents a distinct event, while each character's journey follows its own order and initiates a loop based on the incidence in each space that forces them to explore the story's locations. For instance, one of the characters, Architect, claims to be the creator of the story-world and wanders across the various locations to engage with other characters to proceed with the story that he has written in advance. Tom is a younger version of Architect, who views the entire story-world as different chambers of a location in a timeline and travels to various locations in search of a female character. As he interacts with objects and attempts to visit the female character, he is compelled to repeat his voyage.

The female protagonist distinguishes the stories' historical periods. Her voyage has not been chronological, and only she has been affected by historic times in each location.

She visits Tom in the present timeline and experiences déjà vu, prompting her to repeat the advice she received from the Architect in the past timeline; where, in the next step, she meets him as a stranger who tries to influence her relationship with Tom. Then, in the future timeline, she encounters Architect again as a friend. However, Architect's behaviour similar to Tom's in the present timeline caused her to have déjà vu again, which negatively impacted her relationship with Architect. This non-chronological journey of the female character, which is the cause of déjà vu, has a sensible causal relationship with the order of her historical information in each storyline. It also influenced the journey of the Architect to complete his loop and begin from where he started to locate the source of the second déjà vu.

In this design, the wanderer audiences can navigate the story world with real-body movements and alter their timeline to unfold the story-world layer while folding their own perspective on the order of events. The design of the virtual world places three distinct locations on the interior surfaces of a cube, Thus, all the locations are always visible to wanderer audiences (Fig. 3). It provides wanderer audiences an overview of the whole story-world; however, they are unable to comprehend the entire transformation within the virtual world as they cannot hear the sounds in two other locations. It creates a mental-image by indicating an out-of-field of hearing that elicits a tendency to explore the story-world and discover causality of narratives.

Fig. 3. Screenshot from the Déjà vu's set.

In this structure, the shots are in space, and because the viewer can see all the spaces at once, the shots are separated by the movement of the characters who function as threads to maintain the consistency of the story world. Cinematic cuts occur when characters enter or exit a location. Thus, the characters cannot disappear for a single instant since their disappearance signifies a breach in the story-world's connection and a "block of disappearance" that does not exist in the depth-of-field or imply any out-of-field.

6 Conclusion

This study explores Gilles Deleuze's concepts and terminology to distinguish the concepts that contribute to the construction of a cinematic story world for immersive mediums. The distinction between space-covered by moving objects and dramatic movement and replicating these features for an immersive image aid to redefine an open-world representation of cinematic narrative, considering the wanderer audience as a narrative component who is agent in exploration of a multiplicity of stories.

Additionally, research into the perception process for wanderer audiences states the feeling of duration as an indicator of narrative engagement and demonstrates the active role of audiences in cinematic VR. It suggests the type of emotional contribution to the VR narrative is self-directed emotions, similar to a real-life experience.

In conclusion, the research offers the narrative structure "story-without-end" which provides a foundation for producing infinite stories in a rhizomatic structure as a method of storytelling for open-world cinematic VR. The practice "Déjà vu" proves the feasibility of employing this narrative structure in a VR film, provides a comprehensive cinematic experience.

Further study will be conducted on the "Déjà vu" project to observe the behaviour of the users in using their avatar to investigate the impacts of free-roaming on the feeling of duration. It aids in comprehending the influence of designing agency for a virtual body on the quality of experience and narrative engagement, as reflect by the feelings about the duration.

Acknowledgements. the doctoral project "Interactive Storytelling for Virtual Reality Medium by Real Walking Inside Virtual Story-world" pursued at Staffordshire University's Media and Performance Department, under the supervision of Dr. Melanie LEE and Dr. Lionel JAYARAJ. Technicians and students from the School of Digital, Technology, and Art helped to produce Déjà vu.

References

1. Deleuze, G.: The Time-Image: Cinema 2. University of Minnesota Press, Minneapolis (1989)
2. Deleuze, G.: Immanence: a life? In: Pure Immanence, trans. Boyman A, pp. 25–33. Zone Books, New York (2001)
3. Deleuze, G.: Difference and repetition, Trans P. Patton, p. 208. Athlone, London (1994),
4. Beunmrgson, H.: Matter and Memory, Translated by Nancy Margaret Paul and William Scott Palmer. Zone Books, New York (1991)
5. Ansell-Pearson, K.: The reality of the virtual: bergson and deleuze. MLN **120**, 1112–1127 (2005). https://doi.org/10.1353/mln.2006.0020

6. Sermijn, J., Devlieger, P., Loots, G.: The narrative construction of the self selfhood as a rhizomatic story. Qual. Inq. (2008). https://doi.org/10.1177/1077800408314356

7. Deleuze, G., Guattari, F.: Rhizôme, Introduction. Editions de Minuit, Paris (1976)

8. Gaudenzi, S.: The Living Documentary: from representing reality to co-creating reality in the digital interactive documentary. Ph.D. thesis. London: Goldsmiths, University of London (2013)

9. Deleuze, G., Guattari, F.: Kafka: Toward a Minor Literature. University of Minnesota Press, Minneapolis (1986)

10. Manovich, L.: The Language of New Media. MIT Press, Massachusetts (2002)

11. Deleuze, G., Strauss, J.: The Fold. Yale French Stud. **80**, 227–247 (1986). https://doi.org/10.2307/2930269

12. Deleuze, G.: The Movement-Image: Cinema 1. University of Minnesota Press, Minneapolis (1986)

13. D'Armenio, E.: Beyond interactivity and immersion: a kinetic reconceptualization for virtual reality and video games. New Techno Human. **2**(2), 121–129 (2022). ISSN 2664-3294

14. Pierluigi, F., Basso, F.: L'image du devenir: le monde en Signata chiffre et la passion du monitorage (2019). https://doi.org/10.4000/signata.2261

15. Pinotti, A.: Self-negating images: towards an-iconology. In: Proceedings, vol. 1, p. 856 (2017).

16. Bergson, H.: The Creative Mind. Kensington Pub. Corp., New York (2002)

17. Mazarei, M.: Immersion in VR movies: how non-experienced audiences identify themselves in virtual environment. In: Communication and Communities Conference. Staffordshire University, Stoke-On-Trent (2021)

18. Lessiter, J., Freeman, J., Keogh, E., Davidoff, J.D.: A cross-media presence questionnaire: the ITC sense of presence inventory. Pres. Teleoper. Virt. Environ. **10**(3), 282–297 (2001)

19. Freeman, J., Avons, S.E.: Focus group exploration of presence through advanced broadcast services. In: Proceedings of the SPIE, Human Vision and Electronic Imaging, vol. 3959–3976 (2000)

20. Freeman, J., Avons, S. E., Meddis, R., Pearson, D. E., IJsselsteijn, W.: Using behavioural realism to estimate presence: a study of the utility of postural responses to motion stimuli. Pres. Teleoper. Virt. Environ. **9**(2), 149–164 (2000)

21. Freeman, J., Avons, S.E., Pearson, D., IJsselsteijn, W.: Effects of sensory information and prior experience on direct subjective ratings of presence. Pres. Teleoper. Virtual Environ. **8**, 1–13 (1999)

22. Smith, E., Collins, E.: Dual-process models: a social psychological perspective (2009). https://doi.org/10.1093/acprof:oso/9780199230167.003.0009

23. Smith, E., Coster, M.: Dual-process models in social and cognitive psychology: conceptual integration and links to underlying memory systems. Pers. Soc. Psychol. Rev. **4**, 108–131 (2000). https://doi.org/10.1207/S15327957PSPR0402_01

24. Clark, A.: Being There: Putting Brain, Body, and World Together Again. MIT Press, Cambridge (1997)

25. Mateer, J.: Directing for cinematic virtual reality: how traditional film director's craft applies to immersive environments and notions of presence'. J. Media Pract. **18**, 14–25 (2017). https://doi.org/10.1080/14682753.2017.1305838

26. Martin, W.: "ESSE" AND "PERCIPI" IN "FILM": a 'Note; upon the beckett-schneider 'correspondence'. Samuel Beckett Today/Paris: Aujourd'hui **14**, 533–546 (2004) https://doi.org/10.2307/25781489

27. Charmaz, K.: Constructing Grounded Theory: A Practical Guide Through Qualitative Analysis. SAGE, London (2006)

28. Adams, E.W.: Resolutions to Some Problems in Interactive Storytelling. Ph.D. thesis, Middlesbrough: University of Teesside (2013)

Integrating Narrative Design into the World Economic Forum's Transformation Maps for Enhanced Complexity Comprehension

Breanne Pitt[1]([⊠]) [iD] and Christian Roth[2] [iD]

[1] Trinity College Dublin, The University of Dublin, Dublin D02 PN40, Ireland
pittb@tcd.ie
[2] University of the Arts Utrecht, Lange Viestraat 2B, Postbox 1520, 3500 BM Utrecht, Netherlands
christian.roth@hku.nl

Abstract. The *Transformation Maps,* developed and maintained by the World Economic Forum's Strategic Intelligence Platform, serve as a systems thinking tool aimed at visualizing and analyzing complex global challenges and interconnected factors. While the tool's information curation is impressive, there is still potential to further enhance the tool's effectiveness in facilitating a deeper comprehension of complex systems. To explore the potential of interactive narrative design applied to the maps, we conducted a workshop with the Forum and the INDCOR COST Action group [1]. This paper gives an overview of the workshop methods and outcomes. We propose the integration of narrative into the *Transformation Maps* on the SI platform to improve agency, immersion and transformation, Janet Murray's three pillars of experiential aesthetic qualities [2]. This is particularly relevant when considering improvements in UX/UI, content, and complexity comprehension within the *Transformation Maps* tool. By focusing on these areas, IDN design can foster meaningful and immersive experiences that catalyze transformative understandings of complex systems, helping individuals transcend existing knowledge boundaries. We provide concrete examples about how IDN design can improve understanding, specifically through the integration of personas for multiperspictivity and personalization. Also, the insights and recommendations derived from this workshop emphasize the power of collaborative efforts among stakeholders, in this case industry and academic professionals, in continuously advancing knowledge and fostering meaningful product reflection and growth.

Keywords: Systems Thinking · Complex Problems · Complex Systems · Interactive Digital Narrative (IDN) · Zone of Proximal Development (ZDP) · Constructivism · IDN Design · Transformation Maps · Learning Experience Design

L. Holloway-Attaway and J. T. Murray (Eds.): ICIDS 2023, LNCS 14383, pp. 344–362, 2023.
https://doi.org/10.1007/978-3-031-47655-6_21

1   Introduction

The world is becoming increasingly complex. Until recently, levels of complexity, specifically in social systems, were relatively low. Research has shown that because of the development and adoption of information technologies, levels of complexity have "become a defining feature of the 21st century [3]." However, existing narrative conventions, such as news and social media, are limited in their ability to effectively capture and convey these complex stories. This limitation often results in oversimplification of complex material, including the propagation of fake news, ultimately leading to the polarization of populations. Many pressing issues of our time, such as pandemics, climate change, and the refugee crisis, involve multiple perspectives, diverse stakeholders, and intricate interconnections that challenge the traditional methods of narrative representation.

There is a need for new approaches to capture these complex, multi-perspective stories in order to sustain the public sphere and further democratic discourse. Digital technologies have been suggested as a way to address these concerns by means of their ability to create complex interactive representations [4]. Therefore, our research aims to investigate how advanced digital tools, specifically the World Economic Forum's *Strategic Intelligence Platform* and its *Transformation Map Tool*, can facilitate a clearer understanding of complexity and address polarization.

1.1   Complex Problems

Current social issues are complex, and require systemic understanding. Complex problems have been extensively discussed in academic literature, encompassing various descriptors such as intractable problems, complex challenges/issues, wicked problems/issues, ill-defined problems, and messy problems [5]. A complex problem is described as one that requires a series of operations to find a solution, which Dörner et al. [6] characterized as follows: includes elements that are large in scale (complexity), highly interconnected (connectivity), and subject to dynamic changes over time (dynamics). Neither structure nor dynamics are disclosed (intransparency). For example, battling climate change confronts individuals with multiple goals that need to be prioritized and coordinated when potentially being contradictory or in conflict with one another. In such a complex system, well meant actions can lead to unforeseen negative consequences, making it challenging to find solutions addressing the underlying problems.

1.2   Interactive Digital Narratives (IDNs) and Cybernetic Approaches for Complex Systems

Interactive digital narratives leverage interactive storytelling and active exploration to better enable users to understand complex systems. By making complexity more accessible, tangible, and understandable, users can delve into the intricacies of these systems at their own pace and develop the essential skills to navigate and comprehend complex problems effectively. Through their engagement with IDNs, users can gain a profound comprehension of complex systems and enhance their ability to make sense of the challenges they encounter.

The most current definition of an IDNs states that it is "a narrative expression in various forms, implemented as a multimodal computational system with optional analog elements and experienced through a participatory process in which interactors have a non-trivial influence on progress, perspective, content, and/or outcome" [7]. In this definition, Koenitz presents a systemic perspective on IDNs, as outlined in the SPP model (System, Process, Product) [8, 9], which is considered the most comprehensive model for capturing the fragmented, distributed, and interactive nature of IDNs [10]. According to this model, the digital work, or system, does not explicitly manifest a "story" in the traditional sense. Instead, it contains the protostory, which represents all the potential narratives that can be instantiated through the interactive process. The interactor's engagement with the complex system components leads to the realization of a reordered product, which represents the actual story experienced by the user.

Koenitz's SPP model draws insights from cybernetics. IDNs lean towards the idea of a narrative environment in the form of a cybernetic system [11]. The term "cybernetics" originates from the Greek word "kybernetes," which means rudder or pilot, referring to a device used to steer a boat or support human governance. Plato first used this term in Alcibiades I10 to describe the governance of people. In the 1830s, French physicist Ampere employed it to describe the science of civil government. Norbert Wiener later defined cybernetics as the study of control and communication in both animals and machines. It encompasses fundamental concepts essential for understanding complex systems, including learning, cognition, adaptation, emergence, communication, and efficiency [12]. Specifically, it is the study of "circular causal and feedback mechanisms in biological and social systems," [13]. The World Economic Forum's Transformation Maps can be considered a form of cybernetic systems in the sense that they incorporate elements of feedback and control in their design. They gather information from a variety of sources, including user inputs, expert insights, and data analytics, and use that feedback to refine and update the maps. However, the integration of IDN design into this current tool can further enhance this cybernetic approach to understanding complex problems, including improvements in, cognition, emergence, communication, and efficiency, concepts Marinescu specifically highlighted in his seminal work [13].

1.3   IDNs and Learning Approaches for Complex Problems

IDNs are powerful tools for learning and understanding complex problems. Inherent IDN characteristics align with leading learning theories like constructivism and Vygotsky's Zone of Proximal Development (ZPD) [14]. By leveraging the principles of these theories, IDNs can be effective learning tools for building a deeper understanding in the face of complexity.

Constructivism. Constructivist learning theory refers to a philosophical approach that emphasizes the active role of the observer in constructing their own knowledge and understanding of the world [15]. Using IDNs can be considered a constructivist approach to learning due to their inherent characteristics and the way they align with the principles of constructivism, such as active engagement, personalization and agency, collaboration and social interaction, reflection and sense-making, learner-centered design. Both second-order cybernetics and constructivism share a common perspective, viewing information and knowledge from the standpoint of observing complex systems (second order) rather than the observed complex systems [16, 17]. This means that the focus is on how observers perceive and interpret their experiences, rather than assuming an objective reality. The link between second-order cybernetics and both constructivism and radical constructivism [18] is established through the view of knowledge as "situated knowledge", which highlights the idea that knowledge is shaped by the context and experiences of the knower, forming a correspondence between their understanding and the world they interact with [10]. It's important to note that Constructivist learning does not work without the right amount of guidance [19].

Zone of Proximal Development. According to Vygotsky's Zone of Proximal Development, learning does not occur solely through independent effort. Instead, with the right level of scaffolding and guidance learners can reach higher levels of performance and understanding [14]. A more knowledgeable person, such as a teacher, peer, or parent, can take on the role of a mediator by providing a tailored experience to the learner's specific needs, allowing them to gradually develop their skills and knowledge to reach higher levels of performance and insight. The ZPD also highlights the importance of challenging learners with tasks that are slightly beyond their current abilities, like progressively understanding complex problems. By operating within the ZPD, learners can experience productive and meaningful learning experiences, actively engaging in their own development with the support of an IDN.

The role of a physical mediator can be digitally replicated through the use of narrative design elements, like characters. Characters can help to break down a learner's experience into manageable chunks [36] within their ZPD. They can scaffold the educational experience by offering roles for the learner to assume, objectives to pursue, specific tasks to perform, and feedback for reflection. Characters can inspire learners to understand the significance of the topic and its relevance to the broader context by establishing personal connection. This results in learners building and extending mental models and transferring this understanding to similar experiences in the real world.

1.4 Transformation Maps

A transformation map is a data visual representation or tool that illustrates the changes, shifts, or transitions happening within a system, organization, industry, or society. Variants of these tools are available under different names: "concept mapping", "mind mapping" and "argument mapping". Typically, these types of data visualization tools are used to help impart critical and analytical skills to users, enable interactors to see relationships between concepts, and also as a method of assessment [20]. Transformation maps offer a holistic view of the elements, components, and interconnections involved in the transformation process. They aid in identifying key drivers, challenges, and opportunities, enabling stakeholders to navigate and comprehend the complexities of the transformation journey.

The Strategic Intelligence Platform at the World Economic Forum developed their own *Transformation Map* tool, which combines AI, human curation through an interactive data visualization tool. The goal is to assist users in navigating and comprehending the intricate and interconnected dynamics shaping economies, industries, and global issues. These maps are designed to enhance comprehension and facilitate informed decision-making by visually presenting complex interrelationships. Covering various topics such as technology, economics, society, geopolitics, and the environment, the *Transformation Maps* can capture trends, risks, and opportunities within each domain. Users have access to interactive features such as dynamic visualizations, curated content, expert insights, advanced briefings, and links to relevant reports and publications in a continuously updated knowledge feed.

These maps are used by policymakers, business leaders, researchers, and other individuals interested in gaining insights into global challenges and emerging trends. They provide a valuable resource for scenario planning, strategic decision-making, and staying informed about the evolving landscape in different sectors. Users can also contribute to the maps by suggesting updates, sharing insights, and participating in discussions. This impressive collaborative effort between the forum and its stakeholders helps to foster a dynamic and continuously evolving knowledge platform that represents multiple perspectives across the globe.

1.5   Addressing the Narrative Deficit: Enhancing Meaning Making for Interactors

The World Economic Forum's *Transformation Maps*, which exist on the Strategic Intelligent Platform, are a concrete digital tool that help to convey interconnected information. However, there is potential for further enhancement through additional narrative guidance, which can improve the interactor's capacity to develop a comprehensive understanding and derive meaningful insights.

In this paper we highlight a practical use case of applying interactive narrative design for the representation of complex issues. Our purpose was to combine both approaches, the *Transformation Maps* as a systemic thinking tool and interactive narrative design for the purpose of enhanced meaning-making, creating a deeper transformative learning experience [21].

The most widely circulated narratives involve complex societal issues such as climate change, immigration, war and pandemics. Current business models in social media, search engines, and video streaming platforms are insufficient in capturing the complexity and interconnectedness of these topics.

With evolving mediums, the abundance of online information poses challenges as individuals struggle to navigate it effectively. Thus, understanding the many interconnections between factors is challenging. Ultimately, learners are likely to get lost in the density of information, experience an information overload, which can undermine their motivation to continue. To address this, preliminary research indicates that integrating narratives with data visualization tools can enhance user understanding of intricate phenomena [22].

We present our workshop approach on how we brainstormed solutions as a group consisting of multiple teams with various backgrounds. Together, we tackled the challenge focusing on given use case scenarios and personas. What makes this method special is that we are directly working together with the client, thus bringing together multiple perspectives including various fields in academia and industry.

Consequently, we present tangible concepts for leveraging interactive narrative design to actively engage, guide, and immerse users within extended transformation maps. Furthermore, our objective is to underscore the necessity of collaborative efforts among diverse stakeholders to enhance existing approaches in addressing complex challenges, starting from the initial design phase of novel tools.

2 Methods

The Strategic Intelligence (SI) platform, specifically the *Transformation Map* tool, aims to provide users with an interactive view of global issues and their transformation. The application is designed to enable users to identify key issues and related topics across various countries, regions, industries and global issues. INDCOR, a COST action network of consultants from academia, conducted a collaborative workshop to demonstrate how to apply interactive narrative design for platform improvements based on three personas, namely business, research, and policy making.

2.1 Objective

The objective of the workshop was to identify the strengths and opportunities of the SI platform and to demonstrate how to apply interactive narrative design based on three personas the Forum members indicated working with: business, research, and policy making professionals. When using personas, there are two participants involved: the sender, who creates the persona, and the receiver, who reads and interprets it. Persona presentations share similarities with stories, where they cannot be fully told and some information needs to be inferred by the reader. When trying to understand a story, readers interact by filling in gaps in the narrative using their own personal experiences. This also applies to persona descriptions, where not all information is explicitly provided, and the reader infers missing details during the meaning-making process. The reader's expectations, domain knowledge, and cultural background play a role in filling in these gaps. While storytelling is a shared experience, each reader creates their own individual story during the reception process [23]. These personas were developed by Rudolf Schutte, Head of Growth for the Strategic Intelligence Platform for the purposes of the workshop (Fig. 1).

2.2 Agenda

During the two-day event at the World Economic Forum, the INDCOR group actively participated in a range of activities that were specifically designed to enhance the workshop experience.

Introduction to Strategic Intelligence Presentation (30 min). On day one, Stephan Mergenthaler, Head of Strategic Intelligence (SI) at the World Economic Forum, delivered a comprehensive presentation outlining the origins, objectives, and existing applications of the SI platform. The purpose of this presentation was to familiarize the INDCOR group with the SI platform, enabling them to actively participate in the subsequent workshop discussions and sessions.

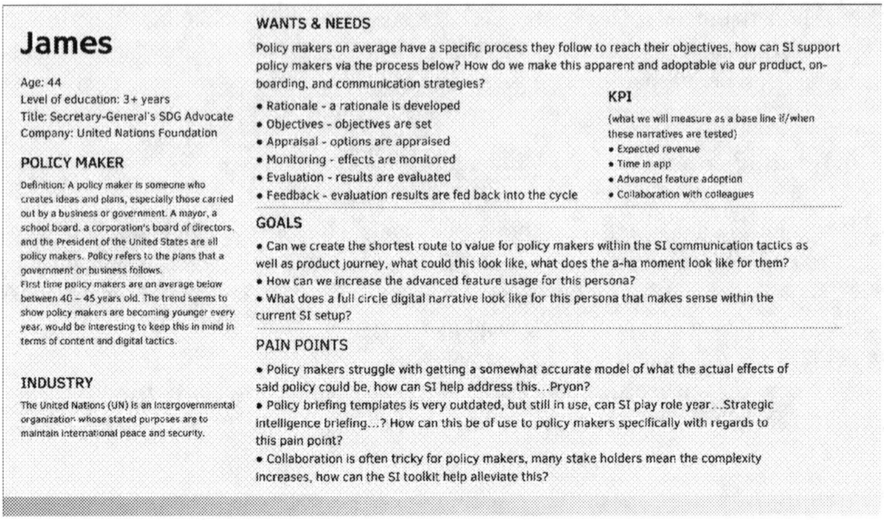

Fig. 1. Persona 1 - Policy Maker, James

Workshop Warm-Up and Introduction (30 min). On day two, Breanne Pitt provided an overview (5 min) of the *Transformation Maps* on the SI Platform. This was followed by an ice-breaker led by Dimitar Uzonov (10 minutes), and an introduction by Breanne Pitt about workshop objectives, task identification and activity explanation. Participants were asked to engage in a brainstorming session aimed at exploring strategies for incorporating narrative elements into the *Transformation Maps*. They were then asked to present a pitch for an IDN idea to the audience, with a prize awarded to the most compelling concept. Hartmut Koenitz, chair of INDCOR, also provided IDN design prompts for the participants. They were as follows:

> *How can the audience experience different perspectives?*
>
> *Translate aspects of the transition maps into decisions and consequences - think of non-obvious choices and consequences from a number of choices.*
>
> *Think of the persona as a playable character and people affected by the persona's decisions as either playable characters or as reactive non-player characters? How would they be experienced?*
>
> *How can live data be transformed into a narrative experience? How can we use replay to deepen understanding?*

Group Activity (30 min). Participants were organized into groups based on assigned personas, which served as a framework for their collaborative work. Leveraging their respective personas, the groups generated innovative ideas on incorporating "narrative" elements into the *Transformation Maps*, aiming to enhance the user's understanding and interpretation of the information presented.

Pitch Presentations (30 Min). Groups presented their proposed ideas and concepts for integrating narrative elements into the *Transformation Maps*. Each group showcased their innovative approaches, highlighting how these enhancements would contribute to a more immersive and meaningful user experience. The pitch session also provided an opportunity for the groups to receive feedback and engage in discussions.

Reflection/Debriefing (30 min). Post workshop, there was a dedicated time for participants to reflect on the activities and engage in a debriefing session. Breanne Pitt asked the group 3 questions, and provided about 10 minutes for participants to write down responses. The questions were:

What are map strengths?

What are map opportunities?

How can you integrate IDN design in a scalable way to leverage identified opportunities?

2.3 Participants

Thirty-two INDCOR members and seven Strategic Intelligence Platform Representatives attended the workshop. INDCOR members consisted of consultants from academia (PhDs, Researchers, and PhD Candidates), game & narrative designers, media psychologists, policy makers, mass media specialists, and UX/UI designers.

3 Workshop Results

To better understand the verbal and written feedback from the workshop on how to improve the existing Transformation Maps with IDN design approaches, we organize the results using Janet Murray's framework [2] and Roth's [24] IDN user experience dimensions.

Janet Murray's influential framework consists of four affordances for digital media, (1) procedural (composed of executable rules), (2) participatory (inviting human action and manipulation of the represented world), (3) encyclopedic (containing very high capacity of information in multiple media formats) and (4) spatial (navigable as an information repository and/or a virtual place). Murray further distinguishes three experiential aesthetic qualities, (1) **agency** (taking meaningful and intentional action and seeing the result of decisions and choices), (2) **immersion** (being transported to an elaborately simulated place or state of mind), and (3) **transformation** (roleplaying and assimilating enacted events as personal experiences). Murray's perspective thus provides comprehensive but abstract top-level categories to describe the user experience in IDN.

Roth's model [24] identifies a series of relevant user experience dimensions for the evaluation of impactful IDN artifacts. Roth and Koenitz [25] map these concrete measurement dimensions to Murray's abstract three experiential aesthetic qualities (Fig. 2). Usability, for instance, is an important prerequisite, which will have a direct impact on the experience of agency. However, according to Roth and Koenitz (2016), this mapping is considered flexible. For instance, certain user dimensions can align with either the broader concepts of agency or immersion to varying degrees.

Figure 2 shows the connection of Roth's [24] user experience dimensions for the analysis of interactive narratives to Murray's aforementioned taxonomy. Here, agency (e.g. making choices within enacted events) and immersion (e.g. role-identification) are prerequisites for transformative experiences.

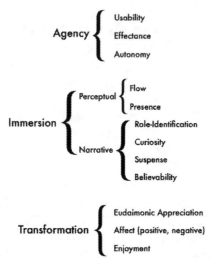

Fig. 2. Roth's IDN user experience dimensions connected to Murray's three experiential aesthetic qualities [25]

This model's framework can guide in the development of a more impactful and seamless user experience, enabling interactors to delve deeper into the *Transformation Maps* and derive greater value from the tool.

3.1 User-Interface (UI) and User Experience (UX)

Participants felt many of the UX/UI elements of the platform were excellent. Specifically, INDCOR members liked the use of a map as a visualization tool to represent interconnections between topics. They felt the map visualization provides a powerful means to explore complex data. More specifically, the amalgamation of all the parts of a system into a visual map helps to raise awareness about the complexity and interconnectedness of select systems. Recognizing complexity is the first step towards fostering a deeper understanding and seeking innovative solutions. It was also agreed that the data visualization method employed stimulates *curiosity*, specifically when surprising connections are made visible that make users aware of their own knowledge gaps. States of curiosity are often associated with a psychological interest for activities or stimuli that are surprising or characterized by a knowledge gap [25]. Golman and Loewenstein highlight the concept of knowledge gaps as a significant driver of curiosity. When users engage with the *Transformation Maps*, they are exposed to complex topics that reveal gaps in their own understanding. Sometimes the connections that are revealed in the maps even *surprise* the user, further contributing to the stimulation of curiosity for the interactor. Overall, this awareness of gaps in knowledge stimulates curiosity and contributes to an immersive experience for users as they explore the surprising aspects of the maps.

However, several opportunities were noted. Many INDCOR members indicated struggles navigating within the system that could be fixed with simple UX improvements. Also, many members reflected that the abundant data presented led to a cognitive overload, preventing participants from experiencing the desired impacts of the tool (Fig. 3). The following recommendations were proposed by INDCOR members to address navigational issues and the experience of "information overload."

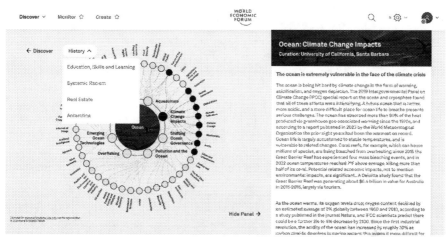

Fig. 3. Above showcases the *Transformation Map* interface on the World Economic Forum's Strategic Intelligence Platform. The content curation is on the right-hand side of the screen, which changes when different key issues are selected on the inner map ring. Also, this image exhibits the **History** and ← **Discover** buttons. In this case, the **History** button has been clicked on, providing a drop down of the path in which the user has explored the maps through clicks. This is how the user can go "back" of "forward" within the tool's interface.

Navigation: Applying Roth's model, we find that effective navigation plays a vital role in ensuring *usability* and better *flow*. It can also support goal achievement, resulting in increased engagement and overall satisfaction. When dealing with complexity, the user interface should be simple. The following suggestion were recommended by INDCOR members to improve the platforms navigation for an enhanced user experience:

Discover Button: For an improved meaning-making symbols need to be intuitive. The ← symbol next to the **Discover** button can cause confusion, leading users to mistake it for a back button within the map navigation. Clarifying the button's purpose as a "home" button would help avoid such confusion.

History Button: Streamline navigation and improve the **History** button: The **History** button should enable users to track and display their navigation path in a visible manner. Simplify the process to a one-click interaction for navigating between maps within the interface. This would reduce friction and enhance user immersion and engagement. Visualizing the history selection process, akin to breadcrumbs used in operating systems, can provide users with a clear representation of their exploration path, while also encouraging reflection on their choices (Fig. 4).

Fig. 4. MacOS Finder Breadcrumbs

Address Information Overload: The feeling of "information overload" can be attributed, in part, to the platforms' excessive *autonomy* and agency resulting from the absence of sufficient guidance. Workshop participants noted the platform was a bit too text and data heavy to have the desired transformative impact (Fig. 5). Figure 5 showcases how the density of the interface. In this example alone, there are over 600 words on the page, which does not include the platform's knowledge feed, which suggests further reading materials. According to a recent study [27], it takes the average reader approximately a minute to read 238 words. That would mean a single node on the map takes approximately three minutes to read. Considering how many maps, key issues and related topics are available, the time needed to thoroughly explore the maps unguided was overwhelming for participants.

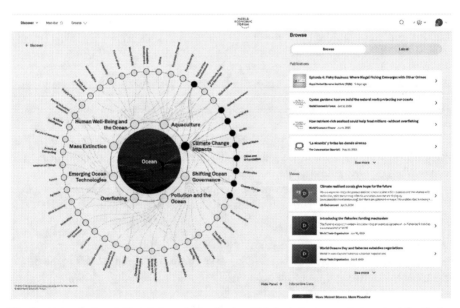

Fig. 5. Above is the platform's knowledge feed, which includes suggested content for further exploration, including videos, publications, and interactive data.

The experience of "information overload" impacts a user's ability to effectively navigate the platform, linking to Vygotzki's Zone of Proximal Development. According to ZPD, if the material exceeds the learner's current capabilities or the learner lacks proper guidance, it can become overwhelming and challenging to comprehend. Complex systems, like the ones presented in the *Transformation Maps*, are outside the ZPD for most people, and therefore necessitate appropriate scaffolding and support to mitigate information overload and facilitate effective learning.

Therefore the platform needs to provide clear guidance and structure to assist users in comprehending the content effectively. The following suggestion were recommended by INDCOR members to counteract the experience of cognitive overload:

Guidance: Introduce design elements that guide users during their exploration and discourage aimless clicking. A suggested approach is visualizing the history selection process, mentioned in the **History** Button improvements above. Improvements to the history button are twofold - they can improve navigation by encouraging guidance in user exploration and can also prompt users to reflect on their chosen path and derive deeper meaning from their journey. By visualizing the **History** button, users are unconsciously prompted to consider questions such as "Why did I take this path?" and "What does it mean?," facilitating a more immersive and reflective and thus transformative user experience.

3.2 Content

INDCOR members expressed high satisfaction with the Strategic Intelligence tool's content, recognizing its relevance and its ability to keep users informed about global trends and potential futures, enabling them to "stay ahead of the curve." The advanced analytics tools that allow users to download dynamic briefings and observe trends over time were particularly appreciated by the group. Furthermore, INDCOR members felt the Forum's commitment to updating the application regularly ensures that users have access to the most current information available. The quality of the content was highly regarded, as it incorporated perspectives from diverse and respected research institutions worldwide.

Similarly, the Forum's dedication to diversity of information and equal representation on a global scale ensures that users have a comprehensive and balanced understanding of the complex interrelations at hand. Complex problems are inherently contentious and transcend the confines of disciplines and nations [28]. The World Economic Forum's approach, which integrates data and insights from diverse research institutions worldwide, promotes a holistic perspective that surpasses regional biases and limitations.

These strengths contribute to the tool's *believability*, enhancing the tool's immersive capabilities. However, INDCOR members identified opportunities to further enhance user agency and immersion within the *Transformation Map* tool, highlighting three specific areas for improvement within the SI platform's content features.

Latest Publications Feature. While users appreciated the option to access related publications from reliable sources, it was unclear how these publications were connected to the interactions in the map. The relevance of some articles was questioned, as they did not address the specific map connections users were exploring. Suggestions include introducing a rating system for articles based on their relevance to the user's interactions, using AI to highlight related keywords in publications, and ensuring the curated text aligns with the keywords and connections in the map. Also, the suggestion was made to highlight keywords to make connections more obvious for the user.

Annotation Capabilities. Enable interactors to annotate insights and reflections with a highlighting and/or notetaking feature so they can journal their experiences and learning questions. Several IDN have an automatic journaling feature. For instance *Firewatch* [29] and *Herald* [30] use a journal to depict significant interactor choices thus making agency more tangible. This also supports constructivist learning theory in that the interactor is playing an active role personalizing and constructing their own knowledge while also engaging in continual reflection and sense-making.

Explore Intersection Feature. The 'Explore Intersection' option lacked functionality and felt incomplete (Fig. 6 left). Users were unable to interact or click on anything, leaving them uncertain about the meaning and purpose of this feature and the intersections. Recommendations include using an intelligent agent or generative AI to assist users in exploring intersections by providing suggested prompts based on user profiles. Additionally, offering the option to chat with an expert could be introduced as an additional paid service or premium features. Lastly, a final suggestion was to have an explore feature, similar to that of the google drive platform (see Fig. 6 right).

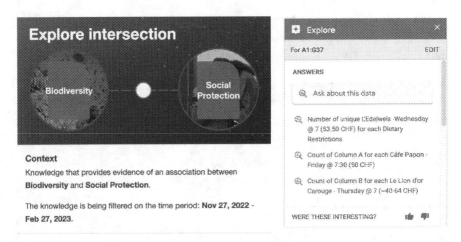

Fig. 6. Current explore intersection field (left) and suggested changes based on google drive feature (right).

3.3 Understanding

Again, INDCOR members noted that the *Transformation Maps* are an excellent tool for raising awareness about the complexity of select systems. However, INDCOR members felt that the platform's ability to foster meaning-making and personal relevance from the data was the platform's biggest opportunity for growth and could benefit from additional development. Therefore, to enhance transformation and immersion within the *Transformation Map* tool, the following were suggestions to enhance the platform's meaning making and personal relevance.

Meaning Making. Meaning can be constructed through story, or narrative, as a dynamic and emergent property [31]. The term meaning making is used in constructivist educational theory to describe the process by which individuals develop their personal epistemology to comprehend and interpret the influences, relationships, and sources of knowledge in their world [32]. Although the map feature aids users in comprehending complex and interconnected topics, there is room for improvement in terms of extracting meaning from the provided information. Questions arise regarding how these maps can contribute to decision-making, planning, risk identification, and opportunity assessment. To address these concerns, the integration of interactive narratives in future iterations holds promise. Interactive narratives have the ability to enhance the platform's capabilities by facilitating engagement, scaffolded learning, and increased learning gains [33], thus assisting users in deriving valuable insights for decision-making processes. The following suggestions were made:

Implement AI-Generated Interactive Scenarios. Utilize AI to develop narratives to explain connections within the map. These narratives can help users with decision-making, planning, risk identification, and opportunity assessment, fostering a more enjoyable and informative experience.

Incorporate Predictive Model Narratives. Integrate predictive models within narratives to showcase potential future developments, build *suspense* and encourage curiosity. Instead of relying on abstract descriptions or trend graphics, these narratives should involve users and stakeholders, providing a more relatable understanding of trends and their implications.

Offer Decision-Making Support Service. Provide a service, possibly as a professional or paid feature, where users can utilize interactive narrative simulations for decision-making support. By connecting role-based scenarios with decision-making options and illustrating potential consequences, users can explore different approaches and make well-informed choices tailored to their specific roles.

Role Identification. Currently, users encounter a tool in which they are not directly represented. They can only indirectly personalize the tool through topic selection or the create map tool, which is an advanced feature. In the world of Interactive Narrative design, Janet Murray [2] introduces the concept of *Scripting the Interactor (StI)*, which casts an interactor into their role by providing context, managing expectations and exposing opportunities for action. This personalization stands firmly on a constructivist paradigm, and also encourages engagement. *Role identification* impacts meaning-making by allowing individuals to engage with different perspectives, experiences, and contexts. When individuals assume roles in interactive experiences, they step into the shoes of a given character or persona, enabling them to explore viewpoints through specific lenses and gain a deeper understanding of complex situations. Effective learning occurs when a user adopts the mindset, behaviors, and values of different identities or roles, which can serve as strong motivators for immersion and meaningful and transformative learning experiences in educational and professional settings [34]. By actively participating in role-playing, individuals can embody different identities, emotions, and motivations, which enhances their capacity for empathy, critical thinking, and reflection. This active involvement enhances the integration of new information and promotes a deeper connection to the content, resulting in more meaningful learning experiences.

Moreover, role playing can foster creativity, problem-solving, and decision-making skills, providing a space for individuals to experiment, test hypotheses, and explore potential outcomes. An IDN example applying multiple perspectives is *The Last Hijack Interactive* in which interactors explore the complex topic of piracy by switching between different roles and thus perspectives [35]. The following suggestions were made for addressing user role representation and engagement:

Empower User Role Creation. Emphasize in the onboarding process that users can create their own roles within the system through completing user profiles. This should allow for greater customization based on individual preferences, encompassing a variety of information types and output formats. Use instructional videos, interactive tutorials, and use case examples to demonstrate the relevance of information in relation to chosen roles.

Employ Interactive Digital Narratives in Onboarding. During the onboarding process, *StI* by presenting interactive scenarios that enable users to define their roles and communicate their needs. Generating user profiles and scenarios based on individual requirements can facilitate role formation and enhance user engagement.

Encourage Role-Taking for Perspective Change. Enable users to adopt different roles for reflection and perspective change. Role-taking facilitates understanding of others' viewpoints, promoting informed decision-making in business and policy contexts. The Forum should explore ways to implement role changes and potentially employ AI-generated narrative scenarios for this purpose.

Foster User Communities. Utilize user profile information to establish communities of users with similar interests, enabling knowledge exchange, insights sharing, and collaborative problem-solving.

Enable User Feedback. Provide users with a platform to contribute insights, success stories, and questions directly into the system. Implement a chat forum-like feature to facilitate communication, allowing users to share their experiences, suggest category updates, propose new developments, and seek clarification from the system.

4   Discussion

The development of *Transformation Maps* by the World Economic Forum enables users to visualize complex systems, and the amalgamation of carefully curated, updated, and monitored expert data has proven to be both impressive and exciting. For the improvement of the *Transformation Maps,* we suggest to integrate knowledge from Interactive Narrative Design as well as from the Learning Sciences and highlight constructivism and ZPD. This interdisciplinary approach can provide designers and researchers with insights into creating effective, immersive, and educational IDNs that align with learners' ZPD and promote engagement throughout the learning experience.

Overall, people found the Transformation Maps to be a great complexity visualization tool, but felt that there were scalable opportunities that could be capitalized. This specifically included integrating role-taking and personalization features, which do not exist on the platform yet. If integrated well, this could potentially help users better understand complexity by offering opportunities to experience multiple perspectives, enabling users to overcome confirmation bias. Looking into the future, narrative design would also be a valuable addition in regard to what-if scenarios and role-taking, ultimately adding simulation aspects to the tool. Some of these features are potentially easier to implement, such as user roles. The inclusion of what-if scenarios requires a more complex simulation capable of representing relevant alternatives, potentially through artificial intelligence.

By integrating some of the design elements indicated in this paper, learners can transcend their existing knowledge boundaries and be encouraged to explore, leading to moments of surprise and insight. By fostering an environment that supports transformative learning experiences, individuals are more likely to develop a systemic understanding of complex issues and engage in thoughtful decision-making processes.

Moreover, the workshop's insights and recommendations highlight the significance of collaborative endeavors involving stakeholders, specifically industry and academic professionals, and also the end-user. Such collaborations play a pivotal role in perpetually advancing knowledge, as well as facilitating substantial introspection and growth in product development.

4.1 Future Work

Based on insights derived from this workshop, we suggest extending the transformation part of Roth and Koenitz' (2016) model, which currently focuses on personal relevance, affect and enjoyment. This extension should incorporate another (cognitive) element, possibly Eureka, or more informally called an "aha" moment, brought about by transformation through (deep) insight and systemic understanding. By recognizing and acknowledging the complexity of a given topic and refraining from forming premature opinions, individuals can avoid trivializing important issues, a common tactic employed by populists. Future work should also analyze the complete learning experience, starting with learners arriving at the maps, their existing knowledge, expectations, and cultural backgrounds, and ending with reflection and evaluation of the learning experience.

4.2 Limitations

Several limitations were identified during the workshop, which should be considered for future improvements.

With regards to time, the duration of the workshop was too short - the allocated one hour was deemed insufficient. Similarly, more time should be devoted to allowing participants to familiarize themselves with the platform and its capabilities. This also includes encouraging participants to explore the platform independently prior to the workshop. Moreover, the initial debriefing session was scheduled for only 15 min, which proved to be too short to provide everyone with an opportunity to express their thoughts. Therefore, the session was extended to 20 min. Ideally, a longer debriefing session of 30 min would allow for more comprehensive discussions.

Another limitation identified was the process of selecting specific maps for each persona. Allowing groups to choose their own maps proved to be time-consuming. To address this issue, it is recommended to assign a dedicated map to each persona, streamlining the selection process and saving valuable time.

Furthermore, it was observed that the guiding questions provided during the workshop influenced participants to some extent, as many groups ended up developing video games as their suggested narrative additions based on the guided question regarding playable characters. This may have limited the diversity of ideas generated. To encourage a broader range of perspectives and outcomes, it is suggested to refine the guiding questions and ensure they do not overly steer participants towards specific solutions.

Lastly, While the Forum sought scalable design strategies, most groups developed video games as their suggested Narrative additions. With 294 actively monitored and updated maps, developing video games was not deemed scalable. As a result, we needed to devote time during the debriefing session to redirect attention to scalability options. To address this issue, it is crucial to communicate the client's expectations more explicitly to the participants, ensuring a clear understanding of the desired outcomes.

5 Conclusion

By combining interactive storytelling techniques with data visualization, interactive narratives could facilitate a more engaging and impactful learning experience. We discussed the potential benefits and challenges of incorporating interactive narrative design approaches into *Transformation Maps* and highlighted their role in fostering inclusivity, perspective change, enhancing meaning making, and driving impactful actions towards sustainable development.

To maximize these benefits, it is essential to consider the importance of user-friendly interfaces, maintaining alignment with the Zone of Proximal Development, guiding personalization, and assigning clear roles for users in knowledge construction. This approach ensures that learners are appropriately challenged, supported, and able to actively engage in the learning process, ultimately enhancing learning outcomes and avoiding cognitive overload.

References

1. INDCOR - Interactive Narrative Design for Complexity Representations. COST ACTION CA18230. https://indcor.eu
2. Murray, J.H.: Hamlet on the Holodeck: The Future of Narrative in Cyberspace. Free Press (1997)
3. Rzevski, G.: Complexity as the defining feature of the 21st century (2015)
4. Rajeski, D., Chaplin, H., Olson, R.: Addressing Complexity with Playable models. Wilson Center, Science and Technology Innovation Program. Washington: Wilson Center (2015)
5. Lönngren, J., Van Poeck, K.: Wicked problems: a mapping review of the literature. Int J Sust Dev WorldSust. Dev. World 28(6), 481–502 (2021)

6. Dörner, D., Kreuzig, H., Reirher, F., Stäudel, T.: On dealing with uncertainty and complexity. Hans Huber, Berna, Suiza (1983)
7. Koenitz, H.: Understanding Interactive Digital Narrative: Immersive Expressions for a Complex Time. Taylor & Francis (2023)
8. Koenitz, H.: Towards a specific theory of interactive digital narrative. In: Interactive Digital Narrative, pp. 91–105. Routledge (2015)
9. Roth, C., Van Nuenen, T., Koenitz, H.: Ludonarrative hermeneutics: a way out and the narrative paradox. In: Interactive Storytelling: 11th International Conference on Interactive Digital Storytelling, ICIDS 2018, Proceedings 11, pp. 11–22. Springer International Publishing (2018)
10. Nack, F.: Interactive digital narrative (IDN)—a complexity case. New Rev. Hypermedia Multimed. **28**(3–4), 69–75 (2022)
11. Wiener, N.: Cybernetics and Society: The Human Use of Human Beings. Houghton Mifflin (1950)
12. Marinescu, D.C.: Complex systems and clouds: a self-organization and self-management perspective. Morgan Kaufmann (2016)
13. Steer, M.D.: Cybernetics: Circular Causal and Feedback Mechanisms in Biological and Social Systems. Transactions of the Seventh Conference, March 23–24, 1950, New York. Heinz von Foerster, Ed. Science, 115(2978) (1951)
14. Vygotsky, L.S.: Play and its role in the mental development of the child. Sov. Psychol. **5**(3), 6–18 (1967)
15. Piaget, J.: The origins of intelligence in children. (M. Cook, Trans.). W.W. Norton & Co (1952)
16. Foerster, H.V.: Cybernetics of cybernetics. In: Krippendorff, K. (ed.) Communication and control in society, pp. 5–8. Gordon and Breach (1979)
17. Foerster, H.V.: Understanding understanding: Essays on cybernetics and cognition. Springer (2003)
18. Von Glasersfeld, E.: An introduction to radical constructivism. Invented Reality **1740**, 28 (1984)
19. Kirschner, P.A., Sweller, J., Clark, R.E.: Why minimal guidance during instruction does not work: An analysis of the failure of constructivist, discovery, problem-based, experiential, and inquiry-based teaching. Educ. Psychol. **41**(2), 75–86 (2010)
20. Davies, M.: Concept mapping, mind mapping and argument mapping: What are the differences and do they matter? (2011)
21. Roth, C.: The 'Angstfabriek' experience: factoring fear into transformative interactive narrative design. In Interactive Storytelling: 12th International Conference on Interactive Digital Storytelling, ICIDS 2019, Proceedings 12, pp. 11–22. Springer International Publishing (2019)
22. Segel, E., Heer, J.: Narrative visualization: Telling stories with data. IEEE Trans. Visual Comput. GraphicsComput. Graphics **16**(6), 1139–1148 (2010)
23. Nielsen, L.: Personas in cross-cultural projects. In: IFIP Working Conference on Human Work Interaction Design, pp. 123–134. Springer, Heidelberg (2009)
24. Roth, C.: Experiencing Interactive Storytelling (Ph.D. thesis). Vrije Universiteit Amsterdam (2016)
25. Roth, C., Koenitz, H.: Evaluating the User Experience of Interactive Digital Narrative. In Proceedings of the 1st International Workshop on Multimedia Alternate Realities (AltMM '16), pp. 31–36. Association for Computing Machinery (2016)
26. Golman, R., Loewenstein, G.: An Information-Gap Theory of Feelings About Uncertainty (2016)
27. Brysbaert, M.: How many words do we read per minute? a review and meta-analysis of reading rate. J. Mem. Lang. **109**, 104047 (2019)

28. Brandt, P., et al.: A review of transdisciplinary research in sustainability science. Ecol. Econ. **92**, 1–15 (2013)

29. *Firewatch.* Campo Santo. (2016). Retrieved June 15, 2023, from http://www.firewatchgame. com

30. *Herald.* Wispfire. (2017). Retrieved June 15, 2023, from http://heraldgame.com/

31. Grove, N.: Story, agency, and meaning making: narrative models and the social inclusion of people with severe and profound intellectual disabilities. J. Religion Disability Health **16**(4), 334–351 (2012)

32. Piaget, J.: The construction of reality in the child (M. Cook, Trans.). Basic Books (1954)

33. Shelton, C.C., Warren, A.E., Archambault, L.M.: Exploring the use of interactive digital storytelling video: Promoting student engagement and learning in a university hybrid course. TechTrends **60**(5), 465–474 (2016)

34. Gee, J.P.: What video games have to teach us about learning and literacy. Comput. Entertainment (CIE) **1**(1), 20 (2003)

35. van Enschot, R., Boogaard, I., Koenitz, H., Roth, C.: The potential of interactive digital narratives: Agency and multiple perspectives in Last Hijack Interactive. In Interactive Storytelling: 12th International Conference on Interactive Digital Storytelling, ICIDS 2019, Proceedings 12, pp. 158–169. Springer International Publishing (2019)

36. Schutt, M.: Scaffolding for online learning environments: instructional design strategies that provide online learner support. Educ. Technol. **43**(6), 28–35 (2003). http://www.jstor.org/sta ble/44428859

Full-Motion Video as Parameterized Replay Stories: Emerging Design Patterns from the Timeline Authoring Platform

Pedro Silva[(✉)]

Georgia Institute of Technology, Atlanta, GA 30332, USA
psilva6@gatech.edu

Abstract. The 1980s saw full-motion video (FMV) titles inaugurate design patterns for a new genre of interactive digital narrative (IDN). Recently, this genre made a resurgence in popularity. Despite the intervening years, FMV's design conventions remain tightly coupled to the affordances of laserdisc technology thanks to streaming platforms like Twitch and YouTube. This paper: (1) employs IDN affordances and aesthetics as a lens to examine modern FMV games, namely the recent works of Wales Interactive; (2) offers a distinction between two story structures commonly employed in FMV design, i.e. event-driven and branching narratives; and (3) leverages research on the emerging conventions of Timeline–an authoring platform for tightly parallel, parameterized stories–to address the challenges of FMV design.

1 Introduction and Background

The popularity of Dragon's Lair [2] spotlighted full-motion video (FMV) as a technique for interactive storytelling. Compared to its contemporaries, the benefits of FMV were clear: pre-rendered video conferred a leap in graphical fidelity, while demanding less computational resources; a game's graphics need not rely on the intensive manipulation of sprites, vectors and 3D models. Early arcade iterations–Dragon's Lair contemporaries like Space Ace [3], Cobra Command [4] and Time Gal [15]–pioneered an emerging aesthetic. They, along with the FMV titles that followed, inaugurated design patterns for a new subgenre of interactive digital narrative.

Bolter [1] describes the aesthetics of a medium "as the way it conditions our senses–how we see, hear, or feel the world" (p. 32). In part, these aesthetics are influenced by a medium's technological characteristics: The aesthetics of FMV are tightly coupled to the limitations and promises of its the laserdisc, a storage medium that affords playback of video files retrievable via random access. FMV's technological affordances promised designers new expressive possibilities, e.g. smoothly animating high-resolution images. FMV also benefited from a readymade vocabulary of filmic language, a reliance that earned the genre the moniker of "Interactive Movie."

L. Holloway-Attaway and J. T. Murray (Eds.): ICIDS 2023, LNCS 14383, pp. 363–373, 2023.
https://doi.org/10.1007/978-3-031-47655-6_22

Leveraging this blend of filmic vocabulary and digital affordances, designers strived for dramatic agency: the pleasure of participating in a responsive and dramatically cohesive system [11]. In particular, the FMV genre excels at replay stories–stories in which the same scenario is offered for replay with variations based on parameters controlled by interactors. These stories "assume a parameterized world in which destiny is open-ended and events can be revisited and changed" [11]. Thus, it is through multiple traversals, as interactors playfully push against the boundaries of a narrative's possibility space, that story threads interleave and give shape to a story's complete causal chain, the assumptions of its storyworld, its themes, and its moral physics.

In addition to its technological affordances, FMV aesthetics are also shaped by the media ecosystem in which they are enmeshed: how a medium relates to the media that came before it, and how it relates to the reality it strives to represent. Laserdisc benefited from photographic video, a far closer representation of reality than the eight-bit sprites and synthesized beeps of its contemporaries. Yet laserdisc's affordances also conferred limitations. FMV decoupled player action from avatar feedback. Scripted and pre-rendered cutscenes limited combinatorial variation, especially compared to its arcade contemporaries, e.g. Super Mario Bros.'s responsive and smoothly scrolling sprites. Similarly, its reliance on filmic language made for challenging interaction design. As FMV evolved, emerging conventions struggled to marry its filmic presentation to digital media's procedural and participatory affordances: Entries often suffered from dead-ends, i.e. shallow branches resulting from a choice that immediately ends the narrative. Ambiguous ties between player choice and narrative outcome often resulted in a lack of dramatic cohesion. Soon, as real-time graphics began matching the fidelity of pre-rendered video, FMV lost its competitive advantage. New entries dwindled.

Lately, this genre has seen a resurgence, popularized by live streaming platforms like Twitch and video archives like YouTube. Wales Interactive, who ranks among the genre's most prolific contemporary publishers, affords interactors a "Streamer Mode" where decision points that are normally time-sensitive are instead paused so that streamers can deliberate choices with their audiences–an accommodation that speaks to the unique pleasure of collaboratively exploring an IDN's possibility space.

Despite the intervening years, FMV's design conventions remain tightly coupled to the affordances of laserdisc technology: User interfaces reveal a single decision point at a time, foregrounding a button-based design that recalls the menu screens of laserdiscs. Additionally, modern FMV entries still struggle to showcase variation without forcing interactors to rewatch scenes that feature (1) no variation or (2) more commonly, variation too subtle to detect or too minor to qualify as narratively meaningful. In more egregious examples, a game may ask interactors to replay an entire experience from start to finish–a tedious "hunt for new content," as described by streamers.

In exploring these design challenges, the Georgia Institute of Technology's Prototype eNarrative Lab has developed the Timeline platform, a system for authoring and navigating parameterized stories. Timeline aims to afford interactors a means of navigating complex, multi-sequential replay stories; and though not designed exclusively for FMV, the platform's emerging design conventions feature productive lessons for meeting the unique challenges of FMV design.

This paper: (1) employs IDN affordances and aesthetics as a lens to examine modern FMV games, namely the recent works of Wales Interactive; (2) offers a distinction between two story structures commonly employed in IDN design, i.e. event-driven and branching narratives; and (3) leverages research on the emerging conventions of Timeline–an authoring platform for tightly parallel, parameterized stories–to address the challenges of FMV design.

2 Authoring Meaningful Repetition: Design Lessons from Timeline

2.1 The Timeline Authoring System

The Timeline platform segments narratives into dramatic beats, each beat visualized as an individual tile. Tiles are assigned a collection of media in the form of video or still images. Example media can include storyboards, animatics, audio clips or title cards. Tiles are arranged horizontally to mimic a timeline while a playhead moves from left to right as the narrative progresses, highlighting the current dramatic segment (see Fig. 1).

At prescribed milestones, tiles are stacked vertically: a choice column, where each tile represents a parameter loosely inspired by Propp's narrative morphemes. In Cooper's Reliving Last Night, for example, a scene in which the protagonist prepares to host a guest includes columns denoting the protagonist's choice of clothing (e.g., formal or casual), choice of drink to offer (e.g., soda or alcohol) and choice of music. By sliding these choice columns vertically and aligning a tile to the timeline, interactors select their desired beat.

As interactors arrange beats, the narrative accommodates these changes, varying the story's trajectory with each choice and generating a number of narrative permutations, which are then punctuated by unique endings. In Stricklin's Now or Forever [14], a time-traveling spouse's choices of whether or not to (1) confront her adulterous partner, (2) text the priest evidence of the affair, or (3) crash the wedding result in eight unique endings. Designed to accommodate multi-sequential narratives, the system's interface encourages playful exploration of a story's permutations; tiles are titled for easy navigation, and interactors can double-click or -tap to jump to any given dramatic segment. The system presents interactors with a single, glanceable timeline. This timeline simultaneously shows a narrative's choice points, possible choices and currently chosen choices.

To facilitate the creation of these parameterized stories, an authoring tool was built alongside the Timeline platform, which allows authors to arrange tiles and choice columns, to assign multiple media to each tile, and finally assign conditions under which a given media should trigger (see Fig. 2). Crucially, each piece of media can be assigned multiple conditionals, playing only if all conditions evaluate as true.

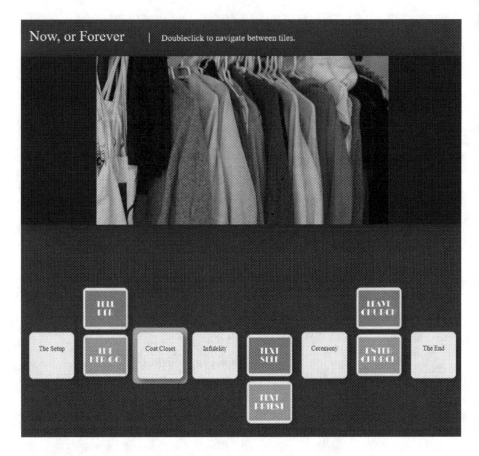

Fig. 1. Stricklin's Now or Forever

Fig. 2. The Timeline Authoring Tool

Timeline was deployed as part of a graduate class in interactive fiction. Students relied on branching diagrams before implementing and tweaking their designs via the authoring tool. Once outlines were implemented via the system's tile interface, students then worked toward producing the video and images that would animate their narrative segments.

A user study was conducted in which 12 participants experienced one of four student-created stories. Participants were asked to answer an explorative questionnaire concerning their experiences of the platform and narrative content. Results from this preliminary usertest highlight that: (1) Stories excel at presenting permutations in which there "are no losing or perfect endings;" (2) interactors were motivated to replay stories in pursuit of other endings; and (3) exposing all choices at the beginning of a story threatens narrative suspense.

2.2   Design Challenges for FMV Authors

Modern FMV entries struggle to showcase variation without introducing frustrating repetition. Interactors are often tasked with rewatching scenes that feature no variation or more commonly, variation too subtle to detect or too minor to qualify as narratively meaningful. Yet replay stories rely on multiple traversals, thus repetition presents a unique design challenge: Parameterized replay stories encourage repeat viewings, but many struggle to foster meaningful replay.

Wales Interactive's Who Pressed Mute on Uncle Marcus [8] introduces design conventions to address this challenge. In this example, interactors are tasked with gathering enough evidence to confront suspected culprits, and each of the narrative's six endings revolve around the accusation of a particular suspect, along with a revelation about the character and the ensuing fallout. Experiencing each requires several playthroughs, and Who Pressed Mute on Uncle Marcus attempts to alleviate unmeaningful repetition by allowing interactors to carry over their collected evidence across playthroughs. This accommodation is an imperfect solution, forcing the diegetic protagonist to leverage evidence collected on previous playthroughs (i.e. information nondiegetic to a given traversal) and thus sacrificing narrative cohesion.

Dead-end story branches remain another common design challenge. In Who Pressed Mute on Uncle Marcus, interactors may accuse the uncle of fabricating his poisoning only to see the narrative abruptly cut to the uncle's funeral: a branch that prooves far less narratively satisfying than had the interactor chosen to continue the investigation. Indeed, streamers label this the bad or false ending, highlighting that designers intended interactors to press onward to "truer" endings. Similarly, a certain combination of parameters in I See Black Clouds triggers the protagonist's death, tasking interactors to begin anew.

This paper argues that in order for repetition to be meaningful, a dramatic beat must: (1) highlight dramatically meaningful variation as contextualized by subsequent traversals; and (2) also be easy to locate within a narrative's larger arc. Here, lessons learned from the design of Timeline prove helpful.

2.3   Parallelism

In Timeline, regardless of an interactor's chosen combination of parameters, the number of dramatic beats that constitute the story neither shrinks nor grows. By retaining its overall structure, this system reinforces a strict sense of parallelism. Narrative branches are required to revolve around readable, orienting milestones. Artifacts such as dead-end story branches are no longer possible.

Maintaining parallelism across all narrative possibilities means choice-points require strict design criteria: Choices must be reframed as the narrative permutates and progresses, but must also remain parallel across branches. In Ramirez's Northbound (2021), the narrative's final choice titled "Alone or Together" undergoes several such reframings, each contingent on the parameters chosen earlier in the story: In one instance, the protagonist must choose to (1) turn herself into border patrol agents to save those who traveled with her or (2) reveal her companions' location, thereby securing entry for her son; in another permutation, the protagonist must choose to (1) leave her son in Mexico in hopes that he can earn asylum into the US, returning to Honduras alone, or (2) be deported back to Honduras together with her son. Though recontextualized, these choices riff on similar dramatic milestones, and both are uniquely encapsulated in the binary "Alone or Together".

Legible milestones serve as important guideposts for navigating a narrative's possibility space. Replay stories require that interactors consider multiple narrative instances, and adding to that cognitive load are stories that play out multi-sequentially. Leveraging the well-known milestones of common rituals or genre archetypes (e.g. the traditions of a wedding ceremony or the sci-fi trope of a rural alien abduction) proves a powerful strategy for authoring these stories. Nayak's An Unexpected Guest [12] opens as a farmer protagonist glimpses a UFO's crash-landing, escalates as the farmer approaches the crash-site and climaxes as the federal authorities arrive for an interview. Likewise, Stricklin's Now, or Forever charts multiple instantiations of a wedding ceremony couched in the trappings of romantic comedy: rice-throwing, a salacious scandal, and an objection speech. In Who Pressed Mute on Uncle Marcus, events are cleverly structured around a family game night, as each round sees the protagonist partner with a member of the family.

2.4   Reframing Agency

FMV conventions task interactors with making choices at predetermined narrative milestones. These choices are presented as button-styled options that recall the menu screens of laserdiscs and DVDs, the buttons labeled with potential actions (e.g. in Who Pressed Mute on Uncle Marcus, interactors may choose who they'd like to pair with for each quiz round). These labels serve to communicate a narrative's affordances for interaction, which in turn promote dramatic agency.

Tenenbaum and Tenenbaum [16] argue that agency is often idealized as freedom and measured by the variability of player options. Often, designers aspire to showcase limitless permutations "with enough variation and emergent moments to support hours of unique play." Instead, Tenenbaum and Tenenbaum's reframe of agency as commitment to meaning–a shift that spotlights expressive intent, and recognizes that constraints are just as ludically and dramatically meaningful as affordances. This reframing is especially productive for the FMV genre.

I See Black Clouds leverages both affordances and constraints in exploring its themes of acceptance. The game's climax sees the protagonist describe a traumatic incident to her therapist, an incident that culminates in interactors choosing between helping a friend in trouble or fleeing from the scene. Choosing to help, however, only results in chiding from the therapist, who reminds the protagonist (and the interactor): "that isn't what happened, is it?" The flashback is rewinded to the same choice point, and interactors are once again confronted with both options. Through replay, the interactor comes to understand that it's only by accepting the truth of events that the protagonist can progress. Crucially, interactors are asked to engage with narrative meaning despite having no strategic choices at play.

Tenenbaum and Tenenbaum rely on speech act theory, scaffolding agency as the product of conversational acts, e.g. assertive, directive and commissive speech acts. As human conversation creates meaning and commits speakers to action, FMV games (as well IDNs more broadly) work as a conversation between designer and interactor. Agency is recharacterized as meaningful commitment that allows interactors to express meaning and be confident that the system interprets those meanings as intended.

These commitments between interactor and designer do not always align: The interactor may instruct the protagonist in what they believes will result in one type of communication, only to see the character perform something unexpected in return. This mismatch between designer affordance and interactor intention occurs when interactors lack enough context to inform their intentions. In Tesla Effect: A Tex Murphy Adventure [5], for example, dialogue options are labeled in film noirish tropes, resulting in affordances for interaction that are difficult to interpret, obscuring the designers' intended affordances and preventing proper commitment to meaning by the interactor. In the The Complex (2020), interactors must decide whether to walk to their boss's office, to pursue an ex-partner down a hallway or to return to their own office; but importantly, while the choices have significant impact on the story's trajectory, the choices as communicated to the interactor fail to convey these dramatically rich possibilities. If the story does not disambiguate between options with careful narrative framing, these choices of direction are devoid of meaning.

3   FMV Through the Lens of IDN

3.1   Distinguishing Event-Driven and Branching Design Patterns

This section proposes a tool for classifying FMV experiences–a spectrum between branching and event-driven story architectures–and examines the affordances and limitations of both.

Branching narratives offer an interactor agency at select decision points. Interactors are confronted with a dramatically compelling scenario and afforded a roster of options in response. Due to the challenges of combinatorial explosion, choice points are normally limited to two or three options. Depending on a an interactor's choice, a narrative is shuttled down one of several possible story branches. Thus, a branching narrative is easily understood via a branching diagram where possible story traversals split and merge on their path toward one of several potential endings. Here, these choice points and selected options operate as story parameters. A single traversal can be described as a series of such parameters, e.g. a list of choice/selected option pairs. Thus, Wales Interactive's The Complex [6], I See Black Clouds [7], Bloodshore (2021) and Who Pressed Mute on Uncle Marcus [8] are branching narratives–and, as elaborated in the following section, so are the stories authored via Timeline.

Conversely, event-driven narratives rely on attributes of the storyworld to trigger dramatic beats. These dramatic beats are composed of preconditions and effects. If the storyworld's configuration meets a beat's preconditions, an interactor may trigger that particular event, which in turn will affect changes to the storyworld's configuration, make a new roster of beats available and close off others. These attributes, for example, may be cast as character traits and inter-character relationships (as in the case of Over the Alps [2020]), inventory items (as evident in classic FMV adventure games like Gabriel Knight II: The Beast Within [1995] or Tex Murphy: Tesla Effect [5]) or keyword gates (as in Barlow's Her Story [2015] and Telling Lies [2019]). Compared to branching narratives, event-driven narratives pose far more challenges when diagraming as traversals are more variable and difficult to predict.

Of note, these two architectures operate as poles of a spectrum rather than dichotomous categories. Wales Interactive's Bloodshore (2021), for example, attempts a mix of event-driven and branching narrative architectures: Screen prompts foreground how each of the interactor's choices affect their portfolio of attributes, e.g. their "Team Morale," "Romance," and "Strength" stats. However, a harmonious blend of both architectures remains a design challenge. Bloodshore obfuscates how these attributes affect the availability of future branches, opting to showcase these stats as an end-of-game scoresheet. Thus, Bloodshore relies on a branching architecture but adorns the interactor's experience with the aesthetics of an event-driven architecture. In response, reviewers cite these player stats as seemingly arbitrary.

In summary, event-driven narratives excel at variability, though often at the expense of dramatic cohesion. On the other hand, branching narratives excel at presenting an authored arc tailored for dramatic tension and release but often offer reduced variability and player agency. Branching narratives thus must rely on choices and options that are well-constrained and narratively motivated. Their dramatic agency relies on transparent interaction conventions mapped onto actions that suggest rich story possibilities. The following section: (1) highlights the challenges of designing for FMV experiences that rely on a branching architecture via the works of Wales Interactive; (2) introduces the Timeline authoring system; and (3) discusses design lessons learned via Timeline's preliminary user study.

3.2   Expanding the Product

Koenitz (2015) models IDNs as an arrangement of three parts: (1) the system: its pre-authored possibility space; (2) the process: the affordances interactors affect in navigating that space; and (3) the product: a fixed instance of a story's telling. Thus, an interactor's traversal becomes an act of narrative instantiation. FMV divides productively into Koenitz's framework. Here, the system encompasses a title's complete archive of possible videos and the parameters that affect their sequence; the process characterizes the act of affecting these parameters in traversing a narrative's possibility space; while the product speaks to the resulting instance, one of many possible.

As Koenitz [9] warns, a product alone is "severely limited as a representation of an IDN work" (p.18). This definition of product is especially narrow when applied to FMV and replay stories. Replay stories encourage multiple traversals through a narrative's possibility space, a playful exploration of its underlying system in order to understand a storyworld's moral physics and themes. This emerging understanding speaks to the IDN aesthetic of transformation [10], i.e. the elaboration of a theme through variation. In pursuit of transformation, interactors may return to previous decision points and enact different choices (as in stories authored for the Timeline platform), or choosing a different character as the focus of a story's narrativity (as in The Invisible Hours [18]). Such experiences are difficult to neatly segment into separate playthroughs.

This paper proposes an expansion of product to include an interactor's total inferences about a storyworld. These inferences are informed by the sum of an interactor's traversals of the system, along with an understanding of an FMV's parameters and affordances for interaction. In other words, product is what the interactor comes to understand of the designer's storyworld, its moral physics, and its themes.

I See Black Clouds [7], for example, follows a protagonist investigating a dangerous poltergeist after her friend's untimely death. However, one of four endings reveals the ghost to be fabricated by the protagonist as a means of coping with post-traumatic stress; and this one ending recontextualizes the others. What begins as a paranormal thriller transforms into a psychological drama. The aesthetic pleasure of replay stories lies in the development of theme through variation. I See Black Clouds elaborates upon the challenges of coping with trauma. Its themes and moral physics reveal themselves via the sequence of choices required for the protagonist's self-discovery. As interactors explore the story's possibility space, they come to understand which decisions plunge the protagonist deeper into denial and which eventually lead to acceptance. Thus, the product of I See Black Clouds reaches beyond a single instantiation and is more productively described as encompassing all of its storyworld inferences.

This expansion of product is especially helpful for FMV design. FMV games are often designed to be replayed, and all potential traversals must (1) be taken in relation to those that came before and those that follow, (2) avoid thematic contradiction, and (3) contribute to a narratively cohesive whole. Each newly witnessed instantiation should reveal more of a storyworld's moral physics, placing in sharper focus "what consequences attach to actions, who is rewarded, who is punished, how fair the world is... how bad a loss characters are allowed to suffer, and what weight is attached to those losses" (Murray, 1997, p. 254). FMV designers must account for their storyworld as a whole, rather than considering story threads and potential traversals in isolation.

3.3   Pushing into Narrativity

Propp [13] originated the terms fabula and syuzhet to distinguish between a story's events, i.e. its fabula, and its sequence of presentation, i.e. its syuzhet. Few narratives are totally linear, most revealing bits of backstory as they move through the narrative action; these backstories then recontextualize events going forward. Detective fiction proves a particularly helpful example. Todorov [17] describes these stories as divided into two layers: the story of the crime and the story of its investigation. Here, the detective's investigation operates as the syuzhet through which the fabula (i.e. the crime) is reassembled and narrativized to the reader.

Videogames often allow interactors agency over both narrativity and enactment. Yet, focus remains squarely on enactment. The procedural and participatory affordances of games provide an alluring capacity for tightly responsive interaction, and these affordances in turn encourage the prioritization of enactment. The genre of FMV, however, lacks such tightly coupled player input and avatar reaction; for FMV, enactment and narrativity are of equal aesthetic importance. Nonetheless, this dominance of enactment over narrativity persists.

The conventions of FMV present an opportunity for exploring narrativity, for syuzhet play, as FMV is unconcerned with the kinetic pleasures of responsive avatar control. I See Black Clouds's narrativity transforms its premise from paranormal thriller to psychological drama. Likewise, Who Pressed Mute on Uncle Marcus [8] sees the protagonist endeavoring to discover who poisoned her uncle in time to administer an antidote. In true detective fashion, the events in the story's fabula, i.e. the poison and poisoner, do not vary; yet, through multiple playthroughs, variations in narrativity continually recontextualize the interactor's inferences about the crime until the protagonist (and interactor) finally uncover the true culprit.

4   Conclusion

This paper employed IDN affordances and aesthetics as a lens to examine modern FMV games, namely the recent works of Wales Interactive. It introduced a two design patterns commonly in the FMV genre: event-driven and branching patterns. It argued for the expanded understanding of IDN product and called for an exploration of playful narrativity. This paper also presented design lessons learned from Timeline, an authoring tool for parameterized stories: These design lessons include the use of parallelism and a reframing of agency as commitment to meaning.

References

1. Bolter, J.D., Engberg, M., MacIntyre, B.: Reality Media: Augmented and Virtual Reality. MIT Press, Cambridge (2021)
2. Cinematronics: Dragon's lair. Game (1983)
3. Cinematronics: Space ace. Game (1983)
4. East, D.: Cobra command. Game (1984)
5. Games, B.F.: Tesla effect: a tex murphy adventure. Game (2014)
6. Interactive, W.: The complex. Game (2020)
7. Interactive, W.: I see black clouds. Game (2021)
8. Interactive, W.: Who pressed mute on uncle marcus? Game (2021)
9. Koenitz, H.: Towards a specific theory of interactive digital narrative. In: Interactive Digital Narrative, pp. 91–105 (2015)
10. Murray, J.H.: Hamlet on the Holodeck: The Future of Narrative in Cyberspace. The Free Press, New York (1997)
11. Murray, J.H.: Inventing the Medium: Principles of Interaction Design as a Cultural Practice. MIT Press, Cambridge (2011)
12. Nayak, S.: An unexpected guest. Game (2021)
13. Propp, V.: Morphology of the Folktale. University of Texas Press, Austin (1928)
14. Stricklin, C.: Now, or Forever. Game (2021)
15. Taito: Time gal. Game (1985)
16. Tanenbaum, K., Tanenbaum, T.J.: Agency as commitment to meaning: communicative competence in games. Dig. Creat. **21**(1), 11–17 (2010)
17. Todorov, T.: The typology of detective fiction. In: Crime and Media, pp. 291–301. Routledge (1966)
18. Works, T.: The invisible hours. Game (2017)

Measuring Narrative Engagement in Interactive Cinematic VR Experiences

Austin Wolfe[✉], Sandy Louchart, and Daniel Livingstone

Wishaw, UK

a.wolfe1@student.gsa.ac.uk, {S.Louchart,D.Livingstone}@gsa.ac.uk

Abstract. This research involves the development of a cinematic VR experience that exhibits narrative engagement and the investigation of possible measurement tools to evaluate that engagement. This is accomplished by the implementation and analysis of standardized self-reporting measures and observational data. The efficacy of these measurement tools is discussed as well as their possible modifications and limitations for storytelling in VR.

Keywords: Immersive Storytelling · Interactive Storytelling · Cinematic VR

1 Introduction

This research investigates a range of measurement tools towards assessing narrative engagement in interactive cinematic VR experiences. This article describes the design of a cinematic VR experience and its evaluation using standardised self-reporting measures.

For the context of this research, cinematic VR describes immersive experiences with limited interactivity and a strong emphasis on storytelling. Therefore, cinematic VR encompasses immersive storytelling applications with fixed or predetermined stories that have a cinematic quality. Cinematic quality can be considered as "VR with media fidelity approaches found in feature film" [1]. Cinematic VR productions are not game-like experiences, but VR narratives based on targeted design and psychological criteria supported by the technology that VR inherently provides.

This research is important as VR is becoming more prevalent in research and personal use. However, the medium still has an untapped potential for immersive storytelling. Additionally, narrative engagement within the VR storytelling experience is both difficult to create and to evaluate, thus it is valuable to investigate work dedicated to VR storytelling as opposed to a game-like experience. Lastly, this work proposes to develop a dedicated high-quality experience expressly for the purpose of investigating narrative engagement.

© The Author(s), under exclusive license to Springer Nature Switzerland AG 2023
L. Holloway-Attaway and J. T. Murray (Eds.): ICIDS 2023, LNCS 14383, pp. 374–394, 2023.
https://doi.org/10.1007/978-3-031-47655-6_23

2   Research Design

2.1   Project Creation

To explore how narrative engagement could be measured in a virtual reality experience, we designed a VR experience focused on narrative engagement and storytelling. The experience created for this study was made based on the recommendations and findings from [2]. This creation comprised three main phases: the Script, the Assets, and Interactivity and immersion.

The Script: Traditional western story tropes might be ill-suited to VR, due to the possibility that the model of the story line would break because of the immersive and interactive nature of VR [3]. With this in mind, a more general outline was chosen for the script. Using a simplified version of Blake Snyder's [3] Beat Sheet as a guide, an initial script was sketched out and was loosely based on an accumulation of varied Scottish folklore books for content. Additionally, the script included the concept of change [4] that was woven into the script early on to assist with engaging the user from the beginning. Moreover, as Richardson et al. [5] postulated that listening was an active process in co-creation, the script was written to be narrated, filling in details that were not present in the world, as well as leaving out details that were.

The Assets: The assets for the project encompassed the concepts of characters, story-world, and curiosity. These assets helped to inform the aforementioned script, as the story plot was character driven. For the character creation, the characters were given a personality based on the FFM [6]. On this scale, the main character was given high scores for openness, conscientiousness, and agreeableness, with low scores for extroversion and neuroticism. This meant that the character's personality was curious, dependable, reserved, empathetic, and calm. This created a blueprint for how the character would look and act, and therefore, was able to be designed based on these personality traits. To emphasise the personality and identity of the character, other assets were created as behavioural residue [7]. An example of such assets were items like a smoking pipe, picture frames, maps, and wine bottles that gave small indications about the character's life, many of which were interactive. To solidify the character, the story-world was then created based on the character's attributes and persona. The world itself was created on an island, with the scenes occurring in various locations around it; this was done so that when scene changes occurred, it would lessen the amount of time it took for the user to reorient themselves in the world, since they could see all the other places they had previously been. To bring the story-world to life, life was added through other assets such as birds, rabbits, sea creatures, grasses, and trees (Figs. 1).

Fig. 1. Example scene from VR experience.

Some of these played multi-purposed roles, contributing not only to the story world and persona of the character but were also employed as curiosity types [8]and diegetic devices [9, 10]. An example of this is a recurring bird whom the user first meets in the menu, and then again in the first scene where it can be interacted with. It is then placed throughout various other scenes to help direct the focus and attention of the player (See Fig. 2).

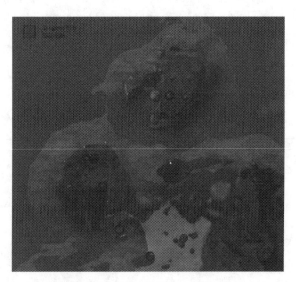

Fig. 2. Example map diegetic placement.

Curiosity played a dual role in both the assets and the interactivity. To et al. [8] defined curiosity as one's inclination toward uncertainty and willingness to balance between the known and unknown. In their research, they defined types of curiosity and levels of uncertainty in games, to encourage game designers to use curiosity types in moments of uncertainty, thus assisting in balancing the knowledge gap.

There are five key types of curiosity: perceptual/attention to something new, manipulatory, curiosity about complex/ambiguous, conceptual/active information seeking, and adjustive-reactive [8]. For example, perceptual and adjustive-reactive curiosity can effectively combat the frustration of players with difficult puzzles or tasks, to keep the game engaging and not frustrating. For the creation of the experience, 4 out of 5 types were employed. Manipulatory was introduced simply by the use of the controller in the experience, with the ability to grab, hold, or throw items. Complex/ambiguous was utilized by making complex objects to interact with. Some of these included objects such as birds or rabbits that were animated and provided haptic feedback when touched. Others were in the form of picture frames that highlighted or changed their image when handled. Perceptual was implemented through music, sound cues from various objects, and visual highlights. And adjustive reactive constituted the items that were simpler and had a common use, such as a violin that the user could play. Conceptual was left out, simply due to the difficulty of executing it within the narrative (Fig. 3).

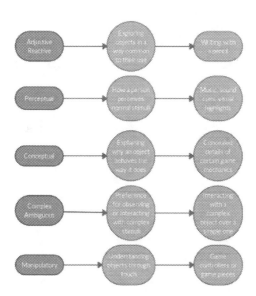

Fig. 3. Example of curiosity types.

Interactivity and Immersion: As stated above curiosity also played a role in interactivity, as many of the "curious" objects were also interactive. Along with this, the use of music, audio cues, and highlights were used to focus/gain the user's attention and increase immersion. In particular, both ambient and spatial sound were used throughout the VR experience [11]. Music and narration were ambient with no discernible source. For narration, as the story was based on Scottish folklore, a local voiceover artist was used to provide the voiceover for authenticity. Likewise, music was also chosen that had a Celtic feel. Specifically, each musical piece was chosen based on the music recommendations regarding tempo/pitch and emotion found in [2]. The spatial sound encompassed everything else. This included elements like waves crashing, bird calls, wind, thunder, rain, and whale calls. Each sound had an individual attenuation radius (the falloff of the source) utilising a natural sound function (See Fig. 5) and employed binaural spatialisation (the sound changed and shifted based on the user's physical orientation towards the sound). These overlapped with each other to create a more natural environment (Fig. 4).

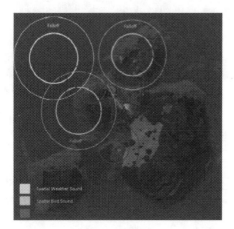

Fig. 4. Example map of spatial sounds.

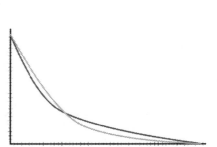

Fig. 5. Natural sound function that determines the rate of attenuation over distance. This models a naturalistic falloff behaviour that is closer to matching reality.

In addition to the spatial and ambient sounds, other interactivity was built into various other assets. As mentioned earlier, examples of some picture frames changed and were highlighted when held, other objects could be collected and thrown or placed down by the user such as vegetables and wine bottles.

2.2   Evaluation Protocol

This section describes the self-reporting measures and the observational methods employed in this study along with a discussion on ethical considerations for these two methods.

Self-reporting Measures
As narrative engagement is a multifaceted concept, several questionnaires can be employed for a well-rounded scope in the context of interactive storytelling VR experiences. For this research, the questionnaires used were based on the following concepts:

- Narrative understanding
- Attention Focus
- Narrative presence
- Emotional engagement
- Suspense
- Curiosity

- Flow
- Presence
- Enjoyment
- Aesthetic pleasantness

For consistency, all scales were measured on a 5-point Likert scale using a combination of forward scoring (**F**) and backwards scoring (**B**), as denoted on the following scales. Forward scoring has numerical values attached to the anchors in a forward direction, with fully agree = 5, and fully disagree = 1. Backwards (reverse) scoring has numerical values attached to anchors in the opposite direction, with fully disagree = 5 and fully agree = 1.

Narrative Engagement Scale

Busselle and Bilandzic's [12] research interpreted four factors for narrative engagement while developing their Narrative Engagement Scale (NES). These were narrative understanding, attentional focus, emotional engagement, and narrative presence. Although it was not developed specifically for VR, it has been a widely used model in research and other VR studies [6, 13, 14] as well as having a Cronbach's α of over .80. For these reasons, it can potentially be adapted for use in interactive VR stories. The NES consists of 12 questions on a 7-point Likert scale and was adapted to a 5-point scale for consistency across all questionnaires.

Narrative understanding

- At points, I had a hard time making sense of what was going on in the experience. (B)
- My understanding of the characters is unclear. (B)
- I had a hard time recognising the thread of the story. (B)

Attentional focus

- I found my mind wandering while the during the story experience. *(B)*
- While in the virtual world I found myself thinking about other things. *(B)*
- I had a hard time keeping my mind on the story. *(B)*

Narrative presence

- During the experience, my body was in the room, but my mind was inside the world created by the story. (**F**)
- The experience created a new world, and then that world suddenly disappeared when the application ended. (**F**)
- At times during the experience, the story world was closer to me than the real world. (**F**)

Emotional engagement

- The story affected me emotionally. (**F**)
- During the experience, when a main character succeeded, I felt happy, and when they suffered in some way, I felt sad. (**F**)
- I felt sympathy for some of the characters in the story. (**F**)

Suspense Scale
Measuring suspense in interactive storytelling is a somewhat novel idea. Knobloch et al. [15] developed a three-item scale for suspense rating media content in terms of being thrilling, gripping, and exciting. Other scales used to measure suspense are context specific [16], but neither of these are in the context of interactive narratives. Based on these studies and his own research, Roth [17] postulated that the measurement of suspense of interactive narratives should be based on the emotional involvement in the story's outcome. He therefore constructed 10 items to capture suspense based on emotional investment in the story specifically in the context of interactive narratives. This scale was later shortened to four items, based on the items with the highest item-total correlations.

- At some moments I was anxious to find out what would happen next **(F)**
- Sometimes I was worried about how the story would develop. **(F)**
- Some moments were rather suspenseful. **(F)**
- I found myself wishing for a particular story outcome. **(F)**

Curiosity Scale
Spielberger et al. [18] determined curiosity as a state, thus the State-Trait Curiosity Inventory (STCI) was developed to measure the intensity of curiosity as a transitory emotional state [19, 20]. The STCI includes 10 items on a 4-point scale asking participants to report how they feel at a particular moment. This was adapted to a 5-point Likert for consistency throughout the other questionnaires, and "in the moment" was rephrased to "during the experience". Additionally, the 10 items were adapted into three based on the recommendations [17].
   During the experience I felt.....

- Curious (F)
- Interested (F)
- Inquisitive (F)

Flow Scale
Csikszentmihalyi [20] proposed eight factors for optimal flow: challenge activity; merging of acting and awareness; clear goals; direct immediate feedback; concentration; a sense of control; loss of self-consciousness; and an altered sense of time. Based on this model, the Flow State Scale (FSS) was developed [21]. Initially, this scale was a 36-item list, and later paired down to 9 items to allow for usage in a wider range of studies. Each item chosen reflected one of the nine higher order factors from the original scale [22]. Findings from the shorter list revealed that it provided a good representation of the long version with high reliability. This was adapted the scale into five items based on the highest item-total correlations.
   During the experience. . .

- . . . I felt competent enough to meet the demands of the situation (F)
- . . . I acted spontaneously and automatically without having to think (F)
- . . . I had a strong sense of what I wanted to do (F)
- . . . I had a good idea while I was performing about how well I was doing (F)
- . . . I was completely focused on the task at hand (F)

Presence Scale

There are currently a few standardised presence questionnaires in circulation for VR applications [23–25]. The IPQ [24] was chosen based on research of the efficacy of presence scales [26] as it provided the highest reliability within a reasonable timeframe. The IPQ is a 14-item list, on a 5-point Likert scale. The items consist of 4 categories: General, Spatial presence (the sense of being physically present in VR), Involvement (measuring the attention devoted to the experience) and Experienced Realism (measuring the subjective experience of realism. Based on these categories, the scale was shorted to contain one item from each category.

- In the experience I had a sense of "being there" (G) **(F)**
- I felt present in the virtual space (SP) **(F)**
- The virtual world seemed more realistic than the real world (ER) **(F)**
- I was not aware of my real environment (INV) **(F)**

Enjoyment Scale

The measuring of enjoyment has proved somewhat problematic. While the concepts of enjoyment have been used in media research, such as amusement, sense of achievement etc. [27]; there is no study available that has attempted to measure it directly [17, 28]. Therefore, a simple short scale consisting of two questions was created.

The experience. . .

- . . . was entertaining (F)
- . . . was enjoyable (F)

Aesthetic Pleasantness Scale

Aesthetic pleasantness in media is often related to the visuals and audio. Aesthetic evaluations may relate to the physical appearance of characters or landscape imagery. Additionally, aesthetic content can relate to the personal background and previous experiences of the recipient. For instance, the depiction of a scene in a movie, can remind the viewer of feelings that resonate with the recipient's mood, thus evoking congruent feelings [29]. Therefore, in this context, it is applied to encompass the elements of story-world, characters, and emotion. For this study, the following questionnaire was used to access aesthetic pleasantness [30].

The experience. . .

- . . . made me think (F)
- . . . made me think about my personal situation (F)
- . . . told me something about life (F)
- . . . was inspiring (F)
- . . . moved me like a piece of art (F)

Self-reporting Limitations

Self-reporting measures to reflect on past experiences can be somewhat limited, as it can be hindered by such things as selective memory, mixing memories of other events, or even exaggeration. However, there is still validity in the use of these methods, as these limitations can be reduced. One such reduction, is the use of standardized questionnaires as they can be backed with research and a high Cronbach α (a reliability coefficient), increasing their validity. Additionally, wording of the questions was kept to the specific standard to avoid confusion or vagueness, with the exception of changing to the phrase "during the experience" across all scales for consistency.

Observation

Observational data for the study was recorded during the experience by the researcher in a nonparticipant role. The data recorded is in a semi-structured format using pre-defined events. The participants were aware that they were being observed, and aware that the researcher would not participate in the experience. The participates were also able to provide open-ended comments after the completion of the post questionnaire. An observational protocol was created for use during the observations. This included the current scene, time, and a record of events (See Table 1).

Table 1. Example of Observation Protocol for Scene 2.

Scene	Time	Description of Events
2	1:10	Interaction with bird
	1:25	Following gaze of character
	1:40	Interaction with character

Observation was carried out via online video (Zoom), with the participant sharing their PC screen. This allowed the researcher to view both the participant and their camera view during the experience.

Limitations of observational data can include the researcher being seen as intrusive. The interruption of the experience to conduct survey or interviews can lead to a disruption of the flow, and thus lead to disengagement [13]. To mitigate this, the observational data recorded was non-invasive; participants were not asked questions during the experience.

2.3   Data Treatment

After the project was completed, 10 participants were recruited to take part in the experiment. All participants were over the age of 18, with little to no experience in VR. Users were recruited via the online XR research platform XRDRN. The data collection was then divided into 2 main phases: *observation* and *reflection*.

Observation Phase. Once the participants had their headset on, they started the program and observations were made and recorded throughout their experience. This data was qualitative in nature.

Reflection Phase. After the completion of the VR experience, participants were invited to complete a set of self-reporting questionnaires. The Narrative Engagement Scale (NES); the Suspense Scale (SS); Curiosity Scale (CS); Flow Scale (FSS-2); Presence scale (IPQ), Enjoyment Scale (ES), and Aesthetic Pleasantness (APS). This data was quantitative in nature.

After completion of the data collection, the data analysis began consisting of three phases: *Analyse Quantitative, Analyse Qualitative*, and *Mixed Methods*. First, the quantitative results were analysed in terms of statistical results. Second, the qualitative database was analysed by coding the data and collapsing the codes into broad themes. The final phase is the mixed methods analysation, which consists of integrating the two databases. The integration of this data uses a data transformation approach; after the qualitative data had been coded into themes, they were counted and grouped, to form quantitative measures. The following sections will discuss the results of the quantitative and qualitative data (Fig. 6).

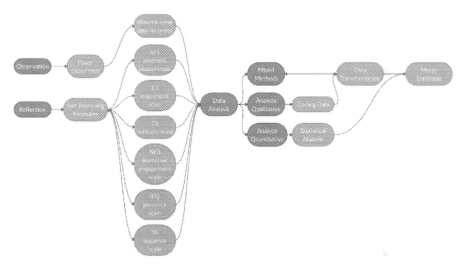

Fig. 6. Phases of Analysis.

3   Results

3.1   Presentation of Quantitative Data

All data was measured on a 5-point Likert scale using a combination of forward and backwards scoring. In this section, the mean and standard deviation are provided for each of the scales. The full record of data is to be published at a later date.

The NES (Narrative Engagement Scale) [14] was considered by the individual factors:

- narrative understanding--the ease in comprehension of the story.
- attentional focus—concept that one should not be aware that one is distracted.
- emotional engagement--feeling for or with the characters.
- narrative presence—sensation that one has left the actual world and entered the story.

Narrative understanding recorded both the highest mean at 4.83, and lowest standard deviation at .37. Likewise, Emotional engagement and Narrative presence also recorded high values with low deviations. Attentional focus saw the lowest data with a mean of 3.60, and the highest variation at 1.57 (See Table 2).

Table 2. Narrative Engagement Scale Data.

	Narrative understanding	Attentional Focus	Narrative presence	Emotional engagement
NES (Narrative Engagement Scale)	M = 4.83 SD = 0.37	M = 3.60 SD = 1.57	M = 4.33 SD = 0.82	M = 4.50 SD = 0.76

Along with the individual factors, the NES was combined with the remaining scales for further analysis. Combined, the overall NES was recorded with a mean of 4.32 and the second lowest standard deviation of .45. The ES (Enjoyment Scale) recorded the highest at 4.75, and lowest deviation at .43. It is also important to note that the lowest scoring scales were the SS (Suspense Scale) at 3.35, with a fairly large deviation at 1.23, as well at the FFS-2 (Flow Scale) at 3.64. Although scoring fairly high comparatively, the IPQ (Presence scale) all showed a larger deviation at 1.25. These results and fluctuations in data will be discussed further during the analysis of this paper (See Table 3).

Table 3. Combined Assessment Data

NES (Narrative Engagement Scale)	M = 4.32	SD = 0.45
SS (Suspense scale)	M = 3.35	SD = 1.23
CS (Curiosity Scale)	M = 4.63	SD = 0.60
FFS-2 (Flow Scale)	M = 3.64	SD = 1.07
IPQ (Presence Scale)	M = 3.92	SD = 1.25
ES (Enjoyment Scale)	M = 4.75	SD = 0.43
APS (Aesthetic Pleasantness Scale)	M = 4.43	SD = 0.83

3.2 Presentation of Qualitative Data

Qualitative data for this study was gathered via observation during the VR experience. The data was hand recorded, then transcribed into documents and coded in to like themes. The coding was recorded and calculated via the program MAXQDA, with the results showing the number of times each code appeared for each participant. This data was coded into the following themes:

- Focus on Characters
- Interaction with Character

- Follow character gaze
- Interact with shell (*meaningful item*)
- Focus on crow (*diegetic item*)
- Aesthetic focus (*environment*)
- Aesthetic focus (*Life*)
- Interaction with other objects

Table 4. Codes at a Glance (%)

Codes	%of participants
Focus on Characters	100%
Interaction with Character	100%
Follow Character gaze	90%
Interact with Shell (Meaningful Item)	100%
Focus on Crow (Diegetic)	100%
Aesthetic focus (Environment)	100%
Aesthetic focus (Life)	100%
Interaction with other objects	80%

Table 5. Codes at a glance (Frequency per participant)

Code System	10	9	8	7	6	5	4	3	2	1	SUM
Interact with other objects	1	1	5	7	1	2		11	3		31
Aesthetic Focus (Life)	4	5	9	8	5	7	8	4	3	3	56
Aesthetic focus (Environment)	7	5	7	2	4	3	7	3	3	4	45
Focus on Crow (Diegetic)	2	1	1	3	1	3	3	1	2	2	19
Interact with Shell (Meaningfull Item)	2	2	2	1	2	1	1	2	4	1	18
Follow Character Gaze	2	1	6	2	1	1	2		2	1	18
Interact with Character	1	1	1	1	1	1	1	4	1	1	13
Focus on Characters	15	11	14	11	10	16	13	11	10	9	120

As Table 4 demonstrates, the majority of the codes appeared for each participant with the exception of follow character gaze, which was reported at 90%, and interaction with other objects which was reported at 80%.

It is important to note that while Table 5 reveals the frequencies of the codes per participant, and their totals, the totals are not necessarily an indication of priority of one code over another, as each code holds a different purpose. For this reason, each code will be evaluated and analysed independently.

Firstly, both the *Focus on Crow* (Diegetic) code and *Interact with shell* (meaningful) code had a max amount of 4 possible occurrences within the experience. The diegetic code revealed the following:

- 30% focused on the object 75% of the maximum allowance.
- 30% focused on the object 50% of the maximum allowance.

- 40% focused on the object 25% of the maximum allowance.

  Whereas the meaning code showed:

- 10% interacted with the object 100% of the maximum allowance.
- 50% interacted with the object 50% of the maximum allowance.
- 40% interacted with the object 25% of the maximum allowance.

Conversely, *focus on characters, Aesthetic focus (life)* and *aesthetic focus(environment)* did not have a set number of occurrences. Therefore, their frequencies and totals are of some importance at 120, 56, and 45 respectively. *Interact with character* only occurs a total of 13 times, however it is important to note that all participants attempted interaction with the character at least once, and that single interaction occurred at the same point during the story. *Interact with other objects* is wildly varied as far as frequencies go and holds a larger SD of 3.37. The final code is the *follow character's gaze*, which held an average of 2 per participant with a deviation of 1.8. With both sets of data presented, the following section will explore a deeper analysis of each, followed by a comparative analysis of the combined results.

4 Analysis

4.1 Self-reporting Analysis

The Narrative Engagement Scale (*NES*) [13] which consisted of 4 separate subcategories:

- narrative understanding
- attentional focus
- emotional engagement
- narrative presence

The data from this scale demonstrated high averages and low deviations for all categories save for one, *attentional focus*. Although the mean was above average (3.60) the deviation was high (1.57). The following statements were used for this subcategory:

- I found my mind wandering while the during the story experience.
- While in the virtual world I found myself thinking about other things.
- I had a hard time keeping my mind on the story.

As demonstrated, these statements primarily focus on the mind: paying attention and not wandering from the subject. The discrepancy for this large deviation of the subcategory can be narrowed into two potential factors. The first possibility is the differences of cognitive capabilities and personalities of each participant. As no baseline was gathered before the experience on each participant's attention level or capabilities, it is difficult to have clarity on the efficacy of this category. Additionally, the other possibility for the large deviation is the manner in which the study needed to be performed. Since observations needed to be completed via video chat and on varying hardware, some individuals experienced technical issues, like stuttering during the experience. This may have been a potential factor in breaking the focus of a participant. However, since the averages in the other subcategories were high with low deviations and overall, the entire scale had a higher average (4.32), this subcategory may not hold as much weight at the others, and either may not be needed, or may need to be modified to eliminate potential discrepancies.

Likewise, the presence scale (*IPQ*) [24] indicated a similar trend. Although the average was above an acceptable range (3.92), like the *attentional focus*, it too suffered a high deviation of 1.25. Also, like *attentional focus*, it is likely that this large deviation was also a product of technical issues. Recall that the four statements used for this scale were:

- In the experience I had a sense of "being there".
- I felt present in the virtual space.
- The virtual world seemed more realistic than the real world.
- I was not aware of my real environment.

These statements are based on the physical presence the participant perceives in VR, and the lack of awareness of their real environment. As mentioned previously, one of the technical issues experienced by some participants was stuttering. This was likely due to participants using varying headsets and graphics cards, as well as having to live stream the experience. Regardless of cause, this would have an impact the user's perception of presence as it breaks the sense of "being there". Additionally, as the observations were conducted in the participants' homes, they had varying physical space in which to move. As this experience was created to move around in a large space, various participants had less room in which to explore; ultimately running out of room and thus become "aware" of their real environment's limitations. To lower the deviations in these scores, these environmental variables must be eliminated.

The suspense scale (*SS*) demonstrated both a lower average (3.35) and a high deviation (1.23). The high deviation of the scale may indicate that the scale may need to be modified further, or that there is a discrepancy in the actual wording of the scale. It is possible that some individuals may perceive the concept of suspense differently than others. Additionally, the use of the words "worry" and "anxious" may be a cause for confusion. Therefore, further research needs to be completed to assess the efficacy of this scale. However, the lower average of the scale indicates a problem with the project itself. The story and the project did not contain clear moments of suspense, and therefore it may have been difficult to identify them. As suspense is an important factor and is closely linked with the concept of curiosity [31], clearer moments of suspense need to be implemented in the project and storyline.

The flow scale (FFS-2) revealed an average of 3.64 and a deviation of 1.07. To review, the concept of flow [20] is the ease in which a user arrives at a pleasant optimal performance. Flow comprises eight specific factors: challenge activity; merging of acting and awareness; clear goals; direct immediate feedback; concentration; a sense of control; loss of subconsciousness; and altered sense of time.

From this perspective, the scale coincides with the eight factors quite well. However, the larger deviation and lower average indicate problems. In past studies, the flow scale was generally used for game-based interactive digital applications [32, 33] as the factors for flow were easier to implement and measure. As this project was a cinematic experience with a linear storyline, there were sufficient opportunities to create flow based on all of these factors. There was no direct instruction or clear task given during the experience for the user to be focused on, nor was there any gauge on which the user could evaluate their own performance. While participants were able to accurately report such statements as "I acted spontaneously and automatically without having to think", the task orientated statements had the largest variation in answers. This is because there was no clear task, and there was no clear task because the participants' actions were unable to affect the storyline in a linear story. This would indicate that either the flow scale is ill suited to cinematic experiences with linear stories, that it needs to be heavily modified to fit this genre, or that the project needs to find a better way to apply this scale without sacrificing its structure.

The curiosity scale (CS) performed well, with an average of 4.63 the low deviation of .60. However, it is important to note that the scale only had three statements that were simplified from the original 10. So, while it is an indication that the project did create curiosity and was able to accurately measure it, it might be pertinent to use the full-scale to get a more accurate view of the curiosity factors in the experience. Additionally, since curious types [8] were used in the project, expanding this scale to target those specific types may also prove beneficial to fine tune the results.

The enjoyment scale (ES) had the highest average of 4.75 and the lowest deviation of .43. Although it only consists of two statements, they were relatively simple, and the participants were able to answer them clearly and accurately. While it would be prudent to continue research to expand the scale, it was effective in relation to this project. This is because, in conjunction with the scale, enjoyment was also able to be observed during the experience. This enjoyment was observed objectively by the researcher in the form of participants smiling, chuckling, laughing, and some dancing.

The aesthetic pleasantness scale (APS) had an average of 4.43 with a deviation of .80. As Sect. 2.5 stated, this scale encompassed the elements of story-world, characters, and emotion. The high average and low deviation indicate that aesthetic pleasantness overall may play a more important role in narrative engagement than initially thought. To explain this assumption, this scale can be directly compared to the qualitative findings discussed in the next section.

4.2 Observational Analysis

First, consider the following codes: *Aesthetic focus (life)*, *aesthetic focus (environment)*, and *focus on character*. The *aesthetic focus (life)* was coded as such to include organic elements within the experience. These included objects such as wildlife, trees, grass, etc. *Aesthetic focus (environment)* included items such as the sky, the waves, and the weather. Combined, these elements make up the story-world, and part of the emotional element as stated in the APS. As mentioned in the previous section both codes had high frequencies throughout the experience, 56 and 45 respectively, with a combined total of 101. Additionally, *focus on the character* (which makes up the character element of the APS) also had high frequencies with a total of 120. This implies that focusing on the aesthetics of the story-world is nearly as important as focusing on the characters in story. As all of these codes are also part of the APS, this further indicates the importance of aesthetic pleasantness overall. Consider that the frequency of these codes combined equals to 221, whereas the rest of the codes combine equals to 99, with an overall total of 320. Based on the number of frequencies for this study, participants spent nearly 70% of their time focusing on the aesthetics (character and story-world).

Another indication of its significance is that of verbal feedback received after completion of the story. Upon completion of the experience, each participant was asked which scenes they had an emotional connection to. With the exception of one outlier, all the other participants named the same two scenes having affected them the most. The first scene identified (Fig. 7) involved the participant standing on the edge of a lighthouse at night with northern lights in the sky, and the lights reflecting on the ocean water.

Fig. 7. First Identified scene by participants

The second scene identified, involved the user being immersed in the ocean, physically flowing through it, with elements and ocean creatures becoming bioluminescent (Fig. 8). Both of these scenes had very strong visual attributes attached to them, which would lead to the possibility of investigating their visual attributes further.

Additionally, the one participant that chose a different scene, chose a scene involving the characters gardening together (Fig. 9). The participant stated that this scene made them feel "nostalgic". This coincides with the postulation that aesthetic content could relate to the personal background and previous experiences of the recipient, evoking congruent feelings in the participant [29].

The next data to analyse is the *interact with shell (meaningful)* code. This code was attached to the specific interaction with an object (shell) during the experience. This object was the only object directly referenced in the experience's narration. Furthermore, it was also used as a physical representation for a "moment of unexpected change" [4] and as an ignition point for the story [4]. It was for these reasons that the shell was deemed a meaningful item [34] as meaning plays a dominant role in guiding attention in scenes of stories. As mentioned earlier, 100% of participants triggered this code. It is interesting to note that although some participants interacted with the shell more than once, all participants interacted with the shell at the same moment the story. This moment happened at the very end of the story when the character interacts with the

Fig. 8. Second scene identified by participants.

Fig. 9. Outlier scene identified by participant

participant. Conversely, the *interact with other objects code* had a more varied response. When comparing the two, while *interact with shell (meaningful)* had a deviation of .87, interact with other objects had a large variation of 3.37. This variation may be attributed to a few things. Firstly, this may connect directly to the sense of flow, as there was no clear direction, instruction, or task given to the participant at any time. Thus, the participant may have been unsure about what they could or should interact with. The exception of this, of course, being the shell, as this was directly used in the story. Personalities differences also may have influenced this variation, as some individuals may be more inclined to be tactile and want to touch and explore things while others may be of a more tentative nature. Although these items were used as curiosity types [8] and behavioural residue [7], it is unclear if they had any true bearing on the narrative engagement of the story as a whole and may need to be assessed individually. However, it can be postulated that the interaction with the shell had a more consistent response because it was a part of the story thus giving it more meaning, whereas the other objects were not. This may imply the that interactive objects require more meaning or purpose to the story in order to have consistent interaction and engagement.

Like the *Interact with shell* code, the *interact with character* code was largely initiated at the very end of the story at the same time for all participants. To clarify, in the final scene the character turns to the participant and gestures for them to come to them and sit down, where the interactable shell is also located. The significance of this is that although the participant had multiple opportunities to interact with the character, 90% of them only did so at the end when the character interacted with them first. This may signify that for a user to engage with an NPC (non-player character), the NPC must first engage with them.

Focus on crow and *follow character's gaze* were both diegetic devices within the experience to gain the attention of the participant and engage them. The crow was purposely made as a focusing diegetic device, while the gaze of the character was an accidental addition. The crow was first introduced in the first scene where the participant could interact with it, and it would appear throughout other scenes using a sound cue to direct the focus of the participant. This proved to be a semi-accurate way to direct focus, as all participants were able to focus on the crow at one point or another. However, the results were not very consistent, which may be because the crow is not a part of the story and holds no other significance.

The *following character's gaze* code was accidental, as it was a product of the character's natural personality. To clarify, the code was initiated whenever the character would point while looking at something, looked out to sea, or was otherwise searching for something. The participant would then follow the gaze and direction of the character. This signifies engagement and connection to the character as well as curiosity, as the user is trying to physically look where the NPC is looking. While the frequencies of this are varied, it appears to add to the engagement of the story, as it is a more natural occurrence than a random appearance of a bird. If purposely controlled, it may prove a more effective device in gaining a keeping attention on the story.

5   Conclusion

5.1   Summary of Research Data

To review the quantitative data, the narrative engagement scale worked moderately well, however the subcategory of attentional focus must either be eliminated or modified to better adapt to cinematic VR experiences and eliminate possible discrepancies due to different cognitive abilities. The flow scale may also not be well suited to certain VR cinematic experiences that follow a linear storyline, as users do not have a specific task assigned to them or have the ability to influence the outcome of the story. The alternative to this is that the gameplay itself would have to change in order to adapt to the concept of flow. The curiosity scale worked successfully and with a reasonable degree of accuracy but was relatively simplistic. Further evaluation and research are needed to develop a more in-depth scale regarding narrative engagement. This also applies to the scale of suspense, with the addition of requiring further development and research on the relationship between curiosity and suspense, as well as to the practical implementation of opportunities to create suspense within the experience.

Regarding qualitative data, aesthetic pleasantness appears to play a significant role in narrative engagement, and therefore needs to be expanded and further explored in depth. Additionally, interactive items may need to hold more meaning for them to be interacted with consistently. Using a diegetic item to focus the attention of the user is potentially an effective way to assist with engagement, but the focus needs to be more purposeful. Finally, meaningful interactions with NPC characters may be dependent on the NPC character initiating interaction first, and that the user is more likely to engage in mirroring the behaviour of the NPC i.e., looking where they are looking.

5.2 Limitations

As this study was conducted via internet, participants needed to have access to their own headsets and VR compatible PCs. This greatly reduced the potential number of participants to only those who had a specific brand of headset. Additionally, although there was nearly double the number of people who expressed interest in the study, only half followed through. This is likely due to the observational requirement needed over Zoom, which some participants were unwilling to do. A small sample size is problematic as in increases the bias and lacks the statistical power to find significant effects in an overall population.

5.3 Recommendations

A larger sample size would give a more accurate representation of populous and eliminate many deviations in quantitative and qualitative data while increasing its validity. Additionally, the study needs to be performed in a more controlled environment. This means the environment needs to use the same hardware, headset, the same graphics card, and have the same room scale. It is also inadvisable to conduct such an experiment online as it introduces other technical issues, such as stuttering or prolonged delays, as well as the inability to accurately see the entirety of the participant's body during observation.

Furthermore, the VR project needs to have more opportunities for suspense, and more research should be explored on other suspense scales, creating suspense, and its definition. This was lacking in both the research and project, and as it is linked with curiosity [31] and since curiosity largely impacts narrative engagement [5, 9, 35], it would be beneficial to have a more in depth understanding of it. Along with suspense, the curiosity scale would also benefit from more exploration into its assessment, concepts, and the relationship of curiosity to narrative engagement as a whole. This would provide a well-rounded data set, increasing accuracy and validity. Finally, additional research should be conducted on the importance of aesthetics in cinematic VR experiences, and aesthetic scale needs to be modified and expanded based upon those recommendations.

The use of the flow scale is probably not appropriate for cinematic VR experience with the linear storyline, therefore either needs to be eliminated from the narrative engagement measurement or heavily modified to better fit with the genre. Likewise, the attentional focus aspect of the narrative engagement scale also either needs to be eliminated or heavily modified to eliminate discrepancies based upon potential cognitive differences, capabilities, or personalities.

References

1. Mateer, J.: Directing for cinematic virtual reality: How the traditional film director's craft applies to immersive environments and notions of presence. J. Media Pract. **18**(1), 14–25 (2017)
2. Wolfe, A. Louchart, S., Loranger, B.: The impacts of design elements in interactive storytelling in VR on emotion, mood, and self-reflection (2022). https://doi.org/10.1007/978-3-031-22298-6_40
3. Koenitz, H., et al.: The myth of 'Universal' narrative models. In: Rouse, R., Koenitz, H., Haahr, M., (eds.) Interactive Storytelling, Springer International Publishing, Cham, pp. 107–125 (2018). https://doi.org/10.1007/978-3-030-04028-4_8
4. Storr, W.: The Science of Storytelling. William Collins, London, UK (2019)
5. Richardson, D.C., et al.: Measuring narrative engagement: The heart tells the story' (2018). bioRxiv. https://doi.org/10.1101/351148
6. McCrae, R.R., Gaines, J.F., Wellington, M.A.: The five-factor model in fact and fiction. In: Handbook of Psychology, 2nd Edn (2012). https://doi.org/10.1002/9781118133880.hop 205004
7. Gosling, S.: Snoop. Bookmarque, London, UK (2008)
8. To, A., et al.: Integrating curiosity and uncertainty in game design. In: Proceedings of 1st International Joint Conference of DiGRA and FDG, pp. 1–16 (2016)
9. Fearghail, C.O., et al.: Director's cut - analysis of aspects of interactive storytelling for VR Films. In: Rouse, R., Koenitz, H., Haahr, M., (eds) Interactive Storytelling, Springer International Publishing, Cham, pp. 308–322 (2018). https://doi.org/10.1007/978-3-030-04028-4_34
10. Brown, S.A., et al.: Capturing user emotions in interactive stories: comparing a diegetic and a non-diegetic approach to self-reporting emotion. In: Bosser, A.-G., Millard, D.E., Hargood, C. (eds.) Interactive Storytelling, pp. 229–242. Springer International Publishing, Cham (2020). https://doi.org/10.1007/978-3-030-62516-0_21
11. Bhide, S., Goins, E., Geigel, J.: Experimental analysis of spatial sound for storytelling in virtual reality. In: Cardona-Rivera, R.E., Sullivan, A., Young, R.M. (eds.) Interactive Storytelling, pp. 3–7. Springer International Publishing, Cham (2019). https://doi.org/10.1007/978-3-030-33894-7_1
12. Busselle, R., Bilandzic, H.: Fictionality and perceived realism in experiencing stories: A model of narrative comprehension and engagement. Commun. Theory **18**(2), 255–280 (2008). https://doi.org/10.1111/j.1468-2885.2008.00322.x
13. Bindman, S.W., et al.: Am I a bunny? The impact of high and low immersion platforms and viewers' perceptions of role on presence, narrative engagement, and empathy during an animated 360° video. In: Conference on Human Factors in Computing Systems – Proceedings (2018). https://doi.org/10.1145/3173574.3174031
14. Schoenau-Fog, H.: 'Hooked! -- evaluating engagement as continuation desire in interactive narratives. In: Si, M., et al., (eds) Interactive Storytelling. Berlin, Heidelberg: Springer Berlin Heidelberg, pp. 219–230 (2011). https://doi.org/10.1007/978-3-642-25289-1_24

15. Knobloch, S., Patzig, G., Mende, A.-M., Hastall, M.: Affective news: Effects of discourse structure in narratives on suspense, curiosity, and enjoyment while reading news and novels. Commun. Res. **31**(3), 259–287 (2004). https://doi.org/10.1177/0093650203261517

16. Hartmann, T., Stuke, D., Daschmann, G.: Positive parasocial relationships with drivers affect suspense in racing sport spectators. J. Media Psychol. **20**(1), 24–34 (2008). https://doi.org/10.1027/1864-1105.20.1.24

17. Roth, C.: Experiencing Interactive Storytelling (2015)

18. Spielberger, C.D., et al.: Preliminary manual for the state-trait personality inventory (STPI). Unpublished manuscript University of South Florida Tampa (1979)

19. Spielberger, C.D., Peters, R.A. Frain, F.S.: Curiosity and anxiety, in Curiosity research: Basic concepts and results (1981)

20. Csikszentmihalhi, M.: Finding flow: the psychology of engagement with everyday life. Choice Rev. Online, **35**(03) (1997). https://doi.org/10.5860/CHOICE.35-1828

21. Jackson, S.A., Eklund, R.C.: Assessing flow in physical activity: The flow state scale-2 and dispositional flow scale-2. J. Sport Exerc. Psychol. **24**(2), 133–150 (2002). https://doi.org/10.1123/jsep.24.2.133

22. Jackson, S.A., Martin, A.J., Eklund, R.C.: Long and short measures of flow: The construct validity of the FSS-2, DFS-2, and new brief counterparts. J. Sport Exerc. Psychol. **30**(5), 561–587 (2008). https://doi.org/10.1123/jsep.30.5.561

23. Slater, M., Usoh, M., Steed, A.: Depth of presence in virtual environments. Presence Teleoperators Virtual Environ. **3**(2), 130–144 (1994). https://doi.org/10.1162/pres.1994.3.2.130

24. Schubert, T., Friedmann, F., Regenbrecht, Holger: The experience of presence: Factor analytic insights. Presence Teleoperators Virtual Environ. **10**(3), 266–281 (2001). https://doi.org/10.1162/105474601300343603

25. Witmer, B.G., Jerome, C.J. Singer, M.J.: The factor structure of the presence questionnaire. Presence: Teleoperators Virtual Environ. (2005).https://doi.org/10.1162/105474605323384654

26. Schwind, V., et al.: Using presence questionnaires in virtual reality. In: Conference on Human Factors in Computing Systems – Proceedings (2019). https://doi.org/10.1145/3290605.3300590.

27. Vorderer, P., Klimmt, C., Ritterfeld, U.: Enjoyment: At the heart of media entertainment. Commun. Theory, **14**(4) (2004). https://doi.org/10.1111/j.1468-2885.2004.tb00321.x

28. Sweetser, P., Wyeth, P.: GameFlow: a model for evaluating player enjoyment in games. Comput. Entertainment (CIE), **3**(3) (2005). https://doi.org/10.1145/1077246.1077253

29. Cupchik

30. Rowold, J.: Instrument development for esthetic perception assessment. J. Media Psychol. **20**(1) (2008). https://doi.org/10.1027/1864-1105.20.1.35. Taylor & Francis Group

31. Hoeken, H., Sinkeldam, J.: The role of identification and perception of just outcome in evoking emotions in narrative persuasion. J. Commun. **64**(5), 935–955https://doi.org/10.1111/jcom.12114. Blackwell Publishing Ltd

32. Isbister, K.: Better game characters by design: a psychological approach, Education (2006)

33. Isbister, K.: How Games Move Us, How Games Move Us (2018). https://doi.org/10.7551/mitpress/9267.001.0001

34. Henderson, J.M., Hayes, T.R.: Meaning-based guidance of attention in scenes as revealed by meaning maps. Nat. Human Behav. **1**(10) (2017). https://doi.org/10.1038/s41562-017-0208-0

35. Loewenstein, G.: The Psychology of Curiosity: A Review and Reinterpretation. Psychol. Bull. **116**(1) (1994). https://doi.org/10.1037//0033-2909.116.1.75

From Playing the Story to Gaming the System: Repeat Experiences of a Large Language Model-Based Interactive Story

Qing Ru Yong and Alex Mitchell[✉] [ID]

National University of Singapore, Singapore, Singapore
e0406308@u.nus.edu, alexm@nus.edu.sg

Abstract. A distinctive aspect of interactive stories is how they enable players to impact the story based on their choices, with repeated playthroughs potentially yielding different stories. While some work has been done to investigate repeat experiences of interactive stories, the focus has mainly been on simpler linear and branching narrative systems. Recent advances in large language model (LLM) systems such as ChatGPT have sparked renewed interest in how users engage with artificial intelligence systems, and how LLM systems could be used in works of entertainment such as games and interactive stories. In this paper, we detail the findings of a qualitative observational study of 10 participants playing and replaying the interactive text adventure game *AI Dungeon* which is based upon the natural-language-generating LLMs GPT-3 and GPT-J. The study provides insights into how the player's mental model of the system shifts from assuming the system is a linear or branching narrative to one with seemingly limitless narrative possibilities. This study also uncovers three related sources of motivations for repeat engagement with an LLM-based interactive story, which are impacted by the player's shifting mental model of the system: narrative closure, narrative incoherence, and expectations for variation between playthroughs. Finally, this study highlights how uncertainty in terms of both how the system works and what objectives the player has could impact the player's choice of actions when engaging with an LLM-based interactive story such as *AI Dungeon*.

Keywords: repeat experience · interactive stories · large language models

1 Introduction

As interactive stories are expected to vary across playthroughs, there is an interest in how players respond to the resulting variations when they repeatedly traverse the work. There has been much work done to understand repeat experiences of non-interactive works [1–3]. Additionally, recent work has investigated the repeat experiences of interactive stories [4–7]. However, previous work has primarily focused on interactive stories with simple systems of linear or branching narratives.

The recent proliferation of large language model (LLM) based systems such as ChatGPT has allowed stories to be procedurally generated based on specific inputs by

L. Holloway-Attaway and J. T. Murray (Eds.): ICIDS 2023, LNCS 14383, pp. 395–409, 2023.
https://doi.org/10.1007/978-3-031-47655-6_24

the player. As a result, interactive story progression need not go in a linear or branching fashion with a fixed set of endings but can instead be contextualized based on the player's input [8]. The interactive text adventures *AI Dungeon* [9] and *The Infinite Story* [10] are examples where this can be seen. Correspondingly, existing theories of repeat engagement with linear and branching narratives may need to be adapted when applied to LLM-based interactive stories with potentially endless narrative possibilities.

Through a qualitative empirical study with 10 participants using the interactive text adventure *AI Dungeon,* this paper investigates the mental models that players form while playing and replaying interactive stories based on an artificial intelligence (AI) system that is not directly and easily interpretable, in this case the LLMs GPT-3 and GPT-J. We also investigate how this shift of mental model might influence players' motivations to replay an LLM-based interactive story, and how their choice of actions differs with repeat engagement.

We observed that when faced with an unfamiliar LLM-based interactive storytelling system, players initially assumed that it has a linear or branching structure, but with repeated engagement, they started to grasp that the system affords seemingly limitless narrative possibilities. Players also constructed a storyworld based on the system output to make sense of their own actions. We observed three related sources of motivations for repeat engagement with an LLM-based interactive story, namely whether a player has achieved narrative closure, whether they encounter narrative incoherence, and the expected level of variation in the storyline. Lastly, we explored the impact of uncertainty on players' choice of actions when engaging and re-engaging with an LLM-based interactive story. Uncertainty in terms of the mechanism of an LLM-based interactive story may motivate players to further engage with the system to understand how it works. When players' objectives shift with repeat engagement, they could also become more certain of how the system works and their actions would also shift based on that. Based on these observations, we suggest that repeat engagement with an LLM-based interactive story is a process of seeking a clearer mental model of the system and that while doing so, players' objectives and motivations shift, resulting in a different set of actions.

2   Related Work

This section surveys the related work in two broad areas: how mental models develop, and the impact of uncertainty on player motivation.

2.1 Development and Shifts of Mental Model

One of the key findings of Mitchell [7] is that people's motivation to replay changes with their shifting understanding of the system of an interactive story. We argue that what Mitchell describes as an understanding of the system is analogous to what Norman [11] calls a *mental model*. The term *mental model* refers to a user's interpretation of how a system or product works based on his/her own beliefs [11]. Users' actions and how they interact with the system are then said to be guided by their mental model [12].

While the concept of a mental model has primarily been used in the field of HCI, its use has expanded to other areas like education and games [13–15]. In their study of the usability and design of real-time strategy games, Graham, Zheng, and Gonzalez [16] refers to a mental model as "an internal representation of a target system [the game] that provides predictive and explanatory power to the operator [the player]" (p. 361). They noticed a shift in the player's mental model, going from initially being based upon the visual features of the AI to accommodating the functional aspects of the AI. In their close readings of interactive stories *Bandersnatch* [17] and *Cultist Simulator* [18], Mitchell, Kway and Lee [5] also suggest that repeat engagement helps players construct a clearer mental model of the playable system.

The concept of a mental model has also been extended into explainable AI. Studies into making AI understandable to the layperson, often termed explainable AI or XAI, can potentially shed some light on how players engage with LLM-based interactive stories. It is believed that people would be more willing to adopt novel techniques and technologies if they could be "directly interpretable, tractable and trustworthy" (p. 83). Discussing how he evaluates the explainability of an AI system, Gunning [19] suggests that users who better understand their own decisions, the overall system model, and what the system could do are said to possess a clearer mental model of the system.

In their survey of related works on player-AI interaction, Villarealle, Harteveld and Zhu [20] found that most existing work focused on how players' mental models are developed *after* interacting with the AI. They highlighted a lack of literature surrounding "mental model development in response to the AI system over time" [p. 5] which they regard as being important in developing human-centered approaches to the design of systems. To address this, their study focused on investigating player experience of a visual-based AI game, *iNNk* [21] where the AI tries to guess the player's drawings. Based on this study, they propose that a player's mental model development can have a *top-down* or *bottom-up* focus and can integrate new information in a *systematic* or *reactive* manner. Noting the potential of their framework in mental model development, we aim to extend their work to LLMs and text-based AI games, through our first research question:

1. **How do the mental models that players have of the system develop and change as they play and replay an LLM-based interactive story?**

2.2 (Un)certainty as a Source of Motivation When Interacting with AI?

Uncertainty has been seen as a major source of motivation in games and interactive stories, as described in works such as Kumari, Deterding and Freeman [22] and Wang, Ang and Mitchell [4]. Despite this, there has been a lack of literature examining how uncertainty (or certainty) might come into play as a source of motivation in works of entertainment backed by an LLM. Uncertainty as a motivator is worth considering given the mechanisms behind LLMs are often opaque to a layperson, potentially giving rise to significant feelings of uncertainty [23, 24].

In their investigation of player motivations in casual games, Kumari, Deterding and Freeman [22] argue that the feeling of uncertainty is an important source of motivation that drives players through what Sicart [25] refers to as the game loop. The feeling of uncertainty encompasses 16 unique motivations, with part of the source of uncertainty consisting of anticipation of new content and anticipation of new goals / opportunities as motivations to play [22]. Suomala and Kauttonen [26] highlight that humans resolve uncertainty in a commercial AI system through contextual information in the system and their own prior experiences. They suggest these prior experiences are based off the users' mental model of the system and the knowledge and skills they acquire over time.

Specifically focusing on interactive storytelling, Wang, Ang and Mitchell [4] further showed that having an incomplete understanding of a game system has been a significant motivation to replay an interactive story in their empirical studies with the interactive story *The Shadows That Run Alongside Our Car* [27]. They suggest that "player reached either narrative or system closure first, continued to replay, and did not feel a need to replay once they reached both forms of closure" (p. 10). Narrative closure here refers to "the phenomenological feeling of finality that is generated when all the questions saliently posed by the narrative are answered" [28, p. 1], while system closure occurs when "a work's structure, though not its plot, is understood" [29, p. 174]. Wang, Ang and Mitchell [4] observed that when presented with an insignificant amount of expected variation, players would lose the motivation to replay, knowing that the shape of the narrative will remain largely the same. Yet, when presented with too much variation, players may experience confusion and frustration, and would likewise lose the motivation to replay.

Significant inroads have been made in exploring the concept of certainty as a crucial criterion in users' use of commercial AI system. There is also existing work done on how uncertainty motivates players in works of entertainment such as games and interactive stories that have linear or branching narratives. However, there is a lack of literature that investigates how uncertainty (or certainty) might motivate players in LLM systems that are entertainment-based and less about achieving a concrete objective.

Therefore, we ask the following second and third research questions:

2. **How do players' shifting mental models (and the attendant reduction in uncertainty) impact their motivations to replay LLM-based interactive stories?**
3. **How do players' choice of actions change with repeat engagements of LLM-based interactive stories?**

3   Methodology

To address these research questions, we conducted a qualitative, observational study of 10 participants repeatedly playing the LLM-based text adventure *AI Dungeon*.

3.1   Materials

The study uses the single-player free-to-play text adventure interactive story, *AI Dungeon*. Based upon the Generative Pre-trained Transformer (GPT) AI model, *AI Dungeon* can generate unlimited content based on the input of the player. GPT is a language prediction models developed by Open AI which take in users' text input to generate human-like sentences through deep learning technologies [30]. The quality of the text is said to be at a level that it may sometimes be indistinguishable from sentences written by humans [31]. The player is provided with a starting prompt (a scenario), and they can type in what they want to do, see, or say in response to that. The system then outputs text in response to what the player types.

3.2 Participants

11 participants were sourced through convenience and snowball sampling. 9 participants were recruited through word-of-mouth via the researchers' social media channels and 2 participants were sourced via the university's research recruitment portal. All but 1 were undergraduate students aged 20–25, stemming from a wide range of disciplines, including communications, economics, business, and engineering. To be eligible, participants were screened to ensure they had not enrolled in interactive storytelling and game studies courses taught by the principal investigator and had not played *AI Dungeon* beforehand. 11 participants took part in the study but only 10 were included in the analysis as P02 had prior exposure to *AI Dungeon*. Most participants did not consider themselves to be gamers, except for P07 who did have significant experience playing computer games. Most participants are also deemed to have no extensive technical background with regards to their understanding of AI, as 9 out of the 10 permissible participants are currently working towards or have university degrees that are not STEM-related[1]. All participants participated in the study before the popularization of LLM-based AI systems such as ChatGPT.

The study was done in 2 phases – 8 participated from January 2021 to March 2021 whilst 2 participated in December 2022. All study protocols were the same, except that the versions of the language model used by *AI Dungeon* were different. The study from January 2021 to March 2021 used the GPT-3 model whilst the study in December 2022 used the GPT-J 6B model. There was no noticeable difference in the output based on our observations as GPT-J performs very similarly to GPT-3 on various zero-shot down-streaming tasks [32].

3.3 Protocol

The sessions took place remotely through video conferencing platform Zoom and was recorded for anonymized transcription. Participation was voluntary and non-remunerated. University IRB approval was obtained before the study was carried out.

Before each session, a demographic questionnaire was administered to understand the gameplay experience of participants. Participants then engaged in one practice playthrough followed by three main playthroughs. The practice playthrough situates players in an empty room to help them familiarize with the controls of *AI Dungeon*. The starting prompt given was:

> *"You woke up and see yourself in an empty room. You tried to get out but the door is locked. There are a couple of drawers and closets lying around."*

The 3 main playthroughs place participants in a fictional world via the following starting prompt:

> *"You are Quill, a noble living in the kingdom of Larion. You have a pouch of gold and a small dagger. You are awakened by one of your servants who tells you that*

---

[1] STEM majors' classification is based on [44].

your keep is under attack. You look out the window and see a group of soldiers approaching."

Various starting prompts were trialed during the pilot studies and the current one was decided upon for two main reasons. Firstly, this current starting prompt was deliberately kept simple with only three sentences to reduce cognitive load for participants. Secondly, as there is still some level of opaqueness in the system model of *AI Dungeon*, we left out detailed information about the setting and scenario as they may potentially bias participants' interpretation of the system.

Each main playthrough lasted 10 to 15 min. At the end of each playthrough, participants were interviewed regarding their objectives, understanding of the system, feeling of narrative closure, strategy taken, and motivations to replay. Care was taken at the end of the first and second playthrough to ensure the questions asked do not encourage the act of replay, such as the need to revisit the storyline in depth. Participants were also not told that they would have to replay with the same starting prompt for three times at the start of the session.

The session culminated with a retrospective protocol analysis [33, 34], similar to the approaches used by Knickmeyer and Mateas [35] and Mitchell, Sim and Kway [36], where participants were shown video footage of their own playthroughs and probed on their thought processes.

3.4 Analysis

The recordings were fully transcribed and anonymized. Analysis was carried out by the first author using thematic analysis [37]. Open coding yielded 233 open codes. Similar codes were then grouped together, resulting in 50 axial codes. 5 themes were identified from the relationships between the axial codes, in discussion with the second author, which were used to structure the next section.

4   Results

Our observations suggest that when players engage with an LLM-based interactive story, their understanding of both the system and their objectives vary across playthroughs. They initially visualize a storyworld on which they base their decisions. At some point, such as upon reaching narrative closure or facing narrative incoherence, players might not wish to further engage with the system. As a result, players might start to test or "game" the system or become more unstructured in what they do.

4.1   Changing Understanding of How the System Generates Content

When asked how they feel the text output by the system relates to what they type, players initially tended to feel the system matches specific keywords to a database or archive and then pulls out relevant information based on that. For instance, P01 states:

"Because they [the system] can't really know how you're going to phrase certain things, so they look at keywords and then match it to the response that is already pre-programmed in."

P09 concurs when they mention:

"I think they try to catch the keywords in the sentence and probably use some algorithms to check online the most common response to all these keywords and respond to it."

In their initial playthroughs, many participants felt that the narrative they have gone through was based upon a pre-defined storyline that either has a linear or branching narrative. P01 described the system as having some form of flowchart, where typing in certain responses will lead her down a specific path in the flowchart. P04 felt that they are reading a story when they are in the first playthrough and is "interested to find out what's next". P08 thought that everything that happens will have to fit within the storyworld, and that when they start to type things that do not fit, the system does not have a reference point to pick up on. This is partially due to the "storyworld" they construct, which will be discussed in 4.2. This is illustrated when P08 says:

"I think maybe because this is an AI, to have an appropriate response, it should have a database of answers. So far, everything has to be within the story of Larion and [the] fictional world."

However, in their second and third playthrough, these same participants start to question their initial assumption of a pre-determined linear or branching storyline. P04, who felt they are reading a storybook in the first playthrough, thought that the story can "go very wild because it is open-ended". In their second playthrough, P08 says "I can just start another story anytime. I won't win the game eventually, there's no end point to the game."

4.2   Perception of Being "in a Storyworld" that the System Understands

This relates closely to how participants thought of the storyworld. We observed that even though *AI Dungeon* is text-based and relies upon a large language model that is meant to generate human-like texts, rather than a storyline, most participants felt they could visualize a storyworld as they played. For instance, when asked if they wish to play *AI Dungeon* again, P03 says they want to play again, and their motivation is that they wish to revisit the characters that are in their current playthrough. P05 feels that whenever they read a story, they are actively visualizing a storyworld, and they shared that they felt that they were doing the same while playing *AI Dungeon*. One participant, P01, felt that in-game elements such as characters or landscapes already existed in the storyworld and were revealed to them rather than being generated on the fly. This is aligned to Herman's [38] proposition of a storyworld in narrative worldmaking where readers rely on textual cues to construct an overall mental representation of a narrative's world, even if these aspects of the world are not fully described in the text itself.

Many of the participants also felt that the system can comprehend and understand the story context and takes that into account before giving a response. For example, P08 felt that the system would attempt to find a course of action it felt will not be very far off from the storyline he is going on. When P06's player character died, they rationalize that the system understands how throwing the gold out of the window exposes his location.

They thought that now that the soldiers knew their location, the system understands death as an imminent possibility.

Some participants also assumed that they are in the same storyworld across playthroughs. As P07 mentions:

> "Even though I chose different choices as an individual, there are things that can't be changed per se like the layout of the land for example."

For instance, when the narrative progresses to a point where they burned down a forest and eventually got a new job on a farmland, P07 felt like they were starting a new game. However, when asked if they felt they were in the same world even though the second playthrough deviated quite significantly from the starting prompt, they thought they still were in the same world, and that they were simply going on another plotline within the Kingdom of Larion.

However, when the narrative becomes incoherent, specifically when participants could no longer incorporate what was happening into the Kingdom of Larion, participants feel they have moved on to another storyworld. Furthermore, when the storyline felt incoherent to participants, they also had a reduced motivation to play on. For example, P04 thought that the appearance of modern-day elements like Coca-Cola and a shopping mall in what he saw as a medieval world (i.e., the Kingdom of Larion) should have triggered some form of error. When asked whether it was incoherent, P04 exclaimed a resolute "yes it is". P04 also shared that because "the game even introduces things like [a] shopping mall as opposed to calling out some new scenarios for me to do new stuff", P04 was confused and did not wish to play on anymore. P04 further clarified that this was because they had "lost a sense of purpose" in the game. The idea of the player's character reviving after dying in the story also felt strange to P06. P06 tried to make sense of this revival by attributing it to either a dream experienced by the player's character, or a plot connected to their previous playthrough. Unable to successfully rationalize this incoherence, P06 felt "there isn't much things to do [anymore]" and no longer wanted to play on.

4.3   Changing Interpretations of Narrative Closure

Participants had different interpretations as to when narrative closure is reached. Some participants felt that narrative closure is reached when the player character achieves the objective suggested by the text. For instance, when probed as to when the game would end P06 said "The end goal is to revive the wife right. When the wife revive [sic], I think it may end there." This was following a sequence where another character, the king, had asked for assistance to revive their dead wife. Many participants also felt that when the player character dies, the game ends when in fact, the game allows players to continue. 8 out of 10 participants mentioned that dying suggests that the game has ended, with P11 observing that if you "kill yourself or die" the game will end. These are perceived end points of the story, after which players did not want to play on.

In later playthroughs, however, when participants realized that *AI Dungeon* is an open system with limitless narrative possibilities, they felt that the game only truly ends if the system disallows them from typing anything. For example, in their second playthrough, when P05 discovers that the system can generate limitless possibilities, they think the game will not end because the system can "keep narrating a new a story. When I want to die, they still continue to revive me." Similarly, P08 states:

> "In the first playthrough, I thought there will be an end. But in the second time, I thought there was no end. I can just start another story anytime."

In their third playthrough, P07 thinks the game will not end as long as the "text box is open for prompts". At this point in the playthrough, they already understood that there is no pre-defined storyline based on a linear or branching narrative. At this stage, some players did not want to play on. For instance, when asked if they wish to replay, P04 said they would not as it was "very messy without any direction." However, other participants were motivated to continue playing on to "game" the system, as we will discuss in Sect. 4.5.

4.4 Shifting Objectives Due to Changing Understanding of the System

Most participants were not clear what they were meant to achieve and what their objectives were in the first playthrough. For instance, P04 thought that because they could not picture their surroundings, most of what they were doing in the first playthrough was to find out what was happening and what places they could go to. Similarly, in their first playthrough, P06 was not sure whether there is any "final endpoint" they need to reach, and hence was not sure what they should do. P07 felt their objective was not very defined in the initial playthrough and that their main goal was to "experience that little adventure" and P08 was just "going where the story is leading [him] to".

After their initial playthrough, participants were generally clearer on what they were trying to achieve. P07 who felt their objective was not very defined in the first playthrough, thought it was clearer in the second playthrough, in the sense that they knew they had to survive and save their people. Similarly, P09 who said they were simply "responding blindly to what the AI says" in the first playthrough, felt that they were working towards killing the King in their second playthrough.

Players who felt they were working towards an objective in the first and second playthrough tended to feel they have their objectives closely linked to what was set out in the starting prompt – to defend the keep and defeat the soldiers. However, when they felt that they had experienced and seen enough of what they felt there was in the storyworld, their objective shifted more to stress-testing the system and figuring out how the system works. For example, in their third playthrough, P04 had completely lost the motivation to explore the storyworld and said they started "coming up with ludicrous scenarios to see how the game responds". Similarly, in their third playthrough, P08 felt they had forgotten about the storyline and instead were typing in random things in their bid to confuse the system. We discuss this further below.

4.5 Gaming the System After Motivation to Replay is Lost

Participants were more focused on figuring out how the system works when they felt they had little motivation to replay. In one case, P08 wanted to see how far they could stretch the system in its ability to comprehend abstract commands and brought in modern day concepts like "Donald Trump", just to see what would happen. While P05 felt they did not have any motivation to explore the storyworld, they were intrigued by how the system would behave when they gave what they thought to be ludicrous input. For example, they typed in "nothing" consecutively and wanted to see at what point the system would "give up and end the game".

This shift to gaming the system occurred in part as the result of perceived narrative closure. When participants felt that they had seen everything that they feel the story can offer, they started to test the system. In their second and third playthrough, when P11 was no longer trying to continue the storyline to achieve the goal set out in the starting prompt, they were testing out how to die. When P10 was no longer focused on the player character's task in their third playthrough, they were focused on "typing out weird answers that seem illogical and see what type of narrative comes up."

Additionally, the shift to gaming the system also resulted from the experience of narrative incoherence. When they didn't understand what was going on in the story, participants' actions tended to be more deliberately bizarre. For instance, when the storyline strayed away from the storyworld and into other contexts in the second playthrough, P07 didn't know what was going on and kept improvising. Similarly, when asked whether they felt like they were working towards a goal, P04 said they were just randomly throwing out ideas after losing their motivation to replay.

5 Discussion

The above findings suggest that while players start with a simple mental model of how the system works, this model changes with repeat engagement. This shift in their mental model is paralleled by a change in their perception of the storyworld. There is also a change in their motivation to replay, and what their objectives are, which in turn impacts their choice of actions during play.

5.1 Development and Shift of Mental Model in LLM-Based Interactive Stories

Mitchell, Kway and Lee [5] suggests that during engagement with an interactive story, players construct a clearer mental model of the system which shifts with repeated engagement. We have observed in finer detail what it means to shift one's mental model when players interact with an LLM-based interactive story. One aspect of this shift in mental model is in players' understanding of how a system works. When faced with an unfamiliar LLM-based interactive story, players may initially think there might be a pre-defined storyline but with repeat engagement, they start to question their initial perception, moving from a model based on linear or branching narratives towards one that suggests unlimited possibilities. This suggests that players largely adopted what Villareale, Harteveld and Zhu [20] would describe as a top-down focus to mental model development, and initially used a systematic approach to assimilating new information.

Another aspect of this development of a mental model is in the construction of a storyworld to help players visualize their actions. Players base this storyworld on the output of the system and rationalize that the system can comprehend the storyworld context in generating a response. However, when the system output is inconsistent with the storyworld that players construct, they might feel they have shifted into another storyworld.

5.2   Potential Reasons for Players' Loss of Motivation in Repeat Engagement

We have identified three points which might influence players' motivations in continuing to interact with an LLM-based interactive story: narrative closure, narrative incoherence, and too much expected variation.

When players felt that all the questions posed by the narrative are answered, such that narrative closure is reached, they are likely to lose their motivation to further engage with an LLM interactive story. Narrative closure can be reached in different scenarios. One such instance is when players felt that they have explored all that is possible in the storyworld that they have constructed, and that further engagement will not yield new, interesting variations. Another instance is when players felt that they have met the objectives they first set out to achieve, they might also not be motivated to further re-engage with the system. Such objectives could be their personal objectives (e.g., to explore the world) or one detailed by the starting prompts given by the system (e.g., to save the kingdom from the invaders).

When players are no longer able to comprehend how the output by the system fits into the storyworld they construct, such that there is a sense of narrative incoherence, they might not wish to further engage with the system. Similarly, when the storyline strays too far away from what it originally started from, they are also less likely to want to continue to play.

Finally, when players' understanding of the system shift from thinking it is a linear or branching narrative to one with limitless narrative possibilities, they might also lose the motivation to replay, as they are not sure what to expect in subsequent playthroughs. This aligns with Wang, Ang, and Mitchell's [4] insight that players feel frustrated and confused in the face of overwhelming variations of storylines in an interactive story with a linear or branching narrative.

5.3   Choice of Actions Shifts with Shifting Understanding of the System

Our observations suggest that uncertainty is a significant determinant of players' choice of actions when they engage and re-engage with LLM-based interactive stories. However, different types of uncertainties and certainties would impact player motivations and their eventual choice of actions differently.

Uncertainty in terms of the opaqueness of the system would motivate players to further engage with the system. Given that the mechanism of an LLM-based interactive story is not immediately clear to players in their initial engagement, players are often motivated to play to figure out how the system works. Their actions tend to focus on gaming the system, trying out different commands that need not necessarily continue the narrative but work towards helping them figure how the system works. This is aligned with Kumari, Deterding and Freeman's [22] insights that when players are uncertain about what new content or new goals they could get out of a repeat engagement, they are likelier to want to continue playing a game. In a similar vein, when players are certain that they have seen everything they wish to see in terms of the narrative, and they have somewhat figured how the system works (i.e. they have reached narrative and system closure), their actions started to become more random and erratic. It became apparent at this point that players would not have motivations to further engage the system, resulting in randomness in their actions. This suggests a shift from a top-down, systematic approach to mental model development, to what Villareale, Harteveld and Zhu [20] would call a more bottom-up, reactive approach.

We also suggest that the shifting objectives players have with repeat engagement with an LLM-based interactive story would impact the type of actions they would take. When players were unsure what they would wish to achieve in their initial engagement, most of their actions and objectives were closely linked to the starting prompt provided by the system. However, in later engagements, after players have spent time figuring out the system, they could again become unsure of their objectives. When they realize that the system affords limitless narrative possibilities, this uncertainty in their objectives would damper their motivations to further engage with it. Once they possess what Suomala and Kauttonen [26] refers to as contextual information of how an AI system work, they either lose their motivations to replay or they start stress-testing the system. We observed that it was through repeat engagements that players' objectives of what they wish to achieve shifted with their changing understanding of the system. And this shift of their objectives was, in turn, a key determinant in their choice of actions. It is also interesting to note that relying on gained understanding of a game system to act may constitute what Garfield [39] refers to as metagaming. Just as practices such as speedrunning are typically considered metagaming [40], the act of using "out-of-character knowledge to make in-character decisions" and the act of stress-testing a game system with this knowledge could also be considered metagaming.

Wang, Ang and Mitchell [4] suggests the need to obtain a balance in the level of expected variations to motivate players to continue to replay interactive stories. Our study concurs by suggesting that while uncertainty due to the opaqueness of the system might motivate players to play on and game the system, uncertainty arising from not knowing what their objectives were might have the opposite impact. In addition, the level of uncertainty players experienced tended to vary based on their changing understanding of how the system works across multiple repeat engagements.

6   Conclusion

This study provides an initial understanding of how players develop a mental model of an LLM-based interactive story, and how this impacts their motivations to replay and their objectives and actions during replay. Through the lens of mental models, we see that, in the face of unfamiliar AI systems, players tended to initially be unclear in their understanding of the system and therefore were unclear of their objectives and what they were doing. Once users perceived themselves to have understood how the system works, with a shift in their mental model of the system from linear or branching narratives to narratives with limitless possibilities, their goals shifted towards testing or gaming the system rather than achieving narrative closure. We also highlight three inter-related sources of motivations for repeat engagement with an LLM-based interactive story: narrative closure, narrative incoherence, and expected variations.

There are some limitations to this study to keep in mind. One participant mentioned that she thought that we (the researchers) had created *AI Dungeon*. This may have affected some participants' willingness to be honest when probed on their motivations to replay. As such, it may have been better to pre-empt participants by making it clear we were not involved with developing the system.

Being a qualitative study of 10 participants with largely homogeneous demographics, this study is not representative and is more exploratory. It should be noted that the educational profile of participants was largely similar (non-STEM) as we were interested in understanding how a typical layperson without technical background would respond to our stimulus. We also used a relatively simple starting prompt of 3 sentences that briefly details the storyworld and starting situation. However, many participant expressed a desire for more context. Hence, future work using a more detailed starting scenario with more information about the character, setting and scenario could potentially yield differing results regarding players' mental models of the system and their response to variation. Future work could also compare our findings with player responses to traditional interactive fiction, using the same story world and story setting, to better understand which user behaviour was due to elements of generative AI.

In addition, most participants had no knowledge about LLMs. With the popularization of LLM-based AI systems such as ChatGPT since this study was conducted, the general layperson may have a different initial understanding of a chat-based AI system. It would be interesting to see how participants with some understanding of AI or experience working with ChatGPT or other generative AI systems would behave.

Finally, the connection between participants' development of a mental model of the system and their sense of the coherence or incoherence of the storyworld highlights the relationship between the concepts of a mental model and a storyworld. It would be interesting to explore this further, particularly in the context of approaches such as curational emergent narrative [41] and narrative instruments [42]. It would also be worth considering what participants are doing not just within but between play sessions from the perspective of metagaming [40], and how this potentially relates to Koentiz's [43] triple hermeneutic of the experience of interactive digital narratives.

This study provides findings on how users make sense of and respond to an LLM-based interactive story, *AI Dungeon*. These insights are especially pertinent at a time where LLM systems like ChatGPT are becoming increasingly prevalent. Understanding the experience of an LLM-based interactive story from a layperson's perspective could provide a foundation from which we might make more general LLM systems understandable to someone without a technical background, and how we can motivate them to repeatedly engage with such a system.

Acknowledgements. This research was funded under the Singapore Ministry of Education Academic Research Fund Tier 1 grant FY2018-FRC2–003, "Understanding Repeat Engagement with Dynamically Changing Computational Media".

References

1. Călinescu, M.: Rereading. Yale University Press (1993)
2. Galef, D.: Second Thoughts: a Focus on Rereading. Wayne State University Press (1998)
3. Brewer, W.: The nature of narrative suspense and the problem of rereading. In: Suspense: Conceptualizations, Theoretical Analyses, and Empirical Explorations. Routledge (1996)
4. Wang, B., Ang, B.H., Mitchell, A.: I need to play three times before I kind of understand: Exploring player motivations for replaying interactive stories. In: Proceedings of CHI Play 2021 (2021)
5. Mitchell, A., Kway, L., Lee, B.J.: Storygameness: understanding repeat experience and the desire for closure in storygames. In: Digital Games Research Association DiGRA 2020, Finland (2020)
6. Mitchell, A., McGee, K.: Reading again for the first time: A model of rereading in interactive stories. In: Proceedings of the International Conference on Interactive Digital Storytelling (2012).https://doi.org/10.1007/978-3-642-34851-8_20
7. Mitchell, A.: Reflective rereading and the simcity effect in interactive stories. In: Schoenau-Fog, H., Bruni, L.E., Louchart, S., Baceviciute, S. (eds.) ICIDS 2015. LNCS, vol. 9445, pp. 27–39. Springer, Cham (2015). https://doi.org/10.1007/978-3-319-27036-4_3
8. Wardrip-Furin, N., Mateas, M.: The future is in interactive storytelling, 4 May 2017. https://theconversation.com/the-future-is-in-interactive-storytelling-76772
9. Latitude, "AI Dungeon" [interactive fiction], Latitude (2019)
10. Mueller, F.: "The Infinite Story" [interactive fiction], Florian Mueller (2019)
11. Norman, D.A.: The Design of Everyday Things, Doubleday Currency (1988)
12. Nielsen, J.: Mental Models, 17 October 2010. https://www.nngroup.com/articles/mental-models/
13. Haig, K.M., Sutton, S., Whittington, J.: SBAR: a shared mental model for improving communication between clinicians. Joint Comm. J. Qual. Patient Saf. **32**(3), 167–175 (2006)
14. Rapp, D.N.: Mental models: theoretical issues for visualizations in science education. Vis. Sci. Educ. **1**, 43–60 (2005). https://doi.org/10.1007/1-4020-3613-2_4
15. Taylor, I., Barker, M., Jones, A.: Promoting mental model building in astronomy education. Int. J. Sci. Educ. **25**(10), 1205–1225 (2003)
16. Graham, J., Zheng, L., Gonzalez, C.: A cognitive approach to game usability and design: mental model development in novice real-time strategy gamers. Cyberpsychol. Behav. **9**(3), 361–366 (2006)
17. Slade, D., Brooker, C.: Black Mirror: Bandersnatch [interactive film], Netflix (2018)
18. Weather Factory, "Cultist Simulator" [PC computer game], Humble Bundle (2018)
19. Gunning, D.: "Explainable Artificial Intelligence (XAI)," Defense Advanced Research Projects Agency
20. Villareale, J., Harteveld, C., Zhu, J.: I want to see how smart this AI really is: player mental model development of an adversarial AI player. In: Proceedings of the ACM on Human-Computer Interaction (2022)
21. Zhu, J., Risi, S.: "iNNk" [computer game], IT University of Copenhagen, Copenhagen
22. Kumari, S., Deterding, S., Freeman, J.: The role of uncertainty in moment-to-moment player motivation: a grounded theory. In: Annual Symposium on Computer-Human Interaction in Play, Barcelona (2019)
23. Vaassen, B.: AI, Opacity, and Personal autonomy. Philos. Technol. **35**(88) 2022. https://doi.org/10.1007/s13347-022-00577-5
24. Bourton, S., Wigley, C., Williams, S.: Embrace the uncertainty of AI, 23 July 2018. https://www.mckinsey.com/capabilities/people-and-organizational-performance/our-insights/the-organization-blog/embrace-the-uncertainty-of-ai

25. Sicart, M.: Loops and metagames: understanding game design structures. In: 10th International Conference on the Foundations of Digital Games, California (2015)
26. Suomala, J., Kauttonen, J.: Human's intuitive mental models as a source of realistic artificial intelligence and engineering. Front. Pyschology **13**, 873289 (2022)
27. Lox Rain, "The Shadows That Run Alongside Our Car" [computer game], Lox Rain (2016)
28. Carroll, N.: Narrative closure. Int. J. Philos. Anal. Tradition **135**(1), 1–15 (2007). https://doi.org/10.1007/s11098-007-9097-9
29. Murray, J.H.: Hamlet on the holodeck: The Future of Narrative in Cyberspace, The MIT Press (1998)
30. Marr, B.: What Is GPT-3 And Why Is It Revolutionizing Artificial Intelligence?, 5 October 2020. https://www.forbes.com/sites/bernardmarr/2020/10/05/what-is-gpt-3-and-why-is-it-revolutionizing-artificial-intelligence/?sh=280bf241481a
31. Sagar, R.: OpenAI Releases GPT-3, The Largest Model So Far, 3 June 2020. https://analytics indiamag.com/open-ai-gpt-3-language-model/
32. Forefront, "GPT-J-6B: An Introduction to the Largest Open Source GPT Model I Forefront," 15 October 2021. https://forefrontai.medium.com/gpt-j-6b-an-introduction-to-the-largest-open-source-gpt-model-forefront-6962eccdfee1
33. Bowers, V.A., Snyder, H.L.: Concurrent versus retrospective verbal protocol for comparing window usability. In: Proceedings of the Human Factors Society Annual Meeting (1990)
34. Kuusela, H., Paul, P.: A comparison of concurrent and retrospective verbal protocol analysis. Am. J. Psychol. **113**(3), 387–404 (2000)
35. Knickmeyer, R.L., Mateas, M.: Preliminary evaluation of the interactive drama façade. In: CHI EA 05, Portland (2005)
36. Mitchell, A., Sim, Y.T., Kway, L.: Making it unfamiliar in the "Right" way: an empirical study of poetic gameplay. In: Digital Games Research Association, Melbourne (2017)
37. Braun, V., Clarke, V.: Using thematic analysis in psychology. Qual. Res. Psychol. **3**(2), 77–101 (2006)
38. Herman, D.: Narrative Ways of Worldmaking," in Narratology in the Age of Cross-Disciplinary Narrative Research, pp. 71–87. Walter de Gruyter, Berlin (2009)
39. Garfield, R.: Metagames. In: Horsemen of the Apocalypse: Essays on Roleplaying, Charleston, IL, Jolly Roger Games, pp. 14–21 (2000)
40. Boluk, S., LeMieux, P.: Metagaming: Playing, competing, spectating, cheating, trading, making, and breaking videogames. University of Minnesota Press, Minneapolis (2017)
41. Ryan, J.: Curating Simulated Storyworlds, Ph.D Thesis, UC Santa Cruz (2018)
42. Kreminski, M.: Narrative Instruments: AI-Based Playable Media for Storytelling, Ph.D Thesis, UC Santa Cruz (2022)
43. Koenitz, H.: Understanding Interactive Digital Narrative: Immersive expressions for a complex time. Routledge, New York (2023)
44. Jones, K.: What Are STEM Degrees?, 29 November 2019. https://www.gcu.edu/blog/engine ering-technology/what-are-stem-degrees

A Board Game *Hootopia*: Biodiversity Education Through Tangible and Interactive Narrative

Yi Zhang[1]([⊠]) [iD] and Zhe Huang[2] [iD]

[1] Beijing Normal University, Beijing, China
sukizhang@mail.bnu.edu.cn
[2] Tsinghua University, Beijing, China

Abstract. This paper introduces *Hootopia*, a tangible interactive board game, aimed at exploring the potential effectiveness of interactive digital storytelling in enhancing children's comprehension of biodiversity and species protection. The game objective is to cultivate a profound connection between players and the imperative of safeguarding animal habitats, aiming for a deeper, experiential understanding rather than the dissemination of specific academic content. In the game, players assume the dual roles of environmental transformers and animal protectors and have a unique opportunity to experience various interests and conflicts among different factions. By immersing players in an enjoyable and engaging narrative, the game seeks to enrich biodiversity education. The study investigates the integration of board game narratives and education, the feasibility of merging gaming and tangible interactive storytelling, and the impact of *Hootopia* on children's engagement, interest, learning outcomes, and attitudes toward biodiversity and species protection.

Keywords: Tangible Narratives · Interactive Storytelling · Tangible interaction · Biodiversity

1 Introduction

Biodiversity plays a crucial role in maintaining the functionality of ecosystems and the well-being of humanity. Unfortunately, our planet is witnessing an unprecedented loss of biodiversity, with a significant number of species at risk of extinction [1]. Recognizing its significance, this paper presents *Hootopia*, an innovative tangible interactive narrative game implemented as a physical-digital hybrid system, incorporating multimodal interactions, and designed for the specific purpose of promoting biodiversity conservation.

Tangible Narratives (TN) is a subset of Interactive Digital Narratives (IDN). According to Daniel Harley and Jean Ho Chu [2], interactive narrative applications involving physical objects typically incorporate physical objects with embedded digital functionalities wherein these physical objects possess manipulability, interactivity, and narrative qualities [3]. Through organizing relevant cases, we found that there are currently

L. Holloway-Attaway and J. T. Murray (Eds.): ICIDS 2023, LNCS 14383, pp. 410–421, 2023.
https://doi.org/10.1007/978-3-031-47655-6_25

three main forms of Tangible Narratives (TN): combining graphic interface with physical object [2, 4–7], embodied interaction with virtual reality environments [8–10], and purely physical object [2, 3, 11]. In general, regardless of the form, all interactive tangible products comprise one or more narrative arcs, the completion of which requires the participation of both individuals and objects. Furthermore, computer components cleverly and appropriately combine narrative perspectives, user behaviors, role-playing, and other narrative elements in this process [2].

Considering that *Hootopia* is primarily targeting a child audience, and in consideration of children's vision health, we have chosen to adopt a purely physical entity kit format. In this paper, we present our design response to the public issue of biodiversity, including our system and story design methods.

2   Related Work

2.1   Biodiversity Education and Habitat Loss

The UN's Sustainable Development Goals (SDGs) were established in 2015 as part of the 2030 Agenda for Sustainable Development, committing to addressing global challenges, and preservation of global biodiversity [12]. Habitat loss has always been and continues to be the greatest threat to biodiversity [13]. Protecting and managing high-value terrestrial and marine habitats are key factors in maintaining biodiversity and are at the core of the 2050 vision of the Convention on Biological Diversity (CBD) [14]. If modern society is to have a chance to reverse our destructive environmental trajectory, there is nothing more important than educating and inspiring future generations to understand and protect biodiversity and to respect the interdependence of all life systems.

Biodiversity education focuses on both the organisms and their habitats. It links the core ideas of environmental education and sustainable development education, including stewardship, local action, and the ability of ecosystems to support life in a sustainable way [15]. However, due to society's limited understanding and respect of biodiversity, as well as the complexity and abstractness of biodiversity education, it is challenging to integrate it into traditional subject-based education models, and there is a gap between expectations and the education sector's ability to address this issue [16].

Based on this research background, in order to bridge this gap, we aim to design an engaging narrative game that goes beyond the classroom and enters into children's daily lives. This game will make the concept of biodiversity more concrete and tangible, helping children better understand the importance of habitat conservation, and cultivating their awareness and capacity to take action in biodiversity conservation.

2.2   Biodiversity Education Game and Tangible Narrative

A Few scientific studies [17–19] have initially confirmed the correlation between digital games and Biodiversity knowledge, particularly regarding the increased motivation of players to learn these concepts. Furthermore, it is widely acknowledged that tangible interaction offers a more beneficial approach for children to learn. Based on the cognitive theory proposed by the renowned developmental psychologist Jean Piaget, emphasizes that touch and perception of the physical environment are important ways to facilitate children's learning and growth. Within the domain of tangible board games related to biodiversity, several notable emerged, including *Wingspan* by Stonemaier Games [20], *Ecosystem* by Genius Games [21], and various educational games developed by One Moment Games [22]. *Wingspan* [20] stands out as a notable example of successfully intertwining gameplay and educational elements, particularly in the context of avian biology.

Tangible interaction in children's education has long been of interest to the interactive narrative community and has become the most widely adopted interactive technology in current children's learning applications [2]. Digital storytelling, which combines traditional storytelling with digital technologies, has become an innovative approach to engage students in deep and meaningful learning [23].

Several studies [11, 24–26] have demonstrated that tangible interactive digital narratives in education can provide a means to transform abstract concepts into tangibility and visibility through storytelling, thereby stimulating children's learning and their ability to understand the surrounding environment. For children, abstract concepts are often difficult to learn and understand, but tangible storytelling as a teaching tool in the domain of abstract problems has three advantages: sensory engagement, accessibility, and group learning [26]. Therefore, tangible interactive narratives can effectively serve as a method to reflect on abstract concepts related to ecological issues and engage in practices for biodiversity conservation, thereby enhancing people's awareness of sustainable development. Our research aims to design tangible interactions that support expression in narratives and the concrete construction of abstract knowledge.

2.3   Balancing Storytelling and Gameplay

Over the past two decades, research has gradually revealed numerous potential similarities between narration and gameplay. However, this has also raised a new question: how to balance narration and gameplay mechanics in games. In our work, we draw insights from scholars in the fields of Interactive Digital Narratives (IDN) and game narratives. In terms of narrative structure, we incorporate some interactive narrative principles proposed by Marie-Laure Ryan [27], including natural interface, integration of user action within the story, and dynamic creation of the story. In terms of interactive game design, we adopt the tangible interaction approach proposed by Michael S. Horn [28] and Bieke Zaman [29], which facilitates children's learning.

Lastly, and most importantly, we draw theoretical insights from the fields of narratology and game studies to provide theoretical guidance for the narrative and gameplay of *Hootopia*. The following key concepts help establish a balance between narration and gameplay mechanics, and we summarize that the framework of narrative in games can be divided into narrative processes and narrative goals.

Narrative Processes. Narrative processes refer to a series of levels and tasks that lead to the ultimate narrative goal. These levels and tasks combine narrative elements and describe the goal rules for players within the narrative plot, specifying what players must do in specific contexts [30]. These levels and tasks contain narrative elements such as events, players, objects, time, and space [31]. When a narrative process is activated, it stimulates a series of player actions, increasing player engagement with the story through interactions with physical objects (narrative objects), the narrative plot, and other players [4].

Narrative Goals. Narrative goals can be divided into author goals, character goals, and player goals [32]. Author goals refer to the goals set by the designer or author for the smooth development of the game. They resemble the worldview constructed by the designer for the game, reflecting the designer's desire for players to experience certain situations with commonalities but potentially presented in different ways. Character goals refer to the goals that characters in the game may have, which drive them to experience the narrative processes (levels and tasks) in the game and propel the narrative forward. Player goals refer to the goals brought by players to the game, which may not necessarily be considered or recognized by the game creators. These goals shape the final narrative that unfolds based on the game's mechanics and gameplay, enhancing the game's playability.

3   Designing *Hootopia*

Hootopia is primarily targeted at children to help them learn and understand the concept of animal conservation through gameplay. *Hootopia* features interactive physical modules with RFID identification, including tiles, animal pieces, and character cards. By providing visual, auditory, and tactile stimulation, children can move and manipulate the physical modules on the tangible map with RFID antennas while experiencing narrative storytelling, inspiring their awareness of biodiversity and species conservation, and piquing their interest in the story.

3.1   Narrative

Hootopia focuses on human management and protection of animal habitats in the real world, condensed into a fast-paced area control tabletop game. Its aim is to allow players to experience the challenges and fun of protecting animal habitats. Additionally, since the animals to-be-protected are from different regions, there is also a game element involving competition with other players, beyond the goal of protecting and restoring animal habitats.

The narrative elements of this tabletop game can be summarized as follows:

Events. First, through a rap poem, players are quickly brought into the game world of saving animals. In this game, human activities threaten the survival environment of animals. Players/agents each play the role of animal saviors from different regions, accompanying animals in a designated protection area called *Hootopia*.

Players/Agents. Each player in the game plays the role of an animal savior. Players need to compete with each other. Of course, players can also choose whether to cooperate or not, while all players/agents bear the mission of protecting animals and their habitats.

Objects/Items. There are two types of objects that players can manipulate in the game. One type is map tiles (see Fig. 1), because the space of *Hootopia* protection area is limited, players can use the map tiles they own to transform the habitat of the protection area to accompany animals. The other type is animals (see Fig. 1), which need suitable habitats, and each animal has different habitat requirements (see Table 1). Players place animals in the corresponding habitat to protect them.

Time. Players take turns to make moves, performing two actions each turn. These two actions can be exploration (flipping over a *Hootopia* card), searching (drawing a map tile card into hand), accompanying (placing an animal in the corresponding habitat of the protection area), transformation or secret transformation (pushing a map tile card into the protection area).

Space/Border. Players complete the mission of protecting animals in the limited space/border of the animal protection area *Hootopia*.

Fig. 1. Objects: Tiles, front and back (upper right)

Fig. 2. Objects: Animal pieces, sizes compared with a tile

The following Fig. 1 is the narrative process and corresponding narrative structure of this board game:

Table 1. Animals pieces and their habitats

Habitat	Animal	Size	Habitat	Animal	Size	Habitat	Animal	Size
Grassland	Hedgehog	1	Polar Region	Penguin	1	Ocean	Turtle	1
	Rhino	2		Seal	2		Jellyfish	2
	Wolf	2		Snow Fox	2		Sea Lion	2
	Giraffe	3		Snow Leoqard	3		Shark	3
	Elephant	4		Polar Bear	4		Whale	4

Table 2. Average rating of player test by group.

No.	Problem Description	Internal (3)	Children (8)	Parents (4)	Teachers (3)	Avg. (18)	Std.
1	How do you find the fun factor of *Hootopia* through gameplay?	4.3	4.5	5.0	4.7	4.6	0.68
2	Do you think the difficulty level of *Hootopia* is appropriate?	4.0	4.1	4.8	4.7	4.3	0.94
3	How do you perceive the strategic elements of *Hootopia*?	4.3	5.0	5.0	5.0	4.9	0.31
4	Can you sense the educational attributes conveyed by *Hootopia*?	3.3	4.1	4.3	4.3	4.1	0.85
5	Would you be willing to play *Hootopia* again?	3.3	4.5	5.0	4.7	4.4	0.90
6	Would you be willing to purchase *Hootopia*?	3.0	4.0	5.0	4.3	4.1	1.20
7	Would you be willing to recommend *Hootopia* to your friends?	3.7	4.4	4.8	4.7	4.4	0.89

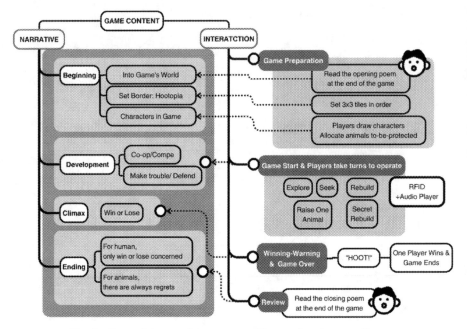

Fig. 3. *Hootopia*'s narrative process and interaction structure diagram

Before the game officially begins, the game's worldview is presented to the players in the form of a doggerel poem, which quickly immerses the players into the game world.

Human actions disturbed nature's calm,
Animals suffered, facing harm,
But fret not, as their savior you stand,
Guiding them back to their wild land!
In limited space, strategic battles engage,
Clever moves arranged, turn the page!
Explore terrains, each unique and rare,
Protect habitats with utmost care!

Then, each player needs to play as an animal protector from a different region, and their respective duties are to protect and restore the habitats of animals. Although they are all pursuing a common goal, and animal protectors do not have hero skills like in other games, the animals they need to protect come from the same regions as the protectors themselves but are different. Therefore, in a limited space, they must engage in strategic competition and gameplay.

During the game, each player can participate in the progress of the story. In each player's turn, they need to perform two actions. They can choose to be a "good person" among the available options, construct advantageous terrain for the animals of all parties in the game, let all parties benefit and co-protect Donghu. They can also choose to be a "devil" by changing the protected area, cutting off the advantageous terrain originally constructed by other players, and impeding the opponent's protection process. Of course, they can also choose to be a silent, ready-to-go "troublemaker", secretly changing the protected area while hoarding cards and handing over the responsibility of exploration and accompaniment to their opponents. Because of the uncertainty of the game, we encourage players to talk, team up, and even counterattack in the game. In the testing process, we did find that players would actively start communication during the opponent's turn, and the interactive narrative mechanism of mutual communication and participation can make players enjoy the fun of the game more.

In *Hootopia* board game, the game's emotions reach a climax when one player wins. Like other competitive games, only one player can win in each round of *Hootopia*. However, unlike other games, *Hootopia* game includes more profound elements besides the competitive aspect. In the endgame phase, players will welcome a highly cohesive summary, allowing players to return to the narrative theme of the game:

With your guidance, animals live in peace,

But human greed and competition brings some unease.

There are winners and losers in the game,

But for the unprotected, it's always the same.

Remorse comes too late for the ones left behind,

Win or lose, the lost animals we cannot find.

This poem underscores a powerful message: regardless of who emerges as the winner, there are animals that have yet to receive the protection they need in "*Hootopia*". This narrative element reinforces the underlying message of protecting animal habitats and fostering a sense of responsibility.

Additionally, it's worth emphasizing that if the zero-sum game mechanics prompt players to reflect on the rationale behind adversarial gameplay, it is indeed aligned with our intended outcome. "*Hootopia*" serves as a unique platform for players to delve into the nuances of competition versus cooperation, thereby enhancing their critical thinking skills and fostering a greater capacity for perspective-taking. This aspect contributes to the game's educational and experiential value, enriching the overall gaming experience.

3.2   Digital Interaction

Feedback holds a pivotal role in shaping the gaming experience. We are acutely aware that traditional board games often lack the immediacy of feedback that digital counterparts offer, which can potentially affect player immersion. In this board game, in order to increase players' auditory interaction, we used RFID components and integrated them into the game components of animal and land cards. In addition, each animal component also carries a small battery and a speaker, achieving specific sound effects (see Fig. 1). Our intention is to provide players with a light-weighted auditory cue to indicate correct or incorrect animal placement in the habitat. Our primary goal is to ensure that the auditory dimension enhances the gaming experience without overwhelming or diverting players' attention from the strategic gameplay. In this section, we will detail the design principles and functions of electronic interaction in the game.

We equipped RFID sensing kits in the game components of animal and land cards, and integrated a small battery and a speaker into each animal component, creating a

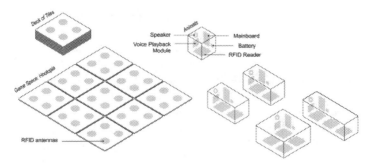

Fig. 4. Layout of the board game and electronic technology schematic diagram.

simple and intuitive interaction. When players place animals on the corresponding land cards in the protected area, the RFID sensing kit inside the animal component will communicate with the RFID antenna on the land card. Once successfully matched, the battery in the animal component will power the speaker, making it emit specific sounds. This interaction design allows players to feel the presence and interaction of animals through hearing, enhancing the immersion of the game.

In terms of sound effects, we designed two different types of sound feedback. The first type is a cheerful animal sound that is emitted when players place animals on the corresponding land cards in the protected area. This conveys the happy state of animals in a safe and harmonious environment, providing positive feedback and making players feel a sense of achievement and satisfaction. The second type is a short, mournful animal sound that is emitted when the habitat of animals in the protected area is cut off. This sound feedback is intended to remind players that the survival environment of animals is threatened, stimulating their desire to protect and their attention to the game situation. Through this sound effect, players can more intuitively perceive the impact of their decisions on animal habitats, increasing the tension and strategic nature of the game.

Overall, the electronic interaction design of the game provides players with a novel way of interaction by combining NFC technology and sound effects. By triggering specific sound effects, players can audibly perceive the presence and status changes of animals, further immersing themselves in the story context of the game, and enhancing their participation and emotional connection. This electronic interaction design enriches the game experience, enabling players to more deeply participate in the challenges and fun of animal protection, enhancing the attraction and interactivity of the game.

This electronic interaction design also has the potential for further expansion and innovation. Through continuous exploration and improvement, more types and diversities of sound effects can be added, as well as more interactive elements and emotional feedback. In addition, other electronic technologies and sensors can also be considered for application in the game to further enhance the player's immersion and interactive experience.

4   Game Testing and Player Feedback

In order to evaluate the gaming experience and playability of *Hootopia*, we conducted a series of game tests that covered all aspects and rules of the game, including internal testing and external testing.

During internal testing, our team played the game multiple times to familiarize ourselves with the rules, adjust game balance, identify potential problems, and improve and rethink the game mechanics based on real-world human activities. These tests played an important role in the initial verification and improvement of the game mechanics.

During external testing, we conducted more extensive testing with a group of real players. We recruited a group of volunteers to participate in game testing and collected their feedback and opinions. The players who participated in each game were children between the ages of 9 and 14 with their parents, as well as some early childhood education teachers aged between 20 and 30. We collected a total of 18 pieces of player feedback.

During the testing process, we collected feedback, suggestions, and observation results from the players. We focused on seven aspects of evaluation: the game's interactive fun, level of difficulty, strategy, education, willingness to play repeatedly, willingness to purchase, and willingness to recommend to friends.

Through analyzing the test results (see Table 1), we found that most players were very satisfied with the overall gaming experience and playability of the game. Players found the game's rules easy to understand, the level of difficulty suitable, and the game full of fun and challenges. In terms of education, the game also received high praise, being recognized as a good way to cultivate children's awareness and interest in the natural environment and wildlife. Additionally, players also offered valuable suggestions and opinions, such as adding new levels, props, and character roles, as well as strengthening social interaction features. We will actively adopt and integrate these suggestions and opinions in the subsequent development process to further improve the game's quality and user experience.

It cannot be denied that there were still immature aspects in the gameplay during internal testing, but through iterative testing and thorough analysis, we were able to make the gameplay both fun and educational. Beyond internal testing, our target audience consisting of children, parents, and teachers have given positive feedback on the game's entertainment value, strategy, and accessibility. Most agree that *Hootopia* does not force feed knowledge, but instead allows players to gain knowledge on animal protection and biodiversity while experiencing the fun of the game. Based on feedback and observation from game testing, we have collected the majority of player evaluations and opinions on *Hootopia*. Some typical player feedback includes: the game rules are easy to understand and even new players can quickly catch on, it has clever strategic and game-play elements which require players to think critically, the map building and animal companion mechanisms make the game highly variable and replayable, introducing advanced game-play increases depth and challenge, and the game subtly raises awareness on animal issues and allows players to empathize with different perspectives when competing with opponents. These positive evaluations reflect the strengths and appeal of *Hootopia*'s rule design, strategic elements, game mechanisms, and experience. Furthermore, we have received valuable feedback and constructive criticism for the improvement and enhancement of *Hootopia*.

5 Conclusion

Our prototype board game, *Hootopia*, presents a distinct approach to educating children about biodiversity without overwhelming them. Through the incorporation of interactive storytelling and digital enhancements, primarily utilizing RFID technology and audio cues, the game offers an immersive experience. By weaving players into a captivating narrative, *Hootopia* aims to enhance children's comprehension of biodiversity and the significance of species preservation, all while ensuring an enjoyable and entertaining learning journey. The study successfully showcases the feasibility of merging tangible gameplay with interactive storytelling. Furthermore, the research outcomes, which encompass children's engagement, interest, learning outcomes, and attitudes towards biodiversity and species protection, have the potential to guide future educational interventions. These findings emphasize the effectiveness of utilizing digital interactive storytelling to foster environmental awareness and promote conservation efforts.

References

1. UN Homepage: Climate change and biodiversity. https://www.un.org/en/climatechange/science/climate-issues/biodiversity. Accessed 23 June 2023
2. Harley, D., Chu, J.H., Kwan, J., Mazalek, A.: Towards a framework for tangible narratives. In: Proceedings of the Tenth International Conference on Tangible, Embedded, and Embodied Interaction. TEI 2016, pp. 62–69. ACM Press, Eindhoven, Netherlands (2016)
3. Echeverri, D., Wei, H.: Letters to José: a design case for building tangible interactive narratives. In: Bosser, A.-G., Millard, D.E., Hargood, C. (eds.) Interactive Storytelling. ICIDS 2020. Lecture Notes in Computer Science, vol. 12497, pp. 15–29. Springer, Cham (2020)
4. Holmquist, L.E., Helander, M., Dixon, S.: Every object tells a story: physical interfaces for digital storytelling. In: Proceedings of the NordiCHI (2000)
5. Mazalek, A., Davenport, G., Ishii, H.: Tangible viewpoints: a physical approach to multimedia stories. In: Proceedings of the tenth ACM international conference on Multimedia, pp. 153–160 (2002)
6. Mayora, O., Costa, C., Papliatseyeu, A.: ITheater Puppets Tangible Interactions for Storytelling. In: Nijholt, A., Reidsma, D., Hondorp, H. (eds.) Intelligent Technologies for Interactive Entertainment, pp. 110–118. Springer, Berlin Heidelberg, Berlin, Heidelberg (2009)
7. Rogerson, J.M., Sparrow, A.L., Gibbs, R.M.: Unpacking "Boardgames with Apps": the hybrid digital boardgame model. In: Proceedings of the 2021 CHI Conference on Human Factors in Computing Systems, pp. 1–17. ACM, Yokohama Japan (2021)
8. Harley, D., Tarun, A.P., Germinario, D., Mazalek, A.: Tangible VR: diegetic tangible objects for virtual reality narratives. In: Proceedings of the 2017 Conference on Designing Interactive Systems, pp. 1253–1263. ACM, Edinburgh United Kingdom (2017)
9. Pietroni, E., Forlani, M., Rufa, C.: Livia's villa reloaded: an example of re-use and update of a pre-existing virtual museum, following a novel approach in storytelling inside virtual reality environments. In: 2015 Digital Heritage. pp. 511–518. IEEE, Granada, Spain (2015)
10. Chu, J.H.: Designing tangible interfaces to support expression and sensemaking in interactive narratives. In: Proceedings of the Ninth International Conference on Tangible, Embedded, and Embodied Interaction, pp. 457–460. ACM, Stanford California USA (2015)
11. Soleimani, A., Green, K.E., Herro, D., Walker, I.D.: A tangible, story-construction process employing spatial, computational-thinking. In: Proceedings of the the 15th International Conference on Interaction Design and Children, pp. 157–166. ACM, Manchester United Kingdom (2016)

12. Assembly, G.: Sustainable development goals. SDGs Transform Our World, 2030 (2015)
13. Brooks, T.M., et al.: Habitat loss and extinction in the hotspots of biodiversity. Conserv. Biol. **16**, 909–923 (2002). https://doi.org/10.1046/j.1523-1739.2002.00530.x
14. Allan, J.R., et al.: The minimum land area requiring conservation attention to safeguard biodiversity (2022)
15. Barker, S., Elliott, P.: Planning a skills-based resource for biodiversity education. J. Biol. Educ. **34**, 123–127 (2000). https://doi.org/10.1080/00219266.2000.9655701
16. Hudson, S.J.: Challenges for environmental education: issues and ideas for the 21st century. Bioscience **51**, 283 (2001)
17. Hwang, G.-J., Yang, L.-H., Wang, S.-Y.: A concept map-embedded educational computer game for improving students' learning performance in natural science courses. Comput. Educ. **69**, 121–130 (2013)
18. Coroller, S., Flinois, C.: Video games as a tool for ecological learning: the case of Animal Crossing. Ecosphere **14**, e4463 (2023)
19. Brewer, C.: Conservation education partnerships in schoolyard laboratories: a call back to action. Conserv. Biol. **16**, 577–579 (2002)
20. Stonemaiergames Homepage, https://stonemaiergames.com/games/wingspan/. Accessed 12 Sep 2023
21. Geniusgames Homepage, https://www.geniusgames.org/products/ecosystem-family-card-game-animals-ecology-habitats-biodiversity. Accessed 12 Sep 2023
22. Onemomentgames Homepage, http://www.onemomentgames.com/. Accessed 12 Sep 2023
23. Robin, B.R.: Digital storytelling: a powerful technology tool for the 21st century classroom. Theory Into Pract. **47**, 220–228 (2008)
24. Horn, M.S., Jacob, R.J.K.: Designing tangible programming languages for classroom use. In: Proceedings of the 1st International Conference on Tangible and Embedded Interaction, pp. 159–162. ACM, Baton Rouge Louisiana (2007)
25. Gil, M., Sylla, C.: A close look into the storytelling process: the procedural nature of interactive digital narratives as learning opportunity. Entertainment Comput. **41**, 100466 (2022). https://doi.org/10.1016/j.entcom.2021.100466
26. Zuckerman, O., Arida, S., Resnick, M.: Extending Tangible Interfaces for Education: Digital Montessori-inspired Manipulatives (2005)
27. Ryan, M.-L.: From narrative games to playable stories: toward a poetics of interactive narrative. Storyworlds: J. Narrative Stud. **1**, 43–59 (2009)
28. Horn, M.S., Crouser, R.J., Bers, M.U.: Tangible interaction and learning: the case for a hybrid approach. Pers. Ubiquit. Comput. **16**, 379–389 (2012). https://doi.org/10.1007/s00779-011-0404-2
29. Zaman, B., Vanden Abeele, V., Markopoulos, P., et al.: Editorial: the evolving field of tangible interaction for children: the challenge of empirical validation. Pers. Ubiquit. Comput. **16**, 367–378 (2012). https://doi.org/10.1007/s00779-011-0409-x
30. Tosca, S.P.: The Quest Problem in Computer Games (2003)
31. Sullivan, A., Salter, A.: A taxonomy of narrative-centric board and card games. In: Proceedings of the 12th International Conference on the Foundations of Digital Games, pp. 1–10. ACM, Hyannis Massachusetts (2017)
32. Cardona-Rivera, R.E., Zagal, J.P., Debus, M.S.: Aligning story and gameplay through narrative goals. Entertainment Comput. **47**, 100577 (2023). https://doi.org/10.1016/j.entcom.2023.100577

Virtual Worlds, Performance, Games and Play

As If They Were Here: The Impact of Volumetric Video on Presence in Immersive Augmented Reality Storytelling

Jessica L. Bitter(✉) ⓘ, Noura Kräuter ⓘ, and Ulrike Spierling ⓘ

Hochschule RheinMain, Wiesbaden, Germany
{jessicalaura.bitter,noura.kraeuter,ulrike.spierling}@hs-rm.de

Abstract. This paper investigates the effects of volumetrically filmed 3D characters on the audience's sense of their presence in immersive interactive augmented reality (AR) narratives. After developing an interactive story with live actors and integrating the volumetrically filmed result into a HoloLens 2 application, we hypothesized that the perceived presence of these virtual characters in real space should be higher than 2D video holograms. In an AB/BA crossover design with 10 participants in each group, we compared the presence effects of the two alternatives in the designed AR play. We used the validated TPI questionnaire, observations, and post-experience interviews. Results show a rejection of the hypothesis that volumetric characters lead to better presence in general. While spatial presence was rated slightly better for 3D characters, social presence was superior for 2D videos. We discuss the results and limitations of the study and discuss lessons for future work.

Keywords: Immersive Storytelling · Volumetric Filming · Head-mounted Augmented Reality

1 Introduction

Volumetric filming involves capturing actors from multiple angles simultaneously and stitching the shots together to create three-dimensional moving shapes. Such three-dimensional vivid characters can enhance interactive narratives in immersive Augmented Reality (AR). Head-mounted displays (HMDs) such as the HoloLens 2 will allow users to move around in a real-world environment, freely choosing their viewing angle and thus experiencing virtual characters as present in the physical world.

Volumetric filming is a nascent field of research. In some early projects with characters in immersive AR storytelling, 2D videos were placed on billboards in the room [3], or 3D modeled characters were used [8]. Recent projects that applied volumetrically captured characters in Virtual Reality (VR) [11] and AR [9,15] did not focus on their use in interactive stories, but on specific aspects

L. Holloway-Attaway and J. T. Murray (Eds.): ICIDS 2023, LNCS 14383, pp. 425–441, 2023.
https://doi.org/10.1007/978-3-031-47655-6_26

like eye-gaze direction, or the combination of volumetric filming and live action. Especially studies about the effect on presence and how this factors into interactive storytelling are scarce.

In this paper, we report on our first steps towards volumetrically filmed characters and their impact on presence in interactive storytelling in immersive AR. We build on previous work in which we developed an interactive scenario with volumetric characters in immersive AR. At that time, we wanted to explore ways to produce volumetrically filmed characters within a tight university budget, as well as design and explore their interactions with users [2]. We now present an evaluation that examined how volumetrically filmed figures for immersive AR affect the presence experience and the feelings associated with immersion. To this end, we compare 2D videos - virtually placed in a physical space and viewed through a HoloLens 2 - to volumetric 3D figures, using a similar scenario that we tested in our previous work (see Fig. 1). We hypothesize that 3D characters as protagonists will lead to a stronger sense of their presence in the same space with users, leading to a more engaging immersive story experience.

In the following, after presenting related work, we describe our volumetric video AR application, our assessment design including the selection of a validated questionnaire, and the results of the data analysis. We discuss the findings with their limitations and preview future work to further explore this topic.

2   Related Work

For our work, both the state of the art for volumetric filming and its incorporation into interactive narratives for immersive AR are relevant. Some researchers directly point to the need for further research to understand the effectiveness of AR storytelling and its potential as a narrative tool [4]. With regard to volumetrically filmed content for AR, projects differ in the degree of depth dimension in the characters. Full three-dimensional characters often result from expensive setups from professional studios like Dimension [9]. While there are advances to more accessible workflows [21], many projects use 2.5D characters for their stories [2,15,22].

Koeck et al. [9] created a mixed media installation for a historic prison in Liverpool. Volumetrically captured characters work in tandem with live actors and projection mapping to create a multi-layered experience. They report on the technical difficulties of performing volumetric captures for the HoloLens, but do not discuss immersion or presence.

O'Dwyer et al. [15] created a volumetric AR character with a film capture method that generated 3D models for each frame. The experience can be alternatively played on a tablet or on a HoloLens 1. The character's movement is not responsive to user interaction. Users can walk around the character while he recounts anecdotes about Trinity's Long Room. The character is positioned into a corner which gives users access to a 270° angle around the character. In their evaluation results, O'Dwyer et al. found that some users were not using the potential to walk around and explore the character, but stayed immobile and watching the character from one place only. Zerman et al. [28] presented an evaluation study on this project to understand user perceptions and preferences concerning AR for cultural heritage, by comparing the two different employed AR platforms (tablet vs. head-mounted display (HMD)). Not surprisingly, they found that the HMD experience was judged to be more immersive than the tablet, but that museum visitors wanted the AR content to interact with them personally.

Schreer et al. [19] describe two VR experiences with volumetric captured characters. Their user evaluation focused on how users navigated the virtual scene, how they perceived the representation of volumetric characters, the nature of the representation compared to classical shapes, and their sense of immersion. In contrast to O'Dwyer et al. they described that users walked around in their scene. Subjects reported experiencing the 3D characters as natural. The results were based on a self-designed questionnaire.

Banos et al. [1] compared three immersive systems (PC monitor, rear projected video wall, and head-mounted display) and two virtual environments, one with emotional content and the other without, to investigate the interactive role of these two media characteristics (form and content). Self-assessments of presence were collected in six groups of 10 participants each. Results indicate that both immersion and affective content play a role in the sense of presence. Another project that focuses on presence and interactive storytelling in immersive AR is presented by Martínez-Cano [12]. He describes the volumetric filmmaking process, which does not span 360°, and suggests parameters that enhance the sense of presence for the user. Without providing a user evaluation, he claims that social presence is enhanced by conversational interaction supported by the character responding to user stimuli.

Sprung et al. [22] present first steps towards an authoring environment for museum curators to create volumetric immersive VR storytelling experiences without programming. They also report evaluation results on the perceived immersion and reception of volumetric video and audio of their application without disclosing a list of questions. They compared three different presentations, from flat 2D video to three-dimensional 2.5D video. Their results show a preference for the visually clearer flat videos over the three-dimensional ones. In one presentation, they added a billboard effect so that the figures automatically faced the user. 60% preferred this version.

In summary, volumetric filming for interactive narrative experiences in immersive AR is just emerging. The motivation is to create more emotionally engaging and immersive experiences than alternative methods for character creation (3D models or 2D video). The extent to which this is feasible and useful is also something we intend to explore in our work.

3   Volumetric Video in an Interactive Immersive Story

To explore immersive AR story experiences with volumetric video, we developed a short interactive narrative play as a kind of participatory theatre. After having shot our previous prototype with only one depth sensor as a 2.5D version [2], we have now filmed an extended version with four sensors to achieve full volumetric figures. The story had once been designed to meet several criteria, such as being short and minimalist for evaluations with head-mounted displays to be passed on sequentially, containing spatial (rather than conversational) interactions for the participants and thus motivating them to change position and explore the space [2].

The piece is about two neighbors on opposite sides who look out of their respective windows and pursue individual activities. One is brushing her shoe, and the other one is reading a book. Suddenly, the shoe falls down. While she is upset about this, the shoe shiner discovers the user and asks for help. The user can pick up the shoe (a virtual 3D object) and hand it back to the woman in the window (Fig. 1). In response, her neighbor becomes jealous and deliberately drops her book and turns to the user. After the user helps again, the neighbors start to argue about their jealousy, but calm down at the end of the story.

Fig. 1. Handing back the virtual shoe: interaction with volumetrically filmed virtual figures appearing in a physical cardboard window frame, captured by a second HMD.

For the 360-degree footage of our actresses, we used four Azure Kinect depth sensors along with Depthkit Studio software, which generated one mp4 file with depth information for each of the four viewing directions. This data was integrated into the Unity game engine and processed for the HoloLens 2 target platform using Depthkit plugins. Additionally, we programmed object interactions using spatial colliders that are triggered when defined distances from the user's hand to the characters are undershot. We also built a physical temporary prototype of the opposing windows out of cardboard, which is scanned by the HoloLens for accurate positioning.

The story was implemented twice for the HoloLens, once with the volumetric videos (see Fig. 1) and once with flat transparent mp4 clips, which we placed in the window frames like the 3D videos (see Fig. 2).

The two versions were then to be compared in an evaluation to determine the advantages of the high expense of volumetric filming for immersive AR storytelling. While volumetric filming as such requires a lot of effort and expensive studio facilities, we wanted to explore mobile and low-cost solutions for AR that could be used in a university setting. Indeed, the prototype captured with only four sensors still contains visible artefacts such as voids and cracks at the borderlines between the viewpoints. Nevertheless, our hypothesis was that our volumetric characters would create a higher sense of spatial presence in immersive AR stories than 2D videos.

Fig. 2. The user interacts with the same scene with 2D video clips. The left image reveals the flat video inserted in a slanted way.

4   Evaluating Immersive AR Experiences

Our aim was to gain insights into the (hopefully positive) effects of the high volumetric filming effort on the feeling of presence in our resulting immersive augmented reality experience. However, presence and immersion are concepts that are not easy to observe or grasp. Different people understand these phenomena differently, also depending on the context, or in turn find different words to express immersion-related feelings. In the context of VR, this has been researched for decades and several validated questionnaires have already been published. In their literature survey about evaluation methods for assessing presence and immersion in games with AR, Marto et al. [13] emphasize the importance of questionnaire validation and discourage the use of custom questionnaires, as participants often confuse immersion and presence. Therefore, we did not intend to develop our own questionnaire, but to reuse an existing validated questionnaire in its given form, also to test possible limitations, thus linking to established research. As a starting point for our selection, we used already existing detailed literature reviews [13,14]. We were mainly interested in questionnaires that focus on presence and/or immersion with HMD-based AR. We filtered out questionnaires that are too tailored to VR, questionnaires that focus on games and questionnaires that contain questions that seem to target older or handheld devices only.

Table 1 summarizes example questionnaires with different concepts. Presence and immersion are described using different scales and subscales that may be relevant to different research domains, such as the constructs of spatial presence, social presence, engagement, or attention. In our case, we implemented an interactive story in immersive AR, and are mainly interested in the spatial presence of the volumetric characters. Hence, we were looking for a questionnaire that captures not only spatial presence but also the social presence of virtual characters in real space, and we decided to use the multidimensional Temple Presence Inventory (TPI) introduced by Lombard et al. [10].

Lombard et al. [10] presented the Temple Presence Inventory (TPI) as a multidimensional measure of telepresence. They emphasised the importance of presence for understanding media experiences, discussed different conceptualisations of presence and stressed the need for further research in this area. The TPI questionnaire captures differences in the perception of presence depending on media form and content. Although initially not designed for AR, we assumed that it can be used to assess the extent of presence experienced with regard to the context of storytelling.

Regarding AR, another validated questionnaire was presented by Georgiou et al. [5]. Their Augmented Reality Immersion (ARI) questionnaire was developed to assess engagement, engrossment, and total immersion in AR applications. It encompasses further subscales such as interest, usability, emotional attachment, attention, presence, and flow, which makes it very comprehensive. The complexity of the psychological measurement of presence concepts in AR is also underlined by Regenbrecht et al. [17], who cite as an example that in AR presence means that virtual objects are experienced as present "in space" and in the real world, but this is different from whether they appear to be real. These are examples of how there are correlating components that are actually distinct. Also Toet et al. [23] propose a general Holistic Presence Questionnaire (HPQ) to cover more psychological processing levels that in their terms mediate the sense of presence, such as affective, cognitive, behavioural and reasoning levels.

We are aware that measuring presence in AR as such is complex and beyond our scope. We integrated filmed characters into our real environment to enhance the feeling of realism as opposed to animated 3D models. Our focus is now on analyzing how the high cost of volumetric filming pays off. Our hypothesis is that a greater sense of presence with the characters in the same space can be achieved compared to 2D videos of the same characters.

The questionnaire that appeared to offer the best balance of differentiated questions on aspects such as spatial presence and different types of social presence is TPI [10]. We therefore decided to use it and test it at the same time. The TPI tries to be platform independent, however there are some issues that restrict

Table 1. Subscales of presence and immersion in applicable questionnaires.

Questionnaires	Subscales	Rating scales
Temple Presence Inventory (TPI) [10]	Spatial presence, Social presence-actor, Passive social presence, Active social presence, Presence as engagement, Presence as social richness, Presence as social realism, and Presence as perceptual realism	7-point
AR Presence Questionnaire (ARI) [5]	Interaction and Immersion, Interference and Distraction, Audio and Tactile Experience, and Moving in Environment	7-point
Immersive Experience Questionnaire (IEQ) [7]	Basic attention, Temporal dissociation, Transportation, Challenge, Emotional involvement, and Enjoyment	5-point
MEC Spatial Presence Questionnaire (MEC-SPQ) [25]	Spatial presence, and Attention	5-point
Player Experience of Need Satisfaction (PENS) [18]	In-game autonomy, In-game competence, Presence, and Intuitiveness of controls	7-point
Immersive Tendencies Questionnaire (ITQ) [26]	Involvement/Control, Natural, Auditory, Haptic, Resolution, Interface quality	7-point
Igroup Presence Questionnaire (IPQ) [20]	Spatial presence, Involvement, and Realism	5-point

to VR or specific devices. Therefore, we also performed a meta-evaluation of the questionnaire to determine which questions are confusing or irrelevant to our use case.

5 Evaluation

5.1 Evaluation Design

To identify an effect of volumetrically filmed content on presence-related feelings, we set up two comparable virtual scenes as AR overlays in the same physical space, one with 3D and one with 2D video, and asked users about their impressions after experiencing both. Our goal was to determine differences in feelings of presence, especially social presence related to the characters.

We used a multi-method design, including the TPI questionnaire after each experience, observations and post-experience interviews. As Toet et al. [23] suggested, a multi-method approach can help when evaluating spatial presence, as one method alone may not cover all aspects. Our observation sheet captured subjects' facial expressions, basic user utterances, and their movements in the scene during the experience. Each participant experienced both versions and completed the TPI questionnaire directly after each run. The first questionnaire also included demographic questions. The final interview asked for qualitative impressions of the differences between 2D and 3D, as well as possible reasons not addressed in the questionnaire. Since the entire evaluation was carried out in the German language, we also translated the TPI questionnaire into German.

The evaluation was conducted with 20 volunteer participants, 13 of whom were female and 7 male. The age range was from 18 to 58, with most of them being students aged around 25. 9 of them had previous experience with AR and 13 with VR. We assumed that our participants would be first-time users who would need an orientation before they could fully engage with our experience [6], as the HoloLens can be challenging at first. To account for a possible habituation effect in our evaluation, we used an AB/BA crossover design with 10 participants in each group, one group of which saw the 2D experience first and then the 3D experience, and the other group vice versa. In this way, we also tried to reduce the influence of the first orientation phase on the perception of the content. When interacting with the story for the first time, attention may initially be focused on understanding what is going on, which is then already known by the second time through.

We also accounted for this effect in our analysis of the data after testing. In our second question of the analysis (see below Table 2), we specifically tested for differences between our two groups, and in the third question, we tested exclusively for the second experience to see if the habituation effect affected the sense of presence.

5.2   Results

Our data features two measuring points, a sample size of N=20 and thus no normal distribution. Therefore, we decided against ANOVA and a T-Test as a method. Instead, we computed our data with two different rank correlations. For an overview of our collected data, see Table 2.

Table 2 shows that most of the TPI subscales were rated below 4: spatial presence, parasocial interaction, and active interpersonal. There is no visible difference between 2D and 3D, i.e. in both cases the presence types are rated rather negatively. Social richness is rated slightly better than 4, and only passive interpersonal is rated around 5, which means that it was perceived as good for both 2D and 3D. Interestingly, the standard deviation is lowest for the highest rated sections. Also noteworthy is the difference between the ratings of passive interpersonal and active interpersonal. Mean scores suggest that participants found it easier to observe the characters' facial expressions, changes in tone of

Table 2. Descriptive key figures of the TPI's sections in our evaluation, using a 7-point Likert scale from 1 to 7. Significance level = 0.05. SP = Social Presence.

	Median	Mean	Standard Deviation
Spatial Presence 2D	3,8012	3,7857	1,23687
Spatial Presence 3D	3,8524	3,8571	1,18186
SP: Parasocial Interaction 2D	3,8583	3,9167	1,04612
SP: Parasocial Interaction 3D	3,5917	3,5833	1,36205
SP: Passive Interpersonal 2D	5,5375	5,7500	0,79998
SP: Passive Interpersonal 3D	5,0625	5,0000	0,94894
SP: Active Interpersonal 2D	2,5000	2,0000	1,51600
SP: Active Interpersonal 3D	2,3667	2,1667	1,35033
Engagement 2D	3,7167	3,6667	1,07074
Engagement 3D	3,5583	3,1667	1,09928
Social Richness 2D	4,7464	4,9286	0,84467
Social Richness 3D	4,5964	4,7143	0,89852

voice, body language, and clothing style than to feel addressed in a way that elicited their active response.

We used non-parametric tests to determine answers to the following questions:

- Is there a general difference between 2D and 3D concerning the different kinds of presence represented in the TPI?
- Is there a difference between the group that experienced 2D first compared to the group experiencing 3D first?
- After the habituation effect, does 3D offer more presence than 2D?

To answer the first question, we used the Wilcoxon test (see Table 3). We computed the significance for each section of the TPI, which showed that in most of the aspects of presence we evaluated, 2D and 3D do not show a significant difference. Only for the parasocial interaction (called "Social presence - Actor within medium" in the questionnaire), a significant difference ($p = 0.031$) is indicated. When comparing the computed Wilcoxon medians of 2D and 3D within the construct of parasocial interaction, there is a hint that while watching 2D, the feeling of presence is higher than while watching the 3D characters (Wilcoxon median 2D = 4.07, Wilcoxon median 3D = 3.36). In addition, we calculated the Pearson correlation coefficient with 0.48. This suggests a high effect size. That said, the Wilcoxon medians for both 2D and 3D range around 4, suggesting that the overall impression of presence in this section was not exceptional.

Secondly, we conducted a Mann-Whitney-U test to determine whether there is a difference between the groups that watched 2D first compared to the group watching 3D first. The figures in Table 4 suggest that only for spatial presence,

Table 3. Key figures of the Wilcoxon test in every section of the TPI, using a 7-point Likert scale from 1 to 7. Significance level = 0.05, Z = Standardized Test Statistics. SP = Social Presence. Significant figures are bold.

	Z	Significance p
Spatial Presence	0.766	0.444
SP: Parasocial Interaction	**-2.155**	**0.031**
SP: Passive Interpersonal	-1.556	0.120
SP: Active Interpersonal	0.806	0.420
Engagement	-0.263	0.793
Social Richness	1.048	0.294

there is a significant difference between the two groups. The calculated Mann-Whitney-U average rank indicates that watching 3D first may lead to a higher feeling of spatial presence than watching 2D first (average rank 3D = 13.75, average rank 2D = 7.25). Here we computed the Pearson correlation coefficient as well, which amounts to 0.55. This again suggests a high effect size.

Table 4. Key figures of the first Mann-Whitney-U test in every section of the TPI, using a 7-point Likert scale from 1 to 7. Significance level = 0.05, U = Mann-Whitney-U Statistics, Z = Standardized Test Statistics. SP = Social Presence. Significant figures are bold.

	U	Z	Significance p
Spatial Presence	**17.5**	**-2.458**	**0.011**
SP: Parasocial Interaction	28.5	-1.626	0.105
SP: Passive Interpersonal	45	-0.381	0.739
SP: Active Interpersonal	42	-0.611	0.579
Engagement	30	-1.515	0.143
Social Richness	48.5	-0.114	0.912

Finally, we attempted to take the habituation effect out of the equation by conducting another Mann-Whitney-U test with the second experiences only. As can be seen in Table 5, there seems to be a significant difference between 2D and 3D which shows only after the habituation phase, in spatial presence and parasocial interaction. When comparing the Mann-Whitney-U average ranks of Spatial Interaction, it hints that 3D offers a better spatial presence experience than 2D (average rank 3D = 13.25, average rank 2D = 7.75). Comparing the same for Parasocial Interaction, it seems to be true here as well. 3D outperforms 2D (average rank 3D = 13.45, average rank 2D = 7.55). The Pearson correlation coefficient here computes to 0.50 which suggests a high effect size.

Table 5. Key figures of the second Mann-Whitney-U test in every section of the TPI, using a 7-point Likert scale from 1 to 7. Significance level = 0.05, U = Mann-Whitney-U Statistics, Z = Standardized Test Statistics. SP = Social Presence. Significant figures are bold.

	U	Z	Significance p
Spatial Presence	**77.5**	**2.08**	**0.035**
SP: Parasocial Interaction	**79.5**	**2.232**	**0.023**
SP: Passive Interpersonal	61	0.839	0.436
SP: Active Interpersonal	57	0.537	0.631
Engagement	66	1.215	0.247
Social Richness	42	-0.611	0.579

In all our tests we found significance and high effect sizes. However, this only became significant once and may have been influenced by the many calculations, so the chance of significance increases. In fact, our evaluation suggests that there is a difference between 2D and 3D, but we cannot confirm this until we have a larger sample.

Additionally, when examining the average results based on individual questions, it was observed that there were obvious differences in the rating of 2D and 3D for specific questions. This could indicate that certain aspects or factors might have influenced users' perceptions and preferences between 2D and 3D character experiences. To that end, we investigated which questions were key to the different results. Table 6 shows the questions in which the participants gave 3D a higher rating than 2D. We excluded questions where the difference was 0.1 or smaller or no difference between positive and negative was queried.

Table 6. Questions where the mean score for the 3D experience is higher than for the 2D experience, using a 7-point Likert scale from 1 to 7.

Questions	3D mean	2D mean
Q17: How often did you smile in response to someone you saw/heard in the media environment?	2.95	2.7
Q18: How often did you want to or did you speak to a person you saw/heard in the media environment?	2.45	2.1
Q22: To what extent did you experience a sensation of reality?	3.4	3.2
Q25d: Please circle the number that best describes your evaluation of the media experience: Dead - Lively	5.4	5.25
Q25f: Please circle the number that best describes your evaluation of the media experience: Unemotional - Emotional	4.85	4.65
Q25g: Please circle the number that best describes your evaluation of the media experience: Remote - Immediate	4.0	3.55
Q29: How was the sound quality during the media experience?	5.1	4.85
Q31: Overall, how satisfying or enjoyable was the media experience you just had?	4.35	4.05

The differences between the ratings listed in the Table 6 are small. For questions 25f, 25g, and 31, the difference is in the middle range around 4. For questions 17, 18, and 22, the difference is in the lower range. This means that 3D, although it outperforms 2D, is still rated rather negatively. Finally, questions 25d and 29 are in the 5 range, which means that both 2D and 3D are rated rather positively, with 3D being perceived as marginally better than 2D.

During the qualitative analysis of the interviews, we found that participants had difficulty deciding whether they preferred 2D or 3D. While 13 of 20 tended toward 2D, it was also found that participants would have preferred 3D if the 3D image quality had been better. Apart from preference for one or the other, feelings of presence were difficult to describe, and sometimes subjects did not know how to express themselves. Factors indicative of a presence experience were paraphrased suggestively.

Seven participants indicated that although the figures in the 2D videos appeared flat, their spatial awareness was not disturbed because they focused primarily on their spatial orientation. "(...) the persons were vividly two-dimensional, but because I look spatially, it made less of a difference for me whether they were really three-dimensional, sticking out of the window or inside, because you were busy orienting yourself spatially anyway and thus had a certain three-dimensionality anyway (...)." For one participant, the characters' posture affected spatial presence in the 3D presentation. Therefore, they found the 2D representation to be more realistic and as if they were really addressing them, "(...) because it was not quite so abstract due to the posture and because we saw each other. So, the conversation was just on-face."

Three participants assumed that their standing position affected their spatial presence in both 2D and 3D. When asked in which experience they felt more like they were in a room together with the characters, they preferred the 2D experience. "2D (was better), because 3D as I said was a bit pixelated and you couldn't see it so well (...); so the first time (2D) she spoke directly to me, I think that was also because I was standing differently. But she just looked me straight in the eye and then I was like, okay she's talking directly to me. And the second time (3D) she just talked past me and then I was like, okay, maybe I should have stood differently. But the first time was a little better."

Another participant expressed the idea that having a marked sweet spot in the room would have been helpful, allowing them to establish eye contact easily with the characters. "I was told I was allowed to move freely in the room and then I stood here and there, but in my opinion, their gaze out of the window was not directed at my glasses, at me, but, I'd say, perhaps at a right angle away from the window. In this respect, perhaps a marked sweet spot in the room would have been appropriate, so that I could really establish eye contact at any time."

They also stated that the sound was helpful for spatial orientation and was key to following the characters' interaction. "I thought the sound was good, so you could locate it. I would call it 3D audio. It was like that, I looked at one window and heard the person from the other window still talking."

The habituation effect was also confirmed in the interviews. For example, it was reported being sensitized by the questionnaire, which carried over to the second experience. "(...) because in the first case I was still too new to the situation, and in the second (...) I consciously paid attention to the appearance of the characters (...) because I had already done the questionnaire and knew what I should pay attention to (...), so of course I was a bit more sensitized, to put it that way."

6 Discussion

6.1 Outcome

The quantitative and qualitative evaluation results presented lead to the rejection of the hypothesis that the volumetrically filmed figures in our example are superior to the inserted 2D video clips in achieving presence-related feelings. The 3D representation did not clearly lead to a higher experience of presence than the 2D inclusion.

Some slight differences could be found as effects. Our quantitative analysis suggests that users seemed to have a higher feeling of spatial presence when watching 3D first. Conversely, our first analytic test showed that when not paying attention to the order of the experiences, 2D seemed to evoke a higher sense of social presence concerning the subscale of parasocial interaction. In addition, feelings of spatial presence and social presence concerning parasocial interaction appeared to be higher overall after the habituation effect. Since we tested for differences between 2D and 3D and between the first and second experience separately, our results should be read as suggestions that need to be confirmed with a bigger sample size. It is also noteworthy that differences in only two of the six tested sections of the TPI became significant in all of our tests. We therefore present our results as initial indications of where influences of different representations on presence and immersion may occur and point to future work in which we plan to continue our research.

Comparing the TPI result with our qualitative analysis (see Sect. 5.2), participants had difficulty deciding which of the two experiences they preferred. 2D was mentioned in terms of visual clarity and familiarity, whereas 3D was perceived as novel and intriguing, but visually unclear: "It was with 2D, so even if they are of course flat, but you're just somehow I think also a bit accustomed by a TV, when you watch TV there it's the same and so got used to it, but maybe that the image was better." Sprung et al. [22] presented similar results. In their study, participants also preferred the visually clearer flat videos inserted in VR over the more spatial 2.5D version with artefacts. We therefore conclude for future work that volumetrically filmed characters must have fewer visual artifacts to add value to an AR story.

The interviews revealed that eye contact was better with the 2D characters. We assume that this is due to traditional filming, where actors look directly at the camera, giving the impression that they are looking at the viewer. A similar effect is difficult to achieve with characters filmed in 3D, as it would require user tracking and calculated responses to viewer's positions.

The observation forms, supported by the interview results, also showed the tendency of participants to remain fixed in a particular location during what should be a spatially variable AR scene. In the interviews, a few indicated that they sometimes felt they were standing in the wrong place and would have liked some indication of where the best viewing position was. This is similar to findings reported by O'Dwyer et al. [15]. We reminded participants during testing that they could move around, but this does not seem to have been sufficient. This suggests that the specific AR story did not contain inherent requirements that would have led to intrinsic motivation to look around more and change location. Increased position changes might have exposed the 2D videos as irritatingly flat.

6.2   Limitations

We deliberately used an existing validated questionnaire on presence, in our case the TPI [10], even though we knew that it was not specifically designed for HMD-based AR. Therefore, at the end of the second questionnaire, we also added questions to get feedback on items that subjects found confusing or irrelevant. The idea behind this was to also meta-evaluate the evaluation method and possibly suggest ways to improve it. The result showed that there were a number of inappropriate questions, e.g. Q10 "How much did it seem as if you and the people you saw/heard both left the places where you were and went to a new place?" was rated as irrelevant. However, we assume that this also depends on the story plot, as this question might be relevant for a different narrative AR setting after all. We suspect that using a specific story can always be seen as a confounding factor, making it difficult to create a unified questionnaire to measure presence and immersion in interactive AR experiences with stories.

Despite the widespread use and recognition of the TPI questionnaire as a valuable presence assessment tool, critical reviews have already been conducted to discover limitations and make potential refinements for the field of AR presence research. Regenbrecht et al. [17] recognized the value of the TPI and presented a modified version tailored to AR environments. Their adaptation demonstrates the adaptability and utility of the TPI questionnaire in different technological contexts. Other researchers such as Yan et al. [27] and Pianzola [16] have underscored the importance of the TPI questionnaire as one of the most widely used presence measurement tools.

Closely related to the composition of the constructs and items, however, is the aspect that each question also depends on the language used. As described, we translated the entire set of questions into German. We cannot exclude that there might have been small differences between the German meaning and the original. Also in our interviews it was difficult for the laypersons to express themselves and to find words to explain their impressions regarding presence and immersion. Above all, immersion is an English term as a metaphor that did not exist in its direct translation into German colloquial language before the introduction of Virtual Reality technology. The dependence on the language used was also highlighted by Vasconcelos-Raposo et al. [24], who translated the TPI into Portuguese and re-validated it to satisfy the equivalent semantics as well as the validity of its concepts. Future work must aim to test the questions in the particular language used.

Finally, the crossover design of the present study would have benefited from a higher number of participants. Without doubt, however, conducting the evaluation with single HMD-based presentation slots, including setup, individual introduction, cleaning, and observation team, was tedious and time-consuming. For future evaluation results, it would nevertheless be beneficial to reduce the habituation effect by inserting an orientation sequence before the actual content to be evaluated.

7   Conclusion

We described an experiment in which volumetric filmed actors were used as characters in an interactive narrative play in immersive augmented reality, which was experienced via a head-mounted display. Mainly, we then focused on evaluating the resulting AR piece by comparing it to a control version where 2D video clips were inserted instead of the volumetric 3D characters. The hypothesis to be investigated was whether the volumetric footage resulted in a higher sense of presence than the 2D videos. We rejected our hypothesis, although there were significant effects in that spatial presence was slightly better with the 3D version, however social presence (parasocial interaction) was rated better with the 2D video version.

We conclude that the simplicity of 2D videos improves clarity and comprehension, while the complexity of 3D visualizations can be cognitively challenging. Our results contribute to existing knowledge about the different effects of 3D volumetric video on the sense of presence in AR narratives. The findings can inform the design and development of immersive AR narratives to create visual representations that meet the needs and preferences of developers and users.

The quantitative analysis indicates that the habituation effect of first-time-users may have had a stronger influence on presence than the difference between the 2D and 3D representations of the characters. Furthermore, our data hinted that the 3D representation outperformed the 2D representation of the characters in terms of spatial presence and parasocial interaction when considering only the second experience in our evaluation.

Our results with the crossover design are limited by the number of participants. For future work, we suggest not only increasing the number of subjects, but also filming the characters with more depth sensors to improve visual quality. In addition, we could first have subjects evaluate the impact of characters detached from the storyline and then compare this to impressions in the context of a story. This could help understand how much a particular interactive narrative affects user experience and presence in immersive AR.

Acknowledgment. We would like to thank Lorena Müller and Leonie Ferdinand, who supported us as actresses during the volumetric shooting. The research on presence has been supported by the LoGaCulture project, funded (in part) by the European Commission under grant agreement LoGaCulture (101094036).

References

1. Baños, R.M., Botella, C., Alcañiz, M., Liaño, V., Guerrero, B., Rey, B.: Immersion and emotion: their impact on the sense of presence. Cyberpsychol. Behav. **7**(6), 734–741 (2004)
2. Bitter, J.L., Senk, G., Spierling, U.: Effects of volumetric video capture on interactive storytelling in immersive augmented reality: a short film experiment. In: 2023 the 7th International Conference on Virtual and Augmented Reality Simulations (ICVARS), March 03–05, 2023, Sydney, Australia, p. 7 pages. ACM, New York (2023). https://doi.org/10.1145/3603421.3603428
3. Bitter, J.L., Spierling, U.: Towards mobile holographic storytelling at historic sites. In: Brooks, E., Sjöberg, J., Møller, A.K. (eds.) Design, Learning, and Innovation, pp. 119–128. Springer, Cham (2022). https://doi.org/10.1007/978-3-031-06675-7_9
4. Calvi, L.: What do we know about ar storytelling? In: Proceedings of the 6th EAI International Conference on Smart Objects and Technologies for Social Good, pp. 278–280 (2020)
5. Georgiou, Y., Kyza, E.A.: The development and validation of the ARI questionnaire: an instrument for measuring immersion in location-based augmented reality settings. Int. J. Hum Comput Stud. **98**, 24–37 (2017)
6. Gödde, M., Gabler, F., Siegmund, D., Braun, A.: Cinematic narration in VR – rethinking film conventions for 360 degrees. In: Chen, J.Y.C., Fragomeni, G. (eds.) VAMR 2018. LNCS, vol. 10910, pp. 184–201. Springer, Cham (2018). https://doi.org/10.1007/978-3-319-91584-5_15
7. Jennett, C., et al.: Measuring and defining the experience of immersion in games. Int. J. Hum. Comput. Stud. **66**(9), 641–661 (2008)
8. Jin, Y., Ma, M., Zhu, Y.: A comparison of natural user interface and graphical user interface for narrative in HMD-based augmented reality. Multimed. Tools Appl. **81**(4), 5795–5826 (2022)
9. Koeck, R.: St George's hall: If these walls could talk (2018)
10. Lombard, M., Ditton, T.B., Weinstein, L.: Measuring presence: the temple presence inventory. In: Proceedings of the 12th Annual International Workshop on Presence, pp. 1–15 (2009)
11. MacQuarrie, A., Steed, A.: Perception of volumetric characters' eye-gaze direction in head-mounted displays. In: 2019 IEEE Conference on Virtual Reality and 3D User Interfaces (VR), pp. 645–654 (2019). https://doi.org/10.1109/VR.2019.8797852
12. Martínez-Cano, J.: Volumetric filmmaking, new mediums and formats for digital audiovisual storytelling. AVANCA| CINEMA, pp. 606–614 (2020)
13. Marto, A., Gonçalves, A.: Augmented reality games and presence: a systematic review. J. Imaging **8**(4), 91 (2022)
14. Moinnereau, M.A., de Oliveira Jr, A.A., Falk, T.H.: Immersive media experience: a survey of existing methods and tools for human influential factors assessment. Quality User Exp. **7**(1), 5 (2022)
15. O'dwyer, N., Zerman, E., Young, G.W., Smolic, A., Dunne, S., Shenton, H.: Volumetric video in augmented reality applications for museological narratives: a user

study for the long room in the library of trinity college dublin. J. Comput. Cult. Herit. **14**(2), May 2021. https://doi.org/10.1145/3425400

16. Pianzola, F.: Presence, flow, and narrative absorption questionnaires: a scoping review. Open Res. Europe **1**(11), 11 (2021)

17. Regenbrecht, H., Schubert, T.: Measuring presence in augmented reality environments: design and a first test of a questionnaire. arXiv preprint arXiv:2103.02831 (2021)

18. Ryan, R.M., Rigby, C.S., Przybylski, A.: The motivational pull of video games: a self-determination theory approach. Motiv. Emot. **30**, 344–360 (2006)

19. Schreer, O., et al.: Preserving memories of contemporary witnesses using volumetric video. i-com **21**(1), 71–82 (2022). https://doi.org/10.1515/icom-2022-0015

20. Schubert, T., Friedmann, F., Regenbrecht, H.: The experience of presence: factor analytic insights. Presence: Teleoperators Virtual Environ. **10**(3), 266–281 (2001)

21. Smolic, A., et al.: Volumetric video content creation for immersive xr experiences (2022)

22. Sprung, G., Egger, A., Nischelwitzer, A.K., Strohmaier, R., Schadenbauer, S.: Virest-storytelling with volumetric videos. In: FMT, pp. 54–59 (2018)

23. Toet, A., Mioch, T., Gunkel, S.N., Niamut, O., van Erp, J.B.: Assessment of presence in augmented and mixed reality: Presence in augmented and mixed reality. In: Conference on Human Factors in Computing Systems, CHI 2021. ACM SigCHI (2021)

24. Vasconcelos-Raposo, J., Bessa, M., Teixeira, C.M., Cabral, L., Melo, M.: Adaptation and validation of the temple presence inventory in a Portuguese population. Int. J. Hum.-Comput. Inter. **35**(6), 441–447 (2019)

25. Vorderer, P., et al.: MEC spatial presence questionnaire **18**(2015), 6 (2004)

26. Witmer, B.G., Singer, M.J.: Measuring presence in virtual environments: a presence questionnaire. Presence **7**(3), 225–240 (1998)

27. Yan, B., Ni, S., Wang, X., Liu, J., Zhang, Q., Peng, K.: Using virtual reality to validate the Chinese version of the independent television commission-sense of presence inventory. SAGE Open **10**(2), 2158244020922878 (2020). https://doi.org/10.1177/2158244020922878

28. Zerman, E., O'Dwyer, N., Young, G.W., Smolic, A.: A case study on the use of volumetric video in augmented reality for cultural heritage. In: Proceedings of the 11th Nordic Conference on Human-Computer Interaction: Shaping Experiences, Shaping Society, pp. 1–5 (2020)

Traversing Space in *The Under Presents* (2019), a VR Game

Kath Dooley(✉) ⓘ

The University of South Australia, Adelaide 5000, Australia
Kath.Dooley@unisa.edu.au

Abstract. This paper reports upon a preliminary investigation of narrative structures embedded within *The Under Presents* (2019), a pioneering VR game produced by independent Los Angeles-based studio, Tender Claws. The narrative experience of the game involves a blend of open-world exploration and quest-based experiences that actively encourage the player's bodily engagement in story creation. With reference to Ryan's notions of emotional and strategic space in digital narratives (2015a), I explore the player's manipulation of space in the game world as an embodied activity that generates narrative, mediated through the VR headset and hand controllers. The malleability of space emerges not only as a central theme within the project but also profoundly influences how players interact with the story world. Further to identifying overlapping emotional or strategic spaces within the game world, I propose the notion of 'corporeal space' to address the constituting role of the player's body in the 360-degree VR environment and in the generation of story. Considering this interplay between space, story and the body, I propose that *The Under Presents* serves as a valuable resource for exploring the potential of narrative experiences within the realm of VR gaming.

Keywords: Virtual Reality · Narrative · Space · Embodiment

1 Introduction

In recent years, virtual reality (VR) technologies have been adopted by the gaming industry to create highly immersive gameplay experiences (Monteiro et al., 2018). The development of the Oculus Rift headset in the early to mid 2010s gave rise to a wave of renewed excitement and investment in VR entertainment, leading to the creation of a range of VR experiences. More recently, the advent of standalone VR head mounted display (HMD) units such as the Meta Quest 2 and HTC Vive Focus has eliminated the requirement for a high-end PC to enjoy VR gaming, resulting in a broader accessibility for players. Popular examples of games that have been developed by major game studios or independent developers include those offering original content (for example *Beat Saber* [Beat Games 2019] or *Job Simulator* [Owlchemy Labs 2016]) or VR reworkings of existing game worlds (for example, *Half-Life: Alyx* [Valve 2020] or *The Elder Scrolls V: Skyrim VR* [Bethesda Game Studio, 2017]). Key to these gaming experiences is the creation of a sense of presence for players- of being 'inside' the 360-degree virtual world of a game- which is fostered by both creative approaches and the technological affordances of VR.

© The Author(s), under exclusive license to Springer Nature Switzerland AG 2023
L. Holloway-Attaway and J. T. Murray (Eds.): ICIDS 2023, LNCS 14383, pp. 442–453, 2023.
https://doi.org/10.1007/978-3-031-47655-6_27

While considerable scholarship has explored narrative structures within games (see for example Aarseth 2001, 2012; Ryan 2009), and narrative theories for virtual reality (Aylett and Louchart 2003; Murray 1997), there is a dearth of literature presenting an analysis of the narrative elements, and the narrative experience, of these contemporary VR games. With this in mind, this paper presents a preliminary investigation of *The Under Presents* (Tender Claws 2019), an innovative VR game that includes both single player and multiplayer game worlds. Offering an array of interactive devices, as well as immersive theater elements, *The Under Presents* transports players to a vaudeville stage that is buried in the sands of a vast desert and asks them to uncover the mystery of a ship and its inhabitants who were stranded in an earlier time. This paper's investigation of narrative elements focuses on space within the VR game, referencing established theories of game narratives, as well as my first-hand experience as a player, to interrogate the way that the player's body is implicated in an experience that unfolds across multiple temporal frames and virtual spaces. The analysis below is drawn from many hours of repeated play of the game, which has involved collaboration with other players and liaison with live-actor non-player characters (NPCs).

After presenting an initial analysis of narrative structures in *The Under Presents*, I consider the interplay between space and embodied experience in VR games more generally, using *The Under Presents* to illustrate how spatial constructs might be manifested. Drawing upon Ryan's examination of the emotional and strategic spaces in digital narratives (2015a), I then argue for the concept of 'corporeal space' in the VR game, this referring to space that is manipulated by, and experienced through, a virtual body positioned at the center of a story world. Consequently, I suggest that *The Under Presents* serves as a valuable resource for understanding the possibilities of narrative experiences in VR gaming.

2 Narrative Structures in *The Under Presents*

The Under Presents offers a rich assortment of narrative elements and structures being a fusion of a quest and puzzle game, and a computer-generated performance space. It was developed by Tender Claws, an independent studio based in Los Angeles, in collaboration with the live performance troupe, Piehole. The game begins with a captivating introductory experience, available as a free download, which lasts for approximately 20 min. This immerses players in a dark, animated wasteland where they must don gold bracelets and a mask before venturing towards a dilapidated nightclub emitting faint strains of music. Guided by the MC, an enigmatic entity sporting a black tuxedo and a misshapen golden mask, players enter the building and traverse rooms teeming with doors and clocks, eventually reaching the coveted 'Main Stage' of the game. This initial segment serves as an onboarding experience, unfolding with minimal direct instruction. As part of this onboarding, players must acclimate themselves to the game's unique method of locomotion that is called the 'Scrunch Teleport,' which entails physically reaching out and pulling space forward.

Within the multiplayer area, the player finds a nightclub venue (The Under), in which a variety of vaudeville stage shows, from musical acts to life coaching, appear on rotation. As shown in Fig. 1, masked players gather here to immerse themselves in the atmosphere, to learn to cast spells, and uncover the world's secrets. Some spells require collaborative efforts among players and can lead to the restoration of ruins in the desert, obtaining new masks, or enhanced mobility for players. Beyond the nightclub, a vast desert stretches out, hosting various structures waiting to be explored. Communication among players is limited as they cannot speak; instead, they rely on hand gestures, movements, or the clicking of their fingers to interact. However, for limited periods of time since the game's release, the multiplayer area has offered an additional drawcard: live actors portraying non-player characters (NPCs) who engage players in improvised performances (see Fig. 2). By interacting with these NPCs and collaborating with fellow players, one can unlock the full potential of the game world.

Fig. 1. Two players congregate in front of the main stage in The Under. (Screen shot taken from a video capture of game play by the author.)

Fig. 2. Players on The Under's dance floor with a live actor NPC. (Screen shot taken from a video capture of game play by the author.)

Some of these NPCs also make appearances in the single-player experience known as 'The Time Boat,' which lies at the core of *The Under Presents*. This scripted narrative revolves around The Aickman, a research vessel that embarks on a mission to recover radiation samples following a nuclear incident in 1958. However, before reaching its intended destination, the ship becomes trapped in ice and sustains damage, leading to the demise of the crew and passengers under various circumstances. The ruins of the ship are buried in the Main Stage area and provide the infrastructure for the night club. By entering photo booths located in the multiplayer arena, players can transport themselves onto the Aickman and experience the narrative as it unfolds across three acts and an epilogue. Within these scenes, players inhabit the ship alongside characters as events gradually take place. Alternatively, they can remove their masks, granting them a god-like perspective of the ship and its occupants. From this vantage point, players can manipulate time by running their finger across their mask, rewinding or fast-forwarding events, allowing for a comprehensive review of the story's progression. While the events aboard the Aickman may seem predetermined, players have the opportunity to intervene at crucial moments during the three acts, leading to the salvation of certain characters from their impending fates.

The Under Presents thus offers a combination of linear (back) story, improvised 'live' moments, and an open-world narrative. The former, as constituted by the Time Boat experience, aligns with Ryan's description of a 'narrative game' thus representing a 'ludus activity' where pre-existing rules lead to states of winning or losing (i.e.: saving characters from death or not saving them) within a narratised world (2009 p. 46).[1] Similarly, according to Aarseth's analysis of narrative events within a game world (2012), this part of the experience is typical of a multipath or quest game, seeing as it features a series of 'dynamic kernels' (p. 132), these being a series of occurrences that are essential to the story, which make it recognisable, and which cannot be replaced or removed without altering the essence of the tale.[2] In this instance, while the player has some ability to influence the outcome of the Time Boat narrative by performing actions at specific points in time, the overall narrative reflects high levels of authorial control.

By contrast, the multiplayer area offers what both Ryan and Aarseth might describe as 'playable story'. For Ryan, this type of game experience involves a narrative that is produced through the action of playing the game, meaning that 'the player's actions are subordinated to narrative meaning' (2009, p. 45). This narrative experience moves away from notions of 'winning' or 'losing' in favour of inducing an aesthetic appreciation of a game world that the player can explore at their leisure. In the context of The Under, one could, for example, find enjoyment by simply observing performances in the night club. In this context narrative is less a chain of predetermined events than it is an experience conjured by the player as they explore the environment and engage with other players or NPCs. For Aarseth, a playable story involves narrative events that can be considered 'dynamic satellites', these being occurrences that can be omitted without altering the core essence of the story (2012, p. 132). One example of the many 'dynamic satellites' in *The Under Presents'* multiplayer area is the rebuilding of an observatory space in the desert surrounding the main stage of The Under. Two or more players working together in this space can restore the building and its contents, obtaining a star mask as reward. However, this activity is not mandatory and presents just one narrative thread that can be followed. Such collaboration with other players results in revelations about the nature of the story world, allowing a narrative to form over time. The intermittent presence of live actors as speaking NPCs in the multiplayer arena also allows for a deeper understanding of the story world while also fostering a sense of intimacy and connection for players

---

[1] Ryan proposes the concepts of 'narrative games' and 'playable stories' to explore the interplay between narrativity and player agency within an interactive digital narrative (2009). She suggests that a narrative game involves 'narrative meaning [...] subordinated to the player's actions' (p. 45). This means that narrative aspects enhance gameplay but are not generated through game play. Ryan cites *Half-Life*, *Max Payne* and *Grand Theft Auto* as examples of a narrative game. She suggests that by contrast, a playable story has less focus on achieving goals and involves exploration of an environment (p. 46). As such, a narrative is generated through the player's experience.

[2] In his 2012 paper titled 'A narrative theory of games' Aarseth presents an analysis of four narrative elements: places (worlds), things (objects), characters (agents), and events, noting how these structures reflect the narrative and ludic emphasis of a game.

who might be directly addressed or engaged in improvisation. In sum, through the immersive Time Boat experience and by engaging in multiplayer exploration, players gain a comprehension of *The Under Presents'* universe as an otherworldly and eternal realm constructed from the remnants of the Aickman. The surreal and liminal multiplayer space transcends conventional notions of time, offering a journey of discovery.

3   Space and Embodied Experience

The distinctive properties of space in video or computer games have been explored by several scholars in recent decades (for example, Aarseth 2001; Jenkins 2004; Nitsche 2008; Ryan 2015a, 2015b; Wolf 2002). Aarseth observes that 'what distinguishes the cultural genre of computer games from others such as novels and movies, in addition to its obvious cybernetic differences, is its preoccupation with space' (2001, p. 161), while for Ryan, video game space 'can be experienced both strategically and emotionally' (2015a, p. 114). On a related note, Nitsche notes the close interconnection of space and narrative in video games, stating that 'narrative elements help to make space meaningful and space helps to situate these elements' (2008, p. 45). Writing on 3D video games, this latter scholar suggests that 'plot' is generated by the player's experience and comprehension of events in space (p. 51), which resonates considering *The Under Presents'* multiplayer experience. Nitsche discusses how virtual game worlds might generate a sense of presence for the player but doesn't fully account for the contemporary head mounted display (HMD) as interface. Unlike a traditional video game, which positions the player in front of a screen, the VR game places their physical body at the virtual centre of a game experience via the HMD, therefore encouraging them to physically turn around, touch and explore a 360-degree landscape. The player might be given a virtual body in the form of an avatar, this fostering what Kilteni et al. describe as a 'body ownership illusion' (2015). Such an illusion can occur when the fake body is presented in an 'anatomical plausible configuration and in presence of congruent visuotactile or visuomotor stimulation' (Kilteni et al. 2015, p. 9). Untethered HMDs such as the Meta Quest 2 offer what Saker and Frith describe as 'coextensive space', which involves an incorporation of 'concrete reality' through emerging design features (2021, p. 1429). In other words, the player's 'real' space and body aligns with the virtual world and virtual body that is presented in the game. For the remainder of this paper, I will explore how the player's movements through and in space foster narrative experience in the world of *The Under Presents*, noting the manipulation of space as an embodied activity. I look to Ryan's notions of 'emotional space' and 'strategic space' as a framework through which to further this investigation.

In her exploration of digital narratives, Ryan proposes two distinct conceptions of space. According to her analysis, the first one, known as emotional space, refers to environments associated with affective reactions. She suggests that 'these reactions can be either positive, such as a sense of belonging, of security, of being home, or negative, such as repulsion, fear, or a sense of being lost' (2015a, p. 106). Ryan proposes that this particular space is most effectively understood when approached from a horizontal perspective, aligning with the ordinary human perception of the world. From this viewpoint, it 'comes closest to the lived, embodied experience that produces emotions' (p. 106).

Consequently, emotional space serves as a realm that stimulates the imagination and encompasses stories and memories that are experienced by the interactor.

While emotional space 'constructs the self as a relation to its environment', strategic space, as described by Ryan, 'constructs the self as possibilities of action' (p. 107) and thus revolves around achieving objectives and solving problems. In light of this, she suggests that strategic space is best depicted in a map view, employing a vertical projection that ensures no object obscures another. This clear visibility of object relationships is crucial for effective strategic planning (p. 107). Ryan illustrates this type of space using squares on a chessboard, which serve as pathways for player actions but hold 'no intrinsic emotional value for the player' (p. 107).

Regarding video games as a form of digital narrative, Ryan proposes that space can be encountered in both strategic and emotional dimensions, involving a dynamic interplay between quest-driven pursuits and the exploration of a world (p. 114). In her discussion of emotional space within open-world games specifically, she draws upon the concept of flânerie, as explored by the French poet Charles Baudelaire. This notion captures the experience of 'free wandering' within the game world, encompassing both serendipitous encounters and movement for the sake of aesthetic appreciation. Ryan highlights that in the design of such worlds, players are not obligated to undertake all the tasks assigned by non-player characters (NPCs) (p. 114). Instead, game space can serve as a platform for social interaction with other players or simply as a captivating landscape to explore. Consequently, open-world games can foster a spirit of flânerie while also offering strategic space to traverse in the pursuit of quests.

This transition between leisurely exploration and quest-driven pursuits resonates with my personal experience of space within *The Under Presents*, indicating a fluid interplay and overlapping of emotional and strategic spaces within the game. As a player, I have dedicated a significant amount of time to simply relishing the atmosphere of the Main Stage or wandering in the desert. The latter has not always been motivated by the need to fulfill specific quests, but rather by a curiosity to gain a deeper understanding of the boundaries and essence of the game's narrative world. Within the realm of the Main Stage and its surrounding desert area, my interactions with other players have held a social component. Although verbal communication has been absent, I have engaged with fellow players through gestures like waving, catching their attention by clicking my fingers, exchanging objects, and even following their lead in terms of exploration (see Fig. 3). In essence, my means of communication, devoid of speech, has relied upon movement and expressive gestures produced by my physical and virtual body in space.

For example, during one of my initial visits to The Under's nightclub, I encountered several players engaging in playful and improvised combat with swords and various tools on the dance floor while a preprogramed performance unfolded on the adjacent stage. Joining in the spirit of this interaction, I removed my mask, held it before me, and attempted to cast magic spells by manipulating objects atop it. This action resulted in the generation of new items, such as onions and other consumables. The experience carried on for a while, during which time I explored the nightclub environment and tested my abilities within that space. When one player departed, I felt a sense of curiosity and followed, eager to discover their intended destination. Outside, in the desert, that player pointed to a piece of paper lying on the ground, which contained a spell formula: an

Fig. 3. A fellow player waves at me in the game's 'Gift Shop' space. (Screen shot taken from a video capture of game play by the author.)

invitation to embark on a quest. After taking note of the formula's details, I wandered back to the nightclub, motivated by the prospect of witnessing another performance.

Even within the most structured narrative sequence of the game (the Time Boat experience), the player is granted the opportunity to engage in flânerie. As a black cloaked avatar, the player can freely explore the ship at their own pace, eavesdropping on conversations among different characters to gain a sense of the unfolding events. This entails traversing the various decks, living quarters, and operational spaces of the Aickman using staircases and portals. When the ship becomes trapped in ice, the player can follow NPCs who venture onto the ice fields. It is not immediately apparent that the player possesses the ability to intervene in the narrative transpiring within this space, and one can progress through the acts purely as an observer. However, as mentioned above, the player has the capability to obtain a god-like perspective of the events unfolding on the Aickman by removing their mask. By doing so, they find themselves positioned in front of a miniature representation of the ship, where they can observe miniature versions of the various characters in the space, including their own static, miniature form holding the mask. While this perspective does not equate to a traditional 'map view' of the scene, it aligns more closely with the vertical projection that Ryan associates with strategic game space. This vantage point, along with the player's ability to scroll through time while occupying it, grants them the ability to isolate specific moments where intervention may yield significant consequences.

As noted above, the player's traversal through space in *The Under Presents* is enabled by the 'scrunch teleport' mechanic. This unique feature entails the player extending their hand and physically drawing space towards themselves, effectively pulling it towards their own body. By embodying this mechanic, players can swiftly navigate through the virtual landscape, actively involving their physical presence in spatial exploration. Samantha Gorman, co-director of the project, explains that this locomotion method is intricately connected to the narrative's time loops and 'tears in space'. She further elucidates on the mechanism's significance, illustrating how it serves as a tangible representation of the game's central themes:

> We landed on a system where the player could reach out and pull the middle portion of the world towards them: as if reality was a spandex cloth you were tugging on. Then when the player lets go, the tugged part stays fixed and the rest of the world snaps toward you. On a technical level, this means that there is always a fixed anchor point in the player's field of vision. Only half of the world moves at once, first the inner field-of-view, and then the outer, so the player remains grounded.

Gorman quoted in Damiani 2019

As this description evidences, the player's engagement with the virtual environment, facilitated by hand controllers and head tracking within the HMD fosters a tangible connection between their 'real-life' body and the manipulation of virtual space. This interaction creates a strong sense of presence within the virtual realm. By utilizing these devices and technologies, the player assumes a pivotal role, acting as the central axis around which the 360-degree game world revolves. The 'scrunch' mechanic employed in this experience doesn't just allow movement through space; rather, it involves the player actively reshaping the space itself. I would suggest that the specificity of this embodied process necessitates a novel understanding of the properties of space in the VR game. While Ryan's concept of emotional space encompasses affective reactions, I would argue that it fails to adequately capture the overtly physical experience of simulated VR space. To capture this, I propose the term 'corporeal space' to describe the space perceived by the player wearing the HMD, who has bodily presence within a 360-degree virtual environment. Although this space may possess emotional or strategic attributes within the context of the game, it primarily constitutes a space that the player, situated at the story world's centre, physically conjures and manipulates through their bodily movements and actions. In the case of *The Under Presents*, this manipulation and exploration of space is driven by the physical movement of the player's body- their head that turns, their outstretched arms and their manoeuvring hands.

Central to this notion of corporeal space in *The Under Presents* is the parallel experience of the player as a physical body in 'real-life' and as a virtual avatar conjuring and experiencing space in 3D, interactive VR. This differs from a non-VR game where, as Ash observes, 'all interactions with the space of the image are foreclosed through the necessary limitations of the control pad' (2009, p. 2116). Rather, in *The Under Presents* the

VR interface gives the conjuring of space over to the player's physical body as controller. Implicated in this phenomenon is Saker and Firth's aforementioned notion of 'coextensive space', which describes 'a symbiotic relationship between physical and digital that is increasingly proximate, extensive and transformative '(p. 1429). This notion suggests that the game spaces mediated through VR technology might simulate an illusion of physicality that approximates the materiality of real space.

There is a long history of non-VR games that incorporate physical bodily movement and experience into their game play including, for example, arcade racing games that place the player behind a steering wheel, the Nintendo Wii (explored by Anderson [2017]), and *Guitar Hero* (explored by Juul [2010]). While it is beyond the scope of this paper to discuss how these games draw upon the player's body as 'the center of the locus of control' (Anderson, p. 24), one can note that the VR game takes this into different territory in the way that the VR hardware facilitates the illusion of the player's body at the centre of an enclosed diegetic world. In the case of *The Under Presents*, as the player 'scrunches' the space around them, the VR hardware tracks their physical movements and changes what they see.

Applied to VR games more generally, this notion of corporeal space foregrounds the role of the player's bodily experience in the generation of narrative as key to storytelling with VR. This standpoint accords with Grodal's suggestion that video games and some forms of VR are 'the supreme media for the full simulation of our basic first-person "story" experience because they allow "the full experiential flow" by linking perceptions, cognitions, and emotions with first-person actions' (2013, p. 133). This line of thought considers video games and interactive VR as simulations of real-life experiences, which involve motor-interaction and encounter in space. Within such simulations, Grodal suggests that the 'motor cortex and muscles focus the audio-visual attention, and provide "muscular" reality and immersion to the perceptions' (p. 133). On a similar note, I would suggest that the specificity of a HMD wearing game player's experience of VR game space sees perceptions, cognitions, and emotions drawn from bodily experience, as is demonstrated through my analysis of *The Under Presents*. Thus, further to positioning the player as the axis around which the story world revolves, the VR game offers interactive devices that foreground the player's corporeality in terms of how they experience and contribute to unfolding narrative threads.

4 Conclusion

Within this paper, I have examined the narrative structures embedded within *The Under Presents*, observing a blend of open-world exploration and quest-based experiences. Moreover, I have argued that the player's manipulation of space in *The Under Presents* is a VR-specific, embodied activity that is mediated through the HMD and hand controllers. The malleability of space emerges not only as a central theme within the project but also profoundly influences how players interact with the story world. Whether it involves utilizing the scrunch mechanic to draw space towards themselves or transitioning between single-player and multiplayer realms, the player's bodily engagement with space shapes their narrative experience.

Further to identifying overlapping emotional or strategic spaces within the game world, I have proposed the term 'corporeal space' to address this constituting role of the player's body in the 360-degree VR environment and in the generation of story. This concept extends existing theories of game space by recognising the specific user experience that is fostered by a HMD, hand controllers and related VR technology. Such an experience involves a narrative journey that is literally controlled by the hands of the player and results from their physical manipulation of spatial components.

This paper's exploration of VR game narratives is limited to a single case study; however, I believe that there is much to be learned here about the potential of VR to create powerful emotional and embodied narrative experiences. Further research might explore the interplay between body, space and story in other contemporary VR games with reference to a broader sample set so as to shed more light on the narrative experiences offered by this immersive medium and further validate the proposed notion of 'corporeal space'.

References

1. Aarseth, E.: Allegories of space: the question of spatiality in computer games. In: Koskimaa, R. (ed.) Cybertext Yearbook 2000. University of Jyväskylä, Jyväskylä, Finland (2001)
2. Aarseth, E.: A narrative theory of games. In Proceedings of the International Conference on the Foundations of Digital Games, pp. 129–133, May 2012
3. Anderson, S.L.: The corporeal turn: at the intersection of rhetoric, bodies, and video games. Rev. Commun. 17(1), 18–36 (2017)
4. Ash, J.: Emerging spatialities of the screen: video games and the reconfiguration of spatial awareness. Environ Plan A 41(9), 2105–2124 (2009)
5. Aylett, R., Louchart, S.: Towards a narrative theory of virtual reality. Virtual Reality 7(1), 2–9 (2003)
6. *Beat Saber*: Designers. Ján Ilavský, Vladimír Hrinčár, Peter Hrinčár. Beat Games, Czech Republic (2019)
7. Damiani, J.: 'The Under Presents' Is A Novel Exploration Of VR And Live Immersive Theatre. Forbes (2019). https://www.forbes.com/sites/jessedamiani/2019/11/19/the-under-presents-is-a-novel-exploration-of-vr-and-live-immersive-theatre/?sh=7dfaa8d87455
8. Grodal, T.: Stories for eye, ear, and muscles: video games, media, and embodied experiences. In: Wolf, M.J.P., Perron, B. (eds.) The video game theory reader, pp. 129–155 Routledge, London (2013)
9. *Half-Life: Alyx* : Designer. Chris Remo. Valve, Washington (2020)
10. Job Simulator.: Owlchemy Labs, Austin, Texas (2019)
11. Juul, J.: A Casual Revolution: Reinventing Video Games and Their Players. MIT Press, Cambridge, Massachusetts (2010)
12. Kilteni, K., Maselli, A., Kording, K.P., Slater, M.: Over my fake body: body ownership illusions for studying the multisensory basis of own-body perception. Front. Hum. Neurosci. 9, 141 (2015). https://doi.org/10.3389/fnhum.2015.00141
13. Monteiro, D., Liang, H.N., Xu, W., Brucker, M., Nanjappan, V., Yue, Y.: Evaluating enjoyment, presence, and emulator sickness in VR games based on first-and third-person viewing perspectives. Comput. Animation Virtual Worlds 29(3–4), e1830 (2018)
14. Murray, J.: Hamlet on the Holodeck: The Future of Narrative in Cyberspace. The Free Press, New York (1997)
15. Nitsche, M.: Video Game Spaces: Image, Play, and Structure in 3D Worlds. MIT Press, Cambridge, Massachusetts (2008)
16. Ryan, M.L.: From narrative games to playable stories: toward a poetics of interactive narrative. StoryWorlds: J. Narrative Stud. 1, 43–59 (2009)

17. Ryan, M.L.: Emotional and strategic conceptions of space in digital narratives. In: Koenitz, H., Ferri, G., Haahr, M., Sezen, D., Sezen, T.I. (Eds.) Interactive Digital Narrative, pp. 106–120. Routledge, New York (2015a)
18. Ryan, M.L.: Narrative as Virtual Reality 2. Johns Hopkins University Press, Baltimore (2015)
19. Saker, M., Frith, J.: Coextensive space: virtual reality and the developing relationship between the body, the digital and physical space. Media, Culture Soc. **42**(7–8), 1427–1442 (2020)
20. *The Elder Scrolls V: Skyrim VR* .: Bethesda Game Studio,Rockville, Mayland (2017)
21. *The Under Presents*.: Dirs. Danny Cannizzaro **&** Samantha Gorman. Tender Claws, Los Angeles (2019)
22. Wolf, M.J.: The Medium of the Video Game. University of Texas Press, Austin (2002)

"It's About What We Take with Us and What We Leave Behind": Investigating the Transformative Potential of Pervasive Games with Various Stakeholders

Adam Jerrett[(✉)] [iD]

University of Portsmouth, Portsmouth, UK
adam.jerrett@port.ac.uk

Abstract. This study investigates the experiences of various stakeholders in *What We Take With Us (WWTWU)*, a wellbeing-focused pervasive game comprised of an alternate reality game (ARG), a room-based game, and game-based workshops. Utilising narrative inquiry, the research explores the perspectives of the game's designer, developer, ARG players, room players, and workshop participants, offering a holistic understanding of a multifaceted game. These narratives highlight unique player experiences including the duality of being both player and creator, how games can catalyse lifechanging decisions, the importance of communities to wellbeing, the benefits of physical play spaces, and questions surrounding the nature of games. Findings align with existing pervasive game design principles, emphasising their ability to generate emergent narratives and benefits, their transformative potential, and their effective community utilisation. However, the findings also underscore challenges faced by creators, such as the need to accommodate diverse player types within such communities, difficulties navigating preconceived notions of game experiences, as well as the need for further research into notions of "space and place" in games. Although insightful, the study's limited sample size and specific geographical context may impact the generalisability of its findings. Future research into *WWTWU* and pervasive games more generally could therefore benefit from diverse sample sizes and deployment in a myriad of broad cultural contexts. Finally, the study underscores that, in the end, games' success relies on the individual experiences of all their stakeholders, what they take with them, and what they leave behind.

Keywords: pervasive games · narrative inquiry · wellbeing · transformative play · emergence

1 Introduction

Pervasive games are unique in their ability to traverse and transform the boundaries, barriers, and borders of the medium. Pervasive games toy with the "magic circle", the distinct space where a game's rules and reality supersede our own, by playing with its borders and expanding it spatially, temporally, or socially into stakeholders' lived realities

L. Holloway-Attaway and J. T. Murray (Eds.): ICIDS 2023, LNCS 14383, pp. 454–471, 2023.
https://doi.org/10.1007/978-3-031-47655-6_28

[32, 33]. This format allows games like alternate reality games (ARGs), escape rooms, and live-action roleplaying games (larps) to tell new kinds of stories. Through emergent narratives – players' individual stories of their experiences [41] – the genre showcases transformative potential through their playful approach to real-world challenges [45].

This study examines *What We Take With Us (WWTWU)* [21], a wellbeing-focused pervasive game comprised of an ARG, a room-based game, and game-based workshops. The research provides a comprehensive view of this multifaceted game by exploring not only the players' experiences across the three formats but also the experiences of the game's designer (and researcher) and developer (and actor). It therefore covers many stakeholders within the game's lifecycle [22]. Examining these five stakeholder perspectives (designer, developer, ARG player, room player and workshop participant), this study highlights the diverse experiences offered by pervasive games. By transforming the boundaries of its magic circle, *WWTWU* sometimes profoundly affected the lives of its stakeholders, emphasising the potential of pervasive games as more than mere entertainment, but as powerful tools for personal progress.

2   Background

2.1   Serious Pervasive Games

"Serious games" are designed with the primary aim to educate, inform, and train players [31]. Initially, such games favoured education over entertainment, and were often bland [11]. The "theory of fun" instead proposes that "fun" in games comes from the learning process inherent in systemic mastery [24].

Merging education with entertainment, "serious" pervasive games apply gameplay to real-world problems within a fictional context to influence behavioural change [25, 26]. Serious ARG, *World Without Oil (WWO)* [16] tasked players with envisioning the repercussions of a global oil crisis. The game epitomised serious pervasive games' transformative potential with its lasting impact, with players longitudinally reporting increased knowledge and changed behaviour [57]. Nordic larps, a subset of live-action roleplaying games, take cues from interactive theatre and drama to often address controversial themes [47]. *Just a Little Lovin'*, for example, is set during the onset of the 1980's AIDS crisis in the USA. It facilitates player engagement with complex themes like death and sexual desire, leading to moments of intense personal reflection for many players [51].

Recent technological advancements have spurred digital pervasive games that diverge from the genre's analogue roots. *Zombies, Run!* turns a jog into a mission to outrun zombie hordes [43], while *Pokémon, Go!* leverages augmented reality technology to encourage players to explore their surroundings and capture virtual Pokémon [36]. Finally, *SuperBetter* utilises gameful mechanics to help players achieve personal health goals through simple behaviour change like drinking a glass of water to defeat the "liquid calories" boss [26].

2.2   Emergent Narratives in Pervasive Play

Game narratives typically fall into two categories: embedded and emergent narratives [41]. While embedded narratives consist of fixed story elements, emergent narratives evolve based on players' interactions with game mechanics [1]. In pervasive games, emergent narratives play a crucial role as reality is integrated into the game, leading to personal and dynamic narrative experiences. Players "do things for real" [34].

ARGs showcase how player behaviours can actively shape the embedded narrative, creating a "puppet master problem" for designers [27]. Within pervasive games, designers must account for the potentiality that players can do anything, which may change the game's designed narrative. During *Go Game,* players literally obliged when prompted to "drop your pants and dance". The phrase was merely meant to signal the start of play. In such games, players' personal journeys often become more significant than the designed narrative, particularly in larps, which are often not about what *happened*, but rather what was *felt* [13].

Pervasive play's inherent unpredictability can also lead to unexpected, emergent benefits. While *SFZero* was not advertised as "serious", its players become more outgoing, creative, and wise by embracing the game's ambiguous design, which tasked players to perform arbitrary tasks like finding some "Things You Can Run Through" [14]. Similarly, players of *The Beast*, an entertainment-focused promotional ARG for the film *Artificial Intelligence*, adopted a playful attitude in attempting to "solve" the mystery of 9/11 [28]. The emergent narratives, and benefit, of pervasive play can fundamentally transform players by providing them with "golden moments" that keep them returning to the genre [4].

2.3   Transformative Play

Transformative play fundamentally alters a game's contextual experience. These changes can apply to the structure of the game itself, how or where it's played, or even shifts in players' thinking or changes to their real-world contexts [41]. Within games, transformative play can be encouraged within four contexts: conformant, explorative, creative, and transgressive play [2]. A related but different form of transformative play, derived from theatre, may also occur as a result of acting and roleplay experiences [49].

Such transformational experiences are increasingly advocated for, with design pillars for transformative digital game experiences being mapped to existential psychotherapy principles, myth and ritual, and the creation of experiential games that "seek to be felt rather than read" [37]. Many of these techniques are already implemented in serious pervasive games, such as the use of ritual, briefing and debriefing, and a focus on dynamics over systems [20].

"Bleed", a key component of transformation in pervasive games refers to the blurring of boundaries between players and characters during roleplay. Aspects of the game can "bleed out" and affect the player, or real thoughts and feelings can "bleed in" and affect the roleplaying experience [46]. Despite potential undesirable outcomes and challenges in managing bleed during gameplay, "playing for bleed" is gaining popularity among players [8, 50]. Intense in-game events can trigger bleed, provoke strong emotional responses, and thus challenge players' preconceived values to catalyse transformative experiences [45]. "Transformative bleed" [5] can therefore allow players to, through their characters, explore personal dilemmas and encourage personal growth [44]. This mirrors the "disorienting dilemma" of transformative learning theories which instigates self-reflection, reassessment of assumptions, and development of new actions based on the reintegration of new knowledge [30].

Bleed can also extend to other pervasive game types, as seen in the player experiences in *World Without Oil* and *The Beast* [28, 57]. By requiring players to perform tasks as themselves in reality, rather than through a digital avatar or roleplayed character, pervasive games can allow bleed to be a potent force for change [20]. When players play *Kind Words* and comfort other players, they are not merely simulating compassion – they are manifesting it, transforming themselves, the game, and the world around them in the process [19].

3   What We Take With Us Overview

WWTWU is a multifaceted game emphasizing "wellbeing" through values-centred design. It is split into three parts: a physical room-based game, an online Discord-based ARG, and a website, each enriching the overall story. This section outlines the game mechanics, describes the narrative, and explains its structure. Lastly, its deployment as a pervasive game is briefly discussed.

3.1   Mechanics

WWTWU, initially conceptualised as an empathy-based escape room, deviated from traditional mechanics by eschewing timers and locked doors, only keeping the genre's fixed location and its narrative framing [35]. The game mechanics were thus concerned with what players would be doing in the room: a series of 11 tasks presented to a single player. These tasks were inspired by wellbeing practices, and included organizing a workspace, acknowledging their feelings, creating art, dancing, telling stories, and engaging in self-talk, among others. The game's tasks were presented on a website [21] (Fig. 1) that evolved through design to be playable anywhere. This allowed for both remote play (which was the impetus for the creation of the ARG), as well as planned location-based play.

In both the ARG and room-based game, players utilise a Discord server where the creator of the server, game protagonist Ana Kirlitz, regularly shares 'past playthroughs' of the game that document her experiences from 2020 to 2023. Room players play *WWTWU* in Ana's abandoned office in Portsmouth, UK, where they can additionally discover epistolary artefacts she has left behind.

3.2   Narrative

WWTWU tells the story of Ana Kirlitz, who relocates to Portsmouth in early 2020 after a breakup (Fig. 2). The new environment allows her career and wellbeing to thrive, aided by her play of the standalone *WWTWU* tasks. However, local lockdowns in the wake of the COVID-19 pandemic plunge her back into depression, which she continues to struggle with throughout the pandemic. In late 2021, her mother dies after contracting COVID-19, leading Ana to return to her childhood home to handle family matters and mourn her loss, abandoning her Portsmouth office (Fig. 3).

Fig. 1. The *WWTWU* game website that showcases the game's tasks.

Fig. 2. Ana Kirlitz, *WWTWU*'s protagonist.

While home, Ana continues playing *WWTWU*, charting her experiences on a private Discord server she uses as a journal. Later, she makes the Discord public, hoping to use the community's game interactions in her PhD research. The ARG begins as players join the server through her invitation. Players learn about Ana's life during the pandemic and accompany her on a journey of personal growth by completing and discussing their tasks on the server (Fig. 4).

Fig. 3. Ana's abandoned office, where the room-based game is played.

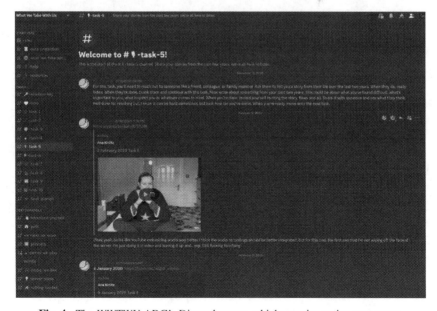

Fig. 4. The *WWTWU* ARG's Discord server, which remains active post-game.

3.3 Game Structure

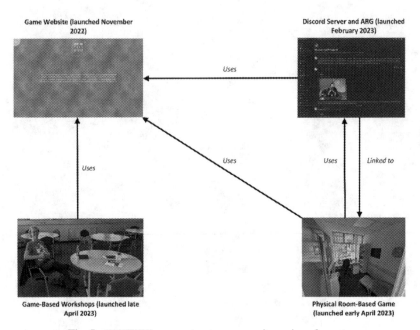

Fig. 5. *WWTWU's* game structure across its various formats.

WWTWU comprises three components: a game website, a Discord-based ARG, and a physical room game. Both the ARG and room game highlight Ana's story. However, as the website focused on *WWTWU's* mechanics, it allowed for standalone workshops. This allowed data to be gathered beyond Ana's narrative while also offering additional research opportunities. Figure 5 illustrates the connections between these components.

3.4 Deployment

WWTWU's game website was launched in November 2022, but was not active until the launch of the ARG in February 2023. During the ARG's run, only a handful of its 50 + players engaged regularly. However, the addition of two new active players towards the game's conclusion highlighted its potential as a wellbeing and community-building tool. The ARG concluded in May 2023.

The room-based game was advertised to potential participants outside the ARG community midway through the ARG's run in early April 2023, and concluded shortly before the ARG in May. As the room was advertised after the ARG had begun, some players (such as Oscar, discussed later) were aware of the ability to participate in either format. The room allowed players to reflect on Ana's narrative while also facilitating players' own wellbeing reflection. Notably, room players were often hesitant to share reflections on the Discord server, despite it being a central component within the room.

Lastly, from April to June 2023, game-based workshops targeted academic environments (e.g., universities, conferences) for additional data collection. Participants in these workshops, like room players, often chose private communication with the researcher over group sharing.

4   Research Methodology

The research focused on understanding the individual experiences of various stakeholders participating in *WWTWU*. Narrative inquiry was chosen as the research methodology due to its emphasis on understanding experience through storytelling. This data is used to understand individual and collective meaning-making processes [12]. Ethnography was considered, due to its prevalence in similar game studies contexts [3, 7], but discarded due to its focus on communal interactions, which contrasted against *WWTWU*'s solitary, introspective player experience. Narrative inquiry instead allowed for a holistic understanding of player experience across stakeholder levels, which resulted in the following research question:

– What are the play experiences of various stakeholders (i.e., designer, developer, players) when playing a serious pervasive game in differing contexts (i.e., an online ARG, room-based game, and game-based workshops)?

Player narratives were constructed using the survey research method, employing questionnaires and interviews as research instruments for each game format [38]. The use of open-ended questions and a semi-structured interview schedule provided richer, nuanced data for analysis [39]. 18 interviews were conducted, covering each stakeholder group: one designer, one developer, six ARG players, seven room participants, and six participants of three game-based workshops. It is important to note that the interviewed designer is also the researcher, who was self-interviewed [23]. The self-interview used the same interview schedule as other participants to standardise data collection across stakeholders.

The study aimed to reach roughly 1000 individuals via Discord, email, and Reddit, hoping to recruit 30–45 players. This is similar to the 2–3% conversion rate typical of ARGs [29]. Ultimately, 28 participated: 26 players across different formats and 2 designer/developers. Of 18 interviewees, most were unfamiliar with their chosen game format, barring the designer, one ARG player (a former ARG designer) and one room player (who played escape rooms). Workshop participants, in particular, lauded WWTWU as a unique wellbeing approach not previously experienced.

One narrative is presented per stakeholder group (designer, developer, ARG player, room player, workshop participant) to showcase a characteristic play experience. The selected player narratives come from participants with no pre-existing knowledge about the game or researcher, ensuring unbiased perspectives. One primary theme per stakeholder group was identified using reflexive thematic analysis [6] and explored in the Discussion section. Additional interviewee experiences are discussed within these themes to highlight its presence across the entire dataset. All participants in the research, including the designer, are referred to by pseudonyms for anonymity.

5   Results

5.1   Designer: Alex

Alex, a 31-year-old white British male, was the sole designer of *WWTWU*. Despite his dual role as creator and player, he found himself deeply immersed in the game's systems and narrative when playing its different formats. While *WWTWU* began as a coping mechanism for pandemic-induced distress, it inadvertently became a therapeutic journey for Alex, despite his reservations about therapy.

Though buoyed by stories shared during the ARG, he was often disappointed by the game's low participation, given his personal connection to it. He nevertheless took pride in creating spaces for people to share their personal experiences. The physical spaces where he played the game also influenced his experience, his new house offering a sense of peace and lightness he hadn't experienced elsewhere.

Music played a significant role in Alex's experience. He was amazed at how engaging with music in the game rekindled his passion for creating and listening to music outside of it – an interest he thought lost. Additionally, the theme of family within the game resonated with him after a familial visit reminded him of the value he placed on such relationships.

The COVID-19 pandemic also had a significant impact on Alex's life and his game experience. *WWTWU* helped him process his pandemic-related emotions, proving to be transformative, albeit challenging. Interacting with the character of Ana, who felt like a separate entity despite being his creation, allowed him to confront emotions he might have otherwise evaded. The emotional impact of the game on other aspects of his life, however, remained to be seen.

One of his most significant takeaways was that personal games, despite their inherent intimacy, should never be made alone. Collaborating with Emily, the actor who physically portrayed Ana, provided much-needed support throughout his experience – one that was incredibly hard but ultimately cathartic. Finally, Alex notes that game development and play are "about what we take with us and what we leave behind". Lessons can always be learned from games, but it's difficult to anticipate what these may be beforehand.

5.2   Developer: Emily

Emily, a 30-year-old white British female and professional actor, was intrigued by *WWTWU* for its focus on mental health and the COVID-19 pandemic's impact. Her involvement in the game, portraying the character Ana, classifies her as a developer within this research.

Emily's play experiences mostly occurred during development, where she immersed herself in the game and its tasks to deeply understand Ana. She experienced multiple emergent benefits, such as adopting new coping strategies like keeping a diary to process her emotions and experiences where she wrote to her past and future selves. This method of self-reflection was revolutionary for her, given her self-reported potential presence on the autism spectrum and previous struggles understanding her feelings. Ana's resilience also affected Emma's own personal habits, leading to her keeping a more organised environment during her performance of the role. Exploring Ana allowed Emily to understand different facets of her personality, emotions, and gain new perspectives on her life.

Her connection to Ana was so profound it resulted in notable transformative experiences during play. Reflecting on Ana's relationship with her father, Emily was inspired to reflect on her own relationship with her beloved deceased grandfather. Memories of her grandfather teaching her practical skills inspired Emily to get her plastering qualifications and start her own business by *WWTWU*'s conclusion.

The game prompted Emily to introspect about her mental health, personal growth, and emotional wellbeing. She discovered her resilience and the ability to evolve in challenging situations. Despite development's often consuming nature, Emily managed to balance her real-life commitments and her dedication to the project, learning valuable lessons about perseverance and the human spirit. This is summarised by her key takeaway from the game: "No matter how much shit you throw at the fan, it will always clear itself – the shit won't stick". Through work and play, *WWTWU* provided Emily insights that significantly affected her which will continue to shape her personal development in the future.

5.3   ARG Player: Chris

Chris, a 19-year-old white South African male computer programmer, discovered the *WWTWU* ARG through a recommendation from an unrelated Discord server. His interest in self-improvement and mental health drew him into the game, despite his late arrival.

Chris viewed the game as therapeutic, engaging mainly with the initial tasks that helped him understand and express his emotions – something he'd always struggled with. His cyclical play experience often involved completing the first four tasks before restarting – a pattern that satisfactorily soothed him. He found tasks involving voicing feelings and giving self-advice particularly beneficial.

Chris's workplace environment, where he played, precluded him from openly doing some tasks. Instead, Chris compensated by heavily engaging with the game's community, often sharing personal details about his life, such as his sexual orientation. He was notably active in the hobbies channel, arranging to obtain craft project materials from another member and regularly posting *Wordle* [52] scores on the server's dedicated thread. These experiences stood out as memorable for him.

Chris also regularly engaged with other players' posts about their emotions. Witnessing other members going through their journeys had a comforting effect, reinforcing that he was not alone. He also frequently interacted with Ana, who he believed to be a Though his late arrival meant limited exposure to her story, he found the revelation that the game was part of an ARG both shocking and exciting.

Chris felt the game would be more challenging without the Discord server. It eased any potential pressure of "bothering" someone when tasks prompted players to reach out to others. The server provided an already receptive audience for such sharing. Chris's key takeaway from the game was "things get better, and there will always be people to support you". The game and its community had a positive influence on him, highlighting the power of games in providing supportive spaces for emotional engagement, personal growth, and community connection.

5.4   Room Player: Oscar

Oscar, a 25-year-old white British male, was intrigued to partake in the room-based game thanks to a fellow student's (Ana's) endorsement. As a Masters student studying games, he appreciates narratives beyond typical gaming norms and aspires to translate such novel experiences into his own games. Upon entering the room, Oscar felt a sense of pleasantness, admiring the neat organisation (aside from an intentionally placed disarray of pens), variety of books, and ambient aesthetics. The environment's calmness, with its minimalistic decor and the comforting presence of plants, he noted, felt conducive to the game's tasks. Oscar was aware of these tasks, having previously lurked on the Discord server, but the room gave Oscar the chance to approach them linearly, which he preferred.

As he played, music was a pivotal part of Oscar's experience. As an ardent music lover, the act of choosing a song and simply listening to it through high-quality headphones was therapeutic. He immersed himself in the experience, culminating in a later game task, where he removed his shoes and sat cross-legged in the provided lounge chair, fully grounding himself within the game.

Oscar's interactions on the Discord server, however, were reserved, despite his admiration for Ana's vulnerability. He found the shared experiences valuable but acknowledged that some, like himself, may simply not be comfortable sharing. Instead, Oscar engaged with the tasks directly within the room. Immersed, he found himself talking aloud, which provided a new perspective and prevented him from falling into negative thought spirals. The story recital task, in which players narrate a story from their past two years, was particularly memorable, as it gave him the freedom to express himself without time constraints.

The reflection the game encouraged, he notes, had a positive effect on his mood. However, while the experience provided perspective, it didn't fundamentally change his mindset. He saw the value of the game in identifying areas to work on, but this didn't spur him into action – this he saw as the purview of therapy.

Finally, Oscar was surprised to learn of Ana's status as a game character, sparking discussion about the distinctions between game and reality in pervasive play. In doing so, *WWTWU* redefined "what defines a game" – Oscar's key takeaway.

5.5   Workshop Participant: Sally

Sally, a 57-year-old white British female, brought a unique perspective to *WWTWU*'s online workshops, fuelled by her deep involvement in early childhood education and wellbeing in both her PhD and role as a university lecturer. Despite joining the workshop to support young children and "the challenges these tiny humans face", she embarked on a personal journey thanks to the game's structure and introspective tasks.

The game's integration of music and introspection was impactful for Sally, leading her to explore personal matters. She started with upbeat songs but was drawn to a Carole King song that resonated with her. Listening to this song "with new ears" in this new context revealed layers of meaning she hadn't noticed before. The workshop provided her time to reflect, helping her realise her propensity for privacy regarding personal matters and highlighting her resilience in dealing with personal disruptions over the past two years. Her privacy concerns were again highlighted in her hesitance initially sharing her workshop experience due to the presence of another unengaged participant, only openly reflecting when engaged privately.

Interestingly, Sally did not perceive *WWTWU* as a game. She had a different concept of what constitutes a game – interactive experiences she would typically observe, rather than participate in. This affected her sharing practice, opting to share on a workshop specific Padlet, rather than Discord. Instead, *WWTWU* felt more like a therapeutic process – a toolset for self-exploration and understanding – due to the presence of activities like free writing and recording. In this regard, she appreciated the freedom the workshop provided. The task involving recording a video message to herself was most memorable – an unfamiliar but thought-provoking activity that led her to consider other areas of her life more deeply.

Sally's key takeaway emphasized the importance of openness to new experiences. Despite her initial scepticism about online gaming and its mental health impact, she recognised *WWTWU*'s potential to provide a sense of community and safety for those struggling with offline interactions. While not entirely within her comfort zone, her experience with *WWTWU* was enlightening and enjoyable.

6   Discussion

To highlight the findings from each individual player experience across the game's various stakeholder levels, a notable theme from each reflexive thematic analysis (conducted on each narrative account) is now presented.

6.1   Designer: Pervasive Games' Emergent Properties

A particular emergent property of Alex's experience with *WWTWU*, given his proximity to the game experience, was his disappointment at the game's engagement level across its three formats. His own play was nevertheless abundant with emergent benefits, corroborating previous findings on pervasive play [14]. His renewed appreciation for music, reinforced understanding of family values, the joy found in his physical play spaces, and the solace he found in his partnership with Emily were all unexpected yet delightful. This sentiment was echoed by other participants, with many highlighting unexpected takeaways. Room players Selma and Jack found joy in playing with stationery and drawing pictures, and ARG player Joe relished the ability to reconnect with old friends while playing.

However, not all emergent properties are beneficial: disengaged room player Zay took "nothing" from his experience – bored throughout – reinforcing the concept that games offer "different fun for different folks" [24]. During briefing, Zay expressed a macabre perspective on the purpose of his life ("my higher purpose is to die"), rooted in religious beliefs. This unexpected response may have affected his play experience negatively. Creators should therefore consider building adaptability into their pervasive game designs that can be altered for different player types to best prepare for a range of emergent player outcomes.

6.2   Developer: Games as Transformation Catalysts

Emily, despite being an actor and developer on the project, played the game repeatedly while embodying Ana, leading to numerous personal transformations. These transformations initially manifested in Emily keeping a personal diary to explore her emotions, which subsequently led to further understanding of her suspected neurodivergence. Most significantly, however, Emily's reflections on her grandfather inspired her to rediscover forgotten practical skills, start her own business, and potentially make a significant career change. Occurring through both roleplay and systemic gameplay, this powerful outcome is consistent with theatrical and game-based understandings of transformative play as well as transformative bleed [2, 5, 41, 49]. Alex, too, experienced profound transformations through play relating to his understanding of the COVID-19 pandemic. Design, deployment, and play of *WWTWU* ultimately helped him overcome pandemic-related fears and start 'returning to normal' in a post-pandemic world.

Some players, like Santiago and Xander, experienced subtler transformations. Santiago used the game's emotional explorations to address fears around emotionally manipulative behaviour. He also introspected on his nationality as a component of his identity which allowed him to embrace these elements and share various game tasks in his native language of Spanish. Xander, in turn, inspired by the ambiance of the game's room setting, decided to create a similar peaceful workspace for himself at home.

To expect all players to undergo profound transformations like Emily or Alex is perhaps unrealistic. While games, pervasive or otherwise, have immense transformative potential, designing for subtle transformative experiences may be a more attainable, yet still highly valuable, goal.

6.3   ARG Player: Community Support Can Transform Solitary Experiences

Chris' *WWTWU* experience was shaped by his participation with the game's Discord-based ARG community. Chris quickly integrated himself in the community, despite joining the game late. He made friends, comforted others, and shared in their triumphs and struggles. Interacting with the community transformed Chris' gameplay experience, allowing him to shape his experience by focusing on community rather than the game's systems or narrative. Were it not for his communal focus, he believed the game would be a lonely experience at odds with the wellbeing it hoped to inspire.

This sentiment was shared by other ARG players who also noted the significant role of the Discord server during play. Diamond mentioned "realising how you feel takes a community", while Shaun expressed excitement over a potential server-wide *Dungeons & Dragons* campaign – a popular topic among players. Shaquille appreciated how one is never alone with their feelings, noting there would always be people willing to help. Such reflections highlight the importance of community when confronting difficult emotions, aligning with *WWTWU*'s design, which drew inspiration from group therapy contexts [54]. As such, community fundamentally transformed many players' experiences with *WWTWU*'s mechanical and narrative contexts.

However, it is notable that many non-ARG players rarely engaged with *WWTWU*'s community, despite often identifying its theoretical value. This may be due to the introversion many players self-reported, which may predispose them towards solitary emotional experiences [9, 55]. Room players Oscar, Ezra, Jack, and Zay, alongside workshop participant Sally mentioned reluctance sharing emotional experiences and difficulties even outside of a game context. Such responses illustrate a potential tension for serious pervasive game experiences: while community is a fundamental aspect of the genre [15, 18], potential players may struggle to fully engage in such experiences due to their individual personality traits. Creators should therefore consider aligning their game communities with the personalities of their expected target audience, potentially with a greater emphasis on psychographics.

6.4 Room Player: The Transforming Role of the Fundamental Physical Spaces in Pervasive Play Experiences

Oscar's interaction with the room-based game greatly influenced him. He quickly noted the intentional design of the room's layout and correctly surmised that any disarray was part of the game. The room provided Oscar with a clearly demarcated space and structure for gameplay, reinforcing the concept of the "magic circle" [32]. Throughout play, physical elements of the game environment – high-quality headphones, the presence of plants, and the room's minimalistic decor – facilitated Oscar's full immersion into the experience. A similar calming experience was evident with many room players. Xander noted a feeling of profound peace, while Ezra appreciated the room's quietness which minimised distractions.

Non-room players also reported that their physical spaces influenced gameplay. Alex noted that his gameplay varied depending on the different environments he played in. In the ARG, Chris felt restricted by playing in his office environment, while Joe desired a solitary physical space to truly engage with their emotions. Workshop participants Jane, Harry, and Anthony's physical spaces also affected their play. Jane's communal workspace took a long time to tidy as part of the game's tasks, making her feel accomplished but exhausted. Harry reflected on university-related topics, given his workshop's academic location. Finally, Anthony had a confronting experience during his workshop, where the messiness of his workspace cast an overwhelming shadow over the rest of his gameplay.

Interestingly, some room players reacted to playing a game located in Ana's abandoned office. Ezra and Jack were wary about being in "someone else's space," refraining from making many changes in case Ana returned. This feeling was intensified for Santiago and Tina when they discovered a letter condoling Ana on the loss of her mother. Their discovery made them feel like they had intruded on something private, making them approach the rest of the game more cautiously. Tina also had an adverse reaction to the room's pandemic-themed elements. As someone who wanted to move on from the pandemic, the game's COVID-19 references caused her discomfort.

The players' experiences align with "space and place" theory, which differentiates between "space" (a physical location that is abstract and foreign) and "place" (a space that has been given personal meaning) – a rarely explored concept in game studies [56]. Some room players felt they were playing in a "space", which significantly impacted their experiences. For others like Oscar and Xander, the unfamiliar "space" of Ana's office became their own "place" as they immersed themselves in the experience. Conversely, non-room players like Alex and Joe found that specific "places" facilitated positive experiences, while others like Jane, Anthony, and Chris found that these places made gameplay more challenging due to their existing personal significance. Consequently, creators are encouraged to consider how physical space is incorporated into their designs, particularly in relation to theories of space and place.

The effects of physical spaces in *WWTWU*'s play suggests an evolution and transformation in how physical spaces are understood within pervasive games. Alex's changing gameplay experience from place to place, or Santiago and Tina's changing relationship to their play space when stumbling upon Ana's private letter suggest that physical location design may be a pivotal design consideration within pervasive games. This differs from existing understandings within escape room design, where a room's visual design primarily supports a narrative theme rather than a specific player experience.

6.5   Workshop Participant: Transforming Conceptions of Game Experiences

Sally's experience with *WWTWU* offers an insightful exploration into how pervasive games can blur the lines between fiction and reality, challenging and transforming pre-existing ideas of what constitutes a game. Rather than seeing *WWTWU* as a game, Sally viewed it as a "tool", possibly due to the tasks being based on existing wellness practices and other artistic interventions traditionally seen as tools or activities, not games [10, 17]. Her perspective could also be related to her self-identified role as an observer, rather than an active participant, in games culture, a notion consistent with discussions regarding self-identification as a "gamer" [42].

This understanding of *WWTWU* as (not) a game was less frequent among other participants but did occur. Notably, *WWTWU* transformed ARG Player Nina's understanding of games with its novel approach to addressing wellbeing. She expected traditional game mechanics like points and leaderboards, so when the game instead mirrored therapy-style questions, she questioned, "where's the game?". Nina was also shocked to find out that Ana was a game character, not a real person, noting that she didn't realize the Discord server was part of an ARG. She attributes this to her use of Discord as a work tool, which meant she did not approach the game with a playful mindset. This suggests that Nina did not fully accept the "lusory attitude" during play, which impacted her understanding of the "magic circle" she was in [32, 48]. Because she did not understand that pervasive games extend the magic circle spatiotemporally, she merely saw the Discord community as a group of players playing a website game – not an ARG that expanded the magic circle onto the Discord server and into players' realities.

Oscar's experience in the room game also helped redefine his understanding of the games medium. These perspectives suggest that the pervasive game genre, though long-standing, is often misunderstood by players who lack genre experience, or have differing expectations about games and play. This presents a dichotomy for creators. While the genre can offer unique experiences that transform players' understanding of games, player unfamiliarity with pervasive games can lead to experiential obstacles. Therefore, creators should consider incorporating techniques such as briefing and debriefing into *all* pervasive game types to better align player expectations.

7 Conclusion and Implications

The study detailed myriad player perspectives on *What We Take With Us*, a hybrid pervasive game implemented across an ARG, a room-based game, and several workshops. The research is unique for incorporating perspectives from the designer and developer, alongside players from each format. This contributes to a holistic understanding of *WWTWU* across the game's multiple formats, combining the insider knowledge of game portmortems [53] with user experience research [40].

The findings reinforce existing perspectives on pervasive game design, emphasising emergent narratives [13], emergent benefits [14], transformative play [44], and effective community utilisation [15]. Yet they also present challenges for creators, such as how to most effectively adapt communities to accommodate diverse player types [55], the influence of concepts like "space and place" on design [56], and the need to resolve tensions surrounding genre unfamiliarity and preconceived notions of game experiences [33].

While the study provides meaningful insights, it is not without limitations. Its modest participant count, specific focus on individual narratives, and the concentrated thematic analysis restrict the breadth of the findings. The specific geographical context (primarily the UK and South Africa), and lack of diversity in the represented narratives may also limit generalisability. Future research could address these limitations by reproducing the study in different cultural contexts, which may yield further insights. Additionally, an in-depth thematic analysis of each game format could provide additional nuances in understanding of pervasive game experiences.

In conclusion, while the study sought to examine the emergent and transformative potential of pervasive games across various formats and stakeholders, the findings reflect a broader truth: games are all about what we take with us and what we leave behind.

References

1. Aylett, R.: Emergent narrative, social immersion and "storification." In: Proceedings of the 1st International Workshop on Narrative and Interactive Learning Environments, pp. 35–44 , Edinburgh (2000)
2. Back, J., et al.: Designing for transformative play. ACM Trans. Comput.-Hum. Interact. **24**(3), 18:1–18:28 (2017). https://doi.org/10.1145/3057921
3. Boellstorff, T.: Coming of Age in Second Life: An Anthropologist Explores the Virtually Human. Princeton University Press, Oxford, NY (2015)
4. Bowman, S.L.: Social Conflict in Role-Playing Communities: An Exploratory Qualitative Study. IJRP. 4, 4–25 (2013). https://doi.org/10.33063/ijrp.vi4.183
5. Bowman, S.L.: The Functions of Role-Playing Games: How Participants Create Community, Solve Problems and Explore Identity. McFarland (2010)
6. Braun, V., Clarke, V.: Reflecting on reflexive thematic analysis. Qual. Res. Sport Exercise Health **11**(4), 589–597 (2019). https://doi.org/10.1080/2159676X.2019.1628806
7. Brown, A.: Awkward: the importance of reflexivity in using ethnographic methods. In: Game Research Methods, pp. 77–92 ETC Press, Pittsburgh, PA, USA (2015)
8. Brown, M.E.: Pulling the trigger on player agency: how psychological intrusions in Larps affect game play. In: The Wyrd Con Companion, pp. 96–111 Wyrdcon, Los Angeles, CA (2014)

9. Cain, S.: Quiet: The Power of Introverts in a World That Can't Stop Talking. Penguin, London (2013)
10. Cameron, J.: The Artist's Way: A Spiritual Path to Higher Creativity. Souvenir Press (2020)
11. Charsky, D.: From edutainment to serious games: a change in the use of game characteristics. Games Cult. (2010).https://doi.org/10.1177/1555412009354727
12. Connelly, F., Clandinin, D.: Stories of experience and narrative inquiry. Educ. Res. **19**(5), 2–14 (1990)
13. Cox, J.: Documenting Larp as an art of experience. Int. J. Role-Play. **9**(1), 24–30 (2019)
14. Dansey, N.: Emergently-persuasive games: how players of SF0 persuade themselves. In: Cases on the Societal Effects of Persuasive Games, pp. 175–192 IGI Global (2014). https://doi.org/10.4018/978-1-4666-6206-3.ch009
15. Dena, C.: Emerging participatory culture practices player-created tiers in alternate reality games. Convergence **14**(1), 41–57 (2008). https://doi.org/10.1177/1354856507084418
16. Eklund, K.: World without oil (2017). https://www.youtube.com/watch?v=M-hzUGFD-Gc
17. Green, S.U.: You Are an Artist: Assignments to Spark Creation. Particular Books (2020)
18. Hellström, M.: A tale of two cities: symbolic capital and Larp community formation in Canada and Sweden. Int. J. Role-Play. **3**, 33–48 (2012). https://doi.org/10.33063/ijrp.vi3.223
19. Jerrett, A., et al.: Developing an empathy spectrum for games. Games Cult. (2020).https://doi.org/10.1177/1555412020954019
20. Jerrett, A. et al.: Practical considerations for values-conscious pervasive games. In: Proceedings of the Digital Games Research Association Conference 2022 Conference: Bringing Worlds Together. Digital Games Research Association, Krakow, PL (2022)
21. Jerrett, A.: What we take with us (2022). https://whatwetakewith.us/
22. Jerrett, A., Howell, P.: Values throughout the game space. In: Proceedings of the ACM. 6, CHI Play, pp. 1–28 (2022)
23. Keightley, E., et al.: The self-interview: a new method in social science research. Int. J. Soc. Res. Methodol. **15**(6), 507–521 (2012). https://doi.org/10.1080/13645579.2011.632155
24. Koster, R.: Theory of Fun for Game Design. O'Reilly Media Inc, California, FL (2013)
25. McGonigal, J.: Reality is Broken: Why Games Make us Better and How They can Change the World. Penguin Press, New York (2011)
26. McGonigal, J.: SuperBetter: How a Gameful Life can Make You Stronger, Happier, Braver and More Resilient. HarperCollins, London, UK (2016)
27. McGonigal, J.: The puppet master problem: design for real-world, mission-based gaming. In: Harrigan, P., Wardrip-Fruin, N. (eds.) Second Person: Role-Playing and Story in Games and Playable Media, pp. 251–264. The MIT Press, Cambridge (2007)
28. McGonigal, J.: This is not a game: immersive aesthetics and collective play. In: Digital Arts & Culture 2003 Conference Proceedings. Melbourne (2003)
29. McGonigal, J.: Urgent evoke: what went right, what went wrong: lessons from season 1 of EVOKE (2015). http://blog.urgentevoke.net/2010/07/26/what-went-right-what-went-wrong-lessons-from-season-1-evoke1/. Accessed 23 Mar 2015
30. Mezirow, J.: Transformative learning theory. In: Contemporary Theories of Learning. Routledge (2018)
31. Michael, D.R.,.Chen, S.L.: Serious Games: Games That Educate, Train, and Inform. Muska & Lipman/Premier-Trade (2005)
32. Montola, M.: Exploring the edge of the magic circle: defining pervasive games. In: Proceedings of Digital Arts and Culture, pp. 103–107 Digital Arts and Culture, Copenhagen (2005)
33. Montola, M., et al.: Pervasive Games: Theory and Design. Morgan Kaufmann Publishers Inc., San Francisco, CA, USA (2009)

34. Montola, M.: Tangible pleasures of pervasive role-playing. In: Proceedings of the 2007 DiGRA International Conference: Situated Play, pp. 178–186 Digital Games Research Association, Tokyo, JP (2007)
35. Nicholson, S.: Peeking Behind the Locked Door: A Survey of Escape Room Facilities (2015). http://scottnicholson.com/pubs/erfacwhite.pdf
36. Paavilainen, J. et al.: The Pokemon GO experience: a location-based augmented reality mobile game goes mainstream. In: Proceedings of the 2017 CHI Conference on Human Factors in Computing Systems. pp. 2493–2498 Association for Computing Machinery, New York, NY, USA (2017)
37. Phelps, A., Rusch, D.C.: Navigating existential, transformative game design. In: Proceedings of DiGRA 2020 Conference: Play Everywhere. Digital Games Research Association, Tampere, FL (2020)
38. Pickard, A.J.: Research Methods in Information. Neal-Schuman, Chicago, IL (2013)
39. Riessman, C.K.: Narrative Methods for the Human Sciences. SAGE Publications Inc, Los Angeles (2007)
40. Rogers, Y., et al.: Interaction Design: Beyond Human-Computer Interaction. Wiley, Indianapolis (2023)
41. Salen, K., Zimmerman, E.: Rules of play: game design fundamentals. MIT Press, Cambridge, MA (2003)
42. Shaw, A.: Do you identify as a gamer? Gender, race, sexuality, and gamer identity. new media & society. 14, 1, 28–44 (2012)
43. Southerton, C.: Zombies, Run! Rethinking Immersion in Light of Nontraditional Gaming Contexts. In: Transmedia Practice: A Collective Approach. pp. 131–141 Brill, Leiden, NL (2014)
44. Spencer, A.R.: The vampire foucault: erotic horror role-playing games as a technologies of the self. Int. J. Role-Play. **13**, 89–97 (2023). https://doi.org/10.33063/ijrp.vi13.312
45. Stark, L.: Leaving Mundania: Inside the Transformative World of Live Action Role-Playing Games. Chicago Review Press (2012)
46. Stenros, J., Bowman, S.L.: Transgressive role-play. In: Role-Playing Game Studies, pp. 411–424 Routledge (2018)
47. Stenros, J., Montola, M. eds: Nordic Larp. Fëa Livia, Finland (2010)
48. Suits, B.: The Grasshopper: Games, Life, and Utopia. University of Toronto Press, Buffalo, NY (1978)
49. Tanenbaum, T.J., Tanenbaum, K.: Empathy and identity in digital games: towards a new theory of transformative play. In: FDG (2015)
50. Toft, I., Harrer, H.: Design bleed: a standpoint methodology for game design (2020)
51. Torner, E.: Just a Little Lovin' USA 2017. In: Axner, J., Waern, A. (eds.) Shuffling the Deck: The Knutpunkt 2018 Printed Companion, pp. 53–61. MIT Press, Pittsburgh, PA (2018)
52. Wardle, J.: Wordle (2021). https://www.nytimes.com/games/wordle/index.html
53. Wawro, A.: 10 seminal game postmortems every developer should read. (2022). https://www.gamedeveloper.com/audio/10-seminal-game-postmortems-every-developer-should-read. Accessed 27 Apr 2022
54. Zamaniyan, S., et al.: Effectiveness of spiritual group therapy on quality of life and spiritual well-being among patients with breast cancer. Iran J Med Sci. **41**(2), 140–144 (2016)
55. Applying the 5 Domains of Play: Acting Like Players. Game Developer's Conference, San Francisco, CA (2013)
56. Dwelling in Animal Crossing: New Horizons. Multiplay Network, Sunderland, UK (2022)
57. World Without Oil (game recap). Disruptive Effects Conference, University of Minnesota (2010)

Communal Ritual Play: Repetition and Interpretation of Game Narratives Across Communities

Bjarke Alexander Larsen$^{(\boxtimes)}$, Nic Junius, and Elin Carstensdottir

University of California, Santa Cruz, USA
{balarsen,njunius,ecarsten}@ucsc.edu

Abstract. Storytelling has always been a communal activity and video games are no different, yet, work on designing story experiences that emphasize the communal elements of storytelling have typically focused on the creation of stories, not communal interpretation of existing ones. This paper draws on communal storytelling rituals from theater and mythology to explore how games and interactive narrative can utilize narrative through communal interactions. From this, several design patterns can be extrapolated from existing games that create communal storytelling rituals. We use Destiny 2, Final Fantasy XIV, and Elden Ring as primary examples to discuss three narrative design patterns for online communal ritual storytelling. These three design patterns are 1) giving players incomplete information, encouraging repetition, 2) not helping players, encouraging community, and 3) building for player expression, encouraging player-stories. All three patterns utilize aspects of rituals and theater to encourage storytelling of their respective games, through encouraging repetition and communal aspects. Games are often repetitive in nature, and harnessing community to strengthen the narrative through this repetition can be a powerful tool to create engaging narratives for players while still relying on repetitive gameplay loops. Designing for communal ritual play is thus a strong way to utilize the advantages of repetitive games and communal narrative.

Keywords: communal storytelling · ritual · interpretation · myth · theater · repetition · games

1 Introduction

Since the beginnings of oral traditions of mythology and ancient theater, storytelling has been a communal activity. Stories in video games are no different. They engage communities as well as individuals, yet, when communal storytelling has been incorporated into narrative design, it has focused on the *creation* of stories as a communal activity [38,57,58,85]. The reading or playing of an existant story of games played by communities instead of individuals, such as the play experience of Terminal Time [61], remains an underdiscussed topic. Drawing on

L. Holloway-Attaway and J. T. Murray (Eds.): ICIDS 2023, LNCS 14383, pp. 472–488, 2023.
https://doi.org/10.1007/978-3-031-47655-6_29

communal storytelling rituals from mythology and theater, we instead focus on the ways communities of players collectively understand and engage with stories.

Communal play and rituals can teach us how to design narratives around the repetition that is exceedingly common in games as well as find ways to encourage players of multiplayer focused games to engage with their narratives. Current games with less traditional single player narrative structures and plots (such as Destiny 2 or Elden Ring) utilize design patterns that encourage communal storytelling instead. These patterns can be extrapolated to create more experiences where the storytelling approach strengthens a community and narrative together, creating more powerful stories that connect people to each other as well as to the work of the narrative.

The single player narrative experience is well researched in interactive storytelling and games [1,5,6,26,43,47,52,60,66,76,84]. One ongoing strand from this direction of research focuses on better understanding the ways players' relationships to games change over repeated playthroughs [42,46,63,64], showing the power of narrative understanding through repetition. The work in this area has largely focused on singleplayer experiences, in the choices of games to analyze and the emphasis on each player's distinct, personal reinterpretation [42,46,63,64]. Interpretation, however, is not exclusively an individual act and entire communities can engage in the practice while playing games, collectively creating new meaning out of (re)experiencing the same story. Not all games are equally suited for this kind of communal retelling and interpretation and certain design patterns lend themselves better to it than others.

To understand the narrative design patterns that encourage collective interpretation of games, we propose *communal ritual play* as a lens to analyze narratively-oriented, multiplayer games. Such a lens allows us to expand the work of studying the ways narrative designs create modes of storytelling that encourage players to engage in interpretation into the ways these designs and approaches encourage the collective sharing and interpretation of in-game experiences. Furthermore, this lens enables us to more deeply understand the way multiplayer narrative design draws players into engaging with these games' stories which are often multimodal and feature hidden or otherwise non-obvious elements, frequently requiring a collective effort to discover in the first place. When narrative elements are used in these multiplayer games they are often told through fractions of a story when experienced a single time, requiring repeated playthroughs or engagement with a community, or sometimes both, to begin understanding the full story being told. Additionally, we focus on *ritual* as the mode of play as rituals, like many multiplayer games, are built for the express purpose of repeated enaction of events and the narrative of multiplayer games rarely exists as a single linear story. These design patterns strongly help foster a community's interpretation of a narrative, yet are rarely connected directly to narrative experience.

To construct the lens of communal ritual play, we turn to theatrical performance practices and literature around ritual and myth. From these, we can form an understanding of what is compelling about revisiting stories which can then be applied to existing multiplayer games, which have communities built around their interpretation. Theatrical performance practices work within the constraints of the play script, which provides a framework for telling a specific story, while performers form their own interpretations of the roles to find novelty and bring the narrative to life [13,56,74]. Likewise, storytelling traditions from mythology are strongly tied to ritual and retellings [26,49], as communities would retell and re-enact myths continously, to both expand their understanding and convey their meaning to the society [34,48,72,78]. By drawing from ritual, myth, and performance practices, we can expand our understanding of how people collectively interpret stories from a small group of specialists to much wider communities of varying expertise levels engaging in this form of novelty seeking and interpretation.

In this paper we describe three narrative design patterns using the lens of communal ritual play: *Incomplete Information*, *Not Helping the Player*, and *Building for Player Expression*. To synthesize these patters, we first identified games with active communities discussing their play and storytelling experiences. Next we searched through public discussions to find repeated topics about game elements with *high player friction*, defined as requiring discussion with at least one other player to be understood. Finally, we constructed categories by grouping these discussions based on commonalities in subjectmatter and play experience. We use the following games as exemplars to discuss these design patterns: *Destiny 2* [15], *Final Fantasy XIV* [81], and *Elden Ring* [31]. Our aim in defining and illustrating these patterns through examples is to allow for more deliberate narrative design of game elments to encourage communal storytelling in repetitive experiences.

2   Related Work

Reinterpretation through repetition is a phenomenon that has been studied in relation to digital games [42,46,63,64], discussed as part of performance practices [13,56,74], and ritual and mythological studies [34,48,51,72,78]. Common to these is communal rituals as a storytelling practice. Communal storytelling is also seen in games, to understand how the creation of stories can be a communal activity [38,57,58,85], something also well known in table-top roleplaying design [24]. Yet, this focus on collaborative *creation* is not the only aspect of communal ritual play, as through a synthesis of ideas from theatrical performance and ritual and mythological studies, a different lens emerges, of considering a collective interpretation of authored stories.

2.1   Replay and Rewind

The work focusing on replaying stories in games has primarily focused on the way individual players interpret singleplayer games and how those games facilitate reinterpretation of their stories [42,46,63,64]. Mitchell and McGee describe the phenomenon of players of interactive stories transitioning between "reading again to reach closure" and "elements after closure" where they move from looking for catharsis in the story in the former to reflecting on their relationship with the story in the latter [64]. When investigating the experiences of players revisiting storygames, Mitchell et al. expand on the idea of reading for closure to encompass both the experience of closure with the narrative and with the game systems, to describe ways players lose interest in replaying a game once the balance between both types of closure is lost [63].

Unlike Mitchell et al.'s focus on player closure, Kleinman et al.'s taxonomy of rewind mechanics describes the way designers facilitate the replaying and recontextualization of the story for the purpose of evaluating games which recontextualize themselves through their mechanics [46]. In a similar vein, Junius et al. propose the concept of theatricality present in games with looping structures specifically designed to recontextualize a game's narrative and invite a player to reinterpret their relationship to story elements within the game [42]. Expanding upon this definition of theatricality, Karth et al. add the notion of story volumes to explain the ways game narratives can be restructured while keeping the same *type* of story and guide players into interpreting the rules governing the storylines [44]. Where communal ritual play diverges from these existing approaches is in its emphasis on the act of reinterpretation as *collective*, even if it still shares the recontextualization focus of rewind mechanics and theatricality.

2.2 Performance

Communal ritual play draws from performance practices to build its lens as theater, from early in its history, has a focus of recontextualizing and retelling stories for different audiences [10]. As performance often operates within the constraints provided by a script, these practices focus on the need to find novel and unique ways of portraying and interpreting a character, lest the performer(s) or audience become bored [56,74]. Nō theater uses the metaphor of a flower as the central aesthetic of performance, something that continuously creates novelty and requires active care to maintain [74]. The novelty seeking described in Nō is an interpretive act, and importantly, a task for each actor to consider on their own [74], similar to the approaches to analyzing replay in games discussed in Sect. 2.1, while also making its practice distinct from more recently developed theatrical practices.

Performance's relationship to the texts it uses to tell stories has undergone numerous re-examinations as new approaches have developed, with some practices viewing the text as dictating every aspect of a production [56,74] and others viewing it as simply another element to be incorporated [9,13,41,53]. When the text of a script is de-emphasized, it invites experimentation in performance and interpretation, finding views of roles, themes, etc. that may have otherwise been missed [13]. This freedom of interpretation informs communal ritual play as, like the work in Sect. 2.1 describes, repeated replaying of sections of multiplayer games will change players' relationship to the game's narrative components and move them beyond simply trying to experience a singular version of the story.

The popular western acting practices of the Method of Physical Actions [56] and the Viewpoints [13] heavily emphasize that performance, novelty seeking, and interpretation must be understood as collective acts. The Method of Physical Actions maintains that every action performed on the stage must in some way motivate a reaction from another character, even if the actor is alone [56]. Additionally, while the rehearsal process fixes some elements of the performance, it is the entire cast's job to explore the spaces between those fixed elements [56], sharing similarities to the way story volumes have been described [44], with the addition that exploring the possibility space is a collective responsibility. The Viewpoints shifts the focus of performance even further towards the collective, not only de-emphasizing the text but also the role of the director, to find an interpretation of a text and performance completely unique to each production [13]. More than anything the Viewpoints is intended to foster collaboration between actors to explore how they can discover actions on stage by indulging in possibilities rather than being restricted under some central authority, including the text of a play [13]. This is still framed within the rather small bounds of a theatrical production and though theatrical performance's understanding of finding novel interpretations within constraints helps to explain the creativity to be found in repetition, by itself it is insufficient to construct the communal part of communal ritual play.

2.3   Myth and Ritual

Early sociologists and myth scholars such as William Smith, E.B. Tylor and Frazer [2, 29, 78] discussed the connection between ritual and traditional mythology. In what has been named the "myth-ritualist theory" the function of myth was seen to make sense of ritual, as a way for societies to explain their customs [78]. Another view is seen in Campbell: "ritual is simply myth enacted" [17, 75]. As Segal [78] notes, the various interpretations differ on whether they consider myth or ritual primary and the other secondary, yet, ritual has long been closely tied to religion and mythological storytelling. See Nagy for a modern interpretation of the myth-ritualist position [68].

Ritual, furthermore has been directly connected to play. Huizinga directly discusses play as a kind of ritual [37], also seen in Wagner [83]. Rettberg [72] discusses how there is a ritual quality to the repetition of play, comparing it to rituals of life such as weddings and funerals. This echoes Krzywinska [48], Geraci [34] and Larsen and Carstensdottir [50,51], who discuss the ritual and mythological quality of MMOs by treating the communal experience of playing a game as a kind of myth. Asimos [4] and Rusch [75] have a more expanded view on how contemporary games can be seen as mythology. Harrington [35] and Cragoe [24] furthermore discuss the connections between mythology and games, and how we play and talk about games can be viewed as a socially constructed and part of larger contexts. Drawing on myth, as a communal storytelling practice that relies on ritual, would be a valuable resource to understand ritual play in games and how it connects to storytelling.

As discussed by structural sociologists, myths can *"teach us a great deal about the societies from which they originate"* [55]. Scholars like Dorson [25], Levi-Strauss [54,55], Bronislaw [59], Campbell [18] or Jung and Eliade [34,78] have all contributed to the modern understanding of myth as useful to building and interpreting communities. And while this has later been challenged and reinterpreted in postmodern scholarship [8,36,45,78] (also seen in game studies [27,28,35]), the connection between mythology and ritual and play are still valuable insights for games because of their repetitive, ritual nature.

Through this lens, we will see how mythological, communal storytelling experiences arise through ritual repetition of play. Thus, by looking at how rituals are formed in games, and how the communities understand, interpret, and maintain these rituals (for themselves and others), we can understand something about how the community interprets the game they are playing. Our view on ritual is informed by Junius et al. [42] and Rettberg [72] as a recurring, repetitive activity that is given contextual, social, or cultural significance, turning mundane activities into more meaningful ways to relate to the world. Rituals in games are informed by the design of the game, its affordances and design constraints, but also in subversion to them, as communities discover optimal strategies and new ways to play unintended by the developers, and thus seeing how the player rituals are formed in relationship with the design of the game is crucial to understanding how design impacts the ritual play of community.

3   Narrative Design Patterns for Communal Ritual Play

The following three narrative design patterns showcase communal ritual play through examples from the following games: *Destiny 2* [15], *Final Fantasy XIV* [81], and *Elden Ring* [31]. Each of these patterns focuses on a different way designs encourage players to form communities around narrative experiences created through ritual play, either through providing players with *incomplete information* 3.1, *avoiding helping them* 3.2, or *letting them express themselves* 3.3.

3.1   Incomplete Information

The design pattern of incomplete information emphasizes not providing a single player with all the information they need to comprehensively understand the game across a single playthrough. Rather, the complete experience is obtained through repetition, wherein players experience new pieces of content, different ways to solve similar problems, or find hidden objectives, making the multiple repetitions a somewhat new experience each time. Players are often given a material reason to re-experience the same content over and over, such as getting new rewards, or new narrative information. Each repetition has set goals and expectations with the potential to uncover a new perspective on the content, much the way new productions of existing theaterical scripts, including historical and ancient texts, are performed today [12,19,74]. This potential for a revelation is what creates the ritual experience, yet within that there is room for flexibility and play because the performance of players collaborating is in focus. The repetition gives leeway for designers to not give a player all the information in a single attempt, as it can be expected they will repeat the ritual multiple times. The existence of secrets or hidden objectives (see *hiding information*) also gives an incentive for players to re-experience it as they know they might find something new. While this approach might contradict traditional game design wisdom, withholding information with intention can help lay the groundwork for players to engage in communal ritual play.

Distributing Information Across Multiple Players or Repetitions. Seasonal activities in Destiny have ritual and repetitive affordances, as they can be done over and over again for rewards, yet the dialogue a player hears can differ. There are many permutations of voice lines that can play at the end of the activity, usually short 30-s dialogue interactions between relevant characters, conversing about current events, providing context, background or humourous insight. The only way to experience the entire story volume[1] [44] is to do the activity multiple times, view video of others completing it, or talk with other players about what they heard. Furthermore, across a season, new dialogue will appear that you could not have heard in the early weeks, reflecting changes in the story. Thus, a player will have to repeatedly engage with the seasonal event, leading to a ritual experience. This model of new dialogue through repetition is also used in Hades to great effect [42].

Destiny also has an example of distributing information across players rather than repetitions. During the "Corridors of Time' event [32]—a giant, community based 5000-piece jigsaw puzzle—each player would get a unique piece of the puzzle, at random. Thus, in order to complete the jigsaw puzzle, the community had to coordinate to gather all the pieces from thousands of players. This is a clear example of distributing information, since no player could hope to complete the jigsaw puzzle by themselves. ARGs[2] have also used similar patterns for similar effect.

Hiding Information. Elden Ring has many secrets hidden in its world. It will rarely make its objectives clear to the player, or only provide cryptic hints on how to complete quests, and sometimes leaving it entirely up to the player to discover. The end of the "Frenzied Flame" questline requires the player to remove all their clothing to be able to enter a door, and there is only one cryptic clue from one NPC to indicate this. Yet, players can leave messages to each other, and this can be used to provide hints directly in the game. Failing that, there is of course out of game information, guides and word-of-mouth. This is a clear design pattern because of how intentionally it is done across Elden Ring. It expects no player to solve everything by themselves and instead learn

---

[1] See Sect. 2.1 and [44].

[2] Alternate Reality Games, see [39].

information from the community. Elden Ring also has several "illusory walls", walls that appear impenetrable until struck. The only way players can know about these is if another player leaves a hint in front of them.[3]

Destiny, too has many open secrets by design. A great example is "Public Events", 5–10 min repeatable events that appear in the open world. Every Public Event has an initial, straightforward goal, e.g. to collect a certain amount of a resource or defend a point. However, every Public Event also has a "Heroic", secret objective, which is never explained in the game. An example is the "Glimmer Extraction" event, where the normal objective is to defeat enemies at 3 separate points. However, if you also blow up a non-assuming generator at each point, the public event will change to have a different objective altogether. This will also complete the event and give you better rewards. However, the only way to know this is a part of the game is to stumble into it accidentally, or—what is more likely—see another player do it. This is an example of how knowledge is shared through the community through repetition. Even something as simple as following the example of other players in the world is achieved because the events have hidden objectives and are repeatable. This kind of knowledge sharing is key to a game community like Destiny's, where these kinds of secrets become small nuggets of shared folk knowledge that can travel across all players organically.

Destiny also has many secret missions, where the developers will deploy a new mission in the game without notifying the players about this. Players will notice there is a new enemy, puzzle, or object leads to a new narrative beat or mission. This is then often quickly posted about on Reddit and Twitter and Discord servers and prominent community members begin to play it on Twitch, thus spreading the new, exciting secret like wildfire, without the game itself ever bringing attention to it.

Repetitive Group Activities Relying on Teamwork and Communication. Some activities, such as dungeons or raids, both in in Destiny and Final Fantasy XIV require teamwork, and/or trial and error. These difficult end-game activities are often designed with difficult mechanics that do not explain themselves to players, but it is up to the group to figure out how they work and overcome the challenge. No part of the games design or UI tutorialize these mechanics to players, but they are nevertheless vital to understand in order to complete the experience. When new players are introduced to these activities, then, it is common practice for the experienced players to take them through it and explain the mechanics (or "sherpa" them, as it is known in the Destiny community). And when a new player has been taught it, if they then join another group of new players, it falls to them to pass the knowledge on.

This is thus the ritual of these activities, as each players' role becomes clear through play and communication, and through the repetition the roles are strengthened, enforced and passed on to new community members. Across

---

[3] Another infamous example from the same developer is how Dark Souls [30] hides a secret area behind two consecutive illusory walls.

all parts of this pattern is the fact that the information gathered by a single playthrough of an experience does not encompass the whole, and one must rely on continual engagement either through repetitive sequential actions or in parallel (by other players) to understand the full breadth of what the game's experience has to offer.

3.2 Not Helping the Player

Another way games can encourage players to be in community with each other is to intentionally inconvenience or trouble them, making it harder to accomplish their goals by themselves. This design pattern focuses on the obfuscation of necessary information, creating friction around basic actions or narrative material. By *not giving guidance to optimal paths* or *distributing the backstory across many fractured instances* it makes it more difficult for an individual player to understand what to do and what is going on. This is not necessarily because the information is secret, such as in the first design pattern 3.1, but rather because the game provides inadequate guidance on how to understand its systems or narrative. By presenting narrative elements to players in pieces and out of order, overwhelming the player with too many disparate pieces of information, or *forcing players through shared difficulties*, one player is not expected to understand the entire experience by themselves, akin to the nature of a play script requiring multiple perspectives and interpretive specialities to collectively transform a script into a finished theatrical work [12,13,19,74]. This is where a player begins relying on the community to map out and collectively understand the connections between each disparate element, as well as optimise strategies for how to play through the game, communally making sense of the mythology of the game.

Not Giving Guidance on Optimal Paths. Elden Ring purposefully does not guide players in how to approach its world or story beyond some very basic explanations for mechanics and highlighting where to go to progress the story and open up new areas. At the game's launch, numerous players went directly to the game's first major dungeon and hit a wall in the first main boss of the game, having ignored the area in the opposite direction to the dungeon. This common experience led to the wisdom of "go south" [31] being passed around the community both in and out of game as the region at the southmost end of the map was designed to help players level up and get better tools to tackle the dungeon with.

Many items in Elden Ring are hidden around the world, and both in Destiny and Final Fantasy, items can require multiple, long quest chains to acquire. Thus it is unlikely a new player will simply acquire all the items they need to play most effectively through a normal playthrough, and they will thus use information gathered from other players about how they should go about gathering the materials and items they need in order to progress.

This also functions through giving an individual player more options than they can easily comprehend by themselves, and avoiding to tell them which of those options is the most optimal for their current situation, instead leaving them to figure it out on their own, or asking their friends.

The (Back)story Is Fractured. Gameplay secrets is not the only element that players need to rely on others to understand. Destiny has millenia of backstory, and furthermore has 9 years of actual history, with events dating back to 2014, many of which are no longer accessible in any way inside the game. This means that if you want to know what happened in the story of the "Red War" which happened in 2017, you will have to rely on other players, either through descriptions or recordings, or so on. This often shows itself through watching recap videos like those by prominent "lore" YouTubers like My Name is Byf [16] or Myelin [67], to understand the past and present story.

And even if you are paying attention, the story itself is difficult to understand, obfuscated through layers of perspectives and metaphors. Outside the immediate cutscenes and dialogue, the story is told through "lorebooks", served in piece-meal chapters that require repeated activity completions (see *distributing information*), and are often told through the perspective of a character, and some of these books have proven themselves to be wrong or willful attempts at misleading the players. It is thus up to the community, collectively, to make sense of the story of Destiny.

This is similar to the story experience of Elden Ring, which is also told in fractured pieces, out of order, and it is up to the community to make sense of it. This heavily relies on *confusion*, giving the players questions and leaving gaps in the narrative, letting players piece patterns out of incomplete or fractured information. This helps build community because it is through people coming together with their disparate pieces of knowledge, ideas and theories that a more complete picture is formed. The worlds of Destiny or Elden Ring are too vast for any one person to keep in their head easily, and thus it relies on the building of a community to comprehend.

Forcing Players Through Shared Difficulties. Compared to Destiny, players of FFXIV have a very different relationship to the main story. The main narrative is all present in 2023 in a form almost identical to how it was in 2013[4]. This means a new player will have to play through story content ranging from 2013 to now in order to be able to see the newest story scenarios their experienced friends are seeing. This is made worse by the fact that the early story is considered too long, slowly paced, and not rewarding by itself [40,70]. However, people are still very much being recommended to play through the "bad parts" to "get to the good stuff" in the later expansions, because the earlier events serve as important setup. Experienced players love seeing new players make it through the story [40,71], and the community in general is very cognizant about not spoil-

---

[4] Small alterations have been made, some superfluous quests have been removed and one optional questline has been made mandatory, but it is structurally almost identical. See https://ffxiv.consolegameswiki.com/wiki/Main_Scenario_Revisions.

ing the experience for newcomers but letting them experience it for themselves, although they are also very aware what a slog it can be to get through.

This leads to a rather specific community relationship towards the story. As a player of FFXIV, you *know* everyone has been through the same gauntlet to get to the current experience, regardless of when they started, and this communally shared experience is part of the bonding of that community. The entire main story is thus a completely *shared* experience for all players, and every member of the community has that shared background of knowing that they too trudged through a slow grind and made it out the other side. It becomes a rather different kind of ritual, a rite of passage, a mythological origin story all players share— echoing the actual origin story of the game itself [69].

While this was likely not the intended experience, it is clear that the developers are adamant about *keeping* the story experience this way, contrasting to many other MMOs like World of Warcraft or Destiny that have either entirely restructured or removed their initial campaigns as newer content has surpassed it in quality. Thus, while this is a very different way of achieving it than the other examples, this too can be seen as an example of not helping the player and thus creating communal ritual play through collective experience of hardship. This method can be quite dangerous as it can repel new players to whom it seems daunting without proper support (often entirely provided by other people). However, on the other side, the shared experience can strengthen a community and bring them closer to each other and the narrative.

3.3   Building for Player Expression

Player expression is a powerful tool to let players experiment and make their own narratives or fun, such as seen in The Sims [62] or Minecraft [65]. In a communal setting, however, player expression can take on a new life and grow beyond an individual player's choices. How players act and dress and customize their characters can become a part of the legend and ritual of playing within the community. This design pattern focuses on letting players' deviant play [23] be used for narrative purpose. By letting players express themselves, use suboptimal strategies or equipment, perform unoptimally or breaking the rules, they can shape their own identity through their play and define their relationship to the game's world and narrative by making concrete decisions about who they are in manners reminiscent of the way actors and productions draw out themes through performance [13,19,56,74]. In communities, these identities then become reinforced in relationships with other people, and through the repetition of play. A game can create folk heroes by letting players help each other, through messages or cooperative play in repetitive trials, where any players' deviance will stand out in subversion to the expected monotony, creating myths. Creating systems for even deeper player expression, such as player-made crafting is a powerful way to allow this expression as well, and can have great communal benefits, letting players create their own ritual experiences and new ways to engage with the fictional worlds.

Folk Heroes. Many multiplayer games have their own legendary community members, who become well known for one thing or another, either in of fame or infamy. The most well known of these across all multiplayer games is likely "Leeroy Jenkins", who became so well known he became a fictional character in World of Warcraft [11,77]. Elden Ring's most well known hero "Let Me Solo Her", became well known as a person able to defeat the game's hardest boss alone, wearing nothing but a loincloth and a pot on his head, which he proceeded to do, repeatedly, as others summoned him for aid [21,79]. The player expression comes through in his strange yet exceedingly confident attire and name, and this was no doubt part of his spreading appeal. Destiny, too, has many local heroes or community members known for various parts of the game, often known for exceptional feats such as "soloing"[5] raids or dungeons, or being exceptionally knowledgable about the lore [16,67].

FFXIV has not just those known for completing hard challenges like well-known raid teams or individuals, but also people known for other, more silly endeavours. The streamer "RubberNinja" became widely known for eating eggs on stream one day [20], as he was gifted a box of eggs and proceed to eat them. Others kept giving him eggs and the stream stayed live with no other content than him eating eggs for several days, prompting the inclusion of an "eating eggs" emote in the game. Destiny, similarly, has introduced elements into the game based on community actions [51]. FFXIV is also an example of the developers themselves not shying away from becoming folk heroes in the game, as several members of the development team have formed a band that plays the game's songs live on stage at fan conventions and celebrations [3]. There is more room for developers to experiment with accentuating interesting player stories through affecting the game or officially supporting it, empowering and encouraging these stories further [22], as also seen in Destiny [14,33,51].

The combination of repetition and player expression is what allow the myths to arise. None of these stories would have become legend if they had only happened a single time and never been retold or re-experienced. Let Me Solo Her became well known because of his persistence. RubberNinja likewise for the length of time he was willing to commit to a repetitive act. The game creates a gap for a larger challenge to be overcome, a fruiful void [7] that players can take upon themselves to fill. It is thus through the repetitions of these ritual activities, that nevertheless allow some form of expression (for example letting players enter raids meant for six people alone or wearing nonsensical outfits) that make them famous.

Crafting and Creating. Finally, one would be remiss to not mention the many ways player expression can be shaped through player-made activities. FFXIV is the greatest example of this. Players can own and customize their own houses, and some sub-communities spend great effort findings ways to bend the rather limited interior decorating toolset to their will. This housing system is also a

---

[5] Completing an activity meant for a group alone.

playground for a variety of player-run scenes, such as sprawling night club, the-atre, or fashion show communities [73,82], the performance of play becoming literal theatrical performance or roleplay, inviting reinterpretation on what play-ing the game can be. These often do exist on a ritual basis, as night clubs and theatres might only be open on certain times. An even grander example of this is "Lunarcon" an player-run convention that exists entirely inside the game [80].

This is all possible because of a flexibility of design of the game. By putting few restrictions on what a "house" can be, players are free to shape the space how they want, turning it into everything from cottages to aquariums [86]. The community then creates their own rituals about these.

4   Conclusion

This paper discussed storytelling in online digital games through the lens of com-munal ritual storytelling, where multiple players create communal storytelling experiences out of repetititive rituals. The lenses of replay and theater perfor-mance was applied to understand how players will change interpretations of a story through performing repetition, and the lens of myth was applied through its comparison with ritual, seeing how we can draw upon narrative meaning within a ritual event. The games Destiny 2, Final Fantasy XIV, and Elden Ring were used as examples to discuss three design patterns, *Incomplete Information*, *Not Helping the Player*, and *Building for Player Expression*, which all utilize rit-ual play and communities to enforce the storytelling of their respective games, through encouraging repetition and communal aspects. These design patterns serve as a first step towards better incorporating narrative in communal game experiences. Games are often repetitive in nature, and harnessing community to strengthen the narrative through this repetition can be a powerful tool to create engaging narratives for players while still relying on repetitive gameplay loops, by intentionally introducing friction into the design and encouraging the com-munity to come together or share stories. Designing for communal ritual play is thus a strong way to utilize the advantages of repetitive games and communal narrative. Future work in this area will focus on more concrete design appli-cations, investigating both the positive and negative applications of communal ritual play for narrative game experiences as well as further discussion of the effects of these design patterns on the form of the textual narrative.

References

1. Aarseth, E., Smedstad, S.M., Sunnanå, L.: A multidimensional typology of games. In: DiGRA Conference (2003)
2. Ackerman, R.: The myth and ritual school: JG Frazer and the Cambridge ritualists, vol. 13. Psychology Press (2002)
3. Aoi, L.: FFXIV meme ascends to official status in special live performance at digital fan festival. https://automaton-media.com/en/news/20210517-840/. Accessed 22 June 2023 (2021)

4. Asimos, V.: Playing the myth: video games as contemporary mythology. Implicit Relig. **21**(1), 93–111 (2018)
5. Aylett, R.: Narrative in virtual environments-towards emergent narrative. In: Proceedings of the AAAI Fall Symposium on Narrative Intelligence, pp. 83–86 (1999)
6. Aytemiz, B., Junius, N., Altice, N.: Exploring how changes in game systems generate meaning. In: DiGRA Conference (2019)
7. Baker, V.: The fruitful void (2005). http://lumpley.com/index.php/anyway/thread/119
8. Barthes, R.: Mythologies. 1957. Trans. Annette Lavers. New York: Hill and Wang, pp. 302–306 (1972)
9. Bass, E.: Visual dramaturgy: Some thoughts for puppet theatre-makers. The Routledge Companion to Puppetry and Material Performance, pp. 54–60 (2014)
10. Bierman, J.: Aristotle or Else. http://tragedy.ucsc.edu/
11. Blizzard Entertainment Ltd.: World of warcraft (2004)
12. Bogart, A., Gay, J.: The art of collaboration: on dramaturgy and directing. In: The Routledge Companion to Dramaturgy, Routledge, pp. 213–216 (2014)
13. Bogart, A., Landau, T.: The Viewpoints Book: A Practical Guide to Viewpoints and Composition. Theatre Communications Group (2005)
14. Bungie: Lore tab of the electronica ghost shell. Lore entry on Ishtar. https://www.ishtar-collective.net/entries/electronica-shell, as well as in Destiny 2. It describes Guardians (players) and how frequently they dance (2017)
15. Bungie and Activision: Destiny 2 (2017), as of 2019, Activision is not affiliated with Destiny. (https://kotaku.com/bungie-splits-with-activision-1831651740)
16. is Byf, M.N.: My name is byf's youtube channel. https://www.youtube.com/mynameisbyf (2011-Now)
17. Campbell, J.: Pathways to bliss: Mythology and personal transformation, vol. 16. New World Library (2004)
18. Campbell, J.: The hero with a thousand faces, vol. 17. New World Library (2008)
19. Chemers, M.: Ghost Light. Sothern Illinois UP (2010)
20. Colp, T.: Final fantasy 14 player is eating thousands of eggs on stream with no plans to stop. Polygon article. https://www.polygon.com/22590564/final-fantasy-14-online-eggs-rubberninja-stream-twitch. Accessed 22 June 2023 (2021)
21. Colp, T.: Gamer of the year 2022: Let me solo her. PC Gamer article. https://www.pcgamer.com/gamer-of-the-year-2022-let-me-solo-her/. Accessed 22 June 2023 (2022)
22. Compton, K., Grinblat, J., Kim, N., Short, E., Short, T.X.: A toolkit for encouraging player stories. https://polarisgamedesign.com/2022/a-toolkit-for-encouraging-player-stories/ (2023)
23. Corneliussen, H., Rettberg, J.W.: Digital culture, play, and identity: A World of Warcraft reader. MIT Press (2008)
24. Cragoe, N.G.: Rpg mythos: narrative gaming as modern mythmaking. Games Cult. **11**(6), 583–607 (2016)
25. Dorson, R.M.: Mythology and folklore. Annu. Rev. Anthropol. **2**, 107–126 (1973)
26. Eladhari, M.P.: Re-Tellings: the fourth layer of narrative as an instrument for critique. In: Rouse, R., Koenitz, H., Haahr, M. (eds.) Interactive Storytelling: 11th International Conference on Interactive Digital Storytelling, ICIDS 2018, Dublin, Ireland, December 5–8, 2018, Proceedings, pp. 65–78. Springer, Cham (2018). https://doi.org/10.1007/978-3-030-04028-4_5
27. Ford, D.: The haunting of ancient societies in the mass effect trilogy and the legend of zelda: Breath of the wild. Game Studies **21**(4), 17 (2021)

28. Ford, D.: That old school feeling (indeterminable year, after 2020)
29. Frazer, J.G.: The Golden Bough. Palgrave Macmillan UK, London (1990). https://doi.org/10.1007/978-1-349-00400-3
30. From Software: Dark Souls (2011)
31. From Software: Elden Ring (2022)
32. Gach, E.: Destiny 2's wild corridors of time puzzle ends with lackluster reward. Kotaku article (2020). https://kotaku.com/destiny-2s-wild-corridors-of-time-puzzle-ends-with-lack-1841112237. Accessed 22 June 2023
33. Gach, E.: They brought back destiny's loot cave, but not the loot. Kotaku article (2020). https://kotaku.com/they-brought-back-the-loot-cave-but-not-the-loot-1845638914. Accessed 30 April 2021
34. Geraci, R.M.: Virtually Sacred: Myth and Meaning in World of Warcraft and Second Life. Oxford University Press, USA (2014)
35. Harrington, J.: 4x gamer as myth: Understanding through player mythologies. In: DiGRA/FDG (2016)
36. Hirschman, E.C.: Movies as myths: an interpretation of motion picture mythology. Marketing and semiotics: New directions in the study of signs for sale, pp. 335–74 (1987)
37. Huizinga, J.: Homo Ludens. Random House (1956)
38. Jacob, M., Zook, A., Magerko, B.: Viewpoints AI: procedurally representing and reasoning about gestures. In: Proceedings of DiGRA (2013)
39. Javanshir, R., Carroll, B., Millard, D.E.: A model for describing alternate reality games. In: Rouse, R., Koenitz, H., Haahr, M. (eds.) ICIDS 2018. LNCS, vol. 11318, pp. 250–258. Springer, Cham (2018). https://doi.org/10.1007/978-3-030-04028-4_25
40. JoCat: So i wanna talk about how it took me 300 hours to like ffxiv (and how you can too in far less time). YouTube video essay (2022). https://www.youtube.com/watch?v=7LM08VrEs6k. Accessed 22 June 2023
41. Jones, B.: Puppetry, authorship, and the UR-narrative. The Routledge Companion to Puppetry and Material Performance, pp. 61–67 (2014)
42. Junius, N., Kreminski, M., Mateas, M.: There is no escape: theatricality in hades. In: Proceedings of the 16th International Conference on the Foundations of Digital Games (2021)
43. Juul, J.: Half-Real: Video Games Between Real Rules and Fictional Worlds. MIT press (2005)
44. Karth, I., Junius, N., Kreminski, M.: Constructing a catbox: story volume poetics in umineko no naku koro ni. In: Vosmeer, M., Holloway-Attaway, L. (eds.) Interactive Storytelling: 15th International Conference on Interactive Digital Storytelling, ICIDS 2022, Santa Cruz, CA, USA, December 4–7, 2022, Proceedings. pp. 455–470. Springer, Cham (2022)
45. Kjellgren, A.: Mythmaking as a feminist strategy: Rosi braidotti's political myth. Fem. Theory **22**(1), 63–80 (2021). https://doi.org/10.1177/1464700119881307
46. Kleinman, E., Carstensdottir, E., El-Nasr, M.S.: Going forward by going back: redefining rewind mechanics in narrative games. In: Proceedings of the 13th International Conference on the Foundations of Digital Games (2018)
47. Koenitz, H.: Towards a theoretical framework for interactive digital narrative. In: Aylett, R., Lim, M.Y., Louchart, S., Petta, P., Riedl, M. (eds.) ICIDS 2010. LNCS, vol. 6432, pp. 176–185. Springer, Heidelberg (2010). https://doi.org/10.1007/978-3-642-16638-9_22
48. Krzywinska, T.: Blood scythes, festivals, quests, and backstories: World creation and rhetorics of myth in world of warcraft. Games Culture **1**(4), 383–396 (2006)

49. Larsen, B.A., Bruni, L.E., Schoenau-Fog, H.: The story we cannot see: on how a retelling relates to its afterstory. In: Cardona-Rivera, R.E., Sullivan, A., Young, R.M. (eds.) ICIDS 2019. LNCS, vol. 11869, pp. 190–203. Springer, Cham (2019). https://doi.org/10.1007/978-3-030-33894-7_21

50. Larsen, B.A., Carstensdottir, E.: Wrestling with destiny: storytelling in perennial games. In: Mitchell, A., Vosmeer, M. (eds.) ICIDS 2021. LNCS, vol. 13138, pp. 236–254. Springer, Cham (2021). https://doi.org/10.1007/978-3-030-92300-6_22

51. Larsen, B.A., Carstensdottir, E.: Myth, diegesis and storytelling in perennial games. In: Vosmeer, M., Holloway-Attaway, L. (eds.) Interactive Storytelling: 15th International Conference on Interactive Digital Storytelling, ICIDS 2022, Santa Cruz, CA, USA, December 4–7, 2022, Proceedings, pp. 634–650. Springer, Cham (2022)

52. Laurel, B.: Computers as Theatre. Addison-Wesley (2013)

53. Lehmann, H.T.: Postdramatic Theatre. Routledge (2006)

54. Lévi-Strauss, C.: The structural study of myth. J. Am. Folklore **68**(270), 428–444 (1955)

55. Lévi-Strauss, C.: Structuralism and myth. Kenyon Rev. **3**(2), 64–88 (1981)

56. Levin, I., Levin, I.: The Stanislavsky Secret. Meriwether Publishing, Colorado (2002)

57. Long, D., Gupta, S., Anderson, J., Magerko, B.: The shape of story: a semiotic artistic visualization of a communal storytelling experience. In: Proceedings of the AAAI Conference on Artificial Intelligence and Interactive Digital Entertainment, vol. 13, pp. 204–211 (2017)

58. Long, D., Jacob, M., Magerko, B.: Designing co-creative AI for public spaces. In: Proceedings of the 2019 on Creativity and Cognition, pp. 271–284 (2019)

59. Malinowski, B.: Magic, Science and Religion and Other Essays. Read Books Limited (1954)

60. Mateas, M.: A preliminary poetics for interactive drama and games. Digit. Creativity **12**(3), 140–152 (2001)

61. Mateas, M., Domike, S., Vanouse, P.: Terminal time: an ideologically-biased history machine. AISB Quart. Special Issue Creativity Arts Sci. **102**, 36–43 (1999)

62. Maxis: The sims (2000)

63. Mitchell, A., Kway, L., Lee, B.J.: Storygameness: understanding repeat experience and the desire for closure in storygames. In: DiGRA 2020-Proceedings of the 2020 DiGRA International Conference (2020)

64. Mitchell, A., McGee, K.: Reading again for the first time: a model of rereading in interactive stories. In: Oyarzun, D., Peinado, F., Young, R.M., Elizalde, A., Méndez, G. (eds.) ICIDS 2012. LNCS, vol. 7648, pp. 202–213. Springer, Heidelberg (2012). https://doi.org/10.1007/978-3-642-34851-8_20

65. Mojang: Minecraft (2011)

66. Murray, J.H.: Hamlet on the Holodeck, updated edition: The Future of Narrative in Cyberspace. MIT press (2017)

67. Myelin: Myelin's youtube channel. https://www.youtube.com/@MyelinGames (2014-Now)

68. Nagy, G.: Greek mythology and poetics, vol. 2. Cornell University Press (1992)

69. Noclip: Final fantasy xiv documentary part #3 - "the new world" (2017), https://www.youtube.com/watch?v=ONT6fxiu9cw. Quote in question is at 16:15, spoken by Michael Christopher Koji Fox

70. Pint: I enslaved my final fantasy 14 guild... YouTube video essay. https://www.youtube.com/watch?v=onrX5ZURtek. Accessed 22 June 2023 (2021)

71. Pint: The secret behind FFXIV's best players... YouTube video essay. https://www.youtube.com/watch?v=qJPKVDZy1vU. Accessed 22 June 2023 (2022)

72. Rettberg, J.W.: Quests in World of Warcraft: Deferral and repetition, chap. 8, pp. 167–184. MIT Press (2008)

73. Reuben, N.: All the realm's a stage: Exploring final fantasy 14's incredible virtual theater shows. https://www.gamespot.com/articles/all-the-realms-a-stage-exploring-final-fantasy-14s/1100-6477641/. Accessed 22 June 2023 (2020)

74. Rimer, J.T., Yamazaki, M., et al.: On the Art of the Nō Drama: The Major Treatises of Zeami; Translated by J. Yamazaki Masakazu. Princeton University Press, Thomas Rimer (1984)

75. Rusch, D.C.: 21st Century Soul Guides: Leveraging Myth And Ritual For Game Design. Transgression, and Controversy in Play, University of Bergen, Norway, DiGRA Nordic Subversion (2018)

76. Ryan, M.L.: Avatars of Story. University of Minnesota Press, 111 Third Avenue South, Suite 290, Minneapolis (2006)

77. Schreier, J.: The makers of 'leeroy jenkins' didn't think anyone would believe it was real. Kotaku article describing the meme. https://kotaku.com/the-makers-of-leeroy-jenkins-didnt-think-anyone-would-b-1821570730 Acessed 5 June 2022. Upload of the original video can be seen at https://www.youtube.com/watch?v=mLyOj_QD4a4 (2017)

78. Segal, R.A.: Myth: A very short introduction. OUP Oxford (2004)

79. Selway, J.: Elden ring - who is let me solo her? Gamerant article. https://gamerant.com/elden-ring-let-me-solo-her-klein-tsuboi-famous-player/. Accessed 22 June 2023 (2022)

80. Shenpai FN et al.: Lunarcon. Convention run inside Final Fantasy XIV. See https://www.lunarcon.net/. Accessed 22 June 2023 (2021-Now)

81. Square Enix: Final Fantasy XIV (2013)

82. Vitelli, J.: Final fantasy XIV's club scene is all the rage. https://primagames.com/featured/final-fantasy-xivs-club-scene-is-all-the-rage. Accessed 22 June 2023 (2022)

83. Wagner, R.: The importance of playing in earnest. Playing with Religion in digital games, pp. 192–213 (2014)

84. Wardrip-Fruin, N.: Expressive processing. MIT Press, Cambridge (2002). Weiberg, B. Beyond Interactive Cinema. Retrieved 9 April 2009 (2009)

85. Winter, R., Salter, A., Stanfill, M.: Communities of making: Exploring parallels between fandom and open source. First Monday (2021)

86. Zheng, J.: The heartfelt story of the Eorzean aquarium, a full-scale FFXIV fish exhibit (2022). https://www.fanbyte.com/games/features/the-heartfelt-story-of-the-eorzean-aquarium-a-full-scale-ffxiv-fish-exhibit/. Accessed 22 June 2023

Bridging the Gap Between the Physical and the Virtual in Tabletop Role Playing Games: Exploring Immersive VR Tabletops

Anastasios Niarchos[1] , Dimitra Petousi[2] , Akrivi Katifori[1,2](✉) ,
Pantelis Sakellariadis[1] , and Yannis Ioannidis[1,2]

[1] National Kapodistrian University of Athens, Zografou, Greece
{sdi1600116,vivi,yannis}@di.uoa.gr
[2] Athena Research and Innovation Center, Marousi, Greece
dpetousi@athenarc.gr

Abstract. Throughout the history of tabletop role playing games (TTRPG), the image most associated with playing are people sitting around a table with notebooks, pencils, and occasionally map grids and miniatures. The Internet, however, especially in the post COVID-19 era, has enabled new ways of distance play and the emergence of virtual tabletop applications. In this work we explore the potential of immersive VR to support remote TTRPG play through a user study based on an immersive VR virtual tabletop application prototype. Using this virtual tabletop as an incentive, we invited 11 TTRPG players to offer their views and perspectives on the strengths and weaknesses of VR to support gameplay. We focus on key TTRPG characteristics and motivations, including shared imagination, creativity and sociality, to inform the design of immersive VR tabletop applications tailored to the needs of remote TTRPG play.

Keywords: Tabletop role playing games · immersive VR virtual tabletop

1 Introduction

The term Role-playing games (RPGs) refers to "the multiple styles of play activities revolving around the rule-structured creation and enactment of characters in a fictional world" [1]. This type of play places emphasis on players creating their own identity and experiencing the game story world from the perspective of this identity. In tabletop RPGs (TTRPGs), game play is managed by one or more human "game masters" (GMs), who act both as storytellers and facilitators and create the story world, also assuming the roles of the non-player characters (NPCs). The players are invited to participate in the adventure by enacting their characters, according to their characteristics defined in a character sheet and their personality and backstory, as they have defined it, in collaboration with the GM.

The most agreed upon starting point for what today is considered the TTRPG phenomenon is the publication of the original Dungeons & Dragons (DnD) fantasy role-playing game rules [2]. The concept of DnD has attracted fans of many different camps,

L. Holloway-Attaway and J. T. Murray (Eds.): ICIDS 2023, LNCS 14383, pp. 489–503, 2023.
https://doi.org/10.1007/978-3-031-47655-6_30

such as war-gamers who were interested in tactical combat or players interested in role playing and the immersion in a fantasy world, influenced by fantasy literature, such as the Lord of the Rings trilogy of books [3]. DnD and its many offshoots created the bedrock for future TTRPG generations, establishing the traditional way of "pen and paper" play as the golden standard for groups. An example TTRPG variation, niche but still well-known, is the practice of Live Action Role Playing (LARP). In this case, players stay in character as much as possible, dressed in appropriate attire and interacting in real-world environments, under the guidance of the GMs and event planners. LARP places much less emphasis on the rules in comparison to TTRPGs.

Through 80s and 90s, the image most associated with playing TTRPGs are people sitting around a table with notebooks, pencils, and occasionally map grids and miniatures, perhaps with some rise in the interest of asynchronous play through mail or the then very much young Internet. Additionally, we notice the rise of computer-based roleplaying games (CRPGs), as ways for players to engage individually in an RPG game, with their computer acting as a GM of sorts.

The Internet, however, has gradually enabled players to communicate more smoothly through long distances, synchronously or asynchronously, thus enabling new ways of distance play beyond the traditional play through correspondence. Groups often opt to play in group chats or through voice calls - pulling elements both from tabletop and correspondence modes of play.

With the new frontier opened in the online space, new digital tools have been created to assist the game experience. Rulebooks in the form of PDFs, online encyclopedias of a game's content, tools to create and organize characters, maps and notes, swiftly moving play towards the digital realm. Digital tools have gradually been introduced to collocated game play, through computers or smart devices that the GM and players bring on the table.

Virtual tabletop applications were conceived [4, 5] for distance play. They combine all of those tools and conveniences to create a welcoming environment for players and emulate the original tabletop experience as much as possible through the computer screen. The COVID-19 pandemic accelerated the use of virtual tabletops as a standard way for people to engage with the game. Even groups committing in collocated play were forced to switch to remote play to continue with TTRPG during the lockdowns. The widespread trend for remote TTRPG play can be seen in interactive livestreaming service platforms such as Twitch, with several on-line TTRPG sessions streaming at the same time [6], and also in services like the "StartPlaying" platform [7], supporting players to find professional GMs for TTRPG through virtual tabletops.

TTRPGs having been established as a remote play activity has been the incentive for new and innovative virtual tabletop applications gradually being introduced in the market, often employing XR with the promise to offer a more immersive digital game experience. Wizards of the Coast has announced its own virtual tabletop application, promising an immersive 3D experience, emulating tabletop gaming [8, 9]. The recent advances in immersive Virtual Reality (VR), towards stable, cost-effective and attractive product solutions have facilitated the wider commercialization of this technology and its wider application in gaming. 3D virtual tabletops, combined with this new hardware will possibly further transform remote play, bringing new interactions and possibilities in the mix.

VR as a medium has been shown to have strong potential for enhancing player engagement and immersion in the game world compared to desktop computer gaming [10]. It is still, however, unexplored whether this potential can be transferred, and in what way, to TTRPG, a game that traditionally has been player on a physical tabletop and based on shared creativity and imagination. In this paper we present an exploratory use study with the research objective to identify the strengths and weaknesses of VR as a means to support virtual TTRPG play, also compared with 2D virtual tabletops. To this end, we have designed and developed an immersive VR virtual tabletop application for TTRPG, combining different features available in existing virtual tabletops. We used it to design a user study, inviting 11 players and GMs with varying gamer profiles and expertise to test it. The study focuses on key game characteristics and motivations, including shared imagination and creativity, sociality, character creation and role identification as well as collaboration, with the ultimate objective to inform the design of an immersive VR tabletop application tailored to the needs of remote TTRPG play.

The next section focuses on relevant research on TTRPG characteristics as well as the potential of VR for gaming, also briefly presenting existing virtual tabletop solutions. Section 3 provides an overview of the immersive VR virtual tabletop. Sections 4 and 5 present the study methodology and results, respectively, while Sect. 6 concludes the paper.

2 Related Work

2.1 TTRPG Key Characteristics and Player Motivations

TTRPGs, collocated and remote, are an inherently social type of game. They involve multiple players who must work together to create and navigate a shared narrative. Thus, communication is essential in TTRPGs to not only build a sense of community but also strengthen teamwork, empathy and communication skills [11, 12].

Previous research has investigated the motivations of TTRPG players that are related to social interactions. According to [13], players engaging in group games develop a sense of belonging as they increase their opportunities for interaction with others. The collaborative nature of the game encourages social interaction and communication among players, resulting in the development of social skills and the establishment of long-lasting relationships. They also develop a sense of safety as the game provides an inclusive environment as they interact without fear of judgment or exclusion [14]. Players are allowed to express themselves creatively, try different roles, and explore different cultures and personalities. RPGs seem to promote tolerance and understanding of diverse backgrounds and lifestyles [15]. Fine [16] explores the world of role-playing games as a form of social interaction and community building and a way to support exploring one's identity and develop social skills.

Bowman [17] determined that TTRPGs benefit participants by facilitating community building and identity exploration. The concept of presence encompasses both psychological and social aspects, which is why it also relates to the Immersion into community [18]. Therefore, being fully immersed in the virtual community requires not only a strong psychological connection but also active engagement with others [17].

Collaboration and communication are key elements of TTRPG game play, and prerequisites to establish shared imagination, shared fantasy and shared experience, concepts also at the core of these games. Players are called to create the world and characters in their minds, relying on each other's creative inputs to develop a shared reality. By building a collectively imagined world, players can use their "agentic imagination", their active ability to shape an identity through immersive imagination [19]. The construction of this identity helps them become more deeply invested in their characters and engage in meaningful ways with the shared game experience [17].

In TTRPGs, the shared imagination between the players and the GM world provides the raw material and constraints that shape the character identities, and provides the setting where the players experience and enact these roles [20]. Worldbuilding involves not just imagining a new world, but also creating materials that instantiate it, such as maps, histories and mythologies, as well as geographical locations including towns and buildings of interest and key persons, important to this imaginary world. This material takes the form of physical or digital 2D and 3D designs, created by the group according to their individual motivations and skills. GMs often keep more or less elaborate notes of the adventure storyline, whereas players may record their perspective of the adventure in, some cases, very detailed and elaborate diaries, most often handwritten. TTRPG story design and play thus include a strong creative element [21], both from the perspective of the GM and the players, who collaborate to create this supporting material.

2.2   Virtual Tabletops and Digital Tools for TTRPG

Along with the emergence of remote TTRPG play, several supporting digital tools have been developed. Popular 2D virtual tabletop applications such as Roll20 [22] and Fantasy Grounds [23] attempt to transfer essential game elements from the physical, tangible TTRPG experience to the virtual. These may include network connectivity (for chat and/or voice communication), catalogs with easy access to rules, digital dice rollers, and digital note organizers (often with helpful formats, such as character sheets). Some additional tools are also provided for GMs specifically, such as placing props in the form of maps and tokens, music players and options to share images, and of course control over non-playable characters and other elements of each scene that players can't (or shouldn't) directly interact with.

Tabletop Simulator [24], designed to support the wider category of tabletop games, puts its users around a shared table and summons the props required for the experience they have chosen, including potentially the necessary components for a TTRPG session. Players control the camera and objects with keyboard and mouse controls, able to view the table freely, and the application also supports an immersive VR mode. The experience does not offer tools tailored for TTRPGs play, such as background environments or avatars for the characters.

VR applications that are targeted specifically to TTRPG experiences roughly take two main paths: Some provide a full set of rules for an established TTRPG or one of their own design, in an effort to substitute the GM role completely. In this manner, the rules and features are tailor made to suit the target experience of the users. For example,

Demeo [25] is a virtual TTRPG that has no need for a GM role, as the application takes on this role. Other applications such as Dungeon Full Dive [26], Quest Haven [27], RPG stories [28] or Tavern Tales [29] are virtual tabletops designed to support remote TTRPG play in VR just like their 2D counterparts.

Apart from virtual tabletop solutions tailored to TTRPG needs, generic multi-user chat applications, such as VR Chat [30] and RecRoom [31] could be considered as possible supporting tools. As they focus on communication and avatar and environment customization they can be consider to offer the possibility to set up a suitable TTRPG environment for TTRPG play, which could also support elements of LARP-ing.

The aforementioned applications offer different possibilities as to the point of view of the player. Some applications (such as Tabletop Simulator and Tavern Tales) place the players in an environment similar to traditional TTRPGs - a table with props, boards and miniatures to emulate the real-life experience. Others, like Demeo and QuestHaven, offer a bird's eye view of the actual game world. In some cases, the perspective might change. As an example, Demeo allows the users to "possess" characters and see the world from their perspective.

Taking into account the aforementioned directions and features of existing tabletop applications for TTRPG, we proceeded with an experience design for an immersive VR tabletop for our study. This prototype offers a virtual tabletop experience where the players can manipulate character sheets, dice and miniatures on the board, as in the physical world. Additionally, however, we provide the GM control of the virtual environment to offer a room-scale "backdrop" or set to the players, relevant to the in-game location their characters are at that point (a forest, a cave, a tavern, etc.), rather than a generic mundane virtual living room. It is amongst our aims to explore how this combination of perspectives, along with rich avatar customization features, is evaluated by the players and GMs, what is its perceived potential and what is the direction and additional features they would wish to see. The VR tabletop is presented in more detail in the following section.

3   The VR Tabletop Application Prototype

Our VR tabletop application prototype brings together different elements of TTRPG in VR. It attempts to reproduce traditional tabletop experience of people sitting around and playing over the same table without the need for them to in the same physical room. The application offers networking connectivity though a server and allows the players to select and customize their character avatar, meet in the virtual room and converse and interact with each other in real time.

The users start with character selection and avatar customization (Fig. 1-a). They select the character class (Fighter, Wizard, Cleric or Rogue) and their equipment. They are then able to customize their avatar features, including hair, skin color, body type, etc., as well as clothing and armor. In this virtual room they can also familiarize themselves with the controls for navigation and interacting with virtual objects, props and miniatures.

Then they can start playing, selecting to join either as a GM or player, and they appear in a virtual room with a table. Each chair acts as a teleportation spot. The table has a screen on one side, indicating the GM's position (which acts as the GM's control panel) (Fig. 2-b). The players can only change their position around the table and they are not allowed to wander around the virtual room, with the exceptions of specific cases, with teleportation points pre-scripted by the GM.

In order to access most of their options in the game, players can summon a floating character sheet that follows their orientation. The sheet includes information on their character and equipment, as well as common options for the VR experience, such as adjusting the sound level. The GM can also see the players statistics in order to make informed decisions during the game. The users can roll dice by pressing buttons, found either on their character sheet (Players) or behind the GM screen (GM), choosing from a selection of dice types, with 4, 6, 8, 10, 12, or 20 sides.

For the needs of the study, the application includes a simplified DnD 5.0 edition rule system, designed to speed up battle resolution scenes and reduce complexity of the character sheets of player and NPC characters. The system can be substituted if needed with that of any other TRPG.

The GM can freely change the virtual environment from a list of presets (including a tavern, a forest, a dungeon, etc.). Some of these environments have special features that the GM can control, such as moveable walls or unique interactable props. The GM, through the GM screen, can also select music that may fit the environment or the situation.

The GM has the option to summon a board on the table in front of the players, where they can organize combat scenes. The GM can place, on the board, miniatures for the NPCs, as well as props, while the players can put their own virtual miniatures. The GM can also change their avatar with a number of pre-made ones to assume the appearance of an NPC.

A list of items is provided for the GM that they can use to award players over the course of a game. These are available in the form of a card that can then be activated by the players to add the item in their equipment inventory (from where they can see the description of the item, roll dice associated with it, or summon a prop of it).

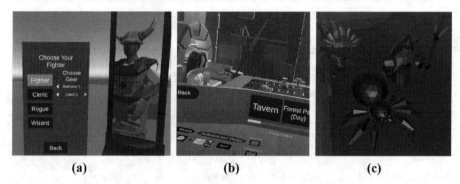

| (a) | (b) | (c) |

Fig. 1. Character customization, (b) GM perspective - GM screen and board and (c) Examples of virtual miniatures for combat scenes on the board

A low poly approach has been taken for the 3D graphics, mainly due to the cost of both the 3D graphics modeling and the hardware that would be needed.

Fig. 2. Example of play testing session. The GM perspective is shown on the screen.

4 Study Objectives and Methodology

Previous research in computer-based games has confirmed the strong potential of VR to enhance immersion and presence, in comparison with desktop gameplay [10, 32], literally offering players the possibility to "be in the game" [33]. However, it still remains unexplored how VR compares both to physical TTRPG play as well as remote gameplay supported by 2D tools. In this exploratory study we aim to examine how specific characteristics of immersive VR in this setting are perceived by players and how VR can be applied to support remote TTRPG gaming.

TTRPGs inherently present a wide diversity in game play, resulting from the freedom of each group to shape their own play experience. There are a multitude of approaches on the storytelling genre and style, the way the story is conveyed, the props used or the management of group interactions. In this sense, there are also conflicting perspectives on remote play and the use of virtual tabletops. Some players place emphasis on sociality, perceiving the game as incentive for the group to spend time together, and consider verbal and nonverbal social cues, including facial expressions and gestures, crucial during game play. Others are more willing to engage in remote play, in some cases using only voice or text chat for communication. There are also different approaches in terms of the props used in the game and its creative potential.

In this study, we focus on (1) sociality, communication and collaboration, (2) immersion and shared imagination and (3) creativity. We invited TTRPG GMs and players to experiment with the prototype and offer their perspectives on the strengths and weaknesses of its different features in relation to the aforementioned aspects, attempting to shape a vision for the future of immersive VR tabletops.

To this end, we made an open call in the authors' personal and institutional mailing lists and social media contacts to invite interested TTRPG players, novice or experienced, engaging in physical or remote TTRPG play. Eleven participants responded to the invitation. As can be seen by the participant profile presented in Table 1, the users had a mix of expertise in TTRPG. There were 6 experienced players, including the 4 GMs. All have been playing the game for several years and have concluded several campaigns. The novice players have participated to up to 5 play sessions, collocated or remote, have a basic understanding of the game and are willing to play frequently but are unable due to different reasons extraneous to the game itself. Most of the participants have extensive experience in computer games. In terms of experience with immersive VR applications, only two users were very experienced (using such applications frequently). Four had little experience (having tried immersive VR 2−5 times), two had no experience and the rest had used immersive VR applications 5−10 times. The participants had played a variety of TTRPG games, including Dungeons and Dragons, World of Darkness, Cyberpunk and others.

Table 1. Study participants profiles. The players with experience as GMs are noted with "GM"

		Age	Experience in TTRPG	Experience with VR	Experience with computer games
P1	GM	18−25	Experienced player and GM, both collocated and remotely	Much	Yes
P2		25−35	Novice player, playing remotely	Little	Yes
P3		18−25	Novice player, collocated	Medium	Yes
P4		35−45	Experienced player, both collocated and remotely	Medium	No
P5		25−35	Novice player, playing remotely	Medium	Yes
P6	GM	18−25	Experienced player and GM, both collocated and remotely	None	Yes
P7		25−35	Novice player, collocated	None	Yes
P8	GM	35−45	Experienced player and GM, both collocated and remotely	Little	Yes
P9		35−45	Experienced player, both collocated and remotely	Little	No
P10		35−45	Novice player, collocated	Much	No
P11	GM	45−55	Experienced player and GM, both collocated and remotely	Little	Yes

The participants were invited to the study location at a pre-arranged date and time, in four groups. They were informed about the study process, introduced to the VR equipment and asked to sign the consent form. They were then guided to join a common play session, with one of the evaluators immersed as a player or GM, to guide the process. The evaluator firstly introduced the functionality and tools, guiding the participants through avatar customization and the main game functionality. The users then participated in a brief play session. This first part of the study lasted about 1 −1.5 h. In the cases where GMs would participate in this role, they were introduced beforehand to the possibilities currently offered by the application, in terms of locations and NPC characters and the game system. They were also presented with an example adventure based on the designed locations, that they could use as is or adapt.

At the end of the play session the group participated in a semi-structured interview, aiming to record in depth, qualitative feedback on their general user experience and the specific study objectives. The study has been approved by the Ethics Committee of the National and Kapodistrian University of Athens.

5   Results

The transcripts of the interviews were analyzed thematically by three researchers which convened to compare their outcomes, before reaching a consensus. We present these outcomes in this section.

5.1   Sociality, Communication and Collaboration

Participants confirmed that a key part of the TTRPG experience is the sense of being together. Social interaction is at the core of the game, expressed by the act of sitting around a table, sharing a story and creating a collaborative narrative. The participants felt that they were truly present in the same shared space, thus effectively creating the illusion of a common place. The shared virtual environment and interactivity were impressive and convincing, allowing them to feel as if they were interacting with their companions in a real space, closely similar to playing in-person. Overall, as indicated by users, this experience seems to effectively foster a sense of connection and socialization among players. Participants with experience with on-line TTRPG gaming unanimously confirmed that this approach is superior to other types of remote TTRPG play. As P9 comments, "in immersive VR, the players are seated beside me, like in the physical world, available but not distracting. In chat-only play co-players are always invisible whereas when video is used, they are always present on the screen. For someone like me who plays in a group with friends living abroad, VR would be a great solution."

The study, however, also highlighted the importance of facial expressions in this context, as nonverbal cues that facilitate communication. The GMs specifically considered the lack of facial features and expressions in the avatars as an important flaw. They felt that it impacted on the level of immersion and realism, as well as on the communication and their ability to understand their players' emotional and mental state: "Missing facial expressions means that you miss out on a very important aspect of the game, that of role playing and theatrical improvisation." (P6) and "For me it is important to observe the players facial expressions during the game. I get feedback on their emotional response to the game, and I am able to adjust accordingly. Otherwise it is too impersonal." (P9).

The majority of the participants also felt that hand interaction with direct hand motion capture and incorporating realistic gestures in the virtual world would allow players to establish a stronger bond with their avatars and facilitate communication and teamwork. Hand gestures are also important as social cues that allow players to express emotions and intentions. Users mentioned that the experience should give them the opportunity to use their whole body to convey their intent, emotions, and reactions, enhancing social presence and creating a more cohesive and engaging game.

Finally, P5, who has experience with playing remotely with groups of players that do not know each other, considers immersive VR as having potential as an ice-breaking activity: "VR and the character avatars make it easier for people to become comfortable with each other, addressing any initial awkwardness or barriers."

5.2   Immersion and Shared Imagination

The users had mixed feelings about the low-poly graphics and aesthetics of the experience. While some believed that low poly graphics were not an issue, others felt that it detracted from the game's overall immersion. P3, P6, P7 and P10 enjoyed the simplicity of the graphics, characterizing the aesthetics as "charming" and "fairytale-like". They felt that it complemented the gameplay, allowing them to focus more on the mechanics. However, others, such as P8 and P11, believed that more realistic graphics would be necessary for a truly immersive experience, as lower quality ones make the environment and characters feel less lifelike and dynamic.

The immersive aspect of the technology was considered a strong aspect. Immersive VR gives a strong impression of "being there", transported in the alternate reality of the game. With its strong visual elements, it conveys the feeling of the location that the GM normally presents by talk and some supporting props. As P4 and P6 explained, this feature is especially helpful for players who may have mild or severe aphantasia (reduced capacity for mental imagery). Additionally, the 3D representation of space allows for a better understanding of the layout, especially useful where players collaborate in exploration or combat scenes.

Four of the more experienced players mentioned that another "side-effect" of immersion is that it supports concentration in the game as it isolates the user from the physical world and its distractions, such as the use of mobile devices or web browsers for activities external to the game.

Directly relevant to immersion is shared imagination, a key aspect of TTRPG. According to P8, the fact that the experience provides a visual and auditory reconstruction of the story world is contradictory to shared imagination. However, all participants agreed that it allows for a consistent experience and reduces the potential for misunderstanding or miscommunication due to differences in interpretation. According to P6, the minimal graphics of this prototype has the potential to stimulate shared imagination. A rough reconstruction of the world is there, and the GM and players can still jointly reconstruct the details of this world. The avatar customization tools at the beginning of the experience were very appreciated by all the players, as they felt that to create and customize their characters can increase player investment in the shared world and foster a greater sense of shared imagination.

Another aspect discussed was the need for embodied interactions. The prototype used controllers for hand interaction and allowed limited interactivity with the virtual environment beyond the use of the virtual tabletop tools and props. The majority of participants appreciated the possibility to experience different virtual environments that correspond to specific game scenes. However, P8 and P11 pointed out that allowing players only to look at the environment while sitting around the table does not really take advantage of the strong immersive qualities of the medium. P11 discussed at length his vision where the GM could alternate between the mode where they all sit around the virtual table and virtual scenes where players can interact with each other and the environment without the game table present. He suggested this more LARP-style play to be available for non-combat scenes, while the players rest and engage in conversation, like in a tavern, around the campfire or even in a dungeon in-between battle: "As the group often has to engage in conversation for decision making and role-playing, I would like to be able to enhance the ambience and feeling of this scene by immersing them in such virtual settings. Directly interacting with the environment and moving around would also work when they solve riddles or explore. I would not propose this for combat scenes as the game would then turn to a computer-based RPG."

5.3 Creativity and Story Execution

All four participating GMs discussed the creativity aspect in relation to the virtual tabletop. P6 and P8, both experienced GMs, mentioned that, although they feel confident for their storytelling skills, they are less proficient in describing, both verbally and visually, locations that the characters find themselves in. As P8 mentions, "It is very difficult for me to vividly describe a building or other locations and with my almost non-existent drawing skills, it is not possible to effectively convey even the layout of the location. I normally rely on terrain elements that I 3D-print and combine with drawing the space layout on the board. Being able to customize the locations in VR will help me complement my storytelling with more vivid settings." P8 and P11 commented positively on the value of being able to present NPCs in VR. P6, when asked if the explicit 3D presentation of the space in VR may affect GM creativity, felt that, on the contrary, having the possibility to customize a 3D space is the digital equivalent to 3D printing, sculpting and painting miniatures and terrain and is equally creative.

Five out of the 6 interviewed experienced players, commented on what they considered an important shortcoming of immersive VR as a TTRPG tabletop. All GMs mentioned that they keep brief, or more elaborate notes for the main story points and structure as well as information including location and NPC names and characteristics, etc. Players also frequently keep notes during game play, to record key points and information, and in some cases, they also engage in keeping journals as first person perspective diaries of their characters (P4, P9 and P11 as player), which often include handwritten maps or drawings of characters and places. These diaries are often hand written during collocated play or kept as notes in different digital mediums, including directly in the chat channels, when playing remotely. These participants expressed their concern on how they would be able to continue this practice in an immersive VR setting.

As shown in Fig. 2, P6 brought his notes for the adventure which were placed in front of him, however they were no longer accessible due to the VR equipment. P9, and P4 even more strongly, consider the difficulty of freely noting down in their diaries an important shortcoming of the experience. P9 proposed a collaborative voice or text note taking system, where the players and the GM would keep some notes on the main events of the story or key information. P8 proposed the use of passthrough VR to be able to continue using an actual notebook whereas P11 proposed voice recording for the player's personal notes.

Another issue discussed by the GMs and the more experienced players was the access to supporting material, such as game rule books, and web resources with clarifications and errata. P11 highlighted the strong need for access to such material, thus making an argument for the GM not being immersed at all, or having the possibility to break immersion. There was also the suggestion to be able to open a web browser window or view other types of files, such as pdf, while immersed.

P8 and P11 proposed automations for combat resolutions or dice rolls, explaining, however, that caution should be placed on not turning the game to a computer-based RPG. P8 also mentioned the common situation where a player character or NPC is bound to die in the game due to a particularly negative dice roll by the GM. The GM in some cases may opt to hide this outcome so as to keep the player alive. This means that the GM should have control on the outcome of these automations so as to intervene when needed.

6 Discussion and Conclusions

The recent boost to remote group experiences, imposed by the COVID-19 pandemic, as well as the availability of cost-effective and stable VR equipment, undoubtedly point to a future where the digital will strongly affect collocated physical tabletop gaming. TTRPGs are not an exception to this trend, with several groups already playing solely on-line and 2D and 3D virtual tabletops becoming more and more widespread. In this work we presented an explorative study towards a deeper understanding of the role of immersive VR in this new digital reality of TTRPG. We focused on three of the game's stronger aspects: sociality, shared imagination and creativity, and invited experienced and novice players for a hands-on demonstration and discussion on the strengths and weaknesses of the medium.

TTRPGs are undoubtedly a very complex type of game, allowing for an infinite variety of the style of play, directly relevant to the player group preferences. Even the exact same game setting, being DnD, Call of Cthulhu or other, may be implemented through variations in balance between storytelling, role play and combat scenes, the interpretation of and emphasis given on the rules, the use of props, or even the inclusion of LARP elements, where players dress-up and act as their characters. The affordances of the immersive VR medium are inherently effective for certain aspects of the game, while they become challenging for others.

Our initial hypothesis was that the GMs would be reluctant with the thought of fixed 3D environments as the settings for their adventures. They were, however, positive, considering this feature as supporting to transform a possibly unclear description of a location to a concise 3D visualization of the location layout and appearance. Physical miniature and terrain features are already used on the physical tabletop anyway, so the GMs did not feel that their virtual counterparts would be detrimental to the creative aspect of the game. They expressed however the need for customization, which makes the inclusion of intuitive authoring tools for such 3D spaces a necessary feature for the immersive VR tabletop. A recognized shortcoming was note or diary keeping in VR.

Sociality is a strong underlying motivation for any type of group game: "Through gaming, people can form strong bonds with others, which can help individuals feel connected and increase their overall well-being" [13]. For TTRPGs, social interaction is a key element, beyond coming together to have fun. The presence of a GM implies the need for group management and leadership skills, as well as conflict resolution. Teamwork is crucial to success, as players, acting as their selected characters, work together to solve problems and overcome challenges, immersed in a story world which is for them an alternate reality with similar rules as their real life. This social experience thus functions at different levels, beyond gaming and towards personal transformation [34]. The challenge of any virtual desktop is to support this process rather than hinder it. The study participants unanimously felt that the medium has significant potential for remote play, in comparison with existing virtual desktops. VR may instill a strong sense of social presence [35], which in this case can enhance sociality both at the level of the player, being together around the table at the same location, as well as that of the character, being able to interact with the other characters in the same virtual location. However, as the interviewed GMs noted, the graphics quality in this case has a significant role: It is important for the avatars to be able to support facial expressions and nonverbal social cues, in general, facilitating communication as well as supporting quality role playing. Humans rely heavily on facial expressions when communicating, including cues such as eye contact, smiles, and frowns, that help convey emotions and establish trust [36, 37]. Without these markers, virtual interactions may feel flat and incomplete, leading to a less immersive experience.

Character customization is also considered essential for role identification. It enables participants to create a character that embodies their unique personality and gaming preferences, empowering them to fully immerse themselves in the game world. This active participation elicits self-expression and increases player engagement, enhancing cooperative collaborations among team members.

The nature of the immersive VR technology can also enhance absorption and concentration in the virtual world and the interactive storytelling, isolating the user from the distractions that are normally present in the physical world. The user thus becomes more present in the game, both at the player and at the character level. Especially for the latter, for the players being able to appear as their character and interact with the story world and each other support a TTRPG direction where the role playing aspect becomes particularly enhanced, moving towards VR-LARP-ing.

One limitation of our study was the small sample pf 11 participants. This limits the generalizability of the findings, and the possibility to explore complex relationships between variables. Therefore, a bigger sample size is needed. Another limitation is the short-term play experience. The participants were not experienced VR users. This means that, on one hand, they needed time and practice to adjust to the medium and interactions, and, on the other, there was the novelty factor of being immersed in VR that may have affected the findings. Also, TTRPGs are typically played over longer periods of time. This means that it is important to understand how immersed gameplay would affect the players after several hours. Low poly aesthetics can also be considered as another limitation, as it has been unappealing to some participants, especially in relation to the lack of facial expressions on the avatars.

Further research is needed to fully understand the different elements of immersive VR game play, as well as identify additional potential uses. AS an example, it may become appealing to the constantly growing audience of viewers of play sessions, computer based or even on-line tabletop ones. Interested individuals could watch live VR-based TTRPG sessions, not only from their computer screen but also being immersed in the same virtual environment as the players, and able to explore and view the live action as "ghosts". The GM could, in this setting, allow selected members of the audience to even participate, playing the role or throwing the dice for one of the NPCs.

As our study confirmed, while immersive virtual reality tabletops are not likely to replace physical collocated gaming in the hearts of TTRPG players, there is still excitement about their potential. The key to their success will be offering features that take advantage of the unique affordances of VR beyond mere replication of the physical tabletop. As a follow-up for this work, we aim to continue looking for design elements that will enhance remote game play with an immersive VR tabletop.

References

1. Deterding, S., Zagal, J.P.: The many faces of role-playing game studies. In: Role-Playing Game Studies: Transmedia Foundations, pp 1–16. Routledge, New York (2018)
2. Michaud, J.: The Tangled Cultural Roots of Dungeons & Dragons. The New Yorker (2015)
3. Collins, N.: The Impacts of Dune and The Lord of the Rings on American Culture. Marquette University, Milwaukee (2022). https://epublications.marquette.edu/english_4610jrrt/27
4. Remote Play and RPGs in 2020: Online Tools for Adventurers in Quarantine (2020). https://ardentroleplay.com/2020/04/30/remote-play/
5. Scriven, P.: From tabletop to screen: Playing Dungeons and Dragons during COVID-19. Societies 11(4), 125 (2021). https://doi.org/10.3390/soc11040125
6. Tabletop RPGs on Twitch. https://www.twitch.tv/directory/game/Tabletop%20RPGs
7. StartPlaying, Tabletop RPGs Run by Professional Game Masters. https://startplaying.games/
8. Jarvis, M.: D&D is getting its own virtual tabletop, and it looks stunning. Dice-breaker (2022). https://www.dicebreaker.com/games/dungeons-and-dragons-5e/news/dnd-virtual-tabletop-revealed
9. D&D Virtual Tabletop: A Closer Look. D&D Beyond (2023). https://www.dndbeyond.com/posts/1474-d-d-virtual-tabletop-a-closer-look
10. Pallavicini, F., Pepe, A., Minissi, M.E.: Gaming in virtual reality: what changes in terms of usability, emotional response and sense of presence com-pared to non-immersive video games? Simul. Gaming 50(2), 136–159 (2019). https://doi.org/10.1177/1046878119831420
11. Spoor, J.R., Kelly, J.R.: The evolutionary significance of affect in groups: communication and group bonding. Group Process. Intergroup Relat. 7(4), 398–412 (2004). https://doi.org/10.1177/1368430204046145
12. Felnhofer, A., Kothgassner, O.D., Hauk, N., Beutl, L., Hlavacs, H., Kryspin-Exner, I.: Physical and social presence in collaborative virtual environments: exploring age and gender differences with respect to empathy. Comput. Hum. Behav. 31, 272–279 (2014). https://doi.org/10.1016/j.chb.2013.10.045

13. Coe, D.F.: Why people play table-top role-playing games: a grounded theory of becoming as motivation. Qual. Rep. **22**(11), 2844–2863 (2017) https://doi.org/10.46743/2160-3715/2017.3071
14. Kawitzky, F.R.: Magic circles: tabletop role-playing games as queer utopian method. Perform. Res. **25**(8), 129–136 (2020). https://doi.org/10.1080/13528165.2020.1930786
15. Goodall, A.M.: Magic, Adventure & Social Participation: Tabletop Role-Playing Games and Their Potential to Promote Social Inclusion and Citizenship (Doctoral dissertation. Université d'Ottawa/University of Ottawa, Ottawa (2021)
16. Fine, G.A.: Shared fantasy: Role playing games as social worlds. University of Chicago Press, Chicago (1983)
17. Bowman, S.L.: Immersion and shared imagination in role-playing games. In: Zagal, J.P., Deterding, S. (eds.) Role-Playing Game Studies: Transmedia Foundations, pp. 379–394. Routledge, New York (2018)
18. Bowman, S.L., Lieberoth, A.: Psychology and role-playing games. In: Zagal, J.P., Deterding, S. (eds.) Role-Playing Game Studies: Transmedia Foundations, pp. 245–264. Routledge, New York (2018)
19. Fuist, T.N.: The agentic imagination: tabletop role playing games as a cultural tool. In Torner, E., White, W.J. (eds.) Immersive Gameplay: Essays on Participatory Media and Role-Playing, pp. 108–126. McFarland, Jefferson (2012)
20. Schrier, K., Torner, E., Hammer, J.: Worldbuilding in role-playing games. In: Zagal, J.P., Deterding, S. (eds.) Role-Playing Game Studies: Transmedia Foundations, pp. 349–363. Routledge, New York (2018)
21. Katifori, A., Petousi, D., Sakellariadis, P., Roussou, M., Ioannidis, Y.: Tabletop role playing games and creativity: the Game Master perspective. In: Proceedings of the 17th International Conference on the Foundations of Digital Games (FDG 2022). Association for Computing Machinery, New York (2022). https://doi.org/10.1145/3555858.3555918
22. Roll20®, The Orr Group. https://roll20.net
23. Fantasy Grounds, SmiteWorks USA LLC. https://www.fantasygrounds.com/home/home.php
24. Tabletop Simulator, Berserk Games. https://www.tabletopsimulator.com/
25. Resolution Games. https://www.resolutiongames.com/demeo
26. Dungeon Full Dive, TxK Gaming Studios GmbH. https://dungeonfulldive.com/
27. QuestHaven. https://www.playquesthaven.com/
28. RPG Stories, Brave Alice. https://www.rpgstories.net/
29. Tavern Tales Tabletop Adventures. https://taverntalesgame.com/
30. VR Chat. https://hello.vrchat.com/
31. RecRoom. https://recroom.com/
32. Brade, J., Lorenz, M., Busch, M., Hammer, N., Tscheligi, M., Klimant, P.: Being there again— Presence in real and virtual environments and its relation to usability and user experience using a mobile navigation task. Int. J. Hum Comput Stud. **101**, 76–87 (2017)
33. Westerman D., Skalski P.D.: Presence and computers: a ghost in the machine? In Bracken C., Sklaski P.D. (eds.) Immersed in Media: Telepresence in Everyday Life, pp. 63–86. Routledge, New York (2010)
34. Mezirow, J.: How critical reflection triggers transformative learning. Adult Contin. Educ.: Teach. Learn. Res. **4**, 199–213 (2003)
35. Oh, C.S., Bailenson, J.N., Welch, G.F.: A systematic review of social presence: definition, antecedents, and implications. Front. Robot. AI **5**, 409295 (2018). https://doi.org/10.3389/frobt.2018.00114
36. Gabbott, M., Hogg, G.: The role of non-verbal communication in service encounters: a conceptual framework. J. Mark. Manag. **17**(1–2), 5–26 (2001). https://doi.org/10.1362/0267257012571401
37. Phutela, D.: The importance of non-verbal communication. IUP J. Soft Skills **9**(4), 43–49 (2015)

Circulation and Narrative in a Virtual Environment

Maarten Overdijk[✉]

HKU University of the Arts Utrecht, Utrecht, The Netherlands
maarten.overdijk@hku.nl

Abstract. Taking the notion of narrative space as a point of departure, this paper looks into possibilities of 'spatializing narrative' in virtual environments based on natural walking. One way to approach the workings of narrative space in virtual environments is through the lens of *circulation*. In 'real-world' architectural environments, the *circulation space* consists of multiple elements that program movement through space, connect spaces in a sequence, and direct the gaze. These circulation elements carry an expressive potential that can be brought into use in the design of narrative spaces. Circulation principles from 'real-world' architecture, however, do not readily translate to virtual environments. In a virtual environment, the notion of circulation itself needs revisiting. This paper examines to what extent, and how circulation principles come into play in an immersive narrative game called Lavrynthos. It examines the tactics that were used to create a continuous circulation space and assesses how circulation is brought into use in the narrative of the game. It identifies several ways in which the circulation space is deployed as a narrative device. The paper, finally, describes a dynamic wherein the circulation space changes as the player moves through the environment, opening up in the direction of movement. This spatial dynamic produces a range of creative possibilities for designing immersive narrative spaces based on natural walking.

Keywords: Narrative Spaces · Virtual Environment · Natural Walking · Dynamic Circulation · Impossible Spaces

1   Introduction

Taking the notion of narrative space as a point of departure [15, 18], this paper looks into possibilities of 'spatializing narrative' [18] in immersive virtual environments based on natural walking. Narrative space has long been recognized as a meaningful and productive dimension in interactive digital narrative [11, 15], in particular in genres such as the walking simulator or the narrative adventure game where the exploration of gamespace produces a narrative experience [13, 24]. The main premise of the notion is that space is not merely a neutral backdrop to narrative events, it is also actively involved in those events [18]. Narrative games, as Whistance-Smith points out [24], use gamespace as a narrative medium. They remediate certain strategies and techniques of spatial expression that are rooted in 'real-world' architecture [13, 18], as well as in cinema [16]. In describing the workings of narrative gamespace, Nitsche [16] – building

© The Author(s), under exclusive license to Springer Nature Switzerland AG 2023
L. Holloway-Attaway and J. T. Murray (Eds.): ICIDS 2023, LNCS 14383, pp. 504–516, 2023.
https://doi.org/10.1007/978-3-031-47655-6_31

on Jenkins [13] – stresses the role of 'evocative narrative elements' that are interpreted and pieced together by the player through a process of 'narrative comprehension'. In order to make sense of the game world, players extract meaning from characters, useful objects or textual clues – as well as from (more abstract) spatial features, thresholds and structures that depend on a spatial-semiotic mode of narrative expression [15, 18, 24]. As players move through space, they encounter these evocative narrative elements, interpret them in the context of the game, and build contextual connections between them [16].

One way to approach the workings of narrative space is through the lens of *circulation*. Circulation – understood as movement through a designed spatial environment – is at the heart of the narrative in genres such as the walking simulator or the narrative adventure game. This becomes apparent in games where the path through space corresponds with a storyline: in this case, movement and interaction with the environment along the path cause a narrative progression [24]. To fully grasp the potential of circulation for narrative gamespaces, it is worthwhile to look into the workings of circulation in 'real-world' architectural spaces. Architectural spaces ranging from landscape garden and themepark to heritage walk and museum build on principles of circulation to evoke a narrative experience [1, 6, 18, 25]. Here, it is important to realize that circulation entails more than a path through space. The *circulation space* of an architectural environment consists of the entirety of elements that program movement through space, connect spaces in a sequence, and direct the gaze [5]. Other circulation elements besides the path per se are involved and may contribute to the experience of narrative, such as the configuration of the path, the path-space relationship or the form of the circulation space [2, 18]. These elements carry an expressive potential, and can be brought into use in the design and analysis of narrative gamespace.

In this paper I explore the circulation space of an immersive narrative game. Recent developments in virtual reality technology have created new possibilities for movement in virtual environments based on natural walking [14, 17]. Here, the player walks through virtual space untethered without sliding or teleporting. This has opened up the opportunity of a walk-in narrative gamespace that builds on the expressive potential of circulation to create an *embodied* spatial experience. However, circulation principles from 'real-world' architecture do not readily translate to a virtual environment. In virtual reality, the notion of circulation itself requires reconsideration. This paper sets out to explore the circulation space of an immersive narrative game called *Lavrynthos* [7]. To my knowledge, Lavrynthos is the first game in virtual reality that creates a narrative experience based on natural walking in a continuous circulation space. Throughout the paper, I examine circulation in 'real-world' architectural space vis-à-vis the immersive narrative space of Lavrynthos. I describe the game in terms of its circulation elements [5] and examine the tactics that were used to create a continuous circulation space. I then assess to what extent, and how, the immersive circulation space in Lavrynthos adds to the narrative of the game. My overall aim is to contribute to the discussion on narrative spaces in the field of interactive digital narrative [11, 15].

2 Circulation and Narrative

To grasp the potential of circulation for narrative games in virtual environments, it is worthwhile to have a look at how circulation works in 'real-world' architecture. Studies of virtual gamespaces often refer to architectural circulation. For example in the appreciation of the *Promenade architecturale* and the *Hôtel particulier* as metaphors to describe the relation of circulation path and player agency in videogame spaces [3]. Or in the book *Virtual Cities* [8], that offers a unique insight in the circulation spaces of virtual game cities from the perspective of an urban designer. And there is the tradition of garden and park-environments that serves as a reference, such as the English landscape garden that 'has an artificial character, and is designed to create a spatial experience that unfolds along a carefully planned route' [10]. Or the themepark, that sparked the notion of 'environmental storytelling' as a perspective on the narrative space of, for example, the walking simulator [4, 13]. In his work on videogame spaces, Nitsche [16] refers to architectural circulation in some detail. In his view, the spaces of video games are *presented* to us in a form that is a hybrid between 'navigable architectural space' and 'cinematically represented space'. The virtual camera makes gamespaces cinematic, he argues, 'and the interaction makes them accessible much like architectural structures' [16]. In videogame spaces, the player takes the camera with them – in the words of Nitsche [16] – to 'enter a continuous navigable diegetic world'. This puts circulation at the heart of the player's experience. And helps to understand the analogy of gamespace and themepark – the latter arguably conceived of as a hybrid of cinema and architecture as well: 'The visitor is the camera', one of Disney's designers famously said, 'and the spatial arrangement of the park is the montage' [25].

In themeparks such as Disney's, 'story' operates on different levels but at the heart of it lies a carefully designed circulation space. Circulation in the themepark is designed to move large amounts of visitors in a controlled fashion through a sequence of scenes. Some of these scenes overlap seamlessly, there's zooming in and out (from the monorail for example) and carefully planned greenery brings elements of the story into focus or keeps them out of sight. Although variations exist, certain circulation elements often appear in Disney parks, such as the radial organization from a central hub that connects different 'worlds' [6]. Each of these 'worlds' is a spatial story that takes place within its own, enclosed area of the park, a tour with a beginning and an end and a plot that unfolds within the hour. Once returned at the central hub, the visitor 'switches' to another channel – television was an important metaphor at the time the park was designed. As an influential and often cited example, the themepark displays some of the intricacies of how circulation works in narrative space: the circulation space of the park directs the gaze of the visitor along a spatial 'montage'; it defines relations between spaces as a narrative sequence, and consequently, programs movement through space as a narrative progression.

Studies have shown various ways in which the circulation space of an architectural environment contributes to, or produces a narrative experience in architectural spaces other than themeparks [2, 18]. Foote and Azaryahu [18] provide the example of a museum with two parallel paths that run through the building in the form a double-helix. At each of the crossings, visitors have a choice which path (read: storyline) to follow: the chronological line, along five successive chapters, or the path along a series of thematically organized rooms. In this example, the configuration of the path structures the story logic of consecutive, chronological 'chapters' and thematical 'rooms' as well as the element of choice. Another, often-mentioned example – described in detail also by Foote and Azaryahu [18] – is the Jewish Historical Museum in Berlin, designed by the architect Daniel Libeskind. Visitors enter this building via an underground passage from the adjacent 'old' museum. Here, below street level, they are confronted with three so-called 'axes': oblique corridors crossing each other with a disorienting effect on the visitor. One path leads to 'the garden of exile' and terminates there, a second path leads to 'the tower of the Holocaust' and terminates in space as well. The third path sends the visitor *through* the spaces of the museum proper in a path-space relationship that represents continuity. Together, the three paths symbolize the history of Jewish life in Germany: exile, death, and survival. The architecture of the museum shows how the design of a circulation space may convey symbolic meaning through its form, path configuration and path-space relationships. Its underground entrance, the oblique form of the corridors and the crossing of the paths show how it may evoke a bodily and affective response. The three axes show how the configuration of a path may structure the narrative as a sequence of episodes or chapters.

A lot can be learned about the potential of circulation for narrative and spatial storytelling by looking into 'real-world' architecture. This can be pinpointed further by examining the elements that make up the architectural circulation space. In the classic text *Architecture: Form, Space, and Order* Frances Ching [5] mentions five elements that jointly describe the circulation space of an architectural environment. Each of these elements, individually or combined, may contribute to a narrative dimension of space. The first element, the *approach*, essentially asks the question: how do we approach the space and what do we see? This alludes to the anticipation of approaching and to what a space reveals about itself from the outside. When there is no approach, and one finds themselves in the midst of a situation, this is significant in terms of storytelling as well. The second element, the *entrance*, marks a transition from one place to another (a passage from 'here' to 'elsewhere' in the case of the themepark entrance). Apart from the 'main entrance' there may be several other spatial transitions within the space – gates, portals, doors or more subtle thresholds that signify a transition from one space (or episode) to the next. The *path*, subsequently, is the essence of the circulation space. A path connects spaces, and its *configuration* influences the way in which we experience these spaces and their relation (as different 'worlds', for example). From a first-person perspective all paths are linear, as Ching points out, but a path can take on different forms. It can be curvilinear or segmented, intersect other paths, have branches or form a loop. The configuration of the path can be radial (like the central hub in Disneyland) or spiral, it can form a grid or a network. The configuration of the path is particularly significant when it comes to the structure of a narrative space. The path, furthermore, may be related in various ways to the spaces it links. A path can *pass by spaces*, it can *pass through spaces,* and it can *terminate in a space* (the latter is often used to endow spaces with symbolic meaning, like in the example of the Jewish Historical Museum). The circulation space, finally, can take on several *forms*. It can be enclosed – like a public passage or a corridor, open on one side – like a balcony or gallery, or open on both sides [5], thus contributing to quite different moments or sequences in narrative space.

3 Circulation in Virtual Environments

Natural walking in virtual reality allows the player an embodied spatial experience that is – potentially – more akin to a 'real-world' architectural experience than navigating conventional gamespace is. However, when it comes to circulation, there are obvious and substantial differences between 'real-world' architecture and immersive virtual environments. Circulation principles from architecture do not readily translate to the virtual spatiality that is produced by the head-mounted display (HMD). In a virtual environment, the notion of circulation *itself* requires reconsideration. Hereto it is useful to elaborate briefly on the nature of the virtual space that is produced by the HMD. In virtual reality, a screen-image is generated that links a stereoscopic view to a 360° panoramic field of vision. This link is possible, as Schröter [20] explains, because the image changes with every movement of the player's head: each change in player position generates a new image, and this creates the sensation of a space that one can move through. Schröter [20] appropriately characterizes this as 'performative actualization', emphasizing that this virtual spatiality is activated by the position and orientation of the player, in a loop of input and feedback. This dynamic is key when considering the possibilities of circulation in an immersive virtual environment. In particular because the virtual image in the HMD does not only represent space as we know it, but can also be programmed to change in specific ways in response to the position of the player. Programmed in a game engine, these changes may pertain to the physics of the environment, the properties of the virtual camera or to the objects in the 3D scene. With respect to circulation an interesting possibility emerges: the circulation space may change as the player moves through the environment.

This ties into what is referred to as the challenge of *natural walking* in virtual reality [14, 21]. Since the virtual environment is often larger than the actual room the player is in, the challenge is to map a large-scale virtual environment onto a room-scale physical space (that is, 2 by 2 m or more) in such a way that a continuous, natural movement along a path becomes possible. Studies indicate that natural walking contributes to a more embodied and immersive spatial experience in comparison to movement mechanics such as teleporting or sliding [12, 14, 21], and this suggests that the same is true for the experience of narrative. As Vasylevska and Kaufmann point out [22], there are several methods to 'compress' a virtual environment into room-scale and allow for natural walking. These methods can be grouped as *sense manipulation* (also known as redirected walking), *rendering manipulation*, and the method we are interested in here, *manipulation of the 3D scene* [22]. Scene manipulation, whereby the circulation space changes as the player walks through the environment, allows one to conceive of a continuous, natural movement in a limited physical space. A particularly promising approach of scene manipulation is the use of *impossible spaces*. The core idea here is to map different parts of the virtual environment onto the same actual space by replacing sections of the environment as the player moves through it. This method allows a continuous path by 'opening up' in specific directions, based on the position of the player.

The challenge is to design the replacement of sections in such a way that the player doesn't notice it is being done. There are several tactics for this, such as masking (blocking the changes out of sight), distracting (having the player look at something else) and the use of deterrents (directing the player onto a specific path) [21, 22]. Each of these tactics is oriented towards keeping manipulation of the scene out of sight. In simulations of architectural circulation – walking through a house or some other type of building – this is often achieved with circulation elements such as corridors or elevators, so-called 'transitioning areas' that allow lay-out changes to be made that are invisible to the user. Such transitioning areas exploit a phenomenon known as 'change blindness' [22], which refers to a failure to notice changes in a scene that have occurred outside the subject's field of view. The use of the elevator in the vr game Tea for God [23] is a well-known example of this. Another type of transitioning area, and the one under consideration here, consists of portals [14, 17]. In this case, subsections of the environment are separated by a pair of portals – an entrance and an exit. However, the player travels *instantly* between the portals through local teleportation and experiences a seamless transition from one subsection to another [14, 17]. Also – and this is crucial – the portal technique allows for a *visual continuity*, meaning that the player is able to look through the portal before entering it – and thus before activating the subsection with their position. One way to achieve this is by using 'render textures', as demonstrated by Lochner and Gain [14], whereby an image of the subsection beyond the portals is projected onto the portal surface – allowing a view forward *and* backward.

In summary, there are several tactics to design continuous circulation spaces in immersive virtual environments based on natural walking. The dynamic of 'performative actualization' [20] is key to an understanding of how they work. Basically, positional tracking cues a replacement of sections of the environment as the player moves through the scene. This *dynamic* circulation space allows one to conceive of a continuous, natural movement along a path in a limited physical space. So far, we have seen the application of this principle in research projects [14, 17, 22] and an FPS game [23]. What could it do when applied in the context of a *narrative* game? To what extend – and how – would it allow to bring circulation space into use as an evocative spatial dimension in the narrative?

4   Case

In order to explore this question I conduct a case-study of a narrative game called *Lavrynthos* [7]. Lavrynthos, which premiered at the 2021 Venice International Film Festival, is a walk-in narrative game in virtual reality that has received much acclaim for its innovative use of natural walking. It implements the principle of *impossible spaces* described above in a work of immersive storytelling. To my knowledge, it is the first narrative game available to the public to do so. I examine the game on basis of first-hand experience from multiple walkthroughs as well as through storyboards and notes made by the designers [26]. With a descriptive analysis I look into the characteristics of the circulation space of Lavrynthos. I describe the space in terms of circulation elements [5] and examine the tactics that were used to create a continuous circulation space based on natural walking. I then assess to what extent, and how this immersive circulation space contributes to the narrative of the game.

4.1 Analysis

Lavrynthos is a walk-in narrative game based on the Greek myth of the Minotaur. The authors departed from the technical possibility of creating a walk-in virtual environment compressed in room-scale, before thinking of any narrative [26]. Soon after came the idea of two characters – one of them the Minotaur, the other a girl named Cora – chasing each other through the labyrinth. The player witnesses the encounter of these two characters and follows them as their quest unfolds. While wandering along the path, the player walks up to scenes that are set in consecutive sections of the labyrinth. There, the story is developed through dialogue between the characters. The player is present in the space, most of the time as a bystander to the dialogue, and is occasionally addressed directly. At all times, the player has the agency to move through space, however, without the ability to intervene or alter the plot. This type of narrative interactivity qualifies as what Ryan [19] has termed internal-exploratory interactivity: the player 'has a virtual body in the fictional world' but their role in this world is 'limited to actions that have no bearing on the narrative events' [19]. The circulation space of the game, as I will point out, plays an active part in the unfolding of the narrative.

The Circulation Space of Lavrynthos

In the opening scene, the player finds themselves on a narrow path deep in the labyrinth. There has been no approach and thus no knowledge of the space from the outside. As the player starts to explore the path that lies in front of them, it appears to extend beyond the walkable play-area. These extending segments of the path are typically hedged of with bars or debris of rock, directing the player onto an intersecting path within the 2 × 2 area (Fig. 1). The labyrinth suggests a multicursal network [3] of branching and intersecting paths, but its circulation space is in fact unicursal: there's (for most of the story) only one direction to walk in – forward along the singular path. The segments of the path that extend beyond the play-area are visible but cannot be entered, making

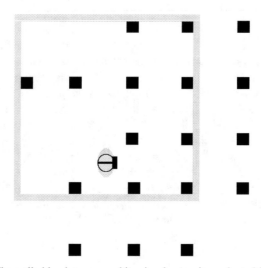

Fig. 1. The walkable play-area and its visual extension, adapted from [26].

the labyrinth appear much larger and more complex than it actually is. This tactic of extending the environment visually is deployed throughout the game.

The lay-out of the environment is based on scene manipulation and impossible spaces. When the player reaches the end of the walkable play-area, the path directs them into turning a corner or pilar. Around the corner or pilar a new section of the environment opens up and replaces a previous one. The use of render textures allows the adjacent section to be seen before it is activated by the player. Figure 2 shows a schematic depiction of 4 sections of the labyrinth, explaining how this is done. The dotted lines indicate the approximate position of the portals. There are two 'textured' portals involved in each transition: one provides a view forward before moving through the portal and one allows the player to look backward when on the other side. This visibility adds to the experience of continuity. However, the portal technique in itself does not reorient the player in the walkable play-area. The orientation of the player may or may not change, depending on how the path continues in the following section. The combination of local teleportation and the ability to see 'through' the portals creates a sensation of continuous, natural movement throughout the circulation space of the labyrinth.

Circulation Space and Narrative
The setting of the narrative, the space that is traversed by the player and where the scenes are enacted, consists of the 'labyrinth proper' and of several locations that are 'hidden' inside the labyrinth. These hidden locations include a classroom, a museum and a classical theatre that extend seamlessly from the space of the labyrinth. This setting is hierarchically organized as a whole through what Ryan [18] refers to as 'a relation of containment': a spatial logic wherein the hidden spaces are perceived as subspaces of the

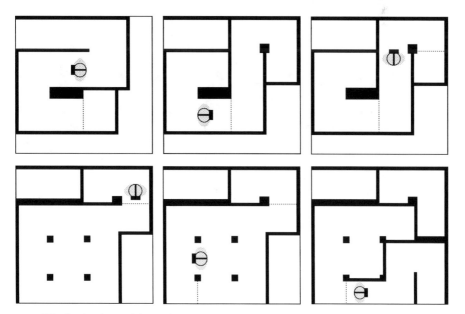

Fig. 2. Sections of the environment and placement of portals, adapted from [26].

labyrinth. Some of the boundaries between these spaces are clear-cut and some are more fuzzy. In terms of the navigability – and presentation – of space, two scenes stand apart. They represent a vision and a memory sequence as seen through Cora's 'mind's eye': the space of thought rather than the space of actual events. These two scenes behave like cut-scenes in the sense that the player is locked into them, but with the ability to move around.

The path through the labyrinth provokes a meandering walk. The player walks the actual distance whereby their body as a whole is brought into play: they have to turn corners, maneuver ledges, and pass through narrow corridors. The path is comprised of twelve segments, each of them positioned between an entrance and an exit. In each of the segments, a scene is enacted. The path, in this way, structures the narrative: it connects the spaces of the labyrinth as a whole, and its configuration in segments defines these spaces as a sequence of episodes. The length of a segment dictates the time it takes to traverse and walk from one episode to the next. The shape of the labyrinth evokes the dramatic structure of the *quest*: a journey through a world whereby successful navigation along the path symbolizes a process of personal growth. In Lavrynthos, the player is essentially a witness to the quest laid upon the two main characters – focused on finding the exit of the labyrinth, and a purpose in life. The dramatic structure is reflected in the circulation space. Between the first episode, where the player finds themselves on a narrow path somewhere in the labyrinth, and the final episode, where they reach the exit, the characters are tested and face their ordeal. The player, following the characters along the path, becomes a fellow-traveler, and because navigating the labyrinth causes a direct bodily and affective response, shares in their disorientation and fear of not being able to escape.

The above shows three general principles as to how the circulation space contributes to the narrative of the game. Basically, the circulation space structures the narrative in time and space, causes a bodily and affective response, and conveys meaning through symbolism and metaphor. Looking closer, we find that – within these principles – the circulation space is deployed as a narrative device in ways that are more specific. To illustrate some of the intricacy of how this is (more or less successfully) done, I elaborate on two episodes in some detail – the second and third, respectively.

At the end of the first episode, after having roamed the labyrinth for some time, the player leaves the 'labyrinth proper' to step out onto a balcony that is part of a classical *scaenae frons*, looking out on what appears to be the audience ring of a theater. This is where the player meets the Minotaur, in first person, who then – by surprise – forces them off the balcony. There's a flash-screen, and the player finds themselves in the audience ring looking towards the balcony. In the same moment, the scale of the environment has changed from 1:1 to dollhouse. The balcony has now become the stage for a dialogue between the two main characters with the player in the audience. In terms of circulation, there's a number of things going on in this episode. Instead of *passing-through* space in true scale, the player now *passes-by* a dollhouse-scaled representation of that same space. With this change in scale and path-space relation, the narrative perspective has changed as well: from first to third person. Instead of being on stage with the characters, the player is now – literally – in the audience, looking at a (now) miniature scene from the outside. The path-space relation, in other words, is used as a device to support a shift in narrative perspective. In the execution of this transition, however, the player is relocated in virtual space. This constitutes a break from continuous circulation: for a brief moment, masked by the flash-screen, the trajectory in virtual space does not correspond to the path in actual space. Because the player hasn't moved in actual space, it is the structure of the stage that, with its change in scale, appears to have moved away from *them*.

The subsequent, third episode starts when the dialogue on the balcony has ended, and the player is invited by the Minotaur to walk into the *porticus post scaenam* – the space behind the stage. As the player enters the porticus, still *passing-by* space in dollhouse-scale, they find that they have in fact left the theatre and entered a space that contains a representation of Cora's parental home. There, Cora's past is narrated in three miniature scenes that are embedded sequentially in the representation of the home. The miniature scenes are presented as *mis-en-abyme*: spatial stories framed within the larger spatial story. The player walks past each of the three flashbacks, enacted in turn, and is then looped back to the *scaenae frons* where the dialogue between Cora and the Minotaur continues in the present time of the narrative. In terms of circulation, the configuration of this segment of the path – a *loop, passing-by* space in dollhouse scale – is used to support the manipulation of narrative time. The loop temporarily diverts the player from the path of chronological progression and constitutes a break from the events as they occur in real-time, offering a glimpse into Cora's past. The fact that the segment loops *behind* the stage, is significant. In this sequence, the front of the stage represents the present time of the narrative, whereas the space behind the stage is deployed to represent a time past. Later in the game, when the player returns to the 'labyrinth proper', they are again *passing-through* space in a 1:1 scale.

5 Discussion

Virtual reality is known to be very compelling, transporting players 'elsewhere' rather than keeping them 'grounded' in actual space. Virtual movement mechanics such as teleporting or sliding may lead to a sense of ground*lessness* and to what Elsaesser [9] qualifies as a 'floating presence': a disembodied spatial experience. Natural walking, in contrast, connects the player to the actual space they are in. In fact, one should look at the circulation space in Lavrynthos as a *composite* of actual and virtual. A situation wherein, as Höfler [12] points out, the sensory and motor perceptions of walking on actual ground connect the body to actual space while it is simultaneously immersed in the virtual space of the HMD. Since the virtual path and the actual path are mostly (except for a brief moment) mutually supportive, the player connects the two in a congruent, embodied spatial experience. And this is key. Natural walking allows an embodied experience of the circulation space. It heightens spatial immersion and strengthens the evocative power of circulation in the narrative.

The circulation space of Lavrynthos contributes to the narrative in three principle ways: it structures its logic in time and space, it causes a bodily and affective response, and it conveys meaning through symbolism and metaphor. These three principles operate in close conjunction. Building on these principles, the authors of Lavrynthos found creative ways to deploy the circulation space as a narrative device. The analysis in this paper illustrates how it was used to shape the episodic structure of the narrative, support a shift in narrative perspective, and to arrange narrative time.

To create a continuous circulation space in a virtual environment, it is crucial to bring certain sections of the environment into the frame at the right moment, or precisely to keep them out of it. Again, a comparison can be made with circulation in architecture. As Gerber [10] points out, the design of the landscape garden – just like virtual gamespace – is about concealing boundaries that are there, but should not be perceived. It's about continuous movement through a space that feels 'open', but really points in specific directions and viewpoints. This is very true for the narrative space in Lavrynthos. The environment may extend visually, but walkable sections can be no larger than the available room space. Obstacles should be used to direct the player onto the right path, and portals must be carefully positioned and oriented for scene manipulation to occur outside the player's field of vision. Portal-pairs are deployed as transitioning areas, providing visual continuity while masking the replacement of sections of the environment. When executed well, this allows the circulation space to be experienced as a continuous and coherent whole, opening up in the direction of movement as the player moves through the game.

It is important to note that, while the path directs the movement of the player through the environment, the position of the player in the environment cues the unfolding of the path. There is, in other words, *a reciprocal relation* of body movement and circulation space: the circulation space shapes the movement of the body, and the movement of the body activates the circulation space, in what can be referred to as *dynamic circulation*. Although the circulation space of Lavrynthos unfolds as the player moves through it, there is only one path to follow. It is not difficult, however, to think of an instance where the spatial dynamics of Lavrynthos could be deployed in a narrative space based on a branched path or a network, offering choice or multiple routes through the narrative.

6 Conclusion

In this paper, I set out to consider circulation and its relation to narrative in a walk-in narrative game. At the heart of such a narrative game lies a carefully designed circulation space that can be described in terms of its elements: entrance, approach, configuration of the path, path-space relationship and form of the circulation space [5]. These circulation elements carry an expressive potential that – individually or combined – may contribute to or produce a narrative spatial experience [2, 18]. Just like in 'real-world' narrative spaces, the circulation space of a virtual environment may contribute to narrative in three principle ways: it may structure the logic of the narrative in space and time, cause a bodily and or affective response, and convey meaning through symbolism and metaphor. Circulation principles from 'real-world' architecture, however, do not readily translate to immersive virtual environments. In virtual reality, the notion of circulation itself needs revisiting. The principle of 'performative actualization' [20] emphasizes that a virtual circulation space is activated by the position and orientation of the player in space. Scene manipulation [22] allows the circulation space to change as the player walks through the environment. This spatial dynamic opens up a range of creative possibilities for designing circulation spaces that enable continuous natural walking and an embodied experience of narrative gamespace. The case of Lavrynthos shows that this holds great promise for the design of walk-in virtual storyworlds.

Acknowledgements. The author would like to thank Rob van Dam and Aaron Oostdijk of HKU University of the Arts Utrecht for their collaboration and support in this study. The research in this paper has been co-financed by the Taskforce for Applied Research SIA, part of the Dutch Research Council NWO.

References

1. Azaryahu, M., Foote, K.: Historical space as narrative medium: on the configuration of spatial narratives of time at historical sites. Geo. J. **73**(3), 179–194 (2008)
2. Bloomer, K., Moore, C.: Body, Memory and Architecture. Yale University Press (1977)
3. Bonner, M.: Piercing all layers of the anthroposphere: on spatialization and architectural possibilism in Hitman. In: Gerber, A., Götz, U. (eds.) Architectonics of Game Spaces: The Spatial Logic of the Virtual and its Meaning for the Real. Transcript, Bielefeld (2019)
4. Carson, D.: Environmental Storytelling: Creating Immersive 3D Worlds Using Lessons Learned from the Theme Park Industry. Game developer (2000). https://www.gamedevel oper.com/design/environmental-storytelling-creating-immersive-3d-worlds-using-lessons-learned-from-the-theme-park-industry. Accessed 13 Aug 2023
5. Ching, F.D.K.: Architecture: Form, Space, and Order. Van Nostrand Reinhold, New York (1996)
6. Clavé, S.A.: The Global Theme Park Industry. Cabi, Cambridge (2007)
7. Delirium XR: Lavrynthos (2021)
8. Dimopoulos, K.: Virtual Cities: An Atlas & Exploration of Video Game Cities. The Countryman Press, New York (2020)
9. Elsaesser, T.: The return of 3-D: on some of the logics and genealogies of the image in the twenty-first century. Crit. Inq. **39**(2), 217–246 (2013)
10. Gerber, A.: The architectonics of game spaces: or, why you should play and design video games to become a better architect. In: Gerber, A., Götz, U. (eds.) Architectonics of Game Spaces: The Spatial Logic of the Virtual and its Meaning for the Real. Transcript, Bielefeld (2019)
11. Hameed, A., Perkis, A.: Spatial storytelling: finding interdisciplinary immersion. In: Rouse, R., Koenitz, H., Haahr, M. (eds.) Interactive Storytelling. ICIDS 2018. Lecture Notes in Computer Science, vol. 11318, pp. 323–332. Springer, Cham (2018). https://doi.org/10.1007/978-3-030-04028-4_35
12. Höfler, C.: Sense of being here: feedback spaces between vision and haptics. In: Feiersinger, L., Friedrich, K., Queisner, M. (eds.) Image - Action - Space: Situating the Screen in Visual Practice, pp. 159–176. Walter de Gruyter GmbH, Boston, MA (2018)
13. Jenkins, H.: Game design as narrative architecture. In: Wardrip-Fruin, N., Harrigan, P. (eds.) FirstPerson: New Media as Story, Performance, and Game. The MIT Press, Cambridge, MA (2004)
14. Lochner, D., Gain, J.: VR natural walking in impossible spaces. In Proceedings of the 14th ACM SIGGRAPH Conference on Motion, Interaction and Games (MIG 2021), pp. 1–9 (2021)
15. Meyer, S.R.: Right, left, high, low: narrative strategies for non–linear storytelling. In: Nack, F., Gordon, A.S. (eds.) ICIDS 2016. LNCS, vol. 10045, pp. 325–335. Springer, Cham (2016)
16. Nitsche, M.: Video Game Spaces: Image, Play, and Structure in 3D Worlds. MIT Press, Cambridge, MA (2008)
17. Overdijk, M., Oostdijk, A., Van Dam, R.: Circulation in virtual media architecture: exploring the spatial logic of a continuous circulation space. In: Proceedings of the 6th Media Architecture Biennale Conference, pp. 1–16. MAB: Toronto (2023)

18. Ryan, M.L., Foote, K., Azaryahu, M.: Narrating Space/Spatializing Narrative: Where Narrative Theory and Geography Meet. Ohio State University Press, Columbus (2016)
19. Ryan, M.L.: Beyond myth and metaphor: the case of narrative in digital media. Game Stud. 1(1) (2001). https://www.gamestudies.org/0101/ryan/
20. Schröter, J.: 3D: History, Theory, and Aesthetics of the Transplane Image. Bloomsbury Academic, New York (2014)
21. Steinicke, F., Visell, Y., Campos, J., Lécuyer, A. (eds.): Human Walking in Virtual Environments: Perception, Technology Applications. Springer, New York (2013)
22. Vasylevska, K., Kaufmann, H.: Compressing VR: fitting large virtual environments within limited physical space. IEEE Comput. Graph. Applicat. 85–91 (2017)
23. Void Room: Tea for God (2019)
24. Whistance-Smith, G.: Virtual wandering: embodied spatial narrativity in walking simulators. In: Punday, D. (ed.) Digital Narrative Spaces: An Interdisciplinary Examination. Routledge, New York (2022)
25. Young, T.: Grounding the myth: themepark landscapes in an era of commerce and nationalism. In: Young, T., Riley, R. (eds.) Themepark Landscapes: Antecedents and Variations. Dumbarton Oaks, Washington DC (2002)
26. YouTube. https://www.youtube.com/watch?v=81PhKa4lf2A. Accessed 28 June 2023

Detecting Player Preference Shifts in an Experience Managed Environment

Anton Vinogradov$^{(\boxtimes)}$ and Brent Harrison

University of Kentucky, Lexington, KY 40506, USA
anton.vinogradov@uky.edu, harrison@cs.uky.edu

Abstract. Players are often considered to be static in their preferred play styles, but this has been shown to be untrue. While this is not an issue in games that only attempt to craft a singular experience for the player, this can become a problem for games that use an Experience Manager (ExpM) to adapt the game to the player. As an ExpM observes the player's actions within the game environment, it makes changes to the environment to bias it towards the player's preferences, but if a player were to shift their preferences then any further ExpM observations are now based on this biased environment. These biased observations may not be able to show the player's true preferences and cause the ExpM to form an incorrect player model. In this situation the ExpM should be able to detect these player preference shifts. In this paper we show that such a shift can be detected using only the observations of the player without further intervention. To evaluate these claims we use a text-based interactive fiction environment created to exhibit this bias caused by an ExpM. We compare our own method to detect such shifts to existing outlier detection methods and find that our method can detect shifts in player preferences.

Keywords: Player Modeling · Experience Management

1 Introduction

An experience manager (ExpM) can serve as an invaluable tool to provide players with a tailored experience, in games and interactive narratives. It acts as an omniscient third party, observing the player's actions and preferences, and utilizing those insights to modify the environment to better suit the player [21]. With the use of a player model in more recent systems, the ExpM has a persistent model that it can use to help make decisions. This player model is generally built over time as the player plays the game, slowly allowing the ExpM to form a better idea of the player's desires and behaviors. This allows for a better balance between authorial intent and player agency, resulting in a more personalized and engaging experience [25].

The ExpM has the ability to make changes to the environment while the player is playing, subtly guiding the player towards a better gameplay path.

© The Author(s), under exclusive license to Springer Nature Switzerland AG 2023
L. Holloway-Attaway and J. T. Murray (Eds.): ICIDS 2023, LNCS 14383, pp. 517–531, 2023.
https://doi.org/10.1007/978-3-031-47655-6_32

This guidance allows the player to take the actions that they want to take and thus can help preserve player agency, while also retaining the author's intent with the game. If the ExpM uses a persistent player model, the changes that it makes to the environment will be to better suit that player model. This biasing of the environment towards a player model is normal and expected but may pose a problem if the player model does not reflect the player's true preferences, such as when a player suddenly changes their preferences.

Take the example of a player that has preferred to fight in a narrative game. The player model would reflect this as the ExpM observes the player choosing combat options when given the chance. Using this information the ExpM can close off paths that the player might take that do not lead to combat scenarios, thereby tailoring the game to the player's preferences. The assumption that the player's preference are static and that further observations should only lead to a refinement of the model is currently being made by recent ExpM methods, but it does not always hold. It has been shown that players do often change their play styles [22] and that dynamic computation needs to be done to accommodate [6].

In the case of a player suddenly shifting their preferences, this can lead to a problem that a normal ExpM may be unable to recover from before the player is disinterested. In the case of our player who prefers fighting, if they were to switch to a completely different preference then further observations of their actions may be influenced by the environmental bias. Since the environment has been changed to better accommodate for a player that prefers fighting, the player will continue to get combat scenarios. The player will then engage with those combat scenarios even if they prefer something else because there is no option to do what they prefer, even though the game may support other scenarios. The ExpM will observe that the player is engaging with these scenarios and it will not be able to recognize that the player preferences have shifted, thus slowing how quickly the player model can change, and souring the player's experience until it does.

In our previous work [23] we have shown that when a player preference shift happens, we can quickly recover the player's preferences using multi-armed bandit algorithms. This process temporarily replaces the ExpM's normal behavior allowing it to focus on recovering the preferences instead of managing the player's experience. Since this is disruptive to the functionality of the ExpM and potentially to the player if done too often we consider it necessary to only trigger this when we are certain that a player preference shift has already happened. In this paper we propose a method to detect when a preference shift has occurred and test it against existing methods for detecting novel and outlier data. We evaluate these methods by looking at two key factors, the accuracy of detecting that a shift has or has not happened, and how soon a shift is detected. We find that our method is more effective in detecting shifts and is significantly more effective at avoiding false positives, while also being quicker to detect shifts compared to existing novelty and outlier detection methods.

2   Background and Related Works

In this section we will discuss some of the previous works in experience management and player modeling and provide a brief overview of novelty and outlier detection.

2.1   Experience Management and Player Modeling

Experience management is the task of having an AI system watch over the player as they interact with the game environment and adapting that environment with respect to some criteria. Often this is used to balance the sense of freedom over which actions players can take (player agency) and the narrative goals of the author (authorial intent) as in the subset field of drama management [8,16,24], but can be used in other areas such as educational games [16,18]. By optimizing the experience to the player, a more personalized experience can be provided.

While there are many ways to manage a game experience it can be represented simply as: the ExpM observing the player, processing this observation, and then modifying the environment based on these observations. Observing the player can be done by recording what actions the player has taken, and how they affect the world, while modifying the environment can be done by adding or removing certain objects or locking and unlocking certain paths. Early experience management systems would process the information that they observed immediately, without forming a persistent model of the player [3,7,10,11,15] while more recent approaches often rely on a player model.

A player model is an abstracted representation of the player, and is not exclusive to experience management. By forming a persistent model of the player the experience manager can take advantage of this knowledge by making decisions based on the model and not only the player's immediate actions. These models often group players together under some preexisting framework, like when used in identifying player types [1,5], detecting player engagement [13], and grouping by player preferences [20,25], but can also be used to cluster player's in an unsupervised manner [4,22]. Player models are an approximate representation of the player that often is assumed to get more accurate with more observations. This has been shown to be untrue [6,22] and that players can shift their preferences over time, either as they learn the game or as they try out new things.

This can pose an issue if an ExpM is confident in its player model and the player shifts their preferences. In this case the player model has been used to modify the environment, but the player may prefer some set of actions that are no longer available. This will lead to any further observations of the player to potentially misinform the ExpM and not allow it to update the player model correctly. Modeling the complex nature of how a player may shift over time would solve this issue, but this is a complex task that can be avoided using other means.

In our 2022 work [23] we have tackled the process of recovering a player's preferences. we found that the past observations of the player's actions cannot be trusted anymore, partly because past data may include their action's before the preference shift, but also observations are limited based on the environmental bias. To remedy this we introduce temporary game objects that help alleviate some of the bias present in the environment, which we call distractions. These distractions also allow us to test the player using Multi-armed Bandit algorithms and successfully recalculate the player model from scratch. This work makes the assumption that a player preference shift can be detected, and thus does not attempt to detect one, or use any of the information from a detected shift in their system.

2.2   Novelty and Outlier Detection

To detect shifts in player preferences we split the ExpM observations into two different distinct parts: observations that are likely to be before a shift, and unclassified observations. This aligns well with the idea of novelty detection, or the task of recognizing and differentiating between data that is similar to what has been seen in the past and data that differs [14]. This is similar to outlier detection, where data needs to be classified as an outlier or not, but novelty detection requires that past data is free from outliers. Both outlier and novelty detection present themselves as one-class classification problems [9], where normal data (i.e. data similar to that used in training) is distinguished from the outlier data. This is different than a two-class classification problem as it does not make the assumption that there are two distinct classes of data, instead it only identifies a single normal class which must be distinguished from all other possibilities.

Novelty detection also takes a step further by distinguishing the data over time. Whereas outlier detection can be applied to a static dataset, novelty detection is focused on separating the data into previously known normal data and new unknown data. This distinction means that novelty detection often has a significant imbalance in training examples, with only normal data being well represented. This is useful when training machine learning models to identify whether or not a given input is likely to be well handled by the model, as a model is more likely to give a correct output when its input is similar to the data used to train it. This also makes it well suited for our own task of finding player preference shifts, as our data has a time component and thus we only have access to known normal data.

We make use of three different novelty and outlier detection methods: Elliptic Envelope [17], Local Outlier Factor [2], and One Class SVMs [19]. One Class SVMs function by finding an optimal separating hyperplane between the classes by taking into account the boundary points. To better separate the data a kernel function is applied, for our methods we use a degree 4 polynomial kernel. Local Outlier Factor method on the other hand calculates to what degree each point in the space is an outlier. Each point is considered local as it takes into account its surrounding neighborhood as opposed to the data as a whole. Elliptic Envelope works by defining an elliptic boundary separating outliers from normal data and is designed for Gaussian distributed data. Both Local Outlier Factor and Elliptic Envelope methods are generally used for outlier detection, but since our data already has a distinction between known normal and unknown data, we treat them all as novelty detection methods.

3 Methods

In this section we will discuss the various parts of the player shift detection system. This will include information about the environment and how we define our player model, and the preference shift detection methods that we use.

3.1 Environment and Player Model

We use a modified version of the environment that we previously introduced in our 2022 work on recovering player preferences [23]. This environment is built in the text based interactive fiction engine Inform7 for its ease of use with artificial agents and humans. In this environment we use seven areas called rooms, which are used to represent a standard fantasy medieval town. These are all traversable using only the commands for cardinal directions: north, south, east, west. This was done to simplify the amount of actions considered by the artificial agents that we use to test our methods.

Within these rooms are a number of objects, for example the *North Gate* room contains a guard and a locked path to a different room, among other things. These objects all have a property called the *action type*, which represents what we think is the primary means of interacting with that object. The action type for the guard is *talk* and in our quest we expect the player to ask the guard for information in their search for the missing cat. Likewise for the locked path the action type is *touch*. There are five of these action types: *look, talk, touch, read,* and *eat*.

Since we are focused on detecting shifts in an experience managed environment, we simulate the effects that the ExpM might have on it. These effects come in the form of biasing the environment so that only certain actions are possible. In our medieval town we consider the *talk* action to be the primary action type, as the quest is centered around doing actions of this type. We also include the *look* and *touch* action types in the environment, but these are not the focus of the quest and thus are less present. The *read* and *eat* action types are missing from the environment, and are limited to locked off portions of the map that we do not include in the environment. The *look, talk,* and *touch* action types together are considered Environmental action types, while *read* and *eat* are considered Missing action types.

These five action types are also the basis for our player model, which we use as a measure of the probability that the player will do these actions. We expect that even when a player has a preference for only a single type of action that they will not be able to complete a quest without doing at least some others. Thus when using this type of player model we never have a probability of zero in any of the action types. Since we are focused on detecting a player preference shift, we do not calculate a player model for our agents, and instead assume that the system would have an accurate measure of the player model before hand.

3.2   Shift Detection

The observations that our system makes can be treated as a type of streaming data, or data that is continuous and comes in at somewhat regular intervals. By treating the data like this we can make these methods work in real time while a player is playing. The observations that the ExpM makes come in the form of the action type that the player has made during the last turn, represented as a one-hot vector, but we apply a 10 turn rolling average to these vectors to make the data more suitable for the methods we test. We include the five action types that we have mentioned and also a sixth, the move action type. This action type is not present in the model and objects cannot have it as a primary means of interaction. Moving around the environment is a necessary action to play the game, but we do not consider this something that a player can prefer to do. For our shift detection we hold on to a sliding window of data rather than considering a single observation at a time, and our operations will be applied to this buffer.

Since we represent our observations as streaming data, we have taken inspiration from novelty detection for this task. Novelty detection is a type of anomaly detection that attempts to classify whether incoming data is an outlier, in this context called novel data. It is well suited for streaming data as it makes a distinction between data used to train the classifier, which it assumes to be uncontaminated, and incoming data, which may be contaminated with outliers. This assumption is necessary for novelty detection, but we also consider it is safe to make as it is already made by the ExpM. Since the ExpM makes changes to the environment that bias it towards a player model, it already makes the assumption that its previously held player model was correct. Any observations that are generated to create the player model already must be uncontaminated, and thus we can assume that before a preference shift has happened the player should be taking actions in accordance to their player model. This assumption is broken when a preference shift happens, but this is the purpose of the shift detection process: to detect a shift in the preferences before the observations of the preference shift are used as training data for the classifiers.

We explore the use of three existing classifiers: Elliptic Envelope [17], Local Outlier Factor [2], and One Class SVMs [19]. Elliptic Envelope and Local Outlier Factor are considered outlier detection methods and thus do not necessarily require that the training data is uncontaminated, while a One Class SVM is considered a novelty detection method and, therefore, does. We use a gap between the training and testing data to ensure that the training data is uncontaminated by keeping it further from the testing data. Each of these methods were given a 50 turn window to use as training data, followed by a 50 turn gap, and finally a variable size testing window ranging from 1 to 20 turns. For the testing window, we also introduced a threshold parameter which governs what percentage of the turns in the testing window need to be considered outliers before we consider a shift to be detected. This is necessary to account for noise in the data leading an outlier without a preference shift happening.

We found in preliminary tests that novelty detection techniques were sensitive to the data and were thus encountering challenges associated with excessive false positives or false negatives. The existing methods have the advantage of being well suited for the general task of detecting novel data, but our task is focused on finding a specific type of shift in the data produced by a player shifting their preferences. We reason that we can take inspiration from how this shift might look and created our own method with the game environment in mind. We expect that a shift in player preference likely consists of a sharp difference in their actions over some period of time, and then staying consistent in those new actions. Thus our method takes 50 turns as the baseline window (P_1) and compares that to another 50 turn comparison window (P_2) to see if the player has a difference in their actions, ignoring the move action type. This creates a mask where 0 represents no increase and 1 represents an increase for a given action type. We amend this mask by setting the highest known preferred action type (according to the player model) to be 0, regardless of its previous value. We do this to ensure that we are not detecting that the player has shifted their preference to an action type that they already prefer. This mask is then multiplied by averaged frequency of action types in the test window (P_3) to get a shift score for each action type, which is then compared to the threshold (Eq. 1). If the shift score for any action type is greater than the threshold, we consider a shift to be detected.

$$ShiftScore = \left(\sum P_1 > \sum P_2 \right) * \overline{P_3} \qquad (1)$$

For each of these methods we fine-tuned the test window size and threshold parameters, and for the existing methods we also fine-tuned any other available parameters. To score the fine-tuned parameters we calculated the f1-score for a single trial, and picked the parameters that resulted in the highest score. We found that our method works best with a test window of 10 and threshold of 40%. For Elliptic Envelope we tuned the test window to 10, the threshold to 90%, and the support fraction to 0.6. For Local Outlier Factor we tuned the test window to 10, and the threshold to 20%, and the number of neighbors to 30. For One Class SVMs we tuned the test window to 13, and threshold to 90%, and also found that the degree 4 polynomial kernel works best.

4   Experiments

In our experiments we use 3 artificial agents, and we test 45 scenarios which we group into 10 categories to examine the differences between them. We measure two different criteria: The turn count when a shift is detected (Table 1), and the percentage of the time that a shift was correctly detected (Table 1). The first criteria helps us find what method is the quickest at detecting a shift, while the second allows us to measure how accurate it is in its detection. Note that for detection we report both detecting a shift when a shift has occurred (true positive rate), and detecting no shift when no shift has occurred (true negative rate) together.

4.1   Agents

Similar to our past work, we make use of artificial agents to test this system [23]. These agents all work on a similar basis, having a set of internal preferences that dictate which actions they want to take and the probability that they will take those actions. On each turn, each of these agents make a decision as to what action type they wish to engage in, then look for an object with a primary action of that type. If they fail to find an object with their chosen action type, they will default to a fallback behavior. If they find an object to interact with, they will interact with it, and if there are multiple objects that match their chosen action type, they will randomly select one with uniform probability, with minor exceptions. The details of the fallback behavior and how they choose a preferred action type is different for each agent, but they share the internal preference distribution system.

The agents that we use are: the Goal focused agent, Exploration focused agent, and Novelty focused agent. We use these three agents so that we can represent a wider set of player behaviors. The inspiration for the Goal and Exploration focused agents come from the Bartle Taxonomy of player types [1], which details 4 different player type quadrants: Explorers, Achievers, Socializers, and Killers. We only try to model the Explorer and Achiever player types as these are focused on how the player interacts with the world on the players-world axis. Since we are using a single player environment, we cannot model the Killers and Socializers. The Goal and Exploration focused agents match up to Achiever and Explorer player types respectively. The third artificial agent is a departure from this taxonomy and is instead based on findings in literature that state that novelty is a key component in user engagement [12]. These three agents allow us to better model the wider variety of how player's may act in a game, but do not cover all possible players and may have overlap between them.

The Goal focused agent first selects an action type that it wishes to interact with, in accordance with its internal preference distribution, then attempts to interact with an object with that action type. When it cannot find such an object, its fallback behavior references an ordered set of required steps needed to complete the quest, and it chooses either to take a step towards completing the quest or moving to a random adjacent room. If the agent is not in the correct room to fulfill a required step, they will instead make a single move action towards that room. The effect of this is that this agent does wander but when it cannot find what it wants to do, it will likely be found near the next required step. This agent also is more likely to take the action that the quest is centered around, even if that action is not one that it prefers, which for our environment and quest is the talk action type.

The Exploration focused agent on the other hand does not reference the required steps. This agent first selects whether it wants to wander to an adjacent room (10% chance) or interact with an object (90% chance). If it does not choose to wander, then it limits which action type it can choose to those that are available in the room. After it chooses an action type, it then randomly picks a matching object to interact with. If there are no objects in the room, it falls back to wandering by picking a random adjacent room to move to. The environment has been designed so that initially each room has an object to interact with, but due to the actions of the agent this can change as they play. This agent is more likely to move from room to room and thus not continue to interact with any given object, and is more likely to act in accordance with its preferences as it has no other systems to modify which objects it interacts with.

The final type of agent is the Novelty focused agent. This agent is more complex in that it first remembers which objects it has interacted with before and uses that information to alter how likely it is to interact with those object. A novelty score is calculated for each action type, with a smaller score for objects that it has interacted with recently, and is averaged with its own preference for that action type. It samples this modified preference distribution to pick an action type, and if there are multiple objects in the room with that type it chooses the one it has interacted with least recently. If an object of that type does not exist, then it defaults to the same behavior as the Goal focused agent, equally split between doing the next quest action and wandering. This has the effect that this agent prefers newer objects, and will tend towards staying in rooms that it either has not been to before or has not been in recently, though this effect is short lived as it interacts with all the objects.

4.2 Scenarios

To test our method we made use of several different kinds of preference switch scenarios. Each of these start with 100 turns of a preference before the shift (pre-preference) and 100 turns of a preference after the shift (post-preference). This allows us to make 50 observations by sliding the train, gap, and test windows by 1 turn until the train window starts to overlap with the post-preference. The pre and post-preferences each selected a single action-type and weighted it at $11/15$, while the other action-types were set to $1/15$. These were chosen to match our earlier work in recovering player preferences [23]. We tested three different rates at which a preference switch happened: an instant switch where the pre-preference switches to the post-preference at turn 100, a slow shift where the preference is linearly interpolated between the pre-preference and post-preference over the course of 20 turns centered on turn 100, and no shift where the preference is not changed. We chose to test both fast and slow shifts to better represent the variability of how a person may play the game. The no shift was included to get a measure of how likely our system is to detect a shift when there is none and thus represents the true negative rate. The fast and slow shifts have 20 different scenarios and the no shift only has 5 for a total of 45 different scenarios.

These scenarios were then categorized into four groups: *Environment to Environment, Missing to Environment, Environment to Missing,* and *Missing to Missing.* These correspond to how we group the action-types into either *Environment* or *Missing*, where *look, talk,* and *touch* are considered Environment action-types as they are present in the environment, and *read* and *eat* are considered Missing action-types since they are missing from the environment. This totals to four grouped fast shifts, four grouped slow shifts, and two grouped no shifts (only

Environment to Environment and Missing to Missing apply to no shift) for ten total groups.

5   Results and Discussion

For our experiments we ran 100 trials for each scenario, agent, and shift speed combination. These were then run through the methods to generate the two metrics, if a shift was detected, and what turn that shift was detected on. The average number of turn to detect a shift is reported in Table 2, with the best in each category highlighted. Likewise the average likelihood that a shift is detected is shown in Table 1, along with the F_1-score to compare the overall performance of each method.

5.1   Scenario Differences

While we have included an exhaustive set of preference shifts, we do not expect that all of these are equally likely to occur in actual gameplay. The *Missing to-* and the *Missing No Shift* scenarios represent a state where environment is already ill suited for the player's preferences, which we consider to be unlikely. Despite this, we have included them to evaluate how the system can handle with these rare circumstances and have found that in some cases it can.

Due to how we have set up the environment the differences between the two missing action types are largely indistinguishable to the shift detection methods and this is reflected in the similarity of results in *Missing No Shift* and *Missing to Missing* scenario groups. These two groups largely mirror each other with the accuracy of detecting a shift in *Missing to Missing* being the inverse of detecting no shift in *Missing No Shift*. It is unlikely that these can be truly distinguished without getting more information from the player, but since these are unlikely this is not a big concern.

For the *Missing to Environment* scenario group we found that each method performs similarly to the *Environment to Environment* group. The observations made when the player prefers a missing action type are often more random, and when used as training data this more uniform distribution of actions taken is easy to distinguish for the novelty and outlier methods. In the case of our method this would show up as a change in the frequency that a specific action is taken between the baseline and comparison windows, as the action type for the post-preference is available in the environment. This contrasts to the *Environment to Missing* group, where our method would not see such a rise as there are no actions with the type that the player prefers in their post-preference. While this is a weakness of our method we still find that it outperforms the others.

We found that there is not much difference between the fast and the slow groups, with the slow shift being only marginally more difficult to detect. The purpose of the gap is to compensate for the shift speed, and it seems that having a gap that is larger than the time it takes for a preference to shift removes the effect of a slower shift. Since the gap does not seem to have a significant effect on the performance, it may be more useful to eliminate it and the sliding training window in favor of using some set of the past data that is known to adhere to the current player model. The sliding training window requires constant retraining of all the methods except our own, which may be prohibitively expensive to run in real time depending on the nature of the game that this system is implemented in. Our method does not have this same drawback, but it too may benefit from a smaller comparison window as it would decrease the number of turns to detect a shift.

5.2 Agent and Method Differences

We found that different agents pose different challenges to different methods. For the *-to Environment* groups the Goal focused agent is the best performing for each method, but this reverses in the *-to Missing* groups. The Goal focused agent's behavior causes it to tend to completing the goal when it does not have its preferred action type. Since the goal of the quest requires environmental actions type, a shift in the preference will likely cause this agent to change its behavior, and this is noticeable to the novelty and outlier detection methods. Since our method works differently and only watches for the frequency of actions of each type, the frequency of environmental action types may not change significantly enough to trigger a detection. This suggests that a combination of our method and existing novelty detection methods may be necessary to cover all types of players.

The Exploration and Novelty focused agents are less likely to follow the quest, with the Exploration focused agent only doing so accidentally. The likelihood that the agent follows the quest seems to be the main contributing factor for the differences between the agents rather than their complexity. Detecting whether the player is engaging with the environment because they are interested in that environment instead of just finishing the quest solely for sake of completion may be useful to improve the ability to detect a preference shift.

For the purpose of comparison, we have included two versions of our method: one with a test window of 1 turn, and another of 10 turns. While other methods require a larger test window as they only categorize each observation in the test data as an outlier or not, our method outputs a score which we can compare against the threshold. We found that attempting to increase window past 10 did significantly decrease the F_1-score in our method, but that decreasing the window did not have such an impact. This allows our method to have an average detection time that is 6 turns sooner than other methods, but also leads to a slight performance hit.

The primary reason that our method outperforms others is that it is significantly better at not detecting a shift when no shift has occurred. This can be seen with the *Environment No Shift* group where our method can correctly identify that no shift has occurred up to 90% of the time for the Goal focused agent, though the results for the other two agents are significantly worse. Compared to Local Outlier Factor which scores a max of 47% only in the Novelty focused agent, our method only scores slightly worse at 46% but all of these have a very

Table 1. The mean and standard deviations of the likelihood that a shift is correctly detected. Bolded are the best performing for each category.

Agent	EE	LOF	SVM	Ours (1)	Ours (10)
Fast					
Environment to Environment Action Types					
Exploration	0.84±0.36	0.91 ± 0.29	0.93 ± 0.25	**0.94 ± 0.23**	0.94 ± 0.25
Goal	**1.00 ± 0.00**	**1.00 ± 0.00**	1.00 ± 0.04	**1.00 ± 0.00**	**1.00 ± 0.00**
Novelty	0.98 ± 0.13	0.95 ± 0.21	0.97 ± 0.16	**1.00 ± 0.06**	**1.00 ± 0.06**
Missing to Environment Action Types					
Exploration	0.89 ± 0.31	0.89 ± 0.32	0.83 ± 0.37	**0.99 ± 0.09**	**0.99 ± 0.09**
Goal	1.00 ± 0.04	**1.00 ± 0.00**	1.00 ± 0.06	**1.00 ± 0.00**	**1.00 ± 0.00**
Novelty	0.97 ± 0.17	0.89 ± 0.32	0.91 ± 0.29	**1.00 ± 0.00**	**1.00 ± 0.00**
Environment to Missing Action Types					
Exploration	0.79 ± 0.41	0.84 ± 0.37	**0.97 ± 0.18**	0.90 ± 0.30	0.87 ± 0.33
Goal	0.99 ± 0.11	**0.99 ± 0.08**	0.96 ± 0.19	0.42 ± 0.49	0.36 ± 0.48
Novelty	0.96 ± 0.19	0.85 ± 0.36	**0.99 ± 0.10**	0.79 ± 0.41	0.75 ± 0.43
Missing to Missing Action Types					
Exploration	0.84 ± 0.36	0.77 ± 0.43	0.92 ± 0.27	**1.00 ± 0.00**	**1.00 ± 0.00**
Goal	0.65 ± 0.48	0.67 ± 0.47	**0.81 ± 0.40**	0.61 ± 0.49	0.53 ± 0.50
Novelty	0.80 ± 0.40	0.58 ± 0.49	0.86 ± 0.34	**0.95 ± 0.22**	0.94 ± 0.23
Slow					
Environment to Environment Action Types					
Exploration	0.84 ± 0.36	0.91 ± 0.28	0.91 ± 0.29	**0.93 ± 0.25**	0.93 ± 0.26
Goal	1.00 ± 0.04	**1.00 ± 0.00**	**1.00 ± 0.00**	**1.00 ± 0.00**	**1.00 ± 0.00**
Novelty	0.98 ± 0.15	0.91 ± 0.28	0.95 ± 0.21	0.99 ± 0.09	**0.99 ± 0.09**
Missing to Environment Action Types					
Exploration	0.86 ± 0.34	0.87 ± 0.33	0.77 ± 0.42	**0.99 ± 0.08**	0.99 ± 0.10
Goal	1.00 ± 0.06	**1.00 ± 0.00**	0.99 ± 0.08	**1.00 ± 0.00**	**1.00 ± 0.00**
Novelty	0.98 ± 0.13	0.88 ± 0.32	0.88 ± 0.32	1.00 ± 0.04	**1.00 ± 0.00**
Environment to Missing Action Types					
Exploration	0.77 ± 0.42	0.83 ± 0.37	**0.96 ± 0.20**	0.86 ± 0.34	0.87 ± 0.34
Goal	0.98 ± 0.15	**0.99 ± 0.10**	0.94 ± 0.24	0.43 ± 0.50	0.39 ± 0.49
Novelty	0.96 ± 0.19	0.83 ± 0.37	**0.98 ± 0.12**	0.81 ± 0.40	0.77 ± 0.42
Missing to Missing Action Types					
Exploration	0.83 ± 0.37	0.80 ± 0.40	0.91 ± 0.29	**0.99 ± 0.07**	0.99 ± 0.07
Goal	0.68 ± 0.47	0.67 ± 0.47	**0.73 ± 0.45**	0.60 ± 0.49	0.54 ± 0.50
Novelty	0.76 ± 0.43	0.58 ± 0.49	0.84 ± 0.37	**0.94 ± 0.23**	0.94 ± 0.25
No Shift					
Environment No Shift					
Exploration	0.28 ± 0.45	0.14 ± 0.34	0.08 ± 0.27	0.43 ± 0.50	**0.45 ± 0.50**
Goal	0.31 ± 0.46	0.34 ± 0.47	0.24 ± 0.43	0.90 ± 0.30	**0.91 ± 0.28**
Novelty	0.21 ± 0.41	**0.47 ± 0.50**	0.21 ± 0.41	0.37 ± 0.48	0.46 ± 0.50
Missing No Shift					
Exploration	**0.19 ± 0.39**	0.19 ± 0.39	0.06 ± 0.24	0.02 ± 0.12	0.01 ± 0.07
Goal	0.38 ± 0.49	0.31 ± 0.46	0.21 ± 0.41	0.43 ± 0.50	**0.47 ± 0.50**
Novelty	0.19 ± 0.39	**0.42 ± 0.49**	0.18 ± 0.38	0.05 ± 0.22	0.06 ± 0.25
F_1-Score					
–	0.69	0.69	0.67	0.71	**0.72**

high variability. Overall the ability to ignore a shift is rather poor and unreliable by all methods but our method shows promise, and this can be further improved with future work.

Table 2. The mean and standard deviations of the turn the shift was detected on. Note that the only cases where a shift was detected are included. Bolded are the best performing for each category (lowest value for Shift, and highest for No Shift).

Agent	EE	LOF	SVM	Ours (1)	Ours (10)
Fast					
Environment to Environment Action Types					
Exploration	129.4 ± 11.1	125.2 ± 09.5	127.9 ± 09.3	**116.8 ± 09.3**	126.3 ± 09.8
Goal	120.4 ± 01.9	120.3 ± 02.0	123.2 ± 01.8	**112.3 ± 03.7**	121.0 ± 03.3
Novelty	124.0 ± 07.0	125.3 ± 09.0	126.3 ± 07.5	**115.7 ± 07.1**	124.6 ± 07.2
Missing to Environment Action Types					
Exploration	129.2 ± 11.1	127.8 ± 11.4	131.5 ± 11.4	**115.1 ± 07.1**	124.6 ± 07.6
Goal	121.3 ± 04.1	120.5 ± 03.0	123.9 ± 04.5	**112.1 ± 03.6**	121.1 ± 03.6
Novelty	124.6 ± 08.0	125.1 ± 09.3	128.6 ± 10.2	**113.3 ± 04.8**	122.2 ± 05.0
Environment to Missing Action Types					
Exploration	130.2 ± 11.2	126.2 ± 10.2	126.2 ± 07.4	**118.3 ± 10.3**	127.3 ± 10.3
Goal	122.7 ± 06.3	**121.8 ± 05.5**	125.9 ± 06.7	123.5 ± 12.4	133.4 ± 12.6
Novelty	125.8 ± 08.9	126.5 ± 09.8	126.0 ± 07.1	**121.3 ± 11.1**	130.4 ± 11.4
Missing to Missing Action Types					
Exploration	129.6 ± 10.7	128.3 ± 11.1	128.6 ± 09.3	**114.9 ± 06.6**	123.8 ± 06.4
Goal	133.5 ± 11.7	129.8 ± 12.1	134.0 ± 12.1	**122.3 ± 11.7**	131.3 ± 11.3
Novelty	131.3 ± 11.4	130.3 ± 11.8	131.0 ± 10.6	**116.7 ± 08.4**	125.5 ± 09.6
Slow					
Environment to Environment Action Types					
Exploration	127.4 ± 10.2	125.4 ± 09.9	127.4 ± 08.6	**116.8 ± 09.2**	125.8 ± 09.4
Goal	120.6 ± 02.5	120.5 ± 02.4	123.2 ± 01.9	**113.1 ± 04.2**	121.6 ± 03.9
Novelty	124.7 ± 07.8	126.4 ± 10.1	126.3 ± 07.2	**116.0 ± 07.7**	125.0 ± 08.3
Missing to Environment Action Types					
Exploration	128.0 ± 10.9	126.8 ± 10.5	131.0 ± 11.1	**114.7 ± 06.9**	124.0 ± 07.3
Goal	121.8 ± 04.6	120.5 ± 02.6	123.7 ± 03.3	**112.9 ± 03.8**	121.4 ± 03.5
Novelty	125.4 ± 08.3	126.9 ± 10.1	128.3 ± 09.3	**113.6 ± 04.8**	122.4 ± 05.0
Environment to Missing Action Types					
Exploration	131.2 ± 11.7	126.4 ± 10.4	126.6 ± 07.7	**121.3 ± 10.4**	129.2 ± 10.9
Goal	122.8 ± 06.0	**122.1 ± 05.6**	126.3 ± 07.2	125.6 ± 11.6	134.7 ± 12.2
Novelty	126.0 ± 08.9	128.0 ± 11.1	125.6 ± 06.1	**121.5 ± 11.0**	130.0 ± 11.3
Missing to Missing Action Types					
Exploration	130.0 ± 10.9	129.5 ± 11.6	129.0 ± 09.5	**115.0 ± 07.2**	123.8 ± 06.6
Goal	133.9 ± 12.0	132.6 ± 12.3	135.1 ± 12.8	**121.5 ± 11.4**	131.3 ± 12.5
Novelty	132.7 ± 12.2	132.6 ± 12.4	131.0 ± 11.0	**116.2 ± 08.2**	125.7 ± 09.0
No Shift					
Environment No Shift					
Exploration	131.1 ± 11.5	129.4 ± 12.0	131.5 ± 11.3	122.3 ± 12.3	**131.7 ± 12.3**
Goal	134.3 ± 11.7	131.2 ± 11.5	134.2 ± 11.8	127.2 ± 13.2	**137.2 ± 14.1**
Novelty	131.6 ± 11.9	131.3 ± 12.8	132.0 ± 10.8	124.6 ± 12.4	**133.4 ± 12.4**
Missing No Shift					
Exploration	**130.8 ± 12.0**	129.1 ± 11.9	127.9 ± 08.3	115.0 ± 07.5	124.5 ± 08.1
Goal	**132.8 ± 11.0**	129.6 ± 12.3	132.7 ± 11.0	121.3 ± 11.3	131.0 ± 11.6
Novelty	131.5 ± 12.1	**131.5 ± 12.4**	131.4 ± 11.3	117.3 ± 09.4	125.7 ± 09.1

6   Conclusion

Experience managed games allow for the player to have a more personalized experience with the game, but can fall short when modeling the player. If a player model cannot take into account how a player's preferences will shift as they play a game, the ExpM will not be able to make accurate observations of the player due to the bias in the environment. Previously it has been shown that recovering a player's preferences can be done quickly, but this relied on the assumption that a preference shift could be first detected. In this paper we show that detecting a shift is possible with a fairly high degree of accuracy and that a lack of shift can be ignored. We develop a means to detect such a shift and show that it is better than existing novelty and outlier detection methods for our data. For future work we plan on expanding this system to include a second stage to confirm a shift exists, as the process of recovering the player's preferences too often may be disruptive to the player. As such, a system that can confirm that a shift has happened with less disruption will allow for a significantly better playing experience, while still being able to adapt to unexpected shifts in the player's preferences.

References

1. Bartle, R.: Hearts, clubs, diamonds, spades: Players who suit muds. J. MUD Res. **1**(1), 19 (1996)
2. Breunig, M.M., Kriegel, H.P., Ng, R.T., Sander, J.: LOF: identifying density-based local outliers. In: Proceedings of the 2000 ACM SIGMOD International Conference on Management of Data, pp. 93–104 (2000)
3. Cavazza, M., Pizzi, D., Charles, F., Vogt, T., André, E.: Emotional input for character-based interactive storytelling (2009)
4. Drachen, A., Canossa, A., Yannakakis, G.N.: Player modeling using self-organization in tomb raider: underworld. In: 2009 IEEE Symposium on Computational Intelligence and Games, pp. 1–8. IEEE (2009)
5. Heeter, C., Lee, Y.H., Medler, B., Magerko, B.: Beyond player types: gaming achievement goal. In: Proceedings of the 2011 ACM SIGGRAPH Symposium on Video Games, pp. 43–48 (2011)
6. Khoshkangini, R., Ontanón, S., Marconi, A., Zhu, J.: Dynamically extracting play style in educational games. EUROSIS Proceedings, GameOn (2018)
7. Lamstein, A., Mateas, M.: Search-based drama management. In: Proceedings of the AAAI-04 Workshop on Challenges in Game AI, pp. 103–107 (2004)
8. Mateas, M., Stern, A.: A behavior language for story-based believable agents. IEEE Intell. Syst. **17**(4), 39–47 (2002)
9. Moya, M.M., Koch, M.W., Hostetler, L.D.: One-class classifier networks for target recognition applications. NASA STI/Recon Technical Report N **93**, 24043 (1993)
10. Nelson, M., Mateas, M.: Search-based drama management in the interactive fiction anchorhead. In: Proceedings of the AAAI Conference on Artificial Intelligence and Interactive Digital Entertainment, vol. 1, pp. 99–104 (2005)
11. Nelson, M.J., Mateas, M.: Another look at search-based drama management. In: AAMAS (3), pp. 1293–1298 (2008)
12. O'Brien, H.L., Toms, E.G.: The development and evaluation of a survey to measure user engagement. J. Am. Soc. Inform. Sci. Technol. **61**(1), 50–69 (2010)
13. Pedersen, C., Togelius, J., Yannakakis, G.N.: Modeling player experience in super mario bros. In: 2009 IEEE Symposium on Computational Intelligence and Games, pp. 132–139. IEEE (2009)

14. Pimentel, M.A., Clifton, D.A., Clifton, L., Tarassenko, L.: A review of novelty detection. Signal Process. **99**, 215–249 (2014)
15. Riedl, M.O., León, C.: Toward vignette-based story generation for drama management systems. In: Workshop on Integrating Technologies for Interactive Stories-2nd International Conference on Intelligent Technologies for interactive Entertainment, pp. 8–10 (2008)
16. Riedl, M.O., Stern, A., Dini, D., Alderman, J.: Dynamic experience management in virtual worlds for entertainment, education, and training. Int. Trans. Syst. Sci. Appl. Special Issue Agent Based Syst. Human Learn. **4**(2), 23–42 (2008)
17. Rousseeuw, P.J., Driessen, K.V.: A fast algorithm for the minimum covariance determinant estimator. Technometrics **41**(3), 212–223 (1999)
18. Sabourin, J.L., Mott, B.W., Lester, J.C.: Early prediction of student self-regulation strategies by combining multiple models. Int. Educ. Data Mining Soc. (2012)
19. Scholkopf, B., Williamson, R., Smola, A., Shawe-Taylor, J., Platt, J., et al.: Support vector method for novelty detection. Adv. Neural. Inf. Process. Syst. **12**(3), 582–588 (2000)
20. Sharma, M., Ontañón, S., Mehta, M., Ram, A.: Drama management and player modeling for interactive fiction games. Comput. Intell. **26**(2), 183–211 (2010)
21. Sharma, M., Ontanón, S., Strong, C.R., Mehta, M., Ram, A.: Towards player preference modeling for drama management in interactive stories. In: FLAIRS Conference, pp. 571–576 (2007)
22. Valls-Vargas, J., Ontanón, S., Zhu, J.: Exploring player trace segmentation for dynamic play style prediction. In: Proceedings of the AAAI Conference on Artificial Intelligence and Interactive Digital Entertainment, vol. 11, pp. 93–99 (2015)
23. Vinogradov, A., Harrison, B.: Using multi-armed bandits to dynamically update player models in an experience managed environment. In: Proceedings of the AAAI Conference on Artificial Intelligence and Interactive Digital Entertainment, vol. 18, pp. 207–214 (2022)
24. Weyhrauch, P., Bates, J.: Guiding interactive drama. Carnegie Mellon University Pittsburgh (1997)
25. Yu, H., Riedl, M.: Data-driven personalized drama management. In: Proceedings of the AAAI Conference on Artificial Intelligence and Interactive Digital Entertainment, vol. 9, pp. 191–197 (2013)

Author Index

Printed in the United States
by Baker & Taylor Publisher Services